Financial Sector Assessment

A HANDBOOK

Financial Sector Assessment

A HANDBOOK

 THE WORLD BANK

 International Monetary Fund

Cover and publication design: James E. Quigley, World Bank Institute.
Original cover photo: Getty Images.

Contents

Chapter 8

Chapter 9

Chapter 10

Chapter 11
Assessing Systemic Liquidity Infrastructure

Appendix H
Assessment of Pension Schemes from a Financial Sector Perspective 449

Boxes

Tables

Figures

Abbreviations and Acronyms

A&A — Accounting and auditing
AML–CFT — Anti-Money Laundering and Combating the Financing of Terrorism
ARIC — Asia Regional Information Center
ATM — Automated teller machine
BAAC — Bank for Agriculture and Agricultural Cooperatives [Thailand]
BCBS — Basel Committee on Banking Supervision
BCP — Basel Core Principles (for Effective Banking Supervision)
BIS — Bank for International Settlements
BRI — Bank Rakyat Indonesia
CAMEL — Capital adequacy, Asset quality, Management soundness, Earnings and profitability, Liquidity, and Sensitivity to market risk
CARAMELS — Capital adequacy, Asset quality, Reinsurance, Adequacy of claims and actuarial, Management soundness, Earnings and profitability, Liquidity, and Sensitivity to market risk
CGAP — Consultative Group to Assist the Poorest
CIDA — Canadian International Development Agency
CPSIPS — Core Principles of Systemically Important Payment Systems
CPSS — Committee on Payment Settlement Systems or Committee on Payments and Settlements Systems
CSD — Central securities depository
CSFB — Credit Suisse First Boston
DB — Defined Benefit
DC — Defined Contribution
DCP — Domestic credit to the private sector
DFI — Development finance institution
DFID — UK Department for International Development
DIS — Deposit insurance system
ECB — European Central Bank
EMDB — Emerging Markets Database

EWS	Early warning systems
FAO	Food and Agriculture Organization of the United Nations
FASB	Financial Accounting Standards Board
FATF	Financial Action Task Force on Money Laundering
FCRA	Fair Credit Reporting Act
FIRST	Financial Sector Reform and Strengthening Initiative
FIU	Financial Intelligence Units
FSAP	Financial Sector Assessment Program
FSIs	Financial soundness indicators
FSLC	Financial Sector Liaison Committee
FSRB	FATF-Style Regional Body
FSSA	Financial System Stability Assessment
FX	foreign exchange
GAAP	Generally Accepted Accounting Principles
GDDS	General Data Dissemination System
GDP	Gross domestic product
GNP	Gross national product
GTZ	Deutsche Gesellschaft für Technische Zusammenarbeit
HI	Herfindahl Index
IAASB	International Auditing and Assurance Board
IAIS	International Association of Insurance Supervisors
IASs	International Accounting Standards
IASB	International Accounting Standards Board
IASC	International Accounting Standards Committee
ICP	Insurance Core Principle
ICR	Insolvency and creditor rights
IDA	International Development Association
IFAC	International Federation of Accountants
IFC	International Finance Corporation
IFCs	International Financial Centers
IFRSs	International Financial Reporting Standards
IFS	International financial statistics
IFSB	Islamic Financial Services Board
IIFS	Institutions offering Islamic Financial Services
IMF	International Monetary Fund
IOSCO	International Organization of Securities Commissions
IPSAS	International Public Sector Accounting Standards
ISA	International Standards for Auditing
KYC	Know-your-customer
LCFI	Large and complex financial institution
LGD	Loss given default
LIBOR	London interbank offer rate
LOLR	Lender of last resort
LSMS	Living Standards Measurement Survey
MFI	Microfinance institution

MFP	Monetary and financial policies
MIX	Microfinance Information eXchange
NBFI	Non-bank financial institution
NCD	Negotiable certificate of deposits
NGO	Non-governmental organization
NPL	Non-performing loans
OECD	Organisation for Economic Co-operation and Development
OFC	Offshore Financial Center
OFI	Other Financial Intermediary
OMO	Open market operations
OTC	Over-the-counter
PAYG	Pay-as-you-go
POS	Point of sale
PSB	Postal savings bank
ROA	Return on assets
ROE	Return on equity
ROSCs	Reports on Observance of Standards and Codes
RSSS	Recommendations for Securities Settlement Systems
SACCOs	Savings and credit cooperative organizations
SDDS	Special Data Dissemination Standard
SIC	Standard Industrial Classification
SIDA	Swedish International Development Co-Operation Agency
SME	Small and medium enterprise
SOE	State-owned enterprise
SRO	self-regulatory organization
TRWA	Total risk-weighted assets
UNCITRAL	United Nations Commission on International Trade Law
UNDP	United Nations Development Programme
USD	U.S. dollars
VAR	Value-at-risk
VAT	Value-added tax
WOCCU	World Council of Credit Unions

Preface

The experience of many countries around the world clearly shows that while financial sector development can spur economic growth, financial fragility and instability can seriously harm growth. Following the financial crises of the late 1990s, there has been increasing interest in the systematic assessment of the strengths and weaknesses of financial systems, with the ultimate goal of formulating appropriate policies to foster financial stability and stimulate financial sector development. The Financial Sector Assessment Program (FSAP), a joint World Bank–IMF program introduced in 1999, represents a response to this demand for systematic assessments. The emergence of various financial sector Standards and Codes and the associated Reports on Observance of Standards and Codes (ROSCs) are further examples of the increased focus on financial sector assessments.

Consequently, there has been an increased demand from financial sector authorities in many countries, as well as from World Bank and IMF staff for information on key issues and sound practices in the assessment of financial systems and in the design of policy responses. This Handbook of Financial Sector Assessment is a response to this demand. The Handbook presents an overall analytical framework for assessing financial system stability and developmental needs, providing broad guidance on approaches, methodologies, and techniques of assessing financial systems.

Although the Handbook draws substantially on World Bank and IMF experience with the FSAPs and from the broader policy and operational work in both institutions, it is designed for generic use in financial sector assessments, whether conducted by country authorities themselves, or by World Bank and IMF teams. It is, therefore, our hope that the Handbook will serve as an authoritative source on the objectives, analytical framework and methodologies of financial sector assessments as well as a comprehensive reference book for training on the techniques of such assessments.

The Handbook was prepared under the general oversight of Messrs. Alexander E. Fleming (Sector Manager, Finance and Private Sector Division, World Bank Institute), Tomás J. T. Baliño (Deputy Director, Monetary and Financial Systems Department, IMF), and Larry Promisel (former Director, Financial Sector Global Partnership, World Bank).

It is the product of intense collaboration among a large number of staff and experts from both the World Bank and the IMF (primary contributors are listed on the next page). The design, drafting, and editing of the Handbook was coordinated by a team consisting of Mr. V. Sundararajan (Lead Project Consultant, Centennial Group Holdings and former Deputy Director, IMF), Mr. Abayomi A. Alawode (Senior Financial Sector Specialist, World Bank Institute), Mr. Mathew Jones (Senior Economist, IMF), and Mr. Martin Čihák (Economist, IMF).

We wish to thank the entire team for their valuable efforts in bringing this project to fruition.

Cesare Calari
Vice-President
Financial Sector Network
World Bank

Stefan Ingves
Director
Monetary and Financial Systems Department
International Monetary Fund

Contributors

Lead Project Consultant: Mr. V. Sundararajan, Lead Project Consultant, Centennial Group Holdings and former Deputy Director, IMF

World Bank Contributors: Rawan Abdelrazek, Ernesto Aguirre, Abayomi A. Alawode, Nagavalli Annamalai, Mehmet Can Atacik, Thorsten Beck, John Bruce, Alexander E. Fleming, Felice Friedman, Joselito Gallardo, Eric Haythorne, Patrick Honohan, Gordon Johnson, Peter Kyle, Margaret Miller, Bikki Randhawa, Dory Reiling, Paul Allan Schott, Vijay Tata, Craig Thorburn, and Fatouma Ibrahima Wane

IMF Contributors: Greta Mitchell Casselle, Martin Čihák, Peter Clark, R. Sean Craig, Nigel Davies, Paulus Dijkstra, Jennifer Elliot, Gilda Fernandez, Mats Filipson, Eva Gutierrez, Geoffrey Heenan, Socorro Heysen, Matthew Jones, Cem Karacadag, Elias Kazarian, Richard Lalonde, Michael Moore, Aditya Narain, Obert Nyawata, Thordur Olafsson, Eric Parrado, Marc Quintyn, Michael Taylor, In Won Song, Kalin Tintchev, Jan-Willem van der Vossen, and Jan Woltjer

Chapter 1

Financial Sector Assessments: Overall Framework and Executive Summary

1.1. Introduction

The design of policies to foster financial system stability and development has become a key area of focus among policy makers globally. This policy focus reflects the growing evidence that financial sector development can spur economic growth whereas financial instability can significantly harm growth and cause major disruptions, as was seen in the financial crises of the 1980s and 1990s (World Bank 2001).This focus also reflects the recognition that close two-way linkages between financial sector soundness and performance, on the one hand, and macroeconomic and real sector developments, on the other hand, need to be considered when designing macroeconomic and financial policies. Moreover, although the development and international integration of financial systems can strengthen access to foreign capital and can promote economic growth, there is a risk of cross-border spillovers of financial system disturbances. Effective surveillance of national financial systems, along with a harmonization and international convergence of key components of financial policies, will help minimize those types of risks and will promote orderly development of the financial system. Thus, financial stability considerations and financial sector development policies are intrinsically interlinked.

Recognizing the need for stronger policies to foster financial stability and development, several entities around the world, including national authorities, multilateral development agencies, regional development institutions, and various standard-setting bodies are focusing on further developing the tools and methodologies of financial sector analysis and assessments. The purposes of those tools have been to monitor financial system soundness and developments, to analyze the linkages between the financial sector and the macro-economy, to assess the effectiveness of various aspects of monetary and financial policies, and to pro-

1

Box 1.1 Financial Sector Assessment Program (FSAP)—A Chronology

The program was developed by the World Bank and the International Monetary Fund to help strengthen financial systems in the context of IMF's bilateral surveillance and World Bank's Financial Sector development work. In consultation with the Bank's regions and the Fund's area departments, the World Bank–Fund Financial Sector Liaison Committee (FSLC)[a] coordinated the initial development of the program and later has helped manage the program. The FSLC has held several outreach meetings on FSAP with concerned country authorities and sought regular feedback on the program from participating countries to adapt the program to country needs and to use the feedback as input into various Board reviews of the programs.

Pilot program launch on May 1999. The managements of the Bank and the Fund inform the Boards that they have decided to launch jointly, on a pilot basis, the IMF–World Bank Financial Sector Assessment Program.

Interim Board discussion of the pilot program, September 1999. Bank and Fund Boards discussed an interim report on FSAP summarizing the early experience of the pilot. Directors provided guidance on scope and procedures of the pilot. The International Monetary and Financial Committee and Development Committee express support for the program in their fall 1999 communiqués.

Comprehensive Board review of the pilot, March 2000. Bank and Fund Boards conducted a comprehensive review of the progress and lessons of the FSAP pilot. Both Boards agreed to continue and expand the program and provided preliminary guidance on how to develop further the FSAP. Guidance covered the scope and pace of the program, links to IMF surveillance and technical assistance, relationship to assessments of standards, confidentiality considerations, and publication and circulation procedures.

Program update, September 2000, and a joint technical briefing on FSAP to both Boards, December 7, 2000. An update of the program was provided to both Boards. The co-chairs of FSLC provided a joint technical briefing for Bank and Fund Boards on the procedures and progress of the program in preparation for a comprehensive program review.

First review of FSAP, December 13, 2000 (Fund), and January 2001 (Bank). Bank and Fund Boards conducted a review of experience with the FSAP and established guidelines for the continuation of the FSAP program for the period ahead; sought priority for systemically important countries in any one year while maintaining broad country coverage; affirmed the value of the Financial System Stability Assessment (FSSA) reports prepared by the FSAP teams as "the preferred tool for strengthening the monitoring of financial systems under the Fund's bilateral surveillance"; and suggested that Bank and Fund staff members should ensure that FSAP assessments are reflected in other aspects of country programming, including appropriate technical assistance.

Second review of FSAP, March–April 2003. Bank and Fund Boards conducted a comprehensive review of the FSAP and provided guidance in streamlining the program; achieving greater selectivity and flexibility in the scope and pace of the program; broadening the range of tools of financial sector surveillance that complement FSAP; increasing the focus on medium-term and structural issues in low-income countries, with a greater role for the World Bank in those countries; and including the anti-money-laundering and combating the financing of terrorism (AML–CFT) assessments in all FSAPs.

Third review of FSAP, February–March 2005. Bank and Fund Boards reviewed the developments in the program since the last review, acknowledged the value of the program, and broadly endorsed the ongoing efforts to strengthen and refine the program, pending the upcoming further reviews of the FSAP by the Fund's Independent Evaluation Office, and the Bank's Operations Evaluation Department, whose recommendations will be considered by the Boards later.

Many Bank-Fund documents relating to the FSAP are available on the Web sites of the IMF (http://www.imf.org/external/np/fsap/fsap.asp) and of the World Bank (http://www.worldbank.org/finance/fsap.html). For details on the March 2005 review of the FSAP by the Bank and the Fund Boards of Directors, see IMF and World Bank 2005.

---

a. The World Bank–Fund Financial Sector Liaison Committee was established in September 1998 by the Boards of the two institutions to improve coordination of Bank and Fund operations related to financial sector stability and development. Among other things, the FSLC helps to coordinate country selection for FSAPs, organizes Bank-Fund teams for FSAPs, and builds consensus on various procedural and policy matters related to financial sector assessment. The activities of the FSLC are reported in periodic progress reports. The FSLC has issued guidance on various FSAP procedures.

mote harmonization and international convergence of key financial policy areas. Those developments have increased the demand for guidance on good practices in conducting financial sector assessments and in designing appropriate policy responses.

In response, this Handbook presents a general analytical framework as well as specific techniques and methodologies for assessing the overall stability and development needs of financial systems in individual countries and for designing policy responses. The stability and state of development of a financial system depend on a broad range of structural, institutional, and policy factors that operate through two channels. First, they affect the attitude of the private sector toward risk taking, the scope and reach of financial services, and the quality of financial sector governance. Second, they influence the effectiveness of financial policies in fostering sound and well-functioning financial institutions and markets. Those considerations are reflected in the organization of the Handbook, which is explained more fully in section 1.2 below.

The Handbook draws particularly on the World Bank–IMF experience in conducting the Financial Sector Assessment Program (FSAP) and on the broader operational and policy development work on financial systems in both institutions. The World Bank and the IMF introduced the FSAP in May 1999 to monitor and help strengthen financial systems in the context of IMF's bilateral surveillance and of the World Bank's financial sector development work and has since become a regular part of Bank and Fund operations (see box 1.1 for a chronology of the FSAP). The FSAP has been built on a range of analytical techniques and assessment tools developed in the IMF, World Bank, Bank for International Settlements (BIS), international standard-setting bodies, and national authorities. Appendix A at the end of this Handbook presents an overview of the current procedures for conducting FSAPs, updates, and follow-up work, including the preparation of relevant Reports on Observance of Standards and Codes (ROSCs) in the financial sector.

A key purpose of this Handbook is to help country authorities to conduct their own assessments of the soundness, structure, and development needs of the financial system. It also can be useful for Bank-Fund teams preparing for FSAP assessments and for country authorities preparing for the Bank-Fund assessments under the FSAP. It is not an expert's handbook designed to provide detailed guidance to sectoral specialists. It is mainly designed to provide broad guidance on methodology and policy design to policy makers, team leaders, and specialists in one sector who are seeking background information on issues and topics in other related areas of assessment work. Detailed guidance for specialist assessors is available from standard-setting bodies and other sources that are referred to in the text.

1.2. Overall Analytical and Assessment Framework—Executive Summary

This section provides the overall analytical framework for financial sector assessments, motivates the structure of the Handbook in terms of this framework, explains how the subsequent chapters fit into the overall framework, and presents a high-level summary of those chapters as a broad guide to policy makers and assessment teams.

1

The objective of financial sector assessments is to achieve an integrated analysis of stability and development issues using a wide range of analytical tools and techniques that include the following:

- Macroprudential analysis, including stress testing, scenario analysis, and analysis of financial soundness indicators and of macrofinancial linkages
- Analysis of financial sector structure, including analysis of efficiency, competitiveness, concentration, liquidity, and access
- Assessment of observance and implementation of relevant international standards, codes, and good practices in the financial sector
- Analysis of specific stability and development issues tailored to country circumstances (e.g., role of public financial institutions, effect of dollarization, reasons for low access or underdeveloped securities markets, etc.)

A broad definition of financial stability and development is used in the assessments. Financial stability refers to (a) an environment that would prevent a large number of financial institutions from becoming insolvent and failing and (b) conditions that would avoid significant disruptions to the provision of key financial services such as deposits and investments for savers, loans and securities to investors, liquidity and payment services to both, risk diversification and insurance services, monitoring of the users of funds, and shaping of the corporate governance of non-financial firms. Financial development is a process of strengthening and diversifying the provision of those services to meet the requirements of economic agents in an effective and efficient manner and thereby support, as well as stimulate, economic growth. Such broad definitions imply that the extent of financial stability can vary from a situation of severe instability to one of sustained overall stability; similarly, the scope of financial development also can vary from being broad based and balanced, covering several financial sector functions and sectors, to being narrowly focused on a specific function or sector. Moreover, overall financial system development could be orderly, with smooth exit and entry of financial service providers and with limited or no interruptions to the provision of financial services and to the real economy, or it could be disorderly, marked by bouts of financial instability and real economic disruption.

The complementarities and tradeoffs between financial stability and development need to be carefully considered in the assessment process. Policies to foster financial stability also support orderly financial development, illustrating the fundamental complementarities between financial stability and development. Nevertheless, in specific contexts, the assessors have to weigh the benefits of stability policies in terms of increased soundness and containment of risks with the costs of regulatory compliance and with the possible side effects of prudential regulations on market functioning and access. Similarly, policies to foster financial development necessarily involve some increase in both macroeconomic and financial risks, which need to be managed. Thus, promoting an orderly process of financial development with stability necessarily involves a proper sequencing and coordination of a range of financial policies.

In line with the broad definitions, a sound and well-functioning financial system is viewed as comprising three pillars that make up the major policy and operational components that are necessary to support orderly financial development and sustained financial stability; the three pillars outlined in the following list also constitute the basis of the assessment framework.

- ***Pillar I***—Macroprudential surveillance and financial stability analysis by the authorities to monitor the impact of potential macroeconomic and institutional factors (both domestic and external) on the soundness (risks and vulnerabilities) and stability of financial systems

- ***Pillar II***—Financial system supervision and regulation to help manage the risks and vulnerabilities, protect market integrity, and provide incentives for strong risk management and good governance of financial institutions.[1] Good practices in most areas of financial system supervision and regulation are reflected in various international standards and codes and the related assessment methodologies; for some areas of supervision and regulation such as microfinance institutions, agreed international standards do not yet exist.

- ***Pillar III***—Financial system infrastructure:

  - Legal infrastructure for finance, including insolvency regime, creditor rights, and financial safety nets
  - Systemic liquidity infrastructure, including monetary and exchange operations; payments and securities settlement systems; and microstructure of money, exchange, and securities markets
  - Transparency, governance, and information infrastructure, including monetary and financial policy transparency, corporate governance, accounting and auditing framework, disclosure regime and market monitoring arrangements for financial and non-financial firms, and credit reporting systems

Those elements of financial system infrastructure constitute the preconditions for effective supervision and regulation that contribute to stability and serve as the foundations for adequate access to financial services and sustained financial development. Again, international standards and guidelines exist to highlight good practices in some areas of infrastructure design (e.g., payment and settlement systems, monetary and financial policy transparency) but not in other areas (e.g., deposit insurance, design of market microstructure).

Elements within all three pillars support both development and stability. The information base for the technical analysis needed for stability assessments and that which is needed for development assessments overlap and provide a common analytical platform for the prioritizing and sequencing of financial sector policy measures. The overall analytical framework for those assessments and the way it is reflected in the organization of the Handbook are described in the following paragraphs.

The first step in the assessment process outlined in the Handbook is to compile a set of key indicators of financial structure, soundness, and state of development of the sector. Chapter 2 provides guidance on key system-wide and sectoral indicators of structure and soundness, including core and encouraged financial soundness indicators (FSIs), market-based indicators of financial soundness, and indicators of access. Key data sources for those indicators are explained in appendix C. The precise scope and content of needed data will be country specific to reflect their structural and institutional circumstances.

1

Nevertheless, chapter 2 seeks to present and motivate some generally useful indicators; more-detailed listing of the sort of quantitative data that may be collected for financial sector assessments are shown in appendix B. Detailed analysis of and processes to determine benchmarks for those indicators is needed to assess financial stability and development. Chapters 3 and 4 form the core of the analytical framework needed for this kind of an integrated assessment, with all other chapters, in effect, providing the specific building blocks for the assessment.

Chapter 3 presents the overall framework of financial stability assessment, which consists of the analysis and assessment of financial sector soundness and its economic and institutional determinants. It encompasses not only quantitative analysis of risks and vulnerabilities but also qualitative assessments of the institutional capacity and financial infrastructure that help manage the risks. The quantitative analysis typically involves monitoring at a suitable level of aggregation; analyzing the economic and institutional determinants for a range of financial soundness indicators (FSIs) of banks, of key non-bank financial sectors, and of relevant non-financial sectors; and examining the impact of various plausible, but exceptional, macroeconomic and institutional shocks on the financial soundness indicators. This type of monitoring and analysis of FSIs—referred to as macroprudential surveillance—includes testing stress levels of the system in response to plausible shocks, which helps identify the key sources of risks and the vulnerabilities to various risk factors. Macroprudential surveillance also encompasses (a) a surveillance of financial markets that helps assess likelihood of economic shocks and (b) an analysis of macro-financial linkages that focuses on the extent to which shifts in financial soundness may itself affect macroeconomic and real sector developments. This combination of approaches captures the two-way linkages between the macroeconomy and financial soundness in formulating an overall stability assessment. In addition, analysis should consider the linkages of domestic financial markets to global markets and the extent to which government policies with respect to taxes, subsidies, monetary and exchange policy regime, and so forth generally affect market discipline and risk taking.

The above analysis should be complemented by information from qualitative assessments of effectiveness of financial sector supervision (Pillar II), and of the robustness of financial sector infrastructure (Pillar III). Such qualitative assessments help identify key elements of the institutional framework and financial stability policies that would mitigate the identified risks and vulnerabilities and thereby help formulate an overall financial stability assessment and identify key policies to foster stability. Chapter 3 motivates and explains the tools of quantitative analysis noted above, including system-wide stress testing of the financial system (elaborated in appendix D), and illustrates how qualitative information on financial supervision and infrastructure can complement the quantitative analysis.

Chapter 4 presents the overall framework for financial structure and development assessment. It consists of an assessment of the functioning of the financial sector, including its scope, concentration, efficiency, competition and adequacy of access, and its institutional and economic determinants. The chapter attempts to analyze the factors behind missing or underdeveloped services and markets, as well as the obstacles in the country that prevent the provision of a broad range of financial services. The goal is to identify policy adaptations and structural changes in financial infrastructure, in supervision and regulation, in governance, and in the broader policy environment designed to strengthen the contribution of the financial sector to economic growth and poverty reduction. This type of assessment involves both quantitative analysis of financial structure and qualitative assessments of a range of institutional and financial policy factors affecting the structure and performance of the sector.

The analysis will typically consider many of the factors already covered under financial stability analysis, notably, the qualitative assessments of key legal and institutional features. However, the analysis will go beyond stability issues and focus on the breadth and efficiency of financial intermediation from a user perspective. Chapter 4 motivates and outlines the tools used in the quantitative benchmarking of financial structure and illustrates how developments in various dimensions of financial sector structure—efficiency, access, scope, and so forth—can be analyzed. The chapter also provides an overview of how those kinds of quantitative analysis can be combined with information from the qualitative assessments of legal and institutional infrastructure as well as from supervisory regimes to formulate an overall development assessment and identify policies to enhance financial development.

Key steps in an integrated analysis and assessment of stability and development can be summarized as follows:

1. *Assess conditions in the non-financial sector* by analyzing financial soundness indicators for those sectors and financial structure and access indicators.

2. *Assess macroeconomic, sectoral and tax-subsidy policies affecting financial stability and development* by analyzing macroeconomic forecasts, early warning indicators, financial market indicators, and tax and sectoral policy. This type of information typically would be drawn from other sources such as local and external official sources as well as data vendors and would help to form a view on the likelihood of shocks to the financial system from the broader economic environment and the way this environment affects financial sector structure and functioning.

3. *Assess financial system risks and vulnerabilities* (a) by analyzing FSIs for banks, insurance companies, the securities market, and key non-bank financial institutions (such as exposures to credit risk, market risk, liquidity risk, and operational risk as well as availability of capital, earnings, and liquid assets that can be used to absorb risk); (b) by monitoring market-based indicators; and (c) by conducting stress tests. The analysis in this step will draw on plausible shocks and linkages identified in steps 1 and 2 above.

4. *Assess financial sector structure and development needs, including its scope, competitiveness, and access,* by conducting quantitative benchmarking and analyzing structural indicators and the data on access (survey-based data, if available). The above analysis will take into account macroeconomic and sectoral conditions affecting financial development and access, drawing on analysis in steps 1 and 2 above.

5. *Assess legal and institutional frameworks and operational effectiveness of financial policies,* both financial supervision and financial infrastructure, including institutional and market development policies (Pillars II and III). This qualitative assessment feeds into step 3 to design policies to foster overall financial stability. This qualita-

1

tive assessment also feeds into step 4 to formulate a program of reforms to foster financial development.

Assessment of legal, institutional, and operational aspects of financial policies involves a wide range of tools, particularly, assessments of observance of international standards and codes as well as of good practices relevant to a stable and well-functioning financial sector. The Handbook provides an overview of the scope, assessment methodology, and assessment experience for those areas of financial supervision and financial infrastructure for which international standards, codes, and good practices exist. A list of international standards used in Bank-Fund operational work is listed in appendix A (box A.2) of the Handbook. For areas of financial policies and institutional design where international standards do not exist, the Handbook provides an assessment framework drawing on good practices identified in operational work and country experience. In some of the areas (e.g., public debt management, bank insolvency regimes, etc.), guidelines based on distillation of country experiences are available. The principles, methodology, and lessons of experience for assessing the legal, institutional, and operational frameworks are presented in chapters 5–11 of the Handbook, and are summarized in the following paragraphs.

Chapter 5 provides an overview describing the process for assessing the effectiveness of financial supervision and regulation of banking, insurance, and securities markets. The assessments are based on the Basel committee's Core Principles for Effective Banking Supervision (BCP); the International Association of Insurance Supervisors' Insurance Core Principles (ICP) and methodology ; and the International Organization of Securities Commissions' Objectives and Principles of Securities Regulations.

Those supervisory standards consist of a set of core principles that can be grouped into four core components:

- *Regulatory governance*—relating to the objectives, independence, enforcement authority, and decision-making arrangements of the regulator
- *Regulatory practices*—consisting of practical application of laws, rules, and procedures
- *Prudential framework*—referring to rules and guidance on internal controls and governance of supervised entities
- *Financial integrity and safety net*—dealing with policies and instruments to promote fairness and integrity of operations of financial institutions and markets as well as safeguards of depositors, investors, and policy holders in times of stress and crises

Chapter 5 outlines the assessment methodology that provides detailed criteria—or practices—for each of the core principles. Those criteria can be compared with country practices to identify significant gaps, if any, in the supervisory regime and to assess the materiality of the gaps from a stability or development perspective. In addition, assessment of observance of each of the core principles will take into account the risk profile and sources of vulnerability of the sector as well as the robustness of infrastructure components (such as accounting and auditing, payments system, insolvency regime) that serve as preconditions for effective supervision. Chapter 5 also explains the basic coverage of legal and institutional frameworks for financial supervision and outlines key issues in designing institutional arrangements for supervision (see appendix F). Special attention is paid to elements of financial safety nets consisting of liquidity support, deposit insurance and policyholder-investor's protection, and crisis management arrangements, including the bank insolvency regime (see appendix G). The chapter also summarizes the main areas of weakness identified in many recent assessments, for example, weak independence and weak legal protection for banking supervisors, weak organization of the supervisory agency and weak supervision of asset risk management in insurance, lack of authority to investigate and the limited enforcement mandate in securities regulation, and weak corporate governance of financial institutions.

Chapter 6 and chapter 7, respectively, discuss assessing regulatory frameworks for other financial institutions (specialized financial institutions and pension funds) and for rural and microfinance institutions. The sectoral and regional significance of many specialized financial institutions (such as housing finance, leasing and factoring companies) and the key role of pension funds in asset allocation and capital markets call for risk-focused and well-tailored regulation that is proportionate and consistent with costs and benefits. Those considerations and the special supervisory issues that arise in leasing, factoring, and pension fund industry are discussed in chapter 6. The provision of financial services to the poor and very poor, particularly those in rural areas, is the purpose of microfinance institutions (MFIs), and the assessment of the regulatory framework for MFIs is part of a broader assessment of adequacy of access. Chapter 7 explains the rationale and scope of regulation of various categories of MFIs as well as the elements of a regulatory framework that are consistent with the MFI functions, risk profile, and operational characteristics.

Chapter 8 considers issues in assessing financial system integrity based on the Financial Action Task Force's (FATF) recommendations for the anti-money-laundering and countering the financing of terrorism (AML–CFT) regime. This chapter covers the scope and coverage of AML–CFT standards, preconditions for effective implementation of those standards, the content of assessment methodology, recent assessment experience, and special topics in AML–CFT assessments such as customer due diligence, financial intelligence units, and scope of UN conventions and Security Council Resolutions.

Chapter 9 discusses key components of the legal infrastructure for the effective operation of financial markets. The legal framework for the financial sector is wide ranging, covering the overall governance and rule of law, laws governing financial infrastructure, and sector-specific laws. It includes the legal framework that empowers and governs the regulator and the rules for the regulation of various institutions and markets as well as the broader legal framework that governs insolvency and the creditor rights regime, ownership, contracts, contract enforcement, accounting auditing and disclosure, and formation of trusts and asset securitization. A review of the overall legal framework should cover both groups of laws. In particular, central banking law, legal foundations of payment system functioning, and government debt management should be reviewed together with the laws governing banking, insurance, and capital markets to ensure that a sound legal basis for macroeconomic policies is available to support stable financial markets. In addition, an overview of company laws, other corporate governance laws, consumer protection laws, and land laws are also important for good governance of financial institutions. Finally, the World Bank's Principles and Guidelines for Effective Insolvency and Creditor Rights regime can help assess enforcement systems for secured and unsecured credit, leg-

1

islative procedures for liquidation and rescue (restructuring), procedures for debt recovery and informal workout practices, and mechanisms for carrying out legal procedures.

Chapter 10 contains an overview describing key components of information and governance infrastructure for finance and explains their role in both financial development and effective market discipline. Those infrastructure components refer to the legal and institutional arrangements that affect the quality, availability, and transparency of information on monetary and financial conditions and policies at various levels as well as the incentives and organizational structures to set and implement policies by regulators, regulated institutions, and their counterparts. The components of this infrastructure consist of the following:

- The framework for Monetary and Financial Policy Transparency, assessed using International Monetary Fund's *Code of Good Practices on Transparency of Monetary and Financial Policies* (chapter 10, section 10.1)
- The accounting and auditing framework that helps to define and validate the information that is disclosure, assessed according to *International Financial Reporting Standards and International Standards for Auditing* (chapter 10, section 10.2)
- Credit reporting and financial information services designed to compile, process, and share information on financial conditions and credit exposures of borrowers and other issuers of financial claims (chapter 10, section 10.3)
- Corporate governance arrangements for financial and non-financial firms, which are assessed according to Organisation for Economic Co-operation and Development (OECD)'s Principles of Corporate Governance and which take into account special considerations that apply to corporate governance of banks and other financial institutions (chapter 10, section 10.4)
- Disclosure practices of financial institutions, determined by the supervisory framework, listing requirements and company laws, which are assessed, in part, according to the disclosure standards under the New Basel Accord (chapter 10, section 10.5)

Chapter 11 presents a framework for assessing systemic liquidity infrastructure. This framework refers to a set of institutional and operational arrangements that have a first-order impact on market liquidity and on the efficiency and effectiveness of liquidity management by financial firms. Key elements of this infrastructure consist of the following:

- Design and operation of payments and settlement systems as well as securities settlement systems, which are assessed according to the Committee on Payment and Settlement Systems' (CPSS's) *Core Principles of Systemically Important Payment Systems*, and International Organization of Securities Commissions (IOSCO)– *CPSS Recommendations for Securities Settlement Systems* (chapter 11, section 11.1)
- Design of monetary policy instruments as well as procedures for money and exchange markets operations, which are analyzed from the perspective of their impact on money market liquidity and on banks' ability to manage short-term liquidity (chapter 11, section 11.2)

- Microstructure of money, exchange, and securities markets consisting of trading systems, price discovery mechanisms, and other institutional determinants of market liquidity and efficiency (chapter 11, section 11.3)
- Public debt and foreign exchange reserve management strategies and operations, which are analyzed according to IMF–World Bank *Public Debt Management Guidelines* and IMF's *Foreign Exchange Reserve Management Guidelines*; both guidelines are supplemented by supporting documents that summarize country experiences (chapter 11, section 11.4)

Chapter 12 provides guidance on sequencing of financial sector reforms. The subject of sequencing of reforms deals with factors that should be considered when setting priorities among a multitude of policy, institutional, and operational reforms that have been identified in a financial sector assessment exercise. Appropriate sequencing and coordination of reforms will facilitate implementation of reforms in support of financial development while avoiding financial instability that could arise from inappropriate sequencing. Thus, appropriate sequencing is an important aspect of financial sector assessments.

Although the assessment framework outlined above is comprehensive, a tailoring of assessments is necessary to reflect country-specific circumstances such as those mentioned in Annex 1.A. Countries with less developed systems will need more attention to medium-term development issues such as institution building and financial market development. Governance, transparency, and legal issues are often at the core of underdeveloped financial systems. In countries that are systemically important, particular attention to contagion and cross-border issues as well as the consequences of globalization and consolidation may be required. Countries also differ in structural features such as extent of dollarization, scope of state-owned financial institutions, the scale of foreign-owned banks, degree of vulnerability to shocks, and the level of market discipline and quality of internal governance. Those differences will affect the assessment priorities, design of policies, and the sequencing of reforms and policy measures.

Annex 1.A   Tailoring Financial Sector Assessment to Country Needs

Countries with less-developed financial systems may need more attention with respect to medium-term development issues such as institution building and financial market development. Coverage of the financial sector in those countries may thus need to focus on specific aspects of financial sector development, including capacity of banking supervision; the legal and regulatory framework for bank and non-bank institutions and payment systems; credit information systems, enforcement of creditor rights, and insolvency regimes; accounting and auditing practices and disclosure rules; the status of the central bank and monetary policy implementation; and bank restructuring. Also, an analysis of factors explaining why markets are missing can help to identify the important structural and capacity building needs for the country.

Systemically important countries need attention to contagion and cross-border issues. Countries particularly vulnerable to a rapid increase in competition from foreign financial institutions may need particular attention with respect to (a) the appropriate sequencing of liberalization, including institutional preconditions, and (b) the ability of domestic

1

incumbents to withstand more intense competition. Of particular note are countries participating in new free-trade arrangements or undertaking substantive financial services commitments in the World Trade Organization. Those types of agreements may facilitate the cross-border provision of services or the establishment of subsidiaries and branches. Countries may commit to dispute settlement provisions and to constraints on their recourse to capital controls. In those cases, emphasis might be placed on (a) the capacity of the regulatory authorities to conduct cross-border consolidated supervision of financial institutions; (b) the conditions that might lead to an unsustainable buildup of short-term financial flows; (c) the dependence of local incumbents, including public service banks, on fee-based and large-customer business that may be particularly vulnerable to foreign competition; and (d) any systemic vulnerabilities that may result from their failure.

In many countries, dollarization poses unique financial risks that need to be addressed. Where available, assessors should provide supporting quantitative information such as shares of foreign currency deposits and loans, the degree of cocirculation, short-term foreign assets and liabilities of the main financial institutions, net foreign assets, and net open foreign currency positions of banks (Gulde and others 2003).

In non-crisis countries with significant financial distress where a large share of banks (or insurance companies or other financial institutions) are undercapitalized and underperforming, the assessors will have to focus on vulnerabilities to various plausible shocks and to resolution measures.[2] Vulnerabilities could be detected through stress testing and estimation of likely macroeconomic consequences. In case a macroeconomic shock were to occur, sufficiently rapid financial restructuring could avert a crisis. This reasoning suggests that the focus of assessment should be on measures to restore normalcy and implementation of resolution strategies, including contingency planning and structural reforms that could bolster the capacity for restructuring and liquidation of banks and non-banks. In cases such as those, FSIs would need to be carefully interpreted, possibly until exceptional resolution arrangements have run their course and normalcy has been fully restored (Hoelscher and Quintyn 2003).

In countries that are part of a currency union, assessors would have to be sensitive to the division of supervisory responsibility between the national and the supranational level (Van Beek and others 2000). In particular, supervisory responsibilities for financial institutions may reside at the national level with varying degrees of harmonization of rules and practices such as loan classification and provisioning as well as licensing and other entry requirements. The degree of control over cross-border transactions in relation to third countries may also differ. By contrast, monetary–exchange rate policy functions in those cases are performed at the supranational level, creating the potential for ambiguities about lender of last resort and crisis resolution arrangements.

In countries with significant presence of Institutions offering Islamic Financial Services (IIFS), assessors would need to consider whether the supervisory framework is adequately adapted to address the specific risk characteristics of IIFS. Risks in IIFS may differ from those in conventional finance because of the contractual design of instruments based on Islamic Law (*Sharia'a*), and the overall infrastructure governing Islamic finance. In the absence of adequate institutional infrastructure and effective risk mitigation, IIFS may be more vulnerable than conventional institutions for a range of risks (operational, liquidity, and market risk—including commodity prices). Where available and appropriate, assessors should also provide quantitative information on the size of the industry; the share of Islamic modes of financing; and FSIs on capital, non-performing loans, provisioning, and earnings for Islamic banks. The definitions of those variables would need adjustments to reflect the specific accounting treatments of Islamic financial contracts. Although some guidance is available in the IMF's Compilation Guide on Financial Soundness Indicators (International Monetary Fund 2004), work in this area is evolving.

Notes

1. For the purposes of the Handbook, a narrow definition of market integrity is used mainly to cover anti-money-laundering initiatives and efforts to counter the financing of terrorism. A broader concept also will cover transparency and governance elements.

References and Other Sources

Gulde, Anne-Marie, David S. Hoelscher, Ize Alain, David Marston, and Gianni De Nicolo. 2003. *Financial Stability in Dollarized Economies.* IMF Occasional Paper 230. Washington, DC: International Monetary Fund.

Hoelscher, David S., and Marc Quintyn. 2003. *Managing Systemic Banking Crises.* IMF Occasional Paper 224. Washington, DC: International Monetary Fund.

IMF (International Monetary Fund). 2004. *Compilation Guide on Financial Soundness Indicators.* Washington, DC: International Monetary Fund. Available on the IMF external Web site: http://www.imf.org/external/np/sta/fsi/eng/2004/guide/appendx.pdf.

IMF (International Monetary Fund), and World Bank. 2005. "Financial Sector Assessment Program—Review, Lessons, and Issues Going Forward." Papers prepared for the IMF and World Bank Board Review. Washington, DC: International Monetary Fund. Available at http://www.imf.org/External/np/fsap/2005/022205.htm.

Lindgren, Carl-Johan, Tomás J. T. Baliño, Charles Enoch, Anne-Marie Gulde, Marc Quintyn, and Leslie Teo. 2000. *Financial Sector Crisis and Restructuring—Lessons from Asia.* IMF Occasional Paper 188. Washington, DC: International Monetary Fund.

Van Beek, Frits, José Roberto Rosales, Mayra Zermeño, Ruby Randall, and Jorge Sheph. 2000. *The Eastern Caribbean Currency Union-Institutions, Performance, and Policy Issues.* IMF Occasional Paper 195. Washington, DC: International Monetary Fund.

World Bank. 2001. *Finance for Growth, Policy Choices in a Volatile World.* New York: Oxford University Press.

Chapter 2

Indicators of Financial Structure, Development, and Soundness

This chapter presents an overview of quantitative indicators of financial structure, development, and soundness. It provides guidance on key system-wide and sectoral indicators, including definitions, measurement, and usage. Key data sources for these indicators are explained in appendix C (Data Sources for Financial Sector Assessments). Detailed analysis and benchmarking of these indicators are discussed in chapters 3 and 4. More detailed data requirements are presented in appendix B (Illustrative Data Questionnaires for Comprehensive Financial Sector Assessments).

2.1 Financial Structure and Development

Indicators of financial structure include system-wide indicators of size, breadth, and composition of the financial system; indicators of key attributes such as competition, concentration, efficiency, and access; and measures of the scope, coverage, and outreach of financial services.

2.1.1 System-wide Indicators

Financial structure is defined in terms of the aggregate size of the financial sector, its sectoral composition, and a range of attributes of individual sectors that determine their effectiveness in meeting users' requirements. The evaluation of financial structure should cover the roles of the key institutional players, including the central bank, commercial and merchant banks, savings institutions, development finance institutions, insurance companies, mortgage entities, pension funds, and financial market institutions. The functioning of financial markets, including money, foreign exchange, and capital markets (including

2

bonds, equities, and derivative and structured finance products) should also be covered. For financial institutions, the structural overview should focus on identifying the number and types of institutions, as well as growth trends of major balance sheet aggregates; for financial markets, a description of the size and growth trends in various financial market instruments (volume and value) would be appropriate. The overview should also reflect new linkages among financial markets and institutions that may be forged from a variety of sources, including innovations in financial instruments, new entrants into financial markets (e.g., hedge funds), and changing practices among financial market participants (e.g., energy trading and investments by financial institutions).

The overall size of the system could be ascertained by the value of financial assets, both in absolute dollar terms and as a ratio of gross domestic product (GDP).[1] Although identifying the absolute dollar amount of financial assets is informative, normalizing financial assets on GDP facilitates benchmarking of the state of financial development and allows comparison across countries at different stages of development. Other indicators of financial size and depth that could be usefully examined include ratios of broad money to GDP (M2 to GDP),[2] private sector credit to GDP (DCP to GDP),[3] and ratio of bank deposits to GDP (deposits/GDP). However, one should be careful in interpreting observed ratios because they are substantially influenced by the state of financial and general economic development in individual countries. Cross-country comparisons of economies at similar stages of development are, therefore, useful in obtaining reliable benchmarks for "low" or "high" ratios.

The description of the number and types of financial intermediaries and markets is also useful, and this information should be supplemented by information on the relative composition of the financial system. Even though many countries do have a wide range of non-bank financial intermediaries (NBFIs), banking institutions still tend to dominate overwhelmingly. In advanced markets and in many emerging markets, NBFIs, particularly pension funds or insurance companies, often play a larger part than do banks in domestic and global asset allocation (and, sometimes, in the providing of credit). Similarly, market participants such as hedge funds play an increased role in financial markets and in the performance of various asset classes. Hence, for one to get a true view of financial structure, it is useful to focus on the share of various sub-sectors (banks, non-banks, financial markets, etc.) in total financial assets by using assets of financial institutions in different sub-sectors and value of financial instruments in different markets as numerators. This type of focus on market shares enables the assessor to get a quick indication of the "effective" structure of the financial system. In addition, the presence of large financial conglomerates—also referred to as large and complex financial institutions (LCFIs)—in the domestic market (either foreign-owned or domestic) would warrant special attention to the scope and scale of their activities, including exposures to other domestic institutions, as well as to intra-group and cross-border exposures, to ascertain their local systemic importance.[4]

Evaluating the overall growth of the financial system and of major sub-sectors is important, and valuable information could be obtained by examining changes in the number and types of financial intermediaries, as well as the growth of financial assets in each sector over time, in both nominal and real terms. Although a description of trends is informative, it is also critical to indicate the driving forces behind (a) observed changes in institutions and their asset positions, and (b) the number of and growth rates of available money and capital market instruments. One factor that has accounted for the observed growth of financial systems in many countries (number of institutions and size of assets) is financial liberalization, especially the softening of entry conditions for banks and other financial institutions and the liberalization of interest rates, which has stimulated financial markets (especially money markets). In addition, changes in prudential regulation and accounting standards often have provided incentives for developing new ways to manage risks (e.g., asset and liability management for insurance company and pension funds) and have led to development of new risk-transfer instruments in capital markets.

2.1.2 Breadth of the Financial System

Data on the financial breadth or penetration often serve as proxies for access of the population to different segments of the financial sector. Well-functioning financial systems should offer a wide range of financial services and products from a diversified set of financial intermediaries and markets. Ideally, there should be a variety of financial instruments that provide alternative rates of return, risk, and maturities to savers, as well as different sources of finance at varying interest rates and maturities. Evaluating the breadth or diversity of the financial system should, therefore, involve identifying the existing financial institutions, the existing markets for financial instruments, and the range of available products and services. The relative composition of the financial system discussed above is a first-cut approach to determining the extent of system diversification. In addition, comparisons between bank and non-bank forms of financial intermediation are useful, for instance, comparisons between banking credit and issues of bonds by the private sector. Often, significant savings and financing through non-bank forms are indicators of financial diversity because bank deposits and loans constitute the traditional forms of savings and credit in many countries. It is, therefore, useful to compare the extent of financial intermediation through banks with the amount of intermediation through insurance, pensions, collective investment schemes, money markets, and capital markets. In particular, the share of various classes of asset holders—specifically, households, non-financial corporations, banks, and NBFIs—within the total capital market instruments or mutual fund assets can provide valuable information on financial diversification.

To supplement the overall indicators of diversity, assessors should also focus on sectoral indicators of financial development. For instance, the development of the insurance industry could be measured by examining trends in the ratio of gross insurance premiums to GDP, which could be broken down further into life and non-life premiums. Similarly, leasing penetration could be measured by the value of leased assets as a percentage of total domestic investment. Table 2.1 shows a few sub-sectors of the financial system and suggests relevant indicators of their size and development. The breadth of the financial system also could be analyzed in terms of the outreach of existing financial institutions. A common indicator related to this outreach is the branch network of the banking system, in particular, the total number of branches and the number of branches per thousand inhabitants. A comparison of the distribution of branches between rural and urban areas or among different provinces could also be useful as an indicator of the outreach of banking outlets.

Table 2.1. Sectoral Indicators of Financial Development

Sub-sector	Indicator
Banking	• Total number of banks • Number of branches and outlets • Number of branches/thousand population • Bank deposits/GDP (%) • Bank assets/total financial assets (%) • Bank assets/GDP (%)
Insurance	• Number of insurance companies • Gross premiums/GDP (%) • Gross life premiums/GDP (%) • Gross non-life premiums/GDP (%)
Pensions	• Types of pension plans • Percentage of labor force covered by pensions • Pension fund assets/GDP (%) • Pension fund assets/total financial assets (%)
Mortgage	• Mortgage assets/total financial assets • Mortgage debt stock/GDP
Leasing	• Leased assets/total domestic investment
Money markets	• Types and value of money market instruments • New issues and growth in outstanding value • Number and value of daily (weekly) transactions in the instruments
Foreign exchange markets	• Volume and value of daily foreign exchange transactions • Adequacy of foreign exchange (reserves in months of imports, as ratio to short-term external debt or to broad money)
Capital markets	• Number of listed securities (bonds and equities) • Share of households, corporations, banks, and NBFIs in the holdings of securities • Number and value of new issues (bonds and equities) • Market capitalization/GDP (%) • Value traded/market capitalization (%) • Size of derivative markets
Colllective investment funds	• Types and number of schemes (unique and mixed funds) • Total assets and growth rates (nominal and as percentage of GDP) • Total number of investors and average balance per investor • Share of households, corporations, banks, and NBFIs, in total mutual funds assets

2.1.3 Competition, Concentration, and Efficiency

Competition in the financial system can be defined as the extent to which financial markets are contestable and the extent to which consumers can choose a wide range of financial services from a variety of providers. Competition is often a desirable feature because it normally leads to increased institutional efficiency, lower costs for clients, and improvements in the quality and range of financial services provided. There are numerous measures of competition, including the total number of financial institutions, changes in market share, ease of entry, price of services, and so forth. In addition, the degree of diversity of the financial system could be an indicator of competition or the lack thereof because the emergence of vibrant non-bank intermediaries and capital markets often have been a source of effective competition for banking systems in many countries. All things remaining equal, an increase in the number of financial institutions or an expansion in available financial market instruments will increase competition by expanding the available sources of financial services that consumers can access. Ease of entry into the system could be judged by looking at the regulatory and policy requirements for licensing, for example, the required minimum paid-up capital.

In many cases, the ownership structure of the financial system can be indicative of competition or lack thereof. For instance, banks of different ownership often have different mandates and clientele, leading to substantial market segmentation. Also, systems dominated by state-owned financial institutions tend to be less competitive than those in which privately owned institutions are very active because state ownership often dampens commercial orientation. In some cases, the shares of domestic- and foreign-owned financial institutions in various financial sub-sectors could be relevant in assessing competition and incentives for financial innovations.

Measures of concentration often have been used as indicators of competition. Concentration is defined as the degree to which the financial sector is controlled by the biggest institutions in the market (as defined by market shares). For example, the three-bank concentration ratio measures the market share of the top three banks in the system, defined in terms of assets, deposits, or branches. Deciding what is concentrated and what is not depends a lot on judgment, and benchmarking becomes critical.[5] A more sophisticated measure of concentration is the Herfindahl Index (HI), which is the sum of squares of the market shares of all firms in a sector. Higher values of the index indicate greater market concentration. When applied to the financial sector, this index uses information about the market share of each bank to obtain a single summary measure.[6] The concept of concentration also could be applied to financial markets, especially by examining the share of different market instruments in the total outstanding value of financial market instruments. For example, the relative shares of money and capital market instruments in total financial assets could give an indication of the extent to which financial markets are positioned between short-term and long-term intermediation. Information on holdings of the instruments by types of investors and by number of issuers of different instruments also helps assess market competition.

The sustainable development of a financial system and the degree to which it provides support to real sector activities depend to a large extent on the efficiency with which intermediation occurs. Efficiency refers to the ability of the financial sector to provide high-quality products and services at the lowest cost. Competition and efficiency of the financial system are related to a large extent because more competitive systems invariably turn out to be more efficient (all other things being equal). Quantitative measures of efficiency that could be evaluated include (a) total costs of financial intermediation as percentage of total assets and (b) interest rate spreads (lending minus deposit rates). Components of intermediation costs include operating costs (staff expenses and other overhead), taxes, loan–loss provisions, net profits, and so forth. Those costs can be derived from the aggregated balance sheet and income statements for financial institutions. However, interest rate spreads sometimes remain high despite efficiency gains because of the need to build loan–loss provisions or charge a risk premium on lending to high-risk borrowers.

For money and capital markets, efficiency implies that current security prices fully reflect all available information. Hence, in an efficient financial market, day-to-day movements of market prices tend to be random, and information on past prices would not help predict future prices. The bid–ask spread (i.e., the difference between prices at which participants are willing to buy and sell financial instruments) is often used as a proxy for measuring the efficiency of markets, with more efficient markets exhibiting narrower

2

Table 2.2. Indicators of Financial System Performance

Sub-sector	Indicator
Competition and concentration	• Total number of institutions • Interest rate spreads and prices of financial services • Intermediary concentration ratios (market share of 3 or 5 of the largest institutions) • Financial market concentration ratios (market share of the largest financial instruments, as a percentage of total financial assets) • Herfindahl index
Efficiency	• Interest rate spreads • Intermediation costs (as percentage of total assets)
Liquidity	• Ratio of value traded to market capitalization • Average bid–ask spread

bid–ask spreads. Because bid–ask spread also reflects market liquidity, as discussed below, additional analysis of the extent of competition in the market and of volatility of price movements would be needed to assess efficiency. In addition, measures of price volatility are sometimes used to substitute for market efficiency, although short-run changes in volatility may reflect shifts in the amount of liquidity in that market.

Two important dimensions of market liquidity should be considered: market depth and market tightness. Market depth refers to the ability of the market to absorb large trade volumes without significant impact on market prices.[7] This dimension is usually measured by the ratio of value traded to market capitalization (turnover ratio), with higher ratios indicating more liquid markets. Another dimension of liquidity is market tightness—ability to match supply and demand at low cost that is measured by the average bid–ask spread. More liquid markets usually have narrower bid–ask spreads. Further discussion of these indicators can be found in section 2.2.4.

Table 2.2 summarizes the indicators of financial system performance that have been discussed in this section.

2.1.4   Scope and Coverage of Financial Services

The financial system provides five key services: (a) savings facilities, (b) credit allocation and monitoring of borrowers, (c) payments, (d) risk mitigation, and (e) liquidity services.

Savings mobilization can be assessed by examining the effectiveness with which the financial system provides saving facilities and mobilizes financial resources from households and firms. The extent of financial savings could be ascertained by examining the level and trends in the ratio of broad money to GDP. As mentioned earlier, this indicator may overstate the true picture if currency constitutes a high proportion of broad money. Other more specific indicators of access to savings facilities include the ratio of bank deposits to GDP and the proportion of the population with bank accounts.

Information on the outreach of the financial system can help interpret developments in financial savings. Hence, indicators such as the total number of bank branches, the population per bank branch, and the distribution of branches and other outlets (e.g., rural or urban) could provide valuable information on the access of the population to saving facilities. Further, it is important to assess the range of saving vehicles that are available because, in many countries, traditional bank deposits are the most common form of financial savings. Saving through non-bank forms of financial intermediation are, therefore, crucial to financial diversity, and development indicators for non-bank intermediaries such as insurance, pensions, and capital markets could be useful in gauging the degree to which the population uses non-bank forms of financial savings. Hence, household and corporate holdings of non-bank financial assets (e.g., bonds) could provide extra information on the degree of access to financial savings.

The ratio of private sector bank credit to GDP is a common measure of the provision of credit to the economy, as well as of banking depth. Often, this indicator is supplemented by information on the ratio of loans to total bank deposits. Where available, the volume of finance raised through the issuance of bonds and money market instruments should supplement information on bank credit. Analyzing trends in those indicators should reveal the overall degree to which the banking sector provides credit to firms and households. It is also useful to assess the sectoral distribution of private sector credit to gauge the alignment of bank credit with the distribution of domestic output. Therefore, the relative proportion of total credit going to agriculture, manufacturing, and services would be relevant information in evaluating the adequacy of the level of credit provided to the economy.

A key function of financial systems in market economies is to offer fast and secure means of transferring funds and making payments for goods and services. The state of development of the payment system is of interest here, especially the focus on the various instruments for making payments, including cash, checks, payment orders, wire transfers, and debit and credit cards. The proportion of payments (volume and value) made with different payment instruments can reveal the developmental status of the payment system, with cash-based economies at the lower end of the spectrum. Some indicators such as the number of days for clearing checks, the number and distribution of clearing centers, and the volume and value of checks cleared could provide general information on the effectiveness of existing money transfer mechanisms. In addition, it is relevant to examine the various risks associated with the payments system, through indicators such as access to settlement credit, size of settlement balances, and so forth, thereby complementing the qualitative information from assessments of Core Principles for Systemically Important Payment Systems.[8]

The major risk mitigation services offered by the financial system include insurance (life and non-life) and derivative markets. The ratio of gross premiums to GDP is a popular indicator of development in the insurance industry, and this indicator could be supplemented with a breakdown of premiums between life and non-life insurance. A deep and well-functioning insurance industry would offer a wide range of products in both the life and non-life business, including motor vehicle, marine, fire, homeowners, mortgage, workers' compensation, and fidelity insurance and life insurance, as well as disability, annuities, medical, and health insurance. In addition, coverage of derivative markets—options, futures, swaps, and structured finance products—where relevant in terms of available instruments, liquidity, and transaction costs, would be important, owing to their role in managing risk and in facilitating price discovery in spot markets.

Liquidity service provided by financial systems is reflected in maturity transformation and secondary market arrangements, which facilitate investment in high-yielding

2

projects. Most high-return projects require a long-term commitment of capital; however, savers are often reluctant to give up their savings for long periods of time.[9] The role of the financial system is to transform liquid, short-term savings into relatively illiquid, long-term investments, thus promoting capital accumulation. The availability of liquidity, therefore, allows savers to hold assets that they can sell easily if they need to redeem their savings.

Against this background, it is important to examine the degree of access that specified target groups (e.g., farmers, the poor, small and medium enterprises, or different geographic regions) have to those financial services. Access is defined as the availability and cost of financial services and could be measured in a variety of ways.[10] First, relevant measures of the supply of financial services includes the numbers of different types of financial institutions, the number of branches and other service outlets, the number of clients served, and the population per outlet. The volume of services (deposits, credit, money transmission, etc.) provided is another useful measure, especially if it is broken down by clientele and size (i.e., in a breakdown by socioeconomic groups or broad sectors or by size distribution). Second, it is also relevant to consider demand-side measures of access. However, demand-side indicators are not easy to construct and often require surveys to collect relevant data. Those surveys have often focused on collecting relevant information such as the savings and credit needs of households and enterprises, the needs relative to the supply, and the ease or difficulty of meeting those needs.[11] Finally, it is important to examine the costs of financial services, usually by examining the level and trends in spreads between the borrowing and lending rates, the general interest rate structure, and the prices of other financial services (e.g., fees and minimum balances for deposits, as well as cost and time of payment services).

In addition, indicators of the functioning of various elements of financial system infrastructure—the insolvency and creditor rights regime, the systemic liquidity arrangements (other than those of payment systems, which have already been covered as a core financial system function), and the information and governance arrangements (e.g., credit reporting, disclosure rules)—can provide useful insights into costs and efficiency of financial transactions. Appendix B (Illustrative Data Questionnaires for Comprehensive Financial Sector Assessment) contains examples of those types of indicators.

2.2 Financial Soundness Indicators

Financial soundness indicators (FSIs) are indicators of the current financial health and soundness of the financial institutions in a country, as well as of their corporate and household counterparts, and FSIs play a crucial role in financial stability assessments. FSIs include both aggregated individual institution data and indicators that are representative of the markets in which the financial institutions operate. FSIs are calculated and disseminated for use in macroprudential surveillance, which is the assessment and monitoring of the strengths and vulnerabilities of financial systems.

FSIs are a relatively new body of economic statistics that reflect a mixture of influences. Some of the concepts are drawn from prudential and commercial measurement frameworks, which have been developed to monitor individual entities. Other concepts

Table 2.3. The Core Set of Financial Soundness Indicators

Indicator	Indicates	Comment
Deposit-taking institutions[a]		
Regulatory capital to risk-weighted assets	Capital adequacy	Broad measure of capital, including items giving less protection against losses, such as subordinated debt, tax credits, and unrealized capital gains
Regulatory Tier I capital to risk-weighted assets	Capital adequacy	Highest quality capital such as shareholder equity and retained earnings, relative to risk-weighted assets
Nonperforming loans net of provisions to capital	Capital adequacy	Indicates the potential size of additional provisions that may be needed relative to capital
Nonperforming loans to total gross loans	Asset quality	Indicates the credit quality of banks' loans
Sectoral distribution of loans to total loans	Asset quality	Identifies exposure concentrations to particular sectors
Return on assets and return on equity	Earnings and profitability	Assesses scope for earnings to offset losses relative to capital or loan and asset portfolio
Interest margin to gross income	Earnings and profitability	Indicates the importance of net interest income and scope to absorb losses
Noninterest expenses to gross income	Earnings and profitability	Indicates extent to which high noninterest expenses weakens earnings
Liquid assets to total assets and liquid assets to short-term liabilities	Liquidity	Assesses the vulnerability of the sector to loss of access to market sources of funding or a run on deposits
Net open position in foreign exchange to capital	Exposure to FX risk	Measures foreign currency mismatch

a. Domestically controlled institutions, that may be grouped in different categories according to control, business lines, or group structure.

are drawn from macroeconomic measurement frameworks, which have been developed to monitor aggregate activity in the economy. A list of FSIs, grouped into a core set and an encouraged set, is presented in tables 2.3 and 2.4 and will be discussed in this chapter. Detailed exposition and guidance on those FSIs can be obtained from the *Compilation Guide on Financial Soundness Indicators* (IMF 2004). It contains a discussion of the distinction between a "core set" for which data are generally available and are found to be highly relevant for analytic purposes in almost all countries and an "encouraged set" for which data are not as readily available and whose relevance could vary across countries.[12]

The list of FSIs discussed herein consists mainly of aggregate balance sheet measures. This type of aggregation of individual institution-level indicators (microprudential indicators) into financial soundness indicators (macroprudential indicators) necessarily involves a loss of information because the distribution of prudential indicators of individual institutions is also a crucial dimension of financial stability. Although aggregation is required for facilitating macroprudential analysis and international comparison, the assessments could be strengthened by allowing some disaggregation through peer groups or through the monitoring of the distributional characteristics of various indicators. In addition, FSIs themselves are either backward-looking or contemporaneous indicators of financial soundness, available often with a lag or low frequency. Therefore, proper interpretation and use of FSIs requires a range of analytical tools (discussed in chapter 3), which includes conducting stress tests of individual institutions and monitoring the

2

Table 2.4. The Encouraged Set of Financial Soundness Indicators

Indicator	Indicates	Comment
Encouraged set[a]		
Corporate sector		
Total debt to equity	Leverage	Provides an indication of credit risk because a highly leveraged corporate sector is more vulnerable to shocks
Return on equity	Earnings and profitability	Indicates the extent to which earnings are available to cover losses
Earnings to interest and principal expenses	Debt service capacity	Indicates the extent to which earnings available to cover losses are reduced by interest and principal payments
Corporate net foreign exchange exposure to equity	Foreign exchange risk	Reveals corporate sector vulnerability to exchange rate movements
Number of applications for protection from creditors[b]		
Capital to assets	Capital adequacy	Broad measure of capital adequacy, which is a buffer for losses
Geographical distribution of loans to total loans	Asset quality	Identifies credit exposure concentrations to particular countries by the banking system
Gross asset position in financial derivatives to capital[c]	Exposure to derivatives	Provides a crude indicator of exposure to derivatives
Gross liability position in financial derivatives to capital[c]	Exposure to derivatives	Provides a crude indicator of exposure to derivatives
Large exposures to capital	Asset quality	Identifies credit exposure to large borrowers
Trading income to total income	Earning and profitability	Indicates the dependence on trading income
Personnel expenses to noninterest expenses	Earnings and profitability	Indicates the extent to which high noninterest expenses reduces earnings
Spread between reference lending and deposit rates	Earnings and profitability	Indicates level of competition in the banking sector and the dependence of earnings on the interest rate spread
Spread between highest and lowest interbank rate	Liquidity	Market indicator of counterparty risks in the interbank market
Customer deposits to total (non-interbank) loans	Liquidity	Assesses the vulnerability to loss of access to customer deposits
Foreign currency-denominated loans to total loans	Foreign exchange risk	Measures risk to loan portfolios from foreign exchange movements
Foreign currency-denominated liabilities to total liabilities	Foreign exchange risk	Measures extent of dollarization
Net open position in equities to capital	Equity market risk	Measures exposure to equity price movements
Market liquidity		
Average bid-ask spread in the securities market[d]	Liquidity	Indicates liquidity in the securities market
Average daily turnover ratio in the securities market[d]	Liquidity	Indicates liquidity in the securities market
Other financial corporations		
Assets to total financial system assets	Size	Indicates size and significance within the financial sector
Assets to GDP	Size	Indicates size and significance within the financial sector
Households		
Household debt to GDP	Leverage	Provides an indication of credit risk because a highly leveraged household sector is more vulnerable to shocks
Household debt service and principal payments to income	Debt service capacity	Indicates a household's ability to cover its debt payments
Real estate markets		
Real estate prices	Real estate prices	Measures trends in the real estate market
Residential real estate loans to total loans	Exposure to real estate	Measures banks' exposure to the residential real estate sector
Commercial real estate loans to total loans	Exposure to real estate	Measures banks' exposure to the commercial real estate sector
Other relevant indicators that are not formally part of the encouraged set of FSIs[e]		

a. See *Compilation Guide for Financial Soundness Indicators* (IMF 2004) for a detailed definition and exposition of encouraged indicators.
b. These may be grouped in different categories based on ownership, business lines, or group structure.
c. May be in notional amounts or market value. The latter provides a better measure of exposure but may be more difficult to obtain.
d. Or in other markets that are most relevant to bank liquidity, such as foreign exchange markets.
e. Other indicators such as additional balance sheet data (e.g., maturity mismatches in foreign currency), data on the life insurance sector, or information on the corporate and household sector may be added.

distribution of stress tests results, as well as examining the determinants of FSIs and forecasting their future course.

In addition, FSIs can be complemented by various market-based indicators, which are forward-looking indicators of soundness and are available with higher frequency. The various categories of FSIs are discussed in the following sections.

2.2.1 FSIs for Non-financial Sectors

Corporate sector indicators tend to focus on indicators of leverage (or gearing), profitability, liquidity, and debt-servicing capacity because of those indicators' demonstrated usefulness in predicting corporate distress or failure.[13] Four commonly used measures of corporate sector health are the debt-to-equity ratio, the return on equity, the cash ratio, and the debt service coverage (or interest coverage ratio). Total debt to equity measures leverage or the extent to which activities are financed out of other than own funds. High corporate leverage increases the vulnerability of corporations to shocks and may impair their repayment capacity. Return on equity is commonly used to capture profitability and efficiency in using capital. Over time, it can also provide information on the sustainability of capital positions. Profitability is a critical determinant of corporate strength, affecting the capital growth, the ability to withstand adverse events, and, ultimately, the repayment capacity. Sharp declines in corporate sector profitability, for example, as a result of economic deceleration, may serve as a leading indicator of financial difficulties.

The cash ratio is a measure of short-term assets held against short-term liabilities, after deductions for inventories and receivables. The cash ratio measures the capacity to absorb sudden changes in cash flows. Debt service coverage measures the capacity to cover debt service payments (interest and principal) and serves as an indicator of the risk that a firm may not be able to make the required payments on its debts. One commonly used measure of debt service coverage is the earnings before interest, taxes, depreciation, and amortization divided by debt servicing costs (principal plus interest). FSIs on the corporate sector can be compiled by aggregating data from the consolidated financial statements of publicly listed corporations and, thus, are a direct analog of the indicators used by shareholders and market participants to monitor the financial health of individual corporations. For the economy as a whole, domestically consolidated data (e.g., data based on National Income Accounts) can be used when corporate financial statements do not provide sufficient coverage.

Household sector indicators of leverage, liquidity, and debt servicing capacity can be useful in monitoring the health of the sector. Two common measures are used: the ratio of household debt to GDP, and the ratio of household debt burden to income. The household-debt-to-GDP ratio measures the overall level of household indebtedness (commonly related to consumer loans and mortgages) as a share of GDP. High levels of borrowing increase the vulnerability of the household sector to economic and financial market shocks and may impair their repayment capacity. The ratio of household debt burden to income measures the capacity of households to cover their debt payments (interest and principal). It is also a potentially significant predictor of future consumer spending growth: a high debt-to-service ratio sustained over several quarters can affect the rate of growth of personal consumption.[14]

Monitoring of the real estate sector tends to focus on indicators of significant swings in prices or volumes of lending and construction because this information often signals future problems in credit quality and collateral. Rapid increases in real estate prices—often fueled by expansionary monetary policies or by large capital inflows—that are followed by a sharp economic downturn can have a detrimental impact on financial sector health and soundness.[15] Ideally, a range of indicators should be analyzed to get a sense of real estate market developments (demand, supply, prices, and links to the business cycle) and to assess financial sector exposure to the real estate sector. If one is to determine the exposure of the banking sector to the real estate sector, it is important to have information on the size of the credit exposure and the riskiness of the exposure. Different types of loans related to real estate may have very different risk characteristics, so it may be useful to distinguish lending according to purpose (e.g., lending for commercial real estate or to construction companies and lending for residential real estate, including mortgages). The level of sophistication of the mortgage market (e.g., mortgage interest rate structure, availability of home equity release products) may also have implications for risk management and financial stability.

2.2.2 FSIs for Banking

Banking sector FSIs can provide useful quantitative information on the stability or vulnerability of the banking system.[16] Banking sector FSIs can be grouped according to six key areas of potential vulnerability in the CAMELS (**C**apital adequacy, **A**sset quality, **M**anagement soundness, **E**arnings and profitability, **L**iquidity, and **S**ensitivity to market risk) framework. Most FSIs are compiled by aggregating microprudential indicators for individual institutions to produce a measure for key peer groups such as domestically owned banks, local branches, foreign subsidiaries, state-owned banks, complex groups, or the entire banking system.[17] Non-bank FSIs (such as those for the corporate and household sectors or those for insurance) can be used to assess credit risks arising for banks from their credit and other exposures to non-bank sectors.

Each of the six subgroups of bank FSIs has a different part in the stability assessment. Indicators of capital adequacy can be used to measure the capacity of the sector to absorb losses. Because risks to the solvency of financial institutions most often derive from impairment of assets, the second category of FSIs is asset quality. FSIs in this category monitor loan quality and exposure concentrations of bank asset portfolios. Indicators of management efficiency are used to capture the importance of sound management in ensuring the health and stability of banks. A variety of data on margins, income, and expenses can be used to measure earnings and profitability because earnings indicate the ability to absorb losses without drawing on capital. In contrast, rapid growth in earnings or profits may also signal excessive risk taking. Measures of liquidity indicate the ability of a banking system to withstand shocks to cash flows. FSIs for liquidity measure the liquid assets available to a bank in the event of a loss of market funding or an outflow of deposits. Market liquidity measures also can be included to monitor the liquidity of the main securities held by banks. Banks are then exposed to market risk from their increasingly diversified operations and positions in financial instruments. Sensitivity to market risk (changes in market prices, particularly interest rates and exchange rates and, occasionally, equity prices) can be measured using information on net open positions, durations, and stress test results.

2.2.3 FSIs for Insurance

Quantitative soundness indicators for the insurance sector can be presented within a CARAMELS (**C**apital adequacy, **A**sset quality, **R**einsurance, **A**dequacy of claims and actuarial, **M**anagement soundness, **E**arnings and profitability, **L**iquidity, and **S**ensitivity to market risk) framework. This framework is analogous to the CAMELS framework for the banking sector. Das, Davies, and Podpiera (2003) propose a set of core and encouraged soundness indicators for the insurance sector (grouped separately for life and non–life insurance). The core indicators presented in table 2.5 are those considered necessary for adequate surveillance of the sector whereas the encouraged set includes additional indicators that are useful in monitoring more specific areas of vulnerability.

2.2.4 FSIs for Securities Markets

The stability of securities markets can be monitored using a range of quantitative indicators that focus on market liquidity because of the important role that liquid securities play

Table 2.5. Insurance Financial Soundness Indicators: Core Set

Category	*Indicator*	*Non-life*	*Life*
Capital adequacy	Net premium/capital	X	
	Capital/total assets	X	
	Captial/technical reserves		X
Asset quality	(Real estate + unquoted equities + debtors)/total assets	X	X
	Receivables/(Gross premium + reinsurance recoveries)	X	X
	Equities/total assets	X	X
	Nonperforming loans to total gross loans		X
Reinsurance and actuarial issues	Risk retention ratio (net premium/gross premium)	X	X
	Net technical reserves/average of net claims paid in last three years	X	
	Net technical reserves/average of net premium received in last three years		X
Management soundness	Gross premium/number of employees	X	X
	Assets per employee (total assets/number of employees)	X	X
Earnings and profitability	Loss ratio (net claims/net premium)	X	
	Expense ratio (expense/net premium)	X	X
	Combined ratio = loss ratio + expense ratio	X	
	Revisions to technical reserves/technical reserves		X
	Investment income/net premium	X	
	Investment income/investment assets		X
	Return on equity (ROE)	X	X
Liquidity	Liquid assets/current liabilities	X	X
Sensitivity to market risk	Net open foreign exchange position/capital	X	X
	Duration of assets and liabilities		X

Note: Relevance to life or non-life segment of Insurance is indicated by X.
Source: Das et al. (2003). The authors also propose a set of encouraged indicators for each of the above categories in order to capture additional dimensions. These include sectoral and geographic distribution of investments and underwritten business, derivative exposures, risk weighted capital ratio, market based indicators (market/ book value, price/ earnings, and price/ gross premium ratios), and measures of Group exposures (group debts/ total assets, proportion of business from group companies (Premium + claims)/ total business.

2

in the balance sheets of financial institutions.[18] Market liquidity can be defined as a measure of volume of securities that can be sold in a relatively short period without having a significant effect on their price. The literature typically recognizes two key dimensions of market liquidity: tightness and depth. Tightness is a market's ability to match supply and demand at low cost. The bid-ask spread FSI may serve as an approximate index of tightness in each market, in that a narrower spread indicates a more competitive market with a larger number of buyers and sellers providing liquidity. Depth relates to the ability of a market to absorb large trade flows without a significant effect on prices. When market participants raise concerns about the decline in market liquidity, they typically refer to a reduced ability to deal without having prices move against them; that is, they refer to reduced market depth. The FSI of market turnover (gross average daily value of securities traded relative to the stock) helps assess the liquidity of banks' balance sheets by giving an indication of the volume of securities that institutions can liquidate in the market. Market depth also can be approximated by other volume variables, quota sizes, on-the-run–off-the-run spreads, and volatilities.

2.2.5 Market-Based Indicators of Financial Soundness

Market-based measures drawn from price and volatility measures of various capital market instruments can provide forward-looking indicators of financial soundness. For example, default probabilities (for banks and non-banks) may be computed on the basis of models of credit risk, using equity prices and balance sheet data. In some cases, volatilities and risk premiums in market prices themselves provide indicators of likelihood of default. Further discussion of those indicators is contained in chapter 3.

2.3 Aggregate Balance Sheet Structure of Financial and Non-financial Sectors—Inter-sectoral Linkages

Analysis of stock variables in countries' sectoral balance sheets (assets and liabilities of financial firms, non-financial firms, households, government, and sub-sectors of those sectors, as appropriate) and the consolidated aggregate balance sheet (for the country) can help highlight inter-sectoral linkages and can provide valuable information on the adequacy of financial structure and on the potential for financial instability. The balance sheet analysis focuses on (a) the determinants and evolution of stocks of assets and liabilities and (b) the likely shocks to the stock variables, both of which can trigger large adjustments in flows (including cross-border capital flows, shifts in holdings of domestic or foreign currency assets, etc.). An approach of this type can, therefore, be a useful complement to the traditional flow analysis that is based on data related to fiscal, balance-of-payments, and financial programming. A classification of claims on and liabilities to any one sector from other sectors can reveal both the extent of access to financial services (in providing savings instruments, in offering credit intermediation, and in providing risk diversification and insurance) and the extent of inter-sectoral linkages that highlight the potential effect of shocks in one sector on the other. In addition, balance sheet data classified by maturity, currency, contractual nature of liabilities (e.g., debt versus equity), and

Box 2.1 The Balance Sheet Approach—An Overview

Applications and Policy Implications

Availability of comprehensive data on sectoral balance sheets permits the analysis of relationship between financial sector and real sectors (households, corporations, etc.) and how the deterioration in one can be reinforced or offset by a strengthening of the other. In particular, capital account crises typically occur because of a sudden loss of confidence in the soundness of the balance sheets of one of the countries' main sectors: the banking system, the corporate sector, the households, or the government. The negative impact of an initial adverse shock to a balance sheet will depend on the existing mismatches in the balance sheet. The currency mismatch (a predominance of domestic currency assets over foreign currency liabilities) or a maturity mismatch (a predominance of long-term illiquid assets over short-term liquid liabilities) can expose the vulnerability of a sector to sharp movements in exchange rate or interest rate or both, which arise from the initial confidence shock, and it can lead to spillover into other sectors, often snowballing in the process. For example, a capital structure mismatch of firms (a predominance of debt over own funds and equity liabilities in the balance sheet) can result in unsustainable debt servicing burden because of an exchange rate or interest rate shock, thus leading to insolvency of firms, and illiquidity and insolvency of financial firms with exposures to the highly leveraged firms.

A loss of confidence in the banking system can lead, in turn, to runs on deposits and flight from currency, thereby exacerbating the initial currency and interest rate shock. Banking crisis also could trigger the realization of contingent liabilities of the government, as well as weaken the government balance sheet and threaten government debt sustainability. This type of interaction among balance sheets could magnify the negative impact of a shock on real output levels. Policy implications of the balance sheet analysis focus on policies to foster a buffering and hedging of private balance sheets, including effective banking supervision to ensure strong risk management by banks, sound public debt and reserve management that effectively balances costs and rollover risks, and promotion of domestic capital markets to ensure currency diversification. Moreover, macroeconomic policy mix would need to take into account the constraints posed by the balance sheet mismatches such as the tradeoff between interest rate and exchange rate adjustments in the presence of maturity and exchange rate mismatches.

The financial sector's balance sheets are key for the resilience of the economy. The relationship between the financial sector balance sheet and the corporate and household balance sheets as well as the impact of shocks on these balance sheets typically are analyzed in financial sector assessments as part of the macroprudential analysis and the related stress–testing exercises. (See chapter 3 for further details.)

Data Availability and Limitations

A comprehensive analysis of sectoral balance sheets is often constrained by a lack of relevant data. The absence of this information often leads to a focus on a few key stock positions in the public sector balance sheet and in listed companies' balance sheets. Therefore, for many countries, balance sheet information beyond what is readily available must be gathered before complete intersectoral analysis is feasible. Some efforts are under way to establish good databases on balance sheets. The efforts to promote the compilation and dissemination of financial soundness indicators focuses on the needs of financial stability analysis. Other ongoing efforts in improving the providing of data to the Fund are designed to strengthen availability of detailed balance sheet data on external and public sector assets and liabilities.

Although it is widely recognized that balance sheet analysis of the corporate sector is key to financial stability analysis, the availability of data poses practical limitations. Typically, data are available only for listed companies; however, a much more comprehensive and differentiated analysis of the sector is needed to understand fully the access to financial services and vulnerabilities to financial risks of this sector.

Financial stability reports published by various countries have increasingly relied on systematic analysis of balance sheet data, thereby creating a demand for strengthened data compilation and dissemination systems. When balance sheet data are not available in sufficient sectoral detail, the flow of funds information (data on changes in assets and liabilities of different sectors) can be a useful alternative because the real and financial transactions that underpin the flow of funds accounts are the means by which balance sheet adjustments take place. Data from sectoral balance sheets and from the flow of funds suffer from a number of measurement difficulties: (a) available information is typically based on book (or transaction) values that may differ sharply from market values, (b) data on off-balance sheet exposures are not well captured, and (c) sharp portfolio adjustments in response to shifts in relative asset prices and new information may render data that are based on historical accounting records to become quickly outdated.

2

Table 2.6. Stylized Framework for Presenting Financial Interlinkages between Sectors in an Economy

Sector A's balance sheet[a]

Assets of Sector A	Liabilities of Sector A
Financial claims on	Financial obligations to
Sector B by currency by maturity	Sector B by currency by maturity
Sector C by currency by maturity	Sector C by currency by maturity
Sector D by currency by maturity	Sector D by currency by maturity
Sector E[b] by currency by maturity	Sector E[b] by currency by maturity
Net worth/net[b] International investment[b]	

Note: A = government sector; B = banking system; C = non-bank financial sector; D = non-financial private; E = rest of world.

a. Similar sectoral balance sheets can be constructed for each sector in line with those in the System of National Accounts (United Nations, Commission of the European Communities, International Monetary Fund, Organisation for Economic Co-operation and Development, and World Bank 1993); the *Monetary and Financial Statistics Manual* (IMF 2000) also provides advice for compilation of accounts with limited data. In practice, presenting information on currency exposures and maturity may be challenging in many countries.

b. When consolidating the sectoral balance sheets into the country's balance sheet, the assets and liabilities held among residents net out, leaving the country's external balance relative to the rest of the world (nonresidents), which is shown as sector E. In the official balance-of-payments statistics, the difference between external financial assets and liabilities is the net international investment position. For other sectors, the difference between financial assets and liabilities is net worth or capital position of the sector.

quality of the assets can help to analyze how balance sheet imbalances in one sector could trigger changes in demand for financial assets of one or more sectors that could trigger financial instability. Recent work on the analytical uses and policy implications of balance sheet data—The Balance Sheet Approach—and some issues in compilation of balance sheet information are highlighted in box 2.1.

Illustrative sectoral balance sheets shown in table 2.6 highlight important information on sectoral interlinkages that will remain hidden in the consolidated country balance sheets. If sectoral balance sheet data can be disaggregated, as shown in the table, to allow the measurement of mismatches in the balance sheet by currency, maturity, and capital structure, then this type of information helps to analyze vulnerability to various shocks.

Some sources of sectoral balance sheet data are noted, as follows. Company finance statistics compiled by Bank of Korea (Financial Statements Analysis) provide balance sheet and income statements for listed and unlisted firms at a detailed level of industrial classification. Annual data on financial assets and liabilities of households in New Zealand are published in Reserve Bank of New Zealand Web site.[19] Those kinds of data help to analyze the effects that macroeconomic shocks have on the soundness of firms and households. The framework for compiling and presenting a government balance sheet is presented in the *Government Finance Statistics Manual* (IMF 2001), and this framework has been applied in several countries (e.g., Ecuador, Uruguay). The issues in the compilation of financial sector balance sheets are discussed in IMF's *Compilation Guide on Financial Soundness Indicators* (IMF 2004). The balance sheet analysis of financial sector is routinely undertaken in all financial sector assessments as part of macroprudential analysis, which is explained in chapter 3.

Notes

1. To get a more useful indication of financial size, central bank assets should be excluded from this calculation.
2. Although this ratio is one of the most popular measures of financial depth, the M2 to GDP ratio could be misleading if currency constitutes a high proportion of broad money.
3. Where available, this ratio should include non-bank forms of intermediation, for example, issues of bonds and money market instruments.
4. For a definition of large and complex financial institutions, see Miles (2002).
5. It is advisable to supplement these measures with other indicators of competition. See chapter 4 for a discussion of model-based indicators of competition.
6. For an example of the computation of the Herfindahl index, see chapter 15 of the *Compilation Guide on Financial Soundness Indicators* (IMF 2004).
7. See chapter 8 of the *Compilation Guide on Financial Soundness Indicators* (IMF 2004).
8. Issued by the Committee on Payment Settlement Systems of the Bank For International Settlements. See Chapter 11 for a detailed discussion of these core principles.
9. See Levine (1997) for more information.
10. See World Bank (2004). Chapter 4 has a brief discussion of access, including an analysis of different approaches to measuring access.
11. See Honohan (2004) for a discussion of various sources of survey data and proposals for basic national access indicators.
12. See also chapter 3.
13. For a survey, see Altman and Narayanan (1997). In the wake of the Asian crisis, numerous authors have demonstrated the close links between poor corporate performance and banking system distress; for example, see Pomerleano (1998).
14. See Debelle (2004) for an overview of household debt and its effect on the macroeconomy and implications for financial stability.
15. See Borio and McGuire (2004), and see Bank for International Settlements (2005) for an overview of housing price dynamics and implications for financial stability.
16. For more details of how to use FSIs to assess banking soundness, see IMF (2004, chapters 6, 8, and 14) and Evans and others (2000).
17. The particular peer groups chosen can be based on the structure of the banking system and the underlying source of weaknesses, so vulnerabilities are not masked but are highlighted by the choice of peer group.
18. See chapter 8 of IMF (2004) for an overview of statistics on securities markets. Two works of the Bank for International Settlements (BIS; 1999, 2001) also provide a detailed discussion of market liquidity, including its measurement and analysis.

19. The Web site for the Reserve Bank of New Zealand is available at http://www.rbnz. govt.nz./statistics/monfin/index.html.

References

Altman, Edward I., and Paul Narayanan. 1997. "Business Failure Classification Models: An International Survey." In *International Accounting and Finance Handbook*, ed. Frederick Choi, chapter 35, 2nd ed. New York: Wiley.

Bank for International Settlements (BIS). 1999. "Market Liquidity: Research Findings and Selected Policy Implications." *CGFS Publication 11* (May), Bank for International Settlements, Basel, Switzerland.

———. 2001. "Structural Aspects of Market Liquidity from a Financial Stability Perspective." A discussion note for the March 2001 meeting of the Financial Stability Forum. Available at http://www.bis.org/publ/cgfs_note01.pdf.

———. 2005. "Real Estate Indicators and Financial Stability." BIS Paper 21, Bank for International Settlements, Basel, Switzerland.

Begum, Jahanara, May Khamis, and Kal Wajid. 2001. "Usefulness of Sectoral Balance Sheet information for Assessing Financial System Vulnerabilities." Computer print-out, International Monetary Fund, Washington, DC.

Borio, Claudio, and Patrick McGuire. 2004. "Twin Peaks in Equity and Housing Prices?" *BIS Quarterly Review 7* (March 2004): 79–96. Available at http://www.bis.org/publ/qtrpdf/r_qt0403.pdf.

Das Udabir S., Nigel Davies, and Richard Podpiera. 2003. "Insurance Issues in Financial Soundness." IMF Working Paper 03/138, International Monetary Fund, Washington, DC.

Debelle, Guy. 2004. "Household Debt and the Macroeconomy." *BIS Quarterly Review*, (March): 51–64.

Evans, Owen, Alfredo Leone, Mahinder Gill, and Paul Hilbers. 2000. "Macroprudential Indicators of Financial System Soundness." IMF Occasional Paper 192, International Monetary Fund, Washington, DC.

Honahan, Patrick. 2004. "Measuring Microfinance Access: Building on Existing Cross-Country Data." UNDP, World Bank, and IMF Workshop on Data on Access of Poor and Low-Income People to Financial Services, World Bank, Washington DC, October 26.

International Monetary Fund. 2000. *Monetary and Financial Statistics Manual*. Washington, DC: International Monetary Fund.

———. 2001. *Government Finance Statistics Manual*. Washington DC: International Monetary Fund.

———. 2002. "A Balance Sheet Approach to Financial Crisis." IMF Working Paper 02/210, International Monetary Fund, Washington, DC.

———. 2004. *Compilation Guide on Financial Soundness Indicators*. Washington, DC: International Monetary Fund. Available at http://www.imf.org/external/np/sta/fsi/eng/2004/guide/index.htm.

Levine, R. 1997. "Financial Development and Economic Growth: Views and Agenda." *Journal of Economic Literature* Vol. 35, (June): 688–726.

Miles, Colin. 2002. "Large Complex Financial Institutions (LCFIs): Issues to Be Considered in the Financial Sector Assessment Program." International Monetary Fund, Monetary and Exchange Affairs Department, MAE Operational Paper 02/3. International Monetary Fund, Washington, DC.

Pomerleano, Michael. 1998. "The East Asia Crisis and Corporate Finances: The Untold Micro Story." World Bank Working Paper 1990 (October). World Bank Group, Washington, DC.

United Nations, Commission of the European Communities, International Monetary Fund, Organisation for Economic Co-operation and Development, and World Bank. 1993. *System of National Accounts*. Series F, No. 2. New York: United Nations.

World Bank. 2004. *Brazil: Access to Financial Services*, Washington, DC: World Bank.

Chapter 3

Assessing Financial Stability

Financial system stability in a broad sense means both the avoidance of financial institutions failing in large numbers and the avoidance of serious disruptions to the intermediation functions of the financial system: payments, savings facilities, credit allocation, efforts to monitor users of funds, and risk mitigation and liquidity services. Within this broad definition, financial stability can be seen in terms of a continuum on which financial systems can be operating inside a stable corridor, near the boundary with instability, or outside the stable corridor (instability).[1]

Financial stability analysis is intended to help identify threats to financial system stability and to design appropriate policy responses.[2] It focuses on exposures, buffers, and linkages to assess the soundness and vulnerabilities of the financial system, as well as the economic, regulatory, and institutional determinants of financial soundness and stability. It considers whether the financial sector exhibits vulnerabilities that could trigger a liquidity or solvency crisis, amplify macroeconomic shocks, or impede policy responses to shocks.[3] The monitoring and analysis of financial stability involves an assessment of macroeconomic conditions, soundness of financial institutions and markets, financial system supervision, and the financial infrastructure to determine what the vulnerabilities are in the financial system and how they are being managed. Depending on this assessment of the extent of the financial system's stability, policy prescriptions may include continuing prevention (when the financial system is inside the stable corridor), remedial action (when it is approaching instability), and resolution (when it is experiencing instability).

3.1 Overall Framework for Stability Analysis and Assessment

The analytic framework to monitor financial stability is centered around macroprudential surveillance and is complemented by surveillance of financial markets, analysis of

3

macrofinancial linkages, and surveillance of macroeconomic conditions. These four key elements play distinct roles in financial stability analysis.

- Surveillance of financial markets helps to assess the risk that a particular shock or a combination of shocks will hit the financial sector. Models used in this area of surveillance include early warning systems (EWSs). Indicators used in the analysis include financial market data and macro-data, as well as other variables that can be used for constructing early warning indicators (see section 3.2).
- Macroprudential surveillance tries to assess the health of the financial system and its vulnerability to potential shocks. The key quantitative analytical tools used for macroprudential surveillance are the monitoring of financial soundness indicators (FSIs) and the conducting of stress tests. Those tools are used to map the conditions of non-financial sectors into financial sector vulnerabilities. The analysis also draws on qualitative data such as the results of assessments of quality of supervision and the robustness of financial infrastructure (see section 3.3).
- Analysis of macrofinancial linkages attempts to understand the exposures that can cause shocks to be transmitted through the financial system to the macroeconomy. This analysis looks at data such as (a) balance sheets of the various sectors in the economy and (b) indicators of access to financing by the private sector (to assess the extent to which private owners would be able to inject new capital to cover the potential losses identified through macroprudential surveillance) (see section 3.4).
- Surveillance of macroeconomic conditions then monitors the effect of the financial system on macroeconomic conditions in general and on debt sustainability in particular (see section 3.4).

Assessing financial stability is a complex process. In practice, the assessment requires several iterations. For example, the effects of the financial system on macroeconomic conditions may produce feedback effects on the financial system. The profile of risks and vulnerabilities (ascertained through macroprudential surveillance) could feed into qualitative assessments of effectiveness of supervision, and those effects, in turn, might influence the analysis of vulnerabilities and overall assessment of financial stability.

3.2 Macroeconomic and Financial Market Developments

An analysis of macroeconomic and financial developments provides an important context for the analysis of financial sector vulnerabilities. The goal of the surveillance of macroeconomic developments and of financial markets is to provide a forward-looking assessment of the likelihood of extreme shocks that can hit the financial system.

The literature on EWSs—which deals with factors that cause financial crises—provides useful guidance for this mode of analysis. EWSs try—in a statistically optimal way (i.e., in a way that minimizes "false alarms" and missed crises)—to combine a number of indicators into a single measure of the risk of a crisis. EWSs do not have perfect forecasting accuracy, but they offer a systematic method to predict crises. Two approaches to constructing EWS models have become common: the indicators approach (Kaminsky,

Lizondo, and Reinhart 1998, and Kaminsky 1999) and limited dependent variable probit–logit models (Berg and Pattillo 1999). Berg and others (2000) assess the performance of those models and find that they have outperformed alternative measures of vulnerability, such as bond spreads and credit ratings. However, although those models can anticipate some crises, they also generate many false alarms.[4]

EWS models are seen as one of a number of inputs into the IMF's surveillance process, which encompasses a comprehensive and intensive policy dialogue. The IMF puts significant efforts into developing EWS models for emerging market economies, which resulted, among other things, in influential papers by Kaminsky, Lizondo, and Reinhart (1998) and by Berg and Pattillo (1999). The IMF uses a combination of EWS approaches, in particular, the Developing Country Studies Division model and a modification of the Kaminsky, Lizondo, and Reinhart model, both of which use macro-based indicators of currency crises (IMF 2002b). It also makes use of market-based models that rely on implied probability of default and balance-sheet-based vulnerability indicators (e.g., see Gapen and others 2004).

In recent years, other institutions and individuals have also developed EWS models. Those efforts included EWS models developed or studied by staff members at the U.S. Federal Reserve (Kamin, Schindler, and Samuel 2001), the European Central Bank (Bussiere and Fratzscher 2002), and the Bundesbank (Schnatz 1998). Academics and various private sector institutions also developed a range of EWS models. The private sector EWS models include Goldman Sachs's GS-watch (Ades, Masih, and Tenengauzer 1998), Credit Suisse First Boston's (CSFB's) Emerging Markets Risk Indicator (EMRI) (Roy 2001), Deutsche Bank's Alarm Clock (Garber, Lumsdaine, and Longato 2001), and Moody's Macro Risk model (e.g., Gray, Merton, and Bodie 2003).

The EWS literature covers three main types of crises: currency crises (sudden, sizable depreciation of the exchange rate and loss of reserves), debt crises (default or restructuring on external debt), and banking crises (rundown of bank deposits and widespread failures of financial institutions). One can distinguish three "generations" of crises models, depending on what determinants the models take into account. The first generation focuses on macroeconomic imbalances (e.g., Krugman 1979). The second generation focuses on self-fulfilling speculative attacks, contagion, and weakness in domestic financial markets (e.g., Obstfeld 1996). The third generation of models introduces the role of moral hazard as a cause of excessive borrowing and suggests that asset prices can be a useful leading indicator of crises (e.g., Chang and Velasco 2001). In general, empirical studies (e.g., Berg and others 2000) suggest that currency crises occur more often than debt crises (roughly 6:1) and that a large portion of the debt crises happened along with or close to the currency crises. Banking crises are hard to identify, tend to be protracted, and, thus, have a larger macroeconomic effect. Banking crises also tend to occur with or shortly after a currency crisis.

Forecasting banking crises is based on three approaches:

- The macroeconomic approach is based on the idea that macroeconomic policies cause crisis, and it tries to predict banking crises using macroeconomic variables. For example, Demirgüç-Kunt and Detragiache (1998) study the factors of systemic banking crises in a large sample of countries using a multivariate logit model and

3

find that crises tend to erupt when growth is low and inflation is high. They also find some association between banking sector problems, on the one hand, and high real interest rates, the vulnerability to balance of payments crises, the existence of an explicit deposit insurance scheme, and weak law enforcement, on the other hand.

- The bank balance-sheet approach assumes that poor banking practices cause crises and that bank failures can be predicted by balance-sheet data (e.g., Sahajwala and Van den Berg 2000; Jagtiani and others 2003).

- The market indicators approach assumes that equity and debt prices contain information on bank conditions beyond that of balance-sheet data. Market-based EWS models are based on the premise that financial asset prices contain information on market beliefs about the future. In particular, option prices reflect market beliefs about the future prices of the underlying assets. This information can be used to extract a probability distribution, namely, the probability of default. The advantage of equity and debt data is that they can be available in high frequency and that they should provide a forward-looking assessment (e.g., Bongini, Laeven, and Majnoni 2002; Gropp, Vesala, and Vulpes 2002).[5]

3.3 Macroprudential Surveillance Framework

Surveillance of the soundness of the financial sector as a whole—which is macroprudential surveillance—complements the surveillance of individual financial institutions by supervisors—which is microprudential surveillance. Macroprudential surveillance derives from the need to identify risks to the stability of the system as a whole, resulting from the collective effect of the activities of many institutions.

Macroprudential analysis also closely complements and reinforces EWSs and other analytical tools for monitoring vulnerabilities and preventing crises. EWSs traditionally focus on vulnerabilities in the external position while using macroeconomic indicators as key explanatory variables. Macroprudential analysis (analysis of FSIs and stress testing) focuses on vulnerabilities in domestic financial systems arising from macroeconomic shocks, whose likelihood and severity can be judged from EWSs. At the same time, information from macroprudential analysis can provide input into assessing macroeconomic vulnerabilities. Analysis of FSIs for individual banks, along with other supervisory information, serves as a form of EWS for the financial condition of individual banks in many supervisory assessment systems (Sahajwala and Van den Berg 2000).

Macroprudential surveillance uses a combination of qualitative and quantitative methods. The key qualitative methods focus on the quality of the legal, judicial, and regulatory framework, as well as governance practices in the financial sector and its supervision. An important part of the qualitative information is often gathered through the assessments of internationally accepted standards and codes of best practice. The quantitative methods include a combination of statistical indicators and techniques designed to summarize the soundness and resilience of the financial system.

The two key quantitative tools of macroprudential surveillance are the analysis of FSIs and stress testing. The analysis of FSIs includes assessing their variation over time and among peer groups, as well as assessing their determinants. FSIs help to assess the vulnerability of the financial sector to shocks. Stress testing assesses the vulnerability of a financial system to exceptional but plausible events by providing an estimate of how the value of each financial institution's portfolio will change when there are large changes to some of its risk factors (such as asset prices).

3.3.1 Analysis of Financial Soundness Indicators

FSIs are used to monitor the financial system's vulnerability to shocks and its capacity to absorb the resulting losses. Work on FSIs has produced a set of core FSIs and a set of encouraged FSIs (see chapter 2).[6]

- The *core set* of FSIs covers only the banking sector, thereby reflecting its central role. Those FSIs are considered essential for surveillance in virtually every financial system and, thus, serve as a small common set of FSIs across countries. Also, the data to compile those FSIs are generally available.
- The *encouraged set* of FSIs covers additional FSIs for the banking system and FSIs for key non-financial sectors because balance-sheet weaknesses in those sectors are a source of credit risk for banks and, thus, help detect banking sector vulnerabilities at an earlier stage. The encouraged set of FSIs are relevant in many, but not all, countries.

The choice of FSIs depends on the structure of a country's financial system and data availability. Although the core set provides an initial prioritization, the choice should not be limited to this set. In bank-dominated systems, the core and some relevant encouraged FSIs may be adequate. FSIs for other types of financial institutions may be needed if those institutions are systemically important. Of course, some countries may have other relevant indicators that are not included in the core or encouraged sets that may need to be monitored. In countries with well-developed markets, with information on key prices, spreads, and price volatility, other market information, including ratings, can be used as market-based indicators to monitor risks in individual sectors and institutions and to help assess the evolution of relative risks, thereby facilitating supervision and macroprudential surveillance (see box 3.1).

The analysis of FSIs typically involves examination of trends, comparison between relevant peer groups of countries and institutions, and disaggregation into various groupings. Control is often an important criterion for disaggregation because it can indicate the sources of outside support that are potentially available to institutions in distress and thus can influence their vulnerability to bank runs, as well as their exposure to cross-border contagion.

Domestically controlled banks are overseen by a country's central bank and supervisor and, in a crisis, would be recapitalized by the banks' domestic owners or otherwise by the state. Within this peer group, public banks, which have a state guarantee, are typically distinguished from private banks, which may fail if losses exceed some minimum level of capital and consequently may be more prone to bank runs. Within the group of domestically owned, private banks, internationally active banks may be grouped into a separate peer group because they are exposed to cross-border contagion. Those banks could entail

3

Box 3.1 Market-Based Indicators of Financial Soundness

Market-based indicators are among the key data sets used by macroprudential analysis, along with aggregated prudential data, macroeconomic data, stress tests, structural data, and qualitative information. They include market prices of financial instruments, indicators of excess yields, market volatility, credit ratings, and sovereign yield spreads.

The market-based indicators have a wide array of uses. In particular, market prices of financial instruments issued by financial institutions and their corporate counterparts can be used to assess financial soundness of the issuers. Sovereign yield spreads are commonly watched indicators of country risk. Market price data from the stock, bond, derivatives, real estate, and other financial markets can be used to monitor sources of shocks to the financial sector. Indicators of market price volatility can help assess the market risk environment. Finally, sovereign ratings and ratings of financial institutions and other firms (as well as the accompanying analysis by the rating companies) are important sources of information to any analysis of vulnerabilities.[a]

Analysis of the market-based indicators complements the analysis of aggregated microprudential data. The use of market-based indicators to monitor financial institutions' soundness is based on the premise that market prices of financial institutions' securities could reveal information about their conditions beyond that of balance-sheet data and other aggregated microprudential data. If this premise is true, then the market-based indicators can usefully complement the FSIs, a majority of which—including all core FSIs—are based on aggregating financial institutions' microprudential data. The key premise is that the asset prices contain information on market beliefs, which, in turn, contain information about the future. In particular, option prices reflect market beliefs about the future prices of the underlying assets. This information can be used to extract a probability distribution, including the probability of default.

An advantage of using market prices rather than prudential data is that the price data are generally available at high frequency. The advantage of equity and debt data is that they are frequent, which allows for more sophisticated analysis, such as the analysis of volatility and covariance. Also, although the accounting measures of risk (such as nonperforming loans [NPLs] and loan loss reserves) are essentially backward looking, market price data should provide a forward-looking assessment (e.g., Bongini, Laeven,

and Majnoni 2002; Gropp, Vesala, and Vulpes 2002). In addition, confidentiality is generally not an issue with market data, which should make it easier for independent analysts to obtain input data and for the results to be publicly shared and verified.

The quality of the market-based indicators depends on the extent and quality of the financial markets. For asset prices to contain useful information, it is important that the market be robust and transparent. If it is not, then asset prices may be substantially affected by factors other than the financial health of the issuer or the underlying quality of the asset. In addition, the usefulness of market-based indicators to assess financial sector soundness may be limited if some financial institutions' securities are not publicly traded or if their trading is limited (as may be the case, for instance, for government-owned banks or family-owned banks). Finally, if relevant information is not publicly disclosed (e.g., loan classification data that are not disclosed in some countries), but if that type of information is collected by supervisors, then prudential data can be superior to market-based indicators in measuring financial sector soundness. However, market-based indicators can still be useful in assessing the potential shocks to the financial institutions arising from or transmitted through financial markets.

Empirical studies show that market prices can be helpful in forecasting bank distress. For example, recent studies for the United States suggest that subordinated yields explain not only bank rating changes but also regulatory capital ratios (Evanoff and Wall 2001), that equity prices provide useful information on bank failure (Gunther, Levonian, and Moore 2001), and that both equity prices and bond yields explain ratings (Krainer and Lopez 2003).

However, early warning systems that combine market information with other data tend to perform better than the nonmodel market-based indicators. Berg and Borensztein (2004) find that "market views," as expressed in spreads, ratings, and surveys, are not reliable crisis predictors, important as they may be in determining market access. They find that early warning system models, which combine a range of indicators, have outperformed purely market-based measures of vulnerability such as bond spreads and credit ratings. Their study was focused on predicting currency crises, but there is even less evidence about the market indicators' efficiency in predicting banking sector crises.

a. When assigning ratings, rating companies typically use a range of analytical approaches and data, including available prudential indicators. Nonetheless, ratings are classified as market-based indicators, thus recognizing that they are produced mainly for use by market participants.

significant risk exposure through their foreign branches and subsidiaries. FSIs should include the activities of those foreign branches and subsidiaries, even though the latter are not part of the domestic activity, because they are a source of risk to the banking system.

For the domestic branches and subsidiaries of foreign-controlled banks, support in a crisis can be expected to come in the first instance from their foreign owners. This type of support may be based (a) on the foreign bank's legal obligation, which generally extends to branches but not to subsidiaries abroad; (b) on broader reputation or operating concerns, which may lead the foreign bank to support its subsidiaries abroad in a crisis; or (c) both of those elements. At the same time, FSIs of the foreign parent banks may also deserve examination because the soundness of the parent bank would influence not only the potential for support to its subsidiaries but also the risk of contagion. Those FSIs are typically produced by the home country of the parent bank. When foreign-controlled deposit-takers play a significant role in the financial system, separate FSIs may need to be compiled for the local subsidiaries of those deposit-takers.

Quantitative information on the structure, ownership, and degree of concentration of the financial system helps to set priorities for analyzing FSIs while also providing a basis for the identification of structural issues and developmental needs. This information indicates the relative importance of different types of financial institutions (e.g., banks, securities companies, insurance companies, pension funds); the relative importance of different types of ownership (private, public, foreign); and the concentration of ownership. It provides a basic understanding of the main components of the sector and its degree of diversification (see chapters 2 and 4 for a further discussion of financial structure and its determinants).

3.3.1.1 Analysis of FSIs for Banking[7]

In most countries, banks form the core of the financial system and, thus, warrant close monitoring for indications of potential vulnerabilities. A range of quantitative indicators can be used to analyze the health and stability of the banking system, including financial soundness indicators (aggregated microprudential indicators), market-based indicators of financial conditions, structural indicators describing ownership and concentration patterns, and macroeconomic indicators. A range of qualitative information is also needed to assess the banking system, including the strength of the regulatory framework (which is based on assessments of the Basel Core Principles, or BCP), the functioning of the payment system, accounting and auditing standards, the legal infrastructure, the liquidity support arrangements, and the financial sector safety nets.

Banking sector FSIs discussed in chapter 2 cover capital adequacy, asset quality, management soundness, earnings and profitability, liquidity, and sensitivity to market risk. An analysis of inter-linkages among those FSIs and their macroeconomic and institutional determinants, together with an assessment of their sensitivity to various shocks through stress tests, provide the basic building blocks of financial stability analysis.[8]

The linkages not only among the various groups of FSIs but also to other variables are derived from accounting and lending relationships within the financial sector and with other non-financial sectors. They also reflect institutional determinants, such as the key parameters of the prudential framework. Topics studied in this area include, for example, determinants of asset quality, links between asset quality changes and capital, and determinants of profitability, all of which are discussed below.

One important topic of study involves determinants of asset quality. Asset quality is affected by the state of the business cycle, the corporate financial structure, and the level of real interest rates, which, together, influence the capacity for debt servicing. Therefore, in empirical work, FSIs of asset quality are typically regressed on various explanatory variables, such as corporate leverage, macroeconomic conditions, and interest rates. In some assessments, those types of regression estimates were based on panel data for banks in a country; in other cases, time series of aggregate data were used. As an example of cross-country time series regression, the IMF (2003c) estimated the relationship between corporate sector FSIs and banking sector asset quality FSIs on panel data compiled from large private databases for 47 countries over 10 years. It found that a 10 percentage point increase in corporate leverage was generally associated with a 1.8 percentage point rise in NPLs relative to total loans after one year. Also, a 1 percentage point rise in GDP growth resulted in a 2.6 percentage point decline in the NPLs-to-loans ratio, reflecting the fact that fewer corporations are likely to experience problems repaying loans during rapid growth.

Links between asset quality changes and capital are also studied. A deterioration in asset quality affects capital (and risk-weighted assets) through additional reserves that banks need to hold against the additional bad assets. The additional reserves reflect the rules in the country involving loan loss provisioning and the application of those rules in banking practice. Therefore, to model this link, one needs to understand well the prudential and supervisory framework in the country in question, which is where the findings of the BCP assessments can be of great help. The link between asset quality (and other risk factors) and capital is typically studied in the context of stress tests (see appendix D on stress testing for references on this issue).

Another important topic of study involves the determinants of profitability. There is a large theoretical and empirical literature on the bank-level and country-level factors determining bank efficiency. This issue is further discussed in chapter 4.

Quantitative analysis of FSIs can be complemented with information from assessments of the effectiveness of financial sector supervision. BCP assessments[9] provide a vast array of contextual information that can be useful in interpreting FSIs. First, they can clarify the definition of data being used to compile FSIs by, for example, indicating the quality of capital. Second, they can help establish the underlying cause of observed movements in FSIs when there are competing explanations, such as whether a fall in the capital ratio might be supervisory action rather than rapid balance-sheet expansion. Third, they provide information on risks, such as operational and legal risk that cannot be captured adequately using FSIs. Fourth, they provide information on how effective the banks' risk management is and, thus, how effectively the banking system is likely to respond to the risk associated with particular values for FSIs. Finally, they indicate the responsiveness of the supervisory system to emerging financial sector problems, which reveals how quickly vulnerabilities identified by FSIs are likely to be corrected. A lack of compliance with many of the BCP would suggest that the banking sector vulnerabilities detected using FSIs may be more serious than in a financial system with good compliance. Assessments of financial infrastructure—corporate governance, accounting and auditing, insolvency and creditor rights regimes, and systemic liquidity arrangements—can also help interpret the liquidity and solvency indicators.

3.3.1.2 *Analysis of FSIs for Insurance*

Insurance is an important and growing part of the financial sector in virtually all developed and in many emerging economies; consequently, insurance sector soundness is important.[10] Insurers help to allocate risks and to mobilize long-term savings (especially retirement savings) by spreading financial losses across the economy. Insurance companies facilitate economic activity in sectors, such as shipping, aviation, and the professional services that are particularly reliant on insurance. The insurance companies can help to promote risk-mitigating activities through their incentives to measure and monitor the risks to which they are exposed. Finally, insurance companies help promote stability by transferring risk to entities better able to evaluate, monitor, and mitigate those risks through specialization.

The risk profiles of insurers and banks differ. Insurance companies generally are exposed to greater volatility in asset prices and face the potential for rapid deterioration in their capital base. Insurance companies typically have liabilities with longer maturities and assets with greater liquidity than banks have, thus enabling the insurance companies to play a larger role in long-term capital markets. Life insurers often have significantly higher exposure to equities and real estate and lower exposure to direct lending than do banks. In some countries, insurers offer products with guaranteed returns, further exacerbating risks for life insurers.

The importance of the insurance sector for financial stability has increased recently because of intensified links between insurers and banks, thereby increasing the risk of contagion. Those links can include cross-ownership, credit-risk transfers, and financial reinsurance. Financial deregulation has caused insurers to diversify into banking and asset management products, thus exposing them to additional risk by making their liabilities more liquid. Insurers have also increased their exposure to equities and complex risk management products in response to deregulation and declining yields on fixed-interest products.

Assessing the soundness of the insurance sector requires good understanding of linkages among, and determinants of, the various financial soundness indicators for the insurance sector discussed in chapter 2. In addition, the analysis of those indicators should be supplemented by information on the quality of risk management in the insurance industry, which will draw on the assessment of observance of relevant supervisory standards (see discussion that follows). Capital adequacy can be viewed as the key indicator of insurance sector soundness. However, analysis of capital adequacy depends on realistic valuation of both assets and liabilities of the insurance sector. Compared with banking, asset side risks for the insurance sector are similar, but liability side risks depend on different factors, such as demographic and sectoral developments. Assessing the stability of the insurance sector should take into account the size and growth of the sector, the importance of banking-type and asset-management-type products, the structure of the industry (including the relative importance of the life sector), and the strength of linkages to the banking sector.

Data quality may be an issue because many countries lack the actuarial expertise, supervisory authority, or capacity to collect sufficient information.

The analysis and interpretation of soundness indicators should draw on an evaluation of the observance of Insurance Core Principles issued by the International Association of Insurance Supervisors (IAIS 2003) (see also chapter 5). This set of principles provides information on the effectiveness of supervision, the structure and characteristics of companies in the sector, and other useful qualitative information that is not always captured by financial ratios.[11] In particular, the specifics of supervisory and regulatory environment affect asset composition, as well as the mix of risks, and should be taken into account in interpreting insurance FSIs.

3.3.1.3 *Analysis of FSIs for Securities Markets*[12]

Securities markets are a major component of the financial sector in many countries. The capitalization of equity and bond markets in many industrialized countries, with savings in securities investments now exceeding savings in deposits, dwarfs the aggregate assets of the banking system. Exposures of households, corporations, and financial institutions to securities markets have increased substantially through investments in primary and secondary markets and through trading of risk in financial markets.

Well-developed securities markets offer an alternative source of intermediation, thus enhancing efficiency in the financial sector through competition. Well-functioning securities markets provide a mechanism for the efficient valuation of assets and diversification of risks, create liquidity in financial claims, and efficiently allocate risks. Those markets help reduce the cost of capital, thereby raising economy-wide savings and investment. They also foster market discipline by providing incentives to corporations and financial institutions to use sound management and governance practices.

The stability of securities markets can be monitored using a range of quantitative indicators measuring depth, tightness, and resilience of markets.[13] Most quantitative indicators focus on market liquidity because of the important role that liquid securities play in the balance sheets of financial institutions. Chapter 2 discusses the FSIs that measure market tightness (bid–ask spreads) and depth (market turnover, measured by gross average daily value of securities traded relative to the stock). The analysis of securities markets' FSIs focuses on trends in those key variables and their determinants, including institutional factors and market structure (for an example of this type of analysis, see Wong and Fung 2002). The analysis also tries to assess resiliency of the market, which refers either to the speed with which price fluctuations resulting from trades are dissipated or to the speed with which imbalances in order flows are adjusted. Although there is no consensus yet on the appropriate measure for resiliency, one approach is to examine the speed of the restoration of normal market conditions (such as the bid–ask spread and order volume) after large trades. For more on the robustness of market liquidity under conditions of stress, see the discussion in section 3.3.2 and in appendix D. For an alternative approach to measuring soundness using market volatility as a financial soundness indicator, see Morales and Schumacher (2003).

Qualitative information drawn from standards assessments and other sources can also help assess stability of securities markets and can help interpret FSIs. The financial market infrastructure (trading systems, payment systems, clearing and settlement systems, central bank operations and other systemic liquidity arrangements, and government foreign exchange reserve and debt management practices) affects financial institutions' access to funding on the liabilities side of their balance sheets, their ability to liquidate positions on the asset side, and their exposure to systemic and operational risk in the clearing and settlement system. This information can be derived from assessments of the Organization of Securities Commissions (IOSCO) objectives and principles (see also chapter 5), the Committee on Payment Settlement Systems (CPSS)–IOSCO recommendations for securities settlement systems (see also chapter 11), the CPSS core principles (see also chapter 11), and other sources such as event studies of past disturbances.

Information on market microstructures and the diversity of funding sources can be used to assess how well financial institutions can maintain access to funding in a crisis. The robustness of market liquidity depends on market microstructure, including whether markets are based on over-the-counter (OTC) or are exchange-based. For OTC markets, information on features affecting the capacity of market makers to make markets—for example, the number and capitalization of market makers and the size of the positions they take—could be useful. For exchanges, information on the trading systems, price transparency, margining rules, and capital committed by the exchange to support trading could be used. For electronic trading systems, an indicator of liquidity is the standard transaction size. Also relevant is the extent to which closely related assets are traded on the different types of markets, which can substitute for one another if one market loses liquidity.

Information on the operation of the payment systems, the clearing and settlement systems, and the safety nets is also useful for interpreting FSIs for securities markets, and it provides insights into access to liquidity in a crisis. Indicators of payment system functioning include the relative size of intraday, inter-bank exposures and daylight overdrafts, the length of settlement lags, the scope of loss-sharing arrangements, the level of reliance on collateral, and the particular markets that have real time gross settlement. All those indicators provide information on the potential credit and settlement risks in the payment system. The safety net and the central banks' providing of liquidity to markets influence the extent to which banks and other market intermediaries can continue to access market liquidity in a crisis. Central bank operating procedures are a key determinant of money market liquidity and of the liquidity of other markets in longer-term paper, where position taking by dealers is supported by access to money markets.

3.3.1.4 *Analysis of FSIs for Nonfinancial Sectors*

Monitoring the financial condition and vulnerabilities of the corporate, household, and real estate sectors can enhance the capacity to assess risks to the financial sector. Loans to the corporate sector typically account for a significant portion of bank loan portfolios; thus, the health of the corporate sector represents a major source of risk to the financial system.[14] Households play an important role as consumers (of goods, as well as financial products and services), as depositors, and as holders of risky assets; hence, changes in their financial position can have significant effect on both the real economy and financial market activity.[15] The real estate sector also has been an important source of risk because of the key role that real estate plays as collateral, but this dimension has proved difficult to monitor because of the paucity of data on real estate prices.[16]

FSIs for the corporate, household, and real estate sectors can serve as early warning indicators of emerging asset quality problems. Shocks to their balance sheets, if significant, are eventually transmitted to the balance sheets of banks and other financial institutions. However, if one is to make effective use of FSIs for those sectors for this purpose, it is necessary to assess the exposure of the financial system to each sector (e.g., using FSIs of the sectoral distribution of lending) and to estimate how a deterioration of the financial condition of nonfinancial sectors, which would be based on FSIs for those sectors, is likely to affect banking sector asset quality. In some assessments, FSIs for corporate and household sectors were made endogenous by estimating the effect on those FSIs of changes in the relative price of debt to equity, level of interest rates, cyclical position, profitability, and unemployment. The prospective evolution of corporate and household leverage can then be projected by using the above variables, and such projections can help assess likely changes in asset quality of financial firms.

3.3.2   System-Focused Stress Testing

Stress testing, in the context of financial sector surveillance, refers to a range of techniques to help assess the vulnerability of a financial system to exceptional but plausible events.[17] It is based on applying a common set of shocks and scenarios to a set of individual financial institutions and subgroups of institutions to analyze both the aggregate effect and the distribution of that effect among the institutions. Stress tests were originally developed for use at the portfolio level so one can understand how the value of a portfolio changes if there are large changes to some of its risk factors (such as asset prices). Those tests have now become widely used as a risk management tool by financial institutions. Gradually, the techniques have been applied in a broader context, with the goal of measuring the sensitivity of a group of institutions (such as commercial banks) or even an entire financial system to common shocks.

System-focused stress testing is best seen as a multi-step process that involves examining the key vulnerabilities in the system and providing a rough estimate of sensitivity of balance sheets to a variety of shocks. This process entails (a) identifying the major risks and exposures in the system and formulating questions about those risks and exposures, (b) defining the coverage and identifying the data that are required and available, (c) calibrating the scenarios or shocks to be applied to the data, (d) selecting and implementing the methodology, and (e) interpreting the results. System-focused stress tests attempt to marry a forward-looking macro-perspective with an assessment of the sensitivity of a collection of institutions to major changes in the economic and financial environment.

The process of conducting a system-focused stress test begins first with the identification of specific vulnerabilities or areas of concern and then with the construction of a scenario in the context of a consistent macroeconomic framework. Isolating key vulnerabilities is an iterative process involving both qualitative and quantitative elements. A range of numerical indicators can be used to help isolate potential weaknesses, including the "big picture" or macro-level indicators, broad structural indicators, and more institution-focused or micro-level indicators. Ideally, a macro-econometric or simulation model should form the basis of the stress-testing scenarios. A working group of selected experts may facilitate the process.

Once a set of adjustment scenarios has been produced in a consistent macro-framework, the next step is to translate the various outputs into the balance sheets and income statements of financial institutions. There are two main approaches to translating macro-scenarios into balance sheets: (a) the "bottom-up" approach in which the effect is estimated using data on an individual institution's portfolios and (b) the "top-down" approach in which the effect is estimated using aggregated data.

A variety of metrics can be used to summarize the results of stress tests. The most common ones use measures that express the effect of a shock as a percentage of capital, assets, or profitability. For example, the estimated decline in the value of assets (or in equity) or a reduction in net income caused by higher loan loss provisions or by interest rate shock can be expressed as a ratio involving either (a) capital or assets or (b) profitability. The dispersion of the effect (the standard deviation of the effect across the sample of banks) is also a key statistic to monitor. Public dissemination of the results of stress tests may present some difficulties, but the publication of results by a broad range of countries has shown that those difficulties are not insurmountable.

Stress tests are useful because they provide a quantitative measure of the vulnerability of the financial system to different shocks. This measure can be used with other analyses to draw conclusions about the overall stability of a financial system. The value added from system stress tests derives from a consultative process that integrates a forward-looking macroeconomic perspective, a focus on the financial system as a whole, and a uniform approach to the assessment of risk exposures across institutions. Recent trends in Financial Sector Assessment Program (FSAP) stress testing show a shift toward greater integration of a macroeconomic perspective, more involvement by country authorities and individual institutions, and greater coverage of the financial sector.

3.4 Analysis of Macrofinancial Linkages

Macrofinancial linkages focus on macroeconomic and sectoral implications of financial instability, and they derive from the many ways in which different nonfinancial sectors rely on intermediation by the financial sector to conduct their activities. Those linkages differ significantly across countries, but they are likely to include (a) the dependence of nonfinancial sectors (e.g., corporate, household, and government sector) on financing by domestic and foreign banks; (b) the deposits and wealth of those sectors placed with the financial sector that would be at risk in a financial crisis; (c) the role of the banking system on monetary policy transmission; and (d) the financial sector's holdings of securities issued by, and loans to, the government so that problems in the financial sector could adversely affect debt sustainability. Thus, the monitoring of financial sector vulnerabilities using FSIs should be combined with an analysis of other data on macrofinancial linkages to assess the effect of shocks on macroeconomic conditions through the financial sector.

3.4.1 Effect of Financial Soundness on Macroeconomic Developments

A key macrofinancial linkage that is important in almost all countries derives from the dependence of nonfinancial sectors on financing provided by banks.[18] The potential effect

3

on macroeconomic conditions of banking soundness problems in the banking sector may be detected using FSIs compiled by local and foreign authorities. Data on nonfinancial sectors' borrowing not only from the domestically controlled banking sector but also from foreign-controlled banks by country are needed for analysis. The data on the former are the same data used to compile the exposure concentration of FSIs. Data on borrowing by the nonfinancial private and government sectors from banks headquartered in BIS-reporting countries can be obtained from the BIS consolidated banking statistics.[19] The coverage of the data is comprehensive because almost all international banking activity is conducted by internationally active banks from those countries. These BIS data indicate the scale of the potential reduction in financing to the domestic private and government sectors that could result from a deterioration in the soundness of the banking sector in that country.[20] The prospects for this type of deterioration can be monitored by examining the FSIs for banking in each BIS reporting country.

An example of this type of macrofinancial linkage is trade finance. IMF (2003d) discusses this linkage in more detail, noting that during recent financial crises, the trade financing to the crisis countries fell dramatically (more sharply than would seem to be justified by fundamentals and risks involved). The paper attributes the decline to the response by banks as leveraged institutions, to the lack of insurance when it was needed, to herd behavior (among banks, official export credit agencies, and private insurers), and to weaknesses in domestic banking systems. Because bank-financed trade credits are typically short-term, are backed by receivables, and are self-liquidating, their performance, transfer, and convertibility risks are considered lower than those for other cross-border lending. The loss of financing to the trade sector appears to have disrupted countries' trade and growth performance, possibly exacerbating the crisis.

Macrofinancial linkages also derive from residents' deposits and wealth placed with domestically owned and foreign-controlled financial institutions, which would be at risk in crises at home or abroad. The importance of this linkage depends on institutional features such as the extent to which the deposits are covered by domestic and foreign deposit insurance schemes. The linkage can be assessed using data on residents' deposit holdings, which, in principle, need to cover both (a) deposits held within the country with domestically owned banks or the local branches and subsidiaries of foreign banks and (b) deposits held abroad, either with domestic banks' branches and subsidiaries abroad or with foreign banks (in both domestic and foreign currency). Data from monetary statistics typically capture the first but miss the second (which can be substantial, especially in dollarized economies). Some information on the latter can be obtained from international investment position data and from the locational BIS international banking data.[21] In this case too, FSIs monitor the soundness of the banking sector while the data on wealth placed with financial institutions give an indication of how much could be lost in the event of a banking crisis (taking into account the extent of protection provided by deposit insurance schemes).

Another linkage results from the effect of banking sector problems on the monetary policy transmission mechanism. Both the domestically owned banks and branches and the subsidiaries of foreign banks play a role in monetary transmission, so a deterioration in banking sector soundness, either domestically or abroad, could alter the effect of changes in monetary policy on the real economy. This linkage implies that it can be useful to analyze FSIs in combination with monetary data to understand how the effect of monetary policy could be affected by the soundness of the financial sector. The analysis would have to take account of financial structure, including the relative importance of market and bank financing, the role of foreign banks in financial intermediation, and the central bank operating procedures.

3.4.2 Effect of Financial System Soundness on Debt Sustainability

Debt sustainability refers to the ability of a borrower to service a given stock of debt, given the anticipated payments of interest and principal. Debt servicing ability depends on the stream of income accruing to the borrower, the stock and residual maturity profile of the borrowers' assets, the stock of debt outstanding, and the agreed terms—chiefly, the interest rate, currency, and time profile.[22]

Developments in financial system soundness can have a significant effect on debt sustainability of households, corporations, and governments; debt sustainability problems in different sectors are mutually reinforcing. The resulting financial instability can impose massive restructuring costs on an economy and can lower overall growth rates, thus undermining the debt servicing capacity of the economy and potentially causing a sovereign default. Debt servicing difficulties in any one sector could arise because of market risk, rollover risk, or liquidity risk—or more fundamentally because of unsustainable debt levels and insolvency risk—and difficulties can spread throughout the system.

Even when sovereign debt is initially at a sustainable level, the realization of contingent liabilities in the event of a crisis can result in deterioration of the government's balance sheet and unsustainable debt ratios. Debt sustainability problems in the nonfinancial sectors can further weaken the financial system by affecting the value of loans and securities held by the financial sector. Sovereign defaults, in particular, have a severe effect on the financial system because of the key role that government securities often play in financial institutions' balance sheets as a risk-free asset, as a store of collateral, and as a liquid asset. In general, doubts about the debt servicing capacity of any large borrower or group of borrowers can cause a loss of confidence by depositors and other holders of securities, thereby prompting a flight to quality or a more widespread run on banks and other institutions. The economic dislocation caused by debt defaults or by a loss of confidence can be magnified by the effect on financial prices as interest rates typically rise and as credit becomes less readily available—unless the monetary authorities take concerted and credible actions. The exchange rate may also come under pressure if domestic assets as a whole become less attractive relative to foreign assets. The effect on financial markets can thus magnify the effect of debt sustainability problems on the macroeconomy.

Assessing debt sustainability and monitoring the two-way linkages between financial system soundness and financial soundness of nonfinancial sectors are key to fostering financial stability. Although it is difficult to specify a precise level at which a given stock of debt becomes "unsustainable," it is possible to detect warning signs of excessive debt accumulation by examining a few key indicators and ratios. At the most simple level, growth rates of the stock of debt provide an indicator of potential problems if the growth rates exceed reasonable estimates of the growth rate of productive capacity, which ultimately determine the ability to repay. The evolution of financial soundness indicators of

3

nonfinancial sectors—including the relative size of the debt stock (e.g., debt-to-GDP or debt-to-equity ratios; see section 3.3.1) and its key determinants—provides some useful information on prospective developments in debt ratios or in debt service capacity. For example, a common rule of thumb for public sector debt sustainability is to relate primary fiscal balance to the real interest rates and real growth rates. Similarly, an analysis of the determinants of corporate debt-to-equity ratios (real interest rates, rate of profit, and real return on equity are likely to be among the determinants) could provide an indication of the dynamics of this ratio.

3.4.3 Effect of Financial Soundness on Growth and Financial Development

The issue of whether financial sector soundness influences growth has received little attention in cross-country empirical research. There is a growing consensus that more finance (i.e., a larger financial sector) causes more growth.[23] Recent empirical evidence suggests that countries with better-developed financial systems indeed tend to grow faster. Specifically, the size of the banking system and the liquidity of stock markets are each positively linked with economic growth. Better functioning financial systems ease the external financing constraints that impede corporate and industrial expansion.[24]

Even though empirical cross-country studies on the issue are limited, there are cases of countries with protracted output losses because of financial sector crises. There is ample case-study evidence (e.g., from the Asian crisis[25] or bank restructuring episodes in the Central and Eastern Europe [CEE] countries in the late 1990s) suggesting that financial sector problems can result in significant or protracted output losses. Although few empirical cross-country studies directly address the issue, there seems to be a consensus that is based on the theory and the analysis of country cases that, in the medium to long run, financial soundness is positively related to economic growth.

In the short run, country authorities may be faced with a tradeoff between economic growth and financial sector soundness. Fast growth can make financial markets vulnerable to shocks, constraining potential output.[26] In particular, rapid credit expansion may, at times, exceed banks' capacity to assess risks, thereby leading to reduced asset quality. At the same time, credit expansions can be only a symptom of rapid financial deepening.[27] In a country experiencing rapid credit growth and rapid output growth, the key is to determine whether the credit growth can be interpreted as a structural and positive development (e.g., if it follows a period of financial liberalization and bank restructuring). Even if credit growth is determined to be the result of structural developments., as has arguably been the case in some transition countries in the late 1990s and early 2000s,[28] policy makers have to evaluate carefully its implications for financial stability and macroeconomic developments. In particular, they need to distinguish to what extent a rapid financial sector growth reflects improvements in access to finance and to what extent the growth reflects a loosening in risk management practices and supervision.

3.5 Special Topics in Financial Stability Analysis

This section deals with selected topics in financial stability, namely,

- The analysis of international financial centers and offshore financial centers and of financial stability
- Key stability issues in the opening of capital accounts
- The implications of dollarization for stability
- Implications of Islamic banking

This list is not an exhaustive list of financial sector issues; it is a list of several issues that are not common to all financial systems and, consequently, were not fully addressed in the general sections, but they are still important in several financial systems.

3.5.1 International Financial Centers and Offshore Financial Centers

International Financial Centers (IFCs) are the primary markets where finance capital and currency are collected, switched, disbursed, and exchanged on a regional or global basis.[29] An IFC's share in the global financial business is disproportionately large relative to its size as measured by area, population, or nonfinancial economic activity. In most rankings, London, New York, and Tokyo (in this order) are the world's three primary IFCs. They are complemented by a range of secondary and tertiary IFCs, which play important roles as regional financial centers or as major offshore financial centers (OFCs). Although IFCs and OFCs are quite distinct in terms of scale and structure, they are treated together in this section for convenience because they have in common certain stability issues that arise as a result of their international operations.

Although there is no generally approved definition of an OFC, a useful one defines it as a center where the bulk of financial sector activity is offshore on both sides of the balance sheet (that is, the counterparties of the majority of the financial institution's liabilities and assets are nonresidents), where the transactions are initiated elsewhere, and where the majority of the institutions involved are controlled by nonresidents. Thus, OFCs are usually referred to in the following ways (the third listed is the most popular):

- Jurisdictions that have relatively large numbers of financial institutions engaged primarily in business with nonresidents
- Financial systems with external assets and liabilities that are out of proportion to domestic financial intermediation designed to finance domestic economies (For most OFCs, the funds that are on the books of the OFC are invested in the major international money-center markets.)
- Centers that provide some or all of the following services: low or zero taxation, moderate or light financial regulation, and banking secrecy and anonymity (Activities of OFCs are centered around international banking and around asset and risk management, including setting up special purpose vehicles and trusts that are aimed at large corporate entities and at high net worth.)

The key defining characteristics of an IFC are (a) the economies of scale and scope in financial activities, (b) the extent of international economic and banking links, (c)

3

the credibility of government policies, and (d) the creditworthiness of the financial sector. Important requirements or prerequisites are economically strong and credible banks within a strong legal system, including property rights, contract enforcement, a functional and credible court system, and bankruptcy processes. Although those conditions are necessary to become an IFC, they are not necessarily sufficient; there are also various historical and other reasons why certain places have become IFCs. Moreover, any financial center requires a long time to establish itself as an IFC. IFCs typically engage in a variety of onshore and offshore financial activities, including foreign exchange trading such as cash, forward, and swap transactions. IFCs also engage in a wide range of equity and debt securities and derivatives trading on the cash, futures, and options markets, not only in organized exchanges and over-the-counter transactions but also in activities such as money management, payments clearing and settlement, merger and acquisition, and securities underwriting. In some cases, some of this activity is carried on in institutions that are favorably treated for tax and other purposes.

Development of an IFC has several potential benefits for the host economy. There is some evidence in the literature quoted earlier that the large presence of foreign banks in IFCs tends to increase competition. More intensive competition, apart from its static benefits, can also widen the range of financial services available to clients. However, there are also cases of IFCs in jurisdictions where domestic markets have failed to overcome some inherent inefficiencies. An important issue to consider is the competition that is taking place among IFCs. From the viewpoint of global welfare, the competition among countries to host offshore banking can result in a gain to a host center that may represent little net gain overall.

At the same time, the presence of an IFC or OFC may be an additional source of instability for the host economy. Financial surveillance needs to analyze not only the complex structure of the key financial institutions operating in an IFC but also the operations in which those institutions are engaged so people can understand the sources of the risks (which are often outside the host jurisdiction) and the transfers of risks within and from the IFC. The effect on domestic financial stability caused by the presence of an IFC or OFC arises from both macro-channels and structural channels. Financial stability would be affected if the domestic economy were more susceptible to shocks than would otherwise be the case, because a segment of the global or regional financial services that are provided takes place in the domestic economy (through the OFC–IFC transactions). Some of those additional factors affecting financial stability follow:

- Additional cross-border business in an IFC or OFC could add to the demands on domestic clearing and settlement systems.
- The presence of an IFC or OFC may make it easier for domestic residents to invest offshore or for nonresidents to invest in securities or claims issued by domestic residents. This condition may improve liquidity in domestic markets and facilitate technology transfer; it may also facilitate excessive risk taking unless restrained by supervision or market forces.
- The effect on domestic economic activity and employment resulting from the presence of an IFC or OFC could be substantial—as is often the case in many OFCs;

hence, shocks to the volume and stability of IFC operations could affect the domestic economy and could indirectly affect domestic financial stability.

- Although foreign institutions operating in an IFC or OFC are supervised by their home regulators, the trading activities among those institutions—particularly in OTC markets occurring in the IFC or OFC—may be largely self-regulated and may call for the involvement of host authorities to achieve stability.
- The global reach, large size, and complexity of transactions of domestic- or foreign-controlled institutions in an IFC or OFC may pose supervisory challenges for both host and home jurisdictions.

The operations of large and complex financial institutions (LCFIs) in an IFC or OFC may have financial stability implications. An LCFI is typically a large player in both wholesale and retail financial markets and has substantial international operations spanning a number of financial activities. The group is likely to be prominent in the local payments, clearing, and settlements structure. The group is likely to encompass many different legal entities, and the link between those and the group's internal management structure may appear complicated or even opaque. The group may not have an overall lead supervisor monitoring its activities at an overall level on a consolidated basis. At the host-country level, responsibility for supervision of an LCFI's local affiliates may reside within a single regulator or several functional regulators. The size of the LCFI and its geographical diversification has the potential to threaten financial stability not only in the IFC but also in several countries and markets. The operations may be of concern not only to its many financial regulators but also to the central banks and insurance or guarantee agencies. The latter group of institutions, in the event of a crisis, could be involved in providing or facilitating liquidity or other official financial support, either to the LCFI itself or to its local counterparties.[30]

The assessment and monitoring of offshore financial centers has increased in recent years, in part, because of heightened concerns about consolidated supervision and money laundering and because of the associated emphasis on cross-border cooperation and information exchange with OFCs.[31] The assessment methodology for OFCs places emphasis on fostering compliance with international standards for supervision and financial integrity. Because they reflect the concerns about consolidated supervision and money laundering or terrorist financing, the assessments generally focus on compliance with the supervisory standards in banking and standards for anti-money laundering and for countering the financing of terrorism. In addition, when warranted, the assessments also include securities and insurance supervision.[32]

Levels of compliance with financial sector standards in OFCs tend to be, on average, higher than in other jurisdictions assessed by the Fund; however, shortcomings remain in the supervisory systems of many of the OFCs. The higher level of financial standards compliance in OFCs reflects, in part, the higher income levels of the OFCs and their concerns to protect their reputation. The shortcomings arise mainly from inadequate resources and expertise in the supervisory agencies located in OFCs with lower per capita income. Those shortcomings are reflected in lower conformity with principles that are concerned with the effectiveness of onsite supervision and in technical areas such as risk management and guidance for financial institutions (IMF 2004c).

The evidence that OFCs pose a risk to financial stability in non-OFC countries is limited. The potential for risk is seen to lie in the following areas:

- Banks have been the most common source of financial instability, and most major OFCs have branches or subsidiaries of globally important banks. Many of those banks are also conglomerates, which pose additional risks. Potential threats to financial instability may increase with weaknesses in consolidated supervision and cross-border consolidated supervision of those institutions.
- The lack of information about the activities booked in OFCs restricts the ability to understand global financial flows and to analyze potential stability effects.
- Hedge funds and reinsurance companies located offshore have the potential to affect stability through their high leverage and exposure to catastrophic events, respectively.

However, an OFC itself may face significant macroeconomic risks, which result from its characteristics as an OFC. Given that financial intermediation in the OFC is typically out of proportion with the size of the domestic economy, most OFCs depend on the financial intermediation as a source of income. Shocks to the volume of financial intermediation (e.g., those caused by shocks to the reputation of the OFC) are likely to have a substantial effect on the domestic macroeconomy.

3.5.2 Capital Account Liberalization

Capital account controls can have a significant effect on the way that external shocks are transmitted to the domestic financial system and on how domestic financial developments affect the macro-economy. When one considers the effect of the capital account on domestic financial stability, it is important to be aware of existing capital controls, including the nature and scope of recent liberalizations and any plans to relax them.[33] Experience has demonstrated that liberalizing the capital account before the home-country financial system has been adequately strengthened can contribute to serious economic problems.[34] For example, studies have shown that a significant number of countries that suffered from a financial crisis have liberalized their financial systems, including their capital accounts, within the past 5 years before the crisis.[35] These experiences have highlighted the importance of (a) appropriate sequencing and coordination when opening capital accounts and (b) domestic financial liberalization policies to preserve financial stability. See box 3.2 and chapter 12 for additional discussion.

3.5.3 Dollarization: Implications for Stability

Dollarization can have important implications for financial stability. A dollarized economy can be defined as one where (a) households and firms hold a fraction of their portfolio (inclusive of money balances) in foreign currency assets, (b) the private and public sector have debts denominated in foreign currency, or (c) both. Dollarization can be "official" when the U.S. dollar is adopted as the legal tender or "partial" when the local currency remains the legal tender, but transactions are allowed to be denominated in dollars, thus effectively allowing a bicurrency system to take hold. It is useful to distinguish among three generic types of dollarization that broadly match the three functions of money: (a) payments dollarization (currency substitution) is the resident's use of foreign currency for transaction purposes in cash, demand deposits, or central bank reserves; (b) financial dollarization (asset substitution) consists of the resident's holdings of financial assets or liabilities in foreign currency (either domestic or external); and (c) real dollarization is the indexing, formally or de facto, of local prices and wages to the dollar.[36] Dollarization can be measured using a variety of statistics, including the ratio of onshore foreign currency deposits to total onshore deposits, the ratio of foreign currency deposits to broad money, the ratio of domestic government debt in foreign currency to total government debt, and the share of private sector debt in total external debt.[37] Additional risks to financial stability resulting from dollarization and the implications for financial policy are discussed below.

Empirical evidence suggests that financial dollarization may increase the vulnerability of financial systems to solvency and liquidity risks. Cross-country estimates of the effect of dollarization on key financial soundness indicators are consistent with the hypothesis that increased dollarization increases financial vulnerability. The variance of deposit growth is positively and significantly correlated with dollarization, suggesting that dollarized financial systems may be more exposed to credit cycles and liquidity risk. A cross-country comparison of estimates of nonperforming loans (NPLs) or a composite systemic risk measure will show that dollarized economies also tend to be more exposed to solvency risk.

The limited backing of banks' dollar liabilities by U.S. dollars and their convertibility at par subjects the financial system to a very specific type of liquidity risk. Systemic liquidity risk arises when the demand for local assets falls because of a perceived increase in country or banking risk, thus prompting foreign banks to recall short-term lines of credit and depositors to convert their deposits into dollars or to transfer them abroad. Unless liquid dollar liabilities are backed by sufficient liquid dollar assets abroad, banks could run out of dollar liquid reserves and could fail to pay off dollar liabilities. Similarly, central banks could run out of international reserves to provide dollar lender-of-last-resort support to distressed banks. When those international reserves are depleted, deposit (or loan) contracts may need to be broken and disruptive or confiscatory measures taken, thereby imposing a heavy cost on the financial system.

Dollar deposits are often more vulnerable to runs than local currency deposits, even in the absence of exchange rate adjustments. In highly dollarized countries, local currency deposits are mostly held for transaction purposes and are less affected by expected yield differentials than dollar deposits, which are predominantly held as store of value and are close substitutes for deposits abroad or dollars cash. Moreover, even when the demand for local currency deposits is affected, the small size of these deposits in the most highly dollarized countries limits the threat they represent for banks' liquidity.

The lack of dollar monetary instruments can further inhibit the scope for interest rate defenses against deposit withdrawals. An interest rate defense may be ineffective once a run has started, because the central bank has limited ability to raise the interest rate on dollar deposits. Banks are often reluctant to raise interest rates on dollar deposits, because of concerns that increasing rates may be interpreted as a sign of weakness, thus further exacerbating deposit withdrawals.

3

Box 3.2 Capital Account Liberalization and Financial Stability

Capital account liberalization exposes the domestic financial sector to greater competition and risk taking. In the absence of appropriate bank supervision, banks can expand risky activities at rates that exceed their capacity to manage them, including the use of derivatives and other complex cross-border transactions that are difficult to monitor and regulate. Large capital inflows can also lead to rapid credit growth, possibly to unproductive sectors of the economy such as real estate and government-supported industries, thus contributing to asset price bubbles and financial sector difficulties.[a] Capital account liberalization can also increase banks' credit risk through aggressive foreign currency lending to unhedged borrowers.

Capital account liberalization may facilitate a faster transmission of economic and financial system shocks, thereby increasing asset price volatility.[b] Exchange rate risks tend to be more pronounced when a fixed exchange rate peg has been maintained for a considerable period of time and if market perception of an implicit exchange rate guarantee has promoted inadequate hedging. If the banking system is weak, the monetary authorities may be reluctant to increase interest rates to stabilize the exchange rate.

The supervisory agency needs to have prudential standards and technical skills to cope with the challenges that accompany capital account liberalization. Experience shows that careful planning of the sequencing and the pace of reforms could be critical to successful liberalization efforts, as further discussed in chapter 12. Before liberalizing the capital account, particular attention should be given to the effectiveness of existing capital controls, the soundness of the macroeconomic environment and consistency of macroeconomic policies, the prudential and supervisory framework, the financial system's level of development, and the ability of both financial and nonfinancial corporations to manage potential risks and shocks that may arise. Successful capital account liberalization requires complementary monetary and financial sector reforms. Policies should be focused on improving internal governance of financial institutions, developing deep and liquid financial markets, and fostering market discipline.

---

a. In Korea, before the 1997 crisis, capital inflows helped finance sectors that subsequently experienced difficulties. In Sweden, the large credit expansion that followed financial deregulation contributed to the asset price bubble in the 1980s.

b. Cross-border contagion may be exacerbated if portfolio managers in developed countries bundle instruments from different countries in the same risk class.

The main solvency risk faced by dollarized financial systems results from currency mismatches in the event of large depreciations. Currency-induced credit risk is generally the key source of vulnerability because borrowers are highly susceptible to defaulting on dollar-denominated loans in the event of a large depreciation. Banks with large domestic dollar liabilities must balance their foreign exchange positions either by extending dollar lending to local currency earners or by holding dollar assets abroad. Thus, to maintain their profitability (especially in light of generally lower rates of return on foreign assets than on local dollar assets) and to satisfy the pent-up demand for loans, banks generally end up lending domestically a large share of their dollar deposits, thus effectively transferring the currency risk to their unhedged clients and retaining the resulting credit risk. Borrowers' currency mismatch is enhanced by the fact that prices and wages may continue to be set in local currency even when financial dollarization is widespread. Counterparty exposure is also amplified if collateral is denominated in domestic currency, and it declines relative to the loan after a depreciation. Banks' direct exposure to currency risk is generally limited by tight regulatory limits on open foreign exchange positions, but off balance-sheet positions (e.g., in derivatives) are often misreported and may cause exposures to be underestimated.

In the event of large depreciations, widespread currency mismatches can have systemic effects that compound the deterioration of banks' financial situation. Because of balance-sheet effects, large devaluations in highly dollarized economies are more likely to be contractionary, further undermining borrowers' capacity to service their debts. Because it impairs the solvency of both borrowers and banks, the credit risk deriving from a large devaluation also increases the scope for a credit crunch and heightens the risk of deposit withdrawals by concerned depositors. Thus, solvency and liquidity risks are closely interrelated.

The interaction between prudential risks and the monetary regime, which instills fear of floating, subjects the financial system to risks similar to those incurred under a rigid exchange rate system. The more financially dollarized an economy is, the more vulnerable to large exchange rate fluctuations it becomes; hence, the less disposed the monetary authorities are to let the exchange rate float. Empirical evidence indicates that both nominal and real (bilateral) exchange rates are less volatile in more dollarized economies (see Gulde and Ize 2004). Instead, interest rates must bear the brunt of the adjustment to shocks, thereby raising interest rate risk both for local currency and for dollar intermediation and then heightening credit cycles. Credit booms are accentuated by the fact that incoming dollar flows feed domestic lending and, through the banking multiplier, boost dollar intermediation.

The dollarization of public debt can be an important collateral source of financial fragility when banks have large holdings of public securities. Sharp exchange rate depreciations can undermine the sustainability of the public debt and, in turn, can undermine the solvency of banks when the latter hold large volumes of public securities.

In countries with a high degree of dollarization, stability assessments should indicate the extent to which dollarization is a potential source of vulnerability and should suggest appropriate measures. Where available, reports also should provide supporting quantitative information such as the degree of co-circulation, shares of foreign currency deposits and loans, short-term foreign assets and liabilities of the main financial institutions, net foreign assets, and net open foreign currency positions of banks.

3.5.4 Islamic Banking—Stability Issues

The provision and use of financial services and products that conform to Islamic religious principles pose special challenges for a stability assessment. Institutions offering Islamic Financial Services (IIFS) and Islamic capital market instruments constitute a significant share of the overall financial system in several countries; in Sudan and Iran, the entire system is based on Islamic finance principles. This situation requires the recognition of the unique mix of risks in IIFS and key aspects of Islamic securities markets not only in stability assessments but also in the design of policies. See box 3.3 for details.

3.6 Key Policy Issues and Policy Priorities to Support Stability

The previous sections of this chapter (3.1–3.5) have described a range of qualitative and quantitative information and techniques that can be used to identify potential strengths

3

Box 3.3 Stability Issues in Islamic Banking

Unique risks in Islamic finance arise both from contractual design of instruments that are based on Sharia Principles and from the overall legal, governance, and liquidity infrastructure governing Islamic finance. The following list[a] summarizes the features that need to be taken into account when assessing stability in a financial system that includes (or is based on) institutions offering Islamic financial services (IIFS).

- Profit-and-loss-sharing (PLS) modes of financing shift the direct credit risk from banks to their investment depositors, but they also increase the overall degree of risk of the asset side of banks' balance sheets because they make IIFS vulnerable to risks normally borne by equity investors rather than by holders of debt. In particular, operational risk is crucial in Islamic finance. It arises from (a) the fact that the administration of PLS modes is more complex than conventional financing (which also makes standardization of the products more difficult to achieve) and (b) the fact that IIFS often have no or limited legal means to control the agent-entrepreneur. Non-PLS modes of financing are less risky and they more closely resemble conventional financing facilities, but they also carry special risks that need to be recognized.
- Sales-based methods of financing often bundle commodity price risks, operational risks, and credit risks in complex ways, making it difficult to price risks.

- Another specific risk inherent in IIFS stems from the special nature of investment deposits, whose capital value and rate of return are not guaranteed. This condition increases the potential for moral hazard and creates an incentive for risk taking and for operating financial institutions without adequate capital.
- Finally, Islamic banks can use fewer risk-hedging instruments and techniques than do conventional banks and can operate in an environment (a) with underdeveloped or nonexistent interbank and money markets as well as government securities and (b) with limited availability of, and access to, lender-of-last-resort facilities operated by central banks.

The above risk factors have historically forced IIFS into holding a comparatively larger proportion of their assets in reserve accounts with central banks or in correspondent accounts than do conventional banks, and those risk factors have also led to reliance mostly on sales-based facilities on the asset side rather than PLS modes. This situation has affected their competitiveness and has increased their vulnerability to external shocks, with potential systemic consequences. Sundararajan and Errico (2002) provide suggestions on how to address the risks inherent in Islamic banking.[b]

---

a. This subsection is based on Sundararajan and Errico (2002).
b. For more on regulatory and risk management issues in Islamic banking, see exposure drafts of various prudential standards in the Web site of the Islamic Financial Services Board (http://www.ifsb.org), an international organization that was established to promote good regulatory and supervisory practices and to develop international prudential standards for institutions offering Islamic financial services.

---

and vulnerabilities in the financial system. Once weaknesses have been identified, the next issues to consider are how this information can be used to help maintain financial stability and how policies can be enacted or changed to minimize the risks to financial stability. The responses to those issues are multifaceted and depend on the nature of the vulnerabilities that have been identified.

Vulnerabilities and the corresponding policy actions can be categorized into four key areas:

- Macroeconomic (such as aggregate imbalance in payments to nonresidents)
- Institutional (relating to weaknesses in particular institutions or classes of institutions)

- Regulatory or supervisory (relating to the design and implementation of regulations and prudential standards)
- Structural (relating to the operational infrastructure of markets, settlement systems, and safety nets)

The mix and the timing of policy tools need to be appropriate for the vulnerability addressed. For example, if rapid credit growth were mainly a result of macroeconomic imbalances, it would need to be addressed primarily by macroeconomic stabilization policies, while prudential tools would play only an auxiliary role. Conversely, if a vulnerability were mainly a result of weaknesses in banking supervision and regulation, then using macroeconomic policies would be second best should reforms of supervision and regulation turn out to be insufficient or slow to yield results. Weaknesses such as these should be addressed in a timely manner through improved prudential supervision and oversight, effective surveillance of individual institutions and markets, and development and maintenance of a robust financial infrastructure. Macroeconomic policy adjustments, even when they are second best, could be crucial, for example, to limit inflationary pressures, credit growth, or bubbles in certain sectors that could substantially affect the financial sector. In addition, by themselves, policies to develop institutions and markets (e.g., money or government securities market development) and to build infrastructure (e.g., design a large value payment system) pose additional financial and macroeconomic risks, which need to be managed through prudential policies and macro-policy adjustments, as further discussed in chapter 12.

The calibration of policies can take into account information obtained from the quantitative macroprudential tools, in particular, stress tests. For example, in the context of macroeconomic policies, stress tests or sensitivity calculations can provide an assessment of how a certain interest-rate and exchange-rate policy mix can affect the financial sector and of what the resulting effect on the economy as a whole would be. Similarly, in the context of regulatory policies, simulations can be used to assess what the effect would be of an envisaged policy change (e.g., an increase in the rate of providing loans) on the health of the financial system. In the context of supervision, stress-test results can be used to direct supervisory attention to those groups of institutions that pose the greatest risk for the system as a whole. Similarly, evolution of financial soundness indicators and information from macroprudential surveillance may call for more intensive supervision in specified areas (e.g., market risks or country risks).

An assessment of the overall stability of the financial system is based on combining the analysis of risks and vulnerabilities with the assessment of various financial policy responses and policy frameworks. If the potential vulnerability to plausible shocks were not high or if the policy framework and policy responses—as seen, for example, from standards assessments—were considered appropriate, then the system would be judged stable. The stability considerations would typically dictate that a range of prudential and market development policies be given high priority.

Notes

1. See Houben, Kakes, and Schinasi (2004, appendix II) and Schinasi (2004) for a discussion of definitions of financial stability.

3

2. Financial stability analysis is intended to assess the stability and efficiency of a financial system as a whole and not of individual institutions. Although a focus on systemically important institutions is needed to assess stability, the analysis cannot be expected to address legal or governance issues such as fraud that pertain to specific institutions.

3. See Borio (2003) for a discussion of this point.

4. For useful overviews of the EWS literature, see Kaminsky, Lizondo, and Reinhart (1998), Berg and others (2000), Altman and Narayanan (1997), and Abiad (2003). See also Altman and Narayanan (1997).

5. See box 3.1 for further details on market-based indicators of financial soundness.

6. See IMF (2004b) for further details of the use of FSIs.

7. This section is based on Craig and Sundararajan (2004), Sundararajan and others 2003, and IMF (2004b, chapters 6, 8, and 14).

8. Several market-based indicators may also be used to analyze the evolution of financial system risks, including credit risks.

9. Basel Core Principles (BCP) assessments examine compliance with 25 basic principles for effective banking supervision. The scope and coverage of BCP are analyzed in chapter 5 and in IMF and World Bank (2002b). For more information on how BCP assessments can provide information that is useful for interpreting FSIs and for a mapping of FSIs with relevant core principles, see IMF (2003c).

10. A general introduction to insurance sector soundness is also provided in International Association of Insurance Supervisors (IAIS; 2000, 2002). This section is based on the discussion in Das, Davies, and Podpiera (2003). Insurance firms often sell pensions or manage pension funds, other mutual funds, and unit trusts. Those in the insurance and pension fund management industry can significantly affect the stability of markets and financial stability generally through their investment behavior. See the IMF *Global Financial Stability Report* for April (2004d) and September (2004e).

11. See Das, Davies, and Podpiera (2003, appendix I) for an explicit mapping of Insurance Core Principles into FSIs for the insurance sector and for examples of core FSIs in a number of countries.

12. This section is based on Craig and Sundararajan (2004), IMF (2004b, chapter 8), and IMF and World Bank (2002a).

13. The basic definitions of the FSIs are provided in chapter 2. See also chapter 8 of IMF (2004b) for an overview of statistics on securities markets, and see BIS (1999, 2001) for a detailed discussion of market liquidity.

14. Chapter 5 of IMF (2004b) reports empirical analysis demonstrating a linkage between corporate leverage and asset quality across a large number of countries. See also Pomerleano (1998).

15. IMF (2005) examines household sector behavior, with a focus on assessing the shifting of market risks to the household sector. See also Debelle (2004).

16. Hilbers, Lei, and Zacho (2001) conclude that unbalanced real estate price developments often contribute to financial sector distress. Also, see chapter 9 of IMF (2004b) for a discussion of real estate price indices. For a comprehensive analysis of real estate indicators, see BIS (2005). See also Borio and McGuire (2004).

17. This section contains a general discussion on stress testing. For more technical details, see appendix D.

18. This section builds on IMF 2003, part I.
19. See the BIS Web site for more information: http://www.bis.org/statistics/consstats. htm.
20. In the limited number of countries where banks from a non-BIS-reporting country have a significant presence, other data must be used. Specifically, the local supervisory authorities may need to ask those banks to report their consolidated lending to the country (if they are not doing so already).
21. The BIS locational international banking statistics are a separate set of data from the BIS consolidated banking statistics that measure banking sector assets and liabilities in foreign countries but are not consolidated on a cross-border basis. See http://www. bis.org/statistics/bankstats.htm for more details.
22. The debt sustainability will also depend on other policy and environmental elements that affect future cash inflows and outflows, such as the expenditure policies of a sovereign borrower. See "Assessing Sustainability," IMF (2002a) for a comprehensive discussion of different concepts of sustainability.
23. See Levine (2003) or Rajan and Zingales (1998), as well as other references in chapter 4.
24. For a further discussion on this subject, see chapter 4.
25. See Ghosh and others (2002).
26. Bell and Pain (2000) review the literature suggesting that banking crises tend to be preceded by credit booms.
27. Gourchinas, Valdes, and Landerretche (2001) find that financial development typically occurs in bouts that are characterized by short periods of intense financial deepening.
28. See Cottarelli, Dell'Ariccia, and Vladkova-Hollar (2003).
29. Analyses of IFCs by economists have been sparse. More attention has been devoted to this area by geographers, who have focused primarily on why IFCs are located where they are. Good reviews of the literature are provided by Choi, Park, and Tschoegl (1990) and Tschoegl (2000).
30. For more on the analysis of risks associated with LCFIs, see Miles (2002).
31. See IMF (2000, 2003b) for a more detailed discussion of rationale and lessons of the OFC assessment program of the IMF. See also Financial Stability Forum (2000).
32. These types of standards assessments are done as part of a broader stability assessment in FSAPs for countries that host an OFC or IFC. A stand-alone assessment of an OFC, however, is limited only to an assessment of observance of relevant international standards.
33. A detailed description of exchange arrangements and restrictions of individual countries is provided in IMF (2003a, 2004a).
34. Ishii and others (2002) provide country examples. For instance, capital account liberalization against a weak and poorly supervised financial sector contributed to the 1994 crises in Mexico and Turkey. Expansionary macroeconomic policies, a weak regulatory environment, and a fixed exchange rate policy together with capital account liberalization fueled the 1992 crisis in Sweden.
35. See Williamson and Mahar (1998) and Kaminsky and Reinhart (1999).

36. See Gulde and Ize (2004) and De Nicoló, Honohan, and Ize (2003) for a discussion of the various forms and consequences of dollarization.
37. These measures may not fully capture the extent of dollarization insofar as dollars are held as cash and used for transactions.

References

Abiad, Abdul. 2003. "Early Warning Systems: A Survey and a Regime-Switching Approach." IMF Working Paper 03/32, International Monetary Fund, Washington, DC.

Ades, Alberto, Rumi Masih, and Daniel Tenengauzer. 1998. *GS-Watch: A New Framework for Predicting Financial Crises in Emerging Markets.* Emerging Markets Economic Research, December. New York: Goldman Sachs.

Altman, Edward I., and Paul Narayanan. 1997. "Business Failure Classification Models: An International Survey." In *International Accounting and Finance Handbook,* ed. Frederick D. S. Choi, chapter 35, 2nd ed. New York: Wiley.

Bank for International Settlements (BIS). 1999. *Market Liquidity: Research Findings and Selected Policy Implications.* CGFS Publications 11. Basel, Switzerland: Bank for International Settlements.

———. 2001. "Structural Aspects of Market Liquidity from a Financial Stability Perspective." A discussion note for a meeting of the Financial Stability Forum, Bank for International Settlements, Basel, Switzerland. Available at http://www.bis.org/publ/cgfs_note01.pdf.

———. 2005. "Real Estate Indicators and Financial Stability." BIS Paper 21, Bank for International Settlements, Basel, Switzerland.

Bell, J., and D. Pain. 2000. "Leading Indicator Models of Banking Crises—A Critical Review." *Financial Stability Review* (Bank of England) 9 (December): 13–29.

Berg, Andrew, and Eduardo Borensztein. 2004. "Assessing Early Warning Systems: How Have They Worked in Practice?" IMF Working Paper 04/52, International Monetary Fund, Washington, DC. Available at http://www.imf.org/external/pubs/ft/wp/2004/wp0452.pdf.

Berg, Andrew, Eduardo Borensztein, Gian Maria Milesi-Ferretti, and Catherine Pattillo. 2000. "Anticipating Balance of Payments Crises—The Role of Early Warning Systems." IMF Occasional Paper 186, International Monetary Fund, Washington, DC.

Berg, Andrew, and Rebecca N. Coke. 2004. "Autocorrelation-Corrected Standard Errors in Panel Probits: An Application to Currency Crisis Prediction." IMF Working Paper 04/39, International Monetary Fund, Washington, DC. Available at http://www.imf.org/external/pubs/ft/wp/2004/wp0439.pdf.

Berg, Andrew, and Catherine Pattillo. 1999. "Predicting Currency Crises: The Indicators Approach and an Alternative." *Journal of International Money and Finance* 18(4): 561–86.

Bongini, Paola, Luc Laeven, and Giovanni Majnoni. 2002. "How Good Is the Market at Assessing Bank Fragility? A Horse Race between Different Indicators." *Journal of Banking and Finance* 26(5): 1011–28.

Borio, Claudio. 2003. "Towards a Macroprudential Framework for Financial Supervision and Regulation?" BIS Working Paper 128, Bank for International Settlements, Basel, Switzerland. Available at http://www.bis.org/publ/work128.pdf.

Borio, Claudio, and Patrick McGuire. 2004. "Twin Peaks in Equity and Housing Prices?" In *BIS Quarterly Review: International Banking and Financial Market Developments*, ed. J. Bisignano, C. Borio, R. McCauley, E. Remolona, P. Turner, P. Van den Bergh, and W. White, 79–93. Basel, Switzerland: Bank for International Settlements. Available at http://www.bis.org/publ/qtrpdf/r_qt0403.pdf.

Bussiere, Matthieu, and Marcel Fratzscher. 2002. "Towards a New Early Warning System of Financial Crises." European Central Bank Working Paper 145, European Central Bank, Frankfurt, Germany. Available at http://www.ecb.int/pub/pdf/scpwps/ecbwp145.pdf.

Chan-Lau, Jorge A., Arnaud Jobert, and Janet Kong. 2004. "An Option-Based Approach to Bank Vulnerabilities in Emerging Markets." IMF Working Paper 04/33, International Monetary Fund, Washington, DC. Available at http://www.imf.org/external/pubs/ft/wp/2004/wp0433.pdf.

Chang, Roberto, and Andres Velasco. 2001. "A Model of Financial Crises in Emerging Markets." *Quarterly Journal of Economics* 116(2): 489–517.

Choi, Sang Rim, Dackeun Park, and Adrian E. Tschoegl. 1996. "Banks and the World's Major Banking Centers, 1990." *Review of World Economics* 132(4): 774–93.

Cottarelli, Carlo, Giovanni Dell'Ariccia, and Ivanna Vladkova-Hollar. 2003. "Early Birds, Late Risers, and Sleeping Beauties: Bank Credit Growth to the Private Sector in Central and Eastern Europe and the Balkans." IMF Working Paper 03/213, International Monetary Fund, Washington, DC. Available at http://www.imf.org/external/pubs/ft/wp/2003/wp03213.pdf.

Craig, R. Sean, and Venkataraman Sundararajan. 2004. "Using Financial Soundness Indicators to Assess Risks to Financial Stability." In *Challenges to Central Banking from Globalized Financial Systems*, ed. Piero C. Ugolini, Andrea Schaechter, and Mark R. Stone, chapter 14. Washington, DC: International Monetary Fund.

Das, Udaibir S., Nigel Davies, and Richard Podpiera. 2003. "Insurance and Issues in Financial Soundness." IMF Working Paper 03/138, International Monetary Fund, Washington, D.C. Available at http://www.imf.org/external/pubs/ft/wp/2003/wp03138.pdf.

Debelle, Guy. 2004. "Household Debt and the Macroeconomy." In *BIS Quarterly Review: International Banking and Financial Market Developments*, ed. J. Bisignano, C. Borio, R. McCauley, E. Remolona, P. Turner, P. Van den Bergh, and W. White, 51–64. Basel, Switzerland: Bank for International Settlements. Available at http://www.bis.org/publ/qtrpdf/r_qt0403.pdf.

Demirgüç-Kunt, Asli, and Enrica Detragiache. 1998. "The Determinants of Banking Crises in Developing and Developed Countries." *International Monetary Fund Staff Papers* 45(1): 81–109.

De Nicoló, Gianni, Patrick Honohan, and Alain Ize. 2003. "Dollarization of the Banking System: Good or Bad?" IMF Working Paper 03/146, International Monetary Fund, Washington, D.C. Available at http://www.imf.org/external/pubs/ft/wp/2003/wp03146.pdf.

Evanoff, D., and L. Wall. 2001. "Sub-Debt Yield Spreads as Bank Risk Measures." *Journal of Financial Services Research* 20: 121–45.

Financial Stability Forum. 2000. *Report of the Working Group on Offshore Centres*. Basel, Switzerland: Financial Stability Forum. Available at http://www.fsforum.org/publications/OFC_Report_-_5_April_2000a.pdf.

Gapen, Michael T., Dale F. Gray, Cheng Hoon Lim, and Yingbin Xiao. 2004. "The Contingent Claims Approach to Corporate Vulnerability Analysis: Estimating Default Risk and Economy-Wide Risk Transfer." IMF Working Paper 04/121, International Monetary Fund, Washington, DC. Available at http://www.imf.org/external/pubs/ft/wp/2004/wp04121.pdf.

Garber, Peter M., Robin L. Lumsdaine, and Paolo Longato. 2001. *Deutsche Bank Alarm Clock: Descriptive Manual, Version 3*. Global Markets Research. London: Deutsche Bank.

Ghosh, Atish R., Timothy D. Lane, Marianne Schulze-Ghattas, Ales Bulir, Javier Hamman, and Alexandros T. Mourmouras. 2002. "IMF-Supported Programs in Capital Account Crises: Design and Experience." Occasional Paper 210, International Monetary Fund, Washington, DC. Available at http://www.imf.org/external/pubs/nft/op/210/index.htm.

Gourchinas, Pierre-Olivier, Rodrigo Valdes, and Oscar Landerretche. 2001. "Lending Booms: Latin America and the World. National Bureau of Economic Research Working Paper No.8249, April 2001.

Gray, Dale F., Robert C. Merton, and Zvi Bodie. 2003. "A New Framework for Analyzing and Managing Macrofinancial Risks of an Economy." Moody's MF Risk Working Paper 1-03, Moody's. Available at http://www.moodys-mfrisk.com.

Gropp, Reint., Jukka Vesala, and Guiseppe Vulpes. 2002. "Equity and Bond Market Signals as Leading Indicators of Bank Fragility." European Central Bank Working Paper 150, European Central Bank, Frankfurt, Germany.

Gulde, Anne-Marie, David Hoelscher, Alain Ize, David Marston, and Gianni De Nicoló. 2004. "Financial Stability in Dollarized Economies." IMF Occasional Paper 230 04/, International Monetary Fund, Washington, DC.

Gunther, Jeffery W., Mark E. Levonian, and Robert R. Moore. 2001. "Can the Stock Market Tell Bank Supervisors Anything They Don't Already Know?" *Economic and Financial Review* (Federal Reserve Bank of Dallas) Issue QII (Second Quarter): 2–9.

Hilbers, Paul L., Qin Lei, and Lisbeth S. Zacho. 2001. "Real Estate Market Developments and Financial Sector Soundness." IMF Working Paper 01/129, International Monetary Fund, Washington, DC. Available at http://www.imf.org/external/pubs/ft/wp/2001/wp01129.pdf.

Houben, Aerdt, Jan Kakes, and Garry Schinasi. 2004. "Toward a Framework for Safeguarding Financial Stability." IMF Working Paper 04/101, International Monetary Fund, Washington, DC. Available at http://www.imf.org/external/pubs/ft/wp/2004/wp04101.pdf.

International Association of Insurance Supervisors (IAIS). 2000. "On Solvency, Solvency Assessment, and Actuarial Issues." IAIS Issues Paper, International Association of Insurance Supervisors, Basel, Switzerland.

————. 2002. "Principles on Capital Adequacy and Solvency." IAIS Principles No. 5, International Association of Insurance Supervisors, Basel, Switzerland.

International Monetary Fund (IMF). 2000. "Offshore Financial Centers." IMF Background Paper, International Monetary Fund, Washington, DC.

————. 2002a. "Assessing Sustainability." International Monetary Fund, Washington, DC. Available at http://www.imf.org/external/np/pdr/sus/2002/eng/052802.pdf.

————. 2002b. "Early Warning Systems Models: The Next Steps Forward." In *Global Financial Stability Report*, chapter 4. Washington, DC: International Monetary Fund. Available at http://www.imf.org/External/Pubs/FT/GFSR/2002/01/pdf/chp4and5.pdf.

————. 2003a. *Annual Report on Exchange Arrangements and Exchange Restrictions.* Washington, DC: International Monetary Fund.

————. 2003b. *Financial Soundness Indicators.* Washington, DC: International Monetary Fund. Available at http://www.imf.org/external/np/sta/fsi/eng/2003/051403.pdf.

————. 2003c. "Financial Soundness Indicators." Background Paper, International Monetary Fund, Washington, DC. Available at http://www.imf.org/external/np/sta/fsi/eng/2003/051403bp.pdf.

————. 2003d. *Trade Finance in Financial Crises: Assessment of Key Issues.* Washington, DC: International Monetary Fund. Available at http://www.imf.org/external/np/pdr/cr/2003/eng/120903.pdf.

————. 2004a. *Annual Report on Exchange Arrangements and Exchange Restrictions.* International Monetary Fund, Washington, DC.

————. 2004b. *Compilation Guide on Financial Soundness Indicators.* Washington, DC: International Monetary Fund. Available at http://www.imf.org/external/np/sta/fsi/eng/2004/guide/index.htm.

————. 2004c. "Offshore Financial Centers: The Assessment Program—An Update." International Monetary Fund, Washington, DC. Available at http://www.imf.org/external/np/mfd/2004/eng/031204.pdf.

————. 2004d. *Global Financial Stability Report* (April). Washington, DC: International Monetary Fund.

————. 2004e. *Global Financial Stability Report* (September). Washington, DC: International Monetary Fund.

————. 2005. "Household Balance Sheets." In *Global Financial Stability Report*, chapter 3. Washington, DC: International Monetary Fund.

International Monetary Fund, and World Bank. 2002a. *Experience with the Assessments of the IOSCO Objectives and Principles of Securities Regulation under the Financial Sector Assessment Program.* Washington, DC: International Monetary Fund. Available at http://www.imf.org/external/np/mae/IOSCO/2002/eng/041802.pdf.

————. 2002b. *Implementation of the Basel Core Principles for Effective Banking Supervision, Experiences, Influences, and Perspectives.* Washington, DC: International Monetary Fund. Available at http://www.imf.org/external/np/mae/bcore/2002/092302.pdf.

Ishii, Shogo, Karl Habermeier, Jorge Iván Canales-Kriljenko, Bernard Laurens, John Leimone, and Judit Vadasz. 2002. "Capital Account Liberalization and Financial Sector Stability." IMF Occasional Paper 211, International Monetary Fund, Washington, DC. Available at http://www.imf.org/external/pubs/nft/op/211/index.htm.

Jagtiani, Julapa, Kolari James, Catherine Lemieux, and Hwan Shin. 2003. "Early Warning Models for Bank Supervision: Simpler Could Be Better." *Federal Reserve Bank of Chicago Economic Perspectives* 27(3): 49–60.

Kamin, Steven, John Schindler, and Shawna Samuel. 2001. "The Contribution of Domestic and External Factors to Emerging Market Devaluation Crises: An Early Warning Systems Approach." International Finance Working Paper 711, Board of Governors of the Federal Reserve System, Washington, DC.

Kaminsky, Graciela. 1999. "Currency and Banking Crises—The Early Warnings of Distress." IMF Working Paper 99/178, International Monetary Fund, Washington, DC. Available at http://www.imf.org/external/pubs/ft/wp/1999/wp99178.pdf.

Kaminsky, Graciela, Saul Lizondo, and Carmen Reinhart. 1998. "Leading Indicators of Currency Crises." *IMF Staff Papers* 45: 1–48.

Kaminsky, Graciela, and Carmen Reinhart. 1999. "The Twin Crises: The Causes of Banking and Balance-of-Payments Problems." *American Economic Review* 89(3): 473–500.

Krainer, John, and Jose. A. Lopez. 2003. "How Might Financial Market Information Be Used for Supervisory Purposes?" *Economic Review*, Federal Reserve Bank of San Francisco, 29–45.

Krugman, Paul. 1979. "A Model of Balance-of-Payments Crises." *Journal of Money, Credit, and Banking* 11(3): 311–25.

Levine, Ross. 2003. More on Finance and Growth: More Finance, More Growth? *Federal Reserve Bank of St. Louis Review* (July/August): 31–46. Available at http://research.stlouisfed.org/publications/review/03/07/Levine.pdf.

Merton, Robert C. 1974. "On the Pricing of Corporate Debt: The Risk Structure of Interest Rates." *Journal of Finance* 29: 449–70.

Miles, Colin. 2002. "Large Complex Financial Institutions (LCFIs): Issues to Be Considered in the Financial Sector Assessment Program." MAE Operational Paper 02/3, International Monetary Fund, Monetary and Exchange Department, Washington, DC.

Morales, R. Armando, and Liliana Schumacher. 2003. "Market Volatility as a Financial Soundness Indicator: An Application to Israel." IMF Working Paper 03/47, International Monetary Fund, Washington, DC. Available at http://www.imf.org/external/pubs/ft/wp/2003/wp0347.pdf.

Obstfeld, Maurice. 1996. "Models of Currency Crises with Self-Fulfilling Features." CEPR Discussion Paper 1315, Center For Economic Policy Research, Washington, DC.

Pomerleano, Michael. 1998. "The East Asia Crisis and Corporate Finances: The Untold Micro Story." World Bank Working Paper 1990, World Bank Group, Washington, DC.

Rajan, Raghuram G., and Luigi Zingales. 1998. "Financial Dependence and Growth." *American Economic Review* 88(3): 559–86.

Roy, Amlan. 2001. "Emerging Markets Risk Indicator (EMRI)." In *Global Emerging Markets Strategy*. London: Credit Suisse First Bank.

Sahajwala, Ranjana, and Paul Van den Berg. 2000. "Supervisory Risk Assessment and Early Warning Systems." Basel Committee on Banking Supervision Working Paper 2, Bank for International Settlements, Basel, Switzerland.

3

Schnatz, Bernd. 1998. "Macroeconomic Determinants of Currency Turbulences in Emerging Markets." Discussion Paper 3/98, Economic Research Group of the Deutsche Bundesbank, Frankfurt, Germany.

Schinasi, Gary J. 2004. "Defining Financial Stability." IMF Working Paper 04/187, World Bank Group, Washington, DC. Available at http://www.imf.org/external/pubs/ft/wp/2004/wp04187.pdf.

Sundararajan, Venkataraman, Charles Enoch, Armida San José, Paul Hilbers, Russell Krueger, Marina Moretti, and Graham Slack. 2003. "Financial Soundness Indicators: Analytical Aspects and Country Practices." IMF Occasional Paper 212, International Monetary Fund, Washington, DC. Available at http://www.imf.org/external/pubs/nft/op/212/index.htm.

Sundararajan, Venkataraman, and Luca Errico. 2002. "Islamic Financial Institutions and Products in the Global Financial System: Key Issues in Risk Management and Challenges Ahead." IMF Working Paper 02/192, International Monetary Fund, Washington, DC.

Tschoegl, Adrian E. 2000. "International Banking Centers, Geography, and Foreign Banks." *Financial Markets, Institutions and Instruments* 9, No. 1 (February): 1–32. Available at http://www.ingenta.com/journals/browse/bpl/fmii.

Williamson, John, and Molly Mahar. 1998. "A Survey of Financial Liberalization." *Essays in International Finance* (Princeton University) 211 (November). Available at http://www.princeton.edu/~ies/IES_Essays/E211.pdf.

Wong, Jim, and Laurence Fung. 2002. *Liquidity of the Hong Kong Stock Market since the Asian Financial Crisis.* Basel, Switzerland: Bank for International Settlements. Available at http://www.bis.org/cgfs/conf/mar02n.pdf.

Chapter 4

Assessing Financial Structure and Financial Development

4.1 Overview

4.1.1 Motivation for Assessing Financial Structure and Financial Development

Extensive evidence confirms that creating the conditions for a deep and efficient financial system can contribute robustly to sustained economic growth and lower poverty (e.g., see Beck, Levine, and Loayza 2000, Honohan 2004a, and World Bank 2001a). Moreover, in all levels of development, continued efficient and effective provision of financial services requires that financial policies and financial system structures be adjusted as needed in response to financial innovations and shifts in the broader macroeconomic and institutional environment.

4.1.2 Scope of Analysis

The goals of financial structure analysis and development assessment for a country are to (a) assess the current provision of financial services, (b) analyze the factors behind missing or underdeveloped services and markets, and (c) identify the obstacles to the efficient and effective provision of a broad range of financial services. The dimensions along which service provision must be assessed include the range, scale (depth) and reach (breadth or penetration), and the cost and quality of financial services provided to the economy. At a high level of abstraction, those services are usually classified as including the following:

- Making payments
- Mobilizing savings

4

- Allocating capital funds
- Monitoring users of funds
- Transforming risk

Thus, the ideal financial system will provide, for example, reliable and inexpensive money transfer within the country, reaching remote areas and poor households. There will be remunerative deposit facilities and other investment opportunities offering liquidity and a reasonable risk-return tradeoff. Entrepreneurs will have access to a range of sources for funds for their working- and fixed-capital formation; affordable mortgage and consumer finance will be available to households. The credit renewal decisions of banks and the market signals coming from organized markets in traded securities will help ensure that good use continues to be made of investable funds. Insurance intermediaries and the portfolio possibilities offered by liquid securities markets will help maximize the risk pooling and the shifting of risk at a reasonable price to entities that are able and willing to absorb it.

The scope of financial structure analysis and of development assessment is fairly extensive—as illustrated in the above list—and those structural issues cannot be simply broken into self-contained segments corresponding to existing institutional arrangements. Structural and development issues arise across the entire spectrum of financial markets and intermediaries, including banking, insurance, securities markets, and nonbank intermediation. They often demand consideration of factors for which well-adapted and standardized quantification is not readily available. Therefore, the challenge is to translate those wide-ranging and somewhat abstract concepts into a concrete and practical assessment methodology.

The suggested approach begins with a fact-finding dimension that seeks to benchmark the existing financial services provided in (and available to) the national economy—in terms of range, scale and reach, cost, and quality—against international practice. Such benchmarking should help pinpoint areas of systemic underperformance, which can then be further analyzed to diagnose the causes of the underperformance against realistic targets. To some extent, the benchmarking can be quantified, but, in practice, quantification must be supplemented by in-depth qualitative information. The question being asked in every case is, if quality or quantity is deficient, then what has caused this deficiency?

Deficiencies will often be traced to a wide range of structural, institutional, and policy factors.

- First, there may be gaps or needed changes in the financial infrastructure, both in the soft infrastructures of legal, information, and regulatory systems and in the harder transactional technology infrastructures that include payments and settlements systems and communications more generally.
- Second, there may be flaws or needed adaptations in regulatory or tax policy (including competition policy) whose inadequacies or unintended side effects distort or suppress the functioning of the financial system to an extent not warranted by the goals of the policy.
- Third, digging deeper, there may be broad governance issues at the national level, for example, where existing institutional structures impede good policy making (especially favoring incumbents over newcomers).

- Fourth, financial sector deficiencies may also be traced to problems in the country's wider economic infrastructures, including the education, transportation, and communications systems. Furthermore, many developing countries are faced with the difficulty that effective finance requires a scale of activity that may be beyond the reach of small economies, populated as they are by a small number of small clients, small intermediaries, and small organized markets (see Bossone, Honohan, and Long 2002). An effective financial system, while contributing to wider economic growth and development, is also somewhat dependent on the wider economic environment—not least the macroeconomic and fiscal environment.

The most distinctive feature of financial structure analysis and development assessment is the focus on the users of financial services and on the efficiency and effectiveness of the system in meeting user needs. Policy reforms that benefit users and that promote financial development are generally favored in such analysis and assessments.[1] The proposed assessment framework is also guided by the presumption, which is based on a sizable body of empirical evidence, that an effective and efficient financial system is best provided by market-driven financial service providers, with the main role of government being to serve as regulator and provider of robust financial infrastructure. Therefore, the establishment of a government-sponsored financial service provider is not seen as likely to be the first-best solution to deficiencies. Instead, the role and effectiveness of financial service providers are assessed regardless of whether they are government owned. Assessment has two phases: information gathering and analytical reporting.

Phase 1: Information-Gathering Phase

To reflect this focus on users and the services they require, the overall assessment needs to adopt a functional approach and not to be confined to a perspective that is based on existing institutional dividing lines between different groups of providers.[2] Nevertheless, much of the information gathering will inevitably reflect those institutional divisions, not the least because national regulatory structures are typically organized along those lines (notwithstanding the trend to integrated supervisory agencies in several countries).

In addition, the adequacy of the legal, information, and payments infrastructures and of other aspects of the overall policy environment are central to the development assessment: each has relevance cutting across any single sector. Yet, information about the effectiveness of the infrastructures and about the unintended and hidden side effects of the policy environment is often obtained only by learning how each sector works. Likewise, the competitive structure, efficiency, and product mix of the various sectors can be explained only on the basis of an understanding of the design and performance of the infrastructures. So the information-gathering phase of the assessment needs to have a sectoral, as well as an infrastructural, dimension. Cross-cutting policy issues such as taxation also need to be kept in mind. Finally, user perspective can be helpful, especially in identifying gaps in providing markets and services, as well as in discovering deficiencies in quality and cost that might not be revealed from analysis of the suppliers.

The information-gathering phase of the assessment is multidimensional. Typical components of the information-gathering phase may include the following:

4

- Quantitative benchmarking of the size, depth, cost and price efficiency, and the penetration (breadth) of financial intermediaries and markets, using internationally comparable data (section 4.2)
- Reviews of legal, informational, and transaction technology infrastructures (section 4.3)
- Sectoral development reviews, providing a more in-depth assessment of service provision, structure, and regulation (Sectors covered will normally include commercial banking and nearbanking, insurance, and securities sectors and may also include some or all of the collective savings institutions and of the financial aspects of public pension funds, specialized development intermediaries, mortgage finance, and microfinance. Those sectors need to refer to the functioning both of the industry [financial services providers] itself and of the regulatory apparatus [section 4.4].)
- Demand-side reviews of access to, and use of, financial services by households, microenterprises, small and medium enterprises (SMEs), and large enterprises (section 4.5)
- Reviews of selected additional cross-cutting aspects of the policy environment (for example, distorting taxation and subsidization of financial intermediation) and of implications for competition of cross-sectoral ownership structures (Those reviews also may mention missing product issues, thus focusing on whether key financial products—such as leasing, factoring, and venture capital—are available and identifying the reasons for their absence [see section 4.6].)

Phase 2: Analytical and Reporting Phases

The relative importance of the components of the information-gathering phase and the scope of their analysis will vary according to country circumstances. This wide-ranging scope of information presents a challenge to assessors who must, in the analytical and reporting phases, synthesize the information to identify the major axes of needed policy reform and of infrastructural strengthening for stability and development. Segments of the financial system that are already active, but for which the benchmarking exercise suggests shortcomings, will deserve more-detailed attention. For segments that are missing or are not very developed, the discussion of needed policies can be confined to the level of broad strategy. How those components can be integrated into a policy framework is discussed in section 4.7.

4.1.3 Stability and Development: Complementarities Despite the Different Perspective

Financial structure analysis and development assessment inevitably overlaps extensively with the stability assessment. Even if adequate from a stability perspective, the existing regulatory framework and the supervisory practices may need reform from the development perspective. Certain areas not normally considered in stability-oriented assessments, such as microfinance and development banking, warrant attention from the development perspective. Moreover, every sector that is relevant to stability can have an important development dimension. Notwithstanding the overlap of themes, the focus of the sectoral and infrastructural development reviews is different from, and complementary to, that of the stability assessment. For each sector, the development review is designed to consider whether policy or legislative changes are needed to enhance the ability and incentive of market participants to deliver financial services.

The types of question asked in analyzing financial structure and development are often different from those that take center stage in the stability assessment. For example, are regulatory restrictions on bank entry and conduct (including interest rate ceilings, ownership, branching, and automated teller machines [ATMs]) unduly constraining, and do they act as barriers to competition and to the extension of financial services to underserved segments? Is the regulation of insurance company investments hampering their contribution to long-term funding of enterprises? Is there an adequate enabling legal framework for the emergence of widely accessed credit registries? Are judicial practice, funding, and skills supportive of speedy and low-cost debt recovery? Does the regulatory framework for payments systems support an efficient and low-cost network of retail payments throughout the country?

The overlap between stability and development raises both practical and conceptual issues for the sectoral reviews: At the practical level, there is the need to coordinate information gathering to avoid duplication of effort. At the conceptual level, there is the need to ensure that the recommendations mesh well together. In practice, the two perspectives—stability and development, reinforce each other in terms of recommendations more often than they create a tension or tradeoff. For example, legal procedures for enhancing creditor rights tend both to reduce the risk of loan losses undermining the soundness of the banking system and to increase the willingness of intermediaries to extend credit. Yet there can be some apparent tension, for example, when entry of foreign-owned banks—although improving the quality and price of services to the rest of the economy—is seen as a threat to the profitability of incumbents (a stability issue). Apparent conflicts must be considered and resolved from a wider perspective of ensuring long-term, stable financial development in the interest of the economy at large. One issue in this context is whether the system is sufficiently robust (stability analysis) to withstand the potential shocks associated with liberalization that will eventually be needed for development reasons. In this sense, the stability analysis can provide some guidance to the timing and sequencing of development-oriented reforms. A detailed analysis of sequencing issues is presented in chapter 12.

4.2 Quantitative Benchmarking

If we are to obtain an overall picture of where the financial sector is, or is not, performing well, then the performance of financial intermediaries and markets—in terms of total assets, scope of activity, depth, efficiency, and penetration—can be compared to a carefully chosen set of comparator countries. National authorities are likely to be interested in countries in the same region, as well as those of a similar size and a similar level or higher levels of per capita income.[3] The type of indicators that would be appropriate is discussed in chapter 2 and summarized in box 4.1.

4

Box 4.1 Quantitative Indicators for Financial Structure and Development Assessment

The measures chosen as quantitative indicators for financial structure and development assessment will naturally include basic indicators of financial depth expressed as a percentage of gross domestic product (GDP). The indicators are proxies for the size of the different components of the financial sector and could include credit to the private sector and broad money (M2) for banking; number of listed equities and bond issues, market capitalization, and value traded of financial markets for financial markets; and insurance premium income and asset size for insurance.

Data on breadth and penetration—which are proxies for the population's access to different segments of the financial sector and, thus, for outreach—of financial markets include bank branch and outlet intensity and deposit and loan size distribution, as well as number of clients in the banking, nearbanking, and insurance sectors. The data gauge the share of the population with access to financial services. Data on market structure—number of banks, concentration in banking, and share of foreign-owned and government-owned banks—are also relevant. Efficiency measures include interest margins, overhead costs or asset indicators, and turnover ratios for capital markets. Indicators of efficiency and quality of payment services include cash-to-GDP ratio, lags in check or payment order clearing, volume and value of checks or payment orders processed in retail and large value payment systems, and number and density of ATMs.

Indicators for size, depth, and efficiency are available for a large cross-section of countries, thus allow-

ing comparison; however, the assembly of breadth and penetration indicators on a cross-country basis is in the beginning stages. There is a clear ranking of cross-country data availability among different sectors, with data on banking, insurance, and stock markets more readily available than on bond markets and microfinance. Quantitative benchmarking may also include some comparisons over time within countries where feasible and should serve as basis for more detailed analysis.

Infrastructural quality measures—contract enforcement (including measures of the effectiveness of the court systems such as the speed of judicial conflict resolution), speed and effectiveness of insolvency procedures, creditor and minority shareholder rights, presence of a credit registry, and firm entry regulations—can be drawn from the World Bank's Doing Business Database. Also informative are user assessments from the World Business Environment Survey.

Finally, the quantitative indicators for financial structure and development assessment can be rounded off by relevant summary economic and social indicators such as GDP per capita, share of the informal economy, illiteracy rate, total population size, and so forth, which can be selected from the World Development Indicators published by the World Bank.

A more detailed presentation of financial structure indicators, including definitional issues and data sources, is contained in chapter 2.

Ideally, given data availability, it may be possible to use the results of research studies that have identified causal factors for cross-country differences in depth, efficiency, and other dimensions of financial development. For example, several studies have attempted to explain differences in average bank margins—key indicators of the price efficiency of banking in terms of policy, institutional, and macroeconomic variables. Those variables include the bank's size, a measure of property rights protection, and other bank- and country-level characteristics, such as bank concentration, output gap, and interest rate level.[4] If those policy and institutional variables are available for the country in question, the results of the studies can be used to throw light on potential improvements that could be achieved through better policies and better institutions. The residual between the expected value of average bank margins in the country predicted by the study and the actual margins, if positive, will point to the need for closer analysis of idiosyncratic features in the country—features that may be contributing to the gap. (For an illustration of this technique in practice in Kenya, see appendix E.) A similar approach can be used for banking depth where macro-variables, such as inflation and the level of gross domestic product (GDP) per capita, are key determinants along with institutional variables, such as shareholder and creditor rights (e.g., see Beck, Demirgüç-Kunt, and Levine 2003).

There are also some cross-country studies of other dimensions, including insurance penetration, stock market capitalization, and turnover, although those studies may not yet be sufficiently well established for heavy reliance to be placed on them for benchmarking purposes. Along with other dimensions, including access to financial services, cross-country research is not yet sufficiently developed to support this kind of benchmarking. In those cases, simple cross-country comparisons against peers can, nevertheless, be informative and can point to areas of deficiency.

4.3 Review of Legal, Informational, and Transactional Technology Infrastructures for Access and Development

The major cross-cutting infrastructures can be grouped under the three headings of legal, informational, and transactional technology.[5] The robustness of legal infrastructures is universally acknowledged as crucial to a healthy financial system. Creditor protection in principle and in practice is central, as is bankruptcy law and its implementation. In both of those areas, reform of the court system is often at the heart of needed reforms. Corporate governance law and practice can also be seen as coming under this heading. Informational infrastructures include accounting and auditing rules and practice, plus the legal and organizational requirements for public or private credit registries and property registries. Other aspects, such as the ratings industry, may be relevant in more-advanced, middle-income countries. Internationally recognized accounting and auditing standards exist, and assessments of their observance, when available, can be useful for both stability and development assessments. The most important transactional technology infrastructures—relating to wholesale payments and settlements—may already be assessed using the Core Principles of Systemically Important Payment Systems (CPSIPS). (See chapter 11 for details of CPSIPS.) The additional dimension required for development purposes is the functioning of the retail payments system: although it is not vulnerable to sudden failure on a large scale, it is not considered "systemically important" in the sense of the CPSIPS. The efficiency with which the legal, information, and transactional technology infrastructures support financial intermediation in the country plays a critical role in access and development. Detailed assessments of those areas are described in chapters 9, 10, and 11 of this handbook, and they provide information on the quality of the infrastructure elements, which are discussed below.

4.3.1 Legal Infrastructure

The efficient functioning of the legal system is indispensable for effective financial intermediation (e.g., see La Porta et al. 1997, 1998, and Levine, Loayza, and Beck 2000). Although discussed in more detail in chapter 9 of this handbook, the following discussion highlights the aspects of the legal system that are important for development assessment.

In addition to the cross-country quantitative evidence mentioned in box 4.1, underlying factual information for this exercise can come both from any completed assessments of formal codes such as the *Principles and Guidelines for Effective Insolvency and Creditor Rights Systems* (World Bank 2001b) and from interviews with banks, enterprises, academics, and other market participants.[6]

The effective creation, perfection, and enforcement of collateral is a cross-cutting issue for financial intermediation and requires assessing the appropriate legislation, the property registries (including stamp duties and notary fees), the court system, and the out-of-court enforcement mechanisms. If collateral taking is limited to certain assets or if high collateral-to-debt ratios are required, this limitation can ration credit to certain sectors or size groups of borrowers. The effectiveness of the collateral process can also affect the terms of lending, such as interest rates, along with the competitiveness of the lending market.

The effectiveness of debt enforcement and insolvency procedures in terms of cost and time it takes, both through and outside the court system, is important for effective and efficient intermediation. Expedited enforcement systems that use private negotiation and out-of-court settlement can be very helpful, if available. The possibility of flexible ways of achieving corporate financial restructuring, albeit without undermining creditors' position, is important. A deficient insolvency framework can restrict the use of the court system overall and can lead to suboptimal out-of-court settlements or even restrictions on the access to, and the terms of, lending.

The functioning of the court system is crucial. The evaluation here could include an assessment of the legal profession along several dimensions, such as education, skills funding, fees, and ethical behavior. The effectiveness of specialized courts in local circumstances can be examined if we bear in mind that those courts can help in situations where complex commercial issues arise and even in situations with less-complex issues, such as loan recovery. The courts may work faster and more consistently than regular courts—though experience here is mixed, and it may be better in the long run to work toward an overall improvement in the functioning of the court system.

The state of corporate governance, including the relationships among management, majority owners, and outside investors, can have an important effect on the ease with which outside investors provide finance and the price thereof. Both the rules and the practice of corporate governance need to be considered; if a formal corporate governance assessment has been carried out, its findings can be drawn upon here.[7]

4.3.2 Information Infrastructures

Asymmetric information between borrowers and lenders and, thus, the transaction costs can be reduced if there is readily available information on the financial condition of borrowers and especially on their history of credit performance. In particular, two areas of the information infrastructure should not be neglected: (a) transparency in borrowers' financial statements enables lenders to assess borrowers' creditworthiness on present and past financial and operational performance, and (b) readily available credit information on borrowers enables lenders to assess borrowers' creditworthiness according to their past performance within the financial system.[8]

Credit registries, if they exist, vary widely in the information that is being collected and that is available to financial institutions; hence, they vary in their effectiveness in improving access. The effect on access is influenced by characteristics such as (a) which financial and nonfinancial institutions provide data and have access to the data (the more the better); (b) whether only negative information (i.e., on defaults and delinquencies) or also positive information, including interest rate, maturity, and collateral, is collected and provided (positive information improves the potential use of the registry for credit appraisal); (c) for what kind of loans is the information collected; and (d) for how long is information kept. While there are reasons to expect privately owned registries to out-perform those operated by public agencies, there are instances of effective publicly owned registries. Local conditions can influence the choice here. Existing credit registries should be evaluated not only on their design features, but also on how they have performed in practice. The legal and regulatory environment is important for existence and effective-ness of credit registries and other financial information vendors. While protection of con-sumer privacy is important, unduly restrictive rules here can hamper information sharing on borrowers to the detriment of their access to credit.

Credit registries may be complemented by other providers of financial information on borrowers. Commercial information vendors, such as Bloomberg or Reuters, trade associa-tions, chambers of commerce, or credit-rating agencies, might also contribute to transpar-ency in the financial market. Finally, there might be private information-sharing agree-ments between financial institutions outside the formal structure of a credit registry.

Accounting and auditing standards and practices are important elements of the infor-mation environment in that they govern companies' disclosure of financial information to the public. A full assessment of the accounting and auditing standards (see chapter 10 for further details on these standards) in this area might not always be practicable, but the standards, nevertheless, represent the overall goals that should be aspired to and can be used as a reference for identifying information-based barriers to enhanced financing for the corporate sector.

4.3.3 Transactional Technology Infrastructures

The effective transfer of money between customers of the same and of different institu-tions is one of the main functions of the financial systems. While the stability assessment of the payment system is mostly interested in wholesale systems, the development assess-ment focuses more on the cost of and access to retail payment services. Development assessment includes evaluating the effectiveness of the check and money transfer system in terms of time and cost. It also entails assessing the access to those services, either directly through banks or indirectly through other financial institutions that use banks as agents. Indicators to assess the effectiveness of the payment system include the cost and time to transfer money. As alternative indicators of access, some studies have surveyed the small numbers of the population and of subgroups who have a transactions banking account, debit card, or credit card, as well as the distribution of travel time to the nearest ATM or money transmission point. Unfortunately, as yet, there is no cross-country dataset for such access indicators.

4.4 Sectoral Development Reviews

Sectoral developmental reviews complement the assessments of regulatory standards. Over the past several decades, extensive institutional change and experimentation in advanced economies have led to the emergence of elaborate regimes of regulation and supervision of the banking, insurance, and securities markets. Those regimes are designed to ensure integrity of the functioning within the sectors and to avoid behavior that is likely to contribute to failure. They have evolved largely in response to the rapid development of the financial sector in advanced economies rather than as a means of promoting the development of the sector—though, in several cases, regulatory liberalization has been influenced by a perceived risk to the competitiveness of domestic financial markets in an increasingly global financial system.

The standards and codes used for those sectors essentially codify what has emerged as the common core of what remains a somewhat diverse set of regulatory institutions. While the standards and codes represent a fairly firm and widely agreed framework for assessment on the prudential side, the mechanics of overcoming barriers to development of what are still unsophisticated financial systems in low- and middle-income countries are not something for which a comprehensive template can be distilled from current practice. Indeed, the standards and codes either explicitly or implicitly assume the presence of much of what is sought in the goal of developing the financial system and at the same time contain (to some extent) principles that guide institutional development and good practices in financial institutions. Promoting institutional development, however, raises issues of sequencing and absorptive capacity in implementing policy reforms. Because of those considerations, conducting the development assessment for any given subsector is necessarily less categorical, more subjective, and arguably more difficult than assessing the relevant standards and codes.

For most low- and middle-income countries, a brief and selective review of development issues provides the information that is needed on the preconditions for a full standards and codes assessment. Where standards and codes for a sector are not being fully assessed, the review of development issues can be accompanied by a less detailed, stability-oriented, regulatory assessment. The assessor should highlight deficiencies in quantity (scale and reach), quality, and price of the services provided and should attempt to identify the infrastructural weaknesses that have contributed to those deficiencies, as well as any policy flaws—including flaws in competition and tax policy—that have likely contributed to the deficiencies. Although some of the needed data are covered in cross-country databases (as mentioned in chapter 2), for many other dimensions in each of the sectors, only noncomparable national sources are currently available. Those dimensions would include aspects such as the stock market free-float, reliance by large firms on international depositary receipts, transactions costs for securities markets, prices of insurance and efficiency of insurance products, and maturity structure of intermediary portfolios. The assessors must use their judgment in evaluating whatever information is available on such matters.

Because competitiveness issues have a pervasive influence on sectoral performance, the issues need to be analyzed in all sectors. The competitive structure of the industry

4

is a multi-dimensional concept in itself. That structure is not merely measured by concentration ratios and by Herfindahl indices, but—in acknowledgment of the distinction between concentration and contestability—also requires an understanding of regulatory influences, including restrictive regulations on branching or cross-regional service provision, on permissible lines of business, on product pricing (e.g., interest ceilings and premium rate floors), or on portfolio allocation (especially for insurance companies, including localization rules, but also including reserve requirements and so forth). Is the market de facto segmented, thereby limiting the pro-efficiency forces of competition? Is ownership of the main intermediaries linked to government or to industrial groups, thereby tending to entrench incumbents rather than enabling new entrepreneurs?

In addition to our looking at the aggregate national position, it is important, though often difficult, to assess the reach of each financial sector along the dimensions of geographic region, economic sector, size of firm, and number of households. Of course, the large and well-established firms in the main cities will have greatest access. The question is whether the gap between those and smaller firms and households in smaller centers and in rural areas is more than it should be. Sources of information on direct access to financial services—with a focus on those at different levels of income—are diverse and scarce. There is a growing appreciation of the importance of compiling data on who has access to what financial services, and efforts are under way to increase systematic coverage of financial issues in surveys of households, business users, financial service providers and their regulators, and national experts. All four types of information are needed for a comprehensive review.[9]

Going beyond aggregate measures of efficiency, availability, and cost of more-advanced products needs to be benchmarked for each of the main sectors. What products do users identify as lacking? How much maturity transformation does each sector achieve? How much is achieved overall through the interaction of the sectors? One may also mention consumer protection legislation, which, though present, is not uniformly at the fore in stability assessments.

Often, the review will reveal that the source of shortcomings is mostly in the policy environment (including the nonprudential or unneeded prudential regulations and taxation and the effects of state ownership) or in deficiencies in the legal, information, or transactional technology infrastructures. Such policy and infrastructural issues will often have a cross-cutting effect on several subsectors and need to be reported as such (see section 4.6).

4.4.1 Banking

The sectoral assessment for banking is at the heart of development issues in finance because of the central role of banking in the financial systems of most developing countries. In addition to what can be quantified on the basis of available statistics, the fact-finding requires broad-ranging discussions with market participants, as well as with the regulators.[10] An effective banking system will be characterized by considerable depth (measured, for example, by total assets); breadth in terms both of customer base (lending to a wide range of sectors and regions, without neglecting the needs of creditworthy borrowers in any sector or region) and of product range (maturities, repayment schedules,

4

flexibility, convenience, risk profile, and nonbanking products where permitted); and efficiency. Overhead costs, interest spreads, and interest margins give an indication of efficiency, though taxes and other requirements can substantially influence the spread, as explained below.

Quantitative Benchmarking

Benchmarking the performance of the banking system needs to go well beyond tabulation of cross-country comparisons of available indicators and should be based on an analysis of factors governing the variations in the indicators. The main indicators need to be looked at in terms of their development over time, in relation to the rest of the national financial system, and in terms of national causal factors. In addition, international comparisons should ideally be made in a more structured way, thus drawing on research findings.

As an example, assessment of bank efficiency and competitiveness requires information on interest rate spreads and margins,[11] which are influenced by both bank- and country-level characteristics. The analysis and decomposition of interest spreads and margins can help assess the existence and severity of deficiencies in the banking sector.[12] A useful device is to use accounting identities to decompose interest rate spreads into five components: (a) overhead costs, (b) loan–loss provisions, (c) reserve requirements, (d) taxes, and (e) (the residual) profits. Decomposition helps identify institutional and legal deficiencies that explain high spreads. Both spreads and margins can be compared across countries and across the underlying factors derived (see appendix E, which is based on Kenya).

Penetration of and access to banking services are important dimensions for which a broad international database is not yet available, but for which national statistics can be very informative. Geographic branch, ATM, and bank outlet data give a first indication of the penetration of banking services across geographic areas of the country. A comparison of bank branch density with other countries can give an indication of bank penetration but has to be treated with care, because it does not include data on nonbank service providers. Similarly, a within-country geographic comparison of penetration should consider other nearbank providers, such as savings banks or cooperatives. Where appropriate, account should also be taken of alternative delivery channels, such as ATMs, phone banking, and Internet banking, plus novel ways of providing access to financial services in more remote areas, such as mobile branches and correspondent banking. There may be regulatory obstacles to penetration: What are the regulatory requirements for opening and closing branches and other delivery channels, and what are the licensing procedures and fees for doing so?

Scope of Activities

If one is to understand the role of the banking system in contributing to the functions of finance in the country being assessed, it is necessary to clarify what are the range and types of financial services being provided by both banks and nearbanks. The institutional organization of the financial service provision varies significantly across countries. On the one extreme might be universal banks that offer not only deposit, loan, and payment services, but also leasing, factoring, insurance, and investment bank products. On the other extreme, one might find a system where banks are restricted to deposit, loan, and payment services and where there is a large number and variety of other banklike and nonbanking institutions that offer leasing, factoring, and mortgage finance. The institutional organization of the financial service provision is often driven by historic development and by the regulatory environment. Even if specialized financial services are offered by specialized financial institutions, there are often ownership links between them and banks. Finally, an institutionally diverse financial system may have converged with nominally different institutions that offer the same services. In this case, it is important to assess whether there is a level playing field between institutions and nondiscriminatory regulatory treatment.

Competition and Market Segmentation

Market structure can be measured using concentration ratios (assets of largest three or five banks to total banking assets), number of banks, and Herfindahl indices. One has to be careful, however, in equating market structure with competitiveness. Contestability of the market—the threat of entry—can be a more important determinant of bank behavior. Regulatory indicators, such as formal entry requirements, share of bank applications rejected over the past five years, and openness of the sector to foreign entrants, can give an indication of contestability of the market. Competition from other financial institutions (such as insurance companies, large credit cooperatives, and capital markets) can play an important role in determining banking system competitiveness. The ownership structure of banks (foreigners, closely held by locals, nonfinancial corporations, government, widely held, cooperative structure, and so forth) can be important for the degree of competition, because banks of different ownership often have different mandates and different clienteles (e.g., see Claessens and Laeven 2004 and box 4.2). In turn, ownership patterns are influenced by regulation and policy on entry, exit, and mergers and acquisitions.

Is the market structure segmented (with less competition than might appear from an overall concentration index) to the extent that different groups of banks deal with different classes of customer (with each customer facing relatively few options)? Evidence on market segmentation is often more anecdotal than quantitative. Interviews with both banks and enterprises often help to determine categories of banks, with competition within each category but with little across categories. There might also be variation in competitiveness across different products. Loan and deposit size distribution data can give supporting evidence for market segmentation, if such data are available. It is also important to assess segmentation between the banking system and other parts of the financial system. This assessment can be important for microenterprises and small enterprises that start their "careers" as borrowers with cooperative or specialized financial institutions; segmentation might prevent them from growing into customers of mainstream banks. If one has established the main features here, it is important to attempt to determine the extent to which they are influenced in a harmful way by inappropriate regulation. This examination could include looking at limits on their lines of business, universal banking, and branching restrictions.

4

Box 4.2 Access to Financial Services from Abroad

Development Role of Foreign Banks

National authorities and local commentators often express concern at the likely development consequences of a growing share of the financial sector coming under foreign control. The typical fears are that small enterprises and remote, rural areas will not be served by foreign-owned banks and that cherry-picking by foreign-owned banks will weaken local banks. In fact, although the client profile of foreign-owned banks often differs sharply from that of locally owned banks (especially when foreign-owned banks have only a limited retail presence because of regulatory restrictions or their own business strategy), it is often observed that an expansion in a foreign-owned bank's share of the total market is associated with a greater emphasis on the small and medium enterprise (SME) sector by local banks. Checking on such dimensions of the competitive dynamics of the sector will help alert national authorities to any shortcomings along those dimensions.

The implicit training provided by the leading international banks both for other market participants and for regulators can represent an almost costless gain for national authorities. The relationship between foreign-owned banks and regulators can be somewhat delicate in that regulators are responsible for local oversight of the foreign entity. Nevertheless, that entity likely enjoys superior risk management practices and other systems and head office scrutiny. By observing and learning from those practices, the local supervisor can accelerate technology transfer to the local market.

Access to Foreign Securities Markets

The tendency of larger companies to take their stock market listings to larger international markets—whether through a primary listing or dual listing abroad, or by issuance of depository receipts—is often seen as an adverse development by local market intermediaries because the intermediaries receive a smaller share of total fees and commissions. Thus, local market liquidity may be adversely affected. However, from the perspective of the economy as a whole, the net benefit is likely to be positive, with not only a lower cost of capital, but also an indirect effect through the importation of enhanced standards of corporate transparency, which are likely to be spread, at least partly, to firms that do not have international listings.

Opening the local equity market to foreign investors is also generally seen as a positive dimension with lower average cost of capital and probably lower net volatility. However, opening nonresident access to domestic financial markets and enhancing resident access to foreign financial markets will require the careful sequencing of capital account liberalization measures as part of a broader financial market development strategy. These considerations are further explained in chapter 12.

Taxation of Banking

Taxation and quasi-taxation issues are important for banking. Among the most prominent are (a) the issue of loan–loss provisioning (can banks deduct provisions allowed by the banking regulator from income before calculating tax?) and (b) the implicit taxes through reserve requirements. The former can affect the incentive to make adequate provisions promptly, while the latter can affect interest spreads, especially in times of high inflation and high nominal interest rates.

Other Issues

Are minimum deposit requirements or fees for customers effectively cutting out the small depositor? What lines of business do banks find most profitable and unprofitable? Are there any pressures from government to do lines of business that are unprofitable? Do banks submit to such pressure? Analyzing the interbank market is important, so one should ask the following: How liquid is the market, is there tiering (another indicator of segmentation), and who are the main takers?

4.4.2 Near-banks

While some nearbanks, such as finance companies, can be seen as an annex to the commercial banking system, some smaller scale near-banks may have sufficient development importance to call for special treatment. Such near-banks consist of specialized microfinance firms, cooperative credit unions, specialized mortgage banks, and government-sponsored specialized development intermediaries. Because of their modest size or the fact that their source of funding is stable and may come from stable external or wholesale sources, they do not raise systemic stability concerns but do expand access to financial services. Some near-banks provide a focused set of services to a broad clientele (e.g., postal savings banks and mortgage banks); others specialize in serving a particular economic sector (e.g., specialized microfinance institutions [MFIs] that may target microenterprises or the poor and near-poor).

Many categories of nearbanks are not operated on a for-profit basis (especially donor-promoted microfinance entities, government-owned development banks, and, to an extent, cooperatively owned entities such as credit unions). This feature generally calls for a distinct regulatory framework, and a review will be appropriate in many countries where those institutions are sizable.[13]

Among the major categories are non-depository finance companies, many of which specialize in particular types of lending such as leasing and factoring. Many of them are captive subsidiaries of banks that have been separately constituted for reasons of legal convenience or in response to regulatory restrictions on banks. The funding of those institutions is typically from the parent bank. Independent finance companies need to find funding in the wholesale markets, typically through private placement of notes, though they may use an organized bond market if one is present. The entities can be important in providing borrowing facilities for SMEs, and obstacles to their effective operation should be monitored.

Mortgage banks (see box 4.3), savings banks, and cooperative credit unions typically concentrate on the needs of households both in terms of deposits and for lending products. However, some savings banks operate as narrow banks, lending their resources to government. To the extent that they are locally or regionally based, their survival increasingly depends on the effectiveness of national umbrella organizations. They also depend on not suffering from tax discrimination (though they will often go further and argue for tax privileges that are hard to rationalize from a welfare point of view). Interviews with those entities will often reveal special environmental challenges that inhibit their effective functioning. Because detailed prudential regulation of the institutions is not cost-effective, they often operate under blanket restrictions that limit their expansion and activities. Judgment must be exercised as to whether such restrictions can safely be relaxed.

Non-deposit-taking microfinance firms (typically donor funded) may not require prudential regulation from the financial authorities, although an element of forced saving is often built into their operations. Increasingly, though, MFIs seek to move into offering deposit services, so the challenge of ensuring that prudential regulation is no more intrusive than is needed arises here also.

4

Box 4.3 Finance of Housing

Financing residential mortgages is a key function of financial systems in advanced economies, thereby accounting for a relatively high share of total financial assets. Traditionally, specialized mortgage intermediaries offering a limited range of other services were the major players in this segment, and they often benefited from fiscal privileges. More recently, the removal of fiscal privileges and the addition of enhanced competition have tended to widen the range of originating intermediaries for mortgage lending. Those intermediaries, in turn, have increasingly securitized much of the mortgages that they originated and have sold them in the wholesale market.

Long-term mortgages entail particular risks whether they are at fixed or floating rates. Fixed-rate mortgages may require high real yields or even may not be able to be sold in a volatile macroeconomic environment. Holders of such mortgages can face advance repayment risk if the general level of market rates falls, unless prepayment penalties can be enforced. Conversely, high inflation rates may shorten the effective duration of conventional mortgages, thus creating a demand for price-index-linked or other low-risk contracts (compare to Jaffee and Renaud 1996).

Availability of long-term mortgage finance enhances the quality of housing, especially for middle-income households. Cross-country experience suggests that macroeconomic stability and financial sector policies are more important in ensuring such availability than is the general level of per capita income. Improved housing finance policy reaches well beyond the financial sector and includes measures to improve the supply of serviced land, building codes, adequate legal framework for land development and real estate, well-targeted subsidies for those who cannot afford adequate housing, and so forth. Because of this wide reach and because mortgage finance has increasingly become part of mainstream finance, a particular focus on the subsector of housing finance may not be warranted for financial sector assessments in most countries.

The indications are that sustained effectiveness of MFIs will require that they should operate on a relatively large scale. If so, policies that encourage larger-scale operation over a proliferation of small entities is to be preferred. Subsidized interest rates offered by MFIs are not compatible with graduation to self-sustaining operation and are generally not to be encouraged, though the limited spillovers into mainstream finance mean that a subsidy need not be considered crucial.

Subsidized lending by larger government-sponsored development banks causes distortions (see box 4.4). Those banks can seriously distort the incentive for a balanced provision of lending products by commercial banks, as well as creating the conditions for corruption. Moving government-sponsored development banks as far as possible either (downstream) toward a commercial operation or (upstream) to become explicitly the lending arm of the fiscal authority (with loans at unsubsidized rates) will, in most cases, seem the optimal direction of policy.

4.4.3 Insurance and Collective Investment Arrangements

As with the banking sector, insurance and collective savings generate financial services on both the asset and the liability side. On the liability side, they provide investment outlets and risk-reduction instruments; on the asset side, they typically represent the most important block of professionally managed long-term funds. Both aspects need to be kept in mind in the assessment. Insurance and fund management industries often overlap, in that insurance firms often sell pensions or manage pension funds, other mutual funds and

---

Box 4.4 Role of Government-Owned Banks

The disappointing performance—not only of government-owned banks but also, more important, of systems in which the banks will play a major part—has been extensively documented in recent cross-country empirical literature (see Barth, Caprio, and Levine 2004 and La Porta, Lopez-de-Silanes, and Shleifer 2002). This performance does not imply that individual countries and individual government-owned banks cannot perform exceptionally well along this dimension, but it does call for special attention to some dimensions along which many government-dominated banking systems are known to underperform.

In the context of development assessment, the effect of government ownership is not simply a question of embedded fiscal costs in a nonperforming or problematic loan portfolio reflecting the inheritance of politically or socially motivated loans. Such fiscal costs can imply a future national tax burden that will tend to slow growth. However, development assessment must pay attention to subsidized and other loans made on other-than-commercial principles insofar as those loans tend to discourage private banks from incurring the cost of developing risk-assessment techniques that are needed to lend into difficult segments, such as small and medium enterprises (SMEs) and rural areas. Government-owned banks often fail to deliver services to their stated target markets—with subsidies often being captured by large, state-owned borrowers or politically connected firms—which can damage the performance of the sector as a whole.

The mission of government-owned banks should, therefore, be examined for compatibility with the competitive provision of financial services generally; their governance structures should also be scrutinized for consistency with the stated mission.

---

unit trusts, and so forth. Some investments of those industries are in the form of bank deposits or other unit trusts, so that a measuring scale in a manner that adequately nets out intersectoral claims can be both important and sometimes difficult in the attempt to benchmark scale. In addition to one's looking at the current position, projections of future developments, especially of pension funds, can be possible and relevant for a view as to the likely contribution of those sectors to funds availability.[14]

The range of products supplied, as well as their pricing (relative to actuarial fairness), is also an area where deficiencies may exist. It is important to determine whether such gaps are attributable to overregulation, to lack of competition (including restrictions on entry), or to lack of organizational capacity and skills in the industries. Because of the diversity of potential insurance products,[15] a comprehensive analysis of cost and availability would be an extensive exercise. Absent such a study, information can, nevertheless, be obtained from market participants. Industry professionals will typically be vocal in identifying policy barriers (including regulatory failure to approve policy design) that inhibit their provision of particular services and products; users will be a better source for identifying others that are unavailable or overpriced because of industry inefficiencies or market power. A similar situation prevails with regard to other collective investment outlets. The tax and regulatory treatment of different insurance, pension, and mutual fund–type products has been a strong influence on the development of the insurance and collective investment sectors, and the whole market can be skewed by distorting incentives that should be avoided as a matter of sound development policy.[16]

Coverage of the subsectors also needs to examine market structure in terms of concentration and ownership. In countries where there is a mandatory private tier to pension provision, issues of competition become especially important, because the rules regarding switching, fee structures, and the like can have a large effect on the net return to pension investors.

The investment policy of insurance firms, pension funds, and other collective savings entities is a key to increasing the availability of term and risk finance to domestic industry. This policy can be subject to severe restrictions (such as ceilings on permissible percentages of the portfolio that can be placed in certain broad categories of investment, such as property or equities), which must be examined for their appropriateness in the context of local capacity. While most of the restrictions are supposedly intended to be prudential in nature, in practice some can have the opposite effect, lowering the return on the funds' overall portfolio without reducing volatility. This effect can be especially true with regard to requirements to hold government securities and prohibitions on international diversification.[17] Requirements to cede reinsurance to a state-owned reinsurance company have similar effects.

The long-term viability of the social security and government employee pension schemes needs some examination. Their wider effects on the economy, including the effects of compulsory contributions, are generally fiscal matters that are beyond the scope of the financial sector assessment. However, it is necessary to be generally aware of those wider dimensions if one is to understand the likely evolution of the system. Some examination of the issues could strengthen the assessment of both the financial structure and development.

The health of the insurance and collective investment sectors is often intertwined with that of the organized securities markets. Those sectors are the major investors in securities, and the level and volatility of asset returns in the sectors depend on the microstructure and soundness of securities markets.

4.4.4 Securities Markets

The sectoral development assessment is to some extent subsumed in International Organization of Securities Commissions's (IOSCO's) Objectives and Principles of Securities Regulation (see box 4.5). Investor protection, fairness, efficiency, and transparency are among the most important prerequisites for the development of organized securities markets. These important elements of effective securities regulation are also covered in the IOSCO objectives and principles. When investors have confidence, the market tends to grow.

In addition, the assessor needs to verify, by looking at the quantitative measures, that the market is, in fact, deep and liquid; that transactions and issuing costs are reasonable; and that an adequate range of both debt- and equity-type instruments are available. The range of instruments would include some derivatives if this inclusion can be supported by the scale of activity and by the technical needs and sophistication of the market participants. The assessor also needs to look at the degree to which the market can provide new funding through public offerings. Benchmarking of the securities markets needs to pay attention to some hidden factors. For instance, in addition to market micro-structure and market size, the liquidity of the securities markets also depends on the degree to which securities are not held in blocks by insiders and, as such, are not normally available for

---

Box 4.5 Standards Assessments and Financial Sector Development

Standards assessments can inform development assessments. Sectoral reviews, plus an understanding of the state of development and the soundness of sectors, are needed to inform standards and stability assessment. The standards, codes, and core principles that are important for the sound and efficient functioning of the financial system cover both financial supervision and financial infrastructure, and they are listed in box A.2.

International standards and codes for financial systems supervision have been designed to promote effective supervision and regulation of individual financial institutions and markets. Those standards (for banking, insurance, and securities market supervision) promulgate a set of objectives, core principles, and good practices that cover regulatory governance, regulatory practices, prudential framework for the operations of financial firms, and financial integrity and safety net arrangements. All supervisory standards recognize that a set of preconditions (outside the scope of those standards) must be met to allow effective implementation of the standards. The preconditions include sound and sustainable macroeconomic policies; a well-developed public infrastructure (accounting and auditing, corporate governance, legal framework, and so forth); procedures for resolving problem institutions; and an appropriate level of systemic protection and safety nets.

A review of preconditions for effective supervision—some of which are covered by their own standards—can clearly help identify gaps in infrastructure and can provide inputs into development assessment. Similarly, assessments of the financial infrastructure as part of development assessment can give information on the adequacy of preconditions for effective supervision. A significant part of financial sector development policies relate to strengthening the public infrastructure. This strengthening not only promotes more efficient financial services with greater depth and access, but also creates conditions for effective supervision.

Standards assessments themselves provide key information needed for development assessment and for a range of policies to implement standards to help improve efficiency of financial firms and to assist with their institutional development.

- All supervisory standards include a set of principles relating to the prudent operations of financial intermediaries covering risk management, risk concentration, capital adequacy, corporate governance and internal controls, customer protection, and prevention of financial abuse. Policies that promote such prudent operations can help strengthen the efficiency of the institutions, strengthen their governance, and enable more effective and appropriately priced delivery of financial services. Information on those matters from standards assessments provides valuable input into development-oriented policy formulation.

- Some development concerns are addressed in IAIS Insurance Core Principle (ICP) 1. ICP 1 sets out preconditions for effective insurance supervision, which represent a subset of the preconditions for a well-developed insurance sector. Prudential insurance assessments can also help in the fact-finding efforts for the development assessment, for example, in relation to investment requirements (ICP 21). Several other useful sets of standards and guidelines have been developed for other elements of this broad subsector (for a compendium, see OECD 2002).

- IOSCO Objectives and Principles of Security Regulations promote robust and efficient financial markets. Thus, IOSCO principles 14–16 aim to ensure that issuers are transparent and fair, principles 17–20 to ensure that collective investment schemes are equally trustworthy, and principle 28 to ensure that secondary market manipulation is inhibited. IOSCO principle 23 deals with standards for the internal organization and operational conduct of market intermediaries to ensure adequate client protection and risk management.

---

trading. Estimates of this free-float can greatly reduce the apparent size of the market and can put its true scale into perspective.

The domestic bond market is often more weakly developed than equities, and causes of this weakness should be reviewed. The reasons typically lie in tax rules; in the systemic dominance of banks, for whom a developed bond market would represent competition; or

4

in crowding out by heavy domestic government borrowing. More generally, government debt management can have a decisive influence on the functioning of the bond market.[18] Effective public debt management can help provide the benchmarks needed to price more risky securities, and the physical and institutional infrastructures for government debt markets could reinforce and complement the needed infrastructure for bond markets generally. The transactions technology infrastructure—in this case, also potentially including such features as privileged market makers—may also be inadequate. These and other prerequisites for bond market development are clearly described in World Bank (2001c), which also notes how sensitive bond market development is to monetary policy management and generally macroeconomic stability—prerequisites that lie beyond the scope of development assessment.

Liquid securities markets require a minimum scale to be cost-effective. Certainly, the cost built into the design of the trading platform and the regulatory burden can become decisive. Overheads of the market itself and of the regulator can also be too heavy to be borne by fees on the existing level of transactions. Where possible, the assessor should attempt to calculate those costs and the degree to which they are being subsidized. This calculation is especially important where consideration is being given to further computerization, a step that often may not be cost-effective or necessary in small exchanges. With many small securities markets, the inherent viability of the brokerage industry needs to be checked, which has been a problem in several countries. In some cases, most brokers are subsidiaries or divisions of banks, an arrangement that may help reduce overheads but may limit the energy with which the brokers develop their services. Of course, the important goal is not survival of the stockbrokers per se, but achievement of an optimal way of giving local firms and investors access to liquid securities markets.

Many securities markets have been subsidized through tax concessions to listing companies, but with limited success. Several countries have forgone substantial revenue in this way with the objective of encouraging the development of the stock exchange but without generating any sizable activity in the market.

The degree to which larger firms are going outside the country to issue shares or depository receipts in advanced stock exchanges should be examined. While such behavior can reduce local market liquidity, it also has the potential to result in the importation of improved transparency and other practices by a demonstration effect. It also results in lower funding costs for the companies that do have such access.

More generally, the question for small countries of whether outsourcing and closer integration with regional or global markets would be more effective than promotion of an onshore securities market must be seriously considered (compare to Bossone, Honohan, and Long 2002).

4.5   The Demand-Side Reviews and the Effect of Finance on the Real Sector

Whereas stability assessments have normally emphasized the regulator and the regulated financial intermediaries and markets with comparatively little focus on the system's users,[19] development assessments are interested in the users and the extent to which the financial services they receive (including from abroad) are adequate to their needs. Development assessments must express a general view on this issue, though in many countries, especially low-income countries, detailed quantification may be beyond the scope of the assessment. Special studies of the finances of the corporate sector or of household, microenterprise, and SME access to finance can be considered where data can be made readily available.

4.5.1 Enterprise Finance

An assessment of demand for and access to financial and especially credit services by enterprises relies on financial information from firms and on surveys and anecdotal evidence from financial institutions, banks, and other market participants. While data on listed companies are often readily available, few developing countries have consistent databases on SMEs. Ideally, corporate data should be combined with bank data to assess both the different sectoral and business line focus of banks and the competitiveness of the banking market (e.g., by considering the number of bank relationships per firm). Such analysis should also be informed by the available data on infrastructure, especially about the legal system and the information environment. The available data could reveal that certain products, such as leasing or factoring, do not constitute valid financing options for enterprises. Factors behind such missing markets would have to be examined.

When one considers financing patterns, in addition to bank or equity finance, it is also important to focus on trade finance, which is an important financing source, espe-

---

Box 4.6 Use of Research-Based Micromodels—Liquidity Constraints in Capital Formation

Several research-based exercises carried out as background for recent financial sector assessment programs (FSAPs) have assessed financing conditions using firm-level data for nonfinancial firms. In a world without financially constrained firms, investment and financing decisions are independent from each other. However, the investment decisions of financially constrained firms often depend on the availability of cash flow (compare to Fazzari, Hubbard, and Petersen 1988).

For the recent Mexican FSAP accounting data for 73 nonfinancial-listed Mexican firms were drawn from WorldScope, a commercial data provider. The exercise estimated the extent to which firm investment depended on cash flow rather than on the marginal profitability of capital. Although WorldScope tends to include only larger firms, it may be assumed that smaller firms are at least as financially constrained. Regressing investment ratios on marginal profitability, financial leverage, and cash flow found cash flow to be a statistically significant variable, which can be evidence of Mexican firms being cash-flow

constrained. In principle—given sufficient data—the exercise could be divided by class, size, or geographical region of firm.

A similar exercise carried out for the Czech FSAP found that firms operating in the utilities, construction, and trading industries invested significantly more than other nonfinancial firms. If the firms are listed and the stock market is sufficiently liquid, marginal accounting profitability can be substituted by Tobin's q-ratio. These kinds of data can throw additional light on firms' financing characteristics. For instance in the Czech FSAP, it was found that trade credit was generally not used as a financing source for investment and that firms that were able to attract new bank loans used them, to a large extent, for purposes other than investment, for example, to repay old loans. The results suggested that the general reduction in the supply of bank credit during 1999 may have increased the financing constraints of firms, especially those of small and highly leveraged firms.

Sources: Financial System Stability Assessments (FSSAs) for Czech Republic and Mexico, respectively.

4

cially for small firms. Trade credit can be both a substitute to and a complement for other external financing sources. Trade credit might vary systematically across size groups, with one group being a net creditor or debtor relative to others. For example, if the small firm group is a net debtor in trade credit, this debtor position might indicate a trickle-down effect, with large firms effectively passing on bank credit to small firms through the trade credit channel. Moreover, many developing countries and emerging markets rely on bank-financed trade credits to support exports at preshipment and postshipment stages, as well as imports. Such financing provided by international banks tend to be channeled to local borrowers through domestic banks and to constitute an important source of working capital.

Development, directed credit, or both might be another important source for certain enterprise groups in many developing countries. While it is typically beyond the scope of a financial sector assessment to produce a detailed cost-benefit analysis of the effectiveness of such programs, an indication of whether those programs reach the target groups and whether they have complementary or crowding-out effects might be interesting.

If appropriate data are available, testing for financing constraints among firms can be an interesting complement (see box 4.5). A further step would be to link firm characteristics, such as size, sector, and profitability, to financing constraints so one can compare access to finance across different firm groups and can test for potential segmentation in the market.

4.5.2 Households, Firms, and Microenterprises

While reliable data for a quantitative assessment of SMEs' access to financial services are hard to come by, it is even more difficult to quantitatively assess households', firms', and microenterprises' access to financial services. There do not seem to be any cross-country databases available, and only a few countries have detailed survey or census data on access to financial services by households, farms, and microenterprises. The World Bank has undertaken Living Standards Measurement Surveys (LSMSs) in several countries, but the finance component is relatively small in most cases.

In other cases, the dearth of data precludes a detailed analysis of households', firms', and microenterprises' access to financial services. However, anecdotal and even limited quantitative evidence can provide some indication of social and geographic variation in access by those groups and can help define follow-up work.

Additional evidence on access may be available from suppliers of financial services. If such evidence is available, for example, one can analyze loan and deposit size distribution data for corporate sectors, household sectors, or both. This analysis would indicate the extent of small loans and deposits, which would show indirect evidence about access by small firms and households. In addition, data from the providers of financial services to those segments—such as microfinance, development finance institutions, or savings banks—can provide further evidence on access. An indication of the outreach and penetration of the different provider groups can help evaluate their effectiveness. Sometimes, quantitative and anecdotal evidence on the competitiveness and possible segmentation of household and microenterprise sector can be obtained. Unlike in the enterprise sector, savings and payment services are often in greater demand in this sector than credit services.

4.6 Reviews of Cross-Cutting Issues

The development assessment draws both on infrastructural assessments (for each of which one or more sets of standards have been developed by the relevant international bodies) and on sectoral assessments. As explained, development dimensions must be added to, or built on, aspects of the sectoral prudential standards. Among the development dimensions that have been highlighted in this regard are the competition issues such as entry and exit policies, the taxation issues, and the distorting or chilling side effects of poorly designed prudential regulation. Some of the issues also arise on a cross-sectoral basis or in respect to undeveloped sectors and segments, which will now be discussed.

4.6.1 Missing Markets and Missing Products

Experience shows that a number of potentially useful products or markets, though readily observed in some low- and middle-income environments, are not present in others. The sectoral and demand analyses of sections 4.4 and 4.5 should detect the absence of key markets or services, and those analyses should be assiduous in discovering the reasons for missing products and markets. Many such products—leasing, factoring, reverse factoring, venture capital and other forms of private equity, and various types of long-term finance—can be provided by commercial banks. Otherwise, they may be provided through finance companies or other specialized banks or nearbanks, which are often nondeposit taking. Insurance and collective savings funds are also important potential providers of those and other products (especially for longer terms and for higher-risk profiles).

It is useful to distinguish between the following underlying causes of underdeveloped or missing markets: macroeconomic or legal. Macroeconomic causes may include an inflation history that impedes long-term contracting at reasonable interest rates. Regulatory impediments may include restrictions on contractual savings institutions to hold private sector assets. Those factors effectively restrict the supply of long-term resources or prohibit financial institutions from entering certain markets. Taxation rules or the lack of clear rules can result in higher costs for certain financing products, such as leasing. While deficiencies in the legal system can impede effective financial intermediation overall, the negative marginal effect may be especially strong for certain products that depend more on its effective functioning, such as leasing. It is important to analyze whether there is a lack of appropriate legislation, a consistent lack of application of the legislation by the court system, or a lack of appropriate registration systems at reasonable costs. But there may also be demand factors; the demand for certain services may not be sufficient to justify the set-up costs.

4.6.2 Taxation Issues

Tax policies are critical to the sound development of most segments of finance, yet taxation is a highly complex and country-specific matter within which the issues relating to

Financial Sector Assessment: A Handbook

4

the financial sector cannot ever be fully isolated. A full analysis of taxation issues will normally be outside the scope of financial sector assessments, but each sectoral review should be alert to particularly important tax aspects and should take a cross-cutting overall view of how urgent or important it is to correct the most prominent distortions (Honohan 2003).

Taxation policies should aim at broad neutrality between similar financial products and services, especially between identical products provided through different institutional forms. The tax burden on financial intermediation should be commensurate with that on other sectors. Tax design should avoid sensitivity to the inflation rate. Financial transaction taxes have been used in several countries with weak fiscal systems as a means of tapping revenue quickly. Though they can be effective in the short run, they should be scrutinized for the degree to which they are being arbitraged away (eventually resulting in transactions costs rather than tax revenue), with the remaining revenue having an unintended and perhaps regressive incidence. Although the application of a value added tax (VAT) to financial services raises administrative complications that are unlikely to be overcome in low- or low-middle-income countries, a theoretical VAT does represent a useful benchmark against which to measure and compare the actual financial tax burden on intermediation and other financial services. This comparison can be especially useful in checking how inflation-proof the financial tax system is.

In some respects, especially through quasi-taxes that masquerade as regulations (such as unremunerated reserve requirements), finance has been overtaxed in many countries. But it is the removal of such special impositions that will be beneficial, not the creation of special privileges. Special pleading by financial sector participants must be treated with a degree of skepticism in this regard: Neutrality, rather than tax-based incentivizing of particular markets or institutions, is preferred. Instead of attempting to use financial sector taxes as "corrective instruments" in this way, the authorities would be well advised to concentrate on making the financial tax system as arbitrage-proof and as inflation-proof as is practicable.

Subsidy of finance creates damaging distortions and can have a chilling effect on the development of more-effective and less-corruptible commercial substitutes for the product or market being subsidized. Such distortions are especially relevant in the context of government-sponsored providers of financial service, providers whose activities may undercut private provision without delivering adequate quality. Detailed examination of credit programs from government agencies will typically be beyond the scope of financial sector assessments, but a general awareness of these and similar subsidies needs to inform analysis of the missing market issue and of the performance of the nearbanks in particular.

4.6.3 Competition Aspects

Effective competition can provide the incentives to expand financial services. Both prudential and competition policies (including licensing and entry, exit and merger policies, and branching and similar regulations) should facilitate the presence of intermediary owners and management that are independent of government and of the major local, nonfinancial groups. Line of business restrictions should avoid the creation of uncompetitive market segments.

The structure of cross-ownership among financial institutions also matters for effective competition. Often seen as complements, banks and markets do compete for financial sector value added. Where banks control the major nonbank financial institutions, competition between the two will tend to be lower, resulting in less variety and higher cost in the provision of financial services. The same may apply to regulation, because a bank-dominated regulator may be slow to sanction desirable institution building on the nonbank side. For example, if the banks own the collective investment institutions, they may discourage measures that tend to open up the development of that sector, to the extent that it would undermine their future profitability. Information on such cross-ownership can be very informative as to the future development prospects of the financial sector as a whole.

4.6.4 Development Obstacles Imposed by Unwarranted Prudential Regulation

Supervision and regulation have important implications for the effectiveness of intermediation and access to financial services, in addition to their roles in fostering stability. Entry regulation and uneven supervisory practices across different groups of financial institutions (either by type or ownership) can hamper competitiveness and, thus, effectiveness. Different regulatory and supervisory standards across different financial institutions that offer similar products and compete directly with each other can negatively affect competitiveness. Heavy regulation of branch openings (as already mentioned) or other delivery channels can limit access to financial services. For example, prudential policies should avoid undue reliance on tools that are likely to disadvantage small and new firms (such as excessive mandatory collateralization requirements for bank loans). Supervision and regulation also impose transaction costs on financial institutions and, ultimately, on the users. The benefit of regulation and supervision in terms of promoting soundness and stability must be balanced with the costs that they may impose in terms of efficiency and access. Given the high fixed-cost component of financial supervision, that balance is especially important for small financial systems and for components of financial systems that are made up of small institutions, such as the cooperative movement or microfinance.

4.7 From Finding Facts to Creating Policies

Once the data gathering and analysis have been conducted (as outlined in sections 4.2 through 4.6), policies and reforms must be identified and prioritized. The task of policy formulation consists of distilling those findings into an overview of the principal strategic issues and development gaps—specifically in terms of the functions that finance is supposed to perform—and of opportunities. The reforms needed to enhance development of the financial system typically fall under the headings of (a) infrastructural strengthening, (b) policy corrections to reduce unintended side effects of regulatory or tax policies, or (c) governance reform. Those reforms must be prioritized and synthesized.

4

A medium-term vision for where the financial sector should be going helps to focus the recommendations and to avoid being distracted by the immediate political imperatives and obstacles that often make progress seem impossible. Because the quantity, term, and price of credit and other financial services are crucial and will generally depend on the efficiency and competitiveness of the sector and on the cost structure facing market participants (including the cost of taxation and regulation), these elements should be among the major dimensions considered in such a vision. Thus, the vision could include an indication of likely ownership patterns: what share to be owned by government and by foreign concerns, how much competition in banking and insurance, what change in the scope of activities allowed to banks, and what degree of subsectoral specialization. The vision could also address the likely growth in the assets of insurance, pension, and contractual savings and how they are likely to be allocated among domestic and foreign equities, bonds, and bank deposits. The institutional prospects for the securities markets, including the potential for collaboration or integration with securities markets abroad, will also be relevant.

Institution building to enhance the soft infrastructure tends to be the least contentious area, though the reforms are not always easy to accomplish in practice. In particular, the infrastructure for payments transactions can usually be strengthened with noncontroversial legislation and with the introduction of cost-effective technology. Credit information and accounting improvements may take longer and may demand the formation of more sustained human capital. Some legal reforms to enhance creditor rights (such as those needed to underpin a leasing industry) are also straightforward, but effective reforms in such areas as bankruptcy and enforcement of collateral tend to be more controversial and difficult to bring into effect.

Shortcomings in regulatory and tax policy design often represent a judgment call relating to some tradeoff (perhaps involving stability against efficiency) and, as such, require careful analysis to arrive at an acceptable compromise. Even then, special interests may have congregated around the regulations (for example, entry restrictions) that hamper reform. Nevertheless, the removal of regulatory and tax barriers to competitive provision of needed financial services is a crucial component of most financial sector development strategies. In some countries, the special interests of incumbent financial service providers (including the employees of government-owned financial agencies) have become entrenched through disproportionate representation in regulatory bodies or even in the legislature. If so, implementation of reforms is likely to be blocked indefinitely. Wider constitutional reforms, such as establishing or strengthening independence of the regulators from such special interests, may be a prerequisite for achieving deep reform of finance and—through that achievement—enhanced growth and poverty reduction. Yet such recommendations are, of course, the most difficult to sell.

Having identified the infrastructural weaknesses and policy flaws, assessors should formulate a clear prioritization and justification of recommendations addressed to senior policy makers and top politicians. The reform program is likely to entail short-term political costs, as well as fiscal outlays, and the program needs to be justifiable in terms of a simple and compelling rationale. In contrast to the stability assessment, where the consensus behind the core principles may be sufficient justification for some policy reforms, the more debatable nature of the development assessment, as well as the often more far-reaching nature of the reforms, calls for reliance on careful justification of policy proposals. For example, if what is needed is greater independence of the regulatory authority or greater liberalization of interest rate spreads, elimination of compulsory reinsurance cessions, commercialization and privatization of the major banks, or liberalization of entry by foreign financial service providers, then this need must be embedded in terms of the vision of the future financial system and of the desired potential benefits.

Reforms will take time, and policy makers need to know what the priorities are—both what is more important and whether specific sequencing is required. Sequencing and coordination of different measures are important to ensure a robust transition path. For example, early liberalization of deposit rates may not be appropriate in a system still dominated by poorly managed state-owned banks whose insiders' apparent goal is market share rather than sustained profit. Similarly in a system with large nonperforming loans and significant corporate financial fragility, some initial bank and corporate restructuring and some strengthening of prudential supervision may be needed before substantive liberalization of interest rates and entry. Thus, the scope and priorities of policy measures would depend both on the state of development of the financial sector and on the initial level of financial stability.

Against this background, rather than (or in addition to) presenting a comprehensive list of reforms, it is suggested that four or five themes may be identified in order of their importance, and the major thrusts of reform under each theme may be explained and prioritized. The particular conditions in each country would determine what those themes should be. No template is offered here nor should one be. Some of the themes might cut across sectors. For example, it could be a needed strengthening of political independence of regulatory authorities in several subsectors, or it could be a lack of competition and contestability reflecting inappropriate regulation in several sectors, or it could be the need for a root-and-branch reform of the tax code. Identifying the fact that such problems crop up in several sectors will help decision makers who are concerned with each sector realize the common position that they are in and may help point to the potential for organizational or legislative approaches that may not seem feasible to those in charge of any one sector. Other themes may be sector specific, such as either inadequate enforcement of stock exchange rules on transparency or a chaotically dysfunctional credit registry. Even if a similar problem exists to a lesser extent in other sectors, pointing the finger at a particularly damaging weakness can help ensure that top policy makers will allocate the financial and political resources necessary to fix it. The design and prioritization of broad themes and specific measures under each theme should help support financial and macroeconomic stability and should facilitate effective implementation. The principles and considerations in sequencing of reforms are more fully explained in chapter 12.

Notes

1. For example, if it is found that some services, such as reinsurance or elements of investment banking, are more effectively provided to a particular small country by foreign markets or firms, then there is a presumption that policies blocking access to foreign provision of those services should be dismantled, even though this dismantling may

damage the interests of local financial firms. Because of their specialist knowledge, incumbent providers are often in a strong position to resist policy changes that, though good for growth and overall financial development in the economy generally, may damage their sectoral interest. For a detailed and instructive account of how bankruptcy professionals, judges, and lawyers systematically blocked bankruptcy reform in the United States throughout the twentieth century, see Skeel (2003).

2. For the importance of the functional approach as opposed to the institutional approach, see Beck and Levine (2002) and Levine (1997).

3. Beck, Demirgüç-Kunt, and Levine (2000) provide a set of benchmark indicators for different parts of the financial system. Research is ongoing to enrich the cross-country data, notably on access.

4. For example, Demirgüç-Kunt, Laeven, and Levine (2003) find a significant role for bank-level variables (such as bank size, equity and liquidity ratios, and fee income), together with national-level variables (such as bank concentration, inflation, GDP per capita, quality of governmental institutions that are based on governance indicators compiled by World Bank), property rights, and restrictiveness of bank conduct and entry regulations).

5. Regulation and supervision are also part of the infrastructure review, here covered in the information-gathering phase on a sector-by-sector basis.

6. Chapter 9 contains a discussion of the scope of the insolvency and creditor rights standards.

7. Chapter 10 contains a discussion of the scope of corporate governance standards.

8. Jappelli and Pagano (2002) present an early study on the positive relationship between the availability of debtor information through credit registries and financial development. Miller (2003) is a collection of papers on different aspects of the issue. Levine, Loayza, and Beck (2000) discuss the importance of accounting standards for financial intermediary development. The Center for International Financial Analysis and Research Inc. provides data for 44 countries on accounting standards.

9. Honohan (2004b) describes of a wide range of data sources, including recent efforts to increase systematic coverage of financial issues in surveys. For example, the World Bank–led Enterprise Surveys have already covered approximately 50 countries since 2002 and are being rolled out at the rate of about 20 countries per year. The World Bank has also surveyed bank regulators in approximately 70 countries about overall access indicators—such as number of branches and ATMs, average loan and deposit size—and provider banks in approximately 60 countries about product and process technology.

10. The Basel Core Principles (BCPs) for Effective Banking Supervision state that "banking supervision is only part of wider arrangements that are needed to promote stability in financial markets" (see chapter 5). Those prerequisites are spelled out in the BCP source document, and they include much of what is needed for efficiency and reach, as well as stability. If a BCP assessment is being conducted in parallel, the assessors will also be gathering information relevant to the sectoral development assessment on banking. For an overview of relation between standards assessments and sectoral reviews, see box 4.5.

11. For recent cross-country studies on interest rate margins, see Demirgüç-Kunt and Huizinga (1999) and Demirgüç-Kunt, Laeven, and Levine (2004).

12. The interest spread studies by the Brazilian Central Bank (http://www.bcb.gov.br/) are a good example.

13. The Microfinance Consensus Guidelines by the Consultative Group to Assist the Poorest (CGAP) (Christen, Lyman, and Rosenberg 2003) provides a useful framework defining good practice for the MFI subsector.

14. International Association of Insurance Supervisors (IAIS)'s Core Principles also address aspects of development issues in Insurance. See box 4.4.

15. Even a listing of broad lines of business would include categories such as auto; employer's liability, product liability, and medical malpractice; marine (including other transport); commercial fire and theft; machinery; flood and other weather-related occurrences such as earthquake, etc.; mortgage protection, export credit, and other credit-related items; homeowners; health and disability; and life and annuity.

16. For example, overly generous tax incentives for life insurance can result in what are little more than tax-avoidance schemes dressed up as insurance policies. Or, onerous regulation of the investment of insurance or pension funds can result in too much being placed in short-term bank deposits, effectively resulting in reverse maturity transformation for the system as a whole. Again, unduly favorable differential tax and regulatory treatment of managed funds can result in a large fraction of investable funds being diverted into inadequately regulated fund management concerns that are sometimes associated with self-dealing.

17. For a discussion of these restrictions and how development and prudential considerations may be balanced, see Vittas (1998). A draft code for the regulation of private occupational pension schemes has been prepared for the Organisation for Economic Co-operation and Development (OECD) (OECD 2003).

18. Indeed, weaknesses in the government's institutional and strategic arrangements for debt management may be the focus of a special side study, for example, using the guidelines recently developed by the IMF and World Bank (2001).

19. Except to the extent that the financial condition of the corporate, household, government, and external sectors has been examined with a view to forming an opinion on the quality of the banks' loan portfolio. See chapters 2 and 3 on the use and analysis of balance sheet-financial soundness indicators of those sectors.

References

Barth, James, Gerard Caprio, and Ross Levine. 2004. "Bank Supervision and Regulation: What Works Best?" *Journal of Financial Intermediation* 13(2): 205–48.

Beck, Thorsten, Aslı Demirgüç-Kunt, and Ross Levine. 2000. "A New Database on the Structure and Development of the Financial Sector." *World Bank Economic Review* 14: 597–605.

———. 2003. "Law, Endowments, and Finance." *Journal of Financial Economics* 70(2): 137–81.

4

Beck, Thorsten, and Michael Fuchs. 2004. "Structural Issues in the Kenyan Financial System: Improving Competition and Access." World Bank Policy Research Working Paper 3363, World Bank, Washington, DC.

Beck, Thorsten, and Ross Levine. 2002. "Industry Growth and Capital Allocation: Does Having a Market- or Bank-Based System Matter?" *Journal of Financial Economics* 64: 147–80.

Beck, Thorsten, Ross Levine, and Norman Loayza. 2000. "Finance and the Sources of Growth." *Journal of Financial Economics* 58: 261–300.

Bossone, Biagio, Patrick Honohan, and Millard Long. 2002. "Policy for Small Financial Systems." In *Financial Sector Policy for Developing Countries—A Reader*, eds. G. Caprio, P. Honohan, and D. Vittas, 95–128. New York: Oxford University Press. See also "Policy for Small Financial Systems," Financial Sector Discussion Paper No. 6. Washington, DC: World Bank, 1991. Available at http://wbln0018.worldbank.org/html/FinancialSectorWeb.nsf/(attachmentweb)/Fs06/$FILE/Fs06.pdf.

Christen, Robert Peck, Timothy R. Lyman, and Richard Rosenberg. 2003. *Microfinance Consensus Guidelines*. Consultative Group to Assist the Poorest: Washington, DC.

Claessens, Stijn, and Luc Laeven. 2003. "What Drives Bank Competition? Some International Evidence." World Bank Policy Research Working Papers No. 3113.

Demirgüç-Kunt, Aslı, and Harry Huizinga. 1999. "Determinants of Commercial Bank Interest Margins and Profitability: Some International Evidence." *World Bank Economic Review* 13: 379–408.

Demirgüç-Kunt, Aslı, Luc Laeven, and Ross Levine. 2004. "The Impact of Bank Regulations, Concentration, and Institutions on Bank Margins." *Journal of Money, Banking, and Credit* 36, (3 Part 2): 593–622.

Doing Business Database. World Bank. Available at http://rru.worldbank.org/DoingBusiness/.

Fazzari, Steven, Glenn Hubbard, and Bruce Petersen. 1988. "Financing Constraints and Corporate Investment." *Brookings Papers on Economic Activity* 1: 141–95.

FSF (Financial Stability Forum). "Compendium of Standards." Financial Stability Forum. Available at http://www.fsforum.org/compendium/about.html.

Honohan, Patrick, ed. 2003. "Avoiding the Pitfalls in Taxing Financial Intermediation." In *Taxation of Financial Intermediation: Theory and Practice for Emerging Economies*, pp, 1–30. New York: Oxford University Press.

———. 2004a. "Financial Development, Growth, and Poverty: How Close Are the Links?" World Bank Policy Research Working Paper 3203, World Bank, Washington, DC. Available at http://econ.worldbank.org/files/32898_wps3203.pdf. See also Honohan, Patrick. 2004. "Financial Development, Growth, and Poverty: How Close Are the Links?" 2004. In *Financial Development and Economic Growth: Explaining the Links*, ed. Charles Goodhard. London: Palgrave.

———. 2004b. "Measuring Microfinance Access: Building on Existing Cross-Country Data." Prepared for the United Nations Development Programme, World Bank, and International Monetary Fund Workshop, "Data on the Access of Poor and Low-Income People to Financial Services," Washington, DC, October 26.

IMF (International Monetary Fund) and World Bank. 2001. *Guidelines for Public Debt Management*. Washington, DC: International Monetary Fund and World Bank. Available at http://www.imf.org/external/np/mae/pdebt/2000/eng/index.htm.

4

————. 2003. "Development Issues in the FSAP." International Monetary Fund and World Bank. Washington, DC. Available at http://www.imf.org/external/np/fsap/2003/022303b.htm.

Impavido, Gregorio, Alberto Musalem, and Dimitri Vittas. 2003. "Promoting Pension Funds." in *Globalization and National Financial Systems*, eds. James A. Hanson, Patrick Honohan, and Giovanni Majnoni. New York: Oxford University Press.

————— "Contractual Savings in Countries with a Small Financial Sector." 2002. World Bank Policy Research Working Paper Series, No. 2841.

La Porta, Rafael, Florencio Lopez-de-Silanes, and Andrei Shleifer. 2002. "Government Ownership of Commercial Banks." *Journal of Finance* 57: 265–301.

La Porta, Rafael, Florencio Lopez-de-Silanes, Andrei Shleifer, and Robert W. Vishny. 1997. "Legal Determinants of External Finance." *Journal of Finance* 52: 1131–50.

————. 1998. "Law and Finance." *Journal of Political Economy* 106: 1113–55.

Levine, Ross. 1997. "Financial Development and Economic Growth: Views and Agenda." *Journal of Economic Literature* 35: 688–726.

Levine, Ross, Norman Loayza, and Thorsten Beck. 2000. "Financial Intermediation and Growth: Causality and Causes." *Journal of Monetary Economics* 46: 31–77.

Jaffee, Dwight M., and Betrand Renaud. 1996. "Strategies to Develop Mortgage Markets in Transition Economies." World Bank Policy Research Working Paper 1697. Washington, DC.

Jappelli, Tullio, and Marco Pagano. 2002. "Information Sharing, Lending, and Defaults: Cross-Country Evidence." *Journal of Banking and Finance* 26: 2017–45.

Miller, Margaret, ed. 2003. *Credit Reporting Systems and the International Economy.* Cambridge, MA: MIT Press.

OECD (Organisation for Economic Co-operation and Development). 2002. *Insurance and Private Pensions Compendium for Emerging Economies.* Paris: Organisation for Economic Co-operation and Development.

————. 2003. *Occupational Pensions Core Principles and Methodology.* Paris: Organisation for Economic Co-operation and Development.

Skeel. David A. Jr. 2003. *Debt's Dominion: A History of Bankruptcy in America.* Princeton, New Jersey: Princeton University Press.

Vittas, Dimitri. 1998. "Regulatory Controversies of Private Pension Funds." World Bank Policy Research Working Paper 1893, World Bank, Washington, DC.

World Bank. 2001a. *Finance for Growth: Policy Choices in a Volatile World.* New York: Oxford University Press.

————. 2001b. *Principles and Guidelines for Effective Insolvency and Creditor Rights Systems.* Washington, DC: World Bank.

————. 2001c. *Developing Government Bond Markets.* Washington, DC: World Bank.

Chapter 5

Evaluating Financial Sector Supervision: Banking, Insurance, and Securities Markets

This chapter looks at the legal, institutional, and policy framework needed to ensure effectiveness of financial sector supervision. It focuses on banking, insurance, and securities markets. Effective supervision, however, depends on a legal and institutional environment that provides the necessary preconditions. Those preconditions include the following:

- The provision and consistent enforcement of business laws—including corporate, bankruptcy, contract, consumer protection, and private property laws—and a mechanism for fair resolution of disputes
- Good corporate governance, including adoption of sound accounting, auditing, and transparency procedures that carry wide international acceptance and that promote market discipline
- Appropriate systemic liquidity arrangements, including secure and efficient payment clearing systems that enable adequate control of risks and efficient management of liquidity
- Adequate ways to minimize systemic risk, including appropriate levels of systemic protection or safety nets and efficient procedures for handling problem institutions

The preconditions complement the legal and institutional framework governing the specific sectors of the financial system (banks, nonbank financial institutions, rural and microfinance entities, securities markets, and insurance providers) and their supervision, which is discussed in section 5.1. The broader legal framework governing the preconditions is covered in chapter 9. Section 5.2 in this chapter focuses specifically on the legal and institutional aspects of financial sector safety nets, one of the key preconditions affecting governance and stability of banking institutions. The scope and content of international standards on financial sector supervision in banking, insurance, and securities markets and the issues in assessing compliance with these standards are taken up in detail in the subsequent sections of this chapter (sections 5.3–5.5).

5.1 Legal and Institutional Framework for Financial Supervision

The legal framework empowering and governing the regulator and the rules used to regulate the various markets and institutional types form the cornerstone of the orderly functioning and development of the financial system. In this respect, the key laws are the law governing the central bank, banking and financial institutions, capital market laws, and insurance laws, and those laws are backed by adequate provisions on the efficient and reliable payment system infrastructure. The provisions are sometimes embedded in the laws or else are governed by separate legislation. The key elements of sound financial sector laws are already part of the existing international standards on supervision. Effective supervision also requires certain preconditions that are embedded in a broader range of laws such as laws on bankruptcy; company laws; contracts laws; and laws governing accounting, auditing, and disclosure, and so forth.

The legal and institutional framework for financial supervision should cover (a) the identity of the supervisor (central bank or separate agency), terms of reference, powers, and authority of the supervisory agency; (b) the authority and processes for the issuance of regulations and guidance; (c) the authority and tools to monitor and verify compliance with the regulations and principles of safe and sound operations; (d) the authority and actions to remedy, enforce, take control, and restructure; and (e) the procedures to delicense and liquidate problem institutions that cannot be restructured.

The legal framework should clarify the roles and responsibilities of different agencies involved in financial supervision. The central bank laws, banking laws, and other laws governing financial sector supervision need to specify the relationships among the supervisory agency, any deposit insurance agency, and other financial sector supervisors. In addition, the relationship with the Ministry of Finance needs to be clear and to provide sufficient operational autonomy to the supervisor. If a country has put in place a unified financial supervisory agency, then this arrangement needs to be laid down in a law, and its autonomy and powers need to be explicit.

The legal and regulatory basis of financial supervision should also support the core components of all financial supervisory standards. Those components consist of the following categories:

- Regulatory governance, which refers to the objectives, independence, enforcement, and other attributes that provide the capacity to formulate and to implement sound regulatory policies and practices
- Regulatory practices, which refer to the practical application of laws, rules, and procedures
- Prudential framework, which refers to internal controls and governance arrangements to ensure prudent management and operations by financial firms
- Financial integrity and safety net arrangements, which refer to (a) the regulatory policies and instruments designed to promote fairness and integrity in the opera-

Figure 5.1. Financial Standards and Their Four Main Components

Regulatory Governance[a]

- Objectives of regulation
- Independence and adequate resources
- Enforcement powers and capabilities
- Clarity and transparency of regulatory process
- External participation

Prudential Framework[b]

- Risk management
- Risk concentration
- Captial requirements
- Corporate governance
- Internal controls

Regulatory Practices[c]

- Group-wide supervision
- Monitoring and on-site inspection
- Reporting to supervisors
- Enforcement
- Cooperation and information sharing
- Confidentiality
- Licensing, ownership transfer, and corporate control
- Qualifications

Financial Integrity and Safety Net[d]

- Markets (integrity and financial crime)
- Customer protection
- Information, disclosure, and transparency

a. Includes BCP 1 and 19; ICP 1; IP: 1, 2, 3, 4, 5, 6, and 7.
b. Includes BCP 2, 3, 4, 6, 16, 17, 18, 20, 22, 23, 24, and 25; ICP 2, 3, 4, 5, 12, 13, 15, 16, and 17; IOP 8, 9, 10, 11, 12, 13, and 29.
c. Includes BCP 5, 6, 7, 8, 9, 10, 11, 12, 13, and 14; ICP 6, 7, 9, and 10; IOP 17, 18, 20, 21, 22, 23, 25, and 27.
d. Includes BCP 15 and 21; ICP 11 and 16; IOP 14, 15, 16, 19, 24, 26, 28, and 30.

BCP—Basel Core Principles
ICP—Insurance Core Principles of International Association of Insurance Supervisors
IOP—International Organization of Securities Commission's Objectives and Principles of Securities Regulation

Note: This four-component framework is based on the paper "Financial Sector Regulation: Issues and Gaps" (IMF 2004a). The allocation of insurance principles into various components is based on the 2000 IAIS standard. For a discussion of specific core principles under each standard, see chapters 5.3–5.5.

tions of financial institutions and markets and (b) the creation of safeguards for depositors, investors, and policyholders, particularly during times of financial distress and crisis

Those four components are illustrated in figure 5.1. For example, in the area of regulatory governance, Insurance Core Principles (ICPs) relating to supervisory objectives and supervisory authority require that insurance legislation include a clear statement on the mandates of the supervisory authority and give authority to issue and enforce rules by administrative means. Many of the other criteria and core principles—such as those relating to independence and accountability—could be part of primary legislation or part of regulations and bylaws issued pursuant to the legislation.

The institutional framework for supervision—and the laws that support it—needs to reflect the financial market structure and the broader institutional and policy environment. The institutional framework should be flexible enough to adapt to the shifts in market structure and in the broader environment to avoid regulatory gaps and to support financial innovation and development. For example, a poorly structured organizational framework for supervision could impede financial innovation or cause overregulation that stifles development. Similarly, an inappropriate organizational structure may cause regulatory gaps and regulatory arbitrage that may allow excessive risk taking and financial instability. An institutional framework for financial stability is, however, quite broad and goes beyond the institutions conducting financial supervision (such as the sectoral supervisor or integrated supervisor or central bank with supervision responsibilities). It includes other institutions and policy authorities that have jurisdictions over the broader financial infrastructure and macroeconomic policies. For example, accounting policies, competition policies, and insolvency regimes are matters outside the jurisdiction of supervision but are critical for financial stability. The broader institutional framework also includes the specific coordinating arrangements to ensure information exchange and policy coordination among all these policy components—supervisory, infrastructure, macroeconomic, and macroprudential—that interact to produce financial stability and financial development. In most cases, the Ministry of Finance will have the overall coordinating powers, and in some cases, there could be specific coordinating committees that bring together representatives of different policy authorities.

The appropriate design of the institutional structure of financial regulation and supervision has become a major issue of policy and public debate in several countries. Although many countries have moved in the direction of a unified agency for prudential regulation and supervision, the case for integrating conduct-of-business regulation and prudential supervision within the same agency is less powerful and considerably less common. Also, the issue of how to tailor the structure of regulation to specific features—operational complexities and transaction characteristics—of regulated institutions has become a pressing issue, for example, in the context of expanding access to the poor or in managing large and complex financial institutions (LCFIs). The issues in assessing the institutional structure are taken up in greater detail in appendix F (Institutional Structure of Financial Regulation and Supervision).

5.2   Aspects of Financial Safety Nets

Financial safety nets consist of three main elements: (a) a framework for liquidity support, (b) deposit insurance plus investor and policyholder protection schemes, and (c) crisis management policies. Each element of the safety net is designed to prevent situations in which the failure or potential failure of individual financial institutions disrupts the intermediation function of financial markets and, thus, the broader economic activity. Facilities for liquidity support attempt to prevent liquidity difficulties in one institution (or market) from being transmitted throughout the financial system. Deposit insurance and other protection schemes are designed to provide confidence to the least-informed depositors and investors with respect to the safety of their funds and thereby avoid spillovers from runs. Crisis management policies are established to minimize the disruption caused by widespread difficulties in the financial sector and thus avoid those difficulties from spilling over into broader economic activity. Therefore, in assessing the adequacy of the financial sector safety net, all three elements, including their legal underpinnings and their interconnections, should be considered.

5.2.1 Frameworks for Liquidity Support

Liquidity support is a key element of the financial sector safety net. Two somewhat distinct functions—one operating at normal times and another in times of crisis—need to be identified. The first is the lender-of-last-resort (LOLR) function, which typically operates in the normal course of day-to-day monetary policy operations. Nearly all central banks have the authority to provide credit to temporarily illiquid, but still solvent, institutions. This kind of support can provide an important buffer against temporary disturbances in financial markets. LOLR actions may help to prevent liquidity shortages in one bank from being transmitted to other financial institutions, for example, through the payment system. LOLR actions are not intended to prevent bank failures but, rather, to prevent spillovers associated with liquidity shortages—particularly in money and interbank markets—from interrupting the normal intermediation function of financial institutions and markets.

All central banks have a LOLR facility in place, but conditions and modalities are often not well defined.[1] Ill-defined conditions may give rise to moral hazard and forbearance, with adverse consequences for the financial system. Thus, an important component in understanding the adequacy of the financial safety net is assessing the adequacy of the central bank's operational procedures for LOLR support.

Somewhat distinct from the normal LOLR function is central bank emergency lending. It is important for central banks to have procedures in place to provide emergency lending, with different modalities and conditions, in times of (imminent) crises. In cases of emergencies, a number of central banks have the legal authority to provide liquidity over and above what is allowed within the normal facility. Having those types of procedures available can be very useful to provide temporary support to the system in times of severe disruptions. However, the very existence of those procedures might lead to moral hazard in banks, causing them to hold less liquidity than they otherwise would do and to take other risks. As a result, the providing of emergency credit is typically at the discretion of the central bank (constructive ambiguity). Nonetheless, internal procedures and policies—a form of contingency planning—should be in place for emergency lending, which should follow sound practices. In particular, the broad principles and the procedures governing the decisions on emergency lending could be established and made transparent.

Key features of emergency lending procedures that should be considered include the following:[2]

- Resources should be made available only to banks that are considered solvent but are coping with liquidity problems that might endanger the entire system (e.g., too-big-to-fail cases).
- Lending should take place speedily.
- Lending should be short term; even then, it should be provided conservatively because the situation of a bank might deteriorate quickly.
- Lending should not take place at subsidized rates, but the rate also should not be penal because it might then deteriorate the bank's position.
- The loan should be fully collateralized, and collateral should be valued conservatively. However, at times of severe crisis, it might be necessary for the central bank

to relax this criterion or to organize government guarantees or to arrange government credit, even if the loan is executed from the central bank's balance sheet.

- Central bank supervisory authorities and the Ministry of Finance should be in close contact and should monitor the situation of the bank.
- Supervisory sanctions and remedial actions should be attached to the emergency lending.

5.2.2 Deposit Insurance

A second key element of the financial safety net is a deposit insurance system (DIS). Although deposit insurance can cause excessive risk taking, a careful design of deposit insurance—complemented by a larger policy package that includes effective supervision, prompt bank resolution methods, and well-designed LOLR procedures—should provide incentives for economic agents to keep the financial system stable.[3]

Good practices that contribute to a proper operation of a DIS include the following:

- The DIS should be explicitly and clearly defined in laws and regulations that are known to, and understood by, the public so bank customers can protect their interests.
- If one is to reduce the probability of moral hazard in banks and to provide incentives for large depositors and counterparty banks to monitor the bank conditions, "large" deposits, including interbank liabilities, should not be covered.
- Ex ante funding schemes are preferable to ex post schemes.
- Membership should be compulsory; insurance premiums should be risk-adjusted, if possible, to moderate the subsidy provided by strong institutions to weaker ones.
- If depositors are to have confidence in the system, the DIS must pay out insured deposits promptly, and it must be adequately funded so it can resolve failed institutions firmly and without delay.
- The DIS should act in the interests of both depositors and the taxpayers who back up the fund. Consequently, it should be accountable to the public, but independent of political interference.
- The DIS should be complemented by effective supervision and well-designed LOLR policies.
- Because the roles of the LOLR, the supervisor, and the DIS are different, it is often advisable in large countries (but impractical in countries facing a shortage of financial skills) to house them in three separate agencies. Regardless, those agencies need to share information and coordinate their actions.
- If the DIS is to avoid regulatory capture by the industry it guarantees, then placing currently practicing bankers in charge of decision making is typically not advisable. However, bankers should be given the opportunity to serve on an advisory board, where they can offer useful advice.
- If a country operates insurance schemes for financial instruments other than (narrowly defined) deposits—including capital market instruments and possibly insurance—then those types of investor and policyholder compensation schemes should

conform broadly to the same standards as deposit insurance, as described in this chapter.

- Although the inclusion or exclusion of foreign currency deposits in deposit insurance would depend on the features of dollarization, adequacy of foreign exchange reserves, and capacity to manage foreign exchange risks, a decision to include foreign exchange deposits should be based on a clear and transparent legal and regulatory framework that specifies who bears the exchange risk.[4]

In a systemic crisis, limited deposit insurance may become ineffective. Other measures such as an extended guarantee (blanket guarantee) could be considered in those circumstances. However, as country experience in systemic crises indicates, a blanket guarantee (a government guarantee for all depositors and certain bank creditors) should be provided only if circumstances are favorable for that guarantee to restore confidence and to stop the crisis from spreading and if there is a credible time-bound exit strategy toward limited guarantee.[5] One crucial condition to restore confidence is that the government's fiscal situation be sustainable.

5.2.3 Investor and Policyholder Protection Schemes

Related to the second element of safety net, deposit insurance, are investor and policyholder compensation schemes, which are designed to promote investor confidence in the functioning of financial markets and to protect policyholders from the failures of financial institutions. They are present in many jurisdictions and form one component of the range of measures adopted by industry associations, self-regulatory organizations (such as stock and futures exchanges), and national authorities. Most schemes are designed to provide some degree of compensation for investors who incur losses from the insolvency or other failure of a member firm; some schemes also provide compensation for losses arising from fraud or other malfeasance on the part of the intermediary or its employees. All schemes have a cap on claims—in absolute terms or as a proportion of the loss incurred or both.

Investor compensation schemes generally cover customer accounts in which a range of investment activities—defined in the respective licensing laws and broader regulatory regimes—take place. Compensation schemes generally do not cover losses on the part of the investor as a result of poor investment advice or management by member firms, although in some schemes, compensation may be available where a causal relationship is established between the poor investment advice or management and the inability of the firm to meet claims made by clients.

In most jurisdictions, the compensation scheme is statutory in nature; however, it may take a variety of forms. Although compensation funds are set up by contract, the obligation to set up and to be a member of one are often in statute. In some cases, schemes are constituted as nonprofit member organizations, whereas, in other cases, the scheme is arranged on the basis of a company operating a fund on behalf of an exchange, the exchange being the principal shareholder of the company. In certain jurisdictions, there are schemes in which trusts—organized on behalf of the various dealer associations and exchanges that are acting as the trust's sponsoring organizations—provide for compensation arrangements. The compensation fund also may be established as a separate company administered by the regulator.

5

The majority of investor compensation schemes are tailored to individual investors and small business; in some cases, institutional investors are afforded equitable treatment under the terms of the scheme. Generally, the claims cap of the scheme is consistent with the type of investor covered by the arrangements; jurisdictions that provide for both retail and institutional claimants in their schemes have caps that are generally higher than those for compensation schemes that are targeted at retail and small business investors. Some schemes provide for a minimum level of compensation, although the majority set limits on the maximum payment in the event of a successful claim.

Funding arrangements for investor compensation schemes rely to a large extent on levies on member firms. Where levies are imposed, they are generally calculated according to factors such as the gross revenue and net capital of member firms. Other factors may also be taken into account in assessing contributions, including the risk profile and level of activity of the firm. Some schemes set a minimum balance for the fund and have specific arrangements to ensure that the minimum balance is maintained. In some jurisdictions, the scheme does not provide for a reserve fund; rather, levies are raised according to projected costs of the scheme in a given year and calculated on an annual basis. Provisions are usually made in the scheme's rules to ensure that additional funds can be raised in the event of a major default or likely shortfall in funds caused by increased claims.

The adequacy of investor protection measures depends on the full range of regulatory responses in place to minimize investor losses and to protect customer assets in the event of the failure of an intermediary. Those measures include (a) procedures to effect the orderly winding up of a failed intermediary, (b) provisions for the regulator to restrain conduct on the part of a failing or failed firm and to direct the appropriate management of assets held by the intermediary, and (c) capital adequacy requirements that are sufficient to facilitate the protection of customer assets in the event of a firm becoming insolvent. Adequate transparency of the regulator—with respect to the steps taken to deal with the failure of market intermediaries—can promote investor confidence.

Some of the emerging good practices of compensation schemes are noted here. Compensation schemes should be independent and transparent in their operations. They should have open and constructive relations with related agencies or functions—such as a supervisor or an ombudsman or any relevant part of the dispute resolution mechanism—and industry representatives. Compensation schemes should be industry-funded to emphasize that prudential and fiduciary responsibility lies with industry participants. The degree of government backing is likely to vary between jurisdictions, but such backing may increase moral hazard to market participants. Prefunded schemes offer greater certainty of compensation, but pay-as-you-go schemes may be perfectly adequate in disciplined markets. The latter type of scheme (and to a lesser extent, the former) may be required to borrow from time to time. The terms and conditions of this borrowing should be subject to clear limits. Funding levies are usually set at a flat percentage of income. The rate may vary from sector to sector, by size of contributor, or by the degree of financial health of the contributor.

Compensation is made on the defined event of failure or almost certain failure of a financial service provider. Compensation is typically subject to an upper limit that is appropriate for the type of product or market and commensurate with the level of funding. Compensation could be limited to retailers or small, unsophisticated commercial consumers, and the extent to which foreign consumers of domestic products should be compensated should be appropriate to the type of market. Most notably, if a market purports to offer products on an international basis, then compensation should be payable to foreign consumers. Finally, the scheme should adhere to good corporate governance practices, follow strict investment guidelines, and be subject to audit.

Policyholder protection funds act as a financial safety net, often after other avenues for redress have been exhausted (e.g., the bankruptcy process). These funds act to maintain public confidence in the industry by protecting the interest of small entities or uninformed customers and by ensuring a smooth exit mechanism for failing companies. Finally, protection funds help to level the playing field across different sectors.[6]

5.2.4 Crisis Management

A third key element of the financial sector safety net includes the policies and procedures in place to manage crises. An assessment of the adequacy of the safety net should consider the readiness of the national authorities to tackle a systemic banking crisis (ideally, to have in place a contingency plan) in case a crisis occurs. Many country authorities may view the prospects for a crisis as highly remote, and thus, assessments of readiness may help raise awareness of the need to have policies and procedures in place to address a crisis.

Some key considerations in assessing the crisis management framework include the following:

- Is the legal framework during "normal times" robust enough to ensure a smooth banking sector restructuring once a crisis has been contained? This question encompasses a wide range of areas, including the banking law, the bankruptcy procedures, the laws on foreclosing assets, and the quality of the judicial system. Adequate bank insolvency law in normal times is critical to ensure smooth bank restructuring in crisis times.

- A high-level policy committee is needed as soon as it is clear that the crisis has taken on systemic proportions. At that point, it is important to act swiftly and decisively, which requires a high-level body. This body should be at the prime ministerial level (or ministerial level) and should include the head of the central bank and the supervisory agency.

- Although it is impossible to have a contingency plan that covers all contingencies (crises come in different shapes and forms), the authorities should have some views with respect to the types of measures that could be taken to contain an emerging crisis. Time is of the essence at that point, and the measures should be of the type to show that the authorities are in control so confidence will return. Some countries occasionally organize crisis management simulations to increase awareness of potential issues and to resolve logistical impediments to the smooth handling of crises.

Additional discussion of those issues is provided in Hoelscher and Quintyn (2003), Lindgren and others (2000), and World Bank and IMF (2004), especially with respect to the legal, institutional and regulatory framework to deal with insolvent banks. See also section 5.3.5 for a more detailed discussion of bank insolvency issues.

5.3 Assessment of Banking Supervision

This section presents the core principles that form the basis for assessing the effectiveness of banking supervision, explains the assessment methodology, outlines the recent assessment experience, and discusses selected key issues in supervision: new capital adequacy standards (Basel II), bank insolvency procedures, supervision of large and complex financial institutions (LCFIs), consolidated supervision, and unique risks in Islamic banking.

5.3.1 Basel Core Principles—Their Scope and Coverage, and Their Relevance to Stability and Structural Development

The Basel Core Principles (BCPs) for Effective Banking Supervision, developed by the Basel Committee on Banking Supervision (BCBS), are the key global standard for prudential regulation and supervision of banks. The BCPs provide a benchmark against which the effectiveness of bank supervisory regimes can be assessed. The BCPs consist of a set of five preconditions for a robust financial system and 25 principles governing aspects of supervision (see box 5.1). The 25 core principles cover various aspects of objectives, autonomy, powers, and resources (Core Principle 1); licensing and structure (Core Principles 2–5); prudential regulations and requirements (Core Principles 6–15); methods of ongoing supervision (Core Principles 16–20); information requirements (Core Principle 21); remedial measures and exit policies (formal powers) (Core Principle 22); and cross-border banking (Core Principles 23–25).

The purpose of the BCPs is to strengthen individual banks by ensuring a sound supervisory framework. Assessments of observance of the BCPs help identify areas that need strengthening and that contribute to stability of the financial system (a) directly by improving good supervision and (b) indirectly by promoting a robust financial infrastructure. The BCPs seek to ensure that the supervisor can operate effectively and that banks operate in a safe and sound manner. The BCPs also define the necessary preconditions, including the legal, accounting, and auditing infrastructure; effective market discipline and resolution of problem banks; public safety nets; and sound macroeconomic frameworks that should be in place for effective supervision. The BCP assessments provide useful qualitative information on the risk environment, on the responsiveness of the supervisor, and on the overall effectiveness of risk management.

The BCPs highlight a set of prerequisites relating to regulatory governance and spell out principles and criteria to govern sound regulatory practices, a prudent operational framework, and financial integrity in regulated firms (box 5.1). In particular, Core Principle 1 lays down a number of prerequisites to the effective exercise of supervision such as clear and legally determined terms of reference, independence of supervisor, powers to address deficiencies, information sharing, and confidentiality and legal protection of the supervisor. What is needed to define the scope of banking supervision is a definition of banking and a licensing system to ensure that only the best-qualified institutions are

Box 5.1 Basel Core Principles for Effective Banking Supervision

The Basel Core Principles comprise 25 basic principles that need to be in place for a supervisory system to be effective. The core principles (CPs) relate to the following:

- Objectives, Autonomy, Powers, and Resources
  - CP 1.1* deals with the definition of responsibilities and objectives for the supervisory agency.
  - CP 1.2 deals with skills, resources, and independence of the supervisory agency.
  - CP 1.3 deals with the legal framework.
  - CP 1.4 deals with enforcement powers.
  - CP 1.5 requires adequate legal protection for supervisors.
  - CP 1.6 deals with information sharing.

- Licensing and Structure
  - CP 2 deals with permissible activities of banks.
  - CP 3 deals with licensing criteria and the licensing process.
  - CP 4 requires supervisors to review—and have the power to reject—significant transfers of ownership in banks.
  - CP 5 requires supervisors to review major acquisitions and investments by banks.

- Prudential Regulations and Requirements
  - CP 6 deals with minimum capital adequacy requirements. For internationally active banks, the requirements must not be less stringent than those in the Basel Capital Accord.
  - CP 7 deals with the granting and managing of loans and the making of investments.
  - CP 8 sets out requirements for evaluating asset quality and the adequacy of loan–loss provisions and reserves.
  - CP 9 sets forth rules for identifying and limiting concentrations of exposures to single borrowers or to groups of related borrowers.
  - CP 10 sets out rules for lending to connected or related parties.
  - CP 11 requires banks to have policies for identifying and managing country and transfer risks.
  - CP 12 requires banks to have systems to measure, monitor, and control market risks.

- CP 13 requires banks to have systems to measure, monitor, and control all other material risks.
- CP 14 calls for banks to have adequate internal control systems.
- CP 15 sets out rules for the prevention of fraud and money laundering.

- Methods of Ongoing Supervision
  - CP 16 defines the overall framework for onsite and offsite supervision.
  - CP 17 requires supervisors to have regular contacts with bank management and staff and to fully understand banks' operations.
  - CP 18 sets out the requirements for offsite supervision.
  - CP 19 requires supervisors to conduct onsite examinations or to use external auditors for validation of supervisory information.
  - CP 20 requires the conduct of consolidated supervision.

- Information Requirements
  - CP 21 requires banks to maintain adequate records reflecting the true condition of the bank and to publish audited financial statements.

- Remedial Measures and Exit
  - CP 22 requires the supervisor to have—and promptly apply—adequate remedial measures for banks when they do not meet prudential requirements or when they are otherwise threatened.

- Cross-Border Banking
  - CP 23 requires supervisors to apply global consolidated supervision over internationally active banks.
  - CP 24 requires supervisors to establish contact and information exchange with other supervisors involved in international operations, such as host country authorities.
  - CP 25 requires (a) that local operations of foreign banks are conducted to standards similar to those required of local banks and (b) that the supervisor has the power to share information with the home-country supervisory authority.

---

* CP 1 is divided into six parts.
Source: BCBS (1999).

permitted into the market. The public needs to be aware of which financial institutions are banks and that, as banks, they are subject to supervision. Consequently, the use of the word "bank" needs to be limited to licensed institutions. Those issues are dealt with in Core Principles 2 and 3.

The quality and integrity of the bank's owners and management are crucial elements in longer-term safety and soundness of the bank, and they need to be vetted by the supervisory authorities. Without clear insight into the structure of the group to which a bank belongs and its acquisitions of interests in other companies, supervisors may not be able to adequately monitor the risks. Core Principles 3, 4, and 5 address those questions. Core Principle 6 requires that banks be subject to rules regulating the adequacy of their capital buffer against risks in the asset portfolio, a key requirement for safe and sound banking. Core Principles 7–11 broadly relate to the quality of lending procedures, the adequacy of provisions (without which capital adequacy figures are overstated), the concentration risks, the risks in lending to connected parties against which contract enforcement may be difficult, and the risks in lending abroad. Core Principles 12 and 13 relate to risks with respect to open positions in securities, currencies, and fixed-income instruments. Good internal systems to monitor and manage risks, as required in Core Principle 14, are also of key importance because bank management is primarily responsible for the stability of the institution and needs to be able to rely on its own information and control systems. Core Principles 16–20 relate to the need for the supervisory authority to have reliable and comprehensive information on the operations and financial condition of a bank. Without this information, monitoring and timely corrective action are not possible. Related to this need, but with a broader objective of informing the markets and the public, is the requirement in Core Principle 21 to disclose audited consolidated annual financial statements that are prepared according to internationally acceptable accounting standards. The supervisory authority must have the means to preempt threats to the stability of financial institutions through timely corrective actions, as envisaged in Core Principle 22. The remaining Core Principles 23–25 relate to the effective monitoring of groupwide risks, the creation of an overview of the financial condition of the group as a whole, and the associated cross-border supervisory cooperation.

Transparency of supervisory framework and policies can contribute to effective supervision. Although the transparency of supervision is not explicitly covered in the BCPs, good transparency practices are covered in IMF Code of Good Practices on Transparency in Monetary and Financial Policies (IMF 2000). Supervisory policies and their implementation need to be disclosed to the public, for instance, through annual reports of the supervisory agency or through dedicated chapters in central bank annual reports. Web sites of supervisory agencies can be used to disseminate annual reports and other periodicals and can serve as a repository for banking laws and regulations. For additional suggestions and guidance on transparency practices, reference is made to the "Supporting Document" of the *IMF Code of Good Practices on Transparency in Monetary and Financial Policies* (IMF 2000).

Good BCP observance has a clear and positive effect on financial sector stability because it helps to ensure that the risks in the banking system—which, in many countries, is by far the most important component of the financial system—are adequately monitored and that tools are in place to manage the risks. If the BCPs are properly implemented and if the preconditions are satisfied, then supervisory authorities have the means to remove weak institutions from the market and to preempt more extensive damage to the banking system. Although risks in banking institutions may also arise from macroeconomic and external shocks (e.g., liberalization-induced credit booms or a foreign exchange crisis), good BCP observance can help manage the effect of the shocks by constraining excessive buildup of exposures to risk factors.[7]

The links between observance of the BCPs and financial development are complex and multifaceted. At one level, the preconditions for observing the BCPs (discussed in section 5.3.2) are also conditions that facilitate financial stability and help to promote financial development. Beyond the preconditions, the observance of best practices of supervision and regulation can also promote strong governance and better risk management, as well as generate more efficient and robust institutions, markets, and infrastructure. In turn, this strengthening of institutions can help promote sustained economic growth. However, the precise mechanism through which this effective operation can occur is far from clear because it also can be the case that developments in the regulatory infrastructure arise in response to financial development. This situation can arise when market participants see that the public good aspects of financial stability outweigh the compliance costs of a stronger regulatory framework so a constituency in favor of a strong regulatory framework emerges.

The key area in supervision that is directly relevant to the ability of banks to contribute to sustainable economic growth relates to implementation of capital adequacy standards and appropriate loan evaluation, as well as provisioning policies and practices. The rules on capital adequacy in a jurisdiction determine the relationship between banks' capital and their loan and investment portfolios and, therefore, limit the amount of loans and investments banks can make against the amount of regulatory capital they hold. When provisions for losses on assets are not adequate, a bank will overstate its capital and thus its capacity to intermediate funds. When a correction needs to be made, the action will instantly decrease the intermediation function of the institution. If this dynamic occurs on a large scale, for instance, as a result of more widespread banking sector problems in an economy, then the result can be a credit crunch, which can have fiscal consequences related to costs of bank resolution, including deposit protection.

Specific institutional features of the banking system need to be taken into account in applying the BCPs and in designing regulatory policies. For example, increasingly, the presence of LCFIs with significant international operations requires an analysis of cross-border exposures to risks and an integrated management of risks across business lines. In some countries, state-owned commercial banks play an important role in the countries' financial systems. In many cases, the weak profitability, governance, and efficiency of those institutions become a cause for concern. The factors may not immediately pose a risk to the banking sector insofar as the implicit guarantee of their liabilities serves to maintain confidence, but they can distort incentive structures and can slow down the growth of a viable commercial banking sector with more rigorous risk-management policies. Better risk-management policies with strong underwriting standards also impose discipline on banks' borrowers to the benefit of the overall quality of the assets portfolio. Also, the balance between the scope of official supervision and the extent of market discipline would vary among countries. The approaches and tools to observe the BCPs may be strongly influenced by the extent to which the overall policy environment and the supervisory policies themselves tend to harness market forces and bring about good governance of banks. For an analysis of the importance of bank supervisory and regulatory policies that facilitate market discipline, see Barth, Caprio, and Levine (2004). In addition, the appropriate balance between official supervision and market discipline could change over time, depending on the extent of stress in the banking system, which might affect the incentives for risk taking.

5.3.2 Preconditions for Effective Banking Supervision

The BCPs include five preconditions for effective supervision. Although preconditions are not formally part of the BCPs because they are normally beyond the jurisdiction of bank supervisors, "weaknesses or shortcomings in these areas may significantly impair the ability of the supervisory authority to implement effectively the Core Principles" (BCBS 1999), the preconditions are as follows:

- Sound and sustainable macropolicies (the precondition that has the most significant effect on risk exposures and capital adequacy)
- A well-developed public infrastructure that covers contract enforcement, a general insolvency regime, an accounting framework, and a corporate governance (all of which affect supervisory powers and enforcement)
- Effective market discipline that is based on transparency and disclosure (which affects the quality of prudential framework)
- Procedures for effective resolution of problem banks
- Mechanisms for providing either an appropriate level of systemic protection or a public safety net (which, along with the preceding precondition above, affects supervision of market conduct and enforcement of corrective actions)

The 2002 evaluation of the experience with the Financial Sector Assessment Program (FSAP) in 60 countries[8] drew attention to the importance of effective preconditions for bank supervision during recent banking crises. In many of the countries experiencing crises, these preconditions were not sufficiently met. It is also noted that "compliance with the BCP is positively correlated to compliance with the preconditions and the stage of development of the financial sector"(IMF and World Bank 2002b). It was stated that developing countries generally are characterized by less favorable preconditions, including unstable macroeconomic conditions, inadequacies of the laws and judicial systems, weak credit culture and accounting systems, low disclosure, and incipient or nonexistent safety nets.

In view of these arguments, the evaluation emphasized the need for assessing the preconditions for effective banking supervision more explicitly in the context of an FSAP process and the BCP assessment. It continued to explain that a more structured approach to their evaluation could improve the analysis of the BCPs. It could furthermore enhance the discussion within an FSAP of linkages between the macroeconomy, the condition of the banking sector and the effectiveness of supervision.

Although an in-depth assessment of some of the preconditions may be beyond the scope of a BCP assessment, an effort should be made to present not only the weaknesses and shortcomings with respect to those preconditions but also the effect they may have on the effectiveness of supervision and on the soundness of the financial system. Emphasis could be placed on the following issues:

- Although the assessment of macroeconomic policies remains in the purview of the broader surveillance, the assessor can focus on identifying vulnerabilities and risks associated with macroeconomic policies both for the financial system and for the effectiveness of bank supervision. Assessors should note whether supervisors have the capacity to assess those vulnerabilities and risks and to what extent the risks can be controlled by supervisors or by banks.

- To assess the adequacy of public infrastructure, the BCP assessors can draw from the conclusions of assessments of financial infrastructure, where available. Using that information, the assessors could note weaknesses in the credit culture, the level of creditor protection, the effectiveness of the judicial system, the bankruptcy procedures, the accounting standards, the auditing profession, and the level of information disclosure to the public.

- An assessment of the strength of market discipline needs to consider (a) issues of transparency, including quality, timeliness, and clarity of the information available to the public; (b) issues of corporate governance; and (c) the role of the government in the financial system and the set of incentives that may weaken market discipline.

- The adequacy of procedures to address problem banks and the effectiveness of the safety net fall within the scope of the BCP assessment and should be examined while assessing Core Principles 1 and 22. In this regard, the assessor should focus on whether supervisors have a sufficient and flexible range of procedures to achieve the efficient resolution of problems in banks, including the capacity to conduct an orderly resolution with respect to problem banks. For the assessment of the safety net, examiners should focus on the existence and design of the deposit insurance and lender-of-last-resort facilities.

In many cases, assessing the weaknesses and shortcomings in the preconditions for effective bank supervision may be time consuming and difficult, demanding a high degree of coordination of different agencies and branches of the government. Important issues of priorities and sequencing arise when trying to prepare a road map to address weaknesses in prudential aspects and preconditions for effective supervision. The question of whether shortcomings in preconditions should be addressed before addressing prudential weaknesses is not a trivial one. Coordination, prioritization, and sequencing of various reforms of infrastructure, supervision, and market and institutional development require careful consideration of the effect on financial stability and the technical interlinkages among various reform components that affect implementation.[9]

5.3.3 Assessment Methodology and Assessment Experience

BCP assessments are a form of peer review that helps to (a) identify regulatory strengths, risks, and vulnerabilities; (b) assess the level of observance of financial sector standards; (c) ascertain the financial sector's developmental and technical assistance needs; (d) prioritize financial sector policies; and (e) provide a reform agenda for improving the supervisory system.[10] Furthermore, standards assessments support the analysis in the context of an analysis of the macroeconomic and structural risks affecting domestic financial systems.

A BCP assessment involves an examination of the adequacy of the legislative and regulatory framework and a determination of whether supervisors are effectively supervising and monitoring all of the important risks taken by the banks. The assessment should follow the guidance provided in the Core Principles Methodology by the Basel Committee on Banking Supervision (BCBS 1999).[11] To achieve full objectivity, compliance with each principle is best assessed by a suitably qualified outside party consisting of at least two individuals with varied perspective so as to provide checks and balances.

Each principle is assigned criteria that are relevant for compliance with it. Two categories of criteria are used: "essential criteria" and "additional criteria." The essential criteria are those elements that should be generally present in individual countries for supervision to be considered effective. Typically, essential criteria specify certain policies and procedures that supervisors are expected to follow to comply with a core principle. The additional criteria are elements that further strengthen supervision and that all countries should strive to implement to improve financial stability and effective supervision. Additional criteria may be particularly relevant to the supervision of more sophisticated banking organizations or may be needed in instances where international business is significant or where local markets tends to be highly volatile.

If one is to achieve full compliance with a core principle, the essential criteria generally must be met without any significant deficiencies. There may be instances, of course, where a country can demonstrate that the core principle has been achieved through different means. Conversely, because of the specific conditions in individual countries, the essential criteria may not always be sufficient to achieve the objective of the principle. Therefore, additional criteria or other measures may also be needed for the particular aspect of banking supervision addressed by the principle to be considered effective. Altogether, there are 227 essential and additional criteria.

As an example of the assessment process and the role of different criteria, consider the case of Core Principle 1. For this principle, each subprinciple is assessed separately. A "compliant" grading for Core Principle 1, for instance, requires that the essential criteria mentioned in the methodology be met, namely, that laws are in place and that responsibilities are clearly defined, that minimum prudential standards are in place, that defined mechanisms exist for coordination, and that those mechanisms are actually used.[12] Furthermore, supervisors should have a role in deciding on resolution of banks, and laws should be updated as needed. Assessment of compliance with those criteria would, for instance, require obtaining and reading the texts of the relevant laws and including the citations in the assessment report. If one is to assess whether responsibilities are, in fact, clear, then information could be obtained on whether agencies cooperate effectively or whether turf issues arise frequently. Do annual reports of various agencies cover the same ground, or are they complementary? Are prudential regulations readily accessible, and do they cover the main prudential areas? If one wishes to review which areas are essential, the list of publications on the Basel Committee's Web site could be consulted to obtain an impression of which areas have been considered important. Coordination mechanisms should be established by a formal decision of the authorities and laid down in some form of decree or similar instrument. This decree should also define the mechanics of coordination, the exchange of information, the procedures for dealing with confidentiality issues, and similar issues. The authorities should provide to the assessors descriptions of how recent bank resolutions were handled, showing, in particular, what role the supervisory authorities had played.

5.3.3.1 Key Considerations in Conducting an Assessment

Consistency to the extent possible, fairness, and objectivity are key, but the primary objective of the assessment remains, not to compare a country's performance with others, but to identify and to address individual countries' strengths and weaknesses. Consistency—defined as a uniform approach to assessments and avoidance of contradictions in assessment grading—is reinforced through the use of assessment methodologies and assessment guidance notes and through the review of draft assessments by other experts. "Calibrating" the BCPs or modifying the assessment criteria to country-specific factors would, however, be contrary to the Basel Committee's intended objective of viewing the BCPs as a standard to be universally adopted and implemented. The quality of the assessment is enhanced when the "four eyes" approach is used—that is, the reliance on two experts with a mix of skills and backgrounds—because it helps mitigate the risk of individual bias.

A well-prepared self-assessment—including the summaries of the relevant legal and regulatory texts, as well as a thorough description of the institutional framework and supervisory practices—is essential. The assessors should meet with the authorities, banks, and other agencies and private sector counterparts. Relevant issues should be discussed not only with the supervisors but also, for instance, with other regulators, the Ministry of Finance, and the representatives from the central bank, as well as from the private sector (e.g., bankers, insurance companies, securities market participants, external rating agencies, and external auditors).[13]

The assessor may need to take into account the countries' level of development while assessing the supervisory prerequisites (Core Principle 1). Differences in prerequisites are likely to have a bearing on the detailed principle-by-principle assessment. For example, when assessing how the collateral value is accounted for in prudential regulations, assessors will have to consider the efficacy of the legal system and whether or not enforcement of regulatory and judicial decisions is problematic. Assessors should reflect the country-specific factors in the "comment" section of the assessment template, and deficiencies can be incorporated in a forward-looking, sequenced action plan. Any considerations relating to the level of development and country-specific circumstances should be reflected fully in the "comments" section of the assessment templates and in the "recommended action plan."

5.3.3.2 Assessment Experience[14]

A review of FSAP experience with BCP assessments reveals areas of strengths and weaknesses (see table 5.1). Notwithstanding better overall performance of industrialized

Table 5.1. Observance of Basel Core Principles for Effective Banking Supervision

Core principle (number and main topic)	Issues raised by assessors
1.1 Framework for supervisory authority/ objectives	Fragmented responsibilities; unclear role of external auditors
1.2. Independence	Political interference in licensing and remedial measures; forbearance; insufficient legal protection; weak autonomy; insufficient staffing.
1.3. Legal framework	Insufficient basis for cooperation and information exchange, also with foreign supervisors.
1.4. Enforcement powers	Legal basis inadequate or overly rigid; forbearance, court intervention, need to consult political authorities.
1.5. Legal protection	Rules on legal protection not explicit, inadequate or absent; no rules on legal expenses; accountability concerns.
1.6. Information sharing	Lack of legal basis or formal agreements; rigid confidentiality constraints, MOUs not implemented in practice.
2. Permissible activities	No authority to act against unauthorized banks; laws unclear on licensing requirements; no protection of the word "bank."
3. Licensing criteria	Reputation of managers not tested; inadequate fit and proper tests, refusal to grant license can be appealed at Ministry of Finance; foreign supervisors not contacted; political interference.
4. Ownership	Prior supervisory approval not required; no fit and proper test for shareholders; no definition of significant ownership, nor qualitative criteria to determine ownership.
5. Investment criteria	No approval authority; inadequate definitions of investments requiring approval; no criteria for impairment of supervision resulting from acquisitions.
6. Capital adequacy policies	No calculation on a consolidated basis; no market risk charges, inadequate risk weightings, inappropriate capital components.
7. Credit policies	Insufficient supervisory guidance on credit policies; no rules on arm's length lending; unclear board and management responsibility for credit policies; no dissemination of policies to staff; insufficient supervisory monitoring.
8. Loan evaluation	Insufficiently rigorous loan classification and provisioning rules, insufficient monitoring, no cash flow based assessment, rules too lenient on use of collateral, restructured or evergreened loans, no tax deductibility for specific provisions, off–balance sheet items not included.
9. Large exposures	Exposures not reported/monitored on a consolidated basis, inadequate and/or overly rigid criteria to establish group connections.
10. Connected lending	Regulations absent or without sufficient legal basis; inadequate/overly rigid definitions of connectedness.
11. Country risk	Absence of regulations, usually because banks have little or no exposure.
12. Market risk	Absence of regulations, or inconsistency with Basel guidance, usually because banks have little or no exposure; no supervision on a consolidated basis, weak or no enforcement.
13. Other risks	Absence or inadequacy of rules on risk management, absence of guidelines on interest rate, liquidity and operational risk; inadequate supervisory capacity.
14. Internal control	Inadequate or no standards, unclear responsibilities of management for internal controls, examination mandate inadequate, no rules on corporate governance.
15. Anti-Money laundering	Inadequate or no legal framework.
16. On-site and off-site supervision	Inadequate frequency of visits, staff shortages, insufficient skills, no risk-based supervision, unclear objectives.
17. Contacts with bank management	Insufficient frequency, no clear procedure to maintaining contact.
18. Off-site supervision	No supervision on a consolidated basis, reporting framework not set by supervisor, non-bank affiliates not covered, inaccurate reporting.
19. Validation of information	Inadequate response to weak audits, no control over external auditors, insufficient frequency of inspections.
20. Consolidated supervision	No requirements on consolidation or consolidated supervision, no legal basis to require consolidated reporting, scope of consolidation too limited, e.g., not covering non-bank affiliates, no reporting of related interests.

Table 5.1. (continued)

Core principle (number and main topic)	Issues raised by assessors
21. Accounting	Standards do not comply with IAS, supervisor has no authority to set bank accounting standards.
22. Remedial measures	Insufficient legal basis, enforcement ineffective, forbearance, limited range of measures, proactive action not possible, court intervention.
23. Global consolidation	Scope too limited, no supervision on a consolidated basis, insufficient authority to oversee foreign banks, insufficient information exchange and MoUs.
24. Host country supervision	No formal arrangements for contacts with home supervisors, little contact in practice, confidentiality constraints.
25. Supervision of foreign establishments	Insufficient exchange of information, insufficient MoUs, no inspection authority for foreign supervisors.

Source: IMF 2004a.

5

countries, similarities in relative strengths and weaknesses exist across all country income groups (industrialized, developing, and emerging). It is significant to note that, in all countries, the broad area of credit risk management has relatively low rates of compliance. Principles relating to the overall foundation for supervision (i.e., the legal and regulatory framework, licensing, and supervisory practices) are relatively well observed when compared with the principles on credit policies, loan evaluation, and risks related to country, market, and other variables. These are areas that affect banks' condition most directly, and their relatively low observance is a matter of concern.

Two crucial areas that are also relatively weak are those of capital adequacy and consolidated supervision. The two areas are connected because, in a number of cases, capital adequacy systems were considered noncompliant or materially noncompliant because capital adequacy was not calculated on a consolidated basis. Also, other prudential standards, such as those related to loan quality and other prudential standards, are much less meaningful if supervision is not exercised on the basis of consolidated reports, accounts, and implementation of remedial action. The principle on anti-money-laundering is also among those that are insufficiently implemented in many countries.

The experience of assessments to date indicates that developing countries generally show lower levels of compliance with the BCPs, whereas many transition countries have intermediate levels of compliance. Advanced economies generally satisfy the preconditions more robustly and achieve the highest level of compliance overall. Compliance with the BCPs is positively correlated with observance of the preconditions and the stage of development of the financial sector.

In general, the main areas of weakness identified by assessments of observance of the BCPs relate to supervisory independence, legal protection for supervisors, and information sharing with other supervisors. Compliance with respect to the principles on credit policies and connected lending, as well as the practices relating to loan classification and provisioning, also appears to be low. Consolidated supervision, especially for large complex financial institutions, is another area of weakness that has been identified in assessments performed to date. The rules on anti-money-laundering and combating the financing of terrorism (AML–CFT) need to be more strongly implemented, as do prompt and effective remedial measures. Finally, systems for managing country risk and market risk were identified as needing improvement in many countries that were assessed.

5.3.4 Basel II

The 1988 Capital Accord (Basel I) introduced capital adequacy measures for credit risk that were based on risk weights assigned to different classes of bank exposures. It was originally intended to be applicable to internationally active banks in the G-10 and other member countries (Belgium, Canada, France, Germany, Italy, Japan, Luxembourg, the Netherlands, Spain, Sweden, Switzerland, United Kingdom, and United States) of the Basel Committee on Banking Supervision. However, the framework was quickly adopted by national supervisors almost universally, making it an international standard. Subsequently, a capital measure for market risk introduced in 1996 has also met with wide acceptance, though it has not been as widely implemented. Nevertheless, significant deficiencies began to surface in the application of Basel I. The use of a uniform 100 percent risk weight for all commercial credits regardless of the risk profile of individual exposures led to distortions. Similarly, the treatment of cross-border and interbank claims also caused biases in credit allocation. Moreover, rapid changes in risk-management technology, including the increasing use of credit risk transfer instruments, needed to be recognized. The factors were among those that led to the development of a new capital accord.

The New Capital Framework (Basel II) represents a significant improvement over the original accord and seeks to provide more risk-sensitive methodologies to align capital requirements with riskiness of banks assets. Under Basel II, the risk weights can be determined using different approaches based on ratings either assigned to bank exposures by external agencies (standardized approach) or internally assigned through supervisor-validated, value-at-risk (VAR) approaches using default probabilities (internal-ratings-based [IRB] approaches). Extensive guidance has also been provided on the expanded credit risk mitigation techniques and their application, as well as on the treatment of securitization and specialized lending. The methodology for market risk capital has been kept almost unchanged while a new capital charge for operational risk has been introduced. Apart from laying out different approaches of varying degrees of sophistication, the Basel II framework also provides for a high degree of national discretion. In addition to laying out methodology to compute minimum capital requirements (Pillar I), the new Basel framework also incorporates guiding principles on the supervisory review of bank risk management (Pillar II) and promotes market discipline through enhanced disclosure requirements (Pillar III).

Member countries of the Basel Committee are expected to implement the Basel framework beginning at the end of 2006. Both the existing and new systems will be run in parallel for a year. While most European Union (EU) countries are expected to implement Basel II in full for their banking systems, many other countries can be expected to implement a mixture of Basel I and Basel II for different parts of their banking systems. Thus, after 2007, assessors can expect banking systems to be applying a bifurcated standard. The assessment of this bifurcated standard will be made further challenging by the fact that there are several different approaches in Basel II for both credit and operational risk, as well as for several areas of national discretion in Pillar I, which could affect cross-institution and cross-country comparisons of capital regimes.

In the period before implementation, national authorities are beginning to examine more closely the various options, as well as the necessity and possibility of applying them. National authorities are also under pressure from the banks in their jurisdictions to refrain from taking actions that would raise capital requirements or increase costs for the system; the banking supervisors are worrying about the lack of capacity to deal with the technical issues in the new Basel framework. International banks face the possibility of being subject to multiple capital regimes through national requirements in different jurisdictions, the resolution of which will require the development of effective systems for cooperation between home and host country supervisors. In contrast, local banks in developing countries are apprehensive about competitive concerns because they fear that foreign banks could gain advantage from using the more advanced approaches that could lower groupwide capital requirements.

Effective implementation of the new capital framework will promote better risk-management practices, more risk-focused bank supervision, and stronger market discipline. However, the framework has been written with the internationally active G-10 banks in mind. Many jurisdictions may not find the proposals easy, or even relevant, to implement. Further, there are other supervisory priorities to be addressed in many countries, and weak implementation may not provide the required comfort but, instead, may divert scarce supervisory and other resources. For this reason, a good level of compliance with the BCPs is considered to be a precondition to considering Basel II implementation.

The Fund, together with the Bank and other international donors, would develop technical assistance programs for countries that seek assistance to implement some or all parts of the new Basel framework within the constraints of available budgets. Finally, countries will not be assessed under the BCPs on the basis of whether or not they have chosen to implement Basel II, but will be assessed against the standard that they have chosen to apply, be it Basel I or Basel II.

5.3.5 Bank Insolvency Procedures: Emerging Bank-Fund Guidelines

Effective bank insolvency procedures form an essential part of the supervisory framework and are also part of a proper financial safety net. Effective procedures help in reducing moral hazard. An analysis of the effectiveness and appropriateness of bank insolvency procedures and exit policies is an important part of BCP assessment. Experience indicates that, in many countries, those types of procedures are weak, opening the door to interference and forbearance.

The World Bank and the IMF have developed a (draft) document titled "Global Bank Insolvency Initiative," (IMF and World Bank 2004),[15] which documents practices around the world in the area of insolvency procedures. Although not a "best practices" document (given the diversity of judicial approaches around the globe, it is premature to develop best practices), this document could certainly be used to check country practices and to provide advice.

5

When authorities face problem banks, the general principle is that the authorities should take prompt action to restore them to health. The supervisors should have the authority to identify unsafe and unsound banking practices and then to require that those practices be halted. Supervisors should be able to apply a series of corrective measures and penalties with increasing severity. If deterioration continues, supervisors should close, merge, or otherwise resolve issues in troubled banks expeditiously before they become insolvent. Increasingly, countries are basing supervisory corrective action on a legal obligation to take specific actions ("prompt corrective action" specifically identified in the law) against a bank as capital levels fall below values established in the law. Prompt action reduces the likelihood that a failing bank will engage in risky and potentially expensive gambles for redemption.

Supervisors need good information on the condition of individual banks so they can take appropriate action. Appropriate disclosure of information to the public would support market discipline. These general issues should come out of the BCP assessment, particularly in Core Principle 22. However, the core principles do not deal specifically with insolvency proceedings other than in the preconditions. That is where the Bank-Fund document on bank insolvency (IMF and World Bank 2004) becomes useful. When making an assessment, assessors should bear in mind that legal and judiciary systems and traditions differ widely among countries. When a bank develops severe financial difficulties, it will have to be either restructured or liquidated. The legal and institutional features that should be in place to allow for orderly restructuring or liquidation are discussed in appendix G (Bank Resolution and Insolvency) and are summarized next. The broader legal environment for effective insolvency procedures is outlined in Annex 5.A.

A special bank insolvency regime, or suitable modifications of a general corporate insolvency regime, is needed to reflect the potential systemic effects of bank failures that call for prompt actions, effective protection of bank assets, and the key role of the banking authorities in bank insolvency proceedings. A typical immediate first step is to have an official authority assume direct managerial control of an insolvent bank (insolvent either in a regulatory sense or in a balance-sheet sense) with the goal of protecting its assets, assessing the true condition, and arranging or conducting either restructuring or liquidation. Official administration continues until the institution has been restored or placed in liquidation. The key principles governing official administration, bank restructuring, and bank liquidation are further discussed in appendix G. One of the key principles is that the authorities should choose the bank resolution option that costs the least. In particular, the cost of bank restructuring should be viewed in terms of net outlays on recapitalization and other assistance operations after deducting the proceeds from reprivatization and asset recoveries. When restructuring is not feasible or when it involves spinning off the viable operations of the bank and, thus, leaving behind only the nonviable part, then the bank will have to be liquidated.

In this process, the supervisory (licensing) agency should have the authority to withdraw a bank's license on the basis of clearly defined criteria. Such criteria include (a) noncompliance with the conditions under which the license was initially granted (in particular, when management is no longer fit and proper), (b) failure to meet prudential requirements, (c) failure to make payments, (d) following of unsafe and unsound banking practices, and (e) criminal activities by the bank. The supervisor could also be given the responsibility to establish the list of qualified liquidators.

Unless the supervisory authorities or some other government agency (such as a deposit insurance fund) is responsible for resolving the problems of insolvent banks, the liquidator will be appointed by the courts, which oversee liquidation. Any deficiency in the court process that could impede bank liquidation should be identified. The authorities should have contingency plans to deal with the emergence of systemic banking problems or large-scale bank closures. Plans should include ways to protect the payments system and to maintain basic banking services. The authorities should also have an idea of how to organize the restructuring efforts, including which institutions would be charged with guiding the restructuring efforts. In addition, the authorities should evaluate the legal framework for bank supervision and regulation to ensure that the authorities have the necessary powers to act quickly and efficiently in the face of a systemic crisis.

5.3.6 Large and Complex Financial Institutions[16]

The activities of large and complex financial institutions (LCFIs)[17] raise issues of cross-sectoral and cross-border transfer of financial risks that are especially relevant to a comprehensive assessment of the strengths and weaknesses of financial systems and their supervision. An LCFI is likely to have the following characteristics:

- An LCFI will be an important player in both wholesale and retail financial markets and in substantial international operations, regionally or globally. In some cases, these operations could dwarf its business in the country under consideration.
- The group may have its headquarters in the country or may be based abroad. In the latter case, it will have a significant local presence in the form of branches or locally incorporated subsidiaries (perhaps including local holding companies). The legal form of its local presence may have important implications for the way it is regulated.[18]
- The group's international and domestic business will span a number of financial activities including commercial banking and other lending, such as the origination and securitization of credit; securities trading, dealing and underwriting, mergers and acquisitions, and other capital market activity; life and general (property and casualty) insurance; and custody and asset management. In some cases, the operations of the wider group may include significant industrial and other nonfinancial activities.
- The group is likely to be prominent in the local payments, clearing, and settlements structure.

As a consequence of the characteristics of an LCFI, the group's liabilities will reflect very diverse sources of local and cross-border funding and reserves, while its assets will include a full range of marketable and nonmarketable financial instruments held locally and abroad. Off-balance sheet items are likely to be particularly prominent and to reflect complex funding, plus hedging and speculative trading strategies, all of which are carried out in both over-the-counter (OTC) markets and on organized exchanges. The group is likely to comprise many different legal entities, and the link between those entities and

5

its internal management structure may appear complicated or even opaque. Complexity or opaqueness in organizational structures could be a potential source of risk, as well as raising issues for supervisory and central bank coordination.

The group's activities may be subject to numerous different national legal and insolvency, accounting, tax, and regulatory regimes, which will influence the management of its business and balance sheet. The group may or may not have an overall lead supervisor monitoring its activities on a consolidated basis. At the host country level, responsibility for supervision of an LCFI's local affiliates may reside within a single regulator or several functional regulators. The size of the group and of its geographical diversification has the potential to threaten financial stability in several countries and markets. Its operations will thus be of concern both to its many financial regulators and also to the central banks and guarantee agencies that could be involved in providing or facilitating liquidity or other official financial support.

The presence of foreign-owned LCFIs in the domestic financial market may not raise particular issues for local financial stability, when their share of local banking, securities, and insurance markets is small and when the nature of their local business is straightforward. While local and foreign affiliates of wider LCFI groups may well be counterparties in foreign exchange and OTC derivatives transactions of local financial institutions, this need not warrant any special analysis, absent any significant concentrations of exposure. Conversely, there may be cases where an internationally active institution has such a large share of the local market or is such a significant counterparty of local financial institutions that its failure could constitute a serious local systemic risk. In such instances of high concentration, an understanding of the wider operations of the group, its reputation, and the risks of its business should be important in assessing potential threats to financial stability.

In relation to LCFIs, there are clearly limits to the scope of assessments at the level of individual countries. Country assessments can be expected to cover only part of the activities of LCFIs, given the international nature of such. Even if local supervision of an LCFI is effective in identifying and mitigating local risks as far as possible and if there is good cooperation with the LCFI's home regulator(s), a host country is unlikely fully to escape the effects of a failure. The assessment process should focus mainly on those aspects over which the countries' authorities can reasonably be expected to exert an influence.

An examination of LCFIs can be approached in three stages, followed by a summary of the main risks identified and recommendations to the authorities:

- Stage I involves the identification of the scope and scale of LCFIs' activities within the local financial system. An assessor will want to seek data on market shares of prominent, internationally active, financial institutions to determine if a focus on LCFI activities is warranted. Where one or more LCFIs have been identified as having particular significance for local systemic stability, more detailed firm-specific information on the legal entity and organizational structures, the nature of intra-group exposures, the main sources of earnings, and so forth may then be needed to provide a sufficiently detailed map of their activities to identify the main channels of systemic risk. For some internationally prominent LCFIs, it may be possible to draw on information gathered from other assessments conducted for other countries.

- Stage II involves an assessment of the major systemic risks arising from the activities of LCFIs. Emphasis should be placed on the extent and nature of both intra-group transactions and the exposures of other domestic institutions to LCFIs. Key concerns will be not only potential direct losses in the event of an LCFI failure but also contagion risks. The approach suggested here is that this assessment be built up by considering credit, technical,[19] liquidity, market, and operational risks from the different businesses of the group. LCFIs' participation in local payment and settlement systems should also form a significant part of the analysis. Drawing on the preceding qualitative identification of risks, the assessor may also want to quantify the risks by considering further stress testing or scenario analyses.

- Stage III involves an assessment of the effectiveness of the authorities' policies and practices in addressing the risks. This stage should include a review of group capital adequacy, the regulation of large exposures and of intra-group transactions, and the extent and effectiveness of information sharing between local and foreign supervisors. Oversight of the role of LCFIs in local payment and settlement systems should also be considered.

Given the potential of LCFIs to be a conduit in the transmission of internal and external shocks, the authorities' approach to surveillance—the identification of potential systemic risks from the activities of LCFIs—should be a prominent part of the assessment. The assessment team may want to assess the effectiveness of stress testing and scenario analyses that are conducted by the authorities and that may be complemented by work conducted by the team itself as part of Stage II. The state of preparedness for managing a crisis arising from a domestically headquartered LCFI that is in difficulties or from the failure of a major foreign, internationally active institution that threatens local financial stability is an important issue for supervisors to consider.

5.3.7 Consolidated Supervision

Consolidated supervision is a supervisory tool that was developed in response to the growing trend in financial institutions of diversifying their activities across national borders and sectoral boundaries through ownership linkages. The creation of diversified financial groups raises additional supervisory concerns, including contagion, conflicts of interest, lack of transparency, and regulatory arbitrage. Supervisory and regulatory arrangements are geared at mitigating those concerns to ensure that risks are properly managed and that they do not threaten the safety and soundness of the financial system.

Consolidated supervision may be broadly defined as a qualitative and quantitative evaluation of the strength of a financial group that consists of several legal entities under common ownership or control. The objective of consolidated supervision is (a) to ensure the safety of the financial system through monitoring and evaluating the additional risks posed to the regulated financial institutions by the affiliated institutions in the financial group and (b) to assess the strength of the entire group. Consolidated supervision should have both quantitative and qualitative elements:

5

- Quantitative consolidated supervision focuses on issues such as asset quality, capital adequacy, liquidity, and large exposures that are measured on a consolidated basis. There is clearly a requirement that the group be able to produce (a) comprehensive on-balance sheets and off-balance sheet data and (b) counterparty information. This input should be in a form sufficient for reliable capital adequacy, liquidity, and exposure concentration calculations to be made. Because different entities in the group may be subject to different accounting regimes, the results of accounting consolidation may need to be treated with caution.

- Qualitative consolidated supervision is closely identified with comprehensive risk-based supervision, which is designed to assess how well management identifies, measures, monitors, and controls risks in a timely manner. This supervision will involve an assessment of the wider risks posed by other group companies in terms of their effect on the regulated entity. This assessment is likely to involve the

---

Box 5.2 Unique Risks in Islamic Banking

Islamic banking poses unique risks to the financial system because of the profit-and-loss-sharing (PLS) modes of financing and specific contractual features of Islamic financial products.[a] PLS not only shifts the risks in the institution to investment depositors to some extent but also makes Islamic banks vulnerable to a range of risks (including those normally borne by equity investors) because of the following features:

- Administration of PLS is more complex, requiring greater auditing of projects to ensure proper governance and appropriate valuation.
- PLS cannot be made dependent on collateral or guarantees to reduce credit risk.
- Product standardization is more difficult because of the multiplicity of potential financing methods, the increasing operational risk, and the legal uncertainty in interpreting contracts.
- Liquidity risks are substantial because of the inability to manage asset and liability mismatches as a result of the absence of Sharia-compliant instruments such as treasury bills and lender-of-last-resort facilities.

The presence of commodity inventories in Islamic bank balance sheets adds to operational and price risks. In addition, for contracts with deferred delivery of products, significant additional price risks arise.

Unique Risks of Islamic Banking

Addressing the unique risks of Islamic banking requires adequate capital and reserves, as well as appropriate pricing and control of risks in a suitable disclosure regime. Because information asymmetries are particularly acute in Islamic banking, the need for strong rules and practices for governance, disclosure, accounting, and auditing rules is paramount. The development of an infrastructure that facilitates liquidity management is also a key priority. The challenge for supervisors in ensuring that this type of framework is in place is made more difficult by the absence of uniform prudential and regulatory rules and standards. Currently, there is no uniformity in income-loss recognition, disclosure arrangements, loan classification and provisioning, treatment of reserves, practices in income smoothing, and so forth, although standards for those elements have been developed—and are in increasing use—by accounting and auditing organizations for Islamic financial institutions.

---

a. The Islamic Financial Services Board (IFSB) was established to adopt regulatory practices and policies to the specific features of Islamic finance and to promote its development. Establishment of IFSB was facilitated by IMF so it can develop prudential standards for Islamic banking and can foster effective risk management. Several IFSB working groups are developing standards and guidelines on capital adequacy, risk management, corporate governance, Islamic money markets, and market discipline and transparency; in addition, draft standards on capital adequacy and risk management have been issued for public comments.

identification of significant activities or business units and an understanding not only of their role within the group but also of the risks to the group posed by their activities.

Some of the key issues and principles governing consolidated supervision are summarized in Annex 5.B.

5.3.8 Unique Risks in Islamic Banking

Islamic banking can be defined as the providing of and use of financial services and products that conform to Islamic religious practices.[20] Islamic financial services are characterized by a prohibition against the payment and receipt of interest at a fixed or predetermined rate. Instead, profit-and-loss-sharing (PLS) arrangements or purchase and resale of goods and services form the basis of contracts. In PLS modes, the rate of return on financial assets is not known or fixed before undertaking the transaction. In purchase-resale transactions, a markup is determined on the basis of a benchmark rate of return, typically a return determined in international markets such as LIBOR (London interbank offered rate). Islamic banks are also prohibited from engaging in certain activities such as (a) financing production or trade in alcoholic beverages or pork and (b) financing gambling operations. A range of Islamic contracts is available, depending on the rights of investors in project management and the timing of cash flows. Special risks in Islamic banking arise because of the specific features of Islamic contracts and the weak environment for effective risk management, thereby reflecting the absence of risk-management tools that are Sharia compatible. Box 5.2 contains further details.

5.4 Assessment of Insurance Supervision

The International Association of Insurance Supervisors (IAIS) has developed the *Insurance Core Principles* (IAIS 2000) as the key global standard for prudential regulation and supervision for the insurance sector. The objective of the Insurance Core Principles (ICPs), from the perspective of the standard setters, is to act as a diagnostic tool to assist in improving supervision globally. To this end, the assessment of ICPs should include prioritized recommendations that can serve as a roadmap for a reform agenda. Fundamentally, insurance supervisors around the world have been concerned about improving insurance supervision and bringing about a basic level of effectiveness in all jurisdictions by facilitating assessments (both internal and external) that are consistent and comprehensive. The global nature of insurance markets (particularly the presence of conglomerates), the expansion of cross-border transactions, the global nature of reinsurance markets, and the presence of active offshore centers all call for some convergence of regulatory practices and norms to ensure effectiveness of regulations and a level playing field.

The ICPs were updated through an extensive process culminating in a new version in October 2003 (IAIS 2003a). This version sets out the key elements of effective regulation and supervision for the insurance sector and elaborates the requirements on the law, the supervisory process, and the functions and operations of market participants so as to deliver an effective and positive contribution from the insurance sector to the wider economy and to the long-term well-being of the population. The October 2003 version of ICP incorporates additional core principles, including adequacy of risk-management operations, AML–CFT (the subject of a separate standard; see later parts of this Handbook), and transparency of insurance supervision policies (also the subject of a separate standard; see later parts of this Handbook). Moreover, the new version contains additional, more specific criteria for assessment purposes as it draws on earlier assessment experience under the Financial Sector Assessment Program and other previously issued guidelines by IAIS outside of the ICPs. For example, the principles also address issues such as management of risk and consumer protection, and they incorporate as essential criteria "principles on capital adequacy and solvency" (IAIS 2002), which was adopted in 2002. The relevance of effective regulation and supervision of insurers for stability and development, the scope of the new ICPs, and their use in assessments and lessons of assessment experience are summarized in the following sections.

5.4.1 Relevance to Stability and Development

Sound and effective regulation and supervision is important in sustaining a sound operating sector that protects and maintains the confidence of policyholders and, therefore, plays an effective role in overall economic development. Supervision of the insurance sector is not an end in itself. Rather, insurance supervision, when properly conducted, plays a critical role in facilitating that sector's contribution to the effective management of risks for the wider economy; the mobilization of long-term savings, particularly in the life insurance sector; and the allocation of investment in long-term fixed interest and equity markets, as well as in infrastructure and venture capital.

Sound regulation and supervision can also guard against the consequences of insurer failure for policyholders. The traditional focus of supervision on policyholder protection is increasingly giving way to broader financial stability concern as activities of insurers in financial markets expand. Failure can have catastrophic consequences for the individual policyholder, particularly because the choice of insurer may not be subject to market forces in all cases (e.g., third-party claimants) and may not be easily diversified. Some insurance contracts are not suitable for the insured party to take out contracts with several providers—in the same way that many hold deposits with several institutions. The ICPs seek to protect policyholders, both as a group (by focusing on the institutional integrity of the insurance companies) and individually (by promoting good marketing practices, adequately disclosing information about contracts to customers and potential customers, and handling consumer complaints). At the same time, the increasing financial market activities of insurers, including a growing role in credit risk transfer, has raised a question about the implications for financial stability arising from insurer's failures and the implications for insurance supervision (see IMF 2002, 2004b).

Insurers have a role to play in guarding against fraud, money laundering, and terrorism financing. The ICPs recognize this role through a comprehensive set of requirements and good practices in the custody and management of assets, corporate governance, and internal controls. Specific obligations with respect to the fitness and propriety of those who act as custodians (in a legal sense or otherwise) of the community's savings are recognized as critical to the maintenance of a sound insurance sector.

5.4.2 The Structure of the ICPs

The ICPs consist of 28 principles in total, grouped into seven categories.[21] The principles cover all aspects of a supervisory framework—from licensing to closure of activities. The seven groupings reflect commonality of purpose among the principles in each group, ranging from preconditions to prudential requirements and market conduct. See Annex 5.C for a summary of the scope of each of the principles.

The first ICP addresses the general conditions needed for effective supervision and is similar in nature to the BCP "preconditions." This ICP addresses elements that are most usually not the direct responsibility of the insurance supervisory authority. The elements relate to the overall policy settings for the financial sector, as well as the infrastructure of financial markets and their efficient operation. Effective policy settings are critical to the supervisors' task because they provide the backdrop against which the institutional risk is assessed. Infrastructure in markets includes not only the broader financial policy aspects but also the legal and professional services that enable the supervisory process to function. The role of accounting, auditing, and actuarial professions shows examples of particular relevance to insurance supervision. The efficiency of financial markets influences the extent to which institutions are exposed to liquidity risk and market risk, as well as the options they have to address those risks. The first ICP is also concerned with the extent to which companies are able to access statistical data to enable those data to assess market risks and liability risks.

The second group of ICPs (ICPs 2–5) deals with the organizational structure and governance aspects of the supervisory authority. Those ICPs cover the objectives of the supervisor, the legal standing of the supervisory authority, the independence, the confidentiality requirements, and the existence of a transparent supervisory process. Information sharing is also covered in this group of ICPs, which makes it consistent with the issue of confidentiality.

The third group of ICPs (ICPs 6–10) focuses on the establishment and operations of the insurance companies as supervised entities. The fundamental licensing obligation and the effective stewardship of the organization under the continuing control of owners with integrity is emphasized through tests for fitness and propriety, as well as through control of changes in ownership and transfers of portfolios.[22] Overall policies and obligations with respect to corporate governance and internal controls also form part of this group.

Ongoing supervision is the focus of the fourth group of ICPs (11–17). The principles in this group set out the process for supervision and its key components at a high level and then elaborate on key elements of the supervisory process. First, to establish the basis for sound assessment of individual institutions and prompt supervisory actions, ICP 11 stresses the role of an overall analysis of the market and identifies the potential risks and vulnerabilities that affect insurance firms and markets[23] and that arise as a result of the overall environment in which they operate. The ICPs that follow cover the reporting obligations of companies, including the regular and ad hoc information requirements; the assessment of returns received by the supervisor; the conduct of onsite inspections; the taking of action through preventative measures; the active enforcement and sanction powers; and, if necessary, the closeout of the insurer. In particular, ICP 12, which focuses on reporting, also establishes the main obligations with respect to external audit and accounting standards. ICP 12 largely focuses on the content and completeness of supervisory reporting[24] and includes a substantive role of offsite supervisory assessment as one of the criteria. ICP 16 includes the definition of insolvency, or at least the point at which intervention is obligated to protect policyholders, and ICP 17 addresses the assessment of groupwide risks.

The group of insurance core principles that cover "prudential requirements" (ICPs 18–23) focuses on insurers' obligations with respect to the key areas of sound risk management, which includes understanding the nature of insurance risks, liabilities, assets, risk instruments, and capital. However, there is no internationally uniform capital requirement or set of rules for assets and liabilities in the insurance sector at this stage. The most important characteristics of a capital adequacy and solvency regime are covered at a fairly high level in the standard. Therefore, a wide range of approaches to capital adequacy and solvency are in use, some of which may be deficient in their ability to identify and require capital for significant risks to financial stability or to the solvency of an insurer. For example, capital required under the regime used in the EU and other jurisdictions does not depend on the composition of the investment portfolio. The IAIS and other organizations are working toward greater uniformity of capital adequacy standard.[25] The ICPs within this group emphasize the need for a sound assessment of risk and adequate resources to meet the risks assessed. The IAIS had already issued other supervisory standards that are relevant and related to these ICPs. Because the ICPs themselves were being revised, the supervisory standards available at the time were incorporated into the ICPs; some guidelines and issue papers were also under preparation at the time of the issuance of ICPs, and those, too, would be relevant for the assessment.[26]

The remaining two groups (ICPs 24–28) deal with markets and consumers (the oversight of insurance intermediaries, customer protection, disclosure to the wider market, and fraud prevention) and with AML–CFT. The oversight of intermediaries (most commonly, insurance agents and brokers) is an important element of insurance sector soundness that does not always have a direct equivalent in other sectors. The failure of an intermediary can have a direct effect on those customers who have dealt with the insurer through the intermediary. The fitness and the propriety of intermediaries are also an important element in the maintenance of a sound system that preserves public confidence in the sector. Customer protection goes beyond the customer's dealings with intermediaries to include (a) the requirements for information disclosure to explain the product and services to the customer and (b) the manner by which a customer may seek to have complaints resolved. Complaint resolution needs to be accessible, to be timely, and not to impose an undue cost, recognizing that customers have relatively limited financial and technical resources available. In some jurisdictions, this role is played by self-regulatory organizations (SROs). In others, it is played by companies with supervisory oversight or even by the supervisors themselves. Wider market disclosure focuses on broader and less-specific disclosure than is involved with individual customers and their individual products. The intent of this wider disclosure is to impose market discipline on companies. Again, it can be more or less effective and needs to reflect the market structures as the system needs to consider all companies, not just those that are publicly listed.

Claims fraud is a key issue in the insurance sector and is addressed in the newly introduced ICP 27. Claims fraud, wherein customers might submit inflated or invalid claims, has an insidious effect on companies and can ultimately bring the solvency of a company into question. As one addresses this issue, the diligence and integrity of the company is emphasized, as well as the linkages between the supervisory and prosecuting authorities.

The principles themselves have been deliberately drafted at a general level, and those principles should be interpreted according to the additional explanation provided for each principle. Each principle is elaborated with an explanatory note and followed by a set of criteria. The explanatory note is intended to provide elaboration and clarification, setting out the rationale for the particular principle and sometimes referring to specific examples. The criteria are divided between the so-called "essential criteria" and "advanced criteria." Essential criteria are considered necessary for all markets to be fully functional and effective. Advanced criteria are considered either for particularly advanced and complex markets or, more likely, to provide a sense of direction for further improvement as markets and practices evolve.

5.4.3 Assessment Methodology and Assessment Experience

ICP assessments are based on a set of essential and advanced criteria, as well as on an assessment methodology. that has been issued as part of the document.[27] The methodology is intended to assist the assessor in his or her goal to be both fair and objective. The document itself speaks of the assessments being "comprehensive, precise, and consistent" (IAIS 2003a). In practice, the methodology and the ICPs themselves include some key nuances that should be understood in carrying out the assessment and in interpreting the results. The following subsections highlight these key issues, without elaborating on every feature of the ICPs and their assessment.

5.4.3.1 Essential and Advanced Criteria—Assessment Process

Assessments are normally carried out against the essential criteria for comparability with other assessments. As noted above, essential and advanced criteria are included in the ICPs. However, it may be necessary or sensible to also consider the advanced criteria in some cases. When considering the advanced criteria, the assessor can prepare the report on the observance of the standards by considering the essential criteria and making further comments or by using the advanced criteria to guide recommendations. Nevertheless, the IAIS methodology indicates that, even where the advanced criteria are considered, the overall assessment of the principle will be based on the essential criteria only for consistency purposes.

There are five categories for the assessment of the criteria. Those categories are defined in the annex to the document as "observed," "largely observed," "partly observed," "not observed," and "not applicable." Procedurally, the assessment process assesses each of the criteria first; only then can the principle be assessed after considering the overall situation with respect to all the underlying criteria. For a principle to be rated as "observed," it needs to have all its related criteria rated as "observed" or "not applicable." Consequently, it is difficult to achieve full observance, particularly for the ICPs that have a larger number of criteria as compared with an ICP that has a smaller number of criteria. Thus, an overall summary that does not identify the criteria but simply summarizes the number of ICPs at each rating will be misleading. ICP 3 is particularly difficult in this context because it has 17 essential criteria and is wide ranging in scope.

A rating of "largely observed" means that the shortcomings are minor and that the authority would be able to achieve observance without an expectation of concern. For example, a shortcoming is recognized and is being addressed effectively. Thus, the assessor has no reason to doubt its successful implementation. However, in situations where, for example, significant industry or political resistance is to be expected and has not yet been overcome in implementing the reform program, then the observance of the relevant core principle would not be rated as "largely observed."

The rating is akin to a temperature reading at a point in time rather than an indication of a future position. The reports provide the opportunity to recognize work in progress through comments, but the rating has to reflect the actual current situation in fact. Differentiating between a rating of "largely observed" and "partly observed" will mean—because of the definitions—that work in progress is influencing the decision to use one or the other of the two ratings.

The assessor can decide to show more than one rating for an ICP depending on the segment of the insurance industry. It may be the case that segments of the industry show a very different result for one or more ICPs. For example, the life and nonlife sectors may be subject to different regulation, and one may be more complete than the other; similarly, reinsurance may not be subject to a particular element but the direct insurance companies may be comprehensively covered. Showing more than one rating can be a useful way to reflect the positive elements of the situation while identifying the segment that may have a missing element.

5.4.3.2 Usefulness of a Well-Prepared Self-Assessment

The authorities should prepare a self-assessment to benefit fully from an independent assessment of observance of ICPs. Self-assessment also helps the authorities to identify the relevant parts of the law and the supervisory practice that will be of interest to the outside assessor.

Sometimes, a supervisory authority may prepare an assessment for another purpose, one that assesses the authority rather than the whole jurisdiction. In those cases, the assessment may rate a particular criterion as "not applicable" where it falls to a different authority in the jurisdiction to undertake that task. Insurance assessment should, however, be carried out in the context of the jurisdiction as a whole rather than for an individual authority. Therefore, the assessor will need to obtain information on the relevant criteria, laws, practices, and oversight from several authorities, including the agency with primary responsibility for insurance supervision. Obtaining this information will require coordinating the assessment process with many agencies.

5.4.3.3 The Insurance Market Assessment

The ICPs can be properly assessed only in the context of an overall analysis of conditions in the insurance sector, including an assessment of the performance of and prospects for the sector. Consequently, it is necessary to analyze and form a view on the adequacy of provisions, profitability, business trends, and capitalization of the sector while using recent data (see chapter 4 for a discussion of sectoral analysis).[28]

A key feature of the assessments made in this context of an overall analysis needs to be the assessment of ICP 1—the conditions for effective supervision. As noted earlier, the elements of this ICP are often outside the control of the supervisor. When a supervisor is doing a self-assessment for other purposes or for an internal examination, then this ICP may be less important. However, within the context of a broader financial sector assessment, it is a critical element because it provides the necessary links to considering development and stability. The ICPs also recognize some steps that the supervisor may take in the face of weaknesses in the conditions.[29] Examples would include the encouragement or sponsorship of statistical studies where they are not being done otherwise. Weaknesses in the asset markets may signal that it is reasonable to impose more onerous or specific obligations on investments. Weaknesses in the legal system may lead to a response to establish separate specific procedures for the sector. Those kinds of steps may be considered in the context of recommendations to strengthen the system as a whole in the face of weak conditions.

5.4.3.4 Flexibility

Another feature of the assessment process is that "the framework described by the Insurance Core Principles is general. Supervisors have flexibility in adapting it to the

---

Box 5.3 Flexibility in Assessments

Core Principle 19 on insurance activity states that "since insurance is a risk taking activity, the supervisory authority requires insurers to evaluate and manage the risks that they underwrite, in particular through reinsurance, and to have the tools to establish an adequate level of premiums." This principle is elaborated through a set of five essential criteria, including supervisory review of adequacy of reinsurance and the requirement that "the insurer has a clear strategy to mitigate and diversify risks by defining limits on the amount of risk retained."

The level of detail and breadth of such a strategy clearly depend on the nature of the risks that the sector underwrites; therefore, the scope of the strategy is a function of the product mix. The level of exposure to natural catastrophes is relevant to property insurance firms, and the level of sophistication in the identification and measurement of catastrophe risks will vary amongst jurisdictions.

In the case where a company insures significant property risks in a jurisdiction where natural catastrophes are material, then it would be expected that the company would take a rigorous approach for establish-

ing limits for each new policy issued by considering the extent to which catastrophe risk is increased or the extent to which concentration becomes a greater concern. Often, for example, this process involves detailed comparison of the distribution of the risks insured in the portfolio with simulation models that help to quantify the risks from the catastrophe. Where a company provides liability insurance, then it would not be sensible to impose or expect similar details in the modeling of catastrophes because aggregation of risk needs to be considered using different techniques.

In the case of a life insurance company, the detailed risk-management systems required for the investment portfolio would vary considerably, depending on the nature of the liabilities and the conditions in the market place, including the access to derivatives and other risk-management instruments. For a company that undertakes investment-linked business, the risk-management focus should be different from that of a company that writes long-term savings contracts with stronger return guarantees.

---

domestic context" (IAIS 2003a, 50). This characteristic leads the assessor to consider whether an element may be inadequate in the context of a more complex aspect of the market, even though it may well be reasonable in another market or may have been reasonable when it was established in times when the market was less complex. Box 5.3 illustrates the application of flexibility in the context of ICP 19, which requires insurers to provide adequate monitoring and evaluation of insurance risks and to ensure adequate premiums and reinsurance to manage the risks.

5.4.3.5 Observance in Law and Practice

The methodology for the assessment of the ICPs calls for observance both in law and in actual practice. For most criteria, it is not sufficient simply to consider whether or not the law or other legal obligations cover the necessary material. "Observance" usually requires the practices to be recognized in the law or legislation and to be enforced effectively. Here is a useful set of questions to consider:

- Is the practice or power specified in the law, the regulations, or both?
- How do the authorities know it is followed in practice?

The assessment is not clear-cut when the desirable practices are in the law but have not been used because the circumstance for their use has not arisen. For example, particular winding-up provisions may appear adequate but may not have had the benefit of any testing. A more clear-cut example arises when a well-constructed solvency margin regulation exists but is not observed by the firms in practice. This situation will not be assessed as "observed," given the lack of implementation of the regulation. Similarly, if a regulation or criterion cannot be monitored or implemented because the financial reporting or supervisory staffing does not permit it, then it would be difficult to rate the mere existence of a rule in the rule book as sufficient for a rating of "observance."

The requirement of clarity of the law, as well as practice, in the current ICPs is onerous; however, it is possible to consider observance by other means (as suggested in IAIS 2003a, 52). This suggestion is intended to bring an additional flexibility to the assessment. It may be that the approach taken in a jurisdiction is not consistent with the wording of the criteria but the effective result is the same in terms of actual results. For example, the principle of establishing clear priority to policyholders in the event of winding-up an insurer is discussed in the explanatory notes to ICP16 (IAIS 2003a, 30), where the alternative priorities for other stakeholders are recognized. At the same time, essential criteria "c" seeks a high level of priority to the policyholder. This example indicates that a low priority in the winding-up provisions of the law may be effectively erased in effect for policyholders by a policyholder protection scheme, which provides additional or alternative protection. Another example of observance by other means could be represented by the operation of custom or by the role of SROs. In those cases, the custom or practice needs to be considered by the assessor. It should be undisputed and robust.

When using the term *legislation*, the ICPs are not taking a prescriptive view on whether or not an obligation is in the primary insurance law or whether it is in a subsidiary regulation, instrument, or circular. This approach provides flexibility within the context of the legal system. There are, however, some places where the use of the word *law* is taken to mean the primary law. In those cases, the ICPs consider that it is of particular importance to include the specified feature in the primary insurance law.

5.4.3.5 *Reinsurers, Policyholders, Beneficiaries, and Customers*

The ICPs depend on the definitions of the terms that the IAIS uses in preparing all of their documents. Most of the terms are defined in the IAIS glossary that is available on the IAIS Web site. Several other important definitions are included in the document, and they influence the scope of the assessment of the criteria and the principle.

The term insurers includes reinsurers. Even though the term generally refers to insurers, the reinsurance sector is also included in all respects unless indicated. The only indication that excludes them is with respect to consumer protection because reinsurance is generally taken to be a market between more informed customers (IAIS 2003a, 41).

A wide definition of the terms *policyholders*, *beneficiaries*, and *customers* is used in the ICP. *Policyholders*, when used, describes not only the owner of the policy but also a beneficiary, for example, a third-party claimant or the widow of a deceased policyholder awaiting claim payment. *Customers* is a term used to also include potential policyholders. The definitions are of most importance when considering the consumer protection in particular. For example, under criterion "e" of ICP 25, the effectiveness or otherwise of an "accessible" complaint handling process will depend on whether or not a claimant can access it regardless of whether or not he or she is the policyholder.

Information and *disclosure* will also need to be interpreted in the context of the definitions but within practical rather than literal bounds. The relevance and timeliness of information provided to the potentially affected parties should be a key consideration. The owner of a policy may need particular information not only before purchase but also during the time the contract is in force. The existence of a complaint scheme may be relevant for general information but will be more pertinent to those who indicate that they have a claim and even more so to those who have had a claim denied by an insurer.

5.4.3.6 *Difficulties That Can Have a Pervasive Effect on Assessments*

An underresourced supervisory body will have difficulty with many of the ratings if it is not able to conduct an effective onsite inspection activity because a number of the criteria will be difficult to verify in the absence of such inspections, formal or otherwise. Where this situation is the case, the commentary can be used to make clear the central reason for the situation.

5.4.3.7 *Reporting*

Ultimately, the ICP assessment is intended to be a diagnostic instrument. As a result, ICP methodology emphasizes that the report (a) summarize the findings to highlight areas for improvement and (b) prioritize them in a sensible order. In addition, the report should explain the priorities.

5.4.3.8 Key Assessment Experience

The experience of assessments to date indicates that the insurance sector generally shows a weaker level of observance of international standards than does the banking sector.[30] Most usually, the reason is reflected in a less well-resourced and less-independent supervisory body and in an insurance law that fails to provide the full range of powers to the supervisor to carry out the task envisioned in the ICPs. It can also reflect, however, a lack of actual soundness in the insurance sector itself. This section considers country experience with individual ICPs and reports the typical difficulties faced in achieving full observance.[31]

Overall, observance differs across core principles, with several weaknesses and strengths. The area in which insurance supervision is most deficient relates to corporate governance of insurance companies. Less than one-third of countries are observant or broadly observant with this core principle. This low level is mainly a result of unclear jurisdiction of the insurance supervisory bodies over corporate governance issues. In general, rules on corporate governance are to be found in corporate law. Also, in the field of internal controls, the supervisory authorities seem to have limited jurisdiction, and the system depends on general corporate laws and regulations.

The major areas of assessed weaknesses are organization of the supervisor and asset risk management. The organization of a supervisory agency needs to be improved in broadly one-third of the countries assessed. In a significant number of cases, the insurance regulator was incorporated into the Ministry of Finance, but insufficient resources (both in numbers and technical capacity) and unclear budgetary autonomy proved to be problematic in many cases. Although observance with respect to risk management is better, it is still weakly supervised with respect to asset portfolio in approximately one-third of countries, mostly concentrated in developing and emerging market countries. As in the banking sector, this weakness is an area of serious concern, mainly because adverse developments in asset values would in all likelihood directly affect the financial viability of the institutions. Deficiencies also occur in supervision of off-balance sheet exposures, notably in derivatives in more than half of the countries assessed. The issues arise mainly in developing and emerging market countries and primarily involve the absence of any regulations in this area.

Other areas of concern relate to market conduct. Rules in many cases were limited to rules on registration of brokers and agents and cross-border operations. The most important issue with respect to this principle relates to deficiencies in the exchange of information with other supervisors.

Creating all the relevant conditions for effective insurance supervision can be a challenge in less fully developed markets. Statistics that can assist companies in correctly pricing and establishing provisions for insurance products may not be widely studied or reported. Asset markets may suffer from a lack of liquidity or may provide insufficient instruments of a duration necessary to match insurance liabilities. Often, the actuarial profession is particularly limited. In many cases, supervisors are able to take action to alleviate such problems, at least in part. Greater difficulties arise if the jurisdiction faces more widespread challenges, particularly if corruption levels are high and extend to the legal system.

Generally, all supervisors have the obligation to protect the interests of policyholders, and this objective needs to be made more clear and transparent. Opportunities still remain, however, to bring transparency practices into line with best practice by elaborating on the objectives in more detail and with more clarity rather than simply relying on the publication of the law itself. Usually, this stronger transparency practice represents an opportunity for the supervisory authority to take a greater leadership role in their public statements and in commentary in annual reports. An issue that is of concern, although not universal, is that the supervisor in some cases has conflicting objectives, for example, policyholder protection and industry growth.

It is difficult for a supervisory office that remains part of a ministry and subject to generic public service rules to demonstrate full observance of the ICP on adequate supervisory authority. Lack of independence from the Ministry of Finance has been a major issue—mainly in developing countries, where more than half of the sample countries exhibit poor implementation.

Transparency of supervisory process is often inadequate. Many supervisors have internal processes that are well structured and understood within the agency. Nevertheless, the transparency of those processes is often inadequate.

Some supervisors have legal constraints that make supervisory cooperation and exchange of information and cooperation (ICP 5) difficult. Others may be able to cooperate in a legal sense, but the effective cooperation among supervisors inside and outside of the jurisdiction may be less than is desirable. In many cases, cooperation was warranted but did not, in fact, occur. Sometimes, in the extreme, cases have been identified in which the local supervisor made every effort to exchange and elicit information, but the counterpart did not respond. This type of case is difficult to assess, given the party that should have participated but did not was outside the jurisdiction. In cases such as these, it is suggested that the authorities' efforts be congratulated explicitly in the report. Every effort to translate the intent of the standards into practical results by the international associations is to be encouraged in this area.

Weaknesses are found in rules concerning fitness and propriety (ICP 7 on suitability of persons). Frequently, the scope of the persons covered by the rules is limited or legal support (for the otherwise effective moral suasion) to remove unsuitable persons is lacking. Less frequently, the law may not have provisions for testing fitness and propriety.

Usually, changes in control and portfolio transfers (ICP 8) are well covered in law, and transactions, when they arise, are given close attention by supervisors. The one weakness that may arise is the ability to look through the corporate structure beyond the immediate parent and, in particular, to examine transactions that take place outside the jurisdiction (e.g., when two international firms merge with a local operation that does not change direct ownership). The intent of the ICP is to protect policyholders from a change of control whether or not there is an intermediate holding company or other corporate structure, so this possible weakness can present an issue. Often, supervisors do not have the legal power to require local change of ownership of a licensed insurer to require shareholder divestment. That type of power would usually enable any concerns to be addressed by changes to proposed ownership arrangements, by conditions being placed on the approach to the management of the local insurer, or by other solutions. This issue

Box 5.4 Key Issues in Ongoing Supervision and Prudential Requirements for Insurance

Ongoing Supervision

Ongoing supervision of insurance (ICPs 11–17) shows different degrees of observance, with developing countries showing more pronounced weaknesses. The stress on macroprudential surveillance of the insurance sector is an important step in strengthening supervision.

- Market analysis (ICP 11) is a relatively new ICP, and experience from assessments remains to be analyzed. This ICP formally recognizes the importance of analyzing market conditions in the sector and macroprudential surveillance of the sector as key inputs into insurance supervision. For a discussion of financial soundness indicators for use in macroprudential surveillance and market analysis, see chapter 3.

- Reporting to supervisors and offsite monitoring (ICP 12) incorporates financial reporting, audit, and offsite analysis. Usual problems include a lack of audit requirements, accounting standards that are adequate for general purposes but short of supervisory needs, or an overly compliance-oriented supervisory approach to the assessment of returns.

- Some supervisors do not have the powers or the resources for onsite inspections (ICP 13).

- Although many supervisors have powers of intervention (ICP 14 on preventive and corrective measures), they may be subject to legislatively imposed trigger points that are too low, thus preventing early intervention with sound legal support earlier in the process.

- A full set of enforcement sanction powers (ICP 15), whether they have been applied in the past in every case or not, is important to the supervisor. Sometimes, they add only to the ability to use moral suasion effectively. The ICP is oriented in this way so the weaknesses tend to reflect certain limitations in the law where the supervisor is provided with powers limited to those that will be expected to be used in practice. Sometimes, the supervisor finds it useful to threaten to use powers even if he or she does not ever use them in fact. In those situations, the full armory is desirable.

- It is usual that the processes of winding-up and exit from the market (ICP 16) are set out in the law but, in some cases, the normal commercial rules apply, which would not provide the necessary policyholder protection. Policyholder protection schemes do not exist in every jurisdiction, and the assessor may wish to take this information into consideration when reviewing the market exit arrangements. In some cases,

the definition of the point of intervention is considered to be open to interpretation and, therefore, gives rise to legal dispute. In cases such as those, the supervisor may be rendered ineffective while his or her intervention is subject to lengthy challenge—an undesirable situation in the interests of policyholders.

- With respect to groupwide supervision (ICP 17), historically, insurance laws have been designed for "ring fencing" the supervised entity and limiting impositions on the rest of the group, whether they be subsidiaries or siblings or parents in the corporate structure.

Observance of Prudential Requirements

Observance relating to prudential requirements must be interpreted with care because the lack of risk sensitivity of the principles and standards renders it possible for almost every jurisdiction to score highly. General levels of observance are high on liability valuation and capital adequacy because the criteria cannot differentiate between stronger and weaker loss reserves (both within a jurisdiction and between jurisdictions) or determine the appropriateness of a capital buffer regime. Weaknesses are more pronounced on asset quality regulation.

- Risk assessment and management (ICP 18) and insurance activity (ICP 19) are new principles, and experience from assessments remains to be analyzed.

- Core principles on capital adequacy and solvency critically depend on realistic and consistent valuations for assets and liabilities. If liabilities are inadequate or if assets are overvalued, then the capital regime is undermined. Asset valuation standards vary greatly among jurisdictions, and liability valuation standards vary both within and among jurisdictions. Significant efforts are under way in a number of countries and regions to develop better standards. Nevertheless, quantitative benchmarks have yet to be developed or proposed by the IAIS, and until this change happens, the lack of differentiation between stronger and weaker prudential regimes will remain a feature of ICP assessments—and will necessitate a more detailed technical analysis.

- The core principle on derivatives and similar commitments (ICP 22) is either observed (having had supervisory attention) or not applicable (where the activity has been prohibited). Many developing and emerging markets commonly lack regulation over this activity.

can also be related to the lack of a full set of sanction powers to facilitate and support the supervisor in its activities.

Corporate governance (ICP 9) and internal control (ICP 10) tend to show strengths or weaknesses together. Where the powers exist, the topics of corporate governance and internal control may have been the subject of recent rules but may not have yet found their way into reliable evidence of effective practice in the institutions; instead, new rules are being formulated on these topics and their robustness remains untested. In addition, where onsite inspections are not carried out, it is difficult for the supervisor to verify the full observance of these requirements.

Ongoing supervision, prudential requirements, and AML–CFT procedures for insurance were generally well observed (according to 2000 standards), but weaknesses were evident in implementation despite strong laws being in place. Some of the core principles in this area (e.g., market analysis, risk management, insurance fraud, AML–CFT) are relatively new; implementation experience at the country level is new, and assessment experience remains to be analyzed. Nevertheless, available evidence suggests that nearly one-third of all sample countries (and the majority of developing countries) demonstrated weak regulation of asset quality, and 60 percent of developing countries insufficiently supervised reinsurance practices of insurance companies. Procedures for orderly winding-up of failed insurers (and securities firms) were missing in a significant number of countries sampled. Approximately, only one-third of the countries had adequate insolvency and bankruptcy regimes. Box 5.4 provides additional details on key weaknesses and issues in the ongoing supervision and prudential requirements for insurance.

Development issues related to the insurance sector will need specific attention in the course of ICP assessments. To this end, the assessor will need to consider the factors that affect the contribution of the insurance sector to overall economic development. The usual starting point is the development of the sector itself. The insurance sector, particularly the life insurance sector, can play a key role as a mobilizer and manager of savings and as a long-term institutional investor. The sector cannot do so, however, if the custody of policyholder funds is at risk or if the population does not have the capacity to invest in the sector's products. Over time, it can be expected that this situation will improve as the sector develops, but limitations may exist. In the long run, a sector that is growing, that acts as an effective investor, and that provides long-term capital will be good for the economy and good for the overall well-being of the population—not just for those who are policyholders—as the economy develops.

Systemic risk should also be considered. In the case of insurance, this kind of risk can arise from two main sources and should be—in a reasonably well-run system—limited. First, the sector itself may be weak. Solvency may be in question or the economic environment may be such that it could reasonably be at risk, which can be serious, particularly if resolution measures are inadequate or if supervisory intervention is restricted. The failure of an insurer leads to significant hardship for those immediately affected[32] and may lead to a loss of confidence in the sector as a whole that could take a considerable period to restore. The second source of risk rests in the linkages, if any, with the banking sector or with securities markets. For example, where an insurance company is owned by a bank, any potential weakness in the insurer may cause difficulty, or at least an imposition, on the capital of the bank. Insofar as the insurance sector is a significant protection seller in credit derivatives markets, weaknesses of insurers could have implications for financial stability. Moreover, when insurance companies are major holders of key instruments traded in the capital market, then market volatility may be significantly influenced by portfolio decisions of insurers.

5.5 Assessment of Securities Market Regulation

Securities markets are a critical component of many economies, and the regulation of securities markets can be fundamental to a country's financial development and integration into the global market. Consequently, securities market regulation is an important element of financial stability. This section looks at the objectives and principles of securities regulation (core principles), which were developed by the International Organization of Securities Commissions (IOSCO)[33] as the key global standard for securities regulation. The section briefly reviews the development of the core principles and examines the ways in which they reflect the broad responsibilities of securities regulators and the nature of IOSCO as a whole. The section then looks at the preconditions for effective securities regulation, which, though fundamental, can be both difficult to achieve and challenging to assess. The section next turns to the IOSCO methodology, which is the principal tool used to assess securities market regulation, and addresses key considerations in conducting an assessment. After reviewing assessment experience to date and discussing some of the key findings, the section concludes by addressing three key topics in securities market regulation and development: (a) demutualization, (b) creation of an integrated regulator or supervisor, and (c) enforcement and the exchange of information.

Securities markets are tremendously varied, both in terms of their legal framework and their level of development. The specific responsibilities of securities regulators are equally varied. Therefore, it is not practical to set forth a single legal or institutional framework suitable for securities market regulation or to identify typical country practice. Indeed, this limitation was a major challenge for the drafters of the IOSCO core principles. Therefore, instead of presenting a single, unified regulatory framework, the core principles identify three key objectives that "form a basis for an effective system of securities regulation" (IOSCO 2003b, 1). Those objectives, which are discussed in greater detail next, are (a) protecting investors; (b) ensuring that markets are fair, efficient, and transparent; and (c) reducing systemic risk. After identifying the three objectives, IOSCO sets forth 30 principles that are intended to give "practical effect" to the objectives. IOSCO then elaborates on the principles through extensive discussion, while noting that, as markets change, the strategies for implementing the principles also will necessarily change. The principles state that "there is often no single correct approach to a regulatory issue. Legislation and regulatory structures vary between jurisdictions and reflect local market conditions and historical development" (IOSCO 2003b, 3). As a result of those factors, assessing securities market regulation can be fraught with numerous challenges. This section seeks to shed light on some of those challenges.

5.5.1 IOSCO Core Principles—Relevance to Stability Considerations and Structural Development

The *Objectives and Principles of Securities Regulation* (the IOSCO core principles) of the International Organization of Securities Commissions is the key global standard for securities market regulation. The IOSCO bylaws state that the organization's members (a) will exchange information about their experiences so they can foster the development of domestic markets, (b) will work together to establish standards and improve market surveillance of international transactions, and (c) will provide mutual assistance to promote market integrity. IOSCO adopted the core principles in September 1998, and they have been identified by the Financial Stability Forum as one of the 12 key international standards. The IOSCO core principles provide evidence of "IOSCO's commitment to the establishment and maintenance of high regulatory standards for the securities industry" (IOSCO 2003b, 2). Over the years, IOSCO has produced many resolutions and numerous technical reports relating to different aspects of securities market regulation. However, before the development of the IOSCO core principles, the organization had never produced a framework statement covering the fundamental aspects of securities regulation.

The purpose of the core principles is to strengthen securities markets by enhancing the regulatory framework. As noted above, the core principles set out three objectives on which securities regulation is based: (a) promoting investor protection; (b) ensuring that markets are fair, efficient, and transparent; and (c) reducing systemic risk. Although each of the principles is presented as equally important, the document underscores the statement in the IOSCO bylaws that IOSCO members should be guided at all times by their concern for investor protection. Investors are to be protected from misleading, manipulative, and fraudulent practices. The most important means for doing so is full disclosure. Regulation should also promote fair and efficient markets with the highest levels of transparency, defined to include both pretrade and posttrade transparency. Finally, the core principles call for regulators to reduce systemic risk. Although regulators cannot prevent firms from failing, the regulations should contain the risks and mitigate the impact of any such failures. The core principles then set out 30 principles of securities regulation that are intended to give "practical effect" to the objectives. Each of the 30 principles is elaborated and explained in significant detail. Because the three objectives are overlapping, it is impossible to link each principle to a specific objective. However, certain principles promote one or two of the objectives in particular.

The IOSCO objectives and core principles (IOP) are stated at a general level—as is the case with other regulatory standards—and permit considerable flexibility in implementation. Each of the 30 principles is supplemented by narrative discussion, illustrating how the objective of the principle might be achieved while simultaneously recognizing that the nature of a particular market will necessarily dictate how the principle is implemented. "The particular manner in which a jurisdiction implements the objectives and principles described in this document must have regard to the entire domestic context, including the relevant legal and commercial framework" (IOSCO 2003b, 3). In addition, the IOSCO core principles were drafted with the recognition that markets change over time and that regulators must have the flexibility to adapt their supervision to changing market conditions. The document notes that there is not a single approach for implementing the principles and that multiple approaches, often depending on the broader legal and regulatory system, may be effective.

The IOSCO core principles also reflect the broad scope of responsibilities possessed by most securities regulators. Securities regulators are responsible for a much broader array of activities than banking supervisors. Like banking supervisors, securities regulators supervise the activities of market intermediaries. However, they also supervise securities markets, collective investment schemes, investment managers or advisers, and issuer disclosure. Some securities regulators also have responsibility for enforcing company law. The core principles thus cover a large range of issues. The 30 core principles, therefore, are grouped into eight subject areas as illustrated in Annex 5.D. Principles 1–5 relate to the regulator and to its powers, resources, independence, and accountability. Principles 6–7 relate to self-regulatory organizations and their supervision. Principles 8–10 relate to enforcement, and Principles 11–13 relate to cooperation, including international cooperation for enforcement and regulatory purposes. Principles 14–16 relate to issuers and the disclosure of information. Principles 17–20 relate to collective investment schemes and their operation. Principles 21–24 relate to the supervision of market intermediaries, and Principles 25–30 relate to how a jurisdiction's overall regulatory structure ensures the integrity of secondary markets, including through robust clearance and settlement function that is addressed in Principle 30.[34]

Because of securities regulators' broad responsibilities for the effective functioning of the markets, the links between (a) observance of the IOSCO core principles and (b) market development and stability are fundamental. As the core principles themselves note, securities markets are vital to the development and strength of national economies. They not only support "corporate initiatives, finance the exploitation of new ideas, and facilitate the management of financial risk" (IOSCO 2003b, 1) but also—with the growth of collective investment schemes—have become increasingly important to individual wealth and retirement planning. Sound domestic markets are important to domestic financial development; with globalization, they have become increasingly important to the strength and stability of the global economy. Indeed, much work has been done to show (a) that financial diversification and development outside of the banking system enhances efficiency, as well as encourages development and promotes stability and (b) that an alternative source of intermediation may help strengthen the banking sector, which, again, will enhance financial development and stability.[35] Improving the quality of regulation and enhancing the supervision and surveillance promotes investor confidence, better risk management, and more efficient and robust institutions and markets. These actions, in turn, will promote economic growth. In addition, the preconditions for a strong securities market, including a well-functioning legal system and observance of contract and property rights, are the institutional factors that promote both financial stability and financial development.

5.5.2 Preconditions for Effective Securities Market Regulation

Effective securities regulation depends on the existence of a number of "preconditions." The IOSCO core principles recognize that "securities law and regulation cannot exist in isolation from the other laws and the accounting requirements of a jurisdiction" (IOSCO

2003b, 8). In particular, the principles note that "there must be an appropriate and effective legal, tax and accounting framework within which the securities markets can operate" (IOSCO 2003b, 8). The preconditions are not formally part of the core principles because they are outside the jurisdictional authority of most securities regulators. IOSCO identifies in an annex to the core principles certain elements of the legal framework that are particularly important for effective securities regulation. These elements include (a) company law; (b) a commercial code or established contract law, including recognition and enforcement of property rights; (c) clear and consistent tax laws, especially with respect to the treatment of investments and investment products; (d) bankruptcy and insolvency laws; (e) competition law; (f) banking law; and (g) a fair and efficient judicial system or other dispute resolution system in which orders can be enforced and illegal behavior sanctioned (IOSCO 2003b, annex III).

Weaknesses in the preconditions can have a significant deleterious impact on the effectiveness of securities regulation and on market development. Investor protection must be grounded in a legal framework for investors to have confidence in the markets. For example, without an effective bankruptcy law, investors will be reluctant to risk investing in a company that may fail because they will be without any legal recourse. Similarly, investors would be reluctant to leave assets in accounts with a securities firm or an asset management company if bankruptcy and property law did not support a clear separation of client assets from the general assets of a firm. Without uniform accounting standards, companies will not be able to present a consistent and meaningful financial picture to investors. The absence of a fair and impartial judicial system that can mediate disputes or enforce sanctions will weaken the credibility and effectiveness of securities regulation.

As part of the IOSCO assessment, it is important to gain an understanding of the relevant preconditions in a particular country, which will require access to information from a wide variety of other sources, including assessments of other financial sector components. Information will be needed from country authorities other than the securities regulator and from market participants. Assessments of the legal system and accounting standards would provide information on shortcomings, if any, that might affect securities regulator's activities. In addition, when considering actions to enhance securities regulation, country authorities will need to determine whether the preconditions themselves should be addressed first to ensure that the proposed action will achieve its objective.

5.5.3 Assessment Methodology and Assessment Experience

The core principles were initially adopted as a stand-alone document, without an accompanying methodology for implementation. When IOSCO adopted the core principles, they were intended as an incentive document, expressing the commitment of IOSCO members "insofar as it is within their authority to use their best endeavors within their jurisdiction to ensure adherence to those principles" (IOSCO 2003b, 3). At the same time, IOSCO also recognized that the core principles could serve as a benchmark or, as IOSCO put it, a "yardstick against which progress towards effective regulation can be measured" (IOSCO 2003b, 2). Therefore, IOSCO began the development of detailed questionnaires to help securities regulators assess the extent to which they were implementing the core principles. The questionnaires included a "high-level" questionnaire and five additional questionnaires that focused on specific areas of securities regulation.

The *Methodology for Assessing Implementation of the IOSCO Objectives and Principles of Securities Regulation* (IOSCO 2003a; hereinafter, the Methodology) has been developed as a tool to provide guidance on assessing the level of implementation of the IOSCO core principles. The core principles were themselves helpful as a starting point for assessing securities market regulation; however, they were drafted at a broad conceptual level to accommodate differences in the laws, regulatory framework, and market structures among IOSCO members. They, therefore, provided little or no guidance to assessors as to how to assess whether they were implemented in practice. Although the self-assessment questionnaires could be used by third-party assessors, they were a cumbersome tool, particularly for those assessors who were less familiar with the market and the regulatory system that they were assessing. As an alternative, the World Bank and the International Monetary Fund developed a guidance note for use by assessors as they worked with the IOSCO core principles. Although helpful, this note was quite general, and IOSCO members believed that more detailed and comprehensive guidance could be of greater assistance. In response, IOSCO set up a task force that was specifically mandated to develop a methodology that could be used by both self-assessors and third-party assessors such as the Bank and the Fund. The task force consisted of IOSCO member regulators from both developed and emerging markets. Staff members from the Bank and the Fund also participated. The Methodology built on the self-assessment questionnaires and the guidance note that were already in existence.

IOSCO developed the Methodology for its own use and for use by third-party assessors. IOSCO intended all along for the Methodology to be used as a tool for conducting self-assessments. At the same time, IOSCO recognized that the Methodology would be used by third-party assessors, some of whom might not be securities regulators. Thus, IOSCO members tried to achieve multiple objectives in drafting the Methodology. To reflect the complexity of regulating a wide variety of types of markets in different stages of development, IOSCO sought to ensure that the Methodology was sufficiently multifaceted. IOSCO also wanted to be sure, however, that the Methodology—and assessments based on the Methodology—would reflect the high standards of regulation that the core principles embodied and would not be watered down or diluted for different markets. IOSCO also sought to ensure a degree of consistency in assessments across different markets. Consequently, the Methodology is a long and complex document, with numerous "key issues" and "key questions" for assessors to draw on and a rather strict benchmarking system. The benchmarking system is intended to add consistency and objectivity to an inherently subjective assessment process while allowing for some flexibility.

The organization of the Methodology follows the format of the core principles. The Methodology groups each of the principles into the eight subject areas used in the presentation of IOSCO core principles. Each grouping of the principles is introduced with an introductory note. It then introduces each individual principle and sets forth that principle's "key issues" and associated "key questions." These descriptions are followed by an elaborate benchmarking system through which IOSCO essentially indicates the relative importance of different aspects of the principles. The benchmarking system recognizes five levels of observance of each principle: "fully implemented," "broadly implemented," "partly implemented," "not implemented," and "not applicable." An explanatory note may accompany these levels. (Annex 5.E illustrates the structure and use of the Methodology for one of the core principles.)

The work of the IOSCO task force reflected the experience being gained in the context of Bank-Fund assessments and country self-assessments. For example, in the Methodology's benchmarking system, IOSCO initially had not included a "broadly implemented" category. However, IOSCO concluded that the benchmarks should be expanded to reflect those situations in which the regulatory system or regulator had implemented nearly all aspects of a particular principle, though not every detail. To reflect this situation, IOSCO incorporated the new category "broadly implemented" into the benchmarking system. Similarly, as a result of feedback from assessors that the application of benchmarks was too rigid, explicit language was included in the instructions to the Methodology to make clear that the benchmarks were intended to be applied in a flexible manner that would take account of the specific regulatory context.

The Methodology represents a compendium of all of IOSCO's work and provides a comprehensive framework for analyzing implementation of the principles. It references in one place many of IOSCO's technical reports, resolutions, statements of good practice, and other relevant materials on securities regulation. It thus is a tremendous resource, giving an assessor the tools to access more in-depth material on a given topic. In addition, the Methodology serves an effective diagnostic and action-planning function. The Methodology is especially strong in establishing the market and regulatory context for the various principles. By organizing the core principles into key issues and key questions and by providing detailed criteria for each topic, the Methodology not only provides a vehicle for analyzing a securities regulatory regime across the entire range of securities regulation but also provides a measure of consistency across markets.

5.5.4 Key Considerations in Conducting an Assessment

An assessment generally begins with an overview of the structure and state of development of securities markets and key institutions in a particular country. Although an in-depth assessment of this information is generally beyond the scope of the assessment of IOSCO core principles, the assessor must understand the effect of the information gathered on the effectiveness of securities regulation in the country being assessed.[36] The nature of the market being assessed and its legal framework must be comprehended fully for the assessment to be well-founded. For example, "markets with a single or a few issuers, that are totally domestic in nature, or that are predominantly institutional, will pose different questions and issues as to the sufficiency of application of the Principles, and as to the potential vulnerabilities likely to arise from their non-application" than markets that feature different characteristics (IOSCO 2003a, 6). In addition, any weaknesses or shortcoming in the preconditions and the effect they have on securities regulation must be considered. Assessors obtain much of this information through the use of a securities markets questionnaire, which seeks data on the structure and performance of securities markets and on the legal and regulatory framework for supervision in the country being assessed (for an example of the sort of quantitative information analyzed, see appendix B, table B.9).

5

An assessment of securities regulation requires the assessor to be familiar with all the relevant laws and regulations, as well as with other key documents and practices. As noted earlier in the discussion of preconditions, effective securities regulation not only is based on the securities law but also is integrally connected to company law. In addition, accounting and audit standards, investment fund law, bankruptcy law, and other parts of the legal framework are critical. In many countries, codes of conduct and other policy documents that may or may not have the force of law may also be important. Consequently, an assessor must be familiar with a wide range of relevant laws and regulations, as well as with other types of government and nongovernment guidance.

A critical foundation of a third-party assessment is a self-assessment completed by the regulator. The availability of a thorough and candid self-assessment is critical to enable a third-party assessor to complete a fair and accurate assessment. A well-prepared self-assessment that includes the summaries of the relevant legal and regulatory texts and a thorough description of the institutional framework and supervisory practices is essential. As noted earlier, before the development of the Methodology, IOSCO members completed a series of self-assessment questionnaires, including a so-called "high-level" assessment and additional assessments covering specific aspects of securities regulation. Those questionnaires are highly informative and, though cumbersome to use, have been helpful to the third-party assessors, especially since IOSCO developed a concordance key to cross-reference specific items in the questionnaires to the Methodology. However, with the adoption of the Methodology, IOSCO members may undertake updated self-assessments directly pursuant to the Methodology. A number of IOSCO members have already started to do so, and some are undergoing "assisted self-assessments" in which they obtain the assistance of other IOSCO members to help them complete the self-assessment. A comprehensive and candid self-assessment prepared pursuant to the new Methodology would serve as a good foundation for developing a complete profile of the market and for assessing how it is regulated, as well as for identifying strengths and weaknesses for further consideration.

Third-party assessors must conduct in-depth discussions with the securities regulator, other relevant authorities, and market participants on the relative strengths and weaknesses of the securities regulator. Assessors should meet with authorities, securities firms, exchanges, SROs, industry groups, depositories, and other agencies and must share the draft assessment with the regulator and discuss comments.

An IOSCO self-assessment and an FSAP assessment follow similar formats. Both types of assessments begin with a discussion of the institutional and market structure of securities regulation in the country being assessed. The information and the methodology used for the assessment are then set forth, followed by a discussion of the sufficiency of the preconditions for effective securities regulation. The heart of the assessment is the principle-by-principle assessment, which contains a detailed discussion of each principle, noting relevant factual information, actual practices that are followed, and effectiveness of oversight. Comments by the assessor are important to document how the assessor arrived at his or her conclusions. Thus, this information should be described in reasonable detail, with reference to the supporting authority as necessary. The assessment concludes with recommended actions and the securities regulator's response.

An assessment must take into account what is actually taking place in practice. The IOSCO methodology explicitly recognizes that there is a significant difference in terms of effective securities regulation between laws and rules that may look good on paper and those that are enforced in practice. The Methodology specifically states that it envisions that assessors will conduct their assessments from two perspectives: first, whether the laws and rules are sufficient and the programs or procedures intended to implement those laws and rules are effective and, second, whether the laws, rules, and programs and procedures are actually implemented in practice. It can be challenging for assessors to gain a realistic understanding of how securities regulation operates in practice, requiring candid discussions with regulators, market practitioners, investor representatives, and others.

5.5.5 Assessment Experience

As of the end of April 2004, 54 IOSCO assessments had been completed in the FSAP process. This number is approximately one-half of the 105 assessments that had been completed or were under way or planned. Not all FSAP assessments include an IOSCO assessment. In April 2002, Bank and Fund staff members issued a report reviewing the experience with the assessment of the IOSCO core principles (see IMF and World Bank 2002a).

Assessors have had some difficulty in applying the Methodology's benchmarks in practice. As the Methodology was being completed, the Bank and the Fund conducted a testing program in which they undertook eight IOSCO assessments pursuant to the Methodology. The eight assessments took place across all geographic regions and in both industrialized and emerging market economies. The assessors comprised World Bank staff members, IMF consultants, and experts nominated by IOSCO. Uniformly, the assessors found that the benchmarking system set forth in the Methodology made it difficult to apply the Methodology with the flexibility they believed IOSCO had intended. Members of IOSCO who had conducted self-assessments pursuant to the Methodology had a similar reaction.

As a result, IOSCO has drafted new instructions on the use of the Methodology to clarify that the Methodology contemplates "the exercise of disciplined flexibility" in the benchmarking process. Assessors are expected to use their discretion in arriving at a rating but must document their conclusions, particularly to the extent they may depart from the benchmarking parameters. Thus, for example, in assessing under Principle 2 whether a securities regulator operates independently from the Ministry of Finance, an assessor must consider whether the regulator must consult with the government ministry on particular matters of regulatory policy. If the circumstances of such consultation include any decision making on day-to-day matters, then under the benchmarking as strictly applied, the regulator would receive a "not implemented" on this principle. However, the assessor may conclude that the matters on which the regulator must consult do not impair the independence of the regulator. In that case, the assessor may give the regulator a higher rating, as long as the reasons for this assessment are well documented. By maintaining the benchmarks but permitting them to be applied with discretion, IOSCO is hoping that the benchmarks will be able simultaneously to bring objectivity to, and a measure of consistency across, assessments while allowing for the flexibility necessary to ensure that the resulting assessment is appropriate for the regulatory system assessed.

Several key conclusions on securities market regulatory practices have emerged from the assessments so far.[37] Weaknesses in the implementation of many of the principles were evident across the range of jurisdictions assessed, although the most marked concerns related to assessments of developing and emerging markets. The assessment experience also highlighted the difficulties in drawing clear connections between the weaknesses identified in the regulation of securities market and financial sector vulnerabilities.

An analysis of completed IOSCO assessments indicates that there are specific areas of weakness in the implementation of the IOSCO principles. Weaknesses in implementation are particularly evident with respect to principles for enforcement of securities regulation (Principles 8–10) and principles for issuers (Principles 14–16). Overall, assessors found that regulators had a lack of authority to investigate; had limited access to time-sensitive data needed for surveillance purposes; had insufficient resources for inspection, surveillance, and investigation; and often had a limited enforcement mandate. With respect to issuers, there is a clear need for more efficient methods to disseminate information to the public and to improve the quality of the information being released. In addition, there is a need to improve the legislative and policy framework relating to the treatment of shareholders, a need to enhance the regulatory regime for auditors, and a need to address the lack of harmonization between international and domestic accounting and auditing standards. Improvements in those preconditions would help improve securities regulation.

In turn, the principles that have relatively higher levels of full and broad implementation are the following: (a) Principles 18–19 (regulation of collective investment schemes, (b) Principles 21 and 25 (regulation of market intermediaries and the secondary market), and (c) Principles 1 and 4–5 (activities of the regulator). Some common deficiencies noted by the assessors in terms of the issues relating to the regulator include the following: a lack of operational independence; limited enforcement powers; and inadequate resources, which thus hamper the ability to perform regulatory functions efficiently and effectively. The lack of operational independence raises particular questions as to control of resources (both human and financial). The lack of a clear mandate—or the lack of clear regulatory powers—also inhibits regulatory functions such as licensing, access to necessary (sometimes confidential) data, and so forth. Other common deficiencies include the need for appropriate regulations dealing with collective investment schemes, the need to expand the scope of the regulator's responsibilities, the need to improve licensing requirements for trading systems, and the need to increase the scope of trading arrangements.

Although assessors are not able to readily consider preconditions, the comments in specific assessments do, nevertheless, allude to the poor state of legal and accounting systems in many jurisdictions. For example, many assessments note the inadequacy of the accounting framework—both in terms of standards and professional arrangements—as being linked to weaknesses in the implementation of the principles for issuers. Likewise, audit issues are commonplace, and aspects of the oversight of auditors feature prominently in many assessments. The insolvency regime is, not surprisingly, often cited as requiring attention in those jurisdictions that exhibit lower levels of implementation of the principles related to market intermediaries. An efficient court system, a highly skilled legal profession, and a set of well-designed administrative review processes would no doubt support strengthening the enforcement of laws in the countries that have been assessed as not having fully implemented the principles relating to enforcement and cooperation (Principles 8–10 and 11–13). (See section 5.5.6 and Annex 5.F for a further discussion of enforcement issues.)

5.5.6 Special Topics in Securities Market Development and Regulation

Three key topics in securities market regulation and development are discussed in this section: (a) demutualization of stock exchanges, (b) creation of integrated regulator or supervisor, and (c) enforcement and exchange of information.

5.5.6.1 Demutualization

The past decade has witnessed tremendous changes in the structure of securities markets as lawmakers, regulators, and market participants try to contend with the effects of globalization and the development of advanced technology. New forms of markets have been created, and traditional markets have struggled to stay competitive. Regulators have been forced to face difficult questions of what constitutes the essential elements of a market and how they should be regulated going forward. The viability of self-regulation, which, in fact, in many countries predated stand-alone securities regulators, has also come into question.

One increasingly common consequence of those developments is a worldwide trend toward the demutualization of stock exchanges. Many stock exchanges began as mutual— or member—organizations where, in exchange for the privilege of membership, an individual or a securities firm was (a) given certain benefits, including the right to trade on the exchange and to make a market in certain securities, and (b) certain responsibilities, including the obligation to act in accordance with the membership rules for the benefit of the exchange at large. This system worked effectively for many years, and, indeed, many would argue that it still does. However, others believe that this membership structure served to constrain the exchanges from competing effectively with their rivals, including fast and efficient electronic systems that could execute trades rapidly at little cost. To marshal greater resources that would enable them to compete more aggressively, a significant number of exchanges decided to transform themselves into for-profit stock companies in which shares would be offered to the public and even, in some cases, listed on the exchange itself. In a number of cases, government authorities initiated the demutualization of domestic exchanges, believing that this action would improve the competitiveness and efficiency of their markets. According to the World Federation of Exchanges, a total of 42 exchanges had demutualized as of March 2003. This figure includes exchanges in both developed and emerging markets, including, for example, the London Stock Exchange, Australian Stock Exchange, Deutsche Borse, Athens Stock Exchange, Philippines Stock Exchange, and Kuala Lumpur Stock Exchange, among others.

The transformation of stock exchanges into for-profit share companies raises significant issues for securities regulators. Although many of the issues exist in the case of traditional stock exchanges, demutualization served to highlight the potential conflicts of interest.[38] In particular, exchanges that have demutualized may have a heightened con-

5

flict of interest between their business and regulatory functions, including in the administration of their own operating rules. For example, when operated by a management team whose main goal is to create a profit, an exchange may have less interest in devoting resources to its regulatory functions. Furthermore, as a for-profit enterprise, an exchange may come into conflict in regulating its own competitors. Regulators have handled those potential conflicts in a variety of ways. Some regulators have removed regulation from the exchange function entirely, giving it to an independent self-regulatory organization or even assuming all or part of the functions themselves. In other cases, improving internal controls at the exchange—coupled with enhanced regulatory oversight or strengthened corporate governance—has been considered sufficient.

From an assessor's perspective, the key issue is to be aware of the market structure that exists in the country being assessed, to recognize the regulatory implications of that structure, and to have a comprehensive understanding of the way in which the regulatory authorities have addressed those implications. When assessing a market with a demutualized exchange, the assessor should consider how the regulatory responsibilities of the exchange are being handled, what procedures the exchange or other parts of the regulatory system have in place to address potential conflicts of interest, and whether the regulator has an effective program of oversight.

5.5.6.2 Creation of an Integrated Regulator or Supervisor—Security Regulator's Perspective

During the past decade, a number of securities regulators in both developed and emerging markets have been merged into or reorganized as an integrated regulator or supervisor.[39] That is, the securities regulator has become part of an organization with the broader mandate of regulating or supervising not only securities firms and markets but also other segments of the financial sector. Thus, securities regulators may now be merged with authorities responsible for banking supervision, insurance supervision, or both or may, in fact, have even broader authority over pensions or other forms of financial activity. The effect of this development on the effectiveness of securities regulation remains unclear. In particular, it is not yet clear whether an integrated supervisor promotes effective implementation of the IOSCO core principles. Some of the fundamental objectives of securities regulation—particularly market conduct and market integrity—are not identical to, and indeed may be inconsistent with, the objectives of other forms of regulatory supervision. This situation may cause a conflict within the integrated supervisor. This possible conflict raises questions relating to whether sectoral integration of supervisory functions should be based on specific objectives of supervision and whether appropriate internal organization of an integrated supervisor could facilitate efficient resolution of conflicts, if any. See appendix F for further details.

From an assessor's perspective, a number of factors are important to consider. What were the reasons that motivated the country authorities to establish a single regulator? Are they being achieved? Is the supervisor effectively monitoring risk transfers among different financial firms in different sectors? Has the supervisor retained personnel and experienced staff members from the securities regulator? Is the investor protection objective of securities regulation being achieved? For example, how would the integrated supervisor handle a situation in which a financial intermediary in that country were to develop a significant problem? How would the supervisor protect investors in such a case?

5.5.6.3 *Enforcement and the Exchange of Information*

Enforcement plays a central part in the operation of well-run capital markets. It is essential for a securities regulator to be diligent in administering the laws and rules and to take effective enforcement action against those who contravene them. Only by taking strong and immediate action can the regulator send a message to the market that wrongdoing will not be tolerated. In many countries that have been assessed, enforcement is very weak, in part because of an inadequacy in resources and insufficient authority.

Enforcement is one area where securities regulation differs markedly from banking supervision. As with bank supervisors, securities regulators are responsible for overseeing market intermediaries and their relationship with their clients. However, securities regulators also are responsible for overseeing the markets more broadly, including the regulation of collective investment schemes and their advisers or operators, as well as the supervision of issuers and listings. Thus, to achieve their investor protection objective, securities regulators must cast a broad enforcement net as they seek to detect and deter fraud, including accounting and financial fraud, in both organized and unorganized markets, between intermediaries and their clients, and in public statements by issuers. In addition, the scope of cooperation and exchange of information among securities regulators for law enforcement purposes is often quite wide ranging, going well beyond the safety and soundness information. Those and other considerations pose challenges in the assessment process. Some of the issues in assessing enforcement are highlighted in Annex 5.F.

Annex 5.A   Legal and Institutional Environment for Effective Bank Insolvency Procedures

Autonomy of Banking Authority

The basic framework for bank insolvency needs to (a) be set out in the law that states the goals to be pursued by the banking authorities when dealing with insolvent banks and (b) empower the authorities to implement the bank insolvency framework. Moreover, the law should grant operational autonomy to official decision makers who are responsible for enforcing prudential rules; initiating and supervising insolvency proceedings; and acting as official administrators, liquidators, or all of the preceding.

To ensure the autonomy of banking authorities, the law should include provisions that do the following:

- Grant security of tenure to high-level officials of the banking authorities. In particular, the law should stipulate who can dismiss the heads or high-level officials of banking authorities and under what conditions. Dismissal should occur only for cause, and the grounds should be limited to, for instance, (a) inability, (b) illness or other forms of incapacitation preventing one from performing one's duties over a significant period of time, (c) willful misconduct, (d) gross negligence, or (e) noncompliance with explicit fitness criteria.

- Grant banking authorities the appropriate degree of budgetary autonomy and flexibility in using its financial resources within the framework of the law, subject always to appropriate accounting and auditing.
- Allow banking authorities to act without interference in their day-to-day operations and decisionmaking, and insulate them from potential pressure from the political establishment and market participants.

Legal Mandate

The legal mandates and functions of each of the official agencies and authorities involved in the resolution of insolvent banks such as (a) the central bank, (b) the supervisory agency, (c) the deposit insurance agency, and (d) the Ministry of Finance should be clearly delineated in a manner that avoids gaps or overlaps. While the legal framework should provide for the exchange of information and coordination, it also should require each agency to exercise its powers independently. A mechanism for the resolution of potential disputes in an open and transparent manner should be provided for in the law.

Appropriate Legal Protection of Banking Authorities and Their Staff Members

Laws should grant legal protection for bank authorities and their staff members to fulfill their responsibilities. Legal protection should be coupled in a balanced manner with the legal accountability necessary to prevent any abuse of power so as not to discourage authorities and officials from taking prompt and decisive action.

Of particular importance is personal protection from civil and criminal liability of senior staff members and other officers or agents of the banking authorities who are involved in the declaration of a bank's insolvency and in the administration of its restructuring, liquidation (including individuals who are appointed as official administrators or liquidators), or both—other than for intentional wrongdoing (e.g., abuse of power, theft, conversion of assets, conspiracy, etc.). This type of protection can be extended (a) by granting express statutory immunity from liability for actions and omissions that the persons concerned have taken in discharge of their legal responsibilities, (b) by making their agency vicariously liable for their faults, (c) by including appropriate indemnification provisions in their contracts of employment, or, perhaps, (d) by a combination of the three mechanisms, depending on the specific legal position of the officials concerned.

Transparency

For a banking authority, the combination of a precise mandate with a high degree of transparency in its implementation is crucial because it reduces simultaneously the opportunities for (a) the pursuit of personal interests on the part of supervisors, (b) the exercise of undue influence over the decision-making process by market participants (so-called "regulatory capture"), and (c) political interference. The legal framework should require agencies dealing with insolvent banks to operate with the maximum degree of transparency compatible with the need to preserve confidentiality.[40]

The transparency of the supervisory function is often difficult to achieve in practice because decisions are typically highly invisible for cogent reasons of confidentiality. This lack of transparency makes supervisory decisions an easy target for interference by politicians and market participants requesting forbearance. The scope for interference can be limited if the decision making relating to supervisory enforcement (including revocation of a license), and the commencement of insolvency proceedings is based on precise rules and on well-specified criteria. In principle, considerations of confidentiality are less likely to justify nontransparency of the official decision makers' evaluations and actions after the commencement of insolvency proceedings.[41] Even where reasons of confidentiality preclude open decision making or the disclosure by an agency of detailed information to the public at large, the provision of more comprehensive information to the politically responsible executive branch of government will still be appropriate.

Accountability and Judicial Review

Banking authorities are subject to various forms of accountability. First, they will need to explain the way in which they conduct their affairs and perform their mandate to the government, the legislature, and the public (and those authorities are thus subject to some measure of hierarchical, political, and public accountability). Second, in certain cases, they are legally accountable in civil and criminal law proceedings, with appropriate legal protection as noted earlier. In addition, they will occasionally need to substantiate before the courts of law the legality of their decisions.

The possibility of judicial scrutiny helps to ensure that administrative decisions are made consistently and on proper grounds. To guarantee the legality of official actions and the protection of the legitimate interests of private parties, affected parties should be able to challenge the decisions made by the banking authorities in administrative law by bringing judicial review proceedings before the administrative courts or by appealing to a special tribunal.[42] Where the external review of decisions takes the form of a special appeals mechanism, it should be entrusted to an independent and impartial tribunal established by law and comprising persons with requisite experience and skills.

At the same time, the mechanisms of legal accountability should not undermine the effectiveness and credibility of the banking authorities' actions. In particular, the banking authorities' margin of discretion should be respected, and a court or appeals tribunal (or both) should not be able to substitute its own policy decisions for those of the relevant authority. Accordingly, the review mechanism should seek only to ensure that the banking authorities act legally and within the limits of their powers and should not allow a reassessment of their actions on substantive grounds. Any reconsideration of decisions on the merits should be confined within the agency and incorporated into its internal operating procedures.

Coordination among Banking Authorities

If one is to deal with an insolvent bank effectively, the following are essential: timely cooperation and coordination between the various banking authorities and other public bodies concerned (e.g., the central bank; the operators of payment and settlement systems; the deposit insurance agency; and, where required, the supervisors of other sectors and jurisdictions, including the securities and insurance sectors).[43] Whenever the

5

restructuring stage is reached (see chapter 5, section 5.3.5), coordination with the officials responsible for the restructuring will be crucial.

At the domestic level, there should be a sound legal basis for the exchange of information and coordination among all the public bodies involved. The law should not impede the sharing of information; in particular, the duties of secrecy owed by official decision makers should not prevent interagency disclosures. Furthermore, means should be clarified for coordination among agencies, particularly with respect to banks that belong to financial conglomerates. In this context, there should be clear principles for determining which supervisory authority bears primary responsibility, and the obligation of each authority to keep other bodies informed should be recognized.

Where an insolvent bank operates in several jurisdictions, the banking authorities should be able to exchange information and to coordinate actions with their foreign counterparts. The operational terms of cooperation should be laid down in bilateral arrangements between the respective national authorities, for example, in the form of memoranda of understanding or through an exchange of letters. A duty of confidentiality should apply to all information shared between the authorities, in accordance with the national legislation of the countries concerned. The flow of information between host and home supervisors should be in both directions.

Annex 5.B Consolidated Supervision

Given the complexities in conducting effective consolidated supervision, it is critical that the supervisory authorities have the necessary tools to carry out their responsibilities. Some of the preconditions and prerequisites for effective banking supervision, which were discussed earlier (particularly, an appropriate legal framework and operational independence of the supervisory agency or agencies), are especially important in the conduct of effective consolidated supervision.

- The legal framework must grant the supervisor the necessary powers to conduct consolidated supervision over the entire span of institutions under its jurisdiction. Supervisors should have (a) sufficient flexibility in licensing and authorization, (b) the power to request information sufficient to effectively assess the banking group's risk profile and the adequacy of its risk management, and (c) sufficient enforcement powers to address technical compliance not only with laws and regulations but also with safety and soundness concerns that may arise within the banking group. In addition, they must have the ability to sanction intragroup transactions that, while strictly legal from a groupwide perspective, have undesirable consequences for the regulated group entities.

- Additional important considerations are the agency's (or agencies') operational independence and adequacy of resources. Issues to be reconciled include reporting requirements and accountability for the agency, as well as its funding and staffing. A supervisory agency that must report to another ministry may suffer political interference, especially when controversial decisions need to be made. Likewise, an agency that is underfunded or that cannot retain qualified staff members will not be able to maintain an effective supervisory program.

- Consolidated supervision allows financial sector supervisors to better understand the relationship among the different legal entities so they can assess the potential for adverse developments in one part of the group that may affect the operation of others. This assessment is done by monitoring and evaluating the additional risks posed to regulated financial institutions by affiliated institutions. It is important to stress, however, that consolidated supervision is a complement to, not a substitute for, single entity supervision. The supervisor responsible for consolidated supervision will, inter alia, have to be cognizant of the effect of the policies of the various supervisors of entities within the group.

Consolidation of accounts is a necessary prerequisite for obtaining meaningful financial information on groups of corporations and for supervising banks on a consolidated basis. Taking into account the groupwide financial exposures and intragroup financial relationships allows a better assessment of the implication of group membership for the financial condition of individual group members.

The consolidation of financial accounts, however, is not sufficient to capture many of the risks facing the bank through group membership. For example, consolidated financial accounts do not provide qualitative information about the group, such as the quality of management or internal controls. Similarly, some group entities, for technical reasons, may not be subject to consolidation in the financial accounts. A robust consolidated supervision program must thus incorporate both qualitative and quantitative analyses of the group's risk profile.

In many other jurisdictions, the concepts of consolidation and supervision on a consolidated basis are still not firmly established. The legal framework is still insufficiently developed; the concept of "group" and the question of how to deal with not only limited liability but also communalities of interest between corporations belonging to a group still need to be clarified. Also, the distinction between consolidation of accounts and supervision on a consolidated basis need to be kept clearly in mind. Those two concepts are clearly connected, but each poses different legal questions.

Effective consolidated supervision requires close cooperation among domestic sectoral supervisors. Similarly, the administrative and management arrangements within the various responsible authorities need to ensure the good coordination and the smooth exchange of information among home or host regulators abroad. Those exchanges will often be conducted within the auspices of a memorandum of understanding (MOU). However, the existence of an MOU will not in itself ensure that relevant information is provided. Much will depend on a relationship of trust being developed between the different regulators so information is exchanged proactively and in a timely manner.

The importance of assessing wider risks from other group members to the regulated entity is stressed in the core principles for banks, securities firms, and insurance companies, although there are differences in emphasis in the respective approaches. Gaps could expose a major bank or other financial institution within the group entity—and, hence, expose the system at large—to unacceptable risks from unregulated group entities. Similarly, overlaps could mean a diversion of scarce regulatory resources, either imposing unnecessary burdens on both regulated firms and taxpayers or, even more seriously, leading to an underfunding of regulatory effort in other areas of potentially high systemic risk.

Annex 5.C   IAIS Insurance Core Principles

The IAIS Insurance Core Principles comprise 28 principles that need to be in place for a regulatory and supervisory system to be effective (IAIS 2003a). The principles relate to the following:

- Conditions for effective insurance supervision help set out the elements of the environment where supervision can be most effective.

  - ICP 1 Conditions for effective insurance supervision include broad requirements in financial policy and financial market infrastructure to support effective supervision.

- The supervisory system deals with the mandates and responsibilities of the supervisor.

  - ICP 2 Supervisory objectives seek clarity in law.
  - ICP 3 Supervisory authority seeks adequate powers, resources, and legal protection.
  - ICP 4 Supervisory process seeks transparency and accountability.
  - ICP 5 Supervisory cooperation and information sharing cover cooperation within the insurance sector and across the financial services sector, as well as nationally and internationally.

- The supervised entity deals with the form and governance of insurers.

  - ICP 6 Licensing calls for requirements for licensing to be clear, objective, and public.
  - ICP 7 Suitability of persons requires ongoing assessment of fitness and propriety of significant owners and key functionaries.
  - ICP 8 Changes in control and portfolio transfers require supervisory approval of changes in significant ownership and control, in mergers, and in portfolio transfer.
  - ICP 9 Corporate governance requires prudent management of an insurer's business on the basis of standards that stress the role of board and senior management.
  - ICP 10 Internal control states the requirements for internal control systems, including internal audit and reporting, as well as compliance functions.

- Ongoing supervision outlines the actual practice of the supervisor.

  - ICP 11 Market analysis requires macro–prudential surveillance of the sector.
  - ICP 12 Reporting to supervisors and conducting off-site monitoring require comprehensive reporting that is done on a solo and a group basis, plus maintenance of an ongoing monitoring framework.
  - ICP 13 Onsite inspection requires comprehensive inspection powers for both the insurer and outsourced companies, plus clarified scope of inspections.
  - ICP 14 Preventive and corrective measures require an adequate, timely, and graduated spectrum of remedial measures.

- ICP 15 Enforcement or sanctions will require measures that are based on clear objective criteria.
- ICP 16 Winding-up and exit from the market will require criteria and procedures for insolvency and calls for priority with respect to policyholders.
- ICP 17 Groupwide supervision calls for consolidated—groupwide—supervision of the insurance group or conglomerate.

- Prudential requirements address the key financial and risk-management processes that should be imposed on and in place within insurance companies.

  - ICP 18 Risk assessment and management state the requirements for risk-management systems and their review by supervision.
  - ICP 19 Insurance activity requires strategic underwriting and pricing policies, as well as limits on risk retained through reinsurance.
  - ICP 20 Liabilities specify supervisory requirements to assess adequacy of technical provisions held against the policy liabilities.
  - ICP 21 Investments require compliance with standards on investment policy, asset mix, valuation, risk management, and asset–liability management.
  - ICP 22 Derivatives and similar commitments cover restrictions on their use and on requirements for disclosures.
  - ICP 23 (capital adequacy and solvency) covers sufficiency of technical provisions to cover expected claims and expenses as well as sufficiency of capital to cover significant unexpected losses.

- Markets and consumers deal with distribution, customer protections, disclosure, and fraud.

  - ICP 24 Intermediaries cover licensing and business requirements for insurance intermediaries.
  - ICP 25 Consumer protection covers requirements on the providing of information to consumers before and during a contract.
  - ICP 26 Information, disclosure, and transparency toward the market call for adequate disclosure by insurance firms.
  - ICP 27 Fraud calls for measures to prevent, detect, and remedy insurance fraud.

- Anti-money-laundering should aid in combating the financing of terrorism.
  - ICP 28 Anti-money laundering and combating the financing of terrorism [AML–CFT]) requires effective measures to deter, detect, and report AML–CFT offenses in line with FATF standards.

Each principle is elaborated through criteria. It is in the criteria that the full meaning of each principle is found in considerable detail. Although those criteria are not reproduced here, they need to be carefully reviewed if one is to gain a full understanding of the meaning and intention of each core principle. The IAIS emphasizes that the criteria are intended to be implemented both in form and in practice. The criteria consist of two distinct groupings:

- Essential criteria—those components that are intrinsic to the implementation of the core principle (all of which should be met for a supervisory authority to demonstrate "observed" status for each principle)
- Advanced criteria—those components that are considered to improve on the essential criteria and thus enhance the supervisory regime (which are not used for assessing observance with a principle but are used when commenting on a jurisdiction's supervisory framework and making recommendations)

Annex 5.D List of IOSCO Objectives and Principles of Securities Regulation

The three core objectives of securities regulation are (a) protecting investors; (b) ensuring that markets are fair, efficient, and transparent; and (c) reducing systemic risk.

Principles Relating to the Regulator

1. The responsibilities of the regulator should be clear and objectively stated.
2. The regulator should be operationally independent and accountable in the exercise of its functions and powers.
3. The regulator should have adequate powers, proper resources, and the capacity to perform its functions and exercise its powers.
4. The regulator should adopt clear and consistent regulatory processes.
5. The staff of the regulator should observe the highest professional standards, including appropriate standards of confidentiality.

Principles for Self-Regulation

6. The regulatory regime should make appropriate use of self-regulatory organizations (SROs) that exercise some direct oversight responsibility for their respective areas of competence, to the extent appropriate to the size and complexity of the markets.
7. SROs should be subject to the oversight of the regulator and should observe standards of fairness and confidentiality when exercising powers and delegated responsibilities.

Principles for the Enforcement of Securities Regulation

8. The regulator should have comprehensive inspection, investigation, and surveillance powers.
9. The regulator should have comprehensive enforcement powers.

10. The regulatory system should ensure effective and credible use of inspection, investigation, surveillance, and enforcement powers, as well as implementation of an effective compliance program.

Principles for Cooperation in Regulation

11. The regulator should have authority to share public and nonpublic information with domestic and foreign counterparts.
12. Regulators should establish information sharing mechanisms that set out when and how they will share both public and nonpublic information with their domestic and foreign counterparts.
13. The regulatory system should allow for assistance to be provided to foreign regulators who need to make inquiries in connection with the discharge of their functions and the exercise of their powers.

Principles for Issuers

14. There should be full, timely, and accurate disclosure of financial results and other information that is material to investors' decisions.
15. Holders of securities in a company should be treated in a fair and equitable manner.
16. Accounting and auditing standards should be of a high and internationally acceptable quality.

Principles for Collective Investment Schemes

17. The regulatory system should set standards for the eligibility and the regulation of those who wish to market or operate a collective investment scheme.
18. The regulatory system should provide rules for governing the legal form and structure of collective investment schemes, as well as the segregation and protection of client assets.
19. Regulation should require disclosure, as set forth under the principles for issuers, which is necessary to evaluate the suitability of a collective investment scheme for a particular investor and the value of the investor's interest in the scheme.
20. Regulation should ensure that there is a proper and disclosed basis for asset valuation, as well as for the pricing and the redemption of units in a collective investment scheme.

Principles for Market Intermediaries

21. Regulation should provide for minimum entry standards for market intermediaries.

5

22. There should be requirements concerning initial and ongoing capital and other prudential requirements for market intermediaries; the requirements should reflect the risks that the intermediaries undertake.

23. Market intermediaries should be required to comply with standards for internal organization and operational conduct that are designed to protect the interests of clients and to ensure proper management of risk; under such standards, management of the intermediary should accept primary responsibility for those matters.

24. Procedures for dealing with the failure of a market intermediary should minimize damage and loss to investors and should contain ways to handle systemic risk.

Principles for the Secondary Market

25. The establishment of trading systems, including securities exchanges, should be subject to regulatory authorization and oversight.

26. Ongoing regulatory supervision of exchanges and trading systems should strive to ensure that the integrity of trading is maintained through fair and equitable rules that strike an appropriate balance amid the demands of different market participants.

27. Regulation should promote transparency of trading.

28. Regulation should be designed to detect and deter manipulation and other unfair trading practices.

29. Regulation should strive to ensure the proper management of large exposures, default risk, and market disruption.

30. Systems for clearance and settlement of securities transactions should be subject to regulatory oversight and should be designed to ensure not only that they are fair, effective, and efficient but also that they reduce systemic risk.

Annex 5.E   IOSCO Methodology—Scope and Use of Principle 8

The IOSCO methodology document (IOSCO 2003a) introduces the group of principles relating to enforcement (Principles 8 through 10) with a preamble that defines the term enforcement and explains each of the core principles in this group. The methodology calls for a broad interpretation of enforcement, covering wide-ranging powers of surveillance, inspection, and investigation. It then explains each of the principles under this group. In particular, it states that Principle 8 deals with preventive measures and with the methods for obtaining information by the regulator. It then clarifies that the scope of those principles encompasses all agencies involved in enforcement and is not limited only to the primary regulator.

Key issues relating to Principle 8 are then listed, which spell out in greater detail specific powers of the regulator that would be needed—including (a) power to require regular reporting or to seek information through inspections of a market participant's business operations and (b) types of documents and records to which access should be required. This list is followed by key questions, which are listed below.

Principle 8

Principle 8: The regulator should have comprehensive inspection, investigation, and surveillance powers.

Key Questions

1. Can the regulator inspect a regulated entity's business operations, including its books and records, without giving prior notice?
2. Can the regulator obtain books and records and request data or information from regulated entities without judicial action, even in the absence of suspected misconduct,
   a. In response to a particular inquiry?
   b. On a routine basis?
3. Does the regulator have the power to supervise its authorized exchanges and regulated trading systems through surveillance?
4. Does the regulator have record-keeping and record-retention requirements for regulated entities?
5. Are regulated entities required
   a. To maintain records concerning client identity?
   b. To maintain records that permit tracing of funds and securities in and out of brokerage and bank accounts related to securities transactions?
   c. To put in place measures to minimize potential money laundering?
6. Does the regulator have the authority to determine or have access to the identity of all customers of regulated entities?
7. Where a regulator outsources inspection or other regulatory enforcement authority to an SRO or a third party?
   a. Does the regulator supervise the outsourced functions of third parties?
   b. Does the regulator have full access to information maintained or obtained by the third parties?
   c. Can the regulator cause changes or improvements to be made in the third parties' processes?
   d. Are the third parties subject to disclosure and confidentiality requirements that are no less stringent than those applicable to the regulator?

Benchmarking Rubric for Principle 8

- *Fully Implemented*—Requires affirmative responses to all applicable questions
- *Broadly Implemented*—Requires affirmative responses to all applicable questions, except to Question 7(c)
- *Partly Implemented*—Requires affirmative responses to all applicable questions, except to Questions 7(c) and 7(d) or, where the regulator must cooperate with other authorities to obtain records of regulated entities, such cooperation is not sufficiently timely

- *Not Implemented*—Inability to respond affirmatively to one or more of Questions 1, 2(a), 2(b), 3, 4, 5(a), 5(b), 5(c), 6, 7(a), or 7(b)

The questions stated earlier serve as a set of criteria by which implementation is graded. For example in the case of New Zealand, the securities commission had affirmative responses to all the questions except 7c; the securities commission cannot require a registered securities exchange—which performs significant inquiry and enforcement functions—to improve its processes or conduct rules. Therefore, a grading of "broadly implemented" was assigned. In another country (an emerging market), although the regulator had comprehensive surveillance and investigative powers and had determined affirmative answers to all questions, the scope of existing regulations relating to Question 4 was assessed as requiring some further improvements. The assessors recommended the preparation of an explicit and comprehensive record-keeping standard for the regulated firms (including information on investment objectives, audit trails, etc.) to facilitate the inspection of the firm's operations. A "broadly implemented" grading was assigned.

Annex 5.F   Enforcement and the Exchange of Information

Securities regulators have a range of enforcement powers. According to the IOSCO core principles and the methodology, securities regulators must, in addition to their inspection and surveillance powers, be able to conduct investigations of possible violations of the securities laws. To conduct those investigations, a securities regulator needs to be able to "monitor the entities subject to its supervision, to collect information on a routine and ad hoc basis, and to take enforcement action to ensure that persons and entities comply with relevant securities laws" (IOSCO 2003a, 37). The methodology makes very clear that the principles envision a broad definition of enforcement in which regulators will be able to demonstrate effective and credible use of their enforcement powers, including taking effective actions to investigate and address misconduct or abuses. "An effective program, for example, could combine various means to identify, detect, deter, and sanction such misconduct. A wide range of possible sanctions could meet the standards according to the nature of the legal system assessed. The regulator, however, should be able to provide documentation that demonstrates that sanctions available (whatever their nature) are effective, proportionate, and dissuasive" (IOSCO 2003a, 37). In many countries, the criminal prosecutor is responsible for prosecuting securities violations, and the regulator will turn over its investigative file to the prosecutor for follow-up. In those situations, effective securities enforcement can be a challenge, particularly if the prosecutor has other priorities.

To implement those principles, a regulator needs to be able to obtain information from the organizations that it regulates, both on a routine and for-a-cause basis, when it believes that a breach may have occurred. The regulator needs also to be able to obtain both bank and brokerage records, even when banks may be subject to the supervision of a different government agency. Those records must include information relating to client identity so the regulator can conduct its investigation. In addition, the regulator must be able to require the production of information from third parties. If the regulator does not have such powers itself, it needs to be able to cooperate effectively with other government regulators and to be able to obtain this information through the competent authority. The powers must be used effectively and credibly for an effective enforcement program to exist.

However, as the principles make clear, because securities transactions are often global in nature and can cross many geographic borders both easily and quickly and because proceeds of securities transactions similarly can be transferred elsewhere, securities enforcement is no longer a purely domestic matter. Rather, securities regulators have to cooperate with their foreign counterparts to conduct an effective domestic enforcement program. As the methodology states, "[E]ffective regulation can be compromised when necessary information is located in another jurisdiction and is not available or accessible" (IOSCO 2003a, 50).

Exchange of information for securities enforcement purposes is also unlike that which occurs for the purposes of banking supervision. Bank supervisors, of course, also operate in a global environment where the banks they supervise may have branches or subsidiaries in another country or, indeed, may be the branches or subsidiaries of banks that are themselves headquartered elsewhere. To ensure effective consolidated supervision, bank supervisors must cooperate with their foreign counterparts and must obtain information about the activities of banks in other countries that have a bearing on the operation of banks under their supervision. Information on safety and soundness is critical. Securities regulators cooperate in a similar fashion for regulatory oversight purposes and maintain similar cooperative regulatory relationships with their foreign counterparts. However, for purposes of enforcement, the type of cooperation and information exchange that takes place is of a different order.

First, for enforcement purposes, securities regulators often need detailed, client-specific information. A securities regulator may need to know what the name of an account holder is, how much money was in the account during a specified time period, where the funds came from, and where they were transferred to if they are no longer in the account. If the client withdrew the funds or securities from the account, the regulator will want to know when and how they were withdrawn and who signed on behalf of the client. Moreover, because of the speed with which evidence can disappear, the regulator may need to know this information overnight. Unlike most bank supervisors, the securities regulator may need this information to conduct a civil or criminal investigation or to support its request for an emergency court order to freeze funds or securities. In addition, unlike bank supervision, the regulator who is receiving the information request may or may not supervise any of the entities in question (neither the account holder nor the entity where the account is located). The target regulator may, in fact, have no interest in the matter whatsoever. Thus, although traditional safety and soundness concerns are important to both bank supervisors and securities regulators, information exchange for securities regulation extends well beyond those concerns.

It can be challenging for assessors to attain a comprehensive and realistic understanding of the effectiveness of a regulator's securities enforcement program because there are few concrete standards of measurement and there is a great diversity in approaches. Bringing a large number of enforcement actions does not necessarily mean that enforcement is effective. Assessors should consider the full range of enforcement powers that the regulator possesses and how it uses those powers to pursue enforcement actions. The assessor should evaluate how the regulator obtains information, from whom it gets information, and what kind of information it can obtain. The assessor must then consider how the regulator then uses this information to build an enforcement case. Can and does the regulator bring enforcement actions that are based on the investigation it has conducted? If not, does the regulator turn this information over to another domestic authority who can bring an enforcement case? Does that authority bring the case? The assessor also must consider whether there are barriers to domestic information exchange and whether there are gateways for information exchange with foreign counterparts. In particular, the assessor must consider whether there are blocking, bank-secrecy, or other types of privacy laws that could interfere with information exchange. The assessor must determine (a) whether the securities regulator can and does obtain information, including client identifying information, on behalf of a foreign counterpart even if it has no underlying interest in the matter; (b) on what conditions, if any, this information is obtained; and (c) how long it will take.

Notes

1. Typical LOLR instruments are a discount window, or a standing facility, often linked to a payment system.
2. The IMF–Monetary and Financial System Department (MFD), Operational Paper OP/00/01, *Emergency Liquidity Support Facilities*, provides a detailed discussion of the various elements of LOLR activities.
3. The details of this type of "incentive-compatible" system are discussed in Garcia (1999, 2000, 2001) and in Beck (2003). The adverse impact of deposit insurance on bank soundness is analyzed in Barth, Caprio, and Ross (2004) and in Demirguc-Kunt and Detragiache (2003). Also note that poorly designed deposit insurance could have a negative impact on financial development, as noted in Cull, Senbet, and Sorge (2001).
4. Nearly two-thirds of the schemes established since 2000 cover deposits in foreign currency.
5. Pros and cons of, as well as country experiences with, blanket guarantees are discussed in IMF Occasional Paper 223, "Managing Systemic Banking Crises" (Hoelscher and Quintyn 2003).
6. For further details on protection funds for insurance companies, see Takahiro (2001).
7. See Sundararajan, Marston, and Basu (2001) for a discussion of empirical evidence on the links between stability and observance of the BCP. For a comprehensive analysis of links between bank regulation and banking performance, see Barth, Caprio, and Levine (2005).
8. See IMF and World Bank (2002b). For a more recent update, see IMF (2004a) on issues and gaps in financial sector regulation.
9. See chapter 9 for a discussion. Sequencing and prioritization of reform programs may require technical assistance in some country circumstances.
10. This section is based on Basel Committee on Banking Supervision (1999).

11. For more detailed guidance on how to perform a self-assessment, see the Basel Committee document (http://www.bis.org/publ/bcbs81.htm) *Conducting a Supervisory Self-Assessment—Practical Application* (Basel 2001).

12. For each core principle, the assessment methodology requires a categorization of practices according to the degree of compliance. Four categories are envisaged: "compliant," "largely compliant," "materially noncompliant," and "noncompliant." Whether or not efforts to achieve full compliance are under way is also noted.

13. In countries with significant cross-border financial services, it is important to meet with supervisory authorities of home countries of major financial institutions to discuss supervisory cooperation, information sharing, and related issues in consolidated supervision.

14. This section is based on IMF and World Bank (2002a) and the IMF (2004a) paper "Financial Sector Regulation—Issues and Gaps."

15. See also World Bank (2001).

16. This section is based on Miles (2002).

17. Another term for an LCFI is *financial conglomerate* (a formal definition of which is being adopted in EU legislation) or, in the United States, *Large Complex Banking Organizations* (LCBOs).

18. For example, for EU member states, a host regulator of a branch of a bank incorporated in another member state has very limited supervisory powers. However, the branch may be a very large player, in both the domestic banking system and capital markets, as well as in international financial market activity conducted from the host country.

19. Technical risk is the risk of a shortfall of an insurance company's technical provisions held against its policy liabilities. The assessment of provisions will take into account the size and timing of expected payments on the policy, future premium receipts, and future investment income.

20. This section is based on Sundararajan and Errico (2002).

21. The earlier version that was adopted in October 2000 consisted of only 17 principles.

22. In the insurance context, portfolio transfers can be particularly relevant because they enable the transfer of obligations through means other than the change of control of the insurer, in effect, changing the control over the policyholder interests without sale of shares in the company. Thus, it is important that the supervisory assessment of change of control also be extended to the processes for portfolio transfer.

23. A quantitative analysis of the market could include, for example, the development in financial markets generally; the number of insurers and reinsurers subdivided by ownership structure, whether a branch, domestic, or foreign; the number of insurers and reinsurers entering and exiting the market; the market indicators such as premiums, balance-sheet totals, and profitability; the investment structure; the new product developments and market share; the distribution channels; and the use of reinsurance (IAIS 2003a, 23).

24. See Essential Criteria C—the last of 7 bullets (IAIS 2003a).

25. For example, see IAIS 2002 on capital adequacy. Also, in the EU, the solvency II project is working toward the development of a harmonized, risk-based, three-pillar approach (similar to Basel II) for use throughout the EU. This effort is part of a broader

initiative of supervisory and multijurisdictional organizations to strengthen capital adequacy and solvency frameworks. For example, the IAIS and the International Actuarial Association are working on a global framework for insurers' insolvency assessment.

26. The IAIS approved the following supervisory guidelines or issues papers in October 2003: "Quantifying and Assessing Insurance Liabilities" (IAIS 2003d), "Stress Testing by Insurers" (IAIS 2003c), "Nonlife Insurance Securitization" (IAIS 2003e), and "Solvency Control Levels" (IAIS 2003b). A guidance paper on investment risk management was issued in October 2004 (IAIS 2004a). The IAIS also prepared "Principles on the Supervision of Insurance Activities on the Internet" (IAIS 2004b), and "Standard on Disclosures Concerning Technical Performance and Risks of Nonlife Insurers and Reinsurers"(IAIS 2004c) was issued in October 2004.

27. The essential and advanced criteria for assessment purposes are integrated with the ICPs into one single document (Takahiro 2003), with the procedural and benchmarking aspects of the assessment process presented in annex 2 of the same document.

28. For a discussion of issues in analyzing soundness and structure of insurance sector, including suggestions on indicators to analyze, see Das, Davies, and Podpiera (2003).

29. See paragraph 1.7. of the explanatory note to ICP 1 (Takahiro 2003).

30. This section is based mainly on a survey conducted in 2002 of assessment experiences of 42 jurisdictions, which were assessed using the ICPs adopted in October 2000. See International Monetary Fund and World Bank (2001), "Experience with Insurance Core Principles—Assessment under the Financial Sector Assessment Program." For an update of information on insurance assessment, see IMF (2004a), "Financial Sector Regulation—Issues and Gaps—Background Paper."

31. For a detailed principle-by-principle listing of typical issues that arise to reach full compliance, see the IMF background paper (IMF 2004a) "Financial Sector Regulation—Issues and Gaps—Background Paper."

32. Insurance company counterparts do not, because of the nature of the product, have the opportunity to diversify credit risk and may often be in situations of hardship in the absence of the insurance claim proceeds in any event.

33. IOSCO was established in 1983 to bring together securities regulators from around the world in an effort to ensure better regulation of securities markets. It was created from its predecessor organization, the Inter-American Regional Association of Securities Regulations that was established in 1974. IOSCO has grown considerably since its inception and currently has more than 180 members. The core principles are presented in IOSCO public document 125 "Objectives and Principles of Securities Regulation," originally issued in September 1998 and last updated in May 2003 (IOSCO 2003b).

34. The assessment of Principle 30 is intended to be supplemented by reference to the IOSCO–CPSS Recommendations for Securities Settlement Systems and the associated assessment methodology.

35. See, for example, Schinasi (2003) and Dalla (2003).

36. See chapter 4 for a discussion of the scope of analysis of securities markets and their structure and functioning as part of the development assessment. See also chapter 2 for a discussion of indicators of structure and performance of securities markets.

5

37. For a detailed principle-by-principle listing of typical issues that arise to reach full compliance, see IMF (2004a).

38. See, IOSCO (2001) and Carson (2003) for a discussion.

39. This subject of integrated supervision is discussed in greater detail in appendix F of this Handbook. See also De Luna Martinez and Rose (2003).

40. The IMF Code of Good Practices on Transparency of Monetary and Financial Policies (IMF 2000) should serve in this context as an important vehicle in promoting good regulatory governance.

41. Even then, however, it would be impermissible for the authority responsible for the official administration or liquidation of the bank to divulge legally protected information relating to the affairs of particular clients. And in the context of bank restructuring, the need to protect the bank's commercial interests could preclude the publication of detailed transactional or operational information.

42. In jurisdictions where bank insolvency proceedings are court-based, the insolvency courts should have exclusive jurisdiction to determine all relevant disputes. Accordingly, the actions of the supervisory authority relating to its participation in the insolvency proceedings—including its decision to commence such proceedings—should not be subject to judicial review by the administrative courts. Allowing parties to challenge the authority's actions by way of judicial review would be unnecessary because the authority cannot make fully determined decisions on the issues but, instead, needs the approval of the insolvency court. Moreover, the possibility of parallel proceedings in insolvency and administrative law could produce conflicts and serious disruption of the insolvency process.

43. Coordination with the Ministry of Finance is also key, especially in those cases that may involve the actual or potential use of public funds.

References

Barth, James R., Gerard Caprio, and Ross Levine. 2004. *Rethinking Bank Regulation and Supervision: Till Angels Govern.* Cambridge: Cambridge University Press.

Basel Committee on Banking Supervision. 2004. "International Convergence of Capital Measurement and Capital Standards—A Revised Framework." June, Bank for International Settlements, Basel, Switzerland.

———. 2001. "Conducting Supervisory Self-Assessment, Practical Application. Bank for International Settlements, Basel, Switzerland.

———. 1999. *Core Principles Methodology.* Basel, Switzerland: Basel Committee on Banking Supervision. Available at http://www.bis.org/publ/bcbs61.pdf.

Beck, Thorsten. 2003. "The Incentive Compatible Design of Deposit Insurance and Bank Failure Resolution—Concepts and Country Studies." World Bank Policy Research Working Paper 3043, World Bank, Washington, DC.

Carson, John W. 2003. "Conflicts of Interest in Self-Regulation: Can Demutualized Exchanges Successfully Manage Them?" Policy Research Working Paper 3183, World Bank, Washington, DC.

Cull, Robert, W. Senbet Lemma, and Sorge Marco. 2001. "Deposit Insurance and Financial Development." World Bank Policy Research Paper 2682, World Bank, Washington, DC.

Dalla, Ismail. 2003. "Harmonization of Bond Market Rules and Regulations in Selected APEC Economies." Manila, Philippines: Asian Development Bank.

Das Udaibir, Nigel Davies, and Richard Podpiera. 2003. "Insurance and Issues in Financial Soundness." IMF Working Paper 03/138, International Monetary Fund, Washington, DC.

de Luna Martinez, Jose, and Thomas A. Rose. 2003. "International Survey of Integrated Financial Sector Supervision." Policy Research Working Paper 3096, World Bank, Washington, DC.

Demirguc-Kunt, A., and Enrica Detragiache. 2002. "Does Deposit Insurance Increase Banking System Stability?" *Journal of Monetary Economics* 49 (7): 1373–406.

Dong, He. 2000. "Emergency Liquidity Support Facilities." IMF Working Paper 00/79, International Monetary Fund, Washington, DC.

Garcia, Gillian G. H. 1999. "Deposit Insurance: A Survey of Actual and Best Practices." Working Paper WP/99/54, International Monetary Fund, Washington, DC. Available at http://www.imf.org/external/pubs/ft/wp/1999/wp9954.pdf.

———. 2000. "Deposit Insurance and Crisis Management." Working Paper WP/00/57, International Monetary Fund, Washington, DC. Available at http://www.imf.org/external/pubs/ft/wp/2000/wp0057.pdf.

———. 2001. "Deposit Insurance: Actual and Good Practices." Occasional Paper 197,,International Monetary Fund, Washington, DC. Available at http://www.imf.org/external/pubs/nft/op/197/index.htm.

Hoelscher, David S., and Marc Quintyn. 2003. "Managing Systemic Banking Crises." Occasional Paper 224, International Monetary Fund, Washington, DC.

International Association of Insurance Supervisors (IAIS). 2000. *Insurance Core Principles.* Basel ,Switzerland: IAIS

———. 2002. *Principles on Capital Adequacy and Solvency.* Basel, Switzerland: IAIS.

———. 2003a. *Insurance Core Principles and Methodology.* Basel, Switzerland: IAIS.

———. 2003b. "Solvency Control Levels." Guidance Paper 6, IAIS, Basel, Switzerland.

———. 2003c. "Stress Testing by Insurers." Guidance Paper 8, IAIS, Basel, Switzerland.

———. 2003d. "Quantifying and Assessing Insurance Liabilities." Discussion Paper, IAIS, Basel, Switzerland.

———. 2003e. "Nonlife Insurance Securitization." Issues Paper, IAIS, Basel, Switzerland.

———. 2004a. "Investment Risk Management." Guidance Paper 9, IAIS, Basel, Switzerland.

———. 2004b. "Principles on the Supervision of Insurance Activities on the Internet." Principle No. 4, IAIS, Basel, Switzerland.

———. 2004c. "Standard on Disclosures Concerning Technical Performance and Risks of Nonlife Insurers and Reinsurers." Standard No. 9, IAIS, Basel, Switzerland.

International Monetary Fund (IMF). 2000. *IMF Code of Good Practices on Transparency in Monetary and Financial Policies.* Washington, DC: IMF.

————. 02002. "The Financial Market Activities of Insurance and Reinsurance Companies." In Global Financial Stability Report, ed. International Capital Market Department of the IMF, 30–47. Washington, DC: International Monetary Fund.

————. 2004a. "Financial Sector Regulations—Issues and Gaps—Background Paper." International Monetary Fund, Washington, DC. Available at www.imf.org/external/np/mfd/2004/eng/081704.htm.

————. 2004b. "Risk Transfer and the Insurance Industry." In Global Financial Stability Report, ed. International Capital Markets Department of the IMF, 77–110. Washington, DC: International Monetary Fund.

International Monetary Fund (IMF) and World Bank. 2001. "Experience with the Insurance Core Principles Assessments under the Financial Sector Assessment Program." IMF, Washington, DC.

————. 2002a. "Experience with the Assessments of the IOSCO Objectives and Principles of Securities Regulation under the Financial Sector Assessment Program." International Monetary Fund, Washington, DC.

————. 2002b. "Implementation of the Basel Core Principles for Effective Banking Supervision: Experiences, Influences, and Perspectives." International Monetary Fund, Washington, DC. Available at http://www.imf.org/external/np/mae/bcore/2002/092302.pdf.

————. 2004. *Global Bank Insolvency Initiative.* Draft report by IMF and World Bank staff, World Bank, Washington, DC.

International Organization of Securities Commissions (IOSCO). 2001. "Issues Paper on Exchange Demutualization." Technical Committee, IOSCO, Madrid, Spain.

————. 2003a. *Methodology for Assessing Implementation of the IOSCO Objectives and Principles of Securities Regulation.* Madrid, Spain: IOSCO.

————. 2003b. *Objectives and Principles of Securities Regulation.* Madrid, Spain: IOSCO. Available at http://www.iosco.org/pubdocs/pdf/IOSCOPD154.pdf.

Lindgren, Carl-Johan, Tomás J. T. Baliño, Charles Enoch, Anne-Marie Gulde, Marc Quintyn, and Leslie Teo. 2000. "Financial Sector Crisis and Restructuring: Lessons from Asia." Occasional Paper 188, International Monetary Fund, Washington, DC. Available at http://www.imf.org/external/pubs/ft/op/opfinsec/op188.pdf.

Miles, Colin. 2002. "Large and Complex Financial Institutions (LCFIs): Issues to Be Considered in the Financial Sector Assessment Program." MAE Operational Paper 02/3, Monetary and Exchange Affairs Department, International Monetary Fund, Washington, DC.

Schinasi, Gary J. 2003. "The Development of Effective Securities Markets." Paper presented November 2003 at the First Annual Asian Bond Forum, Hong Kong.

Sundararajan, Venkataraman, and Luca Erric. 2002. "Islamic Financial Institutions and Products in the Global Financial System: Key Issues in Risk Management and Challenges Ahead." IMF Working Paper WP/02/192, International Monetary Fund, Washington, DC. Available at http://www.imf.org/external/pubs/ft/wp/2002/wp02192.pdf.

Sundararajan, Venkataraman, David Marston, and Ritu Basu. 2001. "Financial System Standards and Financial Stability: The Case of the Basel Core Principles." IMF

5

Working Paper WP/01/62, International Monetary Fund, Washington, DC. Available at http://www.imf.org/external/pubs/ft/wp/2001/wp0162.pdf.

Takahiro, Yasui. 2001. "Policyholder Protection Funds: Rationale and Structure." In *Insurance and Private Pensions Compendium for Emerging Economies, Book 1*, ed. Insurance and Private Pensions Unit; Financial Affairs Division; Directorate for Financial, Fiscal, and Enterprise Affairs, Part 1:2, 1–20. Paris: Organisation for Economic Co-operation and Development (OECD).

Taylor, Michael, and Alex Fleming. 1999. "Integrated Financial Supervision: Lessons of Northern European Experience." Policy Research Working Paper 2223, World Bank, Washington, DC.

World Bank. 2001. "Principles and Guidelines for Effective Insolvency and Creditor Rights Systems." World Bank, Washington, DC. Available at http://www.worldbank.org/ifa/ipg_eng.pdf.

Chapter 6

Assessing the Supervision of Other Financial Intermediaries

6.1 Overview

This chapter focuses on issues in the regulation of a range of non-bank financial institutions (NBFIs), categorized as Other Financial Intermediaries (OFIs). OFIs refer to those financial corporations that are primarily engaged in financial intermediation—that is, corporations that channel funds from lenders to borrowers through their own account or in auxiliary financial activities that are closely related to financial intermediation—but are not classified as deposit takers (IMF 2004a).[1] OFIs include insurance corporations; pension funds; securities dealers; investment funds; finance, leasing, and factoring companies; and asset management companies. This chapter discusses considerations in assessing the regulation and supervision of OFIs (other than insurance companies and security market intermediaries) generally, with a focus on specialized finance institutions, leasing and factoring companies, and pension funds.

Although OFIs are often dwarfed by commercial banks in terms of volume of business and size of assets, OFIs should receive adequate attention during the assessment process for various reasons. OFIs play an important developmental role through their activity in areas and markets where the presence of commercial banks is not fully felt. Moreover, the development of OFIs could increase bank competition, which could lead to greater access to finance. In many countries, pension funds are major contractual savings institutions with a significant effect on financial markets and the macroeconomy.

Specialized financial institutions (such as thrifts, building societies, and mortgage institutions) have emerged in many countries to carry out real estate finance. However, in many countries, other than their specialization in housing finance, those institutions are indistinguishable from deposit-taking institutions such as banks, and they require attention from both the stability and the development perspectives.

Leasing companies engage in relatively simple transactions where the lessee (a business owner) uses the asset (owned by the leasing company) for a fixed period of time, while making payments on a set schedule. At the end of the lease, the lessee buys the asset for a nominal fee, giving the lessee the opportunity to make a capital investment. Leasing companies can serve as a significant source of finance for small firms wanting to invest in equipment, and that investment in leasing companies can yield attractive returns if conditions are right.

Factoring companies are financial institutions that specialize in the business of accounts receivable management. Factoring is an important source of external financing for corporations and small and medium enterprises (SMEs), which receive credit based on the value of their accounts receivables. Under this form of asset-based finance, the credit provided by a lender is explicitly linked on a formula basis to the value of a borrower's underlying assets (working capital), not to the borrower's overall creditworthiness. In developing countries, factoring offers several advantages over other types of lending. First, factoring may be particularly useful in countries with weak secured-lending laws, inefficient bankruptcy systems, and imperfect records of upholding seniority claims, because factored receivables are not part of the estate of a bankrupt SME. Second, in a factoring relationship the credit is primarily based on quality of the underlying accounts, not on the quality of the borrower. Thus, factoring may be especially attractive to high-risk SMEs (Bakker, Klapper, and Udell 2004).

The development of OFIs such as leasing and factoring companies (especially if they were operated by groups that were independent of large banks and insurance companies) increases lending to smaller borrowers. Some practitioners argue that stand-alone OFIs tend to compete more vigorously. For that reason, the International Finance Corporation prefers to finance stand-alone leasing companies despite their disadvantage when competing with leasing subsidiaries of commercial banks, which can tap into low-cost depositors' funding from their parent companies) (International Finance Corporation 1996).

While the small size of the OFI sector in some countries may limit OFI's systemic effect on the rest of the financial sector in case of crisis, stress in OFIs could have systemic effects in specific circumstances. In particular, difficulties in OFIs may have some systemic effect, insofar as they trigger a loss of confidence in deposit-taking activities. For instance, a crisis of confidence can spread from one subsector of the financial system to another subsector, owing to perceived ownership or balance-sheet linkages. Moreover, the lack of effective regulations for OFIs can exacerbate the fragility of the overall financial system through regulatory arbitrage (Herring and Santomero 1999).

In many countries, pension funds are a major source of contractual savings, providing a stable source of long-term investment to support growth and at the same time playing a key role in financial markets through their investment behavior. National pension systems provide retirement income from a mixture of government, employment, and individual savings. Pension funds affect the stability of financial markets and the distribution of risks among different sectors of the economy by their investment behavior and the way they manage their risk.

6.2 Objectives of the Legal and Regulatory Framework for OFIs[2]

Against this background, the assessment of the regulation and supervision of OFIs should not only account for their effectiveness in meeting the traditional objectives of financial supervision, but should also consider whether the regulatory framework helps build a sound environment that fosters the development of those institutions. For instance, an inadequate regulatory framework that promotes regulatory arbitrage in the OFI sector could restrict the potential developmental role of OFIs and at the same time could lead to the buildup of substantial undetected vulnerabilities and risks.

While both competition regulation and conduct of business (including market integrity) regulation apply to all sectors and institutions in the financial system, assessing which type of OFIs warrants prudential regulation is, in practice, a difficult exercise. Three characteristics of financial institutions are critical in judging the scope of prudential regulation: (a) the difficulty of honoring the contractual obligations, (b) the difficulty faced by the consumer in assessing the creditworthiness or soundness of the institution, and (c) the adversity caused by a breach of contractual obligations (see Carmichael and Pomerleano 2002). For instance, banks are subject to systemic liquidity risks that may lead to the breach of obligations, financial conglomerates have complex structures whose soundness and creditworthiness are difficult to assess, and the failure of a large bank or insurance company is likely to generate great adversity. Each group of institutions could be ranked using those characteristics to judge the desirability and scope of prudential oversight.

An appropriate regulatory environment is required to foster the development of OFIs as recognized legal entities that are well integrated with the rest of the financial system. In many emerging economies, the legal and regulatory framework for finance, leasing, and other specialized financial institutions is ambiguous, fragmented, and incomplete. Assembling and analyzing the laws and regulations governing the operations of each group of institutions to ensure clarity and completeness is an important step in the assessment of OFIs. While repressive regulation can retard the growth of OFIs, an inappropriate and poorly designed regulatory structure can create incentives for regulatory arbitrage. However, even when high-quality legislation exists, enforcement is sometimes poor. Those factors are all impediments to the development of the financial system in general, but the impediments become more pronounced in the case of OFIs that, in many emerging economies, are often not supported by a clear legal framework.

Legislation should permit effective enforcement. The legal framework for financial system supervision could be somewhat prescriptive, spelling out specific prudential rules within the scope of the governing law, or could be general, thereby providing guidelines and principles while conferring broad regulatory powers on the regulator. The guidelines approach could provide more discretion and flexibility to the regulator, which may be particularly important for OFIs, because separate laws governing specific types of OFIs and markets often overlap, which gives rise to conflicts and ambiguity regarding the applicable rules. If, however, the regulator's lack of operational independence hampers the effective use of discretion, a more-prescriptive law, if well designed, could provide a workable alternative.

6

6.3   Assessing Institutional Structure and Regulatory Arbitrage

The appropriateness of the institutional structure for supervising OFIs should consider the overall institutional framework for financial supervision and the scope of the OFIs' activities within that framework. The number and size of OFIs (individual and aggregate), as well as their links to banks and other players in the financial system, are major factors influencing the appropriate institutional structure for supervising OFIs. The stage of financial development, the legislative environment generally, and the range of regulators' skills available would also affect the appropriate institutional structure for supervising OFIs.

An institutional structure that is sectorally focused rather than focused on the nature of functions to be regulated may result in gaps in the regulation of OFIs. In some country circumstances, therefore, bringing the regulation and supervision of all types of financial institutions, including OFIs, under a unified supervisory framework would help reduce the possibilities of regulatory arbitrage and regulatory gaps and allow for more-efficient oversight. A unified structure facilitates the adoption of a common set of standards for institutions with the same profile of risk—for instance, uniform application of conduct of business and financial integrity regulations, and adjustments in the scope of prudential regulations according to risk profile. However, under a structure with more than one regulatory body involved in institutional regulation and supervision, special attention should be given to the definition of the legal power of responsible bodies, the identification of conflicting areas of jurisdiction, and the extent of regulatory duplication. This sectorally focused structure is a source of inconsistencies and ambiguities that have created weaknesses in the regulatory and supervisory process in many countries. For instance, this structure's inability to undertake "fit-and-proper" tests and impose minimum capital requirements or other specific guidelines creates loose regulatory and supervisory regimes that allow OFIs to develop their business recklessly and get involved in banking activities.

In countries with separate, sectorally focused regulators, the assessment should focus on verifying the differences in the types of risk posed by various categories of service providers, since the application of different rules to products and services that are functionally equivalent can give rise to increased incentives for regulatory arbitrage (OECD 2002). For instance, institutions assuming the main banking functions should be considered banks and regulated and supervised as such. In some countries, OFIs became an important segment of the financial system as a result of efforts to circumvent prudential norms and exploit loopholes in the banking sector.

Table 6.1 compares the regulatory features of banks and OFIs. Raising the following four questions when completing table 6.1 can help regulators verify the differences in the rules applied to different group of institutions (Carmichael and Pomerleano 2002):

- Can institutions subjected to different regulation provide similar products?
- Is a financial institution capable of choosing among different regulators by altering its corporation form, regulatory jurisdiction, or institutional label? For example, is a parent institution able to reduce its regulatory burden by shifting business into an unregulated subsidiary?

Table 6.1. Main Regulatory and Prudential Aspects of Different Groups of Financial Institutions[a]

Regulation	Commercial banks	Deposit-taking institutions			Non-deposit-taking institutions	
Main regulator/supervisor						
Restriction on loans						
Participation in the clearing/settlement system						
Issuing deposits						
Subject to onsite supervision						
Subject to offsite supervision						
Minimum paid-up capital						
Minimum risk weighted capital/asset ratio						
Liquidity ratio						
Cash reserve requirements						
Required provisions						
Limit to a single borrower						
Insider lending						

a. This table can be adapted to individual country situations.

- Can new OFIs offer banking-type products under a different banner to remain outside the jurisdiction of the main regulator?
- Is there a regulatory structure in which at least one regulator has overall responsibility for financial conglomerates?

In a unified supervisory structure where the number of OFIs is significant but OFIs operate independently from the main players in the financial sector (i.e., banks and insurance companies), establishing a separate department that is exclusively dedicated to the supervision of OFIs is a common practice. In such structure, there are cases where the same regulators are responsible for both onsite supervision and offsite supervision for a group of OFIs, or cases where there is separation between the responsibility for onsite and offsite functions. On the one hand, having the same regulators be responsible for both onsite and offsite functions helps ensure continuity in monitoring events in the sector, as well as coherence in supervision. On the other hand, separating offsite and onsite functions provides a certain degree of specialization in the related processes and procedures. In either case, the regulators' skill levels should be adequate to avoid having inexperienced and unqualified regulators be systematically assigned to supervising OFIs.

In a unified structure where the links between OFIs and banks are significant through investment and ownership, regulators with responsibility for a group of related institutions (including banks and OFIs) help monitor development in related sectors in a consolidated manner. Moreover, specialization helps enhance the regulation and supervision of OFIs. Regulators in charge of supervising banks can usually supervise OFIs, provided they receive adequate training and guidance to specifically deal with OFIs. As stressed in the Basel Core Principles (BCPs) for Effective Banking Supervision, an essential element of banking supervision is regulators' ability to supervise the banking organization on a consolidated basis, which includes their ability to review both banking and non-banking activities conducted by the bank.

6.4   Assessing Regulatory Practice and Effectiveness

The regulatory regime for OFIs should help meet regulatory objectives—effective competition, good conduct of business and financial integrity, and prudent operations—while ensuring that regulations reflect the specific operational characteristics of the OFIs and promote their development. From this perspective, many core principles of effective bank supervision and regulation also apply to OFIs. The general rule is that financial institutions that do not have deposit-like liabilities to the general public do not need to be regulated and supervised as closely as those that do. The tools and techniques for deposit-taking OFIs would follow the standards contained in the BCPs. Financial institutions that are banklike in all but name should also be just as closely regulated and supervised. In several countries, OFIs that were (formally or informally) taking deposits from the general public and were either not required to conform to banking regulations or did not come under the supervision of the main supervisory authority have faced difficulties that necessitated the intervention of the government (World Bank 1999).

Given the diversity of institutions that make up the group of OFIs, certain additional principles and considerations can complement the BCPs and help adapt them to the supervision of OFIs. Such principles and considerations, regardless of the institutional structure (unified or segmented), include modifying prudential rules to accommodate the operational characteristics of OFIs; ensuring consistency in decision making; recognizing the unique risks of OFI; ensuring that supervision is proportionate and consistent with costs and benefits; and maintaining resources and skills sufficient and adequate to face the growth of the OFIs sector. Those principles are similar to those applying to banks, and are further explained in Annex 6.A. Their implementation can be a challenge. For example, housing finance institutions, including building societies, often offer deposit services (not necessarily checking accounts) and may need to be regulated as banking institutions (see box 6.1). In many cases, tailoring regulations to the specific operational characteristics of the OFIs and avoiding overregulation is important for the development of the sector.

For the majority of OFIs where retail deposits and systemic issues are not involved, competition and market conduct regulations—such as entry and disclosure requirements and monitoring association with other institutions—should be sufficient. With regard to entry requirements, the regulator would encourage low barriers to entry into these sectors by ensuring that there are minimal restrictions on the corporate form and ownership structure of OFIs, freedom of entry for foreign firms, and strong antitrust conditions to prevent excessive concentration in the industry. Disclosure of correct and timely information to market participants complements supervision.[3] Regarding the association of OFIs with other institutions, particular attention should be given to OFIs established as subsidiaries of regulated institutions as a means of circumventing the regulation. The dangers of excessive growth in unregulated subsidiaries were highlighted in a number of crises (see World Bank 2001).

Box 6.1 The Case of Financial Institutions Providing Housing Finance

In the housing sector, banks and other specialized financial institutions such as thrifts, mortgage societies, primary mortgage institutions, or mortgage banks often offer the same products. Those institutions face similar risks, including credit risk exposure to the borrowers, liquidity risk from the possible loss of short-term funding, and market risk at the time of maturity.

The conditions under which deposits can be withdrawn from those institutions are often mentioned as differentiating factors between banks and specialized housing finance institutions and are viewed as justification to impose different prudential rules (such as on liquidity). The general rule, however, is that when specialized housing finance institutions solicit deposits directly from the public and when those institutions' deposits are guaranteed implicitly or explicitly by the government, those institutions must be regulated at least to the standards of banks.

Given that the risks of specialized housing finance institutions are sometimes greater than those of

banks, which have more diversified balance sheets, there is even a case for stricter regulation of those institutions. The concentration in housing and real estate finance means that their risks may be highly concentrated, and a large overconcentration can be the source of systemic failures. However, in some countries, the availability of a mortgage-backed securities market may help those institutions manage their risk profile and minimize the concentration of exposures.

In some countries, building societies—which are very similar to banks in terms of the range of financial services offered—are grouped together with other nonbank financial institutions (NBFIs) and are supervised separately, even though they need to be regulated with standards similar to those of banks. More generally, the heterogeneity of other financial institutions often results in inappropriate regulation and supervision of some financial institutions providing housing finance.

When corporate laws are still evolving, however, additional conditions in financial regulation can support the good market conduct and prudent operation of OFIs. Those additional conditions could cover the following:

- *Licensing requirements.* As with any financial institution, the purpose of licensing OFIs should be to ensure adequate capitalization and sound management, not to limit entry or restrict competition. Regulators should have the authority to screen potential owners and managers to prevent those lacking professional qualifications, financial backing, or moral standing from obtaining a license. An OFI license should not become a simple alternative for applicants who could not meet the requirements to be granted a commercial bank license. Liberal entry into the financial system should not mean unqualified entry. Countries with easy entry have often experienced problems with insufficiently regulated, undercapitalized, and poorly managed institutions.

  In some countries, once an OFI has been licensed, it conducts activities that are normally not permissible under the range of activities specified in its license. The balance sheet restrictions for each group of financial institution should, therefore, be closely monitored (e.g., limits on assets and liabilities, prohibition on particular classes of assets or liabilities, restrictions on the types of assets held, and mandated maximum or minimum holdings of particular assets).

- *Minimum capital requirements.* With regard to minimum capital requirements (and all the main rules for the conduct of the institution), the requirements for banks should not be applied to OFIs when not adequately justified. The minimum capital requirement is usually part of the financial institution's licensing requirements, but should not inhibit the start-up of new institutions or act as barrier to competition. The amount of capital appropriate for a group of OFIs or an individual institution is a function of the institution's potential to incur unexpected losses. A higher than necessary limit could restrict the industry's growth.

- *Accountability requirements.* In many countries, accountability requirements, including accounting and auditing practices by OFIs, are inadequate.[4] This deficiency increases the chance that misleading information could cause market instability. Facilitating market discipline and sound practices for accounting and auditing helps reinforce supervisory efforts to encourage OFIs to maintain sound risk management practices and internal controls. As with any financial institution, OFIs need sound accounting standards to achieve satisfactory transparency—public disclosure of reliable information that enables market participants and other users of that information to make an accurate assessment of the institution's financial condition and performance, its business activities, and the risks related to those activities.

- *Risk management practices commensurate with the risk profile in the industry.* Measuring, monitoring, and controlling risks are often issues of concern with OFIs, especially in countries where licenses were granted too liberally. It is important that the OFI put in place a risk management process adequate for the size and the nature of its activities. Regulators should ensure that such a risk management system is not static, but rather adjusted to the OFI's risk profile (concentration, credit, currency, or tax-related risks). This process is not only helpful in identifying potential systemically important OFIs, but also in setting priorities for allocation of limited supervisory capacity, for instance, to determine the frequency of reporting and the depth and focus of onsite supervision.

Building supervisory capacity does not mean that all OFIs need to be supervised, and when they do, they usually do not require the same level of supervision and resources as banks. The supervisory authority must establish priorities for the allocation of regulators' supervisory capacity. There is sometimes little benefit in trying to regularly visit small, dispersed OFIs that, with modest change in regulation (e.g., licensing, minimum capital, accounting, auditing, and disclosure requirements), could present negligible risk.

After establishing supervisory priorities, regulators should also ensure that OFIs (particularly small non–deposit-taking institutions) are not overwhelmed by excessive reporting requirements when they do not present major variations in their portfolios from one period to the other. In most cases, quarterly or even semiannual returns (instead of monthly returns) would be appropriate. For those institutions accuracy and completeness are far more important than frequency. At the same time, more attention should be given to OFIs with substantial assets whose reporting should be more frequent. Other recurrent issues relate to the following:

- Deficiencies with offsite supervision, which weaken early warning systems to identify weak OFIs

- Unreliable and rudimentary working methods, which prevent regulators from efficiently and accurately assessing the OFI's exposure to various risks and, for the most part, its soundness and financial performance
- The lack of internal guidelines or manual for onsite and offsite supervision, which are important to determine the examination procedures and policies for OFIs

An adequate information system and a guideline or manual are useful tools to help address the specific risks inherent to OFIs.

6.5 Selected Issues on the Regulation and Supervision of Leasing Companies

In some circumstances, a separate legal and regulatory framework for leasing companies can be helpful to create a suitable environment for leasing and promote confidence in the industry. Many developed countries, despite their long history of leasing, do not have a separate leasing law (Amembal, Lowder, and Ruga 2000). Those countries usually have well-developed common and civil laws that provide an adequate basis to support leasing transactions. In countries where the leasing industry is still in the very early stages of development, a new legal and regulatory framework could help promote confidence in the efficiency and fairness of the market. Specialized leasing laws may not be necessary, however, provided that existing regulations designed to deal with financial institutions do not discriminate against the industry.[5] When the industry develops, however, it will be important that the fundamental elements of an efficient financial leasing law be put in place. Those elements include the following (see International Finance Corporation 1998):

- Freedom of contract
- Recognition of the three-party structure of the modern financial lease
- Duties consistent with party's role in the transaction

    - Lessee's duty to pay after acceptance
    - Lessor's lack of equipment responsibilities
    - Lessee's recourse against the seller
    - Equipment not liable to other creditor's claims
    - Transfer freedom and restraint

- Default remedies, including the right to accelerate the remaining lease payments
- Expedient repossession and recovery

The rights and duties of the lessor as legal owner of the asset and the rights and duties of the lessee as user of the asset should be clearly stated. The legal owner needs a clear, simple, workable, timely process to reclaim an asset if the terms of the lease are breached by the user, including the automatic right of repossession without lengthy court proceedings and the right to claim payments due and other damages. The lessee must have the right to use the asset unimpeded and gain the full productivity of the asset. In some countries, it may be necessary to clarify that the lessee does not have the right to create a lien on leased assets (International Finance Corporation 1996). One advantage of the leasing

---

Box 6.2 Measures to Develop a Favorable Regulatory Environment for Leasing

Legal Framework

- *Lessor's ownership*. Ownership should be clearly stated, with simple, effective, and timely procedures for repossession if lessee defaults.
- Lessee's rights. Rights should be clear—uninterrupted use of leased asset for the lease period if the lease payments are current.

Regulations

- *Licensing*. Regulation should recognize the existence of leasing. Restricting leasing to licensed institutions (and requiring commercial banks to set up separate subsidiaries to write leasing contracts) may help the industry develop aggressively. Leasing companies should be allowed to mobilize term deposits only.

- *Prudential requirements*. Regulations may have lower minimum capital requirements than many other financial institutions. Other prudential requirements may be less strict than for deposit-taking institutions.

Tax Treatment

- *Lessor*. The lessor should be allowed to depreciate the asset, with lease payments taxed as income and asset depreciation computed over life shorter than or equal to lease contract.
- *Lessee*. The lessee should be allowed to treat lease payments as an expense for tax purposes.
- *Sales tax*. The postcontract sale of the asset should be exempt from sales tax.
- *Capital allowances*. Allowances should be given to lessor or lessee, with equal treatment compared to other financing.

Source: International Finance Corporation (1996).

---

companies over banks is that they own the leased asset. However, physical repossession can still prove difficult. For instance, the mobility of the leased asset has made repossession even more difficult. In its lessons of experience, International Finance Corporation (1996) has identified a set of measures to develop a favorable regulatory environment for leasing (box 6.2).

In many countries, leasing companies are not regulated and supervised because they do not take deposits. However, many leasing companies are bank subsidiaries, and regulators should be interested in such companies for the purpose of consolidated supervision. Moreover, as previously stated, even for NBFIs where retail deposits and systemic issues are not involved and where corporate laws are still evolving, additional conditions—including licensing requirements, minimum capital requirements, accountability requirements, and risk conditions consistent with the risk involved in the industry—can support market conduct.

6.6 Selected Issues on the Regulation and Supervision of Factoring Companies

Factoring companies are financial institutions that specialize in the business of accounts receivable financing and management. If a factoring company chooses to purchase a firm's receivables, then it will pay the firm a prenegotiated, discounted amount of the face value of the invoices (Sopranzetti 1998). A moral hazard problem develops when the seller's credit management efforts are unobservable to the factoring company: Once the entire

---

Box 6.3 Factoring as a Sale and Purchase Transaction Rather Than as a Loan

A key issue for factoring is whether a financial system's commercial law views factoring as a sale and purchase transaction rather than as a loan. If it is a sale and purchase transaction, creditor rights and loan contract enforcement are less important for factoring because factors are not creditors—that is, if a firm went bankrupt, its factored receivables would not be part of its bankruptcy estate because they would be the property of the factor.

Still, creditor rights and loan contract enforcement are not irrelevant to factoring for at least two reasons. First, they define the environment in which the factoring company engages in collection activi-

ties. The strength of the regime for creditor rights will affect underwriting standards because factors must consider the anticipated cost and efficiency of their collection activities when they make credit decisions about which invoices to purchase. Second, under recourse factoring, the factoring company has a contingent claim against the borrowing firm if there is a deficiency in the collection of a receivable. This contingent claim can be secured or unsecured, depending on whether the factoring company filed a security interest in some or all of the firm's assets as a secondary source of repayment.

Source: Bakker, Klapper, and Udell (2004).

6

receivable is sold (factored), the seller has no incentive to monitor that receivable, as the seller no longer bears any credit risk. Factoring is not one homogeneous product. Most factoring companies do not simply provide immediate cash services; they also offer a range of other professional services such as collecting payments, pursuing late payers, providing credit management advise, and protecting clients against bad debts. Factoring companies typically fall under three categories: banks, large industrial companies, or independent factoring companies.

One fundamental issue with factoring resides in recognizing the commercial status of the industry, which in turn determines the oversight structure. In some countries, factoring is recognized as a commercial activity and is, therefore, regulated by commercial law, but it is not unusual in certain countries to see factoring companies undertake the functions of financial intermediation without authorization (see box 6.3 for further details).

The regulatory environment has an important effect on the factoring industry. In some countries, factoring operates entirely outside the purview of any regulatory structure or authority, and in others it is regulated along with other financial services such as banking and insurance. In most countries, however, the level of regulation falls somewhere in between (Bakker, Klapper, and Udell 2004). For countries where factoring is developing, a law setting out minimum standards for the management of factoring companies and specifying the tools to be used to manage key risks in factoring operations could be envisaged. Some countries simply restrict market entry to formally registered financial institutions such as banks or other specialized financial institutions. However, those restrictions could hinder competition by excluding the emergence of independent factors. To address the potential lack of discipline in some markets, International Finance Corporation (1998) recommends that governments consider requiring minimum capital and prudential guidelines as a barrier to entry into the market.

6.7 Selected Issues on the Regulation and Supervision of Pension Funds

National pension systems are typically characterized as multipillar structures that are defined in many ways, depending on the purpose of analysis.[6] From the perspective of analyzing financial stability and development, it is useful to distinguish between (a) state-provided pension schemes, which are a combination of a universal entitlement and an earnings related component; (b) occupational pension funds, which are funded by and organized in the workplace as Defined Benefit (DB), Defined Contribution (DC), or a hybrid; and (c) private savings plans, which are often tax advantaged. As a result of increasing longevity and rising dependency ratios, the funding of promised retirement benefits (in DB plans) has become a challenge in many countries. This funding challenge has led to pension reforms that reduce benefits, increase contributions (i.e., taxes to pay state pensions), redefine risk sharing between sponsors and beneficiaries, and raise retirement age. Increased funding of pension obligations (by both the private and public sectors) and greater retirement savings by individuals are increasingly part of the solution.

While funded pension plans' size and importance vary greatly among countries, in many countries pension funds are among the largest institutional investors. As a result, pension fund asset allocations could affect financial markets and the flow of investment funds quite significantly. As pension funds became increasingly underfunded and shift toward DC and hybrid plans, the issues of appropriate asset liability management and asset allocation have become pressing. As a result, both pension fund management and the approaches to its regulation have changed. The regulatory framework for pension funds is increasingly focusing on risk management, in addition to the traditional focus on protection of pensioner and employee benefits and rights.[7] Key issues in assessing pension funds' regulatory framework from a financial sector perspective and the emerging practices are covered in appendix H.

Annex 6.A   Regulation and Supervision of OFIs: A Few Guiding Principles

As one puts in place a regulatory framework for Other Financial Intermediaries (OFIs), some regulations common in traditional banking must be adjusted to accommodate those institutions. The challenges facing a given country's supervisory agency—and the realistic obstacles to meeting those challenges—must be weighted seriously when examining proposals for the regulation of OFIs.

A. The regulatory framework should minimize adverse effects on competition and encourage competition.

1. Repressive and inappropriate regulation can have a negative influence on the development of OFIs. Examples of repressive regulation include restrictive licensing and pricing and investment regimes. Excessive regulation of banks can stimu-

late the growth of non-banks or the establishment of non-bank subsidiaries as a means to circumvent regulation. Discriminatory tax treatment is an example of inappropriate regulation.

B. The regulatory framework should clearly define the power of the regulator and the permissible activities of OFIs.

2. The regulatory framework should be clear with regard to (a) the establishment and powers of the regulator and (b) the legal existence and the behavior of the entities being regulated. The regulatory frameworks also should be supported by adequate infrastructure such as accounting and disclosure rules, property rights, and contract enforcement.

3. The regulatory framework should define the permissible activities of OFIs, including the regulatory distinction between banks and non-banks, as well as the activities retained solely for banks. There should be no ambiguity as to the meaning of "bank," "lease," "factor," or "deposit" or to what constitutes the illegal acceptance of deposit without a license.

C. Similar risks and functions should be supervised similarly to minimize scope for regulatory arbitrage.

4. "Banklike" financial institutions should be supervised like banks. The supervisory authority should also ensure that no new activity is undertaken without the prior consent of the regulator (e.g., taking deposits).

D. The links between OFIs and other players in the financial sector should be closely monitored.

5. Exposition to risks through investment and ownership linkages (particularly with banks) should be evaluated, because those linkages make each sector vulnerable to adverse development in other sectors.

E. The unique risks of OFIs should be recognized within the supervisory structure and when defining prudential norms.

6. There should be a dedicated focus within the institutional framework to recognize those unique risks of the regulation and supervision of OFIs, whether financial institutions are under a unified or a separate supervisory framework.

7. When appropriate, prudential norms ought to be specifically defined for OFIs. The following set of regulations will commonly require reexamination: minimum statutory capital, capital adequacy ratio, asset classification, provisioning, liquidity, acquisition, and investment.

F. Supervision should be proportionate and consistent with costs and benefits.

8. Simple and less-risky institutions should not be burdened by the full regulatory requirements imposed on more-complex and riskier institutions.

G. Resources and skills should be targeted to the higher-impact and more-complex OFIs.

9. The frequency of offsite supervision and the depth of onsite supervision should consider the scale of the institution to avoid having scarce supervisory resources be wasted or institutions be saddled with unnecessary compliance burdens.
10. Staff members responsible for supervising OFIs should have the resources and skills to understand the specific risk related to those institutions. The methodology used should help identify sources of risks (credit, market, liquidity, operational, legal, and reputation), as well as risk management practice.
11. Supervisory staff members should have guidelines to provide direction to reach appropriate conclusions on a consistent basis.
12. Staff members should have access to training for upgrading their skills to ensure that regulatory and supervisory frameworks meet the industry's needs.

H. There should be a strengthening of the self-regulatory capacity.

13. Associations can play an important role in representing the OFIs' views on appropriate regulatory and supervisory frameworks. They can also voice the opinions of the market participants to government authorities, particularly when there is no regulatory body directly involved with the regulation. Moreover, they can provide educational, promotional, legal, financial, and other services tailored to the needs of the OFIs.

Notes

1. See IMF (2004a) for the definition of deposit taker and Other Financial Corporation (OFC). This Handbook uses the term Other Financial Intermediary (OFI) instead of OFC to avoid confusion with references to Offshore Financial Centers. IMF (2004a) uses the term deposit takers as units that engage in financial intermediation as a principal activity and that have liabilities in the form of deposits payable on demand, transferable by checks, or otherwise used for making payments. Or they have liabilities in the form of instruments that may not be readily transferable such as certificates of deposits, but that are close substitutes for deposits and are included in measures of broad money.
2. This section is partly drawn from Carmichael and Pomerleano (2002).

3. Where the institutions are the beneficiaries of government tax incentives, subsidies, or other privileges, there is a case for imposing reporting requirements, additional disclosures, and even inspections and audit requirements to ensure that the incentives and privileges are not subject to abuse.

4. Comprehensive standards addressing financial instruments are essential if an accounting standards regime is to be credible. The International Accounting Standard (IAS) Board provides guidance for all financial instruments not only on disclosure and presentation (IAS 32), but also on recognition and measurement (IAS 39) at fair value or at amortized cost. See http://www.iasplus.com/standard/ias39.htm and chapter 10, section 10.2.

5. In some countries, the leasing industry is one part of the financial system that is not burdened by heavy government regulations. In the absence of a leasing law, however, leasing regulations are usually fragmented and unclear. Many countries have opted for a separate leasing law to avoid confusion and to clearly define the rights and obligations of the various parties (see International Finance Corporation 1996).

6. World Bank (1994) describes Pillar 1 as noncontributory state pension; Pillar 2, mandatory contributory; and Pillar 3, voluntary contributory. This classification is useful to the discussion of the social safety net, the redistribution of income, and the fiscal aspects of pensions.

7. For a discussion of risk management issues in the pension fund industry, see IMF (2004b).

References

Amembal, Sudhir P., Loni L. Lowder, and Jonathan M. Ruga. 2000. *International Leasing: The Complete Guide*. Salt Lake City, UT: Amembal Associates.

Bakker, Marie H. R., Leora Klapper, and Gregory F. Udell. 2004. *Financing Small- and Medium-Size Enterprises with Factoring: Global Growth in Factoring—and Its Potential in Eastern Europe*. Washington, DC: World Bank.

Bank for International Settlements, 1997. *Core Principles for Effective Banking Supervision*. Basel, Switzerland: Bank for International Settlements.

Carmichael, Jeffrey, and Michael Pomerleano. 2002. *The Development and Regulation of Non-Bank Financial Institutions*. Washington, DC: World Bank.

Herring, Richard, and Anthony Santomero. 1999. "What Is Optimal Financial Regulation." Financial Institutions Center, The Wharton School, University of Pennsylvania, Philadelphia.

International Finance Corporation. 1996. "Leasing in Emerging Markets." International Finance Corporation, Washington, DC.

————. 1998. "Overview of Legislation on Leasing: Recommendations on Legal Framework." International Finance Corporation, Russia Leasing Development Group. Available at http://www2.ifc.org/russianleasing/eng/analit/2/2.htm#num5.

IMF (International Monetary Fund). 2004a. Compilation Guide on Financial Soundness Indicators. Washington, DC: International Monetary Fund. Available at http://www.imf.org/external/np/sta/fsi/eng/2004/guide/index.htm.

————. 2004b. "Risk Management and the Pension Fund Industry." In *Global Financial Stability Report: Markets and Issues, 81–120.* Washington, DC: International Monetary Fund. Available at http://www.imf.org/External/Pubs/FT/GFSR/2004/02/pdf/chp3.pdf.

OECD (Organisation for Economic Co-operation and Development). 2002. "Highlights of Recent Trends in Financial Markets." *Financial Market Trends* 81 (April): 1–47. Available at http://www.oecd.org/dataoecd/19/1/2080704.pdf.

Sopranzetti, Ben J. 1998. "The Economics of Factoring Accounts Receivable." *Journal of Economics and Business* 50 (4): 339–59. Available at http://www.sciencedirect.com/science/article/B6V7T-3X6J8JJ-2/2/989f666d01da736e1ef28877aba328e4#fn1.

World Bank. 1994. *Averting the Old Age Crisis: Policies to Protect the Old and Promote Growth.* World Bank Policy Research Papers. New York: Oxford University Press.

————.1989. *World Development Report: Financial Systems and Development.* Washington, DC: World Bank.

————. 2001. *Finance for Growth: Policy Choices in a Volatile World.* Washington, DC: World Bank.

6

Chapter 7

Rural and Microfinance Institutions: Regulatory and Supervisory Issues

7.1 Overview

The providing of financial services to the poor and the very-poor, particularly in rural areas, is the purpose of microfinance institutions (MFIs), and the assessment of the regulatory framework for MFIs is part of broader assessment of adequacy of access. Access, however, is multidimensional, and assessing its adequacy requires a review of (a) the range of financial services provided—and target groups served—by several tiers of formal, semiformal, and informal financial institutions; (b) the demand for financial services from households, microenterprises, and small businesses at different levels of the income strata; and (c) the different combinations of financial service providers, the users of those services, and the range of services that prevail in different geographical segments of the market. The primary objectives of the assessment of the adequacy of access are (a) to identify the gaps that exist (and that need to be corrected) in the range of products that are available for different layers of households, microenterprises, and small businesses in various geographic markets; and (b) to assess whether the regulatory framework for financial transactions helps expand or restrict access to the needed financial services.

7.2 Rationale for Assessing the Regulatory Framework for Rural Finance and Microfinance Institutions

The core objectives for the regulatory framework are the same for microfinance activities and institutions as for other components and segments of the overall financial system. However, the key principles and standards for the design of a regulatory framework for institutions providing financial services to the rural finance and microfinance sector are likely to be different from those for formal banking and finance institutions, because the design must consider the operational, market, and client characteristics of the rural finance and microfinance sector. This section focuses on the regulatory framework issues that have an important influence on access to financial services for low-income rural households.

The term *financial services* extends beyond the traditional credit products and savings deposits facilities provided to varying degrees by different types of rural finance and microfinance institutions. See section 7.3 and table 7.1 in that section for a listing and discussion of various types of MFIs, including those linked to nongovernmental organizations (NGOs) and various non-bank institutions). The term includes payments, money transfer and remittance services, and insurance and contractual savings products. It is important to focus on access to payments and savings products by different segments of the population and the supply of those products by different institutions. Payment and savings products are often the most important financial services for low-income households. Improved access to savings product can help households achieve higher returns on their savings and smoother cash flows, and can reduce vulnerability to external shocks.

The degree and quality of access to financial services available to low-income rural households and their small businesses is influenced by the quality of the legal and regulatory framework. This framework should be guided by the following core principles of good microfinance: (a) to provide a level playing field among participants in the provision of a range of financial services beyond credit and savings facilities; (b) to allow the institutional transformation of nontraditional and non-regulated MFIs (such as multipurpose and microcredit NGOs) into specialized, regulated, or licensed rural finance and microfinance intermediaries; (c) to promote and reward transparency in financial accounting and transaction reporting; and (d) to foster the exchange and sharing of credit histories of borrowing clients.

Available data and information show that deeper, more-efficient financial markets can contribute to accelerated agricultural growth and better food security. Scaling-up access in rural markets to a wider array of financial services through a varied range of financial intermediaries becomes critical to help low-income rural households smooth consumption and enhance labor productivity, which is the most important production factor controlled by the poor. Also, agriculture has strong forward and backward multiplier effects for the overall economy. Economic growth in agriculture is a key precondition for overall economic growth and poverty reduction, given that most of the world's poor still live in rural areas (Robinson 2001; Zeller 2003).

There are examples of agricultural development banks, MFIs, and credit unions developing strong rural portfolios, while commercial banks do not generally seem to fit this market niche as readily. Some MFIs have tried to transform from nongovernmental status to a regulated, supervised financial institution; however, with notable exceptions, this has not proven to be a reliable route to improved rural outreach of financial services. In general, commercial banks have not entered the rural and agricultural credit markets on a substantial scale in most developing countries, despite incentives designed to encourage downscaling and rural market penetration.

In a few countries, agricultural development banks have succeeded in transforming themselves into more-sustainable institutions by offering demand-driven financial services, building credible lending contracts, and using full-cost recovery interest rates. The experiences of Thailand's Bank for Agriculture and Agricultural Cooperatives (BAAC, Bank Rakyat Indonesia's (BRI) village units in its microbanking system (Yaron and Charitonenko 1999; Zeller 2003), and the revival and restructuring for privatization of Mongolia's Agricultural Bank (Boomgard, Boyer, and Dyer 2003) and of Tanzania's National Microfinance Bank demonstrate that state-owned banks can be transformed into dynamic, profitable, and successful rural-oriented financial intermediaries with business-oriented management reforms. Of course, such transformation of state owned banks can be achieved only with firm political commitment, ownership of reforms, management autonomy, and incentives (Zeller 2003).

Group-based models have built impressive portfolios in rural markets; savings and loan cooperatives and credit unions have grown rapidly in diverse settings.[1] Emphasis on the importance of large-scale operations, internal systems, attractive products, and portfolio quality has contributed to improvements in performance. In addition, the village banking methodology[2] pioneered by FINCA International has shown, in many cases, that rural community-based and self-managed financial entities can become self-sustaining. This model was later adapted with changes by CARE, Catholic Relief Services, World Vision, and even a few commercial banks.

Several MFIs have shown that they can profitably serve large numbers of relatively poor households, microenterprises, and small businesses. Although the client base is typically in peri-urban markets or in off-farm business activities in rural markets, those experiences have renewed interest in the feasibility of reorienting rural finance and microfinance institutions. There is a growing list of MFIs that have moved beyond their initial urban client base to tailor their products to rural clients, including the Equity Building Society in Kenya, CrediAmigo, a bank-affiliated MFI in Brazil and the Development Bank of Brazil (BNDES), MiBanco in Peru, Financiera Calpia in El Salvador, and Basix India Ltd, a micro–credit institution serving the rural poor in India. The experiences of these MFIs point toward the possibilities of adaptation and replication by other MFIs operating in predominantly rural markets.

The rural finance and microfinance sector is small relative to the commercial financial sector, with limited effect on the overall stability of the financial system. In a large number of developing countries, the total loans outstanding in the rural finance and microfinance sector was about 1 percent of broad money supply (M2), with this sector reaching fewer than 1 percent of the population as clients. A handful of countries stand out from the rest with higher levels of microfinance outreach and penetration, especially in Indonesia (6.5 percent); Thailand (6.2 percent); Vietnam and Sri Lanka (4.5 percent); Bangladesh and Cambodia (3.0 percent); Malawi (2.5 percent); and Bolivia, El Salvador, Honduras, India, and Nicaragua (at 1.0 percent or slightly more) (Honohan 2004).[3]

7.3 Institutional Providers of Rural Finance and Microfinance Services

The distinction between microfinance and small and medium enterprise (SME) finance and the recognition of the different types of financial institutions catering to those

7

segments are important to the assessment of the adequacy of access and the effect of regulation. While different categories of borrowers often face similar constraints, lenders commonly distinguish between microfinance, which refers to credit provided to poor households and to informal (i.e., unregistered) microenterprises, and SME finance, which refers to credit given to enterprises registered as large microenterprises, small businesses, and medium-size enterprises.

There are several important differences between the two categories of borrowers. Microfinance is most often provided by non-bank institutions such as NGO MFIs that are often based on the group-lending approach (although numerous microfinance loans may consist of loans to individuals rather than to groups), as well as various membership-based financial cooperatives and mutual-assistance associations. SME finance is provided mainly by banks, building societies, and non-bank financial institutions (NBFIs) and does not use a group-lending approach. Another important difference is security: Microfinance is almost never formally secured, although informal security (i.e., not legally binding) in the form of collateral interest over household goods and tools is commonly used, while SME finance usually allows a firm's assets or personal guarantees to legally secure small business loans. Those differences create a natural separation between the institutions that specialize mainly in microfinance and the institutions that provide small business loans, although some institutions do provide both kinds of finance services.

Institutional providers of financial services to low-income rural households, microenterprises, and small businesses fall into several categories according to the scope of regulation, type of ownership, and type of services offered. The institutions can be differentiated on (a) whether they are required to obtain a license to carry out financial intermediation activities, to be registered with some central agency (but not required to obtain a license) that will provide nondeposit credit-only services, or to be registered as a legal entity; (b) what type of organizational format, including ownership and governance aspects, they have; and (c) what types of financial services are permitted and provided. The principal categories are

- government programs or agencies for rural finance, microfinance, or SME finance
- non-bank, nonprofit NGO MFIs
- membership-based cooperative financial institutions (CFIs)
- postal savings banks (PSBs) or institutions
- development finance institutions
- specialized banking institutions (usually licensed for limited operations, activities, or services to differentiate them from full-service commercial banks) such as rural banks, microfinance banks, and non-bank finance companies
- commercial banks

Key differences in the organization and operation of those different institutions are highlighted in table 7.1. The institutions differ in terms of what products and services they are allowed by law and regulation to offer; whether they are subject to rigorous prudential regulation, internal governance structure, and accountability; and how funds for administrative and business operations are sourced. The differences arise from the applicability of legal and regulatory requirements, and those differences have important

Table 7.1. Institutional Providers of Financial Services

Institutional provider	Organizational format	Ownership	Regulatory status and how regulated	Financial services permitted to be offered
Government rural or micro or SME finance programs or agencies	Trust fund or agency	Government	Not regulated by banking authority	Wholesale or onlending funds to participating institutions
Non-bank/nonprofit/ NGO MFIs	Nonprofit foundation, trust, or association	Private sector entities or organizations	Not regulated by banking authority	Microfinance loans only; no voluntary deposits
Membership-based cooperative financial institutions (CFIs)	Savings and credit cooperative organization (SACCO) or credit union	Members	Not regulated by banking authority, but may be regulated by department in cooperative	Savings and time deposits and loans to members only
Postal savings banks (PSBs)	State-chartered institution	Government	Not regulated by banking authority	Savings and time (fixed) deposits only and money transfers
Development finance institutions	State-chartered institution	Government	May or may not be regulated by banking authority	Wholesale certificates of deposit, loans, and credits
Specialized banking institutions				
Rural banks	Limited liability company	Private sector investors or shareholders	Licensed or supervised by banking authority	Savings and time deposits, loans, and money transfers
Microfinance banks	Limited liability company	Private sector investors or shareholders	Licensed or supervised by banking authority	Savings deposits, microfinance loans, and money transfers
Non-bank finance companies	Limited liability company	Private sector investors or shareholders	Licensed but not necessarily supervised by banking authority	Wholesale certificates of deposit, loans, and credits
Commercial banks	Limited liability company	Private sector investors or shareholders, or state-owned institution	Licensed or supervised by banking authority	Demand and savings and time deposits, loans, credits, money transfers, and foreign exchange; full banking services

7

implications for the outreach and sustainability of the institutions. For indicators of structure, outreach, and performance of MFIs, see box 7.1.

Not all institutional providers of financial services listed in table 7.1 may exist in a given country for a number of important reasons, including the stage of development of the rural finance and microfinance sector. In a number of countries, rural finance and microfinance services may be provided by several types of institutions.

7.3.1 Government Rural Finance, Microfinance, or SME Finance Programs or Agencies

The direct provision of rural finance, microfinance, and SME finance loans and credit facilities by government agencies or programs should be noted and examined in the assessment of adequacy of access. Those government programs usually have an unfair

7

Box 7.1 Benchmarks for Outreach and Financial Performance and Soundness of Rural Finance and Microfinance Institutions

Standards and indicators for the breadth and depth of outreach, the operating and financial performance, and the financial soundness of rural finance and microfinance institutions have been developed by an international network of donors and practitioners. Those standards and indicators have been adopted by prudential supervisory agencies and regulatory authorities in a number of countries. Among the more prominent examples are the standards and indicators developed and detailed in the monitoring systems developed by ACCION International (ACCION "CAMEL"), World Council of Credit Unions (WOCCU "PEARLS") and Microfinance Information eXchange (MIX). For purposes of comparison with and reference to best practices, the benchmarking standards published periodically by WOCCU, MIX (MicroBanking Bulletin), MicroRate, and Microfinance Centre for Central and Eastern Europe (CEE) and the Newly Independent States (NIS) are easily accessible. Those benchmarks can be useful in carrying out the assessment of adequacy of access for rural finance and microfinance institutions, and are summarized here.

- Breadth and depth of outreach
  - number of deposit accounts (because some institutions such as postal savings banks [PSBs] provide only deposit services)
  - number of active borrowers, and as a percentage of total population and of population at or below poverty line

- average loan balance or amount per borrower, and as a percentage of (a) gross national product (GNP) per capita and (b) national poverty income level

- Financial structure
  - ratio of institutional capital to average total assets
  - ratio of equity to debt
  - ratio of average total loans outstanding to average total assets
  - commercial funding (market-price liabilities) as a percentage of gross loan portfolio

- Overall financial performance and soundness
  - adjusted Return on Assets (ROA)
  - adjusted Return on Equity (ROE)
  - operational self-sufficiency (revenue from loans, investments, and other financial services as a percentage of administrative and operating expenses)
  - financial self-sufficiency (revenue from loans, investments, and other financial services as a percentage of financial or interest expenses, loan-loss provisions, and administrative and operating expenses)
  - on-time loan repayment rate
  - portfolio at risk overdue greater than 30 days as a percentage of gross loan portfolio
  - loan–loss reserve as a percentage of portfolio at risk overdue greater than 30 days

---

competitive advantage over and tend to crowd out the private sector-based providers of similar financial services to households, microenterprises, and small businesses. In a number of countries, state-owned development finance institutions or specialized banks are the institutional vehicles used. The key issues to address in the assessment, aside from whether the institutional vehicles are reaching their target sector or client base and have, in fact, contributed to the development and expansion of the target sector, are (a) efficiency of loan collection, (b) incidence of loan defaults and adequacy of loan-loss provisions, (c) claims on budgetary or fiscal resources for loan guarantees and additional capital to cover operating losses, and (d) level of solvency or insolvency.

7.3.2 Non-bank, Non-profit NGO MFIs

Non-bank, non-profit NGO MFIs include (a) mixed-purpose NGOs that have credit provisions in their socially oriented activities and (b) specialized credit-only MFIs. Those MFIs are generally private sector-owned institutions and are typically organized as nonprofit foundations, trusts, or associations. In a number of cases, the MFIs are organized as formally incorporated entities under a country's Companies Act. Some MFIs are stand-alone local entities, while others may be affiliated with or sponsored by international NGOs such as FINCA, CARE, Catholic Relief Services, World Vision, ACCION International, and Women's World Banking. The geographical reach of their operations vary depending on their organizational and legal status and on the type of NGO sponsor, with some MFIs operating only at the district or county level others on a province-wide or region-wide basis, and a few on a nationwide scale.

7.3.3 Membership-Based CFIs

CFIs are (a) multipurpose cooperative associations (e.g., producers, services, marketing, and rural cooperatives) that include savings and credit functions; and (b) single-purpose, membership-based, financial cooperative organizations (e.g., credit unions and savings and credit cooperative organizations [SACCOs]). CFIs, which have been in existence in many countries much longer than non-bank, nonprofit NGO MFIs, are clearly distinguishable from the NGO MFIs in that their financial transactions (deposit taking and credit giving) are generally limited to registered members under a closed- or open-common bond, typically defined by geography (residence), occupation, or place of employment. The rights and privileges of ownership in CFIs are based on the one person–one vote principle, and management is exercised by members–owners. In general, CFIs will outnumber NGO MFIs in many countries, and their combined outreach will tend to be larger as well.

7.3.4 Postal Savings Banks

A PSB has the ability to reach a very large number of depositors for savings and time deposits in generally small amounts, and to provide payments and transfer or remittance services, particularly in the rural areas in a number of countries, including Azerbaijan, Kenya, Pakistan, and Tanzania. However, PSBs are limited to deposit-taking and payment services and do not extend credit. PSBs are intended primarily to provide a safe and secure facility for the small savings of poor and low-income households, especially in rural areas, even though the management and boards of PSBs may be tempted to expand into rural finance and microfinance lending services to improve earnings. In practice, the priority should be on improving efficiency, cost-effectiveness, and governance before broadening the asset portfolio beyond safe assets such as bank deposits and government issues.

7.3.5 Development Finance Institutions

In many countries, Development Finance Institutions (DFIs) have been established and funded by the Government to develop and promote certain strategic sectors of the economy (e.g., highly capital intensive investments, the agricultural sector) and to achieve social goals. DFIs are expected primarily to fill in the gaps in the supply of financial services that are not normally provided by the banking institutions. The DFIs also play a crucial role in the development of SMEs, the housing sector, and in some countries microcredit. The key issue to monitor is the extent to which DFIs are accorded special benefits in the form of funding at lower rates, implicit government guarantees to the institutions's debts, favourable tax treatment etc.

7.3.6 Specialized Banking Institutions

The regulatory framework for banking and finance in a number of countries also covers lower-tier licensed banks that have the legal capability for deposit-taking activities (generally limited to savings and fixed deposits) and for providing loans, but the capability excludes trust and investment services and foreign exchange or trading facilities. In some countries, banking activities may be limited to the geographical market area that is serviced (county or district, province, or region). The limited-service banking institutions, (e.g., rural banks and microfinance banks) are subject to prudential supervision by a country's central supervisory authority, and they are required to comply with reporting requirements and with applicable prudential standards. Non-bank finance companies involved in rural finance, microfinance, and SME finance—which do not take retail public deposits but are permitted to fund their operations and loan portfolios through commercial borrowings and wholesale, large-value, institutional deposits—are generally required to register and to obtain a license. However, those companies may not be prudentially supervised by a country's central supervisory authority.

7.3.7 Commercial Banks

Commercial banks may have direct participation in low-income markets as a result of their complying with directed or credit quota policies of government for targeted sectors. Sometimes, banks have indirect involvement in rural and microfinance as depositories of the operating funds of MFIs and CFIs, or they have involvement through commercially priced wholesale loans and credit facilities to MFIs and CFIs as bank clients. An important area to focus on is the existence of vertical and horizontal business relationships between commercial banks, on the one hand, and MFIs and CFIs, on the other. The importance of this point stems from the synergistic relationships that the smaller MFIs and CFIs can form with the larger commercial institutions from the formal sector, whereby the combination can reach a larger number of clients with resources than may be obtained from the latter large institution at commercial—not subsidized—rates and terms.

7.4 Conceptual Framework for the Regulation of Rural Finance and Microfinance Institutions

The aim of a supportive regulatory framework is to build strong regulated and unregulated institutions of all types (a) to provide services on a sustainable basis under uniform, common, shared performance standards and (b) to encourage the regulatory authority to develop appropriate prudential regulations and staff capacity that are tailored to the institutions' operational and risk profiles. This objective requires defining different tiers of financial institutions with different degrees of regulatory requirements. The requirements could vary from (a) simply registering as legal entities, to (b) preparing and publishing periodic reports on operations and financial results, to (c) observing non-prudential rules of conduct in business operations, to (d) securing a proper license and being subject to prudential regulation by a regulatory authority, prudential supervision, or both by a central supervisory authority. Lower-tiers institutions serving the lower end of the market can enable non-bank microlenders to seek greater formalization without actual licensing.

As the rural finance and microfinance sector grows, adding a licensing tier that permits MFIs to legally mobilize savings and other commercial sources of funds can encourage capacity building and innovation that are aimed at self-sufficiency and greater outreach. Another approach that has been used is to open a special window for micro-lending as a product that enables commercial banks, as well as alternative specialized institutions, to benefit from different cost and regulatory structures. Licensing of rural and community banks can also facilitate the emergence of new types of MFIs that serve specific markets. However, the premature creation of special tiers with easy entry may result in weak institutions, may affect the development of the commercial financial system, and may risk overwhelming inadequate supervisory resources.[4]

Thus, the licensing of MFIs should be designed to balance promotional and prudential objectives. The main potential threats pertaining to deposit-taking MFIs are that (a) deposit-taking MFIs could collapse, thus adversely affecting the commercial system, and that (b) prudential regulation of deposit-taking MFIs could prove to be an administrative burden that distracts supervisors from adequately protecting the safety and soundness of the main financial system. The Consultative Group to Assist the Poorest (CGAP) *Microfinance Consensus Guidelines* (Christen, Lyman, and Rosenberg 2003) takes a balanced view, arguing that deposit taking on a small scale may essentially go unsupervised—especially where the deposits consist of only forced-savings components of the lending product, so that most depositors are net borrowers from the MFI at most times. This approach would leave the supervisory apparatus unencumbered from having to deal in-depth with a profusion of tiny MFIs.

A consensus on the framework for the regulation of rural finance and microfinance institutions has evolved on the basis of country experiences in recent years. This framework (summarized in table 7.2) identifies different categories and tiers of institutional providers of microfinance, and it specifies the thresholds of financial intermediation activities that trigger the need for progressively stronger types of regulation and supervision. The legal and regulatory framework for banking and finance in many countries may not include lower tiers for rural finance and microfinance banks. Some countries may be in the process of establishing the legal and regulatory framework specifically to create new tiers for rural finance or microfinance banks, which usually have a limited geographical coverage specified by law. Regulation of microfinance activities and institutions may take three main forms: (a) simple registration as a legal entity; (b) non-prudential regulations that provide standards of business operations and oversight, such as operating and financial reports to be submitted, to protect the interests of clients or members; and (c) full prudential supervision. Global experience illustrates that the benefits from regulating microfinance may be limited when commercial banking standards are applied to MFIs without adequate consideration of microfinance methodologies.

Non-bank finance companies and other types of registered institutions providing rural finance and microfinance services are not subject to statutory prudential regulation and

Table 7.2. Tiered Structures and Regulatory Triggers by Type of MFI

Type of microfinance institution (MFI)	Activities that trigger regulation	Forms of external regulation	Recommended regulatory authority
Informal savings and credit groups funded by members fees and savings	None	None required	None required
Category A: Nongovernmental organizations (NGOs) funded by donor funds			
Category A1: Funding only from grants	None, if total loans do not exceed donated funds, grants, and accumulated surplus	Registration as a nonprofit society, association, or trust	A registrar of societies or self-regulating body, if any
Category A2: Funding from donor grants and from commercial borrowings or securities issues	Generating liabilities through borrowings to fund microloan portfolio and operations	Registration as a legal corporate entity; authorization by a banking authority or securities commission	A registrar of companies, banking authority, or securities agency
Category B: Financial cooperatives and credit unions funded members' money and savings	Accepting deposits from and making loans to members	Registration as a financial cooperative	A registrar of cooperatives or banking authority
Category C: Special-licensed banks and MFIs funded by the public's money (deposits, investor capital, and commercial borrowings)	Accepting wholesale and retail public deposits for intermediation into loans and investments	Registration as a corporate legal entity; licensing as a finance company or bank (with full prudential requirements)	A registrar of cooperatives or banking authority

Note: This regulatory framework for the classification of MFIs was originally proposed by van Greuning, Gallardo, and Randhawa (1999) and modified by Randhawa (2003). Except for informal groups, MFIs are classified into four categories that are based on the structure of their liabilities (i.e., sources of funding). Cooperatives in category B have a long but inefficient history of regulation. If their deposit taking is small in scale and limited to their members, they should be given low regulatory priority. Category C should not include MFIs that require mandatory savings to secure loans as long as most customers are net borrowers most of the time. Formal banks with a microfinance department are not included in this regulatory framework because they are subject to prudential supervision, even if it is usually not adapted to the specific features of this segment of the financial system.

supervision by a central supervisory authority, because they do not mobilize retail deposits from the public and intermediate those deposits into loans and investments. Nevertheless, such institutions should observe and adhere to a set of rules and standards with respect to the conduct of their business operations to provide protection for their borrowing customers and for third-party providers of wholesale commercial funds, even though commercial fund providers and institutional investors are presumed to be well informed and to be capable of any required due diligence.[5] An overview of desirable standards for conduct of business is provided in box 7.2.

7.5 Assessment of the Regulatory Framework Issues for Rural Finance and Microfinance Institutions

The assessment of the regulatory framework for the rural finance and microfinance sector covers both the institutional aspects and the benchmarks used to evaluate the sector's performance and soundness. The considerations include (a) assessing the need for prudential supervision versus non-prudential regulation and for the technical capacity for supervi-

---

Box 7.2 Conduct of Business Regulations for MFIs

Listed below are basic standards and rules covering the conduct of business operations of "non-prudentially regulated" non-bank finance companies and other types of registered institutions providing rural and microfinance services. Generally, company registration laws and regulations require legally registered companies to prepare and submit audited annual reports and financial statements to the registry agency. Because there may not be any onsite examination or supervision by a regulatory body, the burden of observance and compliance falls substantially on an institution's internal governance structure and, without doubt, on the institutions that may be the sources for wholesale funds.

- adherence to and use of uniform accounting standards and procedures for internal and external reporting of operating and financial results

- annual reports on operating and financial results, which have been reviewed by acceptable external auditors and that include periodic reporting and publication of financial results
- written policies and procedures approved by the institution's board and management covering loan approval and documentation; loan account aging, classification, and provisioning for possible loan losses; loan delinquency control processes; loan loss write-offs; and internal audit and control systems
- observance of industry standards with respect to debt-to-equity ratio, equity-to-risk assets ratio, short-term assets-to-short-term liabilities ratio, portfolio at risk (loans overdue greater than 30 days as a percentage of total loan portfolio), and portfolio at risk coverage (provisions and reserves for loan losses as a percentage of portfolio at risk)

---

sion, as well as the costs of that supervision; (b) determining which agency should carry out the supervision or regulation, and whether delegated or auxiliary supervision may be warranted or justified; and (c) establishing benchmarks and standards for evaluating outreach and for financial performance and soundness. In addition, certain cross-cutting issues—taxes that may obstruct more effective outreach and costs, and credit information-sharing systems that can help MFIs manage loan delinquencies and reduce costs—need to be considered. Also, PSBs and CFIs—though significant components of the rural finance and microfinance sector—are often excluded from the scope of the regulatory framework. However, an analytical evaluation of their outreach, operating performance, and financial soundness—as well as the primary problems they face or may pose to the rest of the sector—may be an important aspect of the assessment of adequacy of access. A discussion of regulatory issues relating to PSBs and CFIs is contained in box 7.3.

Some key questions in assessing the regulatory framework of rural finance and microfinance institutions include the following:

- Is there a need to regulate (but not prudentially supervise) those other institutions? If so, what is the scope of the regulation? Very often the distinctions between broad regulatory oversight (sometimes called *non-prudential regulation*) and detailed prudential supervision are ignored in a number of countries. Inappropriate regulatory approach has led to the misallocation of scarce supervisory and staff resources in the attempt to impose prudential standards and requirements on rural finance and microfinance institutions that are not engaged in mobilizing and intermediating public deposits, a step that poses a systemic risk. Prudential supervision involves the regulatory authorities' verifying the compliance of institutions with mandatory

7

Box 7.3 PSBs and CFIs and the Scope of Their Regulation

Postal savings banks (PSBs) are generally not included in the prudential regulatory framework for banking and financial institutions, which can aggravate weaknesses that often exist in the PSBs' internal governance structure and accountability processes. Individual members' deposits in PSBs are not included in formal deposit insurance or in protection schemes (when those schemes exist), but they are implicitly guaranteed by the government. Thus, the risk exists for potential claims on the government treasury or budget in the event of losses from mismanagement or fraud. Furthermore, savings and time deposits collected by PSBs are not intermediated into rural finance or microfinance loans, but they are often used to help fund treasury or budget operations by the requirement that PSBs' investments be limited to government treasury bills and bonds.

Cooperative financial institutions (CFIs) offer important potential ways to decentralize the access to financial services, particularly in rural areas that banks and commercial microfinance institutions (MFIs) may find too costly to reach. In many countries, CFIs constitute an important and comparatively large segment of the rural finance and microfinance sector in terms of the number of institutions and their membership base. Governments, as well as the donor community,

need to focus more attention on measures to treat CFIs as part of the financial services segment, rather than as part of the cooperative segment. There have been only a few cases of countries adopting specialized laws and regulations for CFIs.

Individual members' deposits in CFIs may be protected when a deposit insurance fund has been established privately by an upper-level regional or national cooperatives federation. While the deposits of a CFI with a commercial bank may be included in formal deposit insurance or protection schemes (when those schemes exist), the recognized legal depositor is the CFI, not the individual members who may own the deposits. There exists the risk of potential claims on the government treasury or budget in the event of losses from mismanagement or fraud, if the CFI segment of the rural finance and microfinance sector is fairly large.

As a closed-circuit financial system, deposits collected by CFIs from individual members are intermediated into rural finance or microfinance loans to members only, but there are instances where CFIs effectively offer deposit services to nonmembers and the general public, because the "common bond" for membership is loosely specified.

---

standards—such as minimum capital levels and adequacy, liquidity management ratios, and asset quality standards—as measures for financial soundness. Prudential supervision of deposit-taking category C institutions (see table 7.2) is aimed at protecting public savings that are being mobilized and lent out or intermediated, which puts public savings at risk of being lost if loans are not repaid. In contrast, for various categories of institutions—institutions in category A2 and similar institutions in category B—may require only non-prudential supervision or regulatory oversight, as outlined in table 7.2.

- Which agency should regulate the institutions? An important issue is the extent to which regulatory authority should be centralized, delegated, or decentralized (see box 7.4 for further discussion). Box 7.5 contains a further discussion of supervision standards, technical capacity and cost considerations that enter into the assessments.

Box 7.4 Critical Issues in Delegating Prudential Supervision

Delegated supervision covers arrangements where the central banking and financial institutions supervisor delegates direct supervision of an identified set of institutions to a body or agency outside the central supervisory authority, while monitoring and controlling that other body's or agency's supervisory work (see Christen, Lyman, and Rosenberg 2003). Limited examples of delegated supervision are being used for microfinance institutions (MFIs); thus, there is little experience to date on the effectiveness of this approach.

If the approach were to be applied even on an interim basis, it is critical to answer the following questions in advance (see Christen, Lyman, and Rosenberg 2003):

- Who bears the costs (which may be substantial) of the delegated or auxiliary supervisory agency and the additional costs of the central supervi-

sory authority's oversight and monitoring of the agency?

- Should the delegated or auxiliary supervision arrangement prove to be unreliable or ineffective, and should the mandate to the delegated or auxiliary supervisory agency need to be withdrawn, does a realistic and practicable fallback or alternative option exist for the central supervisory authority?

- In the event that a supervised institution fails, which agency—the central supervisory authority or the delegated or auxiliary supervisory agency—will have the authority and capability to clean up and rectify the situation by suspension, intervention, or liquidation?

- Does a delegated or auxiliary supervisory agency bear any legal liabilities in the exercise of the delegated or auxiliary responsibilities?

7.6. Some Cross-Cutting Issues Affecting Rural Finance and Microfinance Institutions

Tax issues may present obstacles to rural finance and microfinance institutions from more effectively providing access to financial services. The legal and nonprofit status of non-bank NGO MFIs may sometimes be questioned by tax authorities on the grounds that the credit services they are providing to their clientele are priced at commercial rates, rather than at "charitable" levels, as in the case of NGO MFIs in India. In other instances, licensed specialized banks and non-bank finance institutions may not be permitted by tax accounting laws and regulations to expense provisions for possible loan losses, in spite of prudential regulations issued by the central supervisory authority, as in Tanzania, which creates an unnecessary real economic burden to such specialized banks and non-bank finance institutions. A related problem stems from the requirement by tax authorities that delinquent loans may be written off only when the sale and disposition of collateral securing such a defaulted loan results in recovering a monetary value that is less than the value of the collateral, as in the case of Kenya.

Credit registries allow borrowers to build up a credit history and can assist lenders in assessing risk, thereby reducing the cost of lending and improving access. Credit registries that give easy and reliable access to a client's credit history can dramatically reduce the time and costs of obtaining such information from individual sources and, therefore, can reduce the total costs of financial intermediation. Credit reporting makes borrower quality much more transparent, which benefits good borrowers and increases the cost of defaulting on obligations. It helps borrowers build up a credit history and eases access to credit. Credit registries are especially important for SMEs, because their creditworthiness is more difficult to evaluate and because they have less visibility and transparency relative to large enterprises.

Often, current regulations may provide for the sharing of only negative information (i.e., information on nonperforming loans). It is preferable that regulations allow for sharing of both positive and negative information to improve reliability of credit risk evaluation and to increase competition.[6] Reporting positive information significantly increases the predictability of rating and scoring models used by lenders, thereby translating into lower loss rates, higher acceptance rates of credit applicants, or both (see Staten 2001). Sharing positive information will also allow borrowers to build their credit history, which can especially benefit small borrowers, because it will allow them to establish a good borrowing reputation and to improve their chances to increase borrowings as their business grows. Regulations governing information sharing should also allow for adequate consumer and data protection mechanisms. Allowing all finance providers to share both positive and negative information on their borrowers will allow small business to participate in

---

Box 7.5 Supervision Standards, Technical Capacity, and Cost Issues

In an assessment of the prudential regulatory and supervisory framework for microfinance, the following key questions need to be addressed:

- Are the prudential standards applied to specialized banks and financial institutions in the rural finance and microfinance sector consistent with and adapted to the nature and characteristics of the market clientele they service (e.g., microfinance loans are short term, repeating, and unsecured with group guarantees being widespread practice), or are the prudential standards used the same as those that apply to regular commercial banks?

- Does the central bank or supervisory authority have rural finance- or microfinance-dedicated staff members assigned to the supervision and examination of the specialized banks and financial institutions in the rural finance and microfinance sector? In a number of countries, including Kenya, Pakistan, the Philippines, and Tanzania, the supervisory authority has a separate specialized microfinance section that deals with policy issues (including appropriate standards), but actual examination and supervision of all licensed banks and financial institutions are carried out by technical staff members from the banking supervision department. In other countries, including Ghana, Indonesia, and the Philippines, rural and community banks are examined and supervised by staff members in the rural banking department of the supervisory authority.

- What is the comparative workload (number of licensed institutions, or number of days needed to complete onsite examination or supervision) of supervisory staff members assigned to commercial banks versus that of members assigned to specialized banks and financial institutions in the rural finance and microfinance sector?

- What is the judgmental assessment of the technical capability of staff members and the quality of their examination and supervision of specialized banks and financial institutions in the rural finance and microfinance sector in comparison with technical staff members responsible for commercial banks? Is this a fair comparison?

- Is it possible to estimate and compare the costs associated with the examination and supervision of specialized banks and financial institutions in the rural finance and microfinance sector in comparison with the costs for the examination and supervision of commercial banks? Is this a fair comparison?

- Does the central bank or monetary authority require the commercial banks and the specialized banks and financial institutions in the rural finance and microfinance sector to pay for or to defray the costs associated with examination and supervision? If so, what charges are imposed?

Box 7.6 Findings and Recommendations on Microfinance Regulatory Issues in Selected FSAPs

Case I: A Transition Economy	Case II: A Developing Country
Key Issues	*Key Issues*

Key Issues (Case I)

Access to financial services through microcredit programs is primarily through microfinance institutions (MFIs) and credit cooperative organizations (CCOs) registered with and licensed by the central bank. The microfinance sector is small in terms of total credit volume and number of households and enterprises reached. The most critical issues for development of the microfinance sector are (a) diversification of funding sources, as authorization for mobilizing deposits does not come automatically with licensing, even for CCO members' deposits; and (b) striking a balance between developing a safe and sustainable sector and imposing unreasonable burdens on both the regulated institutions and the regulatory authority.

Policy Recommendations (Case I)

- MFIs and CCOs should be allowed to take deposits from their members or borrowers, provided they meet established prudential norms related to expected financial and operational risks.
- The legal and regulatory environment for MFIs or CCOs that do not take deposits should be reviewed and simplified commensurate to their risk profile.
- Improvement of the regulatory and supervisory framework through better prudential reporting standards and more-effective sanctions could make supervision more effective.

Key Issues (Case II)

The regulatory regime for microfinance is uneven and tilted toward overregulation. The policy direction is unclear as to whether the provision of microfinance and small-scale finance services will depend more on formally licensed banks and institutions reaching down, or will depend on developing the scaling-up of community- or nongovernmental organization (NGO)–based MFIs, including savings and credit cooperative organizations (SACCOs).

Policy Recommendations (Case II)

- The move toward a more systematic and thorough regulatory regime for the few MFIs to be taking more than a specified amount of deposits is commendable, but smaller NGO MFIs and SACCOs able to reach remote rural areas should not be suppressed by excessive regulation.
- The development and strengthening of umbrella organizations and the greater reliance by MFIs on funding from local banks rather than external donors should be encouraged.
- A specialized agency for cooperative financial institutions should be considered for focusing on capacity building and financial infrastructure.

Sources: FSAP reports

the process of reputation building and generation of credit history. It would help facilitate the process of borrowers' graduating from microfinance to bank finance as their business develops. Information sharing among all finance providers could contribute significantly to reducing segmentation and increasing competition.

7.7 Ways to Address Rural Finance and Microfinance Regulatory Framework Issues

The core issues in the legal and regulatory framework for rural finance and microfinance will differ from one country to another because of country differences in the structure and stage of development of the rural finance and microfinance sector and because of the regulatory approach used. This difference is illustrated by highlighting key issues and policy recommendations in selected Financial Sector Assessment Program (FSAP) reports, which are summarized in box 7.6.

7.8 Consensus Guidelines on Regulating and Supervising Microfinance

CGAP published consensus guidelines approved by 29 international donor agencies that support microfinance (Christen, Lyman, and Rosenberg 2003). Those guidelines were approved by CGAP members in September 2002. The consensus guidelines list 21 key policy recommendations on regulation and supervision of microfinance, which create a good checklist of issues to focus on in the assessment of regulatory aspects that pertain to access to financial services. The particular set of key policy recommendations in the checklist that may be applicable to a given situation will vary from one country to another depending, among other things, on the range and variety of institutional providers of rural finance and microfinance services, on the size and relative importance of each type of rural finance and microfinance institution category, and on the size of the rural finance and microfinance sector relative to the formal commercial finance sector. Several of the key policy recommendations are selected for emphasis and are highlighted next:[7]

- Problems that do not require the government to oversee and attest to the financial soundness of regulated institutions should not be dealt with through prudential regulation. Relevant forms of non-prudential regulation, including regulation under the commercial or criminal codes, tend to be easier to enforce and less costly than prudential regulation.
- Before regulators decide on the timing and design of prudential regulation, they should obtain a competent financial and institutional analysis of the leading MFIs, at least if the existing MFIs are the main candidates for a new licensing window being considered.
- Minimum capital needs to be set high enough so that the supervisory authority is not overwhelmed by more new institutions than it can supervise effectively.
- Where possible, regulatory reform should include adjusting any regulations that would preclude existing financial institutions (banks, finance companies, etc.) from offering microfinance services, or that would make it unreasonably difficult for such [regulated and licensed] institutions to lend to MFIs.
- Prudential regulation should not be imposed on "credit-only" MFIs that merely lend out their own capital, or whose only borrowing is from foreign commercial or non-commercial sources or from prudentially regulated local commercial banks.
- As a corollary to the above principle and] depending on practical costs and benefits, prudential regulation may not be necessary for MFIs taking cash collateral (compulsory savings) only, especially if the MFI is not lending out (i.e., not able to intermediate these funds).

- Design of microfinance regulation should not proceed very far without estimating supervision costs realistically and identifying a sustainable mechanism to pay for them. Donors who encourage governments to take on supervision of new types of (licensed) institution should be willing to help finance the start-up costs of such supervision.
- In developing countries, "self-supervision" by an entity under the control of those supervised is not likely to be effective in protecting the soundness of the supervised financial institutions.
- A microlending institution should not receive a license to take deposits until it has demonstrated that it can manage its lending profitably enough so that it can cover all its costs, including the additional financial and administrative costs of mobilizing the deposits it proposes to capture.
- Financial cooperatives (credit unions and savings and credit cooperatives)—at least large ones—should be prudentially supervised by a specialized financial authority, rather than by an agency that is responsible for all types of cooperatives (financial and non-financial).

The Bibliography includes a number of reference works and guidelines that are useful in addressing the above questions—particularly on relevant prudential standards, tools for supervision, and costs of supervision—as well as providing the benefit of lessons from the experience of a number of countries that have had to address similar questions and issues.

Notes

1. Example of rapid growth in cooperatives and credit unions include Burkina Faso, Ecuador, Guatemala, and the Philippines.
2. Village banking is a means of delivering financial services such as small loans and savings products to those people who could not otherwise obtain them. While many agencies and organizations provide small loans to low-income families, not all use the village banking method. Developed by FINCA (http://villagebanking.org/), the village banking method is unique in the responsibility and autonomy given to borrowers in running their banks and in the method's emphasis on community, as well as individual development. The village banking method has been shared widely with 40 voluntary agencies and development organizations that currently operate more than 80 programs worldwide. The village banking method is highly participatory in nature. It gives the beneficiaries a voice and involves them in the development process. Not only do members receive loans, but also they form cohesive groups that manage and collect repayments on those loans, that save diligently, and that decide on ways to invest those savings, and progress together, thus forming networks for mutual support.
3. Data cited as of 2003.
4. See Honohan (2004) for a discussion of this point.
5. In some countries, wholesale borrowings through commercial paper or money market instruments and through medium- to long-term large-value certificates of deposit may require prior authorization from a securities or capital market authority or, where

the institutional investor or lender is an insurance company, from the insurance commissioner.

6. Positive information includes repayment history with amounts and terms of the loans, while negative information includes delays in repayment and defaults.

7. See Christen, Lyman, and Rosenberg (2003). The selected set of key policy recommendations is presented and reproduced verbatim, except for those terms in brackets, which have been inserted for purposes of further clarification, and except for some changes in the order of presentation.

References

Barron, John M. and Michael Staten. 2001. "The Value of Comprehensive Credit Reports: Lessons from the U.S. Experience." In *Making Small Business Lending Profitable—Proceedings from the Global Conference on Credit Scoring*. International Finance Corporation: Washington, DC.

Boomgard, James, Debra Boyer, and James Dyer. 2003. "The Agricultural Bank of Mongolia: From Insolvent State Bank to Thriving Private Bank." Case Study presented at the International Conference on Best Practices titled "Paving the Way Forward for Rural Finance," Washington, DC, June 2003.

Christen, Robert Peck, and Richard Rosenberg. 2000. *The Rush to Regulate: Legal Frameworks for Microfinance*. Washington, DC: Consultative Group to Assist the Poorest.

Christen, Robert Peck, Timothy R. Lyman, and Richard Rosenberg. 2003. *Microfinance Consensus Guidelines*. Washington, DC: Consultative Group to Assist the Poorest.

Fiebig, Michael. 2001. Prudential Regulation and Supervision for Agricultural Finance. Rome: Food and Agriculture Organization of the United Nations (FAO) and Deutsche Gesellschaft für Technische Zusammenarbeit (GTZ), Agriculture Finance Revisited No. 5.

Gallardo, Joselito. 2002. "A Framework for Regulating Microfinance Institutions: The Experience in Ghana and the Philippines" World Bank Policy Research Working Paper No. 2755, World Bank, Washington, DC.

Gallardo, Joselito, Korotoumou Ouattara, Bikki Randhawa, and William F. Steel. 2005. "Comparative Review of Microfinance Regulatory Framework Issues in Benin, Ghana, and Tanzania." World Bank Policy Research Working Paper WPS3585, World Bank, Washington, DC.

Honohan, Patrick. 2004. "Financial Sector Policy and the Poor: Selected Findings and Issues." World Bank Working Paper No.43, World Bank, Washington, DC.

Robinson, Marguerite S. 2001. *The Microfinance Revolution: Sustainable Finance for the Poor*. World Bank: Washington, DC, and Open Society Institute: New York.

Staschen, Stefan. 2003. *Regulatory Requirements for Microfinance—A Comparison of Regulatory Frameworks in Eleven Countries Worldwide*. Deutsche Gesellschaft für Technische Zusammenarbeit.

van Greuning, Hennie, Joselito Gallardo, and Bikki Randhawa. 1999. "A Framework for Regulating Microfinance Institutions." World Bank Policy Research Working Paper No. 2061, World Bank, Washington, DC.

World Bank. 2001. "Finance for Growth: Policy Choices in a Volatile World," World Bank Policy Research Report, World Bank and Oxford University Press, Washington, DC.

World Bank Institute. 2004. *Interactive CD-ROM on Microfinance Regulation.* Washington, DC: World Bank Institute.

Yaron, Jacob, and Stephanie Charitonenko. 1999. "Making the Transition from State Agricultural Credit Institution to Rural Finance Intermediary: Role of the State and Reform Options." Paper prepared for the panel on Strategies for Microfinance in Rural Areas, Second Inter-American Forum on Microenterprise, Buenos Aires, Argentina, June 1999.

Zeller, Manfred. 2003. "Models of Rural Financial Institutions." Lead theme paper presented at the International Conference on Best Practices, "Paving the Way Forward for Rural Finance," Washington, DC, June 2003.

7

Chapter 8

Assessing Financial System Integrity—Anti-Money Laundering and Combating the Financing of Terrorism

Both the World Bank and IMF have long been involved in international efforts to strengthen financial sector supervision and to promote good governance, which, among other things, both contribute to reducing financial crime and enhance the integrity of the international financial system. Since 2001, the Bank-Fund involvement in those issues has been intensified, with a sharper focus on both anti-money-laundering (AML) measures and efforts aimed at combating the financing of terrorism (CFT). Both the Bank and the Fund have worked closely with the Financial Action Task Force on Money Laundering (FATF), the standard setting body in this area, to develop a methodology for assessing the observance of international standards on the legal, institutional, and operational framework for AML–CFT.[1] The Bank and the Fund conduct assessments of AML–CFT regimes as part of the FSAP assessments and, in the case of the Fund, as part of OFC assessments. Assessments are also conducted as part of the mutual evaluations for FATF members, which are done by FATF or FATF-style regional bodies (FSRB).[2]

The FATF standards draw on and complement a wide range of United Nations (UN) conventions and resolutions that promote international cooperation in preventing and containing drug trafficking, organized crime, corruption, and efforts to finance terrorism. In addition, all financial supervisory standards have core principles to enhance know-your-customer (KYC) rules, suspicious transactions reporting, and other due diligence requirements that help to support AML–CFT regimes. Box 8.1 contains an overview of key UN conventions and resolutions that complement FATF standards, and box 8.2 highlights key aspects of financial sector supervisory standards that support an effective AML–CFT regime.

Money laundering is "transferring illegally obtained money or investments through an outside party to conceal the true source."[3] The number and variety of transactions used

---

Box 8.1 United Nations Conventions and Security Council Resolutions in Support of AML-CFT Regimes

The 2004 Methodology (FATF 2004a) identifies three United Nations (UN) conventions and several UN Security Council Resolutions that are incorporated into the requirements of the FATF standards on AML–CFT regimes. UN conventions have the effect of law in a country once that country has signed, ratified, and implemented the convention, depending on the country's constitution and legal structure. Under certain circumstances, the Security Council of the United Nations has the authority to bind all member countries, regardless of other action or inaction on the part of an individual country. This box summarizes the relevant provisions of these United Nations instruments.

- *United Nations Convention against Illicit Traffic in Narcotic Drugs and Psychotropic Substances (1988; the Vienna Convention)*—The Vienna Convention, as it is commonly known, deals primarily with the illicit drug trade and related law enforcement issues. It is the first UN convention to define the concept of "money laundering," even though it does not use that term, and it calls on countries to criminalize the activity. This convention is limited, however, to drug-trafficking offenses and does not address the preventative aspects of the crime.

- *The International Convention against Transnational Organized Crime (2000; the Palermo Convention)*—This convention contains a broad range of provisions to fight organized crime. With respect to money laundering, it requires countries to

  - Criminalize money laundering and include all serious crimes as predicate offenses of money laundering (not just drug-related offenses), plus permit the required criminal knowledge or intent to be inferred from objective facts, not proven individually.

  - Establish regulatory regimes to deter and detect all form of money laundering.

  - Authorize domestic and international cooperation and exchanges of information among administrative, regulatory, law enforcement, and other types of authorities.

  - Promote the establishment of governmental units to centrally collect, analyze, and disseminate information.

- *International Convention for the Suppression of the Financing of Terrorism (1999)*—This convention requires countries to criminalize terrorism, terrorist organizations, and terrorist acts. Under this convention, it is unlawful for any person to provide or collect funds with the intent or knowledge that the funds will be used to carry out any defined acts of terrorism.

- *Security Council Resolution 1373*—This resolution obligates all countries to criminalize actions to finance terrorism. This resolution also obligates countries to deny all forms of support to terrorist groups and to freeze assets of those involved in terrorist acts. It also encourages cooperation among countries for criminal investigations and for sharing information about planned terrorist acts.

- *Security Council Resolution 1267 and Its Successors*—Security Council Resolution 1267 required all countries to freeze the assets of the Taliban and entities owned or controlled by them, as determined by the "Sanctions Committee." Later, Resolution 1333 added the assets of Osama bin Laden and al-Qaeda to the freezing list. Subsequent resolutions established monitoring arrangements (Resolution 1363), merged earlier lists (Resolution 1390), provided some exclusions (Resolution 1452), and improved implementation measures (Resolution 1455). Together, the various lists for freezing assets are maintained and updated by the "1267 Committee" and are published on the UN's Web site.

The UN documents noted above are available at the Web homepages of the United Nations and the United Nations Office of Drugs and Crime: UN conventions are accessible at http://www.undoc.org/undoc/index.html; and the security council resolutions at http://www.un.org/documents/scres.htm.

---

to launder money has become increasingly complex, often involving numerous financial institutions from many jurisdictions, and increasingly using nonbank financial institutions (e.g., bureaux de change, wire remittance services, cash couriers, insurers, brokers, traders), as well as nonfinancial businesses and professions (e.g., lawyers, accountants, and trust and company service providers). Money-laundering methods are diverse and

---

Box 8.2 Core Principles and Guidelines of Financial Sector Supervision in Support of AML–CFT Regimes

The Basel Committee on Banking Supervision (Basel Committee), International Association of Insurance Supervisors (IAIS), and International Organization of Securities Commissioners (IOSCO) have each issued broad supervisory standards and guidelines on a wide range of supervisory issues, including money laundering as it relates to banking, insurance, and securities. FATF incorporates those standards and guidelines in its 40 recommendations.

The Basel Committee

The Basel Committee has issued three documents covering money-laundering issues:

- *Statement on Prevention of Criminal Use of the Banking System for the Purpose of Money Laundering*—This statement contains essentially four principles that should be used by banking institutions:
  - Proper customer identification
  - High ethical standards and compliance with laws and regulations
  - Cooperation with law enforcement authorities
  - Policies and procedures to be used to adhere to the statement
- *Core Principles for Effective Banking Supervision*— These principles set out a comprehensive blueprint for supervisory issues, which cover a wide range of topics. Core Principle 15 deals with money laundering by stipulating that bank supervisors must determine that banks have adequate policies and procedures in place, including strict know-your-customer (KYC) rules.
- *Customer Due Diligence for Banks*—This paper provides extensive guidance on appropriate standards for banks to use in identifying their customers. The paper was issued in response to a number of deficiencies noted on a global basis with regard to the KYC procedures noted above. In addition, the standards go beyond the fight against money laundering and are intended to help protect banks in terms of safety and soundness.

IAIS

This association has issued its Guidance Paper 5, "Anti-Money-Laundering Guidance Notes for Insurance Supervisors and Insurance Entities," which parallels the Basel Committee's statement on prevention. It contains four principles that should be embraced by insurance entities:

- Comply with anti-money-laundering laws.
- Have know-your-customer procedures in place.
- Cooperate with all law enforcement authorities.
- Have internal anti-money-laundering policies, procedures, and training programs for employees.

IOSCO

This organization passed its "Resolution on Money Laundering" to be implemented by securities regulators in individual countries. It consists of seven specific areas for securities regulators to consider in establishing requirements for firms under their jurisdiction:

- The extent of customer identifying information with a view toward enhancing the ability of authorities to identify and prosecute money launderers
- The adequacy of record-keeping requirements to reconstruct financial transactions
- Whether an appropriate manner is used to address the reporting of suspicious transactions
- What procedures are in place to prevent criminals from obtaining control of securities businesses and to share information with foreign counterparts
- Whether means are appropriate for monitoring compliance procedures designed to deter and detect money laundering
- The use of cash and cash equivalents in securities transactions, including documentation to reconstruct transactions
- Whether means are appropriate to share information to combat money laundering

---

8

are constantly evolving. Money launderers may also operate outside financial systems, for example, through alternative remittance systems.

Terrorist acts and terrorists who commit or assist in such acts are defined in various UN conventions and resolutions. Various UN resolutions seek actions to freeze or confiscate funds to designated terrorists. Although the origin of the funds used in support of terrorism may be either legal or illegal, often, the methods used to channel funds for terrorist purposes are the same as those used by money launderers.

This section explains and motivates the main elements of FATF standards for AML–CFT regimes, provides an overview of the underlying assessment methodology, and highlights the main lessons of recent assessment experience. Some special topics that frequently arise in AML–CFT assessments are highlighted in light of their importance for effective AML–CFT regimes. Some of the key elements of AML–CFT regimes are already covered as part of the assessments of financial supervision standards. AML–CFT standards go beyond financial supervision aspects and cover legal, institutional, and law enforcement aspects that go beyond the financial sector and that include certain other businesses and professions.

8.1 AML–CFT Standards—Links to Stability and Institutional Development

Money laundering can have potentially negative consequences for a country's macroeconomic performance, can impose welfare losses, and may also have negative cross-border externalities. For example, it could compromise bank soundness with potentially large fiscal liabilities, could lessen the ability to attract foreign investment, and could increase the volatility of international capital flows and exchange rates. In the era of high capital mobility, abuse of the global financial system makes national tax collection and law enforcement more difficult. Money laundering may also distort the allocation of resources and the distribution of wealth and can be costly to detect and eradicate. Economic damage can arise not only from direct financial system abuse but also from allegations that affect the reputation of a country or from one country's actions against perceived financial system abuse in another economy. Those types of allegations or actions can, through reputational effects, affect the willingness of economic agents—particularly those outside the country in question—to conduct business (e.g., inward investment, banking correspondent relationships) in that country, which can lead to adverse consequences.

Money laundering and terrorist financing may compromise the reputations of financial institutions and jurisdictions, undermine investors' trust in those institutions and jurisdictions, and, therefore, weaken the financial system. Trust underpins the existence and development of financial markets. The effective functioning of financial markets relies heavily on the expectation that high professional, legal, and ethical standards will be observed and enforced. A reputation for integrity—soundness, honesty, adherence to standards and codes—is one of the most valued assets by investors, financial institutions, and jurisdictions.

8.2 AML–CFT Standards—Scope and Coverage

In 1990, the FATF issued a report containing a set of 40 recommendations, which provided a comprehensive plan of action needed to fight against money laundering. Since then, the recommendations have been revised twice, most recently in October 2004 (FATF

2004b) and have been recognized widely as an international standard in this area. The recommendations cover (a) all the measures that national AML regimes should have in place within their legal, criminal justice, and regulatory systems; (b) the preventive measures to be taken by financial institutions and certain other businesses and professions; and (c) international cooperation. The FATF recommendations now apply not only to money laundering but also to terrorist financing. The eight "Special Recommendations on Terrorist Financing" (FATF 2004c), which were adopted in 2001 and most recently updated in October 2004, address ratification and implementation of UN resolutions, criminalization of the financing of terrorism, efforts to freeze and confiscate terrorist assets, reports of suspicious transactions, international cooperation, alternative remittances, wire transfers, nonprofit organizations, and cash couriers. Taken together, the 40 recommendations and the 9 special recommendations provide a comprehensive framework of measures for combating money laundering and terrorist financing.

An effective AML–CFT system requires an adequate legal and institutional framework and law enforcement mechanisms, as outlined in the FATF recommendations. The AML–CFT system should include (a) laws that create money laundering and terrorist financing offenses and that provide for freezing, seizing, and confiscating the proceeds of crime and terrorist funding; (b) laws, regulations, or, in certain circumstances, other enforceable means that impose the required obligations on financial institutions and on designated nonfinancial businesses and professions; (c) an appropriate institutional or administrative framework and effective laws that provide competent authorities with the necessary duties, powers, and sanctions; and (d) laws and other measures that give a country the ability to provide the widest range of international cooperation. It is also essential that the competent authorities ensure that the whole system is effectively implemented. Specific FATF recommendations spelling out the above framework in greater detail are listed in Annex 8.A.

8.3 Preconditions for Effective Implementation of AML–CFT Standards

An effective AML–CFT system also requires that certain structural elements and a general policy framework, not covered by the AML–CFT assessment criteria, be in place. The lack of those elements, or significant weaknesses or shortcomings in the general framework, may significantly impair the implementation of an effective AML–CFT framework. The structural elements include in particular

- Sound and sustainable financial sector policies and a well-developed public sector infrastructure
- The respect for principles such as transparency and good governance
- A proper culture of AML–CFT compliance that is shared and reinforced by government, financial institutions, designated nonfinancial businesses and professions, industry trade groups, and self-regulatory organizations (SROs)
- Appropriate measures to combat corruption
- A reasonably efficient court system that ensures that judicial decisions are properly enforced

- High ethical and professional requirements for police officers, prosecutors, judges, and so forth, as well as measures and mechanisms to ensure that those requirements are observed
- A system for ensuring the ethical and professional behavior on the part of professionals such as accountants, auditors, and lawyers that may include the existence of codes of conduct and good practices, as well as methods to ensure compliance such as registration, licensing, and supervision or oversight

Many of those issues are likely to be covered as part of the assessments of preconditions for other supervisory standards, and information from the other assessments can help inform AML–CFT assessments.

8.4 Assessment Methodology and Assessment Experience

The 40 recommendations and eight special recommendations on terrorist financing have been endorsed by the Executive Boards of the IMF and the World Bank as the AML–CFT standard for which Reports on Observance of Standards and Codes (ROSCs) are prepared (see IMF and World Bank 2002). Coverage of the AML–CFT standard in Fund-Bank work has progressively widened and now encompasses the full scope of the FATF recommendations. Key dates in this evolution are outlined in the following list:

- In April 2001, the Executive Board directed that AML elements in the relevant supervisory standards for the prudentially regulated financial sector be given particular emphasis. Law enforcement aspects and the broader legal institutional framework for AML policies were excluded.
- In November 2001, the Fund developed an action plan that extended IMF work not only to include terrorist financing elements but also to include, for any jurisdiction, the overall legal and institutional arrangements for AML–CFT. The plan also extended beyond such arrangements to support financial supervision per se, but it excluded involvement in law enforcement issues.
- In July 2002, the Bank, the Fund, and the FATF agreed to an AML–CFT assessment methodology for evaluating compliance with AML–CFT standards, and this agreement was endorsed by the Fund's and the Bank's Executive Boards. The methodology delineated those legal, institutional, and supervisory elements of the AML–CFT standard for which the Fund and the Bank would take accountability, as well as those law enforcement and nonfinancial sector elements that should be left to others. A pilot program of assessments that had been based on 2002 methodology was initiated.
- In March 2004, the Fund's and the Bank's Executive Boards reviewed the pilot program and determined that Bank-Fund staff members could take accountability for the full scope of the AML–CFT standard, including effective implementation of criminal justice elements and application of the regime beyond the regulated financial sector.[4]

Box 8.3 Weaknesses in AML/CFT Regimes: Results of Pilot Program Assessments

The assessments undertaken during the pilot program using the 2002 Methodology identified numerous shortcomings in national AML–CFT regimes. This box lists specific types of shortcomings that led to ratings of "materially noncompliant" or "noncompliant" in a fairly high percentage of countries assessed. The shortcomings identified were encountered across a wide range of countries and appeared with varying frequency. Some shortcomings are concentrated in a few countries where compliance is generally weak. Others represent exceptions in regimes where compliance is otherwise strong.

The list below provides an indication of some of the types of deficiencies that needed to be corrected to achieve compliance with the earlier FATF standard; it does not cover topics such as the financial intelligence function and enhanced due diligence that were not yet included in the FATF standard at the time of the pilot program.

Main Weaknesses Identified in AML–CFT Assessments

- Poor assistance provided to other countries' investigations into financing terrorism
- Poor attention given to transactions with higher risk countries
- Poor detection and analysis of unusual large or otherwise suspicious transactions
- No criminalization of the financing of terrorism and of terrorist organizations
- Inadequate systems to report suspicious transactions linked to terrorism
- Inadequate AML programs in supervised banks, financial institutions, or intermediaries and inadequate authority to cooperate with judicial and law enforcement
- Inadequate guidelines for detecting suspicious transactions
- Inadequate measures to freeze and confiscate terrorist assets
- No obligation to take reasonable measures to obtain information about customer identity
- Lack of procedures for mutual assistance (for the production of records, the search of persons, and the seizure and obtaining of evidence for money-laundering investigations and prosecution) in criminal matters
- Inadequate internal policies, procedures, controls, audit, and training programs

- No requirement to report promptly to the Financial Intelligence Units if institutions suspect that funds stem from a criminal activity
- Poor international exchange of information relating to suspicious transactions as well as to persons or corporations involved

The scope of the weaknesses listed above are further explained in the following list:

- General Legal Framework (FTAF 1–3)—In most cases, secrecy laws hindered the effective investigation and prosecution of money-laundering offenses by imposing restrictions on access to customer information or its exchange, whether domestically or internationally.
- Customer identification and record keeping (FATF 10–13)—Deficiencies include not prohibiting anonymous or fictitious accounts, unclear or vague regulations on official documents to be used for identifications, exemptions from identification requirements, and insufficient coverage of recordkeeping requirements.
- Increased diligence of financial institutions (FATF 14–19)—Deficiencies ranged from an absence of clear laws requiring the reporting of suspicious transactions to overly restrictive thresholds for determining suspicion; in some cases, procedures and channels for reporting suspicious transactions were unclear.
- Implementation and role of regulatory and other administrative authorities (FATF 26–29)—In many countries (in the pilot), supervisors and regulators cannot effectively cooperate with each other domestically because of legal impediments to share relevant information or absence of legal gateways; also, authorities have not established adequate guidelines to assist financial institutions in detecting suspicious patterns of behavior by customers, partly reflecting deficiencies in the role of financial intelligence units.
- Criminalization of the financing of terrorism and associated money-laundering(SRII)—In almost a third of the countries, the financing of terrorism was not criminalized in any manner or, even if criminalized, was not made a predicate offense for money laundering.

Source: IMF and World Bank (2004, annex II).

8

8.4.1 AML–CFT Assessment Methodology

Starting in 2002 and as agreed, AML–CFT assessments can be conducted using one of two approaches: either (a) Fund-Bank assessments or (b) FATF or FATF-style regional body (FSRB) mutual evaluations. Under both approaches, assessors will need to use the revised common methodology endorsed by the Fund-Bank Boards and by the FATF in February–March 2004.[5]

The 2004 methodology (revised slightly in February 2005) was developed to reflect (a) the revised FATF 40 recommendations that were adopted by the FATF in 2003 and revised in 2004, (b) the originally eight (now nine) special recommendations to combat terrorist financing adopted in 2001 and revised in 2004, and (c) a number of FATF interpretative notes. The following are key features of the 2004 methodology:

- Although the 2002 methodology was structured both topically and sectorally, the 2004 methodology follows the structure of the revised FATF 40 recommendations. This revision will help in the determination of whether the FATF recommendations have been fully and properly implemented and whether the AML–CFT system is effective.[6] Consistent with the FATF recommendations, all financial institutions are now assessed against the same criteria, thus eliminating the overlap and duplication in criteria in the 2002 methodology, which included specific criteria for different financial sectors.

- The criteria relating to the eight special recommendations on terrorist financing are kept separate from the AML criteria, though, where applicable, they cross-reference the relevant AML criteria.

- The 2004 methodology distinguishes between the mandatory elements (i.e., the essential criteria) and the nonmandatory elements (i.e., the additional elements). The latter are formulated as questions and are based on best practice or guidance issued by the FATF or other international standard setters. The additional elements are not to be taken into account when determining a compliance rating for a recommendation but may be referenced when describing the overall robustness of the system.

- The 2004 methodology further distinguishes between basic requirements that need to be implemented through laws and regulations and through more detailed requirements that may alternatively be implemented through other enforceable means, such as enforceable guidelines issued by competent authorities.

- There is a four-level compliance rating: compliant, largely compliant, partially compliant, and noncompliant. The overall structure and rating system are comparable to assessment methodologies for other standards and codes.

- The 2004 methodology contains more than 200 essential criteria, 20 subcriteria, and 35 additional criteria. In addition, the methodology contains examples and note boxes to help provide guidance to the assessors in their work.

- The 2004 methodology contains a fairly detailed and comprehensive set of assessment criteria, particularly with respect to criminal justice and regulatory systems, preventive measures for financial sector, powers of competent authorities, and international cooperation. The following selected examples illustrate the level of detail in the methodology. The methodology contains, for example, detailed criteria concerning the conduct of customer due diligence (CDD) with respect to the circumstances under which CDD is to be conducted, timing of verification, measures to be taken with respect to existing customers, conditions under which simplified CDD may be allowed, conditions under which a financial institution can rely on third parties and introduced business, and additional CDD measures in certain circumstances such as correspondent banking. The methodology specifies preventive measures that should apply to a designated set of nonfinancial businesses and professions where they prepare for, or carry out, certain types of transactions.[7] Countries are also required to review the effectiveness of their AML–CFT systems on a regular basis and to maintain comprehensive statistics for this purpose.

8.4.2 Assessment Experience

To date, experience in conducting AML–CFT assessments has been gained using an earlier 2002 methodology during a 12-month pilot program that ended in October 2003. During the pilot program, the Fund, the Bank, the FATF, and the FSRBs collaborated to undertake AML–CFT assessments of 41 jurisdictions.[8] Some general observations from the pilot program included the following:

- Overall compliance with the FATF recommendations is uneven across jurisdictions. Many jurisdictions show a high level of compliance with the original FATF 40 recommendations. The most prevalent deficiency is weaker compliance with the eight special recommendations on terrorist financing.
- For many countries, the essential legal elements of an AML–CFT regime are in place; however, important gaps in implementation remain because of insufficient resources and training.
- Poor coordination among government agencies has weakened AML–CFT regimes. In a number of cases, effective working relationships had not been established among the financial supervisors, the financial intelligence unit, the financial investigators, the police, the public prosecutors, and the courts.
- Ineffective law enforcement was observed in several instances. Police, prosecutors, or the courts lacked the skills, training, or resources to investigate, prosecute, or adjudicate money-laundering cases. In addition, law enforcement agencies frequently focused on predicate offenses and neglected the law enforcement strategies that were available under proceeds of crime legislation.
- Weak financial supervision has affected the enforcement of know-your-customer rules, suspicious transactions reporting, and international cooperation and information exchange. In some cases, understaffed and undertrained financial supervisors lacked the skills or capacity to monitor and to enforce compliance with formal AML–CFT requirements. (See box 8.3 for a summary of the results of pilot program of assessments.)

8.5 Special Topics in AML–CFT Assessments

While AML–CFT assessments cover a wide range of issues, certain institutional arrangements play a critical role in the effectiveness of the overall AML–CFT regime and,

8

hence, are analyzed closely in most assessments. These assessments include customer due diligence arrangements and the role of financial intelligence units.

8.5.1 Assessing Preventive Measures: The Example of Customer Due Diligence

FATF Recommendation 5 calls for financial institutions to undertake customer identification measures in a variety of circumstances: when establishing business relations, when carrying out certain occasional transactions, when there is a suspicion of money laundering or terrorist financing, and when the financial institution has doubts about previously obtained identification data.

Recommendation 5 also addresses the types of customer identification measures to be undertaken in various circumstances: using reliable, independent source documents, data, or information; identifying beneficial owners, including the owners and controllers of legal persons and arrangements; obtaining information on the purpose and intended nature of a business relationship; and monitoring transactions on an ongoing basis for consistency with the business relationship, including the source of funds. Recommendation 5 provides that the extent of customer identification measures may be adjusted on a risk-sensitive basis, depending on the type of customer, business relationship, or transaction, with enhanced due diligence required for higher risk transactions.

The corresponding criteria in the methodology state that financial institutions should be required to undertake customer identification in the various circumstances and should use the various measures called for in Recommendation 5. Assessors evaluate compliance at two levels. They confirm that financial institutions (or other covered parties) are subject to binding customer identification obligations—in the form of law, regulation, or other enforceable means—for each of the requirements identified in the methodology. In addition, they verify that supervisory arrangements are in place to monitor and enforce compliance with the formal customer identification requirements. This action requires the assessor to evaluate supervisory procedures for offsite monitoring and onsite examination of financial institutions' customer identification policies and procedures. Typically, assessors also visit with financial institutions to verify that customer identification requirements are being followed and that supervisory oversight is effective.

Assessments undertaken during the 12-month pilot program identified a variety of banks' weaknesses in compliance with FATF's recommendations with respect to customer identification. In some cases, the obligation for banks to undertake customer identification was advisory rather than mandatory. In a number of cases, customer identification obligations were vague and did not address a number of issues covered in the recommendations. In several cases, supervisors did not have an effective program for monitoring and enforcing compliance with customer identification requirements. Failure to monitor compliance frequently occurred because of inadequate supervisor resources.

8.5.2 Financial Intelligence Units

Financial Intelligence Units (FIU) constitute a key element in policies to counter financial crime and money laundering. FIU is a national agency that receives, analyzes, and disseminates to competent authorities the particular financial information and intelligence concerning suspected proceeds of crime or other disclosures required by national laws and regulation.[i] With some variation among jurisdictions, FIUs are statutorily empowered to receive a wide variety of financial information from diverse sources. These sources may include reports by financial institutions of suspicious or unusual transactions—as determined by financial institutions—of some or even all offshore wire transactions or of large cash transactions. FIUs also typically have access to information not only from other domestic governmental sources, including those administering customs, tax, pension, and criminal laws but also from foreign FIUs. A key task of FIUs is to analyze this information (along with information publicly available) to uncover leads on possible financial crime for use in investigations or inquiries conducted by domestic (and often foreign) law enforcement and financial institution regulatory agencies.

Establishment of an FIU is one of the key standards of the FATF, a prerequisite for an effective regime that reports suspicious transactions and for the detection and prevention of money laundering and terrorist financing. Intelligence gathered and disclosed to law enforcement's and financial institutions' regulatory agencies can also assist in investigations on or inquiries into potential predicate crimes, including financial crimes. Because FIUs provide a central gathering point for analyzing a broad range of domestic and foreign financial information, they may be particularly effective at uncovering patterns among large numbers of complex financial transactions that point to a possible financial crime. For example, reports of many FATF member countries conclude that a majority of the financial information received and analyzed by their FIUs does not point to possible money laundering but, rather, to fraud against the financial institutions themselves, including wire and check fraud, credit card fraud, loan fraud, and embezzlement.

FIUs have far greater access than do individual financial institutions to relevant data. For example, FIUs can track suspicious transaction reports from all financial institutions that are required to make such reports and can seek additional information from governmental and other sources with respect to those transactions. In addition, FIUs often develop special expertise to identify patterns among transactions (e.g., offshore wire transfers) that suggest possible laundering or terrorist financing. Combinations of information gleaned in those ways can sometimes uncover complex schemes. If the transactions involve multiple jurisdictions, the ability to share information internationally among FIUs also becomes more important.

Annex 8.A   FATF 40+8 Recommendations for AML–CFT

Forty Recommendations

Legal Systems (in line with UN conventions)

1. Legal systems should specify a broad scope of money-laundering offenses by criminalizing money laundering related to all serious offenses and capturing, at a minimum, the designated range of offenses.

2. Legal systems should establish standards to prove the offense of money laundering and to clarify that criminal, civil, and administrative liability will apply to legal persons (corporations).

3. A country should have authority to confiscate illegal funds and to apply provisional measures, such as freezing or seizing to deal with money-laundering offenses.

Preventive Measures (to be taken by financial institutions and nonfinancial businesses)

4. Secrecy laws should not prevent implementation of the recommendations.

5. Financial institutions and nonfinancial businesses should have an obligation to carry out customer due diligence, including identifying and verifying customer identity.

6. Financial institutions and nonfinancial businesses should have special measures in place for politically exposed persons.

7. Financial institutions and nonfinancial businesses should have special measures in place for correspondent banking.

8. Financial institutions and nonfinancial businesses should have measures in place to address money-laundering threats from new technologies and from business that is not conducted face to face.

9. Financial institutions and nonfinancial businesses should rely on third parties for customer identification and for introduced business.

10. Financial institutions and nonfinancial businesses should adhere to a five-year record-keeping requirement.

11. Financial institutions and nonfinancial businesses should pay special attention to complex, unusual large transactions and to all unusual patterns of transactions.

12. Customer identification should be applied to designated nonfinancial businesses and professions (DNFBPs).

13. Financial institutions and nonfinancial businesses should have an obligation to report suspicious transactions to financial intelligence units.

14. Legal protection should be granted for persons reporting their suspicions in good faith, and prohibitions against tipping off should be established.

15. Financial institutions and nonfinancial businesses should have measures in place for internal controls, compliance, and audit.

16. Requirements for reporting and monitoring suspicious activity should be applied to DNFBPs.

17. A country should have effective, proportionate, and dissuasive sanctions for money-laundering offenses.

18. A country should not allow the establishment of shell banks.

19. Financial institutions and nonfinancial businesses should consider monitoring of cross-border cash transportation and should develop a system for reporting currency transactions above a fixed amount.

20. Financial institutions and nonfinancial businesses should consider applying FATF requirements to other businesses beyond DNFBPs.

21. Special attention should be given to higher-risk countries.

22. AML requirements should be applied to foreign branches and subsidiaries.
23. Financial institutions should be subject to adequate regulation, supervision, and monitoring.
24. DNFBPs need to be subject to regulation, supervision, and monitoring.
25. Competent authority should provide guidelines on reporting, along with feedback on effectiveness.

Institutional and Other Measures

26. A country should have established a financial intelligence unit.
27. A country should have a designated law enforcement authority for money-laundering and financing-terrorism offenses.
28. Law enforcement authority should have adequate legal powers for investigation.
29. Regulators should have adequate legal powers to monitor and ensure compliance with AML–CFT requirements.
30. Competent authorities should have adequate resources, integrity, and training for AML–CFT efforts.
31. Effective mechanisms need to be developed domestically for cooperation.
32. Institutions should maintain statistics on reporting, investigations, prosecutions, and mutual legal assistance.
33. Institutions should establish measures to deter unlawful use of corporations and timely information on beneficial ownership and control.
34. Institutions should establish measures to prevent unlawful use of legal arrangements (e.g., trusts), and ensure timely information on settlor, trustee, and beneficiaries.

International Cooperation

35. Each country should adopt Vienna, Palermo, suppression of financing of terrorism, and other international conventions.
36. Each country should rapidly provide mutual legal assistance.
37. Each country should render assistance notwithstanding the absence of dual criminality.
38. Each country should have expeditious powers to identify, freeze, seize, and confiscate property laundered from money laundering and financing terrorism.
39. Each country should recognize money laundering as an extraditable offence.
40. Each country should provide a wide range of other possible international cooperation.

Special Recommendations for Combating the Financing of Terrorism

SRI   Ratify and implement relevant UN conventions and resolutions.
SRII   Criminalize terrorist financing.
SRIII   Implement measures to freeze and confiscate terrorist assets.

SRIV   Have a suspicious transaction reporting requirement that applies to suspicion of terrorist financing.

SRV   Provide cooperation on proceedings related to financing of terrorism.

SRVI   Implement measures to deter improper use of money- and value-transfer services.

SRVII   Call for countries to require adequate originator information in fund transfers and related messages.

SRVIII   Call for countries to review adequacy of laws and regulations related to non-profit organizations to prevent misuse for terrorism purposes.

SR IX   Have measures to detect physical cross-border transportation of currency and bearer negotiable instruments.

Notes

1. The FATF is an intergovernmental body whose purpose is the development and promotion of policies to combat money laundering and terrorist financing. It was established by the G-7 Summit in 1989. See http://www1.oecd.org/fatf/.

2. These are regional anti-money-laundering, task-force-like organizations that have been created in the Caribbean, Asia, Europe, and Southern Africa. Similar regional groupings are planned for Western Africa and Latin America.

3. Definitions of money laundering have been adopted in common vocabulary (see *Oxford English Dictionary*, 1989, 702). FATF defines money laundering as the processing of criminal proceeds to disguise their illegal origin, and the International Organization of Securities Commissions (IOSCO) defines it as a wide range of activities and processes intended to obscure the source of illegally obtained money and to create the appearance that it has originated from a legitimate source.

4. See IMF and World Bank (2004).

5. See FATF (2004a). In time, the FATF-style regional bodies (FSRBs) are expected also to endorse the revised methodology.

6. The 2002 AML–CFT methodology was organized topically with the legal and institutional framework and effectiveness for criminal justice measures in one part, core preventive measures for all financial institutions in a second part, and sector-specific preventive measures for banking, insurance, and securities in a third part. The organization of the 2002 AML–CFT methodology reflected the evolving nature of its development, beginning with the focus on supervisory measures for prudentially regulated financial institutions, the addition of the legal and institutional framework and CFT, and, finally, the implementation of the criminal justice measures.

7. The designated nonfinancial business and professions are casinos; real estate agents; dealers in precious metals and stones; lawyers, notaries, and other independent legal professions; accountants; and trust and company service providers.

8. Assessments were conducted on the basis of a 2002 assessment methodology. This section is based on the Fund-Bank report titled *Twelve-Month Pilot Program of Anti-Money-Laundering and Combating the Financing of Terrorism (AML–CFT) Assessments* (IMF and World Bank 2004).

9. The definition of FIU has been developed by Egmont Group of Financial Intelligence Units, an international body of government disclosure receiving agencies set up in 1995 so it could enhance cooperation and information exchange to detect and combat money laundering. Egmont Group has issued guidance on information exchange and processing by FIUs.

References

Financial Action Task Force on Money Laundering. 2004a. "Methodology for Assessing Compliance with the FATF 40 Recommendations and the FATF 8 Special Recommendations." FATF Secretariat, OECD, Paris, France. Available to access from the FATF homepage at http://www.fatf-gafi.org; also available at http://www.imf.org/external/np/aml/eng/2004/031604.pdf.

———. 2004b. "The Forty Recommendations." FATF Secretariat, OECD, Paris, France. Available to access from the homepage of http:// www.fatf-gafi.org.

———. 2004c. "Special Recommendations on Terrorist Financing." FATF Secretariat, OECD, Paris, France. Available to access from the homepage of http://www.fatf-gafi.org.

International Monetary Fund (IMF) and World Bank. 2002. "Anti-Money-Laundering and Combating Financing of Terrorism (AML–CFT). Proposals to Assess a Global Standard and to Prepare ROSCs." Paper 27 prepared for the Bank and Fund Boards, World Bank Joint Progress Report on the Work of the IMF and the World Bank, Washington, DC. Available at http://www.imf.org/external/np/mae/aml/2002/eng/071702.htm.

———. 2004. "Twelve-Month Pilot Program of Anti-Money-Laundering and Combating the Financing of Terrorism (AML–CFT) Assessments." Paper for the Bank and Fund Boards, Washington, DC, March 2004. Available at http://www.imf.org/np/aml/eng/2004/031004.htm.

Oxford English Dictionary. 2nd ed. Edited by John Simpson and Edmund Weiner. Oxford: Oxford University Press, 1989, 702.

8

Chapter 9

Assessing the Legal Infrastructure for Financial Systems

9

The legal infrastructure plays a pivotal role in the operation of financial markets, as well as in the efficient intermediation of capital flows and domestic savings. Banks and other financial institutions hold claims on borrowers, the value of which depends on the certainty of legal rights and the predictability and speed of their fair and impartial enforcement. The legal framework that empowers and governs the regulator and the rules for the regulation of the various markets form the cornerstone of the orderly existence and development of the financial markets. In this respect, the key laws are (a) the law governing the formation and operation of the central bank and (b) the law regulating banking and financial institutions and markets.

The key components of an effective legal framework for the regulation and supervision of the financial system are laid out in various international standards for financial sector supervision and are discussed in chapter 5. In particular, the core principles of supervision relating to regulatory governance (box 5.1) explicitly cover the key legal underpinnings. In addition, the effective governance and operations of the regulator and the regulated also depend on the broader legal framework governing insolvency regime and creditor rights, financial safety nets, ownership, contracts, contract enforcement, accounting and auditing, disclosure, formation of trusts and asset securitization, and so forth. The assessment of the legal infrastructure encompasses both the sectoral and the broader components of the overall framework.

9.1 Financial Sector Legal Framework

A review of the overall legal framework encompasses both the laws empowering and governing the regulator and the rules for the regulation of various sectors (such as the central bank laws, banking insurance and capital market laws, etc.), as well as the broader legal framework underpinning the payments system, government debt management, and other infrastructure elements (such as insolvency regime, creditor and land rights, corporate governance, and consumer protection). The scope and coverage of those components of the legal framework are outlined below.

9.1.1 Central Banking Law

The central bank law should provide for the establishment, organization, powers, and duties of the central bank, with a clear definition of its ultimate objectives, and should grant the central bank autonomy to implement monetary policy. The primary objective of a central bank is usually to ensure price stability, as well as sound banking and payment systems. The law must also provide the central bank with the necessary instruments and powers to enable it to achieve its objectives. Extraneous powers and duties are to be avoided, and the bank ought to be protected from outside interference in its operations and be assured of full operational autonomy.

The law should also stipulate the role of the central bank and that of the government in determining foreign exchange policy, for example, who decides on the country's exchange regime, who determines the exchange rate, and who is responsible for foreign exchange operations and reserves management. The responsibilities of the central bank in matters such as exchange control and the management of international reserves need to be clear.

Coordination between the central bank and the Ministry of Finance should be provided for in the law. In addition to the bank's duty to act as the fiscal agent of the government, the law would strive to provide the government with a risk-free depository, with a mechanism for consultation and coordination in the formulation of a country's macroeconomic policies, and with assistance in defining the institutional relationship between monetary and fiscal operations.

Modern central bank laws limit central bank credit to government and do not permit the central bank to perform non–central banking functions. For proper accountability and to protect the ability of the central bank to achieve its monetary policy mandate, developmental and other social policy objectives should be financed through the government's budget. The law should also place limits on government lending and should make transparent the conditions when that type of lending is permitted.

While the law should grant appropriate operational independence to a central bank, it must also specify the arrangements for its accountability and assurances of integrity. The arrangements include those for internal auditing, auditing and publishing its accounts, providing public information services, and making available central bank officials to report to designated public authority on the conduct of monetary policy and on its performance in achieving its objectives.[1]

9.1.2 Banking Law

The banking law typically provides for the formation and operation of banks and, sometimes, nonbank financial institutions. The law should deal with the requirements for the opening of a bank; the minimum share of capital; the fit-and-proper criteria for sharehold-

9

ers, managers, directors, and owners of banks; the provisions with respect to terminating licenses; the powers of banks to accept deposits and to carry on banking business; and the prudential supervision of banks, including the obligation on banks to furnish information on their activities regularly to the banking regulator. The law should also deal with distressed banks and with the power of the regulator to implement a range of remedial measures, to withdraw a license, to impose new management, and to ensure orderly liquidation and restructuring with the goal of maintaining financial stability. In addition, the law should deal with issues of confidentiality and bank secrecy. Anti-money-laundering measures are usually enshrined in separate legislation, but this legislation should be closely linked to the banking law framework. The legal aspects of banking supervision have already been considered in detail in chapter 5. The legal and institutional framework for anti-money-laundering activities and for countering the financing of terrorism are covered in chapter 8.

9.1.3 Payment Systems

Efficient payment systems are critical to the effective functioning of a financial system. Robust payment systems that are resistant to systemic and credit risk are an essential requirement for maintaining and promoting financial stability. Furthermore, in developing countries, an efficient and reliable payment system infrastructure constitutes an essential factor in creating a dynamic market economy. In many developing countries, payment system mechanisms are provided for by way of central bank directives rather than by law. Increasingly, however, the successful operation of payment systems can raise quite difficult issues, and a proper legal basis for such systems is desirable. The legal basis should provide for a variety of systems, including noncash methods of payment such as those relying on electronic debit cards and credit cards. Different types of clearance systems—such as paper-based and electronic clearing and settlement systems that are based on multilateral netting, paper-based gross settlement systems, same-time (intraregion) payment systems, electronic real-time gross settlement systems, and "swift-based terminal" systems—need to be provided for. Issues of confidentiality, supervision, and netting also need to be incorporated in the legislation.

Finality of payment and zero hour rule[2] provisions are important to ensure the safety and soundness of the payment system. These items ought to be provided for in the law. The banking law should also provide that, although banks cannot be liquidated without the consent or knowledge of the central bank, the fact that the payment system also includes other participants whose liquidation cannot be orchestrated by the central bank requires clear and express provisions in the law that provides for the zero hour rule.

9.1.4 Government Debt Management

Government securities usually play an important role in both developed and developing country economies, and the management of those security markets can be crucial for ensuring a robust and stable financial system. The legal regime that deals with this subject should provide for both the primary and secondary market for the securities. The rights and obligations of dealers; the procedures for public auctions, maturities of bills, and registration and transfer of ownership; and the responsibilities of agent banks are all topics that should be covered in the law.

The law needs to provide a clear legal basis for the issue of debt and the statutory designation of the authorities that are empowered to manage government debt. The law that provides for the issue of government securities must contain sufficient provisions to govern the issuance, transfer, and redemption of those securities. To avoid a legal vacuum, those provisions that deal with "physical securities" need to be reviewed and replaced with new rules and procedures that cover book-entry or scripless securities.

The law should provide for registration, structure, and settlement, including those in book-entry form. The law must contain procedures and rules to establish ownership, transfer, and final settlement of debt by the government on the basis of book-entry or scripless form. It is also important for the law to recognize electronic evidence in a court of law to prove ownership and to ensure the legality of transactions affecting rights of parties.

9.1.5 Capital Markets

Laws to establish a securities markets and stock exchanges play a key role in facilitating the providing of financing for domestic investment. Misuse of securities markets has resulted in the need for strict rules governing (a) the issue of securities to the public; (b) the registration and trading of securities; (c) the operation of stock exchanges; (d) the regulation of dealers, brokers, and other persons involved in the securities industry; (e) the strict requirements for prospectuses as well as for disclosure; and (f) the operation of publicly listed companies. A key component of the capital market is the creation and trading of asset-backed securities, which play a critical role in effective risk management by financial institutions and in strengthening access to finance by creating liquidity. However, securitization transactions call for a sophisticated system of laws on secured transactions, negotiable instruments, and creditor rights, as well as effective enforcement systems, as outlined in box 9.1. Legal aspects of securities markets regulation, drawing on IOSCO objectives and principles, are discussed in chapter 5.

9.1.6 Insurance

Insurance needs to be regulated by law and regulations that support the development of the sector and that provide adequate protection to policyholders while containing claims for insurance fraud. The insurance laws should specify the powers and responsibilities of the regulator; the conditions for the formation and registration of companies; disclosure requirements; prudential supervision; management of distressed insurers; and provisions with respect to payment of premiums, events of default, and reserves. Legal aspects of insurance supervision are discussed in detail in chapter 5, in the context of the IAIS Insurance Core Principles.

The development of insurance business has also suffered from repressive regulations by government in many low-income countries. Those regulations have included the creation of state-owned insurance companies, sometimes with a monopoly over all insurance business or for the benefit of state-owned business of state-owned enterprises. In addition, the regulations have included measures (a) to discourage entry by foreign companies,

---

Box 9.1 Legal Framework for Securitization

Securitization is achieved through the creation of asset-backed securities, which are capital market instruments that represent debt, equity, or hybrid interests in a pool of financial assets, which most often are loans (secured or unsecured), or other evidences of indebtedness (such as receivables). A pool of assets is formed and sold in an economic and legal sense to a special purpose vehicle, which then issues securities backed by the asset pool. Securitization permits the shifting of risk from one category of financial intermediaries (usually banks or commercial financial institutions that originate loans or debt instruments), to other financial intermediaries and investors (usually participants in the public or private capital markets). The development of asset-backed securities requires a sound and vibrant commercial finance sector and effective and efficient laws and institutions in the areas of negotiable instruments, secured transactions, and creditors' rights generally. In addition to efficient and reliable enforcement of contracts representing commercial indebtedness, the creation of asset-backed securities requires:

1. A sophisticated secured transactions law that clearly defines the rights and responsibilities of the parties with respect to the collateral in the event [that] the underlying debt is not paid in time
2. A system of laws relating to the creation, transfer, and enforcement of negotiable instruments by financial intermediaries
3. A reliable and effective system of enforcing commercial indebtedness
4. Laws permitting the transfer of secured and unsecured loans and the transfer and assignment of collateral and rights therein
5. Laws permitting the creation and regulation of special purpose financing vehicles with the purpose of isolating and clearly defining the financial risks of pools of assets held by such vehicles, and ensuring the transparency and accountability of the vehicle
6. Laws and regulations relating to governance of financial institutions and special purpose vehicles, which not only ensure fairness, transparency and accountability, but [also] impose appropriate fiduciary standards
7. A comprehensive system of accounting and reporting that permits timely and accurate identification, assessment, measurement, and management of risks involved in the creation of the indebtedness and its transfer of interests in the debt; and the ownership, management, and governance of the special purpose vehicles, as well as a system for assessing and managing the risks of off-balance sheet financial structures from the perspective of commercial financial institutions [that are] originating, holding, or participating in the indebtedness
8. A clear system of regulation and disclosure in the capital markets that permits full and fair assessment of the risks involved in purchasing and holding an undivided interest in a pool of financial assets
9. A system of accounting principles and rules that permit a consistent understanding, assessment, and measurement of the prices, values, and risks involved in the transfer and pooling of financial assets for all participants
10. A system of tax and related laws [that] may be necessary to ensure that the economic effects of securitization are consistent with economic or other policy imperatives of the jurisdiction

---

(b) to set premiums, (c) to control the terms and conditions of offered policies, and (d) to require insurance companies to invest their reserves in low-yielding assets or in social projects of various forms. In many cases, the imposition of minimum local retention ratios (thus discouraging reinsurance with international companies or markets) or the mandated use of a state-owned reinsurance company has acted as an additional constraint on the development of insurance.

Furthermore, insurance business in developing countries often suffers from widespread mistrust between insurance companies and their customers. To protect against fictitious claims and insurance fraud, insurance companies frequently include clauses that limit their liability in cases where material information was not provided at the time an insurance policy was bought. Insurance policies also have exclusion clauses that stipulate that insurance coverage will not be provided under specified .circumstances. However, the exclusion clauses make insurance contracts difficult to understand and give rise to disputes. In some countries, those disputes result in long delays in settling claims, which accentuate the mistrust that clients experience toward the insurance companies.

9.1.7 Financial Safety Nets

A deposit insurance scheme for bank deposits or for policyholder and investor protection schemes that are designed for insurance and capital markets should be explicitly and clearly defined in laws and regulations that are known to and understood by the public, as already outlined in chapter 5. Even if those arrangements are specified in separate laws, the relationship to the supervisory agency and the government, as well as the related coordination arrangements, should be transparent. The operation of lender-of-last-resort—both in normal and crisis times—is normally provided for in central bank laws. The scope of emergency lending, however, is often part of a larger legal and operational framework that provides for cooperation arrangements among agencies for crisis management and financial stability policies.

9.2 Commercial Laws

Key components of commercial laws that affect the sound functioning of financial institutions and markets include laws that define the regime for formation of companies, corporate governance of both financial and nonfinancial firms, and consumer protection in the financial system. The scope of those components is outlined below.

9.2.1 Company Law

A regime for the creation and operation of companies is a key element of any commercial system. Laws providing for the formation and registration of different types of companies—including joint stock, limited liability, closed and open partnerships (limited and special), and other forms of corporate entities—should be in place. Those types of laws should deal with the operation of the company registrar, procedures for registering companies, public access to the register, minimum capital requirements, procedures for the issue and transfer of shares, meetings of shareholders, rights and duties of shareholders, provisions for annual meetings, extraordinary meetings, role of the board of directors, duties of directors, role of auditors and audit procedures, accounting and auditing requirements, and penalties for infringements of the law.

9.2.2 Corporate Governance

Governance of the financial sector has emerged as an important factor in financial stability. Particularly in the transition economies where the legal and regulatory infrastructure is still in need of further strengthening, corporate governance has become recognized as an important factor in establishing trust in the financial system and in ensuring that bank depositors, insurance policyholders, and small shareholders have confidence that their funds have been entrusted to competent and honest administrators. Poor governance erodes customer confidence in banks and financial institutions and deters potential customers from (a) placing deposits with the bank, (b) transferring savings to an investment fund, or (c) purchasing an insurance policy. Poor corporate governance also makes it more difficult for financial institutions to raise additional equity capital, especially from investors outside the group of current shareholders.

A strong corporate governance framework improves the quality of the enterprise sector and is an important issue in determining the quality of a country's investment climate. Well-governed companies are likely to be more creditworthy as bank borrowers. In addition, the equity shares of well-governed corporations can provide solid investments for investment funds, pension funds, and insurance companies. Where weak corporate governance is associated with insufficient competition in the business sector, improved corporate governance practices can open the way for new entrants and increase competition for customers and new markets.

A corporate governance framework encompasses three primary areas:

1. Laws, regulations, and decrees that provide the legal framework for the commercial sector
2. Regulatory agencies responsible for the enforcement of legislation
3. Common marketplace practices (or business culture) that, in some countries, are as important as legislation and institutions

In the financial sector, it is important that the legal framework provide for (a) the ownership structure of banks, (b) appropriate fit and proper provisions for shareholders and key administrators, (c) transparency, and (d) strong regulatory oversight. The law also should provide detailed stipulations for the obligations of directors; directors' duties of care; procedures for the convening, operation, and termination of meetings; the relationship between management and owners; shareholder rights; audit responsibilities; accounting practices; public access to the records of the company registry; ability of the shareholders to obtain copies of shareholder lists; disclosure of shareholdings by public sector officials; fiduciary obligations of members of boards; and presence of codes of corporate conduct.

9.2.3 Consumer Protection

Consumers are an important stakeholder in the financial market. In fact, they are the reason for the existence of markets and, thus, they sustain markets. It is imperative that the legal framework provides for appropriate legal arrangements to safeguard the interest of consumers. Consumer protection in the financial system involves the protection of personal and credit information data; the right to security and safety in electronic and e-commerce transactions; the availability, access, and inexpensive cost of services such as remittances and the opening and maintaining of accounts; and an appropriate mechanism to address grievances in the event of a dispute with a bank. Often, cost-effective and efficient out-of-court dispute settlement arrangements serve a useful purpose in the protection of consumer rights.

Also, banks need to have sound systems in place to ensure that financial data, especially credit information, is secure, is accurate, and is released to relevant parties in accordance with prescribed legal safeguards that are permitted under the law or as agreed to by the customer. The customer has a legal right to require the systems used for electronic transactions, including ATMs and wire transfer systems, to be secure and to not expose the customer to unnecessary risk and loss. In this regard, a fair fees structure and availability of basic services is essential for access to finance by the poor. The consumer protection legislation should also provide for full and adequate disclosure of prices and of retail sale terms and conditions. In addition, an appropriate disclosure regime for financial institutions is a key ingredient of a comprehensive consumer protection regime.

9.3   Creditors Rights and Insolvency Systems

Effective creditor rights and insolvency systems play a vital role in helping to sustain financial soundness, and they promote commercial confidence by enabling market participants and stakeholders to more accurately price, manage, and resolve the risks of default and nonperformance. The extension of credit is predicated on repayment, and its costs are influenced by the risks and potential for default, as well as the associated costs and delays of recovery. Insolvency systems also promote a number of salutary goals: to promote market discipline, as well as good corporate and financial governance; to support optimal resolutions of financial distress for businesses; and to mitigate asset deterioration through swift and reliable enforcement channels. Experience with financial crises has shown that effective creditor rights and insolvency systems also facilitate prompt resolutions and recovery.

Attracting loans and investment requires that repayment risks be reasonable and manageable. Systems of credit protection, resolution, and enforcement will underpin and uphold those expectations in the commercial relationship. Collateral is increasingly significant and quite varied in today's markets. With competitive pressures on domestic and international businesses, those businesses must tap latent asset values to secure financing and capital so they can grow their business. Modern security laws take advantage of current developments in access to security in all of its various forms and shapes. Collateral without reliable enforcement, however, affords little genuine protection. Consequently, the full dimension of broad security must be complemented by effective and efficient enforcement processes.

A modern, credit-based economy requires (a) predictable, transparent, and affordable enforcement of both unsecured and secured credit claims by efficient mechanisms outside of insolvency and (b) a sound insolvency system. The systems must be designed to work in harmony. Commerce is a system of commercial relationships predicated on express or implied contractual agreements between an enterprise and a wide range of creditors and constituencies. Although commercial transactions have become increasingly complex as more sophisticated techniques are developed for pricing and managing risks, the basic rights governing those relationships and the procedures for enforcing the rights have not changed much. Those rights enable parties to rely on contractual agreements, thus fostering confidence that fuels investment, lending, and commerce. Conversely, uncertainty about the enforceability of contractual rights increases the cost of credit to compensate for the increased risk of nonperformance, and in severe cases, uncertainty leads to credit tightening.

The legal framework for creditor rights includes mechanisms that provide efficient, transparent, and reliable methods for recovering debt, including seizure and sale of immovable and movable assets, as well as sale or collection of intangible assets such as debt owed to the debtor by third parties. An efficient system for enforcing debt claims is crucial to a functioning credit system, especially for unsecured credit. A creditor's ability to take possession of a debtor's property and to sell it to satisfy the debt is the simplest, most-effective means of ensuring prompt payment. It is far more effective than the threat of an insolvency proceeding, which often requires a level of proof and a prospect of procedural delay that in all but extreme cases make it not credible to debtors as leverage for payment.

Although much credit is unsecured and requires an effective enforcement system, having an effective system for secured rights is especially important in developing countries. Secured credit plays an important role in industrial countries, notwithstanding the range of sources and types of financing available through both debt and equity markets. In some cases, equity markets can provide cheaper and more attractive financing. But developing countries offer fewer options, and equity markets are typically less mature than debt markets. As a result, most financing is in the form of debt. In markets with fewer options and higher risks, lenders routinely require security to reduce the risk of nonperformance and insolvency.

The legal framework for secured lending should provide for the creation, recognition, and enforcement of security interests in all types of assets—movable and immovable; tangible and intangible, including inventories, receivables, proceeds, and future property and, on a global basis, including both possessory and nonpossessory interests. The law should encompass any or all of a debtor's obligations to a creditor—present or future and between all types of persons. In addition, it should provide for effective notice and registration rules to be adapted to all types of property, and it should set clear rules of priority on competing claims or interests in the same assets.

The legal framework for corporate insolvency should establish a collective process for resolving or adjusting the rights and interests of a variety of stakeholders in a failed business. Each country's system balances a number of policies and objectives as determined by the policy makers within that country. Invariably, a system includes a number of potentially diverging policies and interests that must be balanced and harmonized to make it functional and meaningful within the context of the needs of a particular country. The policies and interests that must be balanced include governmental and political objectives, cultural and social concerns, and economic and commercial interests. A country's system is also defined by three main pillars—the legal, institutional, and regulatory frameworks—each of which is equally important to creating an effective and efficient system for users. The absence or inefficiency of any one of those pillars compromises the entire system.

Though approaches vary, a number of common objectives and goals apply to commercial insolvency systems. They should attempt to

- Provide for timely, efficient, and impartial resolution of insolvencies.
- Integrate with a country's broader legal and commercial systems.
- Maximize the value of a firm's assets and recoveries by creditors.
- Provide for (a) efficient liquidation of nonviable businesses and those where liquidation is likely to produce a greater return to creditors and (b) rehabilitation of viable businesses.
- Strike a careful balance between liquidation and reorganization, allowing for easy conversion of proceedings from one procedure to another.
- Provide for equitable treatment of similarly situated creditors, including similarly situated foreign and domestic creditors.
- Prevent the improper use of the insolvency system.
- Prevent the premature dismemberment of a debtor's assets by individual creditors who are seeking quick judgments.
- Provide a transparent procedure that contains—and consistently applies—clear risk allocation rules and incentives for gathering and dispensing information.
- Recognize existing creditor rights, and respect the priority of claims with a predictable and established process.
- Establish a framework for cross-border insolvencies, with recognition of foreign proceedings.

Where an enterprise is not viable, the main thrust of the law should be swift and efficient liquidation to maximize recoveries for the benefit of creditors. One the one hand, liquidations can include the preservation and sale of the business, as distinct from the legal entity. On the other hand, where an enterprise is viable—meaning it can be rehabilitated—its assets are often more valuable if retained in a rehabilitated business than if sold in a liquidation. The rescue of a business preserves jobs, provides creditors with a greater return on the basis of higher going-concern values of the enterprise, potentially produces a return for owners, and obtains for the country the fruits of the rehabilitated enterprise. The rescue of a business should be promoted through formal and informal procedures.

Rehabilitation should (a) permit quick and easy access to the process, (b) protect all interested parties having a financial stake in the outcome of the process, (c) permit the negotiation of a commercial plan, (d) enable a majority of creditors in favor of a plan or other course of action to bind all other creditors (subject to appropriate protections), and (e) provide for supervision to ensure that the process is not subject to abuse. Modern rescue procedures typically address a wide range of commercial expectations in dynamic markets. Though those types of laws may not be susceptible to precise formulas, modern systems generally rely on design features to achieve the objectives outlined earlier.

Corporate workouts should be supported by an environment that encourages participants to restore an enterprise to financial viability through informal workouts that are negotiated in the "shadow of the law." Accordingly, the enabling environment must (a) include clear laws and procedures that require disclosure of or access to timely and accurate financial information on the distressed enterprise; (b) encourage lending to, investment in, or recapitalization of viable distressed enterprises; (c) support a broad range of restructuring activities such as debt write-offs, reschedulings, restructurings, and debt-equity conversions; and (d) provide favorable or neutral tax treatment for restructurings.

A country's financial sector should promote (possibly with help from the central bank or finance ministry) an informal out-of-court process for dealing with cases of corporate financial difficulty in which banks and other financial institutions have a significant exposure—especially in markets where enterprise insolvency is systemic. An informal process is far more likely to be sustained where there are adequate creditor remedies and insolvency laws.

Strong institutions and regulations are crucial to an effective system for commercial enforcement and insolvency proceedings. The institutional framework has three main elements: the institutions responsible for the proceedings, the operational system through which cases and decisions are processed, and the requirements needed to preserve the integrity of those institutions—recognizing that the integrity of the system is the linchpin for its success.

A sound regulatory framework requires insolvency administrators who are competent to exercise the powers given to them and who act with integrity, impartiality, and independence. Finally, the bodies responsible for regulating or supervising insolvency administrators should be independent of individual administrators and should set standards that reflect the requirements of the legislation and public expectations of fairness, impartiality, transparency, and accountability.

In 2001, the World Bank endorsed the "Principles and Guidelines for Effective Insolvency and Creditor Rights (ICR) Systems"[3] (principles) for use in connection with assessments of creditor rights, commercial enforcement, and insolvency systems under the program to develop reports on the observance of standards and codes (ROSC).[4] The principles provide a framework for comprehensively assessing the effectiveness of insolvency and creditor rights systems against international best practices. The principles contain a set of core principles elaborated under 35 topics in four primary areas: (a) creditor rights and enforcement systems (for secured and unsecured credit); (b) corporate insolvency systems (liquidation and rescue legislative procedures); (c) credit risk management, debt recovery, and informal enterprise workout practices; and (d) effective implementation of legal mechanisms (institutional and regulatory frameworks).

The insolvency and creditor rights assessments have a number of applications for international financial institutions, policy makers, and the private sector. The assessments support diagnostic and strategic work, underpin policy dialogue and lending operations, and provide input to technical assistance and capacity building efforts. Assessments can be seen as building blocks for diagnostic work such as investment climate assessments in which creditor rights and enforcement systems are viewed as pivotal to assessing nonperformance and regulatory risks for lending and investment. They also provide useful inputs into key policy documents, such as sectoral strategies for the private and financial sectors or countrywide development strategies. As in the case of other Bank-led ROSC assessments, their strengths lie both in the systematic standardized coverage and in their ability to benchmark against an internationally recognized standard, and they provide an easy guide to policy dialogue and reform.

9.4 Access to Credit and Land Rights

Land law constitutes an important factor for sustainable development and private sector growth. It creates property rights systems for individuals, businesses, and the state, which, in turn, will create incentives to conserve and produce. It sets out the circumstances in which, and processes by which, rights in land can be transferred, permanently or temporarily, or used to secure loans. It also embodies some limitations imposed by the state on those rights, for instance, zoning rules that limit land use or rules prohibiting transfers of land to foreigners. The legal structures reflect basic allocative decisions of the society and influence the extent of poverty and prosperity in an economy.

Land law provides a critical portion of the legal infrastructure for private sector investment and a modern financial system. Secure land rights allow investors with a safe time horizon to invest and to recoup investments and, thus, are an important element in the incentive structure for investment. Also, marketable land rights allow land to move to those who will use it more efficiently and who are thus willing to pay more for it, increasing its productive use. In addition, mortgageable land rights can be used to raise capital for investments, and those rights can play a key role in capital formation in developing economies.

In many countries, landholders do not enjoy secure and transferable tenure. Often, vast bureaucracies administer systems of tenure, such as long-term leaseholds from the state in which official permission is needed for transactions, and the transactions are subject to onerous taxation. Use controls built into titles may freeze land in what have become inappropriate uses. Mortgaging or real estate development may be flatly proscribed. In such situations, local land administration officials often take full advantage of the rent-seeking opportunities posed by their discretionary power.

Businesses commonly complain of the shortfalls and frustrations of land laws and land administration and of the cost they pose for doing business. The frustrations occur because, even where land law is adequately framed to promote private sector development, reliable proof of titles may be difficult. Land survey services and services to determine and register titles are essential to making land rights effective, and they are often almost as important as the content of the right itself.

On the financial side, mortgageability is the critical characteristic of land. It is vital to allow individuals to be able to raise capital for the capitalization of the economy. Land is the primary form of collateral for credit. Land registration also can provide a link to the owner's credit history, an accountable address for the collection of debts and taxes, a basis for the creation of reliable and universal public utilities, and a foundation for the creation of securities (such as mortgage-backed bonds) that can then be rediscounted and sold in secondary markets.

Secured transaction law can yield significant financial and fiscal benefits. Advanced secured transaction laws provide more credit by reducing the costs of borrowing and thus can increase the amount of available credit in the economy. Any reduction in the costs of borrowing enhances the advantage, thus ensuring that debt offers an advantage to firms. And for public finance, the existence of an adequate system of records of rights in land can provide the basis for land taxation, a relatively simple and easy-to-administer tax

9

that has been critical in many countries to the funding of decentralized local government programs. The land law ought to establish (a) basic property rights, (b) transferability and basic mortgage ability, (c) adequate systems for recording those rights and their transfer, and (d) framework for securities that are based on the value of assets in land.

9.5 The Judicial System

It is widely accepted that economic growth and social development cannot be sustained and promoted in countries where the justice system fails. By consistently enforcing clear rules, an independent and impartial judicial system supports legal reform and promotes economic and social development. An effective judiciary should apply and enforce laws and regulations impartially, predictably, and efficiently.

Whether the legal system is one of civil law or common-law tradition, it is imperative that its structure ensure adequate checks and balances on the three branches of the government—legislative, executive, and judicial. The legislature ought to act as the enabling and enlightened arm that makes, adds, and amends the rules for the regulation of the financial sector. The executive branch needs to be efficient and effective in carrying out the mandate of the legislature, whereas the judiciary ought to act as the guardian of the nation to ensure that the other two arms operate within their mandate.

The process through which laws and regulations are conceptualized, drafted, enacted, publicized, and enforced is the foundation of a society governed by the rule of law. When the law-making process is not effective, the legal system suffers from outdated and badly written laws that do not provide a sound legal basis for executive action. This situation must be avoided because it encourages reversal of policy and practices and it makes executive action and acts of regulatory bodies vulnerable to legal challenge.

The legal and judicial system must provide a method for resolving disputes not only between private agents but also between private agents and the state. Courts are a way to resolve disputes justly. Courts must resolve disputes by judgments that are based on independent fact-finding. Those judgments must be enforced by the state. State enforcement distinguishes courts from alternative forms of dispute resolution. State enforcement also limits potential violence and can improve the business climate. But for courts to be effective, the other branches of government must also comply with the law. The judicial system must provide checks and balances against arbitrary state action. If the judiciary is to fulfill its role as the guardian of the nation, the judiciary and its work must be perceived as fair. Courts must work efficiently, and they should be sufficiently accessible.

The fairness of judicial decisions is determined first by the judges' independence—real and perceived. There must be sufficient safeguards to ensure that judicial decisions are independent of both political decisions and the influence of powerful private parties and that government officials can be made to obey the law. Other branches of government should not override or ignore judicial decisions. When they do, they should be subject to legal action. Judges' independence entails that their decisions are not determined by anything other than the facts in the case and the applicable law.

Fairness of judicial decisions must be safeguarded by adequate procedural provisions. Hearings should be open to the public. Assignment of cases should follow standardized procedures. There must be sufficient guarantees in the law governing civil procedure for party input, oral proceedings, and independent fact-finding. Rules of evidence and standards for evaluating arguments should be in place and should be applied in a predictable fashion. Possibilities for the review of decisions should be adequate because they safeguard the quality of judicial decisions. There should be a three-tiered system in place: (a) a court where the cases are heard initially; (b) courts of appeal, which review cases as to the facts and with respect to the law; and (c) cessation by a final instance court with respect to conformity to existing law.

Judges' independence must be supported by objective selection and career planning and by training. Judges must be selected according to objective criteria. The criteria must be job relevant and merit based. The criteria must also be public. Selection must be done in a transparent manner. Judges should have life or fixed-term tenure. They should be sufficiently trained. Compulsory training at entry should be followed up with permanent education to guarantee judges' independence and the quality of their decisions. Judicial salaries should meet living wage and some reasonable proportion of good wage in the private sector. Existing laws and the body of jurisprudence must be readily available to judges and their staff members and should be regularly updated. Another safeguard for judicial independence is the existence of an independent, competent association of lawyers.

Governance of the judiciary—including its accountability and efficiency—should underpin its independence. Existing institutional arrangements on this point vary considerably. Responsibilities with respect to the budget of the judicial organization; the judicial career, including matters of discipline; the court management; and the other issues should be distributed among the judicial administration body—such as a judicial council, the Supreme Court, and the Ministry of Justice—in such a way that judicial independence is not compromised. Changes in the budget for the judicial organization should be commensurate with the development of the national budget and also should reflect changes in demand for judicial services. Court management should follow set rules, and the management processes should be monitored and audited. The courts' efficiency is defined in terms of the speed, cost, and quality of the judicial decisions, as well as the access that aggrieved citizens have to the court. Those four factors are interdependent. Procedures for resolving a dispute must be proportionate to the value, importance, and complexity of the dispute.

Procedures and the way courts work should facilitate timely judicial decisions. Pretrial settlement of disputes may be encouraged but not enforced. Procedures and procedural law should not be unnecessarily complicated. Procedures should be reasonably efficient, as well as designed and reformulated in the interests of eliminating unnecessary steps and bottlenecks. Judges must have the power to move cases ahead and to punish or deny efforts to create additional delays. Adequate case management systems should be in place. Where there are small claims courts and other specialized courts and where there is the possibility of oral proceedings, trials tend to go faster. A forum for provisional judgment can prevent the need for full proceedings, which take more time.

Cost is an important factor in the courts' ability to provide an adequate service. Courts should be managed in an economic manner. The funding for staffing, equipment, and offices of the courts must be adequate to allow the performance of the courts' duties. Internal resource distribution should be based on need and workload. Court fees are part of the cost, but most of the cost for taking a case to court relates to fees for legal assistance. Low value or simple disputes should be assigned to simpler and faster procedures that consume fewer court resources. For example, disputes over small amounts of money should be handled by small claims courts, where parties can represent themselves.

The judiciary and the courts must be sufficiently accessible. To provide access to justice, courts should be reasonably close to the citizens and not exclusively concentrated in the capital. Courts must be managed in such a way that taking a case to court is not unnecessarily cumbersome. Cost should also not hinder citizens' access to courts. The cost of taking a case to court should not be so high that it prohibits access to justice. There should be sufficient possibilities for low-cost or free legal advice and assistance. Ways of providing legal aid in case of need should guarantee access to courts.

Although judicial review in developing countries is helping to ensure checks and balances, it can also be abused if the law does not lay down the perimeters for the role of court judicial review. The banking law ought to circumscribe the role of the courts in judicial review by defining it in the law and by disallowing a stay of regulatory decisions. A further useful provision is one that confines the relief of the court to compensation. The foregoing will help to prevent vexatious and unwarranted proceedings against regulatory action.

Alternative dispute settlement systems can be designated in relation not only to the disputes between banks and customer and between a bank and another bank but also to the disputes that arise between the banks and the regulator. Experience has shown that installing effective dispute settlement mechanisms for all types of disputes has paid off handsomely. They reduce litigation cost, resolve disputes faster, and instill greater faith in the banking system as far as customers are concerned while also establishing better relationships between banks and between banks and the regulator. In this respect, options such as a banking ombudsman to resolve customer–banker disputes, banking tribunals to deal with differences between the banks and the regulator, and use of arbitration by banks should also be explored.

Notes

1. For a discussion of key elements of central bank autonomy and accountability, see Lybek (1998). Accountability arrangements are also discussed in the Code of Good Practices in Transparency of Monetary and Financial Policy (IMF 1999).
2. The definitions of when a settlement of payment instruction is final in a payment system—settlement finality rules—may come in conflict with the "zero hour rules" in an insolvency regime. In the context of a payment system, zero hour rules make all transactions by a bankrupt participant void from the start (zero hour) of the day of bankruptcy (or similar event). In a real-time system dealing with gross settlements, the effect could be to reverse payments that have apparently already been settled and were thought to be final. In a system with deferred net settlement, such a rule could cause the netting of all transactions to be unwound, with possible systemic consequences. For a discussion of the legal basis of payment systems, see Bank for International Settlement (2001).

3. The principles and guidelines for effective insolvency and creditor rights systems (principles) were developed in collaboration with a number of international partner organizations and numerous international experts who constituted the Bank's task force and working groups. From 1999 to 2000, regional practices were examined, and various drafts of the principles were discussed in regional workshops involving more than 700 public and private sector specialists from some 75 countries. The principles and background papers can be accessed in the Global Insolvency Law Database (http://www.worldbank.org/gild), which has been designed as a research tool to promote access to and awareness of country practices. This broad dialogue process yielded strong international support and consensus on the principles, which establish a uniform framework to assess the effectiveness of corporate insolvency and creditor rights systems. Since April 2001, the principles have served as the basis for formal assessments in countries around the world, including in the context of the financial sector assessment program. The Bank is currently collaborating with the IMF and the United Nations Commission on International Trade Laws (UNCITRAL) to develop unified standards on insolvency and creditor rights systems.

4. The principles on insolvency and creditor rights (ICR) systems have been used in a series of experimental country assessments in connection with the program to develop reports on standards and codes (ROSC).

References

Anderson, Kym. 2004. "Agricultural Trade Reform and Poverty Reduction in Developing Countries." Policy Research Working Paper 3396, World Bank: Washington, D.C.

Bank for International Settlements. 2001. "Core Principles for Systemically Important Payment Systems." Committee on Payment Settlement Systems, Bank for International Settlements, Basel, Switzerland. Available at http://www.bis.org/publ/cpss34.pdf.

Chiquier Loic, Hassler Olivier, Lea Michael. 2004. "Mortgage Securities in Emerging Markets." Policy Research Working Paper, WPS 3370, World Bank: Washington, DC.

European Bank for Reconstruction and Development (EBRD).2004. *Model Law on Secured Transactions*, EBRD: London, England.

Ganslandt, Mattias and James R. Markusen. 2001. "Standards and Related Regulations in International Trade: A Modeling Approach." NBER Working Papers No. 8346, National Bureau of Economic Research: Washington, D.C.

Johnson, Gordon W.1999. "State-Owned Enterprise Insolvency: Treatment of Financial Distress." Paper presented at Symposium on State owned Enterprise Insolvency, April 10, 2000. World Bank, Washington DC.

International Monetary Fund. 1999. "Code of Good Practices on Transparency in Monetary and Financial Policy." International Monetary Fund, Washington, DC.

Lybek, Tonny. 1998. "Elements of Central Bank: Autonomy and Accountability." Monetary and Exchange Affairs Department Operational Paper 98/1, International Monetary Fund, Washington, DC.

Wood, Philip R. 1999. "Insolvency Law and the Legal Framework." Paper presented at the World Bank Symposium on Legal Framework, September, World Bank, Washington, DC.

World Bank. 2001a. "Principles and Guidelines for Effective Insolvency and Creditor Rights Systems." World Bank, Washington, DC. Available at http://www.worldbank.org/ifa/ipg_eng.pdf.

————. 2001b. Reforming Land and Real Estate Markets. World Bank: Washington, DC.

————. 2002a. Court Records Assessment Manual, World Bank: Washington, DC

————. 2002b. Legal and Judicial Reform: Observations, Experiences, and Approach of the Legal Vice-Presidency. World Bank: Washington, DC.

————. 2002c. Legal and Judicial Sector Assessment Manual, World Bank: Washington, DC

————. 2003a. Land Policies for Growth and Poverty Reduction. World Bank: Washington, DC.

————. 2003b. Land Rights for Poor People Key to Poverty Reduction, Growth. World Bank: Washington, DC.

————. 2003c. Legal and Judicial Reform: Strategic Directions. World Bank: Washington, DC.

————. 2004. "Stability and Security." in World Development Report 2005, chapter 4. World Bank: Washington, DC.

9

Chapter 10

Assessing Information and Governance Infrastructure

Information and governance infrastructure for finance provides the foundation for financial development and effective market discipline, and it helps to reinforce official supervision. It refers (a) to the legal and institutional arrangements and structures that affect the quality, availability, and transparency of information on monetary and financial conditions and policies at various levels and (b) to the incentives and organizational structures to set and implement policies by regulators, the regulated institutions, and their counterparties. The information infrastructure includes (a) the framework for monetary and financial policy transparency (discussed in section 10.1); (b) the accounting and auditing framework that helps to define and validate the information that is disclosed to the public and the regulatory authorities (discussed in section 10.2); and (c) the arrangements to compile, process, and share information on financial conditions and credit exposures of borrowers and other issuers of financial claims (credit-reporting and financial information services, discussed in section 10.3).

The governance arrangements for financial and non-financial firms that are publicly listed and traded are of particular interest because they directly affect the functioning of the financial markets where their securities are traded. The corporate governance arrangements and the Organisation for Economic Co-operation and Development (OECD) principles of corporate governance are discussed in section 10.4. The governance of financial firms and of financial sector regulators is covered in different degrees of detail in the standards for financial sector supervision. Selected aspects of financial sector governance are also highlighted in that section.

A key aspect of financial institutions' governance is the institution's disclosure practices, which are determined in part by the supervisory framework, including the listing requirements by securities regulators, and by the company laws. The appropriate scope of financial institutions' disclosure, including the disclosure standards under the New Basel Capital Accord, is discussed in section 10.5.

The disclosure and governance arrangements for financial and non-financial sectors should be seen in the broader context of public sector governance. Within this broader context, there are significant linkages among the governance arrangements for the regulatory agencies (including the central bank), the regulated entities, and the non-financial sector. This governance nexus should be taken into account in assessing the overall information and governance infrastructure.[1]

10.1 Monetary and Financial Policy Transparency

Good transparency practices for central banks and financial agencies in their conduct of monetary and financial policies can contribute policy effectiveness, policy consistency and good governance. The scope of good transparency practices and the issues in assessing their adequacy and effectiveness are discussed in this section.

10.1.1 Code of Good Practices

The concept of transparency of monetary and financial policies refers to an environment in which the objectives of the policy; the policy's legal, institutional, and economic framework; the policy decisions and their rationale; the data and information related to monetary and financial policies; and the terms of agencies' accountability are provided to the public on an understandable, accessible, and timely basis. The *Code of Good Practices on Transparency in Monetary and Financial Policies* (MFP Code) identifies desirable transparency practices for central banks and financial agencies in their conduct of monetary and financial policies. The MFP Code was developed by the IMF in 1999.[2] This document is a distillation of concepts and practices that are already in use and for which there is a record of experience. Together with the *Supporting Document to the Code of Good Practices on Transparency in Monetary and Financial Policies* (Supporting Document; IMF 2000b), the various guidance notes, and the specific templates, the MFP Code serves as the reference material for assessing transparency practices in monetary and financial policies.

The transparency of monetary and financial policies contributes to policy effectiveness, facilitates policy consistency, and strengthens governance. The public's awareness of the goals and instruments of policy, as well as the authorities' credible commitment to meeting the goals, can contribute to good policy making and can improve the effectiveness of policies. Transparency in the mandate, as well as the rules and procedures in the operations of monetary and financial agencies, helps to ensure consistency in cases where conflicts might arise between or within government units. Good governance calls for central banks and financial agencies to be accountable, particularly where the monetary and financial authorities are granted a high degree of autonomy. In the case of monetary policy, transparency about policy process—achieved by providing the private sector with a clear description of the considerations that guide monetary policy decisions—helps ensure that market expectations can be formed more efficiently and, thereby, makes the monetary policy transmission mechanism generally more effective. Through good

10

transparency practices, the central bank can establish a mechanism for strengthening its credibility by matching its actions to its public statements. Similarly, transparency of a regulatory agency's mandate, operations, and regulatory processes is essential in establishing the credibility and effectiveness of financial sector oversight. Although credibility is achieved by meeting the stated objectives and responsibilities, transparency may also limit self-interest on the part of the regulators and may foster increased commitment of regulated firms to regulatory compliance, prudent behavior, proper risk management, and internal control.

The MFP Code lists 17 good practices on transparency of monetary policies by the central bank and 20 good practices on transparency of financial policies, all grouped into four categories. Many of the good practices are further divided into more detailed practices. The four groups of transparency practices and a summary description of each practice are presented in Annex 10.A. The four groups are (1) clarity of roles, responsibilities, and objectives of central banks and financial agencies; (2) the processes for the formulating and reporting of monetary policy decisions by the central bank and of financial policies by financial agencies; (3) public availability of information on monetary and financial policies; and (4) accountability and assurances of integrity by the central bank and financial agencies.

10.1.2 Assessment Methodology and Assessment Experience

The objectives of MFP transparency assessments are to review the effectiveness of current practices and to recommend desirable transparency practices. The assessments, therefore, are designed to

- Allow the authorities to evaluate the transparency of their monetary policy and their financial supervisory and regulatory frameworks.
- Identify and, where appropriate, recommend desirable transparency practices for central banks and financial agencies.
- Provide input into the overall assessment of the vulnerabilities of a country's monetary and financial system.
- Help identify the developmental needs of a country pertaining specifically to transparency issues and to assist in making informed policy decisions about the reforms needed.
- Provide input on the extent to which transparency practices contribute to policy effectiveness and to monetary and financial stability.

The MFP Code is broad and takes into account the varied institutional and legal frameworks that are found in many countries across various stages of financial development. Consequently, the ways in which transparency is applied and achieved—in terms of timing and manner of disclosure as well as the content of reports—may differ, reflecting different institutional arrangements and legal traditions. Assessments should not be conducted in a mechanistic way because practical policy considerations may require that some disclosures not be made in certain contexts.

In particular, benefits of transparency practices have to be weighed against the potential costs, and it may be appropriate to limit the extent of transparency. For example,

10

extensive disclosure requirements about internal policy discussion on money and exchange market operations might disrupt markets, constrain the free flow of discussion by policy makers, or prevent the adoption of contingency plans. Thus, there are circumstances in which it would not be appropriate for central banks to disclose their near-term monetary and exchange rate policy implementation tactics or to provide detailed information on foreign exchange operations. Similarly, there may be good reasons for the central bank (and financial agencies) not to make public specific contingency plans, including possible emergency lending. However, the broad principles and procedures governing the decisions on emergency lending could be established and made transparent while maintaining "constructive ambiguity" about their applicability in specific situations (see chapter 5, section 5.2.1). However, limiting transparency in selected areas needs to be seen in the context of a generally transparent environment. Also, the MFP Code is not designed to offer judgment on the appropriateness or desirability of specific monetary and financial policies or frameworks that countries should adopt.

The assessment of observance of the MFP Code should draw on a wide range of information and should focus on the degree and means of disclosure to the public, as well as on the effect of disclosure practices on a policy's effectiveness. The sources of information needed for the assessment typically include relevant laws, regulations, and instructions, as well as other documentation (reports, studies, public statements, Web sites, unpublished guidelines, directives, and assessments); counterparty agencies and officials with whom assessment-related discussions are held; meetings with other domestic authorities; any relevant government or industry associations (such as bankers' associations, auditors, and accountants); and key market participants and analysts who draw on the information disclosed. The methodology for the assessment consists of examining, for each practice in the MFP code, the various forms of disclosure used, frequency of disclosures, quality or content of disclosure, and modes of disclosure. In addition, a fifth dimension—clarity and comprehensibility of transparency—is also examined. The content, clarity, and accessibility of the information that is disclosed are what transforms "disclosure" into "transparency." An assessment of those five dimensions is based on a broad qualitative judgment drawing on country practices and is not based on any specified list of assessment criteria.

Illustrative country practices are summarized in the Supporting Document,[3] which also provides two- or three-part explanations of each transparency practice:

- "Explanation and rationale" elaborates on what is meant and why it is desirable.
- "Application" indicates where and how the practices are implemented, with some quantification and, where applicable, with some country examples.
- "Implementation considerations" deals with practical considerations—benefits and costs, intended audience, domestic versus international dimensions—where relevant. The supporting document also provides a list of references—academic studies as well as official documents—on transparency and accountability issues. The qualitative judgment of various dimensions of transparency can be informed by the supporting document, and this judgment is used to classify the degree of observance of each practice into five categories: observed, broadly observed, partly observed, non-observed, and not applicable. Detailed guidance on the procedures

and practical considerations in conducting the assessments are available in the guidance note (IMF 2000) for assessing the code.

- A supplementary document providing case studies for 15 countries is under preparation.

So far, the IMF Executive Board has conducted two reviews of experiences with assessments of the MFP Code, drawing on MFP Code assessments for 57 countries.[4] In general, the two reviews indicated a high level of observance of transparency practices among the countries reviewed. Observance was strongest with respect to the public availability of information on monetary and financial policies. Many central banks and financial agencies are making more effective use of various channels of communication to increase the public's access to information. In banking supervision and payment system oversight, transparency was weak in practices relating to clarity of the roles, responsibilities, and objectives of the institutions.

Transparency practices with respect to the accountability and assurance of integrity of the central banks and financial agencies continue to be a challenge for many of the countries (see boxes 10.1 and 10.2). This finding also has been borne out in other Fund initiatives such as the Safeguards Assessments (IMF 2002) and in the assessments of Special Data Dissemination Standards (SDDS) (IMF 2003). Among all financial sectors, banking supervisory agencies had the most-developed transparency practices whereas insurance regulatory agencies had the least-developed transparency practices.

Standard-setting bodies have increasingly included transparency-related criteria in their individual standards and codes. The IAIS standards emphasize the need for transparency by the supervisory agency, and various transparency practices of the MFP Code are embedded in the IAIS Core Principles. The *Core Principles for Systemically Important Payment Systems* (see Chapter 11 for references and discussion) calls for effective oversight of such payment systems by the central bank and, consistent with the MFP code, calls for the central bank to define clearly its payment system objectives and to disclose publicly its role and major policies with respect to systemically important payment systems. The coverage of transparency issues in regulatory standards is, however, rather uneven, and there have been recent efforts to specify transparency practices of regulatory agencies in greater detail as a component of good regulatory governance of those agencies (components of good regulatory governance consist of independence, accountability, transparency, and integrity).

10.2 Accounting and Auditing Assessments

An assessment of accounting and auditing standards is a key part of the evaluation of robustness of a country's financial market infrastructure (the third pillar of the Financial Sector Assessment) and includes financial sector governance. A core component of good corporate governance is an accurate disclosure that is based on high-quality accounting and auditing standards. A comprehensive assessment of those standards presents the strengths and weaknesses of accounting and auditing frameworks. The assessment also analyzes the framework's quality and enforcement, as well as its potential success in changing the effectiveness of supervision and the soundness of the financial system. A sound account-

---

Box 10.1 Main Weaknesses in the Transparency Practices of Central Banks and Monetary Policy

1. Clarity of Roles, Responsibilities, and Objectives of Central Banks

- A general lack of clarity about the hierarchy among a multiplicity of monetary policy objectives and about how potential conflicts among them would be resolved
- Potential conflicts in the policy objectives, as provided for in different statutes
- Lack of clarity in the responsibility over foreign exchange policy
- Absence of specifics and conditions under which governments may override central bank policy decisions
- Existence of legal provisions to use various instruments often encumbered by the need to seek approval from another authority (e.g., the Ministry of Finance)
- Disclosure of certain information that is often limited by strict interpretations of secrecy rules governing operations of some central banks
- Accountability of some central banks weakened by the absence of an explicit legal requirement to report to a legislative body or designated public authority to inform on the conduct of monetary policy and the fulfillment of policy objectives
- Unclear institutional relationships between central banks and governments, as well as associated agency roles and financial transactions

2. Open Process for Formulating and Reporting Monetary Policy Decisions

- Poor or nonexistent explanations for the rationale and functioning of its policy instruments

- Insufficient frequency of disclosures (with some authorities arguing that the guidelines are not clear in that regard)
- Reservations about announcing meeting schedules for policy-making bodies

3. Public Availability of Information on Monetary Policy

- Remaining weaknesses in the availability of specific data templates even through many countries subscribe or plan to subscribe to the International Monetary Fund's data dissemination standard (Special Data Dissemination Standard, or SDDS, and the General Data Dissemination System, or GDDS)
- Timeliness and frequency of publications a common problem
- Concerns about the quality of some of the information that is disclosed

4. Accountability and Assurances of Integrity by the Central Bank

- Deficiencies in some of the procedures in the areas of auditing and accounting
- Many cases of nondisclosure of internal governance procedures, including the standards for the personal conduct of staff members
- Nondisclosure, lack of explicit legal protection for officials and staff members in the conduct of their official duties, or both.

---

ing framework is a precondition for effective supervision; thus, an examination of the accounting and auditing framework—not necessarily a comprehensive assessment—is an essential prerequisite for undertaking assessments of observance of supervisory standards. This chapter explains the rationale of accounting and auditing standards and provides an overview of International Financial Reporting Standards (IFRSs) and International Standards for Auditing (ISA), highlighting the components of the standards that are particularly relevant for financial sector assessments. The chapter then outlines the World Bank's Report on Observance of Standards and Codes (ROSC) program on accounting and auditing standards, highlighting the key lessons of experience.

10.2.1 Role of the Accounting and Auditing Framework: Relevance to Development and Stability

Accounting and auditing standards of high quality provide the basis for reliable and transparent disclosure of information to relevant stakeholders. Disclosure is crucial for informed financial decisions, efficient resource allocation, and effective functioning of markets. Chapter 4 discusses the fact that they form the core of the information infrastructure needed for financial development. Accounting, auditing, and disclosure requirements of high quality for financial institutions are regarded as one of the key basic areas of financial reform necessary to prevent a financial crisis.[5] By contributing to good corporate governance, high-quality accounting and auditing influence perceptions of risk, cost, and

---

Box 10.2 Main Weaknesses in the Transparency Practices in Financial Policies

1. Clarity of Roles, Responsibilities, and Objectives of Financial Agencies Responsible for Financial Policies

- Lack of legal basis for the objectives and responsibilities for some financial agencies
- Lack of documentation spelling out explicit and detailed definition of the institutional oversight role of some central banks with respect to payment systems and its relations with banking activities
- Lack of explicit and clearly defined authority along with the necessary powers to issue and enforce accompanying regulations; little specific focus on the implicit risks of participation in payment systems
- Insufficient published information on objectives, operations, and outcomes of financial agencies
- Legal requirements for submission of reports on developments not sufficiently comprehensive
- Lack of clarity with respect to terms of appointment and dismissal of key officers
- Little information on formal arrangements for cooperation and exchange of information among various supervisory agencies
- Absence of information on investor protection schemes in securities regulations
- Lack of legal underpinning of the regulations and procedures for securities

2. Open Process for Formulating and Reporting Financial Policies

- Absence of public disclosure of the relationships between financial agencies
- Lack of specific requirements for periodic reporting on financial agencies

- Lack of disclosure of information-sharing arrangements among agencies
- Absence of public announcement of changes in payment systems policies

3. Public Availability of Information on Financial Policies

- Inadequate coverage of payment system operations and banking supervision in many annual reports; insufficient discussion of progress on achieving policy objectives in insurance supervisory agencies periodic reports
- Need for the body of applicable laws, regulations, and other guidelines for the insurance sector to be made more user friendly (especially for non-specialists)
- Sparse information on capital market development and processes for market supervision
- Poor disclosure of information on emergency financial support to institutions

4. Accountability and Assurances of Integrity by Financial Agencies

- Accountability of financial agencies not clearly defined in legislation
- Lack of a code of conduct for the staff members performing supervisory functions
- Information on internal control and audit, internal governance procedures, accounting policies, and so forth, not consistently disclosed
- Insurance sector frequently suffers from weak internal arrangements for the resolution of conflicts and disputes settlement processes

---

10

availability of capital, as well as foster financial stability through strengthened market discipline.

Standards such as these are not well implemented in many emerging market and transition economies, and many countries do not require the reporting of key financial data by individual institutions, including their consolidated financial exposure. This gap can hamper the ability to filter out healthy from unhealthy institutions. Moreover, the lack of appropriate information can prevent the effective monitoring of financial institutions and their risk taking.[6] For example, insufficient or incorrect disclosures of credit risks may constrain the ability of investors to assess risks and the ability of supervisors to act in a timely manner (Mishkin 2001). Sound accounting and auditing standards and practices are also important prerequisites for financial liberalization because they form part of the proper institutional framework that places appropriate constraints on risk taking. Accounting and auditing are 2 of the 12 areas of standards that are recognized internationally as key to effective operation of domestic and international financial systems, as already outlined in chapter 1.

10.2.2 Scope and Content of International Accounting and Auditing Standards

International accounting and auditing standards have been developed respectively by the International Accounting Standards Board (IASB) and its predecessor the International Accounting Standards Committee (IASC),[7] and by the International Federation of Accountants (IFAC).[8] IFRSs encompass both the previously adopted—and, in some cases, amended—International Accounting Standards (IASs), as well as newly developed, IASB-issued IFRSs.

The original IASs were issued from 1973 to 2000 by the IASC, which was replaced by the IASB in 2001. The IASB has since amended or eliminated some IASs, has proposed to amend others, has proposed to replace some IASs with new IFRSs, and has adopted or proposed new IFRSs on topics for which there were no previous standards. Thus, standards are continuously changing and being upgraded to reflect the current conditions and needs of financial markets. Narrowly interpreted, IFRSs refer to the new numbered series of pronouncements that the IASB has issued, distinct from the IAS series issued by its predecessor IASC. More broadly, IFRSs refer to the entire body of IASB pronouncements, including standards and their interpretations, as well as to the IASs and their interpretation approved by the predecessor IASC. The standards issued by the IASC, many of which were revised by the IASB in 2004, will continue to be designated as IASs.

Currently, 36 effective IAS–IFRS standards, with 11 interpretations, are accompanied by documents providing the framework for the preparation and presentation of financial statements, as well as guidance on interpretation of standards. The framework defines the objectives of financial statements, identifies the qualitative characteristics that make information in the statements useful, and defines the basic elements of financial statements and the concepts in recognizing and measuring them (e.g., asset, liability, income). The framework addresses the general-purpose financial statements designed to meet the needs of shareholders, creditors, employees, government agencies, and the public at large for information about a public entity's financial position, performance, and cash flows.

Hence, it does not cover special-purpose reporting to tax and regulatory authorities. A complete set of financial statements includes a balance sheet, income statement, cash flow statement, statement of changes in equity, and notes composing the summary of accounting policies and other explanatory notes.[9]

Some of the IASs and IFRSs are particularly important in financial sector assessments. A number of the standards are more relevant for the financial institutions. For instance, IAS 32 and IAS 39 provide requirements on the recognition, measurement, and disclosure of financial instruments, and IAS 30 applies to the disclosures by banks and other similar institutions of their income statement, balance sheet, and contingencies and commitments, including other off-balance sheet items. IAS 1 is also particularly pertinent because it deals with the content of financial statements generally. Boxes 10.3, 10.4, 10.5, and 10.6, provide further details of the scope of IAS 39, IAS 32, IAS 30, and IAS 1, respectively. IAS 39, which seeks the measurement of specified assets at fair value, may have significant effect on the volatility of earnings, levels of provisioning, and various observed prudential ratios, and it has raised concerns among regulators. IAS 32 on financial instruments calls for a range of financial risk disclosures, thus seeking to improve transparency of financial risks, which may pose a challenge for some classes of financial institutions (particularly insurance companies) with traditionally weak risk disclosures. Those considerations highlight the significant challenges in aligning prudential standards with evolving accounting standards and the complexities involved in achieving convergence of national and international standards. Evolving issues in international convergence in major markets are summarized in box 10.7.

There are 33 ISAs, accompanied by a "Code of Ethics for Professional Accountants" and other related engagement standards.[10] The auditing standards provide requirements on a range of issues, including quality control (ISA 220), documentation (ISA 230), responsibility to consider fraud and error (ISA 240), risk assessments of internal control (ISA 400), analytical procedures (ISA 520), and the auditor's report on financial statements (ISA 700).

The IASB and the IFAC's IAASB constantly revise and update the standards to reflect current trends and issues in financial reporting and auditing, which reflect globalization, capital flows, regionalization, technology changes, and so forth. Recent events in industrialized countries relating to corporate business failures and misstatements of financial information have also raised the attention to the role and oversight of the auditing profession, the governance of standard-setting bodies, and the scope of corporate governance as it relates to reporting and disclosure. The IASB has been issuing new standards (IFRSs), and revising current IASs, while IFAC and its numerous committees and have been actively revising ISAs. For example, it recently released proposed revisions to ISA 230 on audit documentation. The IFAC's Public Sector Committee (PSC) focuses on the accounting, auditing, and financial reporting needs of national, regional, and local governments, as well as on related agencies, and it proposes benchmark guidelines. It has also undertaken a multiyear initiative that is focusing on developing International Public Sector Accounting Standards (IPSAS) for government budget reporting that is based on IASs. It has also published a guidance paper on anti-money-laundering.

One issue of particular relevance, especially to developing and emerging market economies, is the role of small and medium enterprises (SMEs) and the need to have

---

Box 10.3 IAS 39: Financial Instruments, Recognition, and Measurement

IAS 39 (revised March 2004) covers a broad range of financial instruments, including the following:

- Cash
- Demand and time deposits
- Commercial paper
- Accounts, notes, and loans receivable and payable
- Debt and equity securities
- Asset-backed securities (collateralized mortgages, repurchase agreements, and securitized receivables)
- Derivatives (swaps, forwards, futures, options, rights, and warrants) and embedded derivatives
- Leases
- Rights and obligations with insurance risk under insurance contracts
- Employers rights and obligations under pension contracts

IAS 39 requires that financial assets be classified in one of the following categories to determine how a particular asset is recognized and measured in financial statements:

- Financial assets at fair value through profit or loss
- Available-for-sale financial assets
- Loan and receivables
- Held-to-maturity investments

The general principle is that available-for-sale financial assets are to be valued at fair value, whereas held-to-maturity may be valued at amortized cost.

IAS 39 recognizes two classes of financial liabilities:

- Financial liabilities at fair value through profit and loss
- Other liabilities measured at amortized cost using the effective interest method

IAS 39 has been a source of debate within financial markets, especially among commercial banks. IAS 39 requires entities to value derivatives, shares, and bonds at fair market value, not at historical costs, but does not recognize macro-hedging and internal-risk transfers. However, banks are heavy users of macro-hedging and inter-group transfers of risks. Not recognizing macro-hedging (see below) would mean that marked-to-market changes in the value of derivative position would be booked to earnings and would raise volatility. If recognized, derivative position would be booked to equity and not earnings. Consequently, a number of European banks, especially in France, have opposed IAS 39 because they believe that it could damage their risk management practice (especially in a fixed interest rate environment) and could lead to earnings fluctuations and, thus, lower share prices. The European Central Bank, prudential supervisors, and securities regulators are also opposed to the fair value option on the grounds that it may, in their view, be used inappropriately (see Europe case below).

IAS 39 permits hedge accounting only under certain circumstances, provided that the hedge accounting meets the following criteria (see IAS 39.88):

- The hedge accounting is formally designated and documented, including the entity's risk management objective and strategy for undertaking the hedge, the identification of the hedging instrument, the hedged item, the nature of the risk being hedged, and the process of how the entity will assess the hedging instrument's effectiveness.
- The hedge accounting is expected to be highly effective in achieving offsetting changes in fair value or cash flows that are attributed to the hedged risk as designated and documented, and this effectiveness can be reliably measured.

In October 2004, the European Union's Accounting Regulatory Committee opposed the adoption of the extant IAS 39 as issued by the IASB. Instead, it adopted a "carved out" version of IAS 39, which (a) removed the fair value option as it applies to liabilities and (b) allowed the use of fair value hedge accounting for the interest rate hedges for core deposits on a portfolio basis. European banks will be able to choose between the original or altered set of rules for hedge accounting.

---

simplified financial reporting requirements for those enterprises. The financial reporting needs of SMEs in both developing and industrial countries are gaining greater attention by regulators. In that regard, the IASB and the IFAC have committed themselves to identifying and addressing the needs of SMEs. The IASB undertook a research project in 2001 in response to the growing call in the field to support a separate set of accounting

---

Box 10.4 IAS 32: Financial Instruments, Disclosure, and Presentation

IAS 32 is closely related to IAS 39 and attempts to enhance financial statement users' understanding of the significance of financial instruments to an entity's position, performance, and cash flows.

The fundamental principle of IAS 32 holds that a financial instrument should be classified from the perspective of issuer as (a) a set of financial assets, (b) a financial liability, or (c) an equity instrument according to the substance of the contract, not the legal form. The enterprise must make the decision at the time that the instrument is initially recognized.

Some financial instruments—compound instruments—have both a liability and an equity component from the issuer's perspective. In that case, IAS 32 requires that the component parts be accounted for and presented separately according to their substance and on the basis of the definitions of liability and equity. The split is made at issuance and is not revised for subsequent changes in market interest rates, share prices, or other events that change the likelihood that the conversion option will be exercised.

Disclosure rules apply to all financial instruments, including risk management and hedges. For each class of financial asset, liability, and equity instrument, the following must be disclosed:

- Information about the extent and nature of the entity's use of financial instruments, including significant terms and conditions that may affect the amount, timing, and certainty of future cash flows
- The accounting policies and methods adopted, including the criteria for recognition and the basis of measurement applied
- The business purposes served by the instruments, the risks associated with them, and the management policies for controlling those risks
- Interest rate and credit risk exposures

10

Box 10.5 IAS 30: Disclosures in the Financial Statements of Banks and Similar Financial Institutions

The goal of IAS 30 is to provide users with information required to evaluate the financial position and performance of banks and to enable them to better understand the special characteristics of banking operations. The standards require a bank to present a balance sheet that groups assets and liabilities by nature and lists them in an order that reflects their relative liquidity, as well as prescribes specific assets and liabilities to be disclosed.

On the income statement, the following specific items should be reported:

- Interest income and expenses
- Dividend income
- Fee and commission income
- Net gains and losses from securities dealings
- Net gains and losses from investment securities
- Net gains and losses from foreign currency dealings
- Other operating income and expenses (including general administrative expenses)
- Loan losses

The following disclosures are included:

- Specific contingencies and commitments (including items not on the balance sheet)
- Specific disclosures for the maturity of assets and liabilities on the basis of the remaining period from the balance-sheet date to the contractual maturity date
- Concentration of assets, liabilities, and items not on the balance sheet (by geographical area, customer or industry groups, or other aspects of risk)
- Losses on loans and advances
- Fair value of each class of financial assets and financial liabilities
- Amounts set aside for general banking risks
- Secured liabilities as well as nature and amount of assets pledged as securities

---

Box 10.6 IAS 1: Presentation of Financial Statements

IAS 1 reflects the broad guidelines set forth in the Framework for the Preparation and Presentation of Financial Statements and is designed to prescribe the basis for presentation of general purpose financial statements and to ensure compatibility both with the entity's financial statements of previous periods and with the financial statements of other entities. It sets out the overall framework and responsibilities for the presentation of financial statements, guidelines for their structure, and minimum requirements for the content of the financial statements. Its main objective is to provide information about an entity's assets; liabilities; equity; income and expenses, including gains and losses; other changes in equity; and cash flows. It should also provide data about key components under each of those items.

The standard requires that statements "present fairly" the financial position, performance, and cash flows of an equity. It requires the faithful presentation of effects of transactions and other events, as well as conditions of assets, liabilities, income, and expenses.

An entity must normally present a classified balance sheet, separating current and noncurrent assets and liabilities. A list of minimum items on the balance sheet is provided.

Other issues that the standard covers include going concern, accrual, consistency, materiality, offsetting, reporting period, income statement, statement of changes in equity, notes, and disclosures about dividends.

---

standards for SMEs. One issue that it encountered in the process, however, was how to accurately "define" SMEs. In June 2004, it published a discussion paper on the proposal to develop separate standards and to set up an advisory panel to monitor the discussion. Going forward, IASB is expected to publish a draft of the SME versions of all existing standards.

Another important issue that arises in many countries with significant presence of Institutions Offering Islamic Financial Services (IIFS) is that the accounting standards designed for conventional types of business are not applicable to these institutions. A number of IASs and IFRSs are not suitable for Islamic financial institutions, and moreover financial statements of IIFS contain items for which there are no applicable IAS/IFRS. To address this problem, Accounting and Auditing Organization for Islamic Financial Institutions (AAOIFI) was established in 1990, as a self regulatory body of IIFS (including also some government and regulatory bodies in the governance structure) to set accounting standards that complement IAS/IFRS and at the same time recognize the specific contractual features of Islamic finance. AAOIFI has issued a number of important accounting and auditing standards for Islamic finance instruments and institutions, as well as some governance and ethics standards relating to Sharia compliance; several countries and IIFS have begun to adopt or draw these standards. For a compilation of these standards see AAOIFI (2004). With growing financial innovations in the Islamic finance industry, and the increased focus on appropriate risk measurement and disclosure in Islamic finance, the financial reporting and governance standards are continuing to evolve, and gaining increasing acceptance among countries and IIFS.

10.2.3 ROSCs and Role of the Bank and the Fund

As part of the FSAP–ROSC initiative,[11] the World Bank has developed a program to assist member countries in strengthening their financial reporting regimes through the implementation of IFRS and ISA. The program's objectives are twofold: (a) an assessment and (b) the development of a country plan. Its assessment activities cover the following:

- Determine the comparability of national accounting and auditing standards with IFRS and ISA, respectively.
- Determine the extent of compliance with established accounting and auditing standards, rules, and regulations, as well as the effectiveness of enforcement mechanisms.
- Identify strengths and weaknesses of the institutional framework in supporting high-quality financial reporting.

The basic premises on which a ROSC accounting and auditing (A&A) diagnostic exercise is carried out are as follows:

- IFRS and ISA are endorsed by the Bank, the Fund, and other international institutions as the primary benchmarks for corporate financial reporting standards. IFRS and ISA should be mandated for all "public interest entities," which are defined by the nature of their business, their size, their number of employees, or their corporate status with a wide range of stakeholders. Examples of public interest entities may include banks and financial institutions, insurance companies, investment funds, pension funds, listed companies, and other economically significant business entities.
- SMEs should be subject to a simplified financial reporting regime given their lesser degree of responsibility with respect to the public. This simplified regime for SMEs typically includes less-stringent accounting and reporting requirements.
- If one considers the distinctive responsibility of independent auditors with respect to a wide array of stakeholders, independent auditors should be subject to adequate public oversight.

10

Box 10.7 International Convergence Process

In September 2002, the U.S. Financial Accounting Standards Board (FASB) and the IASB agreed to reduce existing differences between U.S. Generally Accepted Accounting Principles (GAAP) and IFRS. This "convergence" process is a two-stage approach involving a short-term project and a more difficult long-term one. The short-term project, which is designed to eliminate minor differences by January 2005, has largely been completed; the combination of work programs is under way to eliminate more substantive differences as soon as feasible but it is likely to take several years.

In January 2005, EU-listed companies began to apply IFRS, a move that will bring impetus both to the international convergence process and toward achieving a common financial market in Europe. As with any major change, the move poses many challenges. Switching to international standards will also require companies to invest in new systems and will require governments to adopt their tax policies. On the positive side, it can expand the pool of investors, lower the cost of capital, improve the efficiency of capital allocation, and reduce the expenditure needed to consolidate the accounts of subsidiaries. Switching to global standards will also allow any given company or investor to understand the financial statements of companies outside its jurisdiction. Multinational companies will no longer have to reconcile multiple financial statements.

- Access to the auditing profession should be limited to individuals who have demonstrated academic and professional abilities through a certification process that complies with IFAC International Educational Standards for Professional Accountants.

The assessment of A&A standards is designed (a) to focus on complying with national standards and on fostering a country-led program to make national standards comparable with international standards within a feasible time frame and (b) to develop a sufficient infrastructure to effectively adopt IFRS and ISA. The focus on assisting member countries for improving their institutional capacity to support implementation of high-quality A&A standards is consistent with the Bank's operational activities.

The assessment process places emphasis on country involvement and on efforts to design a country-led program. The program attempts to improve A&A performance, to involve all key stakeholders, and to be linked to progress in related critical areas such as corporate governance and financial sector reform. Detailed A&A ROSCs are done on a stand-alone basis or, occasionally, as part of the FSAP. When detailed A&A assessments are not available, the focus of financial sector assessments is directed to a comparison of national standards with IAS 30, 32, 39; the legal and institutional framework for A&A; the quality of A&A of financial institutions; and a review of disclosure practices applying to financial institutions (see section 10.5).

10.2.4 Focus of A&A Assessments

Assessments of A&A standards address financial reporting by public interest entities, which are defined as such because of their business, size, and number of employees or because their corporate status is such that they have a wide range of stakeholders. Public interest entities include credit institutions, insurance companies, investment firms, pension funds, and listed companies. The assessments cover the following four areas:

- *Institutional Framework*—The ROSC A&A focuses on the current state of the institutional framework and, accordingly, provides policy recommendations for strengthening it. The goal is to enable the framework to promote high-quality A&A practices. The framework assessment includes (a) the laws and regulations[12] (quality of the design of the framework), (b) the history and current state of the A&A profession, (c) the strengths and weaknesses of accounting education and training, (d) the A&A standard-setting process, and (e) the arrangements for ensuring compliance with A&A requirements (enforcement mechanisms).
- *Comparability of National and International Standards*—One key benefit of conformity of any country's A&A standards to IFRS and ISA is the promotion of sound financial reporting that facilitates cross-border usage. Generally, the standards and regulations of different countries have reached various levels of conformity. The methodology for this examination, which helps to identify gaps, is based on IFRS and ISA.
- *Compliance with National Standards*—Enforcement of the standards is a key underpinning of a sound financial reporting environment. Efficient and effective

enforcement is also important because corporate stakeholders depend on access to high-quality financial information.

- *Action Plan*—To strengthen the corporate financial reporting regime, the ROSC's A&A module identifies areas for improvement. Those findings serve as the basis for working with policy makers and other stakeholders to develop an action plan to improve A&A practices.

10.2.5 ROSC A&A Methodology

The World Bank has developed a diagnostic tool to gather and analyze pertinent information for preparing A&A ROSCs. This tool consists of a set of questionnaires under each of the following four components: (a) A&A environment, (b) national accounting standards in relation to IASs, (c) actual accounting practices in relation to national standards, and (d) auditing standards and practices. The process adopts a highly participatory approach, with strong involvement of policy makers and other country stakeholders, and culminates in the creation of a country action plan. The information gathered from the diagnostic tool is supplemented with a due diligence exercise to capture primary experiences of practitioners and other facts on professional accounting and auditing practices in the country. The details of the assessment process, the diagnostic tools and questionnaires, and the ROSC preparation procedure are further discussed in Annex 10.B.

10.2.6 Assessment Experience

By the end of December 2004, 38 A&A ROSCs had been completed, 28 of which have been published, and this process has contributed to progress in implementation. A regional breakdown shows that 15 were completed in the Central and Eastern Europe region, 7 in the Middle East, 7 in Latin America and the Caribbean, 5 in Africa, 2 in East Asia, and 2 in South Asia. The majority (29) of the assessments were conducted in middle-income countries whereas only 7 were done in low-income countries and 2 in high-income countries. It is anticipated that the A&A assessments will be conducted in an increasing number of low-income countries. The program has provided a body of experience that has informed the work of standard-setting bodies and that has facilitated reforms in several countries.

The experience gained in implementing the A&A ROSC program thus far suggests a few key issues and lessons to consider in moving forward:

- Adoption of IFRS and ISA as applicable standards is crucial in all countries, particularly when business entities contribute materially to the economy, the public interest, or both. However, if efficient and effective monitoring and enforcement mechanisms are lacking—which creates an environment of noncompliance—then adoption of the standards is not sufficient. This situation is most often the case in developing countries and emerging markets. Similarly, wholesale adoption of the standards without simultaneously developing the necessary legal and institutional infrastructure and without improving professional skills in auditing and accounting may be an inappropriate solution.

10

- In many developing and emerging market countries, observance of A&A standards is constrained by (a) the lack of access to the standards and related publications by students and professionals; (b) the non-availability of standardized implementation guidelines and practice manuals in a country context; (c) the lack of proper training on the practical application of both standards and the code of ethics for professional accountants and auditors; and (d) a rudimentary academic environment that is illustrated by deficient curriculum, lack of appropriate academic literature, and a shortage of well-trained instructors.

- A greater participation of developing countries in the process of developing and revising the standards is critical to facilitate the design and implementation of standards that reflect the realities in developing countries.

- Reaching an international consensus on a common framework of principles for the regulation and supervision of the A&A profession is important.

10.3 Credit-Reporting Systems and Financial Information Services

The concept of credit-reporting systems in finance is a new subject and has received increasing attention in recent years in light of its key role in improving information available to financial intermediaries for their decisions and, thereby, facilitating improved access to finance. Credit reports are becoming more and more important throughout the world, fueled by demand for that type of data not only from banks and other financial intermediaries but also from private firms, retailers, employers, and others. Bank supervisors and regulators are also increasing their demand for high-quality credit data to more effectively monitor credit risks in supervised financial institutions. Credit-reporting systems are also seen as playing a key role in improving credit risk measurements as envisaged under the New Basel Capital Accord. Given the previous context, government officials, as well as bank supervisors and regulators, are interested in knowing answers to the following questions. What is a credit-reporting system? What does a credit report looks like? What would be good practices of a robust credit-reporting system in terms of the key elements involved?

The discussion of those issues is organized as follows. Section 10.3.1 provides a brief introduction of credit-reporting systems and their role in financial development and stability. Section 10.3.2 describes the fundamental elements of a credit-reporting system and identifies good practices for credit reporting. Section 10.3.3 presents the potential uses of credit registries for strengthening credit risk measurements and the supervisory review process. Section 10.3.4 briefly summarizes the role of credit rating agencies.

10.3.1 Introduction to Credit-Reporting Systems

Credit or consumer reporting firms and other types of public credit information registries provide rapid access to accurate and reliable standardized information on credit history and financial condition of potential borrowers, be they individuals or firms, and help to support a well-functioning credit market. Credit reporting addresses a fundamental problem of credit markets: asymmetric information between borrowers and lenders, which leads to adverse selection and moral hazard. Credit information sharing allows lenders to more accurately evaluate risk and to avoid adverse selection. Similarly, credit-reporting mechanisms strengthen incentives for borrowers to repay and thus reduce moral hazard because late or nonpayment with one institution can result in sanctions from many others. Credit reporting expands access to finance, especially for lower income consumers, micro-enterprises, or small businesses. Credit reporting can also play a key role in improving the efficiency of financial institutions by reducing loan processing costs, as well as the time required to process loan applications.

Some empirical work has been done to provide evidence of the importance of credit registries in credit markets. For example, Jappelli and Pagano (2001) analyze the effect of credit registries—both private and public—and find a positive effect on the volume of bank lending (as a percentage of GDP) and a decrease in credit risk. Barron and Staten (2003) show that greater availability of information reduces default rates and improves access to credit. Kallberg and Udell (2003) demonstrate that data from Dun and Bradstreet Corporation, a private credit information firm, have greater predictive power in calculating probability of default than a firm's financial statements. Galindo and Miller (2001) argue that firms in countries with better credit information are less credit constrained because they rely less on internal funds. Overall, theoretical and empirical analyses show that banks' sharing of information on borrowers helps to curtail the effects of adverse selection and moral hazard, reduces credit risk, improves access to credit markets, and strengthens the stability of the banking system.

10.3.2 Elements of a Robust Credit-Reporting System

Good practices of a robust credit-reporting system are presented in this section to provide broad guidance on issues to consider in establishing a new credit-reporting system and in identifying areas for the improvement in, or the assessing of, an existing credit-reporting system. This section describes several fundamental elements with respect to the structure of a sound credit-reporting system. It is not a comprehensive and complete illustration but a general guideline. The appropriate design of the system in any particular economy may largely vary by its size, the level of penetration of financial services, the degree of competition, and the legal framework. The implementation of Basel II may also affect the design and operation of the systems (see section 10.3.3).

10.3.2.1 Providers and Users of Credit Data

Typically, in a credit-reporting system, the major credit information providers and users include both financial firms and several categories of non-financial firms:

- Commercial banks and other regulated financial institutions
- Non-bank financial intermediaries
- Credit card issuers, insurance firms, automobile finance companies, and mortgage lenders and guarantors
- Retailers (appliance retailers and others)
- Firms providing business-to-business credit and trade credit
- Microfinance institutions

- Other businesses that provide goods or services on credit (utilities, cell phone providers, agribusiness, etc.)

10.3.2.2 Credit-Reporting Institutional Arrangements

Institutional forms for credit-reporting arrangements around the world include both public credit registries administered by central banks and private credit-reporting firms of varied ownership structure. A survey conducted by the World Bank between 1999 and 2001 covers both private firms that specialize in credit data from banks and other financial intermediaries as well as firms that specialize in trade credit, which is typically the most important source of external finance for small businesses. The survey reveals that public and private credit registers are present in a large number of developed and emerging market economies throughout the world (see Miller 2003). Forty-one countries have public credit registers, 44 countries have private credit bureaus, and many have both types. Table 10.1 summarizes the pros and cons of different types of private credit registries and public registries.

10.3.2.3 Quality of the Data Collected and Distributed

The quality and scope of the credit data collected and used is critical to establishing a sound credit-reporting system. The heart of a credit report is the record of the payment history of a consumer or a firm, which summarizes types of loans, current and past, from different creditors and their amounts, including past due amounts and past due history. The following summarizes the key recommendations with respect to the credit-reporting system, drawing on country practices:

Table 10.1. Institutional Arrangements for Private Credit Registries

Institutional Type	Pros	Cons
Private firm with no bank ownership	• All types of data • Independence	• No automatic access to data
Private firm with bank ownership	• All types of data • Special access to specific bank data	• Independence may be questioned
Bank association	• Access to bank data • Integrity	• Only bank data and bank access
Chamber of Commerce	• Retail and nonbank data • Broad cover • Historical record	• No bank data • Limited funds for modernization
Commercial and credit insurance firms	• In-depth data on commercial sector	• Limited coverage • High cost per entry
Industry-specific databases	• In-depth data on single sector	• Limited scope—cannot cross-check data
Public ownership such as a central bank	• Automatic access to credit data	• Only bank data

Source: Miller (2003).

- The credit information database should be an open system rather than a closed network. Majority ownership by a limited group of lenders will discourage a broader database.

- It is advisable to collect both positive and negative information instead of negative information only. In this way, responsible borrowers can document good credit histories and can build their "reputation collateral." A borrower's good name or reputation collateral provides an incentive to meet commitments much the same way as does a pledge of physical collateral, also reducing moral hazard.

- Credit data should be properly maintained for a reasonable time frame, at a minimum, 5 years. And negative data should not be deleted, even when a debt is repaid. Negative data encourage borrowers to honor obligations.

- Data should be inaccessible after a certain amount of time. Time limits may vary by size of loan and type of inquiry. International best practice is to establish time limits on the length of the credit history record available to a lender. Economic research shows that the recent credit payment record is most relevant for predicting future default. Moreover, the fact that, after a certain period of time, information, especially with respect to defaults, will not be distributed to lenders creates additional incentives for the borrower to improve credit repayment behavior and to "clean up" the record. For example, records are available only for 5 years in Australia, Brazil, Germany, Ireland, Peru, and Spain and for 7 years in the United States and Mexico. It is essential that all information in the file is kept for this set period. For example, if a debt is paid, then information on it should stay in the registry for the period prescribed. Deleting either full records or parts of records significantly lowers predictive power of the data in the registry and weakens any stimulating effect that the bureau has with respect to repayment incentive.

- Credit reports should not include highly sensitive information such as political or religious affiliation. Other identifying information such as gender should be carefully evaluated.

10.3.2.4 Legal and Regulatory Framework for Credit Reporting

The legal and regulatory framework for credit reporting is usually governed by several laws and regulations and varies greatly around the world. Those laws include the following:

- Regulations concerning bank secrecy
- Data protection law
- Consumer protection
- Fair credit granting and consumer credit regulations
- Provisions with respect to privacy and personal or corporate secrets in existing laws

Several countries chose to pass a specific law regulating credit-reporting entities: Israel, Kazakhstan (draft version), Korea, Mexico, Peru, Russia (currently in a draft version), Sweden, Thailand, Ukraine (draft version) and United States. In almost all European countries, as well as in Australia, New Zealand, Hong Kong, Taiwan, and Argentina, the focus is on regulating the data management process rather than on credit-reporting agen-

10

cies as institutions. In those countries, major legislation governing operation of a credit registry involves a data protection law.

Economic research shows that the registries are most effective when they are able to collect information from a wide number of sources, including bank and non-bank financial institutions, as well as from firms selling goods on credit. The legal framework should be able to support this type of a system and should not restrict the ability of some creditors to participate in a credit bureau. The Fair Credit Reporting Act (FCRA) in the United States (Federal Trade Commission 2005) and data protection laws in Europe allow information exchange among all types of creditors. There are usually no restrictions on the collection of information from public sources such as court records, bankruptcy filings, and so forth. Credit bureaus create added value by merging information from public sources with the information collected by the credit bureau and by allowing automated access to such records.

An effective legal and regulatory framework for a credit registry should encourage information sharing and should promote competition while achieving a balance between information sharing and privacy and consumer protection. It should include the following characteristics:

- The legal framework should encourage information sharing among lenders; for instance, certain laws may be established or amended to provide legal clarity with respect to acceptable information sharing practices.
- The legal framework should encourage appropriate competition in credit markets.
- The tradeoff between privacy protection and information sharing should be taken into account. Although improper sharing of credit information causes privacy issues, broad privacy or data protection laws may unduly limit credit reporting. Thus, the legal framework should be constructed to achieve a proper balance.
- Consumer protection should also be considered in the legal framework. Customer protection should be enhanced in the law through appropriate access to data and expeditious resolution of credit-reporting issues. Borrowers should have access to their own data and should be notified of adverse actions that result from a credit report. Reports should include information with respect to all the persons who have access to data. Consumer-friendly procedures should be developed to challenge erroneous information in a reasonable time frame. For example, a specific contact would be established to provide "one-stop service" for consumers to resolve credit issues.

One of the key provisions in the credit-reporting and data protection laws is the ability of the subject of the information to view his or her own record. One of the most effective mechanisms for maintaining quality and accuracy of information in the database is ensured by notifying the borrower when credit is refused. The notice informs the borrower that the decision to refuse credit was in whole or in part based on the information obtained from a credit registry, specifying the registry's name. The notice should also state that, according to the law, the borrower can obtain a record from the credit bureau, and the notice should provide contact information for this bureau. In most countries, the consumer is entitled to obtain a free report if he or she has received this type of notice. Alternatively, the price for a report may be set at some low level. Notice of refusal of

10

credit also serves as a good educational tool to inform the consumer of the importance of building a good credit history and of improving one's standing.

The subject of the credit report, whether an individual or a firm, is in the best position to know who has a valid reason for accessing that report. Subjects of such credit reports know where they have requested credit or employment and whether other firms or individuals have a valid reason to request the information. Therefore, one of the best ways to limit unauthorized use of credit information is to develop systems that record all queries for an individual's report. Consumers can review this information if they think their data have been used in an inappropriate manner. This simple reporting tool can greatly help to detect misuse of the data by lenders and others who may request this information, as well as by the staff of a credit-reporting firm.

Procedures, particularly non-judicial dispute resolution mechanisms, should be in place to facilitate challenges to erroneous data. Again, the consumer or firm that is the object of the credit report is in the best position to know whether data in the report are correct or flawed. At the same time, the consumer or firm has an incentive to challenge negative information in the report, even if the individual person or company knows it to be accurate. Those two facts should be balanced in regulations on dispute resolution in credit reporting. Providing access to credit-reporting firms by means of the Internet and by phone can encourage consumers to review their reports and to identify reporting errors. As stated above, it is particularly important that consumers have access to reports when an adverse action has been taken. Clear procedures should be established in regulations that specify the steps in the dispute resolution process and the time frame that credit-reporting firms have to verify and respond to complaints. The regulations may include requirements that credit-reporting firms operate toll-free phone numbers to take complaints or to otherwise facilitate consumer access. If the credit-reporting firm and consumer differ over the validity of the information, the consumer should be able to add a comment to this effect on the credit report. However, consumers should not be able to effectively hamper the functioning of the system by their interaction with the credit-reporting firm. For example, requirements that all consumers get a free copy of their credit report every year, even if they have not requested it, can add great cost to the system. Similarly, allowing consumers to obtain unlimited numbers of free credit reports on themselves can lead to abuse.

Country experience shows that the regulatory framework is usually weaker than the legal framework in developing countries. The following questions should be carefully considered in establishing or improving a regulatory framework:

- Is enforcement strong enough in the regulatory framework? Can—and do—regulators effectively enforce laws and regulations by means of audits, lawsuits, and fines or by reviewing industry codes of conduct?
- Do consumers have the ability to bring complaints outside the judicial system?

10.3.2.5 Consumer Outreach and Education

The role of credit reports is often misunderstood by consumers; thus, appropriate transparency and outreach should be used to foster consumer education. People seldom think about or review their credit report until they have a problem, so the association they have with credit reports is often a negative one. Consumers are unlikely to fully appreciate what role credit reports have in facilitating access to credit or how the consumers may contribute to a more competitive credit market. When there is a problem, consumers may not know either the laws and regulations pertaining to this activity or their rights and responsibilities under those statutes. An important role for the regulator is that of providing outreach and education to consumers, both to ensure that consumers are able to exercise their basic rights and to encourage the development of the industry. The regulator can accomplish this function in many ways, including by making available the laws and regulations pertaining to credit reporting in easy-to-understand formats and through multiple media (e.g., Web sites, printed communication, information distributed at banks, etc.) and by sponsoring or encouraging public service ads and announcements related to credit reporting. The regulator can require that notices of an adverse action that was based on a credit report include information about the consumer's rights under the law. The public outreach function may be particularly important when a credit-reporting system is first established to gain the public's confidence and to maximize participation in the system. Some recommended elements of this outreach effort include the following.

- Enough information should be made available on managing credit and on the rights and responsibilities of borrowers with respect to credit reporting. For example, materials at the appropriate level and language could be provided through the Internet, banks, retailers, and government offices. Also, media communication such as radio and television public service advertisements could play an important role in dissemination efforts.
- Industry should take an active part in providing consumer assistance.
- It is advisable to strengthen not only outreach to lenders with respect to the importance of credit information but also outreach to other interested parties such as judges and microfinance institutions.

10.3.3 Credit Registries, Efforts to Strengthen Credit Risk Measurement, and New Basel Capital Accord (Basel II)

Credit registries possess enormous potential as a key tool in the hands of supervisory authorities that would enable those authorities to face the challenges of implementation of Basel II.[13] Moreover, effective use of the information contained in credit registries, whether public or private, will enable credit institutions to improve the identification and control of their banking risks, thereby helping to pave the way for more advanced risk and capital measurement approaches envisaged in Basel II.

As already explained, credit registries facilitate the sharing of information among lenders and with supervisors—subject to adequate safeguards—on credit history loan characteristics and specified characteristics of borrowers (households and firms separately), which enables each bank to assess the quality of its credit assets and enables the supervisors to monitor credit risk in the entire system. The access to credit information by banks helps to impose discipline on borrowers and fosters greater transparency, as well as more competition.

Information from credit registries can be used to support both onsite and offsite supervision, as well as to facilitate macroprudential surveillance. Because supervisors have access to the entire population of loans granted by each credit institution, they can use this information to construct a range of financial soundness indicators for individual banks, peer groups, and the system as a whole. The information can be used to select samples for more detailed examination in onsite inspection. Also, comparison of the information reported by different credit institutions can help those conducting offsite surveillance to detect the potential of any one bank's systematic overvaluation of credit worthiness of its borrowers or a deterioration in the credit quality of a bank's loan portfolio relative to the rest of the system. The information from credit registries can help when analyzing the dynamics of aggregate credit risk—and bank-specific risks—and its macroeconomic and institutional determinants. Finally, information in credit registries—together with other information outside the registries—can help when estimating (or validating bank estimates for) probability of default of different borrowers, when providing input into estimating loss given default (LGD), and when verifying the bank's estimate of exposure at default.

Credit registries can be a useful tool to validate the bank's own internal ratings and internal assumptions about credit risk modeling. The statistical techniques to verify borrower rating systems are well developed, and it is relatively easy to discriminate among the relative positions of obligors. However, the validation of probabilities of default associated with each rating is more difficult because data are scarce, particularly on defaulted obligors and on the correlation among defaults, which is hard to quantify. In this context, a rating system for borrowers—developed by supervisors and based on data on the entire population of all credit institutions—could provide a yardstick with which to compare and validate ratings and probabilities used by individual institutions. This approach would require credit registries to be managed by supervisors and to contain a certain minimum quantity of information so an overall rating system could be developed.

The estimation of LGD is typically based on market prices of defaulted loans and bonds or on a credit institution's own data on discounted cash flows—revenues and expenses—following default so best estimates of loan losses can be obtained (using both internal and external data). Little progress has been made on the techniques to validate LGD. Information from credit registries can be used to estimate the key determinants of LGD (by means of a regression model), and the possibility of using credit registries to document loan losses offers a realistic option to develop estimation and validation procedures for LGD. Similar observations apply to exposure at Default (EAD). In addition, the transition matrix for the entire credit system, as well as the sectoral and geographic differences in credit quality, can all be monitored using the credit registries. Finally, the broad recognition of credit risk mitigation techniques in Basel II calls for the credit registries to carry precise information on loan characteristics so they can be used to estimate the value of guarantees, collateral, and other risk mitigants accurately.

If they are to harness the potential of credit registries, their information structure should have adequate information to estimate the value of Probability of Default (PD), EAD, LGD, maturity, risk mitigation factors, and loan loss provisions so various parameters of credit risk models can be estimated by banks and validated by supervisors. For this purpose, required minimum information that should be included in the data structure of credit registries should be evaluated so credit registries can contribute to effective implementation of Basel II.

10.3.4 Role of Credit Rating Agencies in Financial Stability and Development

Credit Rating Agencies—or External Credit Assessment Institutions, as referred to in the New Basel Capital Accord—provide independent, forward-looking "opinions" to investors on the credit worthiness—or ability and willingness to service debt in full and in time—of an obligor (debt issuer) with respect to a specific financial obligation, or a class of financial obligations, or a specific financial program such as a commercial paper issuance. Those opinions are expressed in the form of (a) a credit rating for various financial instruments and transactions such as corporate bonds (both financial and non-financial institutions); (b) obligations issued by sovereign (central governments) and sub-sovereign (state and local governments) borrowers, other public institutions, and supra-nationals (multilateral and regional institutions); and (c) structured finance transactions (e.g., asset-backed securities, project finance transactions, collateralized debt obligations).

The ratings are based on current information obtained from the obligors and other sources that the rating agencies consider reliable. Judging credit quality involves analyzing a broad scope of relevant risk factors, often subjective, which are unique to particular industries, issuers, and countries. For a discussion of what methodologies are used in assessing country credit ratings, what the sources of possible biases are in those assessments, and how the rating methodology has evolved in recent years, see Bhatia (2002). Credit ratings may be of long-term or short-term duration, depending on the maturity of the instrument. Rating agencies differentiate the ability to service foreign and local currency debt in their analysis and issue separate ratings by currency. They may be subject to downgrade or upgrade should a rating agency consider that material changes in the financial condition of an issuing entity warrant a rating review.[14]

10.3.4.1 Effect on Development

By providing independent information to investors, rating agencies facilitate access to financing in domestic and international markets and, thereby, enhance growth opportunities. Credit ratings provide a relative ranking of an issuer's creditworthiness under similar stress conditions and, thereby, facilitate determination of the risk premium required to invest in the riskier securities. Historical studies by Moody's confirm that there is a clear pattern of higher probabilities of default (a key input into estimating risk premium) for obligations with a lower credit rating. For instance, from 1970 to 1996, the average 1-year default rate was 0.01 percent for A-rated issuers, 0.12 percent for Baa-rated issuers, 1.36 percent for Ba-rated issuers, and 7.27 percent for B-rated issuers. Default is defined as any missed or delayed disbursement of interest, principal, or both (see http://www.moodys.com).

Thus, development of credit rating agencies, together with sound accounting auditing and other information infrastructure, is a key institutional reform to help develop corporate and sub-sovereign bond markets, as well as asset-backed securities markets and project finance. This reform would complement the development of government securities markets at the central government level, which would help determine a risk-free rate as a benchmark against which the riskier securities could be priced. Also, local governments in emerging and developing economies are increasingly seeking ways to raise debt on private credit markets to finance local investments. For this purpose, development of sub-sovereign credit evaluation—and the associated information system and credit rating arrangements—has become an important topic for investors and policy markers (El Daher, 1999).

Sovereign credit ratings are seen as a fundamental factor in the global financial architecture to facilitate access to foreign capital by developing and emerging markets. Rating agencies rely on a constellation of both qualitative and quantitative factors (economic structure and growth prospects, macroeconomic policies, contingent liabilities, financial sector health, political factors, etc.) in arriving at a "sovereign credit rating" as a forward-looking estimate of default probability (Beers, Cavanaugh, and Ogawa 2002). Ratings assigned to entities in each country are most frequently the same as the sovereign's or lower, but they may be higher (because of specific structural features). Several developing countries have received official assistance to obtain credit ratings as a step toward strengthening their access to international capital markets (IMF 2003a).

10.3.4.2 Effect on Financial Stability

Rating agencies contribute to enhancing financial stability through two channels. First, by summarizing a large and diverse amount of information for the benefit of investors and by acting as a monitor of default prospects and default events, rating agencies provide market incentives for improved governance by issuers. Second, bank regulators increasingly use rating information in assessing capital adequacy. The standardized approach of the New Basel Capital Accord spells out six criteria that supervisors can use to evaluate external credit assessment institutions before allowing their ratings to be used as the basis for assigning risk weights on banks' exposures.

The recognition criteria consist of (a) objectivity (use of rigorous rating methodology that is subject to validation and back testing); (b) independence (free-form political or industry pressures); (c) international access and transparency of assessments (ratings should be disclosed and should be available to both domestic and international investors); (d) disclosure (of assessment methodology, including definition of default, time horizon, and the meaning of each rating); (e) resources (sufficient to carry out high-quality assessments); and (f) credibility (wide acceptance and integrity of the process). See Basel Committee on Banking Supervision (2004).

Rating agencies may weaken financial stability through the effect of rating changes on market perceptions. Recent experience has also highlighted that "procyclical" behavior of ratings agencies may have contributed to financial instability because of asset price changes arising from upgrading in good times and downgrading in bad times; rating changes also have significant spillover effects on other asset markets, including in neighboring developed and developing countries (Kaminsky and Schmuckler 2002).

10.4 Corporate Governance Assessments

The state of corporate governance can have an important effect on the availability and cost of capital for all firms, and good corporate governance of financial firms plays a key role in fostering financial stability. Corporate governance constitutes a set of relationships among a company's management, its board, its shareholders, and other stakeholders. Those relationships define, among other things, the property rights of shareholders, the mechanisms of exercising and protecting those rights, and the way of ensuring a fair return. Corporate governance also provides the structure through which it sets the objectives of the company, as well as determines the means of attaining those objectives and monitoring performance. Good corporate governance (a) should provide proper incentives for the board and management to pursue objectives that are in the interests of the company and its shareholders and (b) should facilitate effective monitoring. This section first discusses the rationale and the role of corporate governance issues in financial sector assessments and then outlines the principles of corporate governance developed by the OECD, which is the international standard for practices in this area. Finally, this section also summarizes the corporate governance assessments by the World Bank under the ROSC initiative and the main lessons of assessment experience so far.

Detailed assessments of corporate governance standards are typically undertaken on a stand-alone basis as part of World Bank's ROSC Program. They are not normally undertaken as a component of FSAP, except occasionally when the related issues have been given priority in financial sector policies.[15] Nevertheless, all financial sector assessments look at certain core corporate governance issues as part of the review of preconditions for effective supervision and as part of assessing the observance of IOSCO objectives and principles of securities regulation. For example, IOSCO principles for issuers are, in effect, a requirement that issuers pursue good corporate governance policies in terms of transparency, disclosure, and fair and equitable treatment of holders of securities. This requirement is typically enforced both through corporate governance clauses in listing requirements and through provisions of company laws. Moreover, all financial sector supervisory standards include principles and criteria of varying depth that seek to ensure adequate governance of supervised entities. In addition, the institutions of financial markets and individual financial institutions themselves together play a critical role in fostering good governance of non-financial firms through the monitoring by financial institutions of their counterparties as part of risk management and through investment guidelines that reward good governance of issuers.[16]

10.4.1 Rationale for Good Corporate Governance?

A good corporate governance regime is central to the efficient use of capital. First, it promotes market confidence; helps to attract additional long-term capital, both domestic and foreign; and fosters market discipline through good disclosure and transparency. Second, good corporate governance helps to ensure that corporations take into account the interests not only of a wide range of constituencies but also of the communities within which they operate and that their boards are accountable to the company and the shareholders.

Those actions, in turn, help to ensure that corporations operate for the benefit of society as a whole.

The experiences of economic transition and the financial crises in many developing and emerging market economies have confirmed that good corporate governance practices can strongly contribute to financial market development and financial stability. Good corporate governance helps to bridge the gap between the interest of those who run a company and the shareholders who own it, thereby increasing investor confidence and making it easier for companies to raise equity capital and to finance investment. Good corporate governance also helps ensure that a company honors its legal commitments and forms value-creating relations with stakeholders, including employees and creditors (OECD 2003).

Empirical evidence[17] suggests that good corporate governance will do the following:

- Increase the efficiency of capital allocation within and across firms.
- Reduce the cost of capital for issuers.
- Help broaden access to capital.
- Reduce vulnerability to crises.
- Foster savings.
- Render corruption more difficult.

10.4.2 OECD Principles of Corporate Governance

In response to a call by the OECD council meeting at the ministerial level on April 27–28, 1998, to develop a set of corporate governance standards and guidelines, the OECD issued in 1999 the *OECD Principles of Corporate Governance* after extensive consultations. Since then, the principles have formed the basis for corporate governance initiatives in both OECD and non-OECD countries alike. Hence, they represent the minimum standard that countries with different traditions could agree on, without being unduly prescriptive. In particular, they are equally applicable to countries with a civil and common-law tradition, different levels of ownership concentration, and models of board representation. Moreover, they have been adopted as one of the 12 key standards for sound financial systems by the Financial Stability Forum. They have been endorsed by the Bank and the Fund executive boards, and they form the basis of the corporate governance component of the World Bank–IMF ROSCs.

The OECD principles were reviewed and revised by the OECD Steering Group on Corporate Governance under a mandate from OECD ministers in 2002. This review and the subsequent revisions were supported by a comprehensive survey of corporate governance practices and by information on practices outside the OECD area derived from regional corporate governance round tables. The revised OECD principles were issued in April 2004.

The OECD principles have been devised with four fundamental concepts in mind: responsibility, accountability, fairness, and transparency. The OECD principles allow for diversity of rules and regulations and are primarily concerned with listed companies. A set of 32 principles is organized into six sections that ensure the following: (a) the basis for an effective corporate governance framework, (b) the rights of shareholders, (c) the

10

**Box 10.8 OECD Principles of Corporate Governance:
Overview of the Main Areas of the OECD Principles**

1. The Basis of an Effective Corporate Governance Framework

The corporate governance framework should promote transparent and efficient markets, be consistent with the rule of law, and clearly articulate the division of responsibilities among different supervisory, regulatory, and enforcement authorities.

There are four core principles under this category, including the requirement that "supervisory, regulatory, and enforcement authorities should have the authority, integrity, and resources to fulfill their duties in a professional and objective manner. Moreover, their rulings should be timely, transparent, and fully explained" (OECD (2004).

2. Rights of Shareholders and Key Ownership Functions

The corporate governance framework should protect and facilitate the exercise of shareholders' rights. Seven core principles in this category spell out the various rights of shareholders and call for effective shareholder participation in key corporate governance decisions. This category requires, among other things, that the equity component of compensation schemes for board members and employees be subject to shareholder approval; that market for corporate control be allowed to function in an efficient transparent and fair manner to protect the rights of all shareholders; and that the exercise of ownership rights by all shareholders, including institutional investor, be facilitated, for example, through disclosure by institutional investors of overall corporate governance and voting policies with respect to their investments.

3. Equitable Treatment of Shareholders

The corporate governance framework should ensure the equitable treatment of all shareholders, including minority and foreign shareholders. All shareholders should have the opportunity to obtain effective redress for violation of their rights. This category comprises three core principles, including the requirements that insider trading and abusive self-dealing should be prohibited and that members of the board and key executives should be required to disclose material interest in any transaction or matter affecting the corporation.

4. Role of Stakeholders in Corporate Governance

The corporate governance framework should recognize the rights of stakeholders established by law or through mutual agreements and should encourage active cooperation between corporations and stakeholders in creating wealth, jobs, and sustainability of financially sound enterprises. Six core principles make up this category, including the requirements that effective redress be made for violation of stakeholder interest protected by law and that the corporate governance framework should be complemented by an effective, efficient insolvency framework and by effective enforcement of creditors' rights.

5. Disclosure and Transparency

The corporate governance framework should ensure that timely and accurate disclosure is made on all material matters with respect to the corporation, including the financial situation, performance, ownership, and governance of the company. Six core principles in this category spell out the types of material information that should be disclosed and call for not only high-quality accounting and disclosure standards in preparing the reports, annual audits, and accountability of external auditors but also effective channels of communications. The principles call for effective promotion of analysis and advice by analysts, brokers, rating agencies, and others who are free from material conflicts of interests that might compromise the integrity of their analysis or advice.

6. Responsibilities of the Board

The corporate governance framework should ensure the strategic guidance of the company, the effective monitoring of management by the board, and the board's accountability to the company and the shareholders. The six core principles in this category call for board members to act on a fully informed basis, treat all shareholders fairly, and apply high ethical standards; spell out eight key functions of the board (e.g., ensuring the integrity of the corporation's accounting and financial reporting systems); and require the board to exercise objective and independent judgment on corporate affairs. The exercise of board functions might require a sufficient number of non-executive directors and sufficient access to accurate, relevant, and timely information.

Note: Information in this box is based on OECD (2004).

equitable treatment of shareholders, (d) the role of stakeholders in corporate governance, (e) the disclosure and transparency, and (f) the responsibilities of the board. The scope of the OECD principles is summarized in box 10.8.

The recent revisions to the principles covered four main areas: (a) a new set of principles on the development of regulatory framework to underpin corporate governance framework and mechanisms for implementation and enforcements; (b) additional principles to strengthen the exercise of informed ownership by shareholders, particularly those calling on institutional investors to disclose their corporate governance policies and those strengthening the rights of shareholders to choose Board members; (c) strengthened principles to reinforce Board oversight and enhance Board members' independent judgment; and (d) new and strengthened principles to contain conflicts of interest through enhanced disclosure and transparency (e.g., on related party transactions), thus making auditors more accountable to shareholders and promoting auditors' independence.

The principles have been framed to keep in mind primarily non-financial firms, but the core principles apply equally well to financial firms. However, additional safeguards and controls apply to financial institutions' governance as reflected in various financial supervisory standards. The key issues in financial sector governance are highlighted in Annex 10.C.

10.4.3 World Bank ROSC Corporate Governance Assessments

10

As part of the ROSC initiative, the World Bank has established a program to assist its member countries in strengthening their corporate governance frameworks. The objectives of this program are to accomplish the following:

- Benchmark the country's corporate governance framework and company practices against the OECD Principles for Corporate Governance.
- Assist the country in developing and implementing a country action plan for improving institutional capacity with a view to strengthening the country's corporate governance framework.
- Raise awareness of good corporate governance practices among the country's public and private sector stakeholders.

Participation in corporate governance ROSC assessments is voluntary, and the World Bank conducts the assessments at the invitation of country authorities, sometimes in the context of an FSAP assessment. The World Bank has developed a template to gather pertinent information for preparing the Corporate Governance ROSC as a diagnostic instrument. The template gathers both quantitative and qualitative information on ownership and control structure of listed companies, capital market structure, legal and institutional factors affecting corporate governance, rights and obligations of listed companies, intermediaries and investors in a given country, relevant disclosure practices, and functions and responsibilities of governing bodies of the corporation. Although the assessments are relevant to all countries, they are particularly pertinent in middle-income countries seeking to build strong capital markets. They are also a useful instrument for transition economies, where mass privatization has created a large pool of listed companies with thousands of shareholders, and for low-income countries seeking to attract international portfolio investors.

The assessments are also a tool for communication between policy makers and domestic and international investors to reach a common understanding in an environment where countries are grappling with the establishment of a market for corporate control and are competing to attract capital. Assessments do not advocate a single model of corporate governance but do promote choice for issuers and investors.

Box 10.9 Methodology and Format of Corporate Governance Assessments

The World Bank has developed a questionnaire in the form of a template that is available on its Web site.* An updated template, following the 2004 revision of the OECD principles, has been prepared and will be available on the same Web site to assist in assessments. It is structured along the six chapters of the OECD Principles and seeks to gather both quantitative and qualitative information on capital markets, listed companies, and enforcement of securities and corporate laws. The objective of the updated template is to facilitate the gathering of information necessary to formulate a diagnosis of the institutional framework underlying corporate governance, as well as the prevailing practices and enforcement. For each OECD Principle, a set of questions has been prepared to assess the compliance of the country under assessment.

The updated template includes a section on the ownership structure of the assessed country because this structure is an important determinant of corporate governance practices. It endeavors to identify pyramid structures, cross-shareholdings, and business groups, and it gathers information on the divergence between cash flow rights and voting rights. Although the OECD Principles are mainly concerned with the rights of shareholders and stakeholders, disclosure, and responsibilities of insiders, the updated template also addresses the issue of institutional capacity.

A first template was produced at the beginning of 2000 as a pilot template, and it was revised into a second version in the same year and was vetted by the OECD, IMF, and SEC. Consultation took place for the preparation of the third generation expanded template in 2003. The fourth and current version, reflecting the revisions to the OECD Principles in 2004, is being finalized. In addition, special template modules have been developed that focus on financial institutions' governance, including governance of banks and non-bank financial institutions (insurance companies, pension funds, and mutual funds),

drawing on lessons learned from previous assessments. The modules have been pilot tested in the Czech Republic (mutual funds, bank, and insurance modules), and the Slovak Republic (pension funds). A new module is under development to assess the governance of state-owned enterprises (SOEs); the module is based on the OECD Guidelines on the corporate governance of SOEs.

The format of the assessment reports is elaborated in the operational guidelines for ROSC reports issued by the World Bank and the IMF. The content has evolved over time. It started with a 15-page narrative describing corporate governance practices of the assessed country, plus a matrix benchmarking the adherence to each OECD Principle. In a second phase, policy recommendations were added. The latest format attempts to differentiate between compliance of the legal and regulatory framework and actual practices of market participants and includes a chapter on institutional strengthening. For FY2005, the format was enhanced with the multiple goals of (a) enhancing readability and clarity, (b) adding further standardization, and (c) developing themes that cut across the various OECD Principles. The new format has (a) a short (5-page) discussion that focuses on key issues and policy recommendations and is in a form similar to commercial brokerage research and (b) a 15-page principle-by-principle assessment that presents the issues in more detail.

The corporate governance country assessment is conducted as an "external" assessment. The World Bank is responsible for researching and drafting the assessment. A local consultant is typically commissioned to complete a "template" (questionnaire) that was designed to capture a country's corporate governance legal and regulatory framework, as well as information on corporate governance practices. World Bank experts then visit a country to meet with government officials, market participants, investors, and issuers, and to draft an assessment report.

---

* A copy of the template can be downloaded from http://www.worldbank.org/ifa/CGTemplate_0603.doc.

The assessment team works closely with stakeholders and makes recommendations that can lead to a country action plan. The World Bank publishes the ROSC report on its Web site with permission of the country authorities.[18] The published reports are accessible at http://www.worldbank.org/ifa/rosc_cg.html. The procedures and format of the corporate governance assessments are further explained in box 10.9.

The format of the assessments allows for systematic benchmarking across countries and regions. It is divided into five parts: (a) an executive summary, (b) a report on key corporate governance issues and major recommendations, preceeded by a capital markets profile, (c) a table of assessment ratings by principle, (d) a principle-by-principle review, and (e) a set of specific technical recommendations.

Each OECD principle is evaluated on the basis of quantitative and qualitative standards. "Observed" means that all essential criteria are met. "Largely observed" means that only minor shortcomings are observed—deficiencies that do not raise any questions about the authorities' ability and intent to achieve full observance within a reasonable period of time. "Partially observed" means that, although the legal and regulatory framework may be fully compliant with the OECD principle, practices and enforcement diverge. "Materially not observed" means that, despite progress, the shortcomings are sufficient to raise doubts about the authorities' ability to achieve observance. "Not observed" means that no substantive progress toward observance has been achieved.

The assessments are complementary to private sector rating activities in this field. The World Bank assessments focus on country analysis, whereas some rating agencies have started to focus on corporate governance of companies. Standard & Poor's and Moody's have begun rating companies in emerging markets. Other similar exercises are carried out by specialized firms such as Pensions Investment Research Consultants in the United Kingdom or Deminor in Belgium and France. New rating companies for corporate governance have emerged in Russia and South Korea.

10.4.4 Key Findings from Country Assessments

The work of Fremont and Capaul (2002) reviews the lessons of corporate governance assessments and its findings are discussed in this section. None of the assessed countries comply with the OECD principles in all respects. Yet all countries surveyed have undertaken or are currently undertaking reforms to bring their legal and regulatory frameworks in compliance with the OECD principles. In most countries surveyed, there is a growing interest toward improving corporate governance practices. A large number of countries, including Brazil, Croatia, the Philippines, and Romania have developed their own corporate governance codes of best practice. The World Bank corporate governance assessments also have been a catalyst to trigger interest and reform.

Some of the key policy issues that have arisen in corporate governance assessments include the following:

- A Code of Corporate Governance should be developed at the country level to provide more detailed guidelines to complement existing laws and regulations, and foster good practices.
- Director-training facilities should be promoted.

- Further legal reforms are needed to ensure additional rights to shareholders, particularly protection of minority shareholders, and to promote more comprehensive governance policy, including effective exercise of voting rights by institutional investors acting in fiduciary capacity.
- Institutional framework for corporate governance requires further strengthening to avoid duplication and overlap (and to promote better coordination) among multiple regulators with oversight responsibilities for listed companies (e.g., overlap and coordination issues could arise among agencies overseeing company law enforcement, securities regulatory agencies, and other law enforcement and regulatory agencies).
- Enforcement of corporate Governance Laws needs to be strengthened in several areas, including listing rules, content of disclosure, shareholders' rights and equitable treatment of shareholders.

In most countries surveyed, business transactions have traditionally taken place on the basis of personal relationships and trust, and little attention has been paid to publicly available information. Corporate governance reform is a way to extend this trust to all market participants by enforcing shareholders' rights, as well as other rules and practices underlying good corporate governance. The OECD principles assume that countries have an efficient legal and regulatory framework in place and that securities regulators have the means and capabilities to enforce the rules and regulations of their capital markets. However, experience from the countries surveyed demonstrates that this assumption is often not the case. Typically, courts are underfinanced, unmotivated, unclear as to how the law applies, unfamiliar with economic issues, or even corrupt. Moreover, securities regulators have little direct power to enforce penalties. Enforcement of prevailing rules and regulations is mostly the responsibility of the courts, which consequently leads to poor enforcement of the rules and regulations underlying corporate governance. In countries with weak judicial enforcement, concentrated enforcement through the market regulators may be preferable to enforcement through the courts.

The legal framework and corporate governance arrangements should recognize various forms of organizing companies when incorporating and policy makers should offer issuers different corporate governance options (in terms of disclosure and governance standards). This "menu of options" approach to corporate governance standards would facilitate reforms and enhance the relevance of the OECD principles for developing countries and transition economies. This approach provides a means for issuers and investors to choose the markets and the companies that are most appropriate to their specific risk profile. At the same time, standardization of options is desirable to lower transaction costs for issuers and investors alike.

10.5 Disclosure Regime for Financial Institutions

The evolving regulatory practices for banks and other financial institutions, in particular the New Basel Capital accord, places a strong emphasis on harnessing market forces, through adequate disclosure and enhanced transparency of financial institutions. The strengthening of transparency and market discipline is designed to complement the capital requirements and supervisory review and other tools of official supervision in promoting soundness. This section highlights key issues in assessing the adequacy of disclosure regime for financial institutions.

10.5.1 Current Practices and Evolving Standards

Public disclosure practices of banks are typically governed by banking laws in some countries and by the listing requirements for publicly traded companies under the countries' securities regulations and the applicable company laws. This type of disclosure of financial information on banks and other financial institutions helps to enforce prudential standards and to protect investors and creditors by promoting market discipline. Market discipline is an effective tool to limit excessive risk taking by banks, particularly in countries with a generous government safety net.[19] Market discipline becomes even more fundamental because supervisory approaches are increasingly shifting from hard prudential limits toward a more risk-based supervisory review. In this framework, banks establish their own policies with respect to risk tolerance and risk management while supervisors validate those policies and procedures, supported by harnessing market forces to foster sound risk management policies. In support of enhanced market discipline, additional disclosure requirements are being introduced as one of the pillars (Pillar III) in the New Capital Accord (Basel II).[20]

The New Basel Capital Accord (Basel II) provides a new international standard on disclosure practices for banks, although elements of it are already covered in the IFRS, in the national listing requirements, and to some extent in Basel Core Principles (e.g., Core Principle 21). The Basel Core Principles, however, do not explicitly require disclosure of banks' financial information.[21] Nevertheless, disclosure practices consistent with the spirit of the principle should be taken into account in BCP assessment. For example, the New Zealand financial supervisory framework relies to a large extent on market discipline, with only a limited recourse to prudential limits and onsite inspections. Therefore, the effectiveness of mandatory disclosure requirements was considered and taken into account in the assessment of several core principles.[22]

The Basel Committee has issued several papers with guidelines for supervisors to enhance disclosure and has described best practices in disclosure of specific banks' activities such as lending and derivatives.[23] In addition, the BIS survey of disclosure practices by banks contains a detailed list of disclosures and provides a benchmark for comparing the practices of domestic banks in the different categories (e.g., disclosure of capital elements, asset quality, derivative activities). The benchmark provided is the level of disclosure in those areas by international banks.[24] Given that the survey looks only at the type of items that are disclosed, conclusions with respect to the comprehensiveness of domestic banks' practices—as compared with those of international banks—should be qualified to take into account the adequacy of the underlying accounting practices.[25]

Countries adopting risk-based supervision frameworks should considerably enhance the disclosure of banks' risk exposures and risk management techniques in line with the new accord requirements. A detailed example of a rather comprehensive disclosure

10

requirement on banks' risk exposures is the requirements imposed on bank holding companies by the U.S. Securities and Exchange Commission (SEC).[26] The recommended disclosure templates of Pillar III (see section 10.5.2) are more detailed in several areas and more focused on specific types of risks, and they complement the SEC requirements. In addition, supervision could become more effective if national authorities disclose aggregate information on the level and trends in risk exposures of the system.[27]

10.5.2 Pillar III and Market Discipline

Pillar III (market discipline) of the New Basel Capital Accord is intended to complement the minimum capital requirements laid out in Pillar I and the supervisory review (of capital) process laid out in Pillar II of the New Basel Capital Accord.[28] This development is an important one because it recognizes the role of market discipline in supplementing the efforts of supervisors in monitoring the safety and soundness of banks. It also places the responsibility for promoting transparency, hitherto largely in the ambit of accounting and corporate governance standards, into the formal framework of banking supervision.

Disclosure under Pillar III, however, is limited in scope to those items that have a direct bearing on the computation of capital adequacy of the institution. Thus, under Pillar III, a bank would have to disclose information material using the approach that it has adopted under Pillar I. However, this limitation in scope does not limit the amount of information that is required to be disclosed, and the suggested disclosures are still substantial and comprehensive, as discussed below.

To facilitate disclosure, Pillar III provides 13 templates. They cover the following: (a) scope of application, (b) capital structure, (c) capital adequacy, (d) credit risk (general), (e) credit risk (standardized approach), (f) credit risk (IRB approach), (g) equity (banking book) positions, (h) credit risk mitigation, (i) securitization, (j) market risk (standardized approach), (k) market risk (internal models approach), (l) operational risk, and (m) interest rate risk in the banking book. Each template, in turn, breaks up the disclosure requirements into (a) quantitative and (b) qualitative disclosure. For example, under credit risk (standardized approach), banks are required to disclose not only the percentage of a bank's outstandings in each risk bucket that is covered by each agency's ratings but also the names of the rating agency and the agency's role.

Pillar III disclosure is to apply only to the top consolidated level of the banking group to which Pillar I applies. Hence, individual banks within the banking group need not separately meet those requirements. However, the Total and Tier I capital ratios of individual banks within the group are to be disclosed separately by the Pillar III entity in the template on capital adequacy.

The disclosure has to be detailed at the portfolio level, where applicable. Thus, for example, if the bank implements a foundation internal ratings–based approach, then in the template for credit risk, it should disclose for each of the five portfolios a broad overview of the model approach with a description of the definitions of the variables and with methods for estimating and validating the variables as part of the quantitative disclosure. For the quantitative disclosure, it should disclose for each of the portfolios exposures across different probability of default (PD) grades and should supplement this information with (a) historical data on actual loss experience in the preceding period for each portfolio, (b) analysis of how these data differ from past experience, and (c) a discussion of the factors that affected the loss experience.

The purpose of such detailed disclosure is to enable concerned market participants to make their own assessments of the risk exposures and risk assessment processes and, hence, to develop a truer picture of the capital adequacy of the institution. The structured presentation will allow for a consistent framework across institutions, which will enhance comparability. This development is particularly important because, under some approaches in Basel II, banks would be using internal methodologies and data sources for computing capital instead of supervisor-defined risk weights, as in the past.

The frequency of the Pillar III disclosures is intended to be generally semiannual, though an underlying expectation is that all material information should be published as soon as practicable. Further, there is also an expectation that all large internationally active banks and the significant banks would disclose information on their Tier I and total capital adequacy ratios and their components on a quarterly basis. Similarly, all information on risk exposure that is prone to rapid change should also be disclosed quarterly. However, qualitative disclosures of a general nature, which are not subject to this frequency of change (e.g., those that deal with risk management objectives and policies), need to be reported only on an annual basis.

The incentive, location, and manner of disclosure are left to the jurisdictions. An important consideration in the design of the disclosure has been that the framework does not conflict with the requirements under the accounting standards, which are much broader in scope. Hence, the medium and location of the disclosure could vary and would also depend on the method used by supervisors to effect the disclosure. Thus, the disclosure could be affected by making it mandatory under the accounting regime or the listing requirements. In other cases, it could be built into a supervisory regulation or reporting requirements. In some cases, it may be influenced by pure moral suasion or may be voluntarily adopted to maintain competitive equality. Further, in some cases (e.g., credit risk mitigation techniques and credit derivatives, asset securitization, and internal ratings), the incentive for disclosure is provided by virtue of its being a qualifying criterion for the recognition or use of those techniques under the New Basel Capital Accord.

There is a presumption of validation built into the disclosure, especially where the disclosure forms part of the accounting requirements, which are generally audited because they should be consistent with the audited statements. In case the disclosures are part of the supervisory reporting requirements that are subsequently made public, there is a presumption that the information is reliable. When it is published by the bank on a stand-alone basis or on the bank's Web site, then banks should ensure that this information has undergone some verification before being posted.

However, Pillar III stops short of requiring that the disclosure be audited by an external or independent party, unless, of course, this step automatically forms part of the regime under which the disclosure is made. The additional reporting burden is a clear disincentive for banks to voluntarily adopt Pillar III. Supervisors will have to find effective means

10

of ensuring reliability of disclosure, especially in circumstances where this disclosure takes place outside their purview. Nevertheless, it can be expected that the markets would be quick to penalize any incorrect disclosure ex post. While one is interpreting the disclosure, care will have to be exercised to take into account the different items of national discretion that have been applied in the particular jurisdiction because this information could affect comparability across countries.

Annex 10.A Code of Good Practices on Transparency in Monetary and Financial Policies

The Code of Good Practices on Transparency in Monetary and Financial Policies (MFP Transparency Code) consists of a set of good transparency practices for central banks and monetary authorities (I–IV) and for financial agencies (V–VIII), which are outlined in this Annex.

1. Clarity of Roles, Responsibilities, and Objectives of Central Banks for Monetary Policy

1.1 calls for the ultimate objectives and institutional framework to be clearly defined in law or regulation, including responsibilities, modalities of accountability, and procedures for appointments and overriding decisions.

1.2 deals with the institutional relationship between monetary policy and fiscal operations, including disclosure of advances to the government, bond market participation, and profit allocation.

1.3 deals with the agency roles performed by the central bank on behalf of the government, including debt and reserves management.

2. Open Process for Formulating and Reporting Monetary Policy Decisions

2.1 covers the framework, instruments, and targets used by the central bank and calls for explanation and disclosure of rules and procedures.

2.2 deals with the composition, structure, and functions of the policy-making body and calls for disclosure of meeting schedules.

2.3 calls for the timely explanation of changes in monetary policy settings with a pre-announced maximum delay.

2.4 calls for periodic reporting on the macroeconomic situations and progress toward achieving objectives.

2.5 calls for public consultations over proposed changes in regulations.

2.6 calls for disclosure of regulations on data reporting by financial institutions.

3. Public Availability of Information on Monetary Policy

3.1 calls for adherence to IMF data dissemination standards.

3.2 calls for public disclosure of balance sheet information and aggregate market transactions on a frequent and pre-announced schedule. It also includes disclosure of detailed balance sheet information and aggregate information on emergency financial support.

3.3 calls for the maintenance of public information services, including an annual report.

3.4 calls for disclosure of texts of regulations.

4. Accountability and Assurances of Integrity by the Central Bank

4.1 calls for public appearances of officials to report on monetary policy conduct.

4.2 calls for disclosure of audited financial statements on a pre-announced schedule and disclosure of internal governance arrangements.

4.3 calls for annual disclosure of information on expenses and revenues.

4.4 calls for disclosure of standards of conduct for staff members (including conflict of interest rules) and legal protections.

5. Clarity of Roles, Responsibilities, and Objectives of Financial Agencies Responsible for Financial Policies

5.1 calls for the objectives and institutional framework to be clearly defined in law or regulation and publicly disclosed and explained, including responsibilities, procedures for appointment, and modalities of accountability.

5.2 calls for disclosure of the institutional relationship between financial agencies.

5.3 calls for disclosure on the role of oversight agencies with respect to payment systems.

5.4 calls for disclosure of the relationship between financial agencies and self-regulatory agencies.

5.5 calls for similar transparency practices to govern the oversight of self-regulatory agencies.

6. Open Process for Formulating and Financial Policies

6.1 calls for disclosure of information on the regulatory framework, regulations, fees, and information-sharing arrangements for financial agencies.

6.2 calls for timely disclosure of significant changes in policies.

6.3 calls for periodic reporting on progress toward achieving objectives.

6.4 calls for a presumption of public consultations over proposed changes in regulations.

7. Public Availability of Information on Financial Policies

7.1 calls for periodic public reporting of major developments in the sector.

7.2 calls for public disclosure of aggregate data on a timely and regular basis.

7.3 calls for the disclosure of balance-sheet information of financial agencies, including emergency liquidity support.

10

7.4 calls for the maintenance of public information agencies, as well as periodic and annual reports.

7.5 calls for disclosure of the text of regulations.

7.6 calls for disclosure of information on guarantees, including their nature, funding, and performance.

7.7 calls for disclosure of oversight of consumer protection arrangements.

8. Accountability and Assurances of Integrity by Financial Agencies

8.1 calls for public appearances of officials to report on the conduct of financial policies and their objectives.

8.2 calls for disclosure of audited financial statements on a pre-announced schedule and for disclosure of internal governance arrangements.

8.3 calls for annual disclosure of information on expenses and revenues.

8.4 calls for disclosure of standards of conduct for staff members (including conflict of interest rules) and legal protections.

Annex 10.B Methodology for Assessing Accounting and Auditing

At the inception of the assessment, policy makers identify the relevant stakeholders who have an interest in accounting and auditing matters. The stakeholders may include securities market regulators, banking regulators, NBFI regulators, accounting and auditing firms, professional associations, institutional investors, and officials from the Finance Ministry. A National Steering Committee (NSC) composed of those selected stakeholders is then formed and chaired by a high-ranking government official. Throughout the ROSC process, the NSC provides input on all of the issues being reviewed. It also acts as the World Bank's counterpart in preparing the ROSC report and country action plan, as well as the intermediary with the government in securing approval for the publication of the final report. Finally, it oversees implementation of the action plan. However, the actual degree and manner of the NSC's involvement in the assessment phase varies across countries and is stipulated at the outset within the terms of reference. NSC members can, for example, assist Bank staff members through regular meetings as the Bank staff complete the questionnaires or can fill in the questionnaires themselves. The assessment is conducted by using the four-part diagnostic tool (described in the following four sections) and is carried out by means of prepared and standardized questionnaires.

Part I: Assessment of the Accounting and Auditing Environment

This assessment involves gathering data on the following areas (this detailed list is not all-inclusive) and essentially provides an overview of the country's institutional framework.

- *Statutory Environment:* Companies Act, Commercial Code, securities market, and banking and NBFI regulations, as well as accounting and auditing laws

- *Public Accounting Profession:* regulations, professional bodies, certifications and licensing arrangements, public perceptions, and liability and indemnity insurance
- *Academic and Professional Education and Training:* academic and professional programs, examinations, and experience requirements
- *Accounting and Auditing Standards:* standards, code of ethics, and independence
- *Monitoring and Enforcement:* respective regulatory authorities for banking, securities markets, NBFIs, insurance and the auditing profession, and the stock exchange
- *Quality and Availability of Financial Reporting:* availability of reporting
- *Various Issues:* country data, securities markets, financial institutions, forms of business enterprises, and the accounting profession

Part II: Assessment of National Accounting Standards with Reference to IAS

This assessment involves gathering data to determine the framework for the preparation and presentation of financial statements and the major gaps between national and international accounting standards. The preparers also interview national experts, including those with jurisdiction over setting national standards. To assess the gaps, the assessment asks the following three questions (plus follow-up questions) for each of the 41 IAS and IFRS:

- Has the respective standard been adopted as a national standard?
- Are the following accounting treatments and disclosures (as they pertain to that IAS) specifically mandated by the national standards?
- What is the effect of any difference between national standards and IFRS on the relevance and reliability of the financial statements for external users?

Part III: Assessment of Actual Accounting Practices (Review of Compliance with Selected Local Accounting Requirements)

This process reviews sample sets of financial statements of public interest entities, including the listed companies, to determine the level of compliance with existing national standards. The review, which requires the involvement of independent reviewers with appropriate technical knowledge, also focuses on institutional arrangements underpinning the quality of auditing and accounting practices. The response to the questionnaire is supplemented by a due diligence review that is conducted by members of the assessment team. The questionnaire addresses 18 topics, including components of financial statements; presentation of balance sheets, income statements, cash flows, and changes in equity; consolidated statements; interest; foreign currency translation; and income taxes. For each given topic, it presents the applicable IFRS requirement and asks the following three questions:

- What is the equivalent national accounting requirement?
- Do financial statements comply with the national accounting requirements?
- If no, then how has the item been treated?

Part IV: Assessment of Auditing Standards and Practices

The objectives of this component are (a) to determine the conformity of local auditing standards and requirements with ISA and the related IFAC Code of Ethics for Professional Accountants and (b) to assess the degree of compliance with local auditing standards and requirements. The questionnaire is supplemented by a due diligence review that is conducted by the assessment team, including a facilitated discussion among local professional accountants in public practice. Observance of the 33 ISAs is reviewed by means of the following format. A brief outline of the ISA is provided, followed by the following questions:

- Has this standard been adopted as a national standard, or are there local standards addressing all requirements of this standard?
- Has the local body issued guidance to facilitate the implementation of the standards? If yes, what are the key effects of such guidance?
- Are the following concepts (of the ISA) addressed in local standards?
- Have local standards on matters of relevance in the country (that are not covered by ISAs) been developed on the basis of the conceptual framework embedded in the standard?
- To what extent, if any, does practice tend to differ from the strict wording of the written local standard or standards addressing the requirement of this standard?
- What are the difficulties faced by professional accountants in public practice to fully comply with this standard?

Due Diligence and Final Report

After the assessment is completed, the assessment team conducts an extensive due diligence review on the basis of all the data collected. This process involves the following steps:

- A detailed review of the findings arising from the diagnostic tool
- An inception and closing meeting with the NSC
- Meetings with representatives of the Ministry of Finance, respective regulator of the securities industry, banking sector, insurance and other NBFIs, professional accounting bodies, listed companies, financial institutions, other public interest entities, and institutional investors
- A roundtable with the major auditing firms to discuss the issues faced in the conduct of audit engagements
- Interviews of knowledgeable in-country stakeholders, especially financial statement users

Final Report

The assessment team then presents a final report outlining its factual findings and puts forth policy recommendations to help the country enhance its accounting and auditing standards and practices. The report is reviewed by the NSC. The team may also organize workshops whereby various national stakeholders discuss the report's findings and policy recommendations. Those deliberations should lead to improved policy recommendations.

Development and Implementation of a Country Action Plan

The action plan is prepared by the NSC on approval of the final report by the authorities. The World Bank, on request by the authorities, may assist in developing the plan. The action plan addresses the most significant areas for improvement and focuses on specific, realistic, and achievable goals. Its implementation may be overseen by the NSC. Combined with the country report, the action plan can contribute to the design of loans, assist in the preparation of key policy documents, and provide benchmarks for the design and monitoring of technical assistance and capacity building programs. The World Bank may, if requested by the government, assist in gathering resources for implementation of the plan. However, long-term developmental programs are necessary for achieving results from accountancy reform initiatives.

Annex 10.C Financial Sector Governance—Selected Issues

Financial sector governance refers to (a) corporate governance of financial institutions and other market participants (e.g., issuers, service providers), as well as governance arrangements for financial sector regulatory agencies, and (b) the nexus of relationships among institutions whereby quality of governance of one institutional segment affects the other. Although quality of financial sector governance will ultimately be conditioned by the overall public sector governance, several key issues arise in assessing and strengthening financial sector governance. First, how well have the components of existing supervisory standards that deal with regulatory governance been implemented in practice? And what is the effect of regulatory governance on the overall effectiveness of supervision and soundness of the financial system? Second, has the governance of financial institutions (particularly banks) required additional controls and safeguards over and above the normal corporate governance practices and standards that apply to non-financial firms? Third, how should regulatory governance and regulatory policies in individual sectors be adjusted to help strengthen and reinforce corporate governance of financial institutions? This last issue has been given prominence in a recent research (see Barth, Caprio, and Levine 2004). Finally, how should policy makers encourage regulated financial institutions to exercise greater focus on the quality of governance of their counterparties (financial and non-financial firms, household, and government)?

Regulatory agency governance can be defined, similar to the definition of public sector governance in Kaufman (2002), as (a) the capacity of the agency to manage resources efficiently and to formulate, implement, and enforce sound policies and regulations and (b) its ability to carry on its mandate consistent with the broader goals and policies of the government and legislature. Regulatory agency governance can be assessed in terms of four key attributes that determine its "capacity" and "ability" to carry out its objectives effectively. Those attributes are independence, accountability, transparency, and integrity.

In the presence of several regulatory agencies and oversight bodies, the overall regulatory governance (not simply the internal governance of a single agency) will also depend on interagency governance arrangements, including division of responsibilities among oversight agencies, as well as information exchange and communication arrangements. The existing supervisory standards cover those elements in varying degrees of depth. The clarity of its mandate, the ability to carry out its mandate through appropriately designed instruments without undue interference, and the legal identity of the agency are among the factors that govern independence. Accountability of the agency to the body that had delegated the responsibility—the government or the legislature—and to the courts and the public (stakeholders) helps to add credibility and reinforce independence.

Transparency means that the agency's objectives, frameworks, regulatory processes and accountability arrangements, and internal processes to ensure integrity are all disclosed to the public in a comprehensive, accessible, and timely manner. Integrity of the agency is ensured by mechanisms such as procedures for appointment and removal of management, internal audit arrangements, standards for the conduct of staff members' personal affairs to prevent conflicts of interest, and the legal protection for staff members in discharging their official duties in good faith. Finally, the combination of information exchange and coordination arrangements among various sectoral supervisors and oversight bodies raises issues relating to the optimal design of institutional arrangements for supervision, as discussed in appendix F, Institutional Structure of Financial Regulation and Supervision.

Recent experience with assessments of observance of the core principles relating to regulatory governance across sectors shows that, in most countries, the principles are well implemented, except in the case of the insurance sector, where compliance was relatively low compared with other sectors (banking and securities). Main weaknesses observed were related to regulators' independence; lack of clarity of regulators' objectives and accountability arrangements; regulatory forbearance, sometimes reflecting lack of legal protection for the regulator; and lack of clarity with respect to the responsibilities of the regulatory body and self-regulatory organizations (see IMF 2004). Also, quality of regulatory governance affects financial system soundness, as illustrated in Das, Quintyn, and Chenard (2004).

In light of the systemic stability concerns associated with the commercial banking functions, supervisory authorities typically place emphasis on additional safeguards to enhance corporate governance of banks. For example, the Basel Committee on Banking Supervision has issued a range of guidance documents, including "Enhancing Corporate Governance for Banking Organizations" (Basel Committee on Banking Supervision 1999b), that bear directly on various aspects of internal governance of banks. The relative emphasis on official regulation and supervision, on the one hand, and corporate governance and market discipline aspects of supervised institutions, on the other hand, varies among countries, in part, reflecting the structure and state of the financial system and, sometimes, the level of systemic stress in the system. Thus, the supervisory approach toward enhanced corporate governance of banks varies over time and across countries. Similarly, the appropriate approach to strengthening governance of non-bank financial institutions is a recurring theme in the design of regulatory policies for non-bank financial sectors, including securities markets and their institutions (see Litan, Pomerleano, and Sundararajan, 2002). In addition, emphasis on disclosure standards for banks under Pillar

III of the New Basel Capital Accord is designed to strengthen governance of, and market discipline on, banks.

Several regulatory authorities, notably the Reserve Bank of New Zealand, place great emphasis on adjusting their supervisory approaches to ensure that corporate governance of banks and market discipline are strong. Those adjustments have been achieved through the following means:

- Holding directors responsible and requiring them to attest to accuracy of disclosures and to quality of regulatory compliance
- Ensuring adequate representation of non-executive independent directors, with a separation of board chairman and chief executive
- Requiring directors to avoid individual and collective conflicts of interests
- Ensuring rigorous internal and external audit arrangements, with external auditors having a measure of independence
- Enforcing regular, timely, comprehensive, meaningful, and reliable financial and governance disclosure
- Promoting incentives for market scrutiny of banks through contestable banking; equal competition between banks and non-banks; limited (or absence of) deposit insurance; and equitable loss sharing among all creditors, depositors, and shareholders

10

The extent to which financial institutions exercise influence on corporate governance of counterparty institutions, particularly non-financial corporations, also will vary a great deal across countries, but certain policies can make a difference. First, sound principles of risk management and asset selection promoted by the regulator could include adequate attention to corporate governance of counterparties. Second, corporate governance policy that is used by major institutional investors in guiding their asset allocation could be highly effective. Finally, the insolvency and creditor rights regime and other supporting institutional arrangements for bad debt resolution and asset management could provide powerful incentives for banks to exercise due diligence on counterparty credit risk and for debtor institutions to exercise good governance. The governance arrangements and governance nexus would, of course, change in times of crises, with relative roles of regulatory and oversight agencies, as well as the intrusiveness of official supervision and regulation changing rapidly to ensure stability.

Notes

1. See Litan, Pomerleano, and Sundararajan (2002) for a discussion of financial sector governance and the broader governance nexus.
2. See IMF (1999) for further details.
3. See IMF (2000b), the supporting document of the MFP Code.
4. See IMF (2003b).
5. See Mishkin (2001).
6. This possibility highlights the importance of risk disclosures, an issue addressed in the New Basel Capital Accord. See also section 10.5.

7. The IASB is an independent, privately funded organization that is based in London and that sets accounting standards. The board members come from nine countries and have a variety of functional backgrounds. The IASB is committed to developing—in the public interest—a single set of high-quality, understandable, and enforceable global accounting standards that require transparent and comparable information in general-purpose financial statements. For additional information, see http://www.iasb.org.

8. The IFAC is an international organization for the accountancy profession. It works with 157 member organizations that represent 2.5 million accountants in public practice, industry and commerce, government, and academia. Its stated overall mission is to serve the public interest, to strengthen the worldwide accounting profession, and to contribute to sound economies by establishing and promoting adherence to high-quality professional standards, thereby furthering the international convergence of such standards, and by speaking out on public interest issues where its expertise is relevant. International Standards for Auditing (ISAs) are issued by the International Auditing and Assurance Board (IAASB), which functions as an independent setter of standards under the auspices of IFAC (see http://www.ifac.org).

9. See IASB (2004) for a list of IASs with summary descriptions of each standard.

10. See IFAC (2004) for a full listing of code of ethics ISAs and other engagement standards.

11. The ROSC Web site posts details of the accounting and auditing assessment tools and published country modules and these are available at http://www.worldbank.org/ifa/rosc.html.

12. Currently, no international regulatory standards exist for A&A, although efforts to address this gap are under way. In the absence of regulatory standards, Bank staff members draw on their own experiences and international best practices.

13. This section is based on Artigas (2004), a paper from Financial Stability Institute.

14. For example, Standard & Poors may put a country on "credit watch," whereas Moody's puts a country "on review for possible upgrade/downgrade," and Fitch issues "alerts."

15. For a recent example of corporate governance assessment undertaken as part of FSAP, see IMF (2003c).

16. This governance nexus—whereby the broader governance arrangements, financial supervisory policies (affecting governance of supervised financial entities), and policies of supervised financial entities themselves (affecting nonfinancial firm governance) interact with one another—is explored in Litan, Pomerleano, and Sundararajan (2002).

17. Fremont and Capaul (2002); for empirical evidence that investors would be prepared to pay a premium for companies exhibiting high governance standards, see Newell and Wilson (2002) and Bhojraj and Sengupta (2003).

18. When ROSCs are prepared in the context of an FSAP, they may also be published—at the initiative of the authorities—as part of the FSSA report of the IMF.

19. See, for example, Nier and Baumann (2003).

20. See section 10.5.2 for a discussion of disclosure standards in the new capital accord.

21. Compliance with Basel Core Principle 21 requires that the supervisor has the authority to hold management responsible for ensuring that the financial statements issued annually to the public receive proper external verification. However, it does not

indicate that the supervisor has the authority to require that the financial statements be disclosed. An additional criterion indicates that the supervisor promotes periodic public disclosures of information that are timely, accurate, and sufficiently comprehensive to provide a basis for effective market discipline. Therefore, at most, if financial statements are not disclosed, assessors would note it in the comments to the principle. See Basel Committee on Banking Supervision (1999a).

22. See "New Zealand: Financial System Stability Assessment" (IMF 2004b).

23. See, for example, Basel Committee on Banking Supervision (1998), Basel Committee on Banking Supervision (1999c), and Basel Committee on Banking Supervision (1999d).

24. See Basel Committee on Banking Supervision (2003b).

25. For example, compliance with Core Principle 21 may be affected, even when the supervisors exercise comprehensive powers to enforce wide-ranging disclosures, if the underlying accounting standards were to deviate from international norms.

26. See United States Securities and Exchange Commission (2001) and United States Securities and Exchange Commission (1997).

27. See Section 10.1 on MFP transparency code of good practices for a discussion of transparency of aggregate information. The Financial Stability Reports published by various central banks (see, e.g., http://www.bankofengland.co.uk/financialstability/index.htm) include aggregate information on regulated financial firms.

28. See Basel Committee on Banking Supervision (2003a).

References

Accounting and Auditing Organization for Islamic Financial Institutions (AAOFI). 2000. *Accounting, Auditing and Governance Standards for Islamic Financial Institutions*. AAOFI, Manama, Bahrain.

Artigas, Carlos Truchartem. 2004. "A Review of Credit Registers and Their Use for Basel II." A Report for the Financial Stability Institute Bank for International Settlements, Basel, Switzerland.

Barron, John M., and Michael Staten. 2003. "The Value of Comprehensive Credit Reports: Lessons from the U.S. Experience." In *Credit Reporting Systems and the International Economy*, ed. M. J. Miller, 273–310. Cambridge, Massachusetts: MIT Press.

Barth, James, Gerard Caprio, and Ross Levine. 2004. "Bank Supervision and Regulation: What Works Best?" *Journal of Financial Intermediation* 13 (2): 205-48.

Basel Committee on Banking Supervision. 1998. "Enhancing Bank Transparency." Basel Committee Publications 41, Bank For International Settlements, Basel, Switzerland.

———. 1999a. "The Core Principles Methodology." Basel Committee Publications 61, Bank For International Settlements, Basel, Switzerland. Available at http://www.bis.org/publ/bcbs61.htm.

———. 1999b. "Enhancing Corporate Governance for Banking Organisations." Bank For International Settlements, Basel, Switzerland. Available at http://www.bis.org/publ/bcbs56.pdf.

———. 1999c. "Sound Practices for Loan Accounting and Disclosure." Basel Committee Publications 55, Bank For International Settlements, Basel, Switzerland. Available at http://www.bis.org/publ/bcbs55.htm.

———. 1999d. "Recommendations for Public Disclosure of Trading and Derivatives Activities of Banks and Securities Firms." Basel Committee Publications 60, Bank for International Settlements, Basel, Switzerland. Available at http://www.bis.org/publ/bcbs60.htm.

———. 2003a. "The New Basel Capital Accord." Third Consultative Paper, Bank For International Settlements, Basel, Switzerland.

———. 2003b. "Public Disclosures by Banks: Results of the 2001 Disclosure Survey." Basel Committee Publications 97, Bank For International Settlements, Basel Switzerland. Available at http://www.bis.org/publ/bcbs97.htm.

———. 2004. "International Convergence of Capital Measurement and Capital Standards—A Revised Framework," June 2004, Bank For International Settlements, Basel, Switzerland.

Beers, David T., Marie Cavanaugh, and Takahira Ogawa. 2002. "Sovereign Credit Ratings: A Primer." Available at the Standard and Poors Web site: www.standardandpoors.com (reprinted from Ratings Direct).

Bhatia, Ashok V. 2002. "Sovereign Credit Ratings Methodology and Evaluation." IMF Working Paper 02/170, International Monetary Fund, Washington, DC.

Bhojraj, Sanjeev, and Partha Sengupta. 2003. "Effect of Corporate Governance on Bond Ratings and Yields: The Role of Institutional Investors and Outside Directors." *Journal Of Business*, Volume 76, Issue 3, pp. 455–476, University Of Chicago Press, Chicago, Illinois)

Das, Udaibir S., Marc Quintyn, and Kina Chenard. 2004. "Does Regulatory Governance Matter for Financial System Stability? An Empirical Analysis." IMF Working Paper 04/89, International Monetary Fund, Washington, DC.

El Daher, 1999. "Credit Ratings: An Introduction and the Case of Subsovereign Ratings." Infrastructure Notes, Urban FM.8c, World Bank, Washington, DC.

Fremont, Olivier, and Mierta Capaul. 2002. "The State of Corporate Governance: Experience from Country Assessments." World Bank Policy Research Working Paper 2858, World Bank, Washington, DC.

Galindo, A., and M. J. Miller. 2001. "Can Credit Registries Reduce Credit Constraints? Empirical Evidence on the Role of Credit Registries in Firm Investment Decisions." In *Annual Meeting, Inter-American Development Bank*, 1–26, Inter-American Development Bank, Washington DC.

International Accounting Standard Board (IASB). 2004. "Summaries of International Financial Reporting Accounting Standards."

International Federation of Accountants (IFAC). 2004. "Handbook of International Auditing, Assurance, and Ethics Pronouncement."

International Monetary Fund (IMF). 1999. *Code of Good Practices on Transparency in Monetary and Financial Policies: Declaration of Principles*. Washington, DC: International Monetary Fund.

————. 2000a. "Guidance Note for Assessing the Code of Good Practices on Transparency in Monetary and Financial Policies." Washington, DC: International Monetary Fund.

————. 2000b. *Supporting Document to the Code of Good Practices on Transparency in Monetary and Financial Policies.* Washington, DC: International Monetary Fund.

————. 2002. "Safeguards Assessments—Review of Experience and Next Steps," February 15, International Monetary Fund Washington DC.

————. 2003a, "Fifth Review of the Fund's Data Standards Initiative," June 18, 2003, International Monetary Fund, Washington DC.

————. 2003b. "Access to International Capital Markets for First Time Sovereign Issuers." Washington, DC: International Monetary Fund.

————. 2003c. "Assessments of the IMF Code of Good Practices on Transparency in Monetary and Financial Policies—Review of Experience." Paper prepared by the Monetary and Financial Systems Department, International Monetary Fund, Washington, DC.

————. 2003d. "Financial System Stability Assessment on the People's Republic of China–Hong Kong Special Administrative Region." IMF Country Report 03/191, International Monetary Fund, Washington, DC.

————. 2004. "New Zealand: Financial System Stability Assessment, Including Reports on the Observance of Standards and Codes." Country Report 04/126, International Monetary Fund, Washington, DC.

Jappelli, T., and M. Pagano. 2001. "Information Sharing, Lending, and Defaults: Cross-Country Evidence." *Journal of Banking and Finance* 26 (10):2023–54.

Joint Forum. 2004. "Financial Disclosure in the Banking, Insurance and Securities Sectors: Issues and Analysis." Basel, Switzerland: Joint Forum.

Kallberg, Jarl G., and Gregory F. Udell. 2003. "Private Business Information Exchange in the United States." In *Credit Reporting Systems and the International Economy*, ed. M. J. Miller, 203–28. Cambridge, Massachusetts: MIT Press.

Kaminsky, Graciela, and Sergio Schmuckler. 2002. "Emerging Markets Instability: Do Sovereign Ratings Affect Country Risk and Stock Returns?" *World Bank Economic Review* 16 (2):171–95.

Kaufman, D. 2002. "Public and Private Misgovernance in Finance: Perverse Links, Capture, and their Empirics." In *Financial Sector Governance: The Roles of the Public and Private Sectors*, ed. R. E. Litan, M. Pomerleano, and V. Sundararajan, Washington, DC: Brookings Institution Press.

Litan, Robert E., Michael Pomerleano, and V. Sundararajan, eds. 2002. *Financial Sector Governance: The Roles of the Public and Private Sectors.* Washington, DC: Brookings Institution Press.

Miller, M. J. 2003. "Credit Reporting Systems around the Globe: The State of the Art in Public Credit Registries and Private Credit Reporting Firms." In *Credit Reporting Systems and the International Economy*, ed. M. J. Miller, 25–81. Cambridge, Massachusetts: MIT Press.

Mishkin, Frederick. 2001. *Financial Policies and the Prevention of Financial Crises in Emerging Market Economies.* World Bank Policy Research Working Paper No. 2683, World Bank, Washington, DC.

10

Nier, Erlend, and Ursel Baumann. 2003. "Market Discipline, Disclosure and Moral Hazard in Banking." Paper presented at BIS workshop Banking and Financial Stability: A Workshop on Applied Banking Research, Rome, March 20–21, Basel, Switzerland.

Organisation for Economic Co-operation and Development (OECD). 2003. "Experiences from the Regional Corporate Governance Round Tables."

———. 2004. "The OECD Principles of Corporate Governance." OECD Policy Brief, Organisation for Economic Co-operation and Development, Paris.

United States Securities and Exchange Commission (SEC). 1997. "Disclosure of Accounting Policies for Derivative Financial Instruments and Derivative Commodity Instruments and Disclosure of Quantitative and Qualitative Information about Market Risk Inherent in Derivative Financial Instruments, Other Financial Instruments, and Derivative Commodity Instruments." SEC Final Rules, Release 33-7386, January 31, Securities and Exchange Commission, Washington, DC.

———. 2001. *Securities Act Industry Guide 3: Statistical Disclosure by Bank Holding Companies.* Washington, DC: Securities and Exchange Commission.

10

Chapter 11

Assessing Systemic Liquidity Infrastructure

Systemic liquidity infrastructure refers to a set of institutional and operational arrangements—including key features of central bank operations and of money and securities markets—that have a first-order effect on market liquidity and on the efficiency and effectiveness of liquidity management by financial firms (see Dziobek, Hobbs, and Marston 2000). Key features of financial market infrastructure and financial policy operations that affect liquidity management include the following:

- Design and operation of payment systems and securities settlement systems
- Design of monetary policy instruments and procedures for money and exchange markets operations
- Public debt and foreign exchange reserves management strategies and operations.
- Microstructure of money, exchange, and securities markets

Those infrastructure elements are important for the effective implementation of monetary and fiscal policy, but their effect on the efficient functioning of financial markets, the soundness of financial institutions, and the broader systemic stability is a key focus of assessing systemic liquidity infrastructure. Another equally important consideration is to examine the extent to which limitations on the availability of infrastructure pose a constraint on the development of money and securities markets and on sound and profitable operations of financial institutions. The remainder of this chapter highlights the key issues to consider in assessing the above-listed infrastructure elements.

11.1 Payment and Securities Settlement Systems

The role and types of payment systems and securities settlement systems, key principles and practices to govern the sound operations of these systems, and the methodology for assessing the observance of these principles are discussed below.

11.1.1 Payment Systems

Payment systems (and securities settlement systems discussed in section 11.1.2) play an essential role in the functioning of financial markets, the maintaining and promoting of financial stability, and the facilitating of economic development. In the past decade, a broad international consensus has developed on the need to strengthen those systems by promoting internationally accepted standards and practices for their design and operation. This section briefly reviews the Core Principles for Systemically Important Payment Systems (CPSIPS) developed by the Committee on Payment and Settlement Systems (CPSS 2001) of the central banks of the Group of 10 countries, the systems and issues they cover, and the way they can be assessed.

Payment systems are characterized by a set of rules, procedures, and mechanisms for transferring money between two or more financial institutions and their customers. The principal mechanisms in a payment system are (a) the payment instruments, (b) the network arrangements for communication between the participants and the system provider, and (c) the facilities for clearing and for settlement operated by the system provider. Payment instruments can vary from a simple written order on paper to very complex electronic devices in e-money schemes. In modern systems, the use of paper documents is practically eliminated. To promote efficiency and to reduce the settlement cycle, payment orders are sent electronically through an international communication network like SWIFT or through a proprietary network that is specifically constructed for the relevant payment system. Also, Internet technology is used for communications that entail, in addition to payment orders, information exchange on statements of accounts, lists of settled payments, queued payments, and so forth. The facilities for clearing and settlement can vary considerably in complexity, depending on the way the settlement takes place, the availability of queuing mechanisms, the liquidity management and credit facilities, the links to other payment systems and securities settlement systems, and so on. However, in countries with very low amounts of inter-bank payments, clearing and settlement are sometimes done manually.

Payment systems can be divided into (a) large-value systems that are used for inter-bank payments, financial market transactions, and execution of monetary policy, and (b) systems for the clearing and settlement of retail payments. Large-value payment systems are mostly characterized by a relatively low volume of payment orders, whereas the amounts settled are often huge. On an annual basis, the turnover in a large-value system can be a multiple of the gross domestic product (GDP) in the country—in some highly developed markets up to 100 times or more of GDP. In retail payments, it is the other way around. The number of transactions (volumes) is huge, while, normally, the turnover (value) is modest. The separation of large-value and retail payment flows is not always clear-cut, and often in developing countries the same system is used for both inter-bank and retail payments, especially when checks are the main instrument used to transfer money.

Systems can settle on (a) a net basis, in which case an agreed bilateral or multilateral offsetting of positions or obligations by participants takes place, or (b) instruction-by-instruction (gross) basis. In a multilateral netting system, a participant's net credit position (the amount to receive) or net debit position (the amount to pay) is calculated as the sum of the value of all payment transfers it has received during a certain period of time, less the value of all transfers it has sent to all other participants in the system. Netting reduces the amount of liquidity needed to settle the payment flows between participants substantially. However, the underlying payments will be settled with finality if, and only if, all participants with a net debit position are able to fulfill their obligations to pay at the end of the settlement cycle. If there are no adequate safeguards in the form of liquidity and loss-sharing arrangements, the netting result has to be unwound, deleting some or all provisional transfers that the participant is unable to settle. Such a procedure has the effect of transmitting liquidity pressures to other participants and may, in extreme cases, result in significant and unpredictable systemic risk. Such potential systemic consequences might lead to strong pressure on the central bank to intervene and to bail out the participant involved. In a gross settlement system, the unwinding risk does not exist. In a Real-Time Gross Settlement (RTGS) system, payments are processed on an individual basis as they arrive during the day and are settled with finality in real time whenever the participant has a sufficient balance in its account with the settlement bank. If the participant has insufficient funds, the payment is queued and settled later with the proceeds of incoming payments. In a real-time environment, participants have to manage their payment flows and balances in their accounts actively and can influence the throughput by obtaining intraday liquidity from the central bank or by borrowing funds in the inter-bank money market.

The intraday finality in an RTGS system means that the receiver can immediately use the funds for settling its own obligation. Intraday finality reduces risk and facilitates:

- Urgent inter-bank payments
- The settlement of intraday and overnight credit transactions with the central bank—for instance, fine tuning operations. (Because those operations are most often collateralized, an effective link with a securities settlement system should be in place to ensure delivery versus payment [DVP] on a gross basis.)
- The settlement of money market transactions
- The delivery of cash collateral
- Payment versus payment (PVP) in cross-border arrangements. (For instance, to ensure that in foreign exchange transactions, the payment in one currency will be settled at the same time as the corresponding transaction in another currency to avoid the settlement risk when the payment of one part of the currency transaction is delayed [due to time zone differences].)

In the past decade, hybrid systems have been developed and have combined elements of RTGS systems and netting systems. A hybrid system is most often an RTGS system with special bilateral and multilateral netting facilities. Participants may have payments intended for each other in their individual queues. In an RTGS system, if no participants have sufficient funds in their accounts to settle the individual queued payments, there is no throughput. Hybrid systems, however, will have procedures in place that will try to settle the queued payments (or part of them) on a bilateral netting basis. Within this framework, the system tries to identify groups of payments that can be settled simultaneously, most often on a bilateral basis but sometimes on a multilateral basis. The procedures enhance throughput in the system substantially.

In some countries, two parallel systems exist for large-value payments, one netting and one RTGS system. In such a situation, the outcome of the clearing process in the netting system is settled in the RTGS system. In almost all countries, retail payments are cleared and settled on a netting basis. A retail system can be dedicated to the settlement of a specific instrument such as checks or card payments. In such a situation, there might be two or more retail payment systems in a country, each operating on a netting basis and completed by an RTGS.[1]

There are often links between the main payment system of the central bank and the so-called ancillary systems, most often netting schemes for large-value or retail payments operated by the private sector to settle in central bank money. Furthermore, the payment system of the central bank is often linked to securities settlement systems inside or outside the central bank to ensure DVP. DVP eliminates principal risk—the risk that the seller of securities will deliver the securities but will not receive a payment, or the risk that the buyer will make a payment but will not receive delivery.

The more links that are established, the greater the risk of contagion. An operational failure—or any other problem—in one system can prevent the timely settlement of a transaction—the delivery of cash of securities—in another system, thus spreading the problem across markets, and perhaps countries, and potentially magnifying its scale and effect.

Good descriptions of payment and securities infrastructure in specific countries can be found in publications of the Bank for International Settlements (Red Books) and the European Central Bank (Blue Books), which also provide statistical information.[2] Also within the framework of payments initiatives of the World Bank in different regions, descriptions of the infrastructure, legal background, and regulation or oversight in a specific country in that region are published periodically (Yellow Books for countries in Latin America and the Caribbean, and Green Books for countries in southern Africa).[3]

11.1.1.1 Relevance to Structural Development and Stability Considerations

The availability of an effective set of non-cash payment instruments and a well-designed payment system are essential for the development of the economy. Non-cash payment instruments can enhance the efficiency in the economy by reducing the cost of making payments and reducing risks.

Large-value payment systems support the development and functioning of sophisticated financial markets. The systems are also the channel for the implementation of monetary policy and liquidity management of commercial banks. With the development of financial markets, the call increases for a more-sophisticated payment and securities settlement infrastructure that relies fully on electronic payments, intraday finality, DVP, and PVP.

The payment infrastructure is one of the first places where financial stress from credit and liquidity problems manifests itself. Liquidity problems can easily lead to contagion and domino effects, where the failure of one institution to meet its required obligations causes other participants or financial institutions to be unable to fulfill their obligations. Well-designed payment systems contain the effects and prevent spillovers to other participants or systems. Weaknesses in the design and operational reliability of a payment system may expose the financial system to systemic risk, impair the effectiveness of monetary policy instruments, and jeopardize effective liquidity management by banks. Thus, an assessment of the soundness, safety, and efficiency of payment systems is a crucial element of any assessment of stability and financial sector development.

11.1.1.2 The CPSS Core Principles

The CPSS has defined 10 core principles and 4 central bank responsibilities with respect to payment systems. The core principles are intended to apply to a wide range of circumstances and types of systems, and can be considered as universal guidelines to encourage the design and operation of a safe and efficient payment infrastructure. The core principles cover (a) legal issues, (b) effective risk management, (c) electronic data processing (EDP) audit aspects, (d) efficiency and level playing field, and (e) governance, and are summarized in box 11.1.

The core principles apply to any system whose role in the economy is so critical that it is regarded as a systemically important payment system (SIPS). A system is regarded as systemically important if it (a) is the only payment system in the country or the principal system of aggregate value of payments, (b) handles mainly payments of high individual

---

Box 11.1 Summary of the CPSS Core Principles

Legal Foundation

I.   The system should have a well-founded legal basis under all jurisdictions.

Risk Management

II. The system's rules and procedures should enable participants to have a clear understanding of the system's effect on each of the financial risks that they incur through participation in it.

III. The system should have clearly defined procedures for the management of credit risks and liquidity risks, which specify the respective responsibilities of the system operator and the participants and which provide appropriate incentives to manage and contain those risks.

IV.* The system should provide prompt final settlement on the day of value, preferably during the day and at a minimum at the end of the day.

V.* A system in which multilateral netting takes place should, at a minimum, be capable of ensuring the timely completion of daily settlements in the event of an inability to settle by the participant with the largest single settlement obligation.

VI. Assets used for settlement should preferably be a claim on the central bank; where other assets are used, they should carry little or no credit risk and little or no liquidity risk.

Security and Operational Reliability, plus Contingency Arrangements

VII. The system should ensure a high degree of security and operational reliability, and should have contingency arrangements for timely completion of daily processing.

Efficiency and Level Playing Field

VIII. The system should provide a means of making payments that is practical for its users and efficient for the economy.

IX. The system should have objective and publicly disclosed criteria for participation, which permit fair and open access.

Governance of the Payment System

X. The system's governance arrangements should be effective, accountable, and transparent.

---

* Systems should seek to exceed the minimum in those core principles.
Source: CPSS (2001).

> **Box 11.2 Responsibilities of Central Banks in Applying the CPSS Core Principles**
>
> A. The central bank should clearly define its payment system objectives and should publicly disclose its role and major policies with respect to systemically important payment systems (SIPS).
>
> B. The central bank should ensure that the system it operates complies with the CPSS Core Principles.
>
> C. The central bank should oversee compliance with the CPSS Core Principles by systems it does not operate, and it should have the ability to carry out this oversight.
>
> D. The central bank, in promoting payment system safety and efficiency through the CPSS Core Principles, should cooperate with other central banks and with any other relevant domestic or foreign authorities.
>
> *Source:* CPSS (2001).

value, or (c) is used for the settlement of financial market transactions or for the settlement of other payments in the same currency.[4] Although retail payment systems are normally not seen as systemically important because they settle in large-value systems that fulfill the criteria for systemic importance, they can influence the function of the latter systems.

The responsibilities of central banks with respect to payment systems center on the effective oversight of payment systems, focusing on the compliance of the SIPSs with the 10 CPSS Core Principles and on crisis management (see box 11.2 for a listing central bank responsibilities). Crisis management deals with major problems in the systems—for instance, the bankruptcy of a participant, the technical problems in the systems itself or in the system of a larger participant, or the major liquidity problems. Crisis management often requires coordination between different authorities—for instance, between the payment system overseer and the banking supervisor and between the payment overseer and the securities regulator. Coordination with monetary policy departments is also necessary, because the payment system is the main channel for the transmission of monetary policy, and the decisions on liquidity support in the payment system will also influence monetary policy. Clear procedures for who should be involved, how decisions should be made, how the exchange of information is organized, and so forth should be in place. Preferably, scenarios should be developed in advance for dealing with specific problems. Cooperation, coordination, and exchange of information among the different supervisory authorities in the country, as well as with relevant foreign authorities, are often worked out in a memorandum of understanding (MOU).

In addition to an oversight role, a central bank might have other roles in the payment area such as a developmental role (designer of the strategy with respect to the development and international positioning of markets and infrastructure) and an operating role (system provider or owner of payment systems or securities settlement systems). Sometimes conflicts of interest might arise between the different roles. One way to make this potential for conflict clear is to enhance transparency of the different roles and the goals and objectives of a central bank in the payment area.

Oversight of payment systems is a core task of a central bank, and often a payment system department is charged with the function. If it is to avoid conflicts of interest with respect to the compliance of the systems operated by the central bank itself, the oversight unit, at a minimum, should be separated from the operational section.

The payment system oversight policy should comply with the International Monetary Fund (IMF) Code of Good Practices on Transparency in Monetary and Financial Policies. Transparency practices relate to (a) the roles, responsibilities, and objectives of a central bank or financial agency; (b) financial policy formulation and reporting; (c) public availability of information; and (d) accountability and assurances of integrity. The central bank responsibilities in the CPSS Core Principles document (CPSS 2001) include those good transparency practices.

11.1.1.3 The Assessment Methodology and Assessment Experience

A CPSS assessment of core principles seeks to identify the strengths and weaknesses of the SIPS, including its potential to transmit shocks (also originating in other countries), as well as risks to the monetary system or financial markets or across the economy more generally. The methodology for the assessment and the structure and scope of the assessment report are explained in detail in the guidance note prepared by the IMF and the World Bank in consultation with CPSS (IMF and World Bank 2001). It contains guidelines for the assessment of the individual core principles by providing a short explanation and the assessment criteria, as well as additional aspects that should be evaluated in this context. Ideally, before an assessment takes place, the central bank of the country first provides a list of systems in the country that are deemed systemically important and then conducts self-assessments of those systems. The self-assessments are reviewed by the assessor, and they provide a basis for the discussions with the stakeholders in the payment system such as the central bank, system provider(s) in case systems that are privately operated, and any relevant governmental and private sector entities (including bankers associations, card companies, clearinghouses, and securities market operators).[5]

Experience with assessing the core principles of the CPSS has shown that the principles provide a useful and robust framework for assessing the reliability and efficiency of SIPSs and formulating policy recommendations (see IMF 2002). The assessments suggest that there are substantial weaknesses in many payment systems. Payment systems in advanced economies and, to a large extent, in transition economies observe most of the core principles. In developing countries, a significant majority of the systems suffers shortcomings of varying importance in design and operation that may expose the systems to risks in the events of a problem.

In many systems, the awareness of risk and the possibilities for the participants to manage and control those risks are insufficient. A significant majority of the net settlement systems have no adequate safeguards in place to ensure the timely completion of daily settlements in the event of a default. Nearly 70 percent of all systems give evidence of an uncertain legal basis, mainly from the absence of legal recognition of netting and finality, and from unclear rules and regulations governing the systems. The effectiveness of the governance structure could be improved in more than 60 percent of the systems. In around half of the systems, the operation reliability is not addressed in full and may

11

be vulnerable to failures that can prevent the daily settlement from being completed in time. Assessment of transparency of central banks' policy on payments shows that the objectives and institutional framework for oversight are not always transparent and that some central banks do not disclose the general policy principles for the oversight of payment systems.

The assessments, as appropriate, recommend changes or reforms to the SIPS. They also help make the authorities aware of those aspects of their SIPS that should be kept under review as the economy and financial markets develop. In practice, some assessments have used the core principles as a basis for more widely assessing the whole payment infrastructure of a country and the risks arising from interrelation between various payment systems (IMF 2002, p. 7, paragraph 12). While such wider assessment may be helpful, especially in developed financial systems where there are links between several systems domestically and sometimes abroad, a decision to assess the whole system must take into account the resource intensity of also assessing systems that are not systemically important.

The level of observance of the CPSIPS in the countries assessed highlights some key policy areas that require attention in many payment systems. The requirements to ensure prompt final settlement on the day of value (CPSS Core Principle IV) and the need to settle a net settlement system even if the largest single obligor fails (CPSS Core Principle V) were not fully observed in many countries that were assessed. This weakness was compounded by legal uncertainty, weak governance, and insufficient operational reliability in a significant number of countries. In light of this, policy recommendations have focused on the following:

- Reviewing procedures to deal with settlement problems, including loss-sharing and risk control systems, information to system participants, and provision of intraday liquidity
- Strengthening bankruptcy law (including the laws on bilateral and multilateral netting), ensuring finality of payments, and clarifying laws on pledges and collateral
- Establishing backup processing sites and testing contingency procedures, including procedures against potential liquidity problems through cross-sectoral and cross-border exposures
- Establishing transparent access criteria and reviewing cost structures and pricing policies, including full cost recovery, to improve efficiency

Assessments have also highlighted factors that could have potential negative impacts on the liquidity situation in payment systems in different countries. This negative impact is the result of (a) arrangements for resolution of troubled banks, (b) nontransparent systemic liquidity arrangements provided by the central bank, (c) liquidity that is concentrated among only a few of the banks in a country in which there is currently no intraday liquidity available from the central bank, and (d) settlement risks in the securities and the foreign exchange markets caused by the lack of DVP and PVP facilities, respectively. In many countries, it is implicitly assumed by most participants that the central bank would, in practice, cover liquidity shortages, even failures, to avoid any systemic effects (IMF 2002, p. 4, paragraph 4).

11.1.2 Securities Settlement Systems

The term *securities settlement systems* is defined to include the full set of institutional arrangement for confirmation, clearance, and settlement of securities trades and safekeeping of securities.

11.1.2.1 Recommendations for Securities Settlement Systems

In November 2001, the CPSS and the Technical Committee of the International Organization of Securities Commissions (IOSCO) issued Recommendations for Securities Settlement Systems (RSSS) as a benchmark to assess the soundness and effectiveness of securities settlement systems (see CPSS and Technical Committee of the IOSCO 2002). The 19 recommendations are considered to be minimum standards intended to reduce risks, increase efficiency, provide adequate safeguards for investors, and enhance international financial stability (see box 11.3). Those recommendations recognize the importance of securities settlement systems for the infrastructure of the global financial markets, and they note that weaknesses in securities settlement systems can be a source of systemic risks to securities markets and to other payments and settlements systems.

The recommendations are designed to cover securities settlement systems for all securities, including equities, corporate and government bonds, and money market instruments. They provide detailed descriptions of the institutional arrangements for confirmation, clearance, settlement, and safekeeping of securities. They also address specific topics and issues, including the legal framework for securities settlements, risk management, access, governance, efficiency, transparency, and regulation and oversight. Ensuring safe and reliable securities clearing and settlement systems requires a clear understanding of the various risks involved in the process of securities transactions. The recommendations describe those risks and provide a wide range of measures to address them. The main risk related to settlement activities is credit risk, which is the possibility that a counterparty to a trade may fail to settle its obligations when due or at any time thereafter. Liquidity risk—which is the possibility that a counterparty may not be able to meet its obligations when due but may settle at a later stage—is another relevant risk. Other risks involved in settlement activities are legal risk, custody risk, operational risk, and the risk of a settlement bank's failure.

The reduction of pre-settlement risks is considered crucial to ensure the timely settlement of securities transactions. In this context, the recommendations define some rules for trade confirmation, settlement cycles, central counterparties, and securities lending. In particular, the recommendations require that trade confirmation take place on the same trade date and that settlement cycles—the time of exchanging securities against cash—be no more than three days after trade execution. To reduce settlement failure, the recommendations advocate cost-benefit analysis for the introduction of a central counterparty (CCP) and encourage securities lending and borrowing.

The recommendations discuss the sources of settlement risks and provide several measures to address them. For instance, a recommendation on central securities depository (CSD) requests that securities be immobilized or dematerialized and then transferred by book entry in a CSD. By centralizing the procedures of issuance and safekeeping,

11

Box 11.3 Summary of the RSSS

Recommendation 1 deals with legal soundness.

Recommendation 2 requires confirmation of trade details between market participants within the same trade day.

Recommendation 3 requires that final settlement occurs no later than T+3

Recommendation 4 requests cost-benefit analysis for CCPs.

Recommendation 5 encourages the use of securities lending and borrowing to reduce settlement risk.

Recommendation 6 deals with dematerialization and immobilization of securities and book-entry transfer in CSDs.

Recommendation 7 requests securities transfers to be based on DVP.

Recommendation 8 requires settlement finality to occur no later than the end of the settlement day.

Recommendation 9 requests CSDs to put in place adequate risk control measures to deal with liquidity and credit risks.

Recommendation 10 deals with the cash settlement assets and expresses preference for central bank money.

Recommendation 11 requires CSDs and CCPs to identify and minimize operational risk, and it deals with outsourcing of clearing and settlement activities.

Recommendation 12 requires the employment of account practices and safekeeping procedures to protect customers' securities.

Recommendation 13 deals with governance structure of CSDs and CCPs.

Recommendation 14 requires CSDs and CCPs to have objective and fair access criteria.

Recommendation 15 requires settlement systems to be cost-effective in meeting the requirements of the users.

Recommendation 16 encourages the use of internationally recognized communication procedures and standards.

Recommendation 17 requires CSDs and CCPs to provide market participants with sufficient information to identify and evaluate the risks and costs with clearing and settlement activities.

Recommendation 18 requests transparent and effective regulation and oversight, and it encourages central banks, securities regulators, and other relevant public authorities to cooperate within and outside the country.

Recommendation 19 deals with the risks related to cross-border links between CSDs.

Source: Adapted from CPSS and Technical Committee of the IOSCO (2001).

---

one can reduce costs through economies of scale. The centralizing would also affect the risk positively by reducing the number of intermediaries involved in the process of issuance and custody. To eliminate the risk that securities are delivered but payment is not received (principal risk), one recommendation requires that the transfer of securities and the cash payment are linked in a way that achieves delivery versus payment (DVP). It is also crucial that the finality of the settlement occurs during the settlement day. The recommendations also require that CSDs put in place risk control measures to address the failure of the participants. The use of unwinding—excluding the default participant and recalculating the outstanding positions—as a risk control tool is discouraged. The CSDs should instead use a combination of limits and collateral requirements.

The operational risk is defined as the risk that deficiencies in information systems or internal controls, human errors, or management failures will result in expected and unexpected losses. To reduce operation risk, the recommendations require CSDs to identify and minimize the source of operational risk through the development of appropriate systems, controls, and procedures. Furthermore, the system should be reliable and secure and should have adequate scalable capacity. Moreover, contingency plans and backup facilities should be established to allow for timely recovery of operations and completion of the assessment with a high degree of integrity.

The recommendation on assets protection requires the entities holding securities in custody (custodians) to put in place measures that fully protect customers' securities. In particular, custodians should use adequate accounting practices and safekeeping procedures. Investors' securities should be protected against the claims of custodians' creditors.

Cross-border settlement arrangements also pose special challenges for regulation and oversight. For those reasons, cross-border links established by settlement systems should observe all relevant recommendations. In addition, a specific recommendation addresses the risks in cross-border links between CSDs.

The recommendations identify the key mechanisms to promote market efficiency. They consider competition as an important mechanism to achieve efficiency. However, because of the particular features of securities settlement industry such as economies of scale and economies of scope, the recommendations emphasize other mechanisms for ensuring efficiency such as fair and objective access criteria, appropriate governance arrangements, and regulation and oversight.

A specific recommendation addresses the regulation and oversight of securities settlement systems. It calls for transparent and effective regulation and oversight to ensure the safety and efficiency of such systems, and for cooperation between central banks and securities regulators to avoid unnecessary cost and to promote adequate information sharing. Furthermore, the central banks that operate the systems should ensure that those systems are compliant with the recommendations.

The recommendations recognize that some functions critical to the settlement of securities transactions are performed by institutions other than securities settlement systems. For instance, the confirmation of trades can be performed by a stock exchange or trade association, or bilaterally by counterparties. Thus, securities regulators and central bank overseers need to cover the relevant aspects of stock exchanges when assessing compliance with the recommendations.

11.1.2.2 Assessment Methodology and Assessment Experience

As a follow-up to the recommendations, the CPSS and Technical Committee of the IOSCO (2002) have developed a comprehensive assessment methodology. The purpose of the methodology is to provide a uniform guidance to assessors, thereby contributing to consistency across assessments. The primary responsibility for the implementation of the RSSS lies with the designers, owners, and operators of the systems. However, the report stresses the need of national authorities—central banks, securities regulators, and other relevant public authorities—to promote implementation by carrying out self-assessments or peer reviews. The authorities should also identify steps to be undertaken in the event that the recommendations are not fully observed. The report is intended to serve as guidance for the Financial Sector Assessment Program (FSAP) assessments and for technical assistance.

The assessment methodology is composed of key questions to be addressed to operators of settlement systems. Some questions are also addressed to securities regulators, central banks, and other relevant public authorities. The replies to the key questions need to be summarized and translated into an assessment grade. There are four assessment grades: observed, broadly observed, non-observed, or not applicable. It is important that the assessor focuses on the system as it is at the time of the assessment and not on any plans and new systems to be introduced in the future. However, plans to enhance the soundness and efficiency of the system could be described in the general section of the report or in sections where the assessor provides comments on planned future actions. The results of the assessment, including recommendations to improve the system, should be summarized in a table.

When carrying out the assessment, one should consider whether there is a single system for all securities or several systems such as a securities settlement system for equities and another system for interest-based instruments. In the event that there is more than one system in the country, it is important to clarify the range of securities to be covered by the assessment. In some cases, it may not be possible to assess all securities settlement systems at the same time; therefore, there is a need to set priorities. From a systemic risk perspective, priorities should be given to the systems that settle the highest average daily value trades, because weaknesses in such systems will affect the smaller ones. Another consideration to be taken when setting priorities is to see which systems are used for monetary policy operations such as settling repurchase agreement (repo) or delivering collateral for central bank credits. Such securities settlement systems should be given priority because any disturbance will negatively affect the execution of monetary policy.

The RSSS were not designed to be applied to derivatives or to address in a comprehensive manner the risk management procedures of a CCP. A CCP interposes itself between counterparties to financial contracts traded in one or more markets, becoming the buyer to every seller and the seller to every buyer. A CCP has the potential to reduce risks to market participants significantly through more-robust risk controls and multilateral netting, but it requires strong risk management to avoid systemic risks. Therefore, the CPSS and the Technical Committee of the IOSCO (2004) has recently published a consultative report on recommendations for CCP that deals with several aspects of CCP, including risk management. For this reason, the RSSS should not be used to assess the CCP risk management, but only to evaluate the costs and benefits of a CCP because this issue will not be addressed by the new recommendations on CCPs. However, some other institutions such as major custodian banks may settle significant shares of securities transactions within their own books. Those entities should be considered as systemically important, and authorities may consider assessing the policies and procedures of the custodians against some of the recommendations dealing with DVP, finality, settlement assets, securities lending, and operational reliability.

11.2 Monetary and Foreign Exchange Operations—Instruments and Effectiveness

The prevailing monetary operations framework is based on monetary policy instruments and operating procedures, money and foreign exchange markets, and payment settlement system. Its design bears directly on banks' ability to manage short-term liquidity. The three structural components are closely interlinked, and they strongly influence and reinforce each other so that the design and framework of one will affect the characteristics that need to be given to the others.

The design features of monetary policy instruments affect liquidity management by banks. First, rules on averaging and maintaining reserve requirements and the rules of access, as well as volume, maturity, and rates of interest on standing facilities, all affect demand and supply of reserves and liquid assets by commercial banks. Second, those and other policy instruments influence and sometimes restrict banks' asset and liability management. Third, central banks' operating procedures in money markets can influence liquidity and efficiency of the markets in which they operate and of other related markets.

Usually banks operate in more than one currency and must, therefore, include foreign exchange considerations in their liquidity management. Access to liquidity in foreign exchange is affected by a number of factors that are different from those affecting liquidity in domestic currency. In this regard, banks operating in highly dollarized economies are faced with particular challenges. For example, deposits in domestic currency may prove less stable than those denominated in dollars. In addition, specific market and institutional factors affecting foreign exchange liquidity include (a) efficiency and liquidity of local foreign exchange markets, (b) foreign exchange intervention procedures of central banks, and (c) linkages between local and external financial markets, which will also have an important effect on liquidity in the local foreign exchange market.

Technical and institutional characteristics of payment and settlement arrangements strongly influence short-run liquidity management by commercial banks. For example, at least three factors help reduce the need for precautionary balances (Borio 1997): design of settlement procedures, access to money markets, and access to central bank facilities. First, if settlement procedures are designed to allow banks to borrow and lend among themselves toward the end of the day after settlement positions are known or can be estimated with a comparatively small margin of error, then the need for precautionary holdings of reserves is reduced. Second, provided the inter-bank market among participants works smoothly, the institutions can be reasonably confident of obtaining funds at the going market rate, and this expectation of being able to finance imbalances at a rate with no penalty also reduces demand for excess reserves. Finally, both the central bank operating procedures, including practices that discourage banks from turning to the central bank, and the market operations that smooth liquidity will encourage the development of inter-bank markets.

The ability of financial institutions to access liquid funding markets and their use of effective techniques for liquidity management will contribute to financial sector resilience. Without ready access to markets that recycle liquidity, market participants would

---

Box 11.4 Liquidity Forecasting Frameworks

Liquidity forecasting enables a central bank to decide on how much liquidity to provide to or withdraw from the market with the objective of smoothing undesirable fluctuations that could distort the implementation of monetary policy and could result in excessive market volatility. Liquidity forecasting involves the centralization of a wide range of information on financial transactions that affect the main items of the central bank's balance sheet, including the sources of base money creation that are not under the control of the central bank (autonomous factors), and those that are under its direct control (policy position). The supply of bank reserves can be derived as

$$
\text{Supply of bank reserves} = \left. \begin{array}{l} \text{Net foreign assets} \\ + \text{ Net credit to the government} \end{array} \right\} \begin{array}{l} \text{Autonomous} \\ \text{factors} \end{array}
$$
$$
\begin{array}{l} + \text{ Other items net} \\ - \text{ Currency in circulation} \\ + \text{ Lending to banks} \end{array} \left. \vphantom{\begin{array}{l}a\\a\end{array}} \right\} \begin{array}{l} \text{Policy} \\ \text{position} \end{array}
$$

The first four items are beyond the control of the central bank in the very short run or—more generally—not related to monetary policy actions (autonomous factors). When the central bank acts as a banker to the government, the ability of the government to prepare accurate cash-flow projections and to share them with the central bank is vital for liquidity forecasts, because variations in the net position of the government often account for the most significant changes in liquidity supply.

In contrast, the policy position consists of central bank lending to banks through a standing facility, and net lending through discretionary money market operations.

Note: Further details can be found in Schaechter (2000).

---

be severely constrained in managing payments, transforming maturities, and managing interest rate risk, hence undermining prudent intermediation. Sound arrangements provide confidence to the market that liquidity can be mobilized and repaid on demand in a predictable and transparent manner.

Effective liquidity management by central banks—management that is based on anticipating liquidity conditions in money markets and acting at their own initiative to smooth liquidity—is essential both for monetary policy implementation and for a well-functioning money market that provides access to liquid funds. Forecasting the banking system's liquidity situation is a key element of a central bank's liquidity management framework (box 11.4). The main purpose of the framework is to create an information set that puts the central bank in a position to decide on the size of the central bank's operations in the money market, and to smooth changes in liquidity conditions in the money market at its own initiative to create stable liquidity conditions and to steer the central bank's operating target effectively.

For effective liquidity management, central banks rely on a wide range of monetary and foreign exchange instruments, in accord with the legal provisions governing the conduct of monetary policy. The mix of instruments that a central bank relies on varies from country to country and from time to time, depending on the state of development of financial market and monetary policy objectives (see box 11.5). The central bank may choose to regulate monetary and credit expansion by using administrative measures that set limits on the price (interest rate controls) or the quantity (credit ceilings) of bank borrowing and lending operations. Alternatively, it may seek to exploit its monopoly in the creation of base money to regulate overall liquidity conditions in the economy

Box 11.5 Monetary Policy Instruments

Rules-Based Instruments

Rules-based instruments include reserve requirements (RRs), liquid asset ratios (LARs), and standing facilities. Unlike money market instruments (which are market-based), rules-based instruments are based on the regulatory power of the central bank.

RRs are requirements for a bank to hold minimum reserves with the central bank, typically as a percentage of its liabilities. When averaging provisions are allowed, banks can fulfill RRs on the basis of average reserve holdings during the maintenance period. RRs serve the following functions: a buffer function for short-term money market rates when averaging provisions apply, a liquidity management function, and a seignorage function when they are not remunerated or remunerated at below-market rates. Efficient cash management requires that sufficient liquid assets are held to meet normal business requirements. Where this voluntary demand for liquid assets coincides with the requirement for reserve holdings, the requirement does not constitute a problem for banks if they are generally able to mobilize these RRs for liquidity management purposes. If RRs are set very low, banks have less leeway through averaging to manipulate their reserve positions without the risk of incurring the penalty of noncompliance. In such cases, banks would have to voluntarily maintain higher levels of reserves.

LARs require a bank to hold minimum amounts of specified liquid assets, typically as a percentage of the bank's liabilities. Where government securities qualify as the main eligible asset, the restrictions (if binding) limit the volume of securities that can be readily used to realize liquidity in the short run. Some countries impose restrictions on banks' loan portfolios by stipulating proportions to be lent to particular sectors or by setting absolute quantitative ceilings on outstanding credit. In the former case, the restriction limits the ability of banks to sell loans affected by the stipulation, while in the latter case, income is constrained and so reduces the incentive to sell those assets in the event that liquidity is needed. Ceilings on loan rates or interest spreads reduce the flexibility to price loan assets for sale.

Standing facilities are policy instruments that may be used at the initiative of banks and that bear a prespecified interest rate. Refinance standing facilities allow banks to borrow from the central bank; deposit standing facilities allow banks to deposit funds with the central bank. In settlement facilities and in some rediscount arrangements, credit is provided at market or below-market rates. In the latter case, many central banks establish volume limits on access to this window or alternately limit usage through moral suasion. For commercial bank liquidity, the management, the rules of access, the volume of credit allowed, and the maturity and rates of interest on the credit available are all relevant design features. In this regard, many countries operate standing credit facilities, most often with unlimited volumes of credit at market or above-market rates. In the case of rediscount operations, the bulk of credit is restrained by penalty rates of interest rather than volume restrictions. Some countries restrict the number of banks that can access the overnight standing facilities, the frequency of access, and the intervals between access.

Money Market Operations

These operations are transactions in money market instruments initiated by the central bank and operated through a competitive mechanism that aims at adding (liquidity providing operations) or withdrawing (liquidity absorbing operations) reserves to and from the system, respectively. Money market operations include the following:

- Open market operations (OMO). Those operations are conducted by the central bank as a participant in regular markets. They involve (a) buying and selling assets outright on the secondary market, and (b) buying and selling assets under a repurchase agreement in the repo market or foreign exchange swaps.
- OMO-type operations. Those operations are conducted using a specific central bank instrument. OMO-type operations involve (a) lending and borrowing against underlying assets as collateral, (b) primary market issuance of central bank securities or government securities for monetary policy purposes, (c) accepting fixed-term deposits, and (d) auctions of foreign exchange (as a tool for both foreign exchange and liquidity management).
- In their market operations, central banks may use various auction techniques. With volume tenders, banks bid only for volumes supplied by the central bank at a preset interest rate. With interest rate tenders, banks bid for the amount and the rate; the central bank charges the rates offered (multiple-rate auction) or the cutoff rate (uniform-rate auction).

Note: Further details can be found in Balino and Zamalloa (1997).

11

by influencing the underlying demand and supply conditions for central bank money. It does so by exchanging financial assets (domestic assets or foreign exchange) for its own liabilities (hereafter referred to as money market operations), or by requiring banks to maintain minimum balances with the central bank (reserve requirements). All of those measures are aimed at influencing the balance sheet of the commercial banks, either directly (through administrative measures) or indirectly (through the balance sheet of the central bank and its money market operations and reserve requirements). The operations, in turn, allow the central bank to influence the liquidity of money and financial markets and to facilitate the achievement of its objectives.

Industrial countries started moving from reliance on credit or interest rate controls toward reliance on money market operations in the 1970s, in view of the increasing inefficiency of the former controls in a context where financial markets had become more integrated both domestically and internationally. In addition, allowing market forces to distribute financial resources was associated with increased economic efficiency and growth. While the instruments used have varied on the basis of country circumstances, the following common trends can be observed: (a) lesser recourse to open-ended or standing facilities that banks may use at their discretion to place funds with, or borrow funds from, the central bank under certain pre-established conditions; (b) increased use of market-based operations conducted at the discretion of the central bank to add or withdraw liquidity from the system; and (c) reduced reliance on reserve requirements. Concomitantly, governments have ceased to rely on the central bank to finance their needs, relying more on the markets to fund their operations.

Central banks in emerging market economies and developing countries have also moved toward reliance on money market operations. At the same time, they have maintained a high reliance on reserve requirements and, at times, liquid asset ratios, which create a captive demand for qualifying assets (typically government securities). Frequently, the central bank has continued to act as banker to the government. The move toward money market operations was the counterpart in the monetary area to the trend toward enhancing the role of price signals in the economy. It has involved reducing direct government intervention in the economy, improving the capacity of financial institutions to mobilize domestic savings, and strengthening the role of market forces in the allocation of financial resources.

As one carries out financial sector assessments, therefore, it is important to assess the functioning of money and foreign exchange markets and to evaluate central banks' monetary operating procedures from the perspective of systemic liquidity management. One objective of assessing systemic liquidity infrastructure is to provide an input in formulating recommendations that will enhance the liquidity of funding markets and will improve access to such markets, thereby helping increase financial sector resilience. Another key objective of assessments is (a) to examine whether monetary operating procedures are efficient and adequate to foster efficient and liquid markets and (b) to help contain interest rate and exchange rate volatility along with the associated risks and vulnerabilities in the system.

11.3 Monetary and Foreign Exchange Markets—Microstructure and Functioning

Market microstructure refers to the mechanics of price formation and liquidity provision, whereas market functioning is about the effectiveness and reliability of those mechanics.[6] A well-functioning market is one where trades can be executed quickly and with minimal costs and where prices adjust to market-clearing levels in an orderly way. In most cases, a well functioning market requires some combination of market making or a system of order queuing arising from the market microstructure. In other words, the functioning of the market is determined by its microstructure.

The microstructure and functioning of money and foreign exchange markets differ from that of other financial markets because of the singular role of the central bank.[7] The central bank is usually the regulator of those markets and is responsible for the development of market institutions. The central bank frequently serves as market maker and dominant supplier of liquidity, particularly in less-developed markets. In a context of shallow markets, the central bank faces the challenge of establishing operating procedures to guide its interventions that balance the need to achieve its policy objectives with the need to promote market development.

Markets may be organized as dealer markets, where market makers provide liquidity by holding inventory and where they aid in price discovery by quoting prices ahead of transactions. In deep markets in which the central bank does not intervene, dealers will adjust their price quotes in response to changes in order flow. In this way, prices will move in response to market fundamentals. However, when markets are shallow or the central bank seeks to control the interest rate or the exchange rate, the central bank often acts as a market maker by providing price quotes and liquidity to the market. Central banks may seek to encourage the deepening of markets by designating authorized or primary dealers to act as market makers. It is important that those dealers have sufficient capital to absorb losses arising from market making and have access to liquidity (including through repo or swap operations with the central bank) to fund their positions.

Central banks also conduct auctions of short-term instruments, repo contracts, and central bank credit; such auctions centralize market activity and concentrate order flows over a short period of time. The central bank may choose to refrain from participating in the auction directly and may allow prices to adjust to clear the market. However, the central bank could actively manage price outcomes by participating in the auction or by imposing cut-off prices.

The functioning of the markets should be assessed by examining the following:

- *Market Liquidity.* Indicators of liquidity include what the bid–ask spread is, whether large trades can be executed without significant price movements and how quickly they can be executed, and whether order imbalances lead to lasting price movements. Liquidity may differ among market participants, especially if there are exchange restrictions. Further, the withdrawal of dealers from the market during times of crisis can lead to sudden stops in liquidity provision.
- *Immediacy of Trades.* This immediacy is crucial in money markets because it underpins effective liquidity management and the operation of the payments system.

The presence of dealers or the access to central bank liquidity facilities is important in ensuring that transactions in the money market can be quickly executed.

- *Efficiency.* Transaction costs in those markets affect the efficiency of financial intermediation and international payments.
- *Transparency.* The regular and reliable supply of information on market activities facilitates orderly price adjustment and better risk management, and the information can be used to inhibit anticompetitive behavior by market participants.
- *Market Participants and Their Behavior.* The entry of different participants (hedge funds, pension funds, and insurance companies) and the consolidation of existing participants that has occurred as markets have been liberalized and developed has implications for market functioning. Risk management and trading strategies have also evolved and have led to shifts to market liquidity over time.[8]
- *Transmission of Policy.* The effectiveness of market makers, be they the central bank or primary dealers, is a key component for the implementation of monetary policy using indirect instruments and for effective intervention in the foreign exchange market.
- *Electronic Trading.* The introduction of electronic trading has sharply reduced transaction costs and has led to a mingling of the inter-dealer marker and the dealer-customer market.

11.4 Public Debt Management and the Government Securities Market[9]

Sovereign debt management is the process of establishing and executing a strategy for managing the government's debt in order to raise the required amount of funding; achieve its risk and cost objectives, such as ensuring that the government's financing needs and its payment obligations are met at the lowest possible cost over the medium to long run, which is consistent with a prudent degree of risk; and meet any other sovereign debt management goals that the government may have set, such as developing and maintaining an efficient market for government securities.

A government's debt portfolio is usually the largest financial portfolio in the country. It often contains complex and risky financial structures, and it can generate substantial risk to the government's balance sheet and to the country's financial stability. Sound debt structures help reduce government exposure to interest rate, currency, and other risks.

Risky debt structures are often the consequence of inappropriate economic policies—fiscal, monetary, and exchange rate—but the feedback effects undoubtedly go in both directions. Poor structures in relation to the maturity profile and the interest rate and currency composition of the debt portfolio have often contributed to the severity of an economic and financial crisis. However, if macroeconomic policy settings are poor, sound debt management may not by itself prevent any crisis. The Fund's balance sheet approach (Allen et al. 2002) has also highlighted the risks involved in inappropriate debt structures that are tilted toward foreign currency and short-term debt and are not matched by assets with similar structure, while underplaying the role of inflation indexed debt (see also IMF

2004). Consequently, poor debt structures could be obvious signs of weakness in the debt management framework, particularly in the risk management framework.

The Guidelines for Public Debt Management (IMF and World Bank 2003a) could be used as a framework to review debt management framework and practices. Note, however, that the guidelines should not be viewed as a set of binding practices or international standards against which countries are to be assessed. Instead, the guidelines should be viewed as a tool in assisting governments in designing debt management reforms. According to the structure of the Guidelines for Public Debt Management, a review should focus on the following aspects:[10]

- Debt management objectives and coordination

  - Are objectives well spelled out, and do they give adequate weight to risk over cost?
  - Do debt managers and fiscal and monetary policy makers understand the ways in which their policy instruments interact, and are mechanisms in place to facilitate the exchange of information?
  - Are contingent liabilities such as the bail-out costs of the banking sector and other key liabilities such as guarantees for public enterprises covered?

- Transparency and accountability

  - Are the roles and responsibilities for agencies responsible for debt management clear and disclosed to the public?
  - Is information on debt management policies and the regulations and procedures for the primary and secondary markets of government securities publicly disclosed?
  - Are debt management activities annually audited?

- Institutional framework

  - Is the legal authority to undertake financial transactions on the government's behalf clear? Are institutions responsible for public debt management identified?
  - Are mandates and roles in debt management activities well divided and articulated?
  - Are internal operational controls well managed according to international best practices? Do debt management information systems generate accurate debt records?
  - Do debt managers receive appropriate legal advice, and do transactions incorporate sound legal features?

- Debt management strategy and risk management framework

  - Does the debt manager have access to useful methodologies and models to assess costs and risks (for example, the IMF's debt sustainability templates)?
  - Are risks—such as interest rate, rollover, and exchange rate risks—taken into account in borrowing decisions? Is the risk of the currency composition of

debt carefully considered, especially against the potential movements in the exchange rate that are a function of the size of the external deficit and of how closed the economy is? Is the risk of short-term or floating rate debt (especially under fixed exchange rate regimes) appropriately assessed? Is the risk of increased cost of debt management and its effect on interest rates and debt sustainability reviewed? Are debt structures reviewed for "lumpiness" in cash flows? Are put options and covenants avoided that make it likely that a large number of payments will come due when the timing is unfortunate?

- Are stress tests regularly conducted?

- Development and maintenance of an efficient market for government securities

  - Are debt management operations in the primary market transparent, predictable, and, to the extent possible, on the basis of market-based mechanisms?
  - Are the development of secondary markets and a broad investor basis being promoted? Are investors treated equitably?

11.5 Foreign Exchange Reserve Management

Countries hold official reserves to meet a range of objectives that will vary from country to country. Typically, reserves are held to limit external vulnerability by maintaining foreign currency liquidity (a) to absorb shocks; (b) to provide a level of confidence to markets that a country can meet its external obligations, including the government's ability to repay its external debt; (c) to maintain confidence in policies for monetary and exchange rate management; and (d) to maintain a reserve for national disasters or emergencies.

Specifically, reserves play a key role in preventing the cascading of sectoral liquidity problems into national liquidity and even solvency problems (through the effect on interest rates). Claims on reserves can arise from public and private sector risk and liquidity management. The size of short-term (by remaining maturity), economy-wide, external debt in relation to available international reserves is typically the starting point in determining reserve adequacy for emerging market countries. However, in the absence of effective capital controls, short-term foreign currency debt between residents can also result in pressures on reserves. Therefore, with flexible exchange rates, overall maturity mismatches in foreign currency are the chief concern as they can spill over into claims on reserves and national liquidity problems (see IMF 2004). When exchange rates are fixed and capital controls are weak, all domestic private sector liquidity problems can spill over into national liquidity problems: Domestic claims that fall due or are available on demand can be turned into claims on the limited foreign exchange reserves.

In all cases, reducing currency mismatches,—and for banks also maturity mismatches in the foreign currency book—and more generally strengthening private sector risk management through improvement in the quality of prudential supervision can contribute to mitigating external vulnerabilities by decreasing the chances of confidence and liquidity crises. Reducing the mismatches might also reduce the need for holding large stocks of international reserves by the monetary authorities. Generally, maturity mismatches in foreign currency are the chief concern because they can spill over into claims on reserves and national liquidity problems. Policies to contain this mismatch include both prudential supervision and macroeconomic debt management policies.[11]

The overriding objective of reserve management is to ensure that an adequate level of foreign exchange reserves is available for meeting a defined range of objectives and that the security and liquidity of those reserves are safeguarded. The generation of a reasonable return is usually subordinated to such considerations. The Guidelines for Foreign Exchange Reserve Management (IMF 2001a) spells out the objectives and good practices in meeting those objectives.[12] The guidelines could be used as a framework to review reserve management practices, although the guidelines are not an international standard against which country practices are to be assessed. Key issues regarding the reserves' adequacy, transparency, and accounting and measurement of reserves are also covered in IMF's work on Article IV surveillance and on the Safeguard Assessments. Measurement and disclosure issues are also dealt with in the Data Template on International Reserves and Foreign Currency Liquidity. The guidelines provide additional focus on whether existing reserves are effectively managed so that they are available to monetary authorities in the event of crises, and the guidelines avoid reputational risk to the central bank that could undermine its authority (see section 1–4 of the guidelines). The guidelines spell out a range of institutional and operational practices that are based on a wide range of country experiences and that encompass (a) the clear objectives for management of reserves; (b) a framework of transparency that ensures accountability and clarity of reserve management activities and results; (c) the sound institutional and governance structures; (d) the prudent management of risks; and (e) the conduct of reserve management operations in efficient and sound markets. The following aspects of the guidelines would merit special attention:

- Reserve management strategy and coordination

  - Are their clear investment guidelines? Are the degrees of freedom of the various decision-making levels to deviate from the strategic asset allocation appropriate, or do they provide too much leeway for taking market risk at low levels in the organization?
  - Are methodologies to establish the strategic asset allocation appropriate in light of the objectives of holding reserves? The currency composition is especially important, but so is also the maturity, credit, and liquidity profile.[13]

- Transparency and accountability

  - Is there a clear allocation of reserve management responsibilities and roles between the government, the reserve management entity, and other agencies, and is that allocation publicly disclosed?
  - Is the conduct of reserve management included in the annual audit of the financial statements, and is the audit performed by independent external auditors? Is the auditors' opinion publicly disclosed?
  - Is information on official foreign exchange reserves publicly disclosed on a preannounced schedule? Does information on the pledging of assets and the use of

11

derivatives relative to domestic currency need to be officially disclosed? Is there any such activity taking place?

- Institutional framework

    - Are the reserve management entity's responsibilities and authorities clearly established through a legislative framework?
    - Are general principles for internal governance to ensure the integrity of the reserve management entity's operations in place? More specifically, is there a clear decision-making hierarchy, and are operational responsibilities adequately separated, preferably between a front office (initiating transactions), a middle office (performing measurement, management, and reporting of risks), and a back office (arranging settlements of transactions)?

- Risk management framework

    - Is there a framework for identifying and assessing the risks of reserve management operations?
    - Are risk exposures monitored continuously to warrant that exposures stay within acceptable limits?

11.6 Microstructure of Securities Markets—Trading Systems, Price Discovery, and Determinants of Market Liquidity and Efficiency

The microstructure of secondary markets for equity and debt securities will have an effect on liquidity and efficiency of price discovery in the markets. Microstructure refers to the type of trading systems used, the rules governing execution of trades on those markets, and the nature and role of intermediaries in the markets. Liquidity can be defined as the relative ease (cost) of selling a security in the market or converting it to legal tender, and liquidity can be vastly different in normal conditions and in times of stress.[14] Liquidity is a "self-fulfilling phenomenon" in that liquidity (investor confidence) is attracted by the perception of an already liquid market. Price discovery is the market's ability to determine pricing of an asset (security), and the more-efficient price discovery mechanisms are, the more reliable the market price will be, thereby reducing volatility.

Organized markets can be stock exchanges—using electronic or physical trading systems—or bulletin boards, over-the-counter markets, or other alternative trading systems such as electronic communications networks.[15] Trading systems may be either auction (or order-driven) markets, wherein orders are entered into the system and compete directly with each other for execution, or dealer markets, wherein market makers post bids and offers and directly execute incoming orders. Many trading systems incorporate elements of both markets. Many jurisdictions maintain anticompetitive rules disallowing competition between markets, which is achieved by refusing to license alternative trading systems or by maintaining rules that require execution on a particular market. Competition between markets provides incentives to cut the costs of trading, but in some markets, fragmentation of liquidity pools between competing markets can make price discovery less efficient and can increase execution costs for large orders.

Trading systems have different levels of transparency; in most major electronic auction markets, there is a depth of transparency for price and volume of pre-trade bids and offers, as well as full post-trade transparency (real time volume and price, and identity of executing dealer). Over-the-counter markets (usually used for less-liquid equity markets, government securities, and corporate debt) would have less transparency, sometimes only post-trading. While transparency is generally encouraged, in some markets it has a reverse effect on liquidity because transparency can drive up impact costs for large trades.[16]

Trade execution rules include obligations to execute on a particular market or exchange, obligations to get the best price for a customer, and limitations on "internalization" of orders—orders never see the exchange floor but are filled inside the dealer by matching one customer's order against another. In general, dealers should be required to get the best price for customers, although the best execution rule, as this requirement is called, can arguably interfere with the timely execution of an order. Parochial requirements for execution in a regional market, for example, should not be allowed to inhibit best execution. Internalization of order flow is a controversial issue in most markets—dealers and banks will execute client orders either against their own trading books or against each other, rather than exposing the orders to the market. In some markets, internalization can drastically reduce perceived liquidity in the market (because executed trades are not transparent), but there are many arguments that customer orders are more efficiently executed at a fair price when internalized. Policy decisions to prohibit internalization are not necessarily the answer—it is far from clear whether exchanges (particularly as they become privatized) should be afforded a monopoly on liquidity as a matter of policy.

Quality of intermediation—how well dealers, asset managers, and advisers operate—in the market will also affect price discovery and liquidity. Intermediaries should be a reliable source of information (thus reducing asymmetry concerns) through their research function and should, along with a sound payment and settlement system, ameliorate settlement risk. Without a strong research and advisory element in the market place, investors (especially minority investors) will not have sufficient confidence in the accuracy and completeness of disclosure by public issuers. Of course, adequate accounting and auditing standards are the foundation for research, analysis, and disclosure. Without adequate prudential standards, intermediaries will not mitigate settlement risk,[17] and weak or absence of prudential standards will damage investor confidence and inhibit liquidity. Lack of prudential standards also may rule out margin lending and securities lending—contributors to liquidity (Group of Thirty, 2003)[18]—because of the risk involved. Lack of ability to short sell and to invest in derivatives prevents investors and intermediaries from using hedging strategies or acting on all their information,[19] and this situation, too, inhibits liquidity. As with rules governing trade execution, regulation of market intermediaries and disclosure regulations should be transparent and predictable in order to attract liquidity (State Street, 2001).

Market integrity (which promotes liquidity) requires entry standards that will protect the market by allowing only "sound" participants; however, unreasonable impediments to entering or exiting the market for either foreign or domestic investors will have a negative impact on liquidity. Transaction, infrastructure, and tax costs will also have an effect on liquidity. Investors need assurance that holdings can be liquidated when the need arises, without encumbrance or disruption in the market (market failure) and at a reasonable cost. Barriers for cross-border trading, including transaction taxes and reserve requirements, will reduce liquidity. However, once firms are allowed to cross-list on large international markets, trading will be attracted to the larger liquidity pool, leaving smaller, less-developed markets with reduced liquidity.

Notes

1. For example, checks, because of the way they have to be presented and processed, are relatively costly and time-consuming to settle when compared with credit transfer instruments such as payment orders. The credit and liquidity exposures in a check system are substantially more difficult to manage. Although some arrangements can be devised to manage the interbank risks, systemic risk almost inevitably remains in check systems if they are used to channel large-value payments. Therefore, countries with such systems usually establish a dedicated RTGS system to take large-value and time-critical payments out of the check-clearing system. However, an RTGS system might not always be cost-effective in a smaller country.

2. See http://www.bis.org/publicpss53.pdf and http://www.ecb.int/pub/html/index. en.html.

3. See http://www.bis.org/cpss/paysysinfo.htm.

4. See CPSS (2001, paragraph 3.0.2) for a discussion of what constitutes a SIPS. The definition in the text is based on IMF and World Bank (2001), which provides guidance on how to conduct assessments.

5. When a self-assessment is not available or contains significant information gaps, a questionnaire is sent to the central bank of the country in that bank's capacity as the payment system overseer.

6. The definitions are from Barth, Remolona, and Woodbridge (2002).

7. The microstructure literature has mostly focused on securities markets. However, there has been recent research on the role of microstructure on exchange rate determination and central bank intervention (see Lyons 2001).

8. See Barth, Remolona, and Woodbridge (2002) for a further discussion of the issues.

9. The section is based on IMF and World Bank (2003a).

10. For more detailed discussions and guidance, see IMF and World Bank (2003a, b).

11. For a comprehensive discussion of policy framework to assess reserve adequacy and to manage foreign currency liquidity, see IMF (2004). Also, required reserves on foreign currency deposits in foreign, rather than domestic, currency can help discourage such mismatches in the foreign book.

12. See IMF (2001a). For an elaboration of the guidelines that are based on country practices, see IMF (2003).

13. For more detailed discussions, see IMF (2001b).

14. Definitions of liquidity are discussed in Sarr and Lybek, (2002). For a recent discussion of modeling liquidity, see von Wyss (2004). Many econometric models are available, and none are absolutely conclusive.

15. For a description of various microstructure choices see Glen (1994) and Dattels (1997).
16. For an analysis of pre-trade and post-trade transparency, see Ganley, Holland, Saporta, and Vila (1998)
17. By limiting access to the clearing and settlement of trades to properly regulated and well-capitalized intermediaries, the risk that a party to a transaction will default is significantly reduced.
18. The Group of Thirty (2003) advocates removal of tax and regulatory barriers to securities lending. Another barrier may be weak prudential regulation, which creates risks in such activities and causes regulators to disallow lending practices. See also CPSS and Technical Committee of the IOSCO (2001).
19. Selling short provokes strong responses from policy makers. While it should be regulated appropriately, prohibiting short selling will act against liquidity and price discovery. Without the ability to sell short, a trader without a position can only buy and cannot act on information that indicates that price will drop. If a trader cannot act on negative information, the price discovery mechanism will be distorted.

References

Allen, Mark, Christoph Rosenberg, Christian Keller, Brad Setser, and Nouriel Roubini. 2002. "A Balance Sheet Approach to Financial Crisis." IMF Working Paper 02/210, International Monetary Fund, Washington, DC. Available at http://www.imf.org/external/pubs/ft/wp/2002/wp02210.pdf.

Balino, Tomas. J, and Lorena M. Zamalloa. 1997. *Instruments of Monetary Management: Issues and Country Experiences*. International Monetary Fund, Washington, DC.

Barth, Marvin J , Eli M. Remolona, and Phillip D.Wooldridge. 2002. "Changes in Market Functioning and Central Bank Policy: An Overview of the Issues." BIS Papers No. 120, Bank for International Settlements, Basel, Switzerland.

Borio, Claudio. 1997. *Monetary Policy Operating Procedures in Industrial Countries*. Basel, Switzerland: Bank for International Settlements.

Committee on Payment and Settlement Systems (CPSS). 2001. "Core Principles for Systemically Important Payment System." CPSS Publications No. 43, Bank for International Settlements, Basel, Switzerland.

Committee on Payment and Settlement Systems (CPSS) and Technical Committee of the IOSCO (International Organization of Securities Commissions). 2001. "Recommendations for Securities Settlement Systems." Consultative Report, CPSS Publications No. 42, Bank for International Settlements, Basel, Switzerland. Available at http://www.bis.org/publ/cpss42.pdf.

———. 2002. "Assessment Methodology for 'Recommendations for Securities Settlement Systems'." CPSS Publications No. 51, Bank for International Settlements and International Organization of Securities Commissions, Basel, Switzerland. Available at http://www.bis.org/publ/cpss51.pdf.

———. 2004. "Recommendations for Central Counterparties." Consultative Report, CPSS Publications No. 61, Bank for International Settlements, Basel Switzerland. Available at http://www.bis.org/publ/cpss61.pdf.

Dattels, Peter. 1997. "Microstructure of Government Securities Markets." In *Coordinating Public Debt and Monetary Management*, eds. V. Sundararajan, P. Dattels, and H. J. Blommestein, Washington, DC: International Monetary Fund.

Dziobek, Claudia, J. Kim Hobbs, and David Marston. 2000. "Toward a Framework for Systemic Liquidity Policy." IMF Working Paper 00/34, International Monetary Fund, Washington, DC.

Ganley, Joe, Allison Holland, Victoria Saporta, and Anne Vila. 1998."Transparency and the Design of Securities Markets." *Financial Stability Review*, Spring 1998, Issue 04, pp. 8–18, Bank Of England, Threadneedle Steet, London

Glen, Jack. 1994. "An Introduction to the Microstructure of Emerging Markets." International Finance Corporation Working Paper Number 24, World Bank, Washington, DC.

Group of Thirty. 2003. "Global Clearing and Settlement: A Plan of Action." Group of Thirty, Washington, DC.

International Monetary Fund (IMF). 2001a. "Guidelines for Foreign Exchange Reserve Management." International Monetary Fund, Washington, DC. Available at http://www.imf.org/external/np/mae/ferm/eng/index.htm.

———. 2001b. "Issues in Reserves Adequacy and Management." International Monetary Fund, Washington, DC. Available at http://www.imf.org/external/np/pdr/resad/2001/101501.pdf.

———. 2002. "Experiences with the Assessment of Systemically Important Payment Systems." SM/02/129, International Monetary Fund, Washington, DC.

———. 2003. "Guidelines for Foreign Exchange Reserve Management: Accompanying Document." International Monetary Fund, Washington, DC. Available at http://www.imf.org/external/np/mae/ferm/2003/eng/index.htm.

———. 2004. "Liquidity Management." SM/04/149, International Monetary Fund, Washington, DC.

International Monetary Fund and World Bank. 2003a. "Guidelines for Public Debt Management—Amended." International Monetary Fund and World Bank, Washington, DC. Available at http://www.imf.org/external/np/mfd/pdebt/2003/eng/am/120903.pdf.

———. 2003b. "Guidelines for Public Debt Management: Accompanying Document and Selected Case Studies." International Monetary Fund and World Bank, Washington, DC. Available at http://www.imf.org/external/pubs/ft/pdm/eng/guide/pdf/080403.pdf.

Lyons, Richard K. 2001. *The Microstructure Approach to Exchange Rates*. Cambridge, Massachusetts: MIT Press.

Sarr, Addourahmane, and Tonny Lybek. 2002. "Measuring Liquidity in Financial Markets." IMF Working Paper 02/32, International Monetary Fund, Washington, DC.

Schaechter, Andrea. 2000. "Liquidity Forecasting." MAE operational paper/00/7, International Monetary Fund, Washington, DC.

State Street Corporation. 2001. "Securities Lending, Liquidity, and Capital Market-Based Finance." A State Street White Paper (December 2001), State Street Corporation.

Sundararajan, V., Peter Dattels, and Hans J. Blommestein, eds. 1997. "Microstructure of Government Securities Markets." In *Coordinating Public Debt and Monetary Management*, Washington, DC: International Monetary Fund.

von Wyss, Rico. 2004. "Measuring and Predicting Liquidity in the Stock Market." Dissertation Number 2899, University of St. Gallen.

11

Chapter 12

Sequencing Financial Sector Reforms

The development of a financial sector necessarily involves a wide range of policy actions, and structural and institutional reforms. Those actions and reforms cover the design of instruments and operational arrangements for markets; the licensing and restructuring of institutions; and the development of the associated legal, information, and liquidity infrastructure. Given the multitude of policy actions and operational reforms to be implemented, the following question naturally arises: What principles and criteria should be considered in setting policy priorities among various policy and institutional reforms? All financial sector assessments present the findings in priority, showing high-priority actions of some urgency for the short term and then listing medium- and long-term structural measures. How should such priorities be set?

Sequencing is the setting of priorities among financial sector measures, and the appropriate sequencing and coordination of reforms is important for the following reasons:

- Inappropriate sequencing of reforms could cause excessive risk taking and financial instability.[1]
- Limited institutional capacity necessarily requires some prioritization of reform elements.
- Given the numerous policy and operational reforms in each area of financial policy, setting priorities could facilitate and encourage the adoption of reforms; hence, this aspect of financial sector assessments is important.

The sequencing of financial sector policies assumes great importance when issues of capital account liberalization (capital account opening) are under consideration. Recent experience with financial crisis clearly suggests that the mistaken sequencing of capital account liberalization contributed to the speed and severity of crisis in many countries

(World Bank 2001). While there is no consensus on the net effect of capital account liberalization on growth, poverty, and volatility, there is consensus that (a) the effect of financial liberalization (financial opening) on growth depends on institutional quality; (b) the growth effects of financial liberalization could be large and statistically significant for a wide range of countries (in the middle range of incomes and institutional quality); and (c) the development of adequate institutional capacity appears to be an important and necessary precondition for coping with volatility and reaping net gains from liberalization (Obstfeld and Taylor 2004). However, building institutions raises issues of institutional design and of the scope of reform strategies—priorities and sequencing—that need to be understood (IMF 2003a). Thus, sequencing of financial sector reforms is among the core elements of reaping the benefits of capital account opening. Key considerations in such sequencing are discussed in this chapter.

12.1 Development with Stability: The Role of Sequencing[2]

Long-term economic growth hinges on sound financial institutions and deep financial markets to mobilize savings and allocate resources. The liberalization of financial institutions, markets, and cross-border capital flows that are aimed at deepening financial intermediation and capital markets, however, increases risks that often result in financial distress and crisis. As new institutions, instruments, and markets emerge, risks evolve in complexity and magnitude.

The goal of the orderly sequencing of financial sector reform is to safeguard monetary and financial stability during financial liberalization and financial sector development. Strategies to develop local financial markets and intuitions must revolve around mitigating risks injected in the financial system as markets develop and become more sophisticated. Risks consist both of financial risks faced by financial intermediaries and market participants, and of macroeconomic risks that may be triggered by financial liberalization (e.g., loss of monetary control or excessive interest rate volatility following liberalization measures). Thus, market development and liberalization measures would need to be bolstered by parallel measures to mitigate both financial and macroeconomic risks. Financial development policies should also be sequenced to allow adequate buildup of risk management capacity and its associated infrastructure.

The different markets (e.g., money, exchange, bond, equity, and derivatives) and various financial products and services (e.g., credit to target groups and financial services to the poor) that need to be developed may be hierarchically ordered according to the types and complexity of risks to be managed when particular markets or products develop and expand, and on the scope of institutional preparations needed for good governance. This ordering helps set broad priorities among various financial sector segments that need further development, and it constitutes a key preparatory step in sequencing. The top row of figure 12.1 illustrates this key step by presenting various goals for the development of market and financial services in a hierarchical order (see section 12.4 for a further discussion). This hierarchy primarily reflects the complexity of risks that need to be addressed and other short- and medium-term priorities that are country specific. In particular, building and strengthening short-term money markets and risk management

Figure 12.1. Financial Development: Stylized Sequencing of Reforms

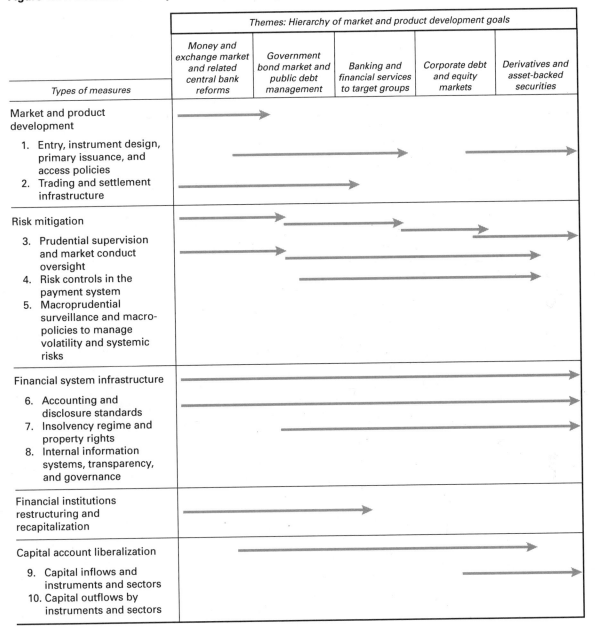

Note: Arrows represent the listing measures under each theme.

Source: Karacadag, Sundararajan, and Elliott (2003).

in such markets can set the stage and can facilitate the development and effective risk management—both financial and macroeconomic—of longer-term and more-risky securities. Measures to develop government bond markets, such as promoting primary dealers to provide market-making services, are generally facilitated by the availability of active money markets that are based on treasury bills or other instruments. The development of government bond markets and of a structure of risk-free yields provides the benchmark for pricing corporate bonds and other more-risky securities and derivative products, thus facilitating risk management. Measures to strengthen the access of target groups such as rural areas and small firms to financial services are medium-term goals that follow a strengthening of the basic banking, money, and government securities markets that help manage macroeconomic risks.

Domestic and external financial reforms thus need to be pursued in a manner that builds the capacity of regulators and financial institutions to monitor and manage the risks associated with a wide range of financial markets, permissible financial transactions, investable instruments, and loanable funds, particularly the following:

- Capital market development-cum-financial stability hinges on establishing the institutional infrastructure for controlling both macroeconomic and financial risks. Macroeconomic risk management requires effective instruments and institutions for monetary and exchange policy implementation, including well-functioning money, exchange, and government debt markets (Ishii and Habermeier, 2002). Financial risk management depends on high standards in corporate governance, accounting, and disclosure, and in prudential regulation and supervision. Those institutional reforms are critical to fostering an environment in which capital markets can grow without undermining financial stability.
- Developing sound financial institutions is a critical component of building capital markets and financial risk-management capacity. Both bank and non-bank financial institutions are the key counterparties in financial markets. They often create and transmit risks. As such, establishing good governance structures—including effective internal controls and risk-management systems—in financial institutions is among the most critical of market reforms.
- Reforms in financial system infrastructure—including the insolvency regime, creditor rights, and accounting and disclosure—and prudential regulation and supervision should start early in the process of market development, given the time needed to implement the reforms and their importance to financial institution restructuring and good corporate governance.
- Capital account liberalization and domestic financial reforms should be approached in an integrated manner (Johnston and Sundararajan 1999). Capital account liberalization by instruments and sectors should be sequenced in a manner that reinforces domestic financial liberalization and allows for institutional capacity building to manage the additional risks, as further explained in the next section.

12.2 Strengthening Access to Foreign Capital

Effective strategies to enhance access to private foreign capital can provide a significant boost to economic growth and poverty reduction, but the benefits of such access can be realized only in proportion to a country's level of institutional development.[3] The rule of law, shareholder protection, adequate prudential regulation and supervision, and financial transparency are significant determinants of whether capital account openness—to enhance access to foreign capital—is beneficial or harmful.

Enhanced access can be achieved by a combination of two approaches:

- Attracting foreign investors and lenders to a domestic market by promoting foreign direct investment, foreign portfolio investment, bank financing from abroad, and infrastructure financing through public–private partnerships.
- Facilitating access to international capital markets by domestic entities, a move that requires certain preconditions of policy environment and institutional preparedness, including credit rating and investor relations.

In addition to sectoral reforms, implementation of those approaches will require financial sector policies that strengthen access to financial services domestically by developing markets, institutions, and infrastructure; that improve investment climate, information provision, and governance; and that are well designed and properly sequenced for capital account liberalization.

Foreign capital can play an important role in developing local financial markets. The timing and use of foreign capital, however, should be selected in a manner that supports its contribution to domestic market development and that limits the cost of additional risk. Accordingly, foreign capital is often best used first to facilitate real sector and institutional reforms, including banking and corporate sector restructuring through privatization (Johnston and Sundararajan 1999). Capital account liberalization should start with the liberalization of foreign direct investment, which helps import the superior technology and management expertise needed to implement operational reforms in financial institutions and corporations. Foreign technology and ownership also promote competition and export growth.

Foreign investors also can serve as an important source of demand for local securities. Liberalizing portfolio investment in equity securities widens and diversifies the investor base for local markets, and it enhances market discipline on issuers in particular and on macroeconomic management more generally (Sundararajan, Ariyoshi, and Ötker-Robe 2002). Opening up to portfolio inflows, however, may increase volatility in market prices, at least for emerging-market economies in the short run (Kaminsky and Schmukler 2003). If one is to limit rollover risk, it is often better to liberalize market for longer-term debts before shorter-term maturities.

However, capital account liberalization should closely complement the domestic market development strategy. For example, allowing short-term capital flows for certain instruments and sectors—with adequate prudential safeguards—can support money and exchange market development. Similarly, the well-planned opening of inflows of foreign portfolio investment can add to the liquidity of domestic equity markets.

Well-developed risk-management capacities of local investors and financial institutions can help domestic financial markets benefit from foreign capital without subjecting markets to excessive stress. Cross-border capital flows, in essence, amplify the wide array of risks already prevailing in liberalized domestic financial markets, including credit, liquidity, market, interest rate, exchange rate, and operational risks. Thus, the risk management capacities of financial institutions and domestic investors have to be strong and sophisticated enough to assess and manage higher degrees of risk in all areas. For example, in hindsight, financial institutions and corporations in South Korea and Thailand (before the Asia crisis) did not adequately assess and manage the risks associated with foreign bor-

12

rowing and lending. Increased openness to cross-border capital flows also requires a closer monitoring of macroprudential risks to assess the effects of shocks on financial system soundness, and adjustments in macroeconomic policies to limit volatility in key prices.

In addition, it is often desirable to achieve some level of depth in domestic financial markets before exposing markets to potentially volatile capital flows (Ishii and Habermeier 2002). In the presence of a solid domestic institutional investor base, local money, equity, and bond markets are likely to be more resilient against economic and financial shocks that may trigger capital outflows. Potential market volatility and high interest rates resulting from a withdrawal of foreign capital are more manageable and short lived when domestic investors can act as counterparties to foreign investors. Thus, an adequate base of domestic investors can serve to cushion the effect of external shocks, particularly when the nature of the shock is a foreign, rather than a domestic, contagion, thereby fostering greater financial stability. This observation once again highlights the importance of developing institutional investors as a critical component in the sequencing of financial market reforms and development.

12.3 Principles of Sequencing

Risks in developing the specific types of markets, the hierarchy of markets, the demands that markets place on risk management and information requirements, and the various considerations discussed in sections 12.1 and 12.2 can be summarized in the form of certain principles and benchmarks on sequencing and coordinating domestic financial sector reforms (see box 12.1) and these principles are further illustrated in figure 12.1. The principles also apply to capital account liberalization, where the key challenge is to identify precisely how and when foreign capital can enhance market development.

Figure 12.1 highlights and illustrates the principles of sequencing and shows that market development measures need to be combined with measures to manage the risks in developing each area of market development, thereby combining development and stability considerations into prioritized action plan. The top row in figure 12.1 lists various themes—in relation to market and product development goals—according to a hierarchy that is based on risk implications and broader policy considerations, such as restoration of stability and confidence in the midst of a shock or strategic focus on strengthening access to target groups. The themes are ordered from left to right at the top in decreasing order of priority, starting with the themes of highest priority requiring implementation in the short term to ensure stability and effective implementation, and moving right toward more medium-term and structural goals. This hierarchical ordering (i.e., setting priorities) is, as already discussed, based on the complexity of risks and broader policy significance of each theme. That is, markets and themes that involve more complex forms of risk and that require a stronger infrastructure may need to be implemented later than markets and themes that involve simpler and more traditional complement of risks.

The first column lists the broad financial policy areas that must be tackled to achieve the specific market and product development goals under each theme. The types of financial policies listed in the first column of the figure distinguishes between five types of policy actions: (a) market and product development, (b) risk mitigation, (c) financial

Box 12.1 Selected Principles of Sequencing

Principles of sequencing domestic financial liberalization are as follows:

- Liberalization is best undertaken in the context of sound and sustainable macroeconomic policies.
- Capital market development-cum-financial stability hinges on establishing the institutional infrastructure for controlling both macroeconomic and financial risks. Financial system reforms that support and reinforce macroeconomic stabilization and effective conduct of monetary and exchange rate policies should be accorded priority. This principle entails giving priority to central banking reforms to develop monetary policy instruments and money and foreign exchange markets.
- Financial liberalization and market development policies should be sequenced to reflect the hierarchy and complementarity of markets and related institutional structures. Market development policies should be comprehensive. Technically and operationally linked measures should be implemented together, and linkages among markets should be considered.
- Capital market development requires a careful sequencing of measures to mitigate risks in parallel with reforms to develop markets. Policies to develop markets should be accompanied by prudential and supervisory measures, as well as by macroprudential surveillance, to contain risks introduced by new markets and instruments.
- The pace of reforms should consider the initial financial condition and soundness of financial and nonfinancial firms, as well as the time needed to restructure them.

- Institutional development is a critical component of building capital markets and financial-risk management capacity. Establishing good governance structures in financial institutions, including internal controls and risk management systems, is among the most critical of markets reforms.
- Similarly, the operational and institutional arrangement for policy transparency and data disclosure need to be adopted to complement the evolving sophistication of financial markets.
- Pacing, timing, and sequencing also need to take account of political and regional considerations that could strengthen ownership of reforms.
- Reforms that require long lead times for technical preparations and capacity building should start early.

The following are additional principles for external financial liberalization:

- The liberalization of capital flows by instruments and sectors should be sequenced in a manner that reinforces domestic financial liberalization and that allows for institutional capacity building to manage the additional risks.
- Reforms need to consider the effectiveness of controls on capital flows in place or the implicit restrictions on capital flows from the ineffectiveness or absence of markets.
- Transparency and data disclosure practices should be adopted to support capital account opening.

Source: These principles are drawn in part from Ishii and Habermeier (2002) and from Sundararajan, Ariyoshi, and Ötker-Robe (2002).

12

system infrastructure, (d) financial institution restructuring and recapitalization, and (e) capital account liberalization. The presentation of policy actions in this matrix, which is based on the core principles of sequencing, helps develop a well-coordinated road map of reforms and emphasizes the importance of implementing a critical mass of reforms under each theme that combines market development and risk mitigation. In practice, countries are likely to be in the midst of various stages of market development and risk mitigation, which will be out of synch with any stylized hierarchy of market development themes and the associated sequencing shown in figure 12.1. Nevertheless, the proposed approach in figure 12.1, which is based on principles outlined in box 12.1, can help prioritize future financial reforms, regardless of patterns of market development in the past, and can ensure that, at each stage, critical reforms are implemented to safeguard stability in the course of market development.

Notes

1. See Johnston and Sundararajan (1999) for some empirical evidence.
2. This section is based on Karacadag, Sundararajan, and Elliott (2003).
3. Issues in facilitating access to international capital markets are discussed in greater detail in IMF (2003b).

References

International Monetary Fund (IMF). 2003. *A Global Financial Stability Report*. Washington, DC: International Monetary Fund.

———. 2003a. *World Economic Outlook, April 2003: Growth and Institutions*. World Economic and Financial Surveys. Washington, DC: International Monetary Fund.

———. 2003b. "Access to International Capital Markets for First-Time Sovereign Issuers." IMF Policy Paper, International Monetary Fund, Washington, DC.

Ishii, Shogo, and Karl Habermeier. 2002. "Capital Account Liberalization and Financial Sector Stability." IMF Occasional Paper No. 211, International Monetary Fund, Washington, DC. Available at http://www.imf.org/external/pubs/nft/op/211/index.htm.

Johnston, R. Barry, and V. Sundararajan, eds. 1999. *Sequencing Financial Sector Reforms: Country Experiences and Issues*. Washington, DC: International Monetary Fund.

Kaminsky, Graciela Laura, and Sergio L. Schmukler. 2003. "Short-Run Pain, Long-Run Gain: The Effects of Financial Liberalization." IMF Working Paper 03/34, International Monetary Fund, Washington, DC. Available at http://www.imf.org/external/pubs/ft/wp/2003/wp0334.pdf.

Karacadag, Cem, V. Sundararajan, and Jennifer Elliott. 2003. "Managing Risks in Financial Market Development: The Role of Sequencing." IMF Working Paper No. 03/116, International Monetary Fund, Washington, DC. Available at http://www.imf.org/external/pubs/ft/wp/2003/wp03116.pdf.

Obstfeld, Maurice, and Alen M. Taylor. 2004. *Global Capital Markets—Integration, Crisis, and Growth*. Cambridge: Cambridge University Press.

Sundararajan, V., Akira Ariyoshi, and Inci Ötker-Robe. 2002. "International Capital Mobility and Domestic Financial System Stability: A Survey of Issues." In *Financial Risks, Stability, and Globalization*, ed. Omotunde E. G. Johnson, Washington, DC: International Monetary Fund.

World Bank. 2001. "Finance for Growth: Policy Choices in a Volatile World." A World Bank Policy Research Report, World Bank and Oxford University Press, New York.

Appendix A

Financial Sector Assessment Program—Objectives, Procedures, and Overall Framework

A.1 History and Objectives

The Financial Sector Assessment Program (FSAP) was launched in May 1999 jointly by the managements of the World Bank and International Monetary Fund (IMF) on a pilot basis. It was a response to calls by the international community for more intense international cooperation (a) to reduce the likelihood, severity, or both of financial sector crises and cross-border contagion and (b) to foster growth by promoting financial system soundness and financial sector diversity. The program aims at contributing to those objectives through the preparation and delivery to national authorities of comprehensive assessments of their financial systems. Those assessments are intended to

- Identify strengths, vulnerabilities, and risks
- Ascertain the sector's development and technical assistance (TA) needs
- Assess observance and implementation of relevant international standards, codes, and good practices
- Determine whether this observance addresses the key sources of risks and vulnerabilities
- Provide a robust infrastructure for financial development
- Help design appropriate policy responses

This joint Bank-Fund program was seen as a vehicle to bring the linkages between financial sector soundness and performance, on the one hand, and macroeconomic and real sector developments, on the other hand, to the core of both institutions' work. This joint program, together with the involvement of experts from national authorities and standard-setting bodies, also was expected to optimize the use of scarce expert resources, to avoid duplication of efforts, and to promote consistency of advice on financial sector issues through an integrated analysis of both development and stability issues. Although country participation in the FSAP is voluntary, the program has been structured from the outset as a means to strengthen the monitoring of financial systems in IMF's bilateral surveillance through Article IV consultations (which is mandatory) and as a means to promote economic development and to reduce poverty through the World Bank's development work to strengthen the financial sector.

After intensive discussions by both Bank and Fund Boards on the lessons from the pilot program, the program was made a regular feature of Bank and Fund operations in a comprehensive review of the program in December 2000 and January 2001. The program was further streamlined in the subsequent reviews of the program by both Boards in March/April 2003 and in February/March 2005. See box 1.1 of chapter 1 for a brief history of FSAP.

A.2 Operational Procedures for FSAP, FSAP Updates, Follow–Up Technical Assistance, and Relationship to Bank-Fund Operations

The operational procedures for carrying out financial sector assessments and updates under the joint Bank-Fund FSAP have been developed by the Bank-Fund Financial Sector Liaison Committee (FSLC). Those procedures have been designed to reflect the following considerations:

- To feed into the IMF's Article IV consultation process through close linkages with IMF's surveillance activities
- To serve as input into Bank's social and structural reviews, country assistance strategies, and other operations of the World Bank
- To serve as a program of peer review of observance of relevant international standards in the financial sector
- To ensure uniform and consistent treatment of countries and economies through adequate quality control and review
- To minimize duplication and overlap when moving from the joint team output of FSAP missions to the separate reporting and accountability requirements of each institution
- To balance the voluntary nature of participation in the FSAP with the need to give priority to some countries and to encourage the countries to participate on the basis of both stability and development considerations
- To ensure adequate consultations within the Fund and the Bank and with the authorities both in country selection and on the scope and focus of work
- To ensure confidentiality of data on individual financial institutions and other market sensitive information provided to the team by the authorities, while facilitating adequate transparency of policy analysis and assessments to the Bank and Fund Boards, as well as to the markets on a voluntary basis
- To facilitate documentation, contacts with authorities, internal review processes, appropriate mission staffing, and adequate Bank-Fund coordination in those areas

Table A.1. Institutions Cooperating in the FSAP

Country	Cooperating official institution
Argentina	Central Bank of the Republic of Argentina
Australia	Reserve Bank of Australia Australian Prudential Regulation Authority Australian Securities and Investment Commission
Austria	Austrian National Bank Financial Market Authority
Belgium	National Bank of Belgium Banking and Finance Commission
Brazil	Central Bank of Brazil
Canada	Bank of Canada Office of the Superintendent of Financial Institutions
Chile	Central Bank of Chile Superintendency of Banks and Financial Institutions
Colombia	Bank of the Republic
Czech Republic	Czech National Bank
Denmark	Denmark National Bank Danish Financial Supervisory Authority
Finland	Bank of Finland Financial Supervision Authority
France	Bank of France Banking Commission
Germany	Deutsche Bundesbank German Banking, Securities and Insurance Supervison Authority [BAFin]
Hong Kong (China)	Hong Kong Monetary Authority
Hungary	National Bank of Hungary Hungarian Financial Supervisory Authority
India	Reserve Bank of India
Ireland	Central Bank of Ireland
Israel	Bank of Israel
Italy	Bank of Italy Italian Securities Commission
Japan	Bank of Japan Financial Services Agency
Malaysia	Bank Negara Malaysia
Mexico	Bank of Mexico Banking and Securities Commission
Morocco	Central Bank of Morocco
Netherlands	Bank of Netherlands Securities Board of the Netherlands Netherlands Pension and Insurance Supervisory Authority
New Zealand	Reserve Bank of New Zealand Securities Commission of New Zealand
Nigeria	Nigerian Deposit Insurance Corporation
Norway	Bank of Norway Banking, Insurance and Securities Commission
Peru	Central Reserve Bank of Peru
Poland	National Bank of Poland

A

Table A.1. (continued)

Country	Cooperating official institution
Portugal	Bank of Portugal Portuguese Securities Market Commission
Saudi Arabia	Saudi Arabian Monetary Agency
Singapore	Monetary Authority of Singapore
South Africa	South African Reserve Bank Financial Services Board
Spain	Bank of Spain National Securities Commission
Sri Lanka	Central Bank of Sri Lanka
Sweden	Bank of Sweden Financial Supervisory Authority
Switzerland	Swiss National Bank Swiss Federal Banking Commission
Thailand	Bank of Thailand
Tunisia	Central Bank of Tunisia
Turkey	Central Bank of the Republic of Turkey
United Kingdom	Bank of England Financial Services Authority Financial Supervision Commission, Isle of Man
United States	Federal Reserve System Office of the Comptroller of the Currency Federal Deposit Insurance Corporation
ECB	European Central Bank Standard Setting Bodies
BCBS	Basel Committee on Banking Supervision
CPSS	Committee on Payment and Settlement Systems
IASB	International Accounting Standards Board
IAIS	International Association of Insurance Supervisors
IOSCO	International Organization of Securities Commissions Other Institutions
AfDB	African Development Bank
BIS	Bank for International Settlements
IADB	Inter-American Development Bank
COBAC	Banking Commission of Central African States (COBAC).
BEAC	Central Bank of Central African States (BEAC)
BCEAO	Central Bank of West African States (BCEAO)

Source: Documents for 2005 Board review of FSAP, available on the web sites of the IMF and the World Bank.

The principle of joint Bank-Fund missions in which the mission members work as a team remains integral to the program regardless of the type of assessment—assessments for the first time, reassessments, or FSAP updates—and regardless of whether it is Bank led or Fund led. However, for countries that are not Bank clients, the Fund will be solely responsible for both the leadership and output of the FSAP missions, whereas the Bank may provide staff members to cover specific areas of those missions' work.

A

The *FSAP Procedures Guide* developed by the FSLC reflects the considerations mentioned here. It is intended for use by Bank and Fund staff and other FSAP team members and also is of interest to countries participating in FSAP. The *FSAP Procedures Guide* covers the following:

- Country selection and scheduling process
- Selection of team leaders, formation of teams (including selection of experts from cooperating official institutions), and preparation of mission terms of reference (including its review, clearance, and distribution)
- Contacts with the authorities
- Preparatory work at headquarters
- Confidentiality protocol
- FSAP documentation and its preparation, review and clearance, transmission and distribution, and related publication policies
- Links to follow-up activities—TA, ongoing surveillance, and Article IV follow-up

Some key elements of those procedures are highlighted in the following paragraphs. Guidance on some of the follow-up activities—for example, TA, ongoing surveillance, and Article IV missions—are at various stages of development, and an overview of those activities is provided in this section.

FSAP is an international cooperative effort that involves a number of cooperating official institutions and all major standard setting bodies. The cooperating institutions provide experts to conduct the assessments (particularly assessment of observance of standards and codes) and the standard-setting bodies develop the methodologies for the assessments, in part drawing on the FSAP experience. Some standard setters also facilitate the expert selection process. The list of cooperating official institutions as of June 30, 2004, is shown in table A.1.

A.2.1 Country Selection Process—Selection Criteria

The participation in the FSAP is voluntary, and countries routinely volunteer to participate. In addition, Bank and Fund staff and management select countries for participation in FSAP (new assessment or an update) on the basis of a set of criteria and procedures (summarized here) and seek their participation in the FSAP. When warranted, the Boards of the IMF (and World Bank) may remark—in the context of the consideration of relevant country report—on the desirability of the country participating in the FSAP. The country selection criteria were discussed and agreed on by both Boards. The criteria include systemic importance of the country (regionally and globally); its external sector weakness or vulnerability; the nature of its exchange rate and monetary regime; the likelihood, or ongoing implementation, of major reform programs with bearing on financial stability and development; and the desire to achieve a geographic balance in the countries covered.

Within any given year, higher priority is accorded to countries judged to be systemically important; the length of time elapsed since the country volunteered for an FSAP is also a factor in the scheduling of FSAP work in any specific year. However, countries that face imminent financial crisis or that are in the midst of crisis are not eligible for

Figure A.1. FSAP Process: Key Steps and Outputs

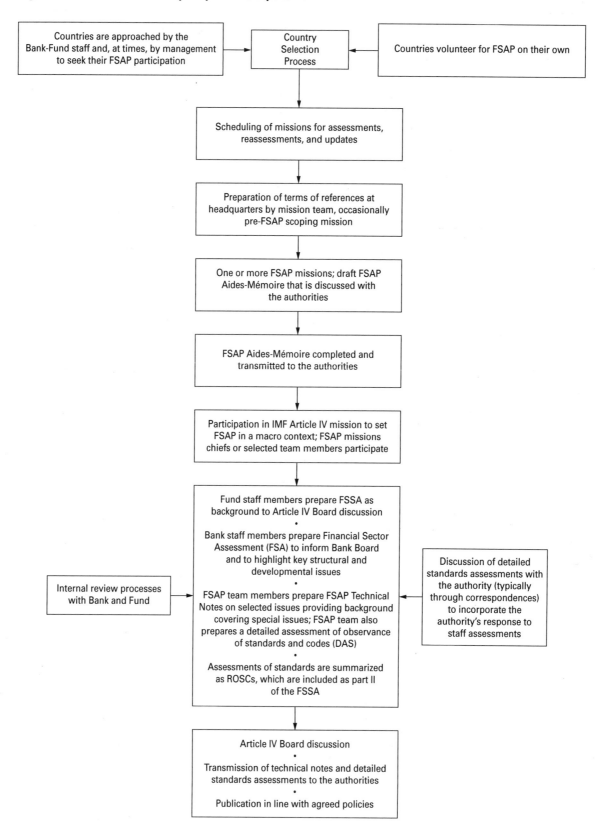

Table A.2. FSAP Confidentiality and Publication Policy at a Glance

Document	Confidentiality	Publication
Aide-Mémoire	Confidential	No
FSSA/FSA	Confidential or not for public use	Voluntary in the case of FSSA
ROSCs	Confidential or not for public use	Voluntary publication
FSAP Technical Notes	• Confidential • Exception: Notes that contain sensitive institution-specific information (e.g., stress tests results) must be classified "strictly confidential"	• If part of Article IV background material, it follows publication policy on article IV and related reports (i.e., voluntary publication). • Stress tests and individual institution information are omitted. • If not part of Article IV background material, it follows practice applied to TA reports.
FSAP Standard and Codes Appendices	Confidential or not for public use	• Voluntary • Follows TA publications policy

Note: All FSAP documents prepared for countries that participated in the pilot phase of the program cannot be published.

FSAP, which is focused on crisis prevention as a purpose and is diagnostic in its approach. Country selection typically strives to achieve a balance in coverage between systemically important countries and developing countries so that development issues are adequately addressed in the program.

Key steps in country selection process are as follows:

- Bank regions and Fund area departments, in collaboration with Fund's Monetary and Financial Systems Department and the World Bank's Financial Sector Vice Presidency, prepare a country list that indicates priorities for participation in FSAP (high, medium, low) on the basis of agreed-upon criteria. The country list takes into account the existing pipeline of countries awaiting FSAP participation.
- FSLC coordinates the priorities between Bank and Fund and proposes a scheduling of missions.
- Bank-Fund management approves the country priority list.
- Countries are contacted, and their participation—if not yet volunteered—is sought.
- Mission schedule is periodically adjusted to take into account the response of the authorities to Bank-Fund requests for FSAP participation and the inflow of new volunteers. When a country volunteers for an update or new assessment, the relevant Bank region and Fund area department are consulted on priorities.

The structure of FSAP documentation, the mission procedures, and the publication policies—all facilitate the link to Article IV surveillance and World Bank operations; they also provide sufficient technical details to the authorities to help formulate priorities within the financial sector policy. The main steps of the FSAP process and the key documents produced at each step are shown in figure A.1. The associated publication policies in the Fund and Bank and the related confidentiality classification of documents are summarized in table A.2.

A

A.2.2 Publication Policies

The publication and distribution policies for FSAP documents are based on decisions of the Bank and Fund Boards after the 2003 review of the FSAP by both Boards, and after the Fund Board's review of transparency policy. The current publication policy for FSAP documents—summarized in table A.2—is as follows.

- Publication of Aides-Mémoires left by FSAP teams with the authorities is not permitted.

- Financial System Stability Assessment (FSSA) [and Reports on Observance of Standards and Codes (ROSCs)] publication remains *voluntary*. ROSCs may be published even when the authorities decide not to publish the FSSA, but not vice versa. Publication is by the Fund on the Fund's external Web site.

- FSAP technical notes that raise issues of sufficient relevance to surveillance can be included in the background material (selected issues paper) for Article IV consultations. In this (to date rare) circumstance, the documents would then be subject to the Fund's circulation and publication policy for Article IV and related publications (i.e., publication is voluntary, but with a presumption of publication, unless indicated otherwise by the authorities). Publication is by the Fund on the Fund's external Web site. Whenever such notes are prepared jointly with the World Bank staff, their circulation and publication are coordinated with the World Bank.

- Technical notes that are not circulated to the Fund Board as background documentation for Article IV consultations, as well as detailed assessments of financial sector standards and codes, fall under the publication policy applied to staff technical documents (which are not Board documents).

- Publication is voluntary by the authorities and is undertaken by them. However, the approval of Fund and Bank management (or only Fund management, if FSAP was for an industrial country) is required. Management approval is normally automatic.

- If authorities request publication of such documents and if management consents, then the FSAP technical notes are circulated to the Fund Board for information before publication. They may also, but are not required to, be published on the Fund's external Web site.

- Requested deletions by the authorities, or partial publishing of some technical notes and not others or of some detailed standards assessments and not others, need to be reviewed internally by concerned Bank-Fund departments before a staff member can make a recommendation for management decision.

A.2.3 Confidentiality and Other Distribution

Assessment of financial system vulnerabilities necessarily involves discussion with the authorities of sensitive information on prudential policies and financial soundness. To ensure that sensitive information that is provided by national authorities to FSAP teams is appropriately protected, the Fund and Bank have drawn up a confidentiality protocol (see 2000 FSAP review documents and Fund-Bank documents on records and information security). This protocol brings together the already-existing confidentiality policies in the two institutions in one document to facilitate understanding by national authorities, the Bank-Fund staff members, and the experts who may be FSAP team members from cooperating institutions. All such experts are required to certify that they are familiar with the policies set out in the protocol.

The protocol outlines the levels of classification for sensitive information—not for public use, confidential, and strictly confidential—and the procedures for handling each classification. The main elements of the protocol are summarized in the following discussion, and each FSAP document's classification is presented in table A.2. FSAP team leaders are responsible for the confidentiality classification of FSAP information. The confidentiality classification is decided in consultation with the provider of the sensitive information.

Documents that contain sensitive information must be marked with the same security classification as the original information. The presumption is that FSAP documents are classified *Confidential*, although in some cases they may be classified *Not for Public Use*, which is the least strict of the three classifications available. However, certain elements of data and information (e.g., stress tests results, information on specific institutions, and highly market-sensitive information) must be classified as *Strictly Confidential*. Strictly confidential information is restricted solely to persons with a specific need to know and is not circulated for review, except as prescribed in the confidentiality protocol.

The basic principle followed in determining confidentiality classifications, as well as circulation of documents within the Bank and Fund, is that of "need to know." Staff members who have a legitimate interest in specific FSAP documents or in groups of documents, as part of their work responsibilities should be permitted access. For example, Bank and Fund staff members and experts working on the country should be permitted access, if they request it through proper channels, to all FSAP documents with the only exception being any highly sensitive information that they do not specifically need to know.

Similarly, a staff member undertaking research in connection with Bank and Fund operations, such as preparing a Board paper by reviewing detailed assessments of one or more financial sector standards, should be given access to the relevant documents. In general, it would be expected that individual countries' experiences would not be identified by name in any such documents unless the authorities have agreed or the information is available in published documents. The staff members to whom documents are made available should be informed at the time as to the confidentiality classification of those documents and, further, that they should not provide the documents—or copies of them—to any other third parties in the Fund or outside without appropriate authorization. Guidance to the Bank-Fund staff on how to apply the confidentiality protocol and the related review and clearance procedures are contained in various internal memoranda (see FSAP intranet sites of the Bank and Fund).

A.2.4 Review and Clearance of FSAP Documents

All FSAP documents are subject to rigorous internal review and clearance processes within the Bank and the Fund on the basis of guidance and procedures that are specific to each institution. The purposes of the review process are to ensure uniform and consistent treatment of countries in assessments and to exercise quality control on the scope and content of policy analysis with the view toward ensuring that it draws on international good practices and on the available institutional experiences on key issues.

For FSAP documents for the Fund Board, the review process combines an internal expert review within the MFD with the review by Fund's area departments and the Policy Development and Review Department. The FSAP documents for the World Bank Board are similarly subject to a peer review process. All other documents are subject to expert review that is organized differently within each institution to reflect the respective organizational structure. Often, input from selected experts from cooperating official institutions is sought to ensure effective quality control of standards assessments.

This review of country documents is complemented by periodic expert meetings to review cross-country experience with standards assessment process and periodic analysis of the results and lessons of FSAP assessments of different standards, as further explained in section A.4.

A.3 Selectivity and Tailoring of Assessments

One of the key messages of the 2003 FSAP review by Bank and Fund Boards was to exercise greater selectivity in the numbers of standards and topics assessed in detail so as to reduce the average resource costs while tailoring the assessments to country-specific circumstances. The detailed principle-by-principle assessments of international standards and codes is resource intensive for both staff members and authorities. The number and types of standards assessed requires careful consideration of country circumstances, while taking into account their relevance for stability and development concerns and seeking to minimize the risk of missing key vulnerabilities. It was acknowledged that FSAP should remain comprehensive in the coverage of topics spanning both stability and development aspects, but the exercise of selectivity was related to the number of detailed assessments of standards or to the scope of detailed analysis of specific development and stability topics. One idea was to spread out the assessments over time so that some of the standards or topics not initially assessed in the first FSAP engagement could be taken up as part of future FSAP updates. Those assessments could be scheduled as part of a medium-term surveillance program or other work program with the country. Some of the considerations in exercising selectivity of topics and standards in FSAP, drawing on FSAP experience, are outlined as follows:

- When the relevant sector, market, or infrastructure is nascent, or when a high degree of noncompliance is expected, a detailed assessment of the corresponding standard may not be needed. Similarly, when the legal and institutional framework is in its very early stages of being built or implemented, the corresponding standard can be assessed at a later stage—after some experience is gained in implementation.
- In more complex financial systems, a set of interrelated standards may need to be assessed together owing to synergies in the assessment process and interlinkages among the sectors. In such circumstances, the scope for distributing the work on some topics and standards over time, including in the context of either planned future FSAP updates or other Bank-Fund operations, should be considered.

Box A.1. Assessing Observance of Financial Sector Standards When There Are Supranational Authorities

The spirit of the standards assessment under FSAP is to evaluate the quality and resilience of supervision in a country. Because supranational authorities, by definition, cover more than one country, such an approach cannot involve assessment of observance only from the perspective of the supranational authority. In each case, therefore, how supervision works in the country must be evaluated regardless of the institutional arrangement. This evaluation becomes all the more important if consideration is given to the fact that even when supranational arrangements exist, several aspects of implementation and enforcement remain with the individual countries.

Against this background, the following procedures should be adopted:

- The first FSAP undertaken within a grouping should commence a detailed assessment of the supranational authority, along with the implementation aspects in the country concerned.
- Before the assessment, the mission should approach the supranational authority, outline the proposed strategy, and obtain its agreement to participate in the assessment. If the supranational authority does not agree to participate, a detailed assessment of observation of that standard cannot be undertaken.
- The detailed assessment of the relevant standard should be included in the FSAP volume on "Detailed Assessment of Standards," and a ROSC module relating to observance of that standard in that particular country should be produced.
- Subsequent FSAP assessments in other countries within the grouping should use the work already done in the earlier FSAP and should only review and update the assessment of the supranational authority. Each successive FSAP within the grouping will presumably require less involve-

ment of the supranational authority, although, in each case, the supranational authority should be contacted and kept informed. When material institutional, legal, or regulatory changes have taken place in the intervening period, a detailed reassessment may become necessary. In any case, the assessment will continue to be in the context of the country that is going through the FSAP.

- If for any reason the supranational authority does not wish to undergo a detailed assessment, the assessment outputs mentioned here will not be produced. There will, therefore, be no detailed assessment write-up in the FSAP "Detailed Assessment of Standards," and no ROSC module will be prepared.

An overall assessment of the country-specific regulatory and supervisory issues in the relevant area would still be undertaken, using the relevant standard as a guide only. The qualitative evaluation would then be brought out in the main FSAP/FSSA/FSA or in the form of an attachment wherever the issues are evaluated as being of significance and needing to be detailed.

For an assessment to qualify as applicable to the grouping as a whole, the following considerations are important:

- Assessors must make a judgment on compliance with relevant supervisory preconditions, as well as the supervisory and enforcement infrastructure within all the members of the grouping.
- Assessors must take into account the size, structure, and risks of the relevant parts of the financial system within the grouping in which the regulated entities operate.
- Assessments must involve the supranational authority and all relevant national authorities.

A

- Although the choice of topics should reflect their macroeconomic significance or significance for real economic growth or poverty reduction, insofar as selected development and stability topics can be covered in other Bank-Fund operations (e.g., TA, Article IV) ahead of FSAP or in future FSAP updates, such coordination of work over time can greatly facilitate the effectiveness and value of FSAP assessments.

- Standards such as corporate governance, accounting and auditing, and insolvency regime, which have a much broader application than in the financial sector, will not normally be covered in detail in an FSAP assessment.
- Following the recent Board guidance, anti-money-laundering and countering the financing of terrorism (AML–CFT) issues will be assessed in all countries participating in the FSAP (and in offshore financial center [OFC] assessments). Given the large scope of those assessments—covering financial supervision, legal and institutional frameworks, and law enforcement and criminal justice system, which often require three or more assessors—those assessments are typically undertaken separately ahead of, or following, the main FSAP assessment work. Where feasible, such assessment could be undertaken by a financial action task force (FATF) style regional body.
- The selecting and tailoring of assessments and topics to country-specific circumstances will also depend on the state of financial development and the specifics of financial structure. Features such as extent of dollarization, systemic importance, size (smallness) of the system, links to currency union, prevalence of institutional types, extent of offshore/cross-border banking, extent of financial stress, and so forth will clearly influence both the scope and content of FSAP assessments (see box 1.2 in chapter 1 for a discussion of tailoring assessments to the structural features of the countries). Also, assessments of countries in a currency union, sharing a supranational monetary or supervisory authority, pose special issues that call for adaptations in FSAP procedures (see box A.1).

A.4 Relationship to Standards and Codes Initiative—Role of Standards Assessments in FSAP

The initiative dealing with International Standards and Codes is one of a series of reforms initiated by the international financial community, including, among other things, the introduction of FSAP, to promote a more stable financial system in the aftermath of the crises of the late 1990s. The initiative aims to promote sound regulation; greater transparency; more efficient and robust markets, institutions, and infrastructure; better informed investment and lending decisions; improved market integrity; accountability and policy credibility; and reduced vulnerability to crises. It seeks to achieve this goal by

- Encouraging the development of internationally recognized standards in the areas enclosed by the Executive Boards of the Fund and Bank as useful to their work
- Encouraging members' adoption and implementation of standards, including through TA
- Assessing members' observance of those standards and, with their consent, producing and publishing ROSCs

The Boards of the Fund and Bank have endorsed a list of 12 areas of international standards and codes as useful to their operational work and for which assessments, using ROSCs as the principal tool, will be undertaken as appropriate. The 12 standards are listed in box A.2, and they are grouped into three categories: (a) transparency standards,

---

Box A.2. List of Standards and Codes and Core Principles Useful for Bank and Fund Operational Work and for Which ROSCs Are Produced

Transparency Standards

- Data Transparency: the Fund's *Special Data Dissemination Standard/General Data Dissemination System* (SDDS/GDDS)
- Fiscal Transparency: the Fund's *Code of Good Practices on Fiscal Transparency*
- Monetary and Financial Policy Transparency: the Fund's *Code of Good Practices on Transparency in Monetary and Financial Policies* (usually assessed by the Fund and the Bank under the Joint Fund-Bank FSAP)[a]

Financial Sector and Financial Integrity Standards[b]

- Banking Supervision: Basel Committee's *Core Principles for Effective Banking Supervision* (BCP)[a]
- Securities: International Organization of Securities Commissions' (IOSCO) *Objectives and Principles for Securities Regulation*[a]
- Insurance: International Association of Insurance Supervisor's (IAIS) *Insurance Supervisory Principles*[a]
- Payments and Settlement Systems: Committee on Payment and Settlement Systems' (CPSS)

Core Principles for Systemically Important Payments Systems and the Committee on Payments and Settlements Systems and IOSCO's Recommendations for Securities Settlements Systems[a,c]

- Anti-Money Laundering and Combating the Financing of Terrorism: Financial Action Task Force's (FATF's) *40+8 Recommendations*[a]

Financial Infrastructure Standards[d]

- Corporate Governance: OECD's *Principles of Corporate Governance*
- Accounting: International Accounting Standards Board's *International Accounting Standards* (IAS), currently called *International Financial Reporting Standards* (IFRS)
- Auditing: International Federation of Accountants' *International Standards on Auditing*
- Insolvency and Creditor Rights: World Bank's *Principles and Guidelines for Insolvency and Creditor Rights System* and United Nations Commission on International Trade Law's (UNCITRAL) *Legislative Guide on Insolvency Law*

---

a. These standards are assessed mainly under the FSAP.
b. Sometimes the term financial integrity is used in a broad sense to cover both AML and CFT, as well as corporate governance, transparency, accounting and insolvency regime, and the like. In this Handbook, integrity is used in a narrow sense of avoidance of financial crime, particularly money laundering, and financing of terrorism.
c. The payment and securities settlements standard covers supervisory elements, as well as design of payment settlement system, and may well be placed under financial infrastructure grouping.
d. These infrastructure standards are mainly assessed by the Bank.

A

(b) financial supervision and financial integrity standards, and (c) financial infrastructure standards.

ROSCs summarize the extent to which countries observe certain internationally recognized standards and codes. ROSCs are typically summaries of the detailed principle-by-principle assessments undertaken on the basis of agreed methodology. ROSCs covering the financial sector and integrity and the monetary and financial policy transparency are usually prepared within the framework of the FSAP. Under the FSAP, detailed assessments of observance of relevant standards are undertaken jointly by Bank and Fund (Fund alone, with staff or expert participation from World Bank as needed, in countries that are not eligible to borrow from the World Bank), and detailed assessment reports (DARs) are given to the authorities. Summaries of those assessments (ROSCs) are included as part of the FSSAs that are presented to the IMF Board in the context of Fund surveillance,

---

Box A.3. Assessing Offshore Financial Centers

In view of the large financial claims on OFCs and the potential vulnerabilities stemming from weaknesses in the financial system of offshore centers, Fund initiated in June 2000 a program to assess—on a voluntary basis—44 jurisdictions known to have significant cross-border business or those with separate offshore financial legislation.[a] The OFC program sought to assess the risks that OFCs could pose to the international financial system when one considers the weaknesses in prudential supervision and financial integrity concerns. The OFC program offers a set of uniform assessment options.

In addition to providing TA to conduct self-assessments by the jurisdictions themselves (module 1 assessments), the program offers stand-alone assessments by a team of specialized supervisors of jurisdictions' compliance with supervisory and regulatory standards (module 2 assessments). This program includes a review and assessment of AML–CFT practices. The third option (module 3 assessments)

is simply an FSAP for OFCs that are Fund members or a comprehensive vulnerability assessment including standards assessments for nonmembers. Such assessments are complemented by TA to improve compliance with standards. Given the OFC's links to major "offshore" financial centers, where major banks and conglomerates maintain balance sheet and operational exposures in OFCs, the FSAP work in many countries has to pay particular attention to such exposures and to consider aspects of the supervisory process—consolidated supervision, supervisory cooperation, and information sharing—relevant to mitigating the associated risks. Among the 44 OFC jurisdictions, assessments have been completed or are ongoing in 33 jurisdictions, of which 8 were done as part of the FSAP. In addition, the FSAPs in countries with important bank representation in OFCs have examined closely the home country's consolidated supervision and supervisory cooperation issues.

---

a. An OFC is a location where the bulk of financial activity is offshore on both sides of the balance sheet (i.e., the counterparties of the majority of financial institutions' liabilities and assets are nonresidents), where the transactions are initiated elsewhere, and where the majority of the institutions involved are controlled by nonresidents.

A

and they are issued as ROSCs. This procedure is designed to help set the standard assessments in a broader context of risks and vulnerabilities that affect the financial system, to assess the extent to which standards compliance contributes to mitigating the risks, and to formulate an overall stability assessment. Gaps in compliance with standards also provide an input into identifying development needs and desired structural reforms to strengthen institutions, markets, and infrastructure. For those reasons, standards assessments are an integral part of the FSAP.

Detailed assessments of financial sector standards are undertaken outside the FSAP only occasionally as part of technical cooperation and assistance programs. However, standard assessments are routinely undertaken as part of IMF's Offshore Financial Centers Assessments Program (see box A.3). Such detailed assessments are designed to assist countries in identifying areas of institutional reforms and related TA needs and are not issued as ROSCs that feed into surveillance. They are, however issued as detailed assessment reports (DARs) and can be published voluntarily by the authorities with the concurrence of Fund and Bank management. The DARs prepared under OFC's program have been routinely published (see http://www.imf.org/external/np/ofca/ofca.asp). Several countries that serve as major international financial centers or that operate separate offshore financial centers have chosen to be assessed under the FSAP (in those countries), instead of under the OFC program whose objectives are more narrowly focused on strengthening and harmonizing supervision and regulation and on fostering cross-border cooperation among supervisors.

Standards for the financial system infrastructure are typically assessed on a stand-alone basis by the World Bank, and, when appropriate, one or more of those assessments may be conducted in the context of FSAP. When stand-alone assessments of infrastructure standards are available, FSAP work will draw on them, but it will generally focus on financial sector aspects of corporate governance, accounting and auditing, and insolvency regime, as part of the assessment of preconditions for effective supervision.

Following the recent pilot program for conducting AML–CFT assessments, assessments of AML–CFT are considered a regular part of the Bank-Fund work and are included as part of all FSAP and OFC assessments. In addition to assessments done jointly by Bank and Fund (Fund alone in the case of OFCs and selected other countries), financial action task force (FATF) and FATF-style regional bodies (FSRBs) also conduct assessments that are based on the commonly agreed methodology; ROSCs are prepared on the basis of those outside assessments. Therefore, country assessments have required close collaboration and coordination with the FATF and FSRBs on assessment schedules.

FSAP and the standards and codes initiative have reinforced each other to achieve the shared objectives. The experience with the assessment of standards under the FSAP has been periodically reviewed at a technical level, as well as at a broader policy context,

---

Box A.4. Periodic Review of Standards Assessment Process

1. Coordinating meetings of experts from cooperating official institutions, representatives of standard setters, and concerned Bank and Fund staff members and experts were held on various dates (as listed below) to review assessment experience in individual standards and to provide feedback to standard setters.

   - Technical reviews of BCP/ Core Principles of Systemically Important Payment Systems (CPSIPS), and IOSCO with assessors and standard setters in November 2001
   - Technical review of BCP in May 2003

   In addition to their streamlining the operational processes in conducting the assessments, the reviews highlighted components of various standards where additional guidance was needed from standard setters.

2. In addition, financial sector standards assessments conducted in FSAP were periodically reviewed to identify key areas of weak or strong compliance, as well as lessons for the assessment methodology and for the core principles that constitute the standard. These reviews were reported to the Fund Board,

and all are available on the IMF external Web site. The list of the Board documents includes the following:

   - Experience with the Assessment of Systemically Important Payment Systems (April 19, 2002)
   - Experience with the Assessments of the IOSCO Objectives and Principles of Securities Regulation (April 18, 2002)
   - Implementation of the Basel Core Principles for Effective Banking Supervision, Experience, Influences and Perspectives (October 4, 2002)
   - Experience with Basel Core Principles Assessments (April 28, 2000)
   - Experience with the Insurance Core Principles Assessments Under the Financial Sector Assessment Program (August 21, 2001)
   - Assessments of the IMF code of Good Practices on Transparency in Monetary and Financial Policies–Review of Experience. (December 23, 2003)
   - Financial Sector Regulation—Issues and Gaps (August 5, 2004) and Financial Sector Regulation—Issues and Gaps—Background paper (August 18, 2004)

A

to strengthen the consistency of the assessment process and to inform standard setters on the lessons of assessment experience for both the content of the standards and for its assessment methodology. Box A.4 contains the list of technical and policy reviews of the standards assessment process conducted in the FSAP context. The policy reviews also served to inform the periodic Board reviews of the standards and codes initiative.

A.5 Selected Organizational Issues

The *FSAP Procedures Guide* covers both assessments and updates. In addition, assessments (countries and economies that have not yet participated in the program) and reassessments (when the passage of time or the pace of the reform process in a country indicates that comprehensive updating of the initial FSAP assessment is desirable) are complemented by focused updates (including updating of stability and standards and codes assessments). More detailed guidelines to implement specific aspects of the procedures—confidentiality, country selection, mission formation and scheduling, contacts with authorities, contacts with cooperating official institutions, document preparation, review process, publication, and the like—have been issued within the Fund and Bank in line with the respective internal procedures of each institution.

This section highlights certain aspects of the internal guidelines and of the procedures designed to facilitate appropriate tailoring of assessments to country circumstances, to ensure consistency of assessments, and to increase efficiency of the assessment process. Certain considerations in the organization and design of FSAP teams are important for appropriate coverage and for tailoring the development and stability assessments. The composition of a FSAP team should reflect the scope of work, which, in turn, is governed by the level of development of the sector, as well as by specific structural features (as outlined in box 1.2 in chapter 1). Those considerations are further explained in the following sections.

A.5.1 Organization and Team-Design: Issues for the Development Assessment

Because of the diversity of issues and the multiplicity of topics that need to be considered, staffing of the development component of the assessment needs to be designed with great care.

A first challenge is the choice of sectors and infrastructural aspects to be examined in detail. Here the balance that needs to be struck is between (a) the need to assess performance in relation to services and sectors that are already well established in the country and (b) the exploration of the reasons for gaps and missing markets. For example, an extensive study of securities markets may not be appropriate if only a handful of securities are listed on the stock exchange, yet the scope for improving corporate access to equity may need to be evaluated. Likewise, in many cases, it proves impracticable to carry out full accounting, auditing, or corporate governance assessments in the context of a financial sector review, yet those issues are important for the legal and information infrastructure assessments.

A second challenge is ensuring that the cross-cutting issues are adequately addressed from a developmental perspective. This challenge calls for very clear terms of reference to be given to sectoral assessors. The sectoral assessors will need to generate some of the input for the infrastructural reviews and other cross-cutting aspects (e.g., legal and informational deficiencies, problems with the payments system, specific taxation problems, and so forth). Much can be obtained in this context from the corporate sector assessment (if one is scheduled).

It will normally be advisable to include in the team a lawyer who is specifically charged with assembling and collating the legal infrastructural review of the development assessment. Because there is no agreed-on standard for assessing the legal infrastructure, specific detailed terms of reference for the lawyer's work need to be elaborated. In addition, it will be important to ensure that the legal infrastructural review remains focused on the development issues, plus supporting the Basel Core Principles (BCP) for effective banking supervision and other aspects of the stability assessment.

A.5.2 Multitasking for the Sectoral Reviews

Having separate experts for sectoral stability and development analysis will overburden the country and impose excessive administrative costs. It will also result in a team that is too large to allow for adequate synthesis of what are indeed overlapping issues. Therefore, there seems little merit in including a large team of "development specialists" alongside prudential specialists. In the case of many sectors, such as insurance and capital markets, the same expert who analyzes stability aspects should also be able to assess developmental aspects. This arrangement will not only avoid duplication but also guarantee consistency across the two dimensions. Staffing the assessment of the sectors should be designed with this multitasking in mind.

In the case of banking, always the most important sector, FSAP missions have typically included two BCP assessors and one or two persons working on stress testing. Teams for low-income countries also should include banking specialists who can provide adequate analysis of the competitive structure of banking, the range of services provided, and the cost and efficiency of their provision.

A.5.3 Organization and Team Design for Stability Assessments

The issues are broadly similar to the case of development assessment discussed earlier. Exercising selectivity in the standards and sectors to be assessed in detail should be based on both the size of the sector and its likely systemic effect over the medium term. Often, even if the overall size of a sector (e.g., securities markets) is not significant, its linkages to key institutions, as well as its critical role in overall financial sector reform, may warrant a detailed assessment of the sector from a developmental perspective and may require a close attention to volatility and liquidity of the markets. The concern is to ensure medium-term stability in the course of financial market development, even though the size of the sector does not pose a threat to short-term stability.

Once a set of supervisory standards for detailed assessment has been chosen, some of the preconditions for effective supervision may be covered as part of detailed assessments

A

of infrastructure standards either by other specialists or by the sectoral assessors themselves, who should look into key elements of the infrastructure affecting the effectiveness of supervision and risks management. For example, instead of conducting detailed assessment of financial policy transparency, the sectoral expert could be asked to cover transparency practices of regulatory authorities dealing with that sector at a high level of aggregation. If, however, a decision were made to conduct a detailed assessment of monetary and financial policy (MFP) transparency, a separate staff member or expert should be assigned to work with the sectoral supervision experts to put together the detailed MFP transparency assessment.

It will normally be advisable to include in the team a financial economist—or a financial policy specialist with some quantitative background—to conduct macroprudential analysis and stress testing. It is important that sectoral supervision experts work closely with the economist in this exercise so that the risk profile is used to guide the depth of supervisory standards assessment and so that information from standards assessment helps to shape the design of macroprudential analysis.

For example, in systems with significant exposure to a specific risk factor (e.g., cross-border lending or borrowing that produces vulnerability to external shocks), the supervisory guidance on sovereign risk management and foreign exchange exposure management should be examined in depth. Similarly, when compliance with a particular supervisory core principle (e.g., connected lending) is weak, macroprudential analysis should pay particular attention to the level and distribution of loans to single customers and to "insider" loans and their evolution over time. Such close coordination of vulnerability assessment with standards assessment is critical to deriving a proper overall stability assessment.

A.6 Follow-Up Issues—FSAP Updates, On-Going Surveillance, and TA

Although comprehensive FSAP assessments and reassessments can take place once in 8 to 9 years, additional tools are used to monitor the financial sector on a more continuous basis, to update FSAP findings in a more selective way, and to provide needed TA. In the Fund, efforts have been under way to develop and promote compilation of financial soundness indicators. Monitoring those indicators on a regular basis—along with other information, particularly market-based indicators—can be used as input in ongoing financial sector surveillance.

In many cases, FSAP updates have been used to focus on key development and stability issues and to update the assessments of one or two selected standards to update the ROSCs. On some occasions, factual updates of developments in implementation of standards have been prepared in the context of Article IV missions, pending the completion of FSAP reassessments, updates, or both. The scope and content of FSAP updates have varied, but they primarily reflect the scope of reforms undertaken by the authorities since the previous FSAP assessments. In some cases, areas of standards that were not assessed in detail in the previous assessment (e.g., AML–CFT) were assessed. In all cases, the macroprudential analysis was updated, with occasional updating of stress tests and with selective updates of previously assessed standards. The updates help to show the extent to which the overall stability has improved or weakened.

A

TA is a key tool to assist countries to follow up on FSAP recommendations and to strengthen financial stability policies and implement orderly development programs. Both the Bank and Fund have stressed the importance of effective and systemic follow-up to support countries in implementing key FSAP and ROSC recommendations. Both the Bank and Fund have collaborated with a group of bilateral donors to establish a multidonor facility called Financial Sector Reform and Strengthening Initiative (FIRST). FIRST is a joint initiative that provides grants to low- and middle-income countries for financial sector projects with the key objectives of facilitating systematic follow-up of the recommendations from the Bank-Fund FSAP and ROSCs. In addition, FIRST supports eligible countries in strengthening their financial systems and implementing recognized standards and codes in advance of participation in FSAP and ROSC programs.

A

Appendix B

Illustrative Data Questionnaires for Comprehensive Financial Sector Assessment

This appendix complements chapter 2 and provides some additional guidance on the sort of quantitative data that should be collected to facilitate the analysis of different aspects of financial stability and of financial structure and development. The precise scope and content of data needed will be country specific to reflect its structural and institutional circumstances. Nevertheless, the appendix seeks to present a generally useful set of indicators and tabular formats and to present the sort of additional indicators that could be useful to capture differences in financial structure and in the state of financial development. The sequence in which the questionnaire—or list of data needed—is presented reflects the organization and coverage of the Handbook. The broad coverage of the questionnaire is as follows:

- General data on the financial system, covering financial structure and its development
- Data and tables for financial system stability assessments
- Data on ownership structure, concentration, exposures, profitability, and costs of banking system in the aggregate and for different peer groups of banks
- Data on the structure and operation of insurance companies, security markets, pension funds, and other financial institutions
- Data on the functioning of money, exchange and government debt markets, payment settlement systems, financial safety nets, insolvency regime, and corporate governance arrangements
- Country-specific data on specific subsectors, markets, or issues for in-depth analysis (taxation of financial services and assessing adequacy of access are presented as examples)

Qualitative information on legal institutional and operational arrangements for financial sector supervision and financial system infrastructure are covered mostly as part of the templates for assessing observance of standards and are not covered in this appendix.

The general questionnaire on the financial system seeks to compile data on the structure, composition, and interrelationships in the financial system, and on the key components of aggregate balance sheet and income statements of major categories of institutions, including various peer groups of banks and banks in the aggregate. Tables B.1, B.2, and B.3 illustrate the data sets typically presented to characterize the recent evolution of financial structure (such as the number of institutions, shares in total assets, or share of assets to GDP) and key balance sheet and performance indicators for the banking system as a whole.

Table B.4 provides measures of financial system interconnectedness.

Table B.5 shows financial soundness indicators for banking—both core and encouraged sets—as defined in the International Monetary Fund's *Compilation Guide on Financial Soundness Indicators.*

Additional data on ownership, concentration, exposures, profitability, and costs are compiled as needed, depending on relevance to country circumstances. Such data are listed in table B.6.

Data needed for stress testing, as characterized in table B.7, will vary widely, depending upon the scope and depth of the exercise, as well as on the stress testing approaches used (see the technical note on stress testing that accompanies chapter 3). These data will generally depend on the size and complexity of the financial system and on the types of risks it is facing. For small systems with few sophisticated financial tools, rudimentary stress tests can be carried out with bank-by-bank data about financial soundness indicators. For most systems, however, additional data may be needed, for example, on the maturity and repricing structure of assets and liabilities. Data needs will generally be much higher in complex financial systems. Having financial institutions carry out the actual calculations that are based on common scenarios and methodologies may help reduce the data that need to be collected and processed in one place. In most systems, the input data will need to cover the basic types of risk (such as credit risk); however, in some systems, additional data on specific risks may be needed (e.g., commodity price risk in systems where the preliminary analysis suggests that this may be an important issue). Construction of scenarios for stress testing and the analysis of financial soundness indicators typically require a range of macroeconomic, as well as financial markets data.

Data to assess the structure and performance of insurance companies (table B.8) are provided separately for life insurance and non–life insurance business. They cover major balance-sheet items, which are classified by type of instruments and maturity, key components of incomes and expenditures, and information on the structure of the industry in terms of the following: number of companies, their distribution by asset size, or their premium income (or gross written premiums, for non–life insurance businesses) and related indicators of performance, solvency, and concentration.

Data needed to formulate an overview of capital markets, as well as the structure performance and efficiency of the markets, including its stocks exchanges, are indicated in table B.9. Such data are also needed in the context of both corporate governance

B

assessments, as well as assessments of *International Organization of Securities Commissions Objectives and Principles* for the regulation of securities markets.

Data needed to assess the structure and performance of pension funds and mutual funds make up table B.10.

Data needed for the analysis of other financial institutions, including nonbank financial institutions (other than security firms, insurance, and pension funds) and specialized finance companies, make up table B.11.

Data on systematic liquidity infrastructure, including money, exchange, and government debt markets and operations, plus payment settlement systems, make up tables B.12 and B.13.

Data on legal, governance, and information infrastructure, including financial safety nets and insolvency regime, make up table B.14.

Data to assess financial sector taxation and access to financial services are shown in tables B.15 and B.16, respectively.

B

Table B.1. Financial System Structure

	Annual data for recent period		
	Number	Assets billion local currency)	Percent of total assets
A. Depository institutions			
Commercial banks—total			
Large domestic banks			
Major foreign banks			
Other banks			
Development banks			
Credit unions and cooperative			
Microfinance institutions			
Building societies			
Other non-bank depository institutions			
B. Non-depository intermediaries			
Insurance companies			
Life and retirement			
Non-life			
Pension funds			
Collective investment schemes			
Money market mutual funds			
Finance companies (including leasing and venture capital)			
Securities firms			
Other (specify)			
C. Total financial system			
Memorandum items:			
Banks that are more than 50 percent owned by government			
Banks that are foreign owned or controlled			
Subsidiaries of foreign banks in country Y			
Branches of foreign banks in country Y			
Subsidiaries of country Y's banks abroad			
Branches of country Y's banks abroad			

B

Table B.2. Aggregate Balance Sheet for the Banking System

Annual data for recent periods

A. Assets

1. Cash (domestic notes and coins)
2. Balances at central bank and other banks
3. Placements (including overnight lending)
4. Government securities
5. Investments
6. a) Local currency advances (gross)
   b) Foreign currency advances (gross)
   c) Total advances (gross)
   d) Less the provision for bad debts
   e) Advances (net)
7. Other foreign assets
8. Fixed assets
9. Other assets
10. Total assets

B. Liabilities

11. Local currency deposits (including interbank borrowing)
12. Foreign currency deposits (including interbank borrowing)
13. Accrued interest
14. Other foreign liabilities
15. Other liabilities
16. Total liabilities
17. Net assets and liabilities

C. Capital and reserves

18. Paid up or assigned capital
19. Shareholders' loans
20. Revaluation reserves
21. Other reserves
22. Profit and loss account
23. Less additional provisions recommended
24. **Total shareholders' funds**

    Other items
25. Contingent liabilities (off-balance sheet items)
26. NPLs
27. Core capital
28. Supplementary capital
29. Total capital
30. TRWA
31. Other nonperforming assets
32. Investments in subsidiaries
33. TEAs

    Average net advances

B

Table B.1. (continued)

Average placements

Average government securities

Average investments

Average other earning assets

Average net earning assets

Average deposits

Average other liabilities

Average capital

D. Performance indicators

Measures of capital adequacy

34. Gearing ratio: [(24 – 32 – 75 percent of 20) / (11 + 12 + 13)][a]

35. Core capital / total deposits [27 / (11 + 12 + 13)]

36. Core capital / TRWA (27 / 30)

37. Total capital / TRWA (29 / 30)

Measure of liquidity

38. Liquidity ratio (per liquidity statement)

39. Cash ratio

Measure of asset quality

40. NPLs and gross advances (26 / 6c)

41. (NPLs – provisions for bad debts) / gross advances [(26 – 6d) / 6c]

42. Provisions for bad debts / NPLs (6d / 26)

43. Advances / deposits [6c / (11 + 12 + 13)]

44. NPAs / assets ratio [(26 + 31/10 + 6d)]

Note: NPLs = nonperforming loans; TRWA = total risk weighted assets; TEAs = total earnings assets; NPAs = nonperforming assets.

a. Numbers indicate line numbers in the table.

B

Table B.3. Profit and Loss Analysis for the Banking System

Annual data for recent periods

A. Income

51. Interest on advances
52. Interest on placement
53. Dividend income
54. Interest on government securities
55. Foreign exchange gain (loss)
56. Other interest income
57. Other income
58. Total income

B. Expenses

59. Interest on deposits
60. Other interest expenses
61. Occupancy expenses
62. Director's emoluments
63. Bad debts charge
64. Salaries and wages
65. Other expenses
66. Total expenses
67. Profit before taxation
68. Number of employees
69. Number of branches

C. Performance indicators

70. Yield on earning assets [(51 + 52 + 53 + 54 + 56) / 33][a]
71. Cost of funding earning assets [(59 + 60) / 33]
72. Interest margin on earning assets
73. Yield on gross advances (51 / 6c)
74. Cost of deposits (59 + 60) / (11 + 12)
75. Return on assets (including contingencies) 67 / (10 + 6d + 25)
76. Return on shareholders funds (67 / 24)
77. Overheads (noninterest expenses) / total income (61 + 62 + 63 + 64 + 65) / 58
78. Bad debts charge / total earnings (63 / 58)

a. Numbers indicate line numbers in the table.

Table B.4. Measures of Financial System Interconnectedness

(units in local currency)

	Annual data for recent periods
Banking system lending (exposure) to shareholders[a]	
On-balance sheet	
Off-balance sheet	
Banking system lending (exposure) to	
Insurance companies	
Finance companies	
Securities firms	
Pension funds	
Banking system equity investments in	
Insurance companies	
Finance companies	
Securities firms	
Pension funds	
Gross interbank lending (exposure) to[b]	
Domestic banks	
Foreign banks—parent or related company	
Foreign banks—unrelated	

a. Banking system is defined here to include banks and all quasi-banks formally classified as nonbank financial institutions.
b. For these data, domestic banks are defined as all banks operating in the country (i.e., including foreign-owned banks).

B

Table B.5. Financial Soundness Indicators for the Banking Sector

(in percent, unless otherwise indicated)

	Annual (or quarterly) data for recent periods
Capital adequacy	
Regulatory capital to risk-weighted assets[a]	
Regulatory tier I capital to risk-weighted assets[a]	
Capital (net worth) to assets	
Asset composition and quality	
Sectoral distribution of loans to total loans[a]	
Sector A—please list the 5 to 10 most important sectors	
Sector B	
Sector C	
Sector D	
Sector E	
Geographical distribution of loans to total loans	
Country A—please list three most important countries	
Country B	
Country C	
FX loans to total loans	
NPLs to gross loans[a]	
NPLs net of provisions to capital[a]	
Large exposures to capital[a]	
Gross asset position in derivatives to capital	
Gross liability position in derivatives to capital	
Sector E	
Earnings and profitability	
ROA[a]	
ROE[a]	
Interest margin to gross income[a]	
Noninterest expenses to gross income[a]	
Personnel expenses to noninterest expenses	
Trading and fee income to total income	
Spread between reference loan and deposit rates	
Liquidity	
Liquid assets to total assets[a]	
Liquid assets to total short-term liabilities[a]	
Customer deposits to total (noninterbank) loans	
FX liabilities to total liabilities	
Sensitivity to market risk	
Net open positions in FX to capital[a]	
Net open positions in equities to capital[a]	

Note: FX = foreign exchange; NPL = nonperforming loans; ROA = return on assets; ROE = return on equity.

a. Included in the "core set" of financial soundness indicators.

B

Table B.6. Data on Ownership, Exposures, Profitability, and Costs in Banking

(in percent, unless otherwise indicated)

Annual data for a recent period
Share in total assets, or in the assets of the 10 largest banks of state-owned financial institutions
Share in the capital of all banks or of 10 largest banks of industrial or financial agglomerates
Classification of assets into normal, precautionary substandard, doubtful, and loss and the associated provisioning amounts
Value of connected lending for banks in the aggregate and for peers groups
Value of loans to large customers (regulatory definition that is based on specified thresholds for each bank)
Holdings of real estate by financial institutions—not related to provision of banking services
Deposits and claims of all banks held abroad classified by country; deposits in related banks by foreign owned banks
Unused lines of credit and guarantees provided by banks against different types of counterparties:
Domestic nonfinancial firms
Foreign banks
Foreign nonfinancial firms
Domestic government and states
Off-balance-sheet exposures to various types of derivative contracts in domestic and foreign currency units
Sources of revenue for all banks and peer groups of banks:
Lending
ATM/Deposit account services
Trust
Security underwriting and market making
Proprietary trading
Fees on investment and other traditional off-balance sheet activities
Data on interest rate spread (average yield on loans minus average cost of deposit) for both dollar and domestic currency intermediation by various peer groups of banks

Note: ATM = automated teller machine.

B

Table B.7. Stress Testing of Banking Systems: Overview of Input Data[a]

(all data should be bank-by-bank)

	Annual data for recent periods

General

Basic balance sheet and income statement data, in particular capital, assets, risk-weighted assets, profits, net interest income

Credit risk

Breakdown of total loans by classification categories

Loan loss provisions (total or by the above classification groups)

Breakdown of loans by currency of denomination (and by classification)

Breakdown of loans by sectors (and by classification)[b]

Interest rate risk[c]

Maturity or repricing structure of assets and liabilities and off–balance sheet positions

Holdings of debt securities by banks, duration of these holdings

Exchange rate risk[d]

Currency breakdown of assets, liabilities, and off-balance-sheet positions

If substantial off-balance-sheet positions, other information (such as deltas of FX options) may be needed

Interbank contagion risk

Uncollaterized lending (and similar) exposures between bank i and j, for all pairs of banks

Other risks

Depending on the features of the financial system, may include more detailed data on exposures such as equity holdings, real estate exposures (including collateral), commodity exposures

Other data

Selected macroeconomic indicators (e.g., interest rates, exchange rates, output growth rates)

Selected data on borrowers (e.g., corporate sector leverage, by economic sector)

Note: FX = foreign exchange.

a. The input data shown here are for a simple stress test in a small, noncomplex system with a large role of banks facing a standard set of interest rate, exchange rate, and credit risks. The data requirements will generally be much higher for complex financial systems. They also may be different for systems in which preliminary analysis suggests substantial exposures to specific risks, such as commodity price risk or real estate price risk. In systems with substantial role of nonbank financial institutions, additional data may be included for those.

b. The sectors may be defined by main activity (e.g., agriculture, manufacturing) or by residency or legal form (e.g., residents or nonresidents, households/firms).

c. These items are only direct interest rate and exchange rate risks, respectively. Data on indirect risks (i.e., interest or exchange rate induced changes in credit risk) are under credit risk.

B

Table B.8. Statistics on Structure and Performance of Insurance Companies

Annual data for recent periods

Structure and concentration

Number and total assets of insurance companies by type of ownership:

Joint stock

Mutual

State-owned

Foreign-owned or controlled

Number and total assets of branches and subsidiaries of different types of insurance companies operating domestically and abroad

Number and total assets of domestic and foreign reinsurance companies operating domestically

Frequency distribution of asset size or premium incomes or new business of insurance companies and concentration indicators such as the shares of three or five largest insurance companies in terms of the chosen indicator

Ownership structure of insurance sector, such as the share of capital of all insurers or largest insurers, held by government, overseas insurance group, mutual, bank, other financial services or industrial group, and the like

Operation and performance

Gross and net (of reinsurance) domestic premium income reported (earned for nonlife insurance)—in currency and as percentage of GDP

Domestic policy holder liabilities (as a percentage of GDP) and as a percentage of domestic commercial and savings bank deposits

Capital and surplus (life) or net assets (non-life) as a percentage of net policy holder liabilities

Net nondomestic premium income reported (earned for nonlife insurance)

Investment portfolio net of investment in subsidiaries

Percentage of gross written and net written premium for each main type of insurance product

Number of insurer new entrants and exits in the past 10–15 years

Distribution costs, operating expenses, commissions, and reinsurance premiums for major insurance products and lines of business as a percentage of sales (new business for life, gross written for nonlife insurance)

Surplus or profit—before and after tax—as a percentage of beginning capital and surplus or shareholder's funds, as a percentage of annual premiums and of average total assets

Gross rate of return on investment and total assets

Asset composition and investment policy of different insurers (e.g., life, property, casualty, which is based on amounts [and shares] invested in various asset classes [e.g., short-term paper, long-term paper government bonds, corporate bonds, corporate equities (listed and unlisted), real estate, loans to private sector] foreign assets also classified by type of securities, and currency of denomination

Liability composition in terms of various asset classes, including insurance reserves and own funds, both domestic and foreign

Contingent and off-balance-sheet accounts, including derivatives and asset swaps.

Actual solvency margins, required minimum solvency margins, separately for life and nonlife business, and for large insurance groups on a consolidated basis.

Note: GDP = gross domestic product.

Table B.9. Capital Markets Overview and Their Structure and Performance Selected

Annual data for recent periods

Overview and structure security of markets

Number of stock exchanges (list of country's stock exchanges and other regulated markets, including junior and OTC markets)

Number of listed companies (official lists of publicly traded companies)

Ownership ratios of domestic and foreign investors in listed companies

Share of most actively traded (top three to five equities) shares in total traded value

Market capitalization of listed companies

    as percentage of GDP

    as percentage of all companies including privately held and state owned

Number and value of transactions in each major market and for companies in major indices

    Turnover ratio

    Total Number of shares outstanding

    Percentage of closely held stocks and "float"

Value and number new issues

    Value as a percentage of total fixed capital formation

Number of delistings and their value

Number and size of merger transactions

Classification of number and market capitalization of listed companies by industrial sectors (according to SIC codes)

    Number of companies in each sector

    Market capitalization of the sector

    Maximum, minimum, and medium market capitalization in each sector

    Average price earnings ratio in each sector

    Return on equity (over 3 years, assuming dividends are reinvested)

Assets under management (bonds and equity separately of pension funds, mutual funds, banks, insurance companies, retail investors, foreign)

Number and total assets held and total capital of market markers, primary dealers, and brokers in the bond and equity markets

Number and list of credit rating agencies and their range of services

Number and list of clearing and settlement facilities, including securities depositories and the range of their services

Cost of new issues, cost of trading, including settlement cost, in secondary markets, including OTC markets

Fixed income securities

Government bond holdings and trading volume of different classes of investors (e.g., pension funds, primary dealers, retail investors, banks)

Maturity profile of outstanding government debt and non-government debt separately.

Outstanding amounts and new sales of government bonds by type of instruments, selling techniques (auction, and on tap), and frequency or timing of issues

Market value, interest rate, face value, and new issues of nongovernment bonds by type and maturity

Cost of new issues and cost of trading non-government debt

Outstanding volume by rating category (AAA, AA+, AA, BB), average (or maximum and minimum) size of capital of the issuer in each rating grade, total number of issuers, average maturity, percentage of face value that is guaranteed (if applicable)

Trading volume, average number of trades per trading day (for most active and least active issues), average quote size, bid–ask spreads, and quarterly standard deviation of price or yield change

B

Table B.9. (continued)

	Annual data for recent periods
Holdings of corporate bonds by various classes of financial institutions	
Outstanding amount and issuance of various types of securitized assets, by maturity, and type of issuing institutions; holdings of securitized assets by different types of financial institutions	

Derivatives

Number and types of guaranteed derivative contracts
Annual and daily average volume of trading in guaranteed derivative contracts and their notional and market values
Volume of trading in derivatives classified by type of investor
Number and types of OTC contracts; annual and daily average turnover in OTC contracts and their notional and market values

Note: OTC = over the counter; GDP = gross domestic product; SIC = standard industrial classification.

Table B.10. Structure and Performance of Pension and Investment Funds

(annual data for selected periods)

	Annual data for recent periods
Mandatory pension schemes	
Number and total assets of pension funds	
Holdings by categories of assets (e.g., government bonds, equities, loans, deposits) and an indication of applicable investment rules for each category	
Value of derivatives and asset swaps in the portfolio	
Capitalization and amount of deposited funds in each pension fund	
Returns on pension fund assets and return on pension fund deposits, and other financial performance indicators	
Disclosure requirements and related data	
Occupational pension schemes	
Number and total assets of pension funds	
Holdings by categories of assets (e.g., government bonds, equities, loans, and deposits) and an indication of applicable investment rules for each category	
Value of derivatives and asset swaps in the portfolio	
Capitalization and amount of deposited funds in each pension fund	
Returns on pension fund assets and return on pension fund deposits, and other financial performance indicators	
Disclosure requirements and related data	
Investment funds	
Number and total assets of all licensed investment and mutual funds	
Number and total assets of different types or classes of mutual funds (e.g., bonds, equity, mixed, money market)	
Number of mutual fund families and types of sponsors (foreign owned or connected with foreign financial institutions and domestically sponsored)	
Size distribution of mutual and investment funds (and mutual fund families) including the share of total net assets of the three largest mutual funds and the largest three fund families	
Data on composition of assets (distinguished between short-term paper, longer-term instruments, overseas securities, and loans to private sector) of all mutual funds	
Data on total foreign assets of mutual fund and investment companies	
Data on volume of purchases and redemptions of mutual funds	
Data on returns, entry (or exit) commissions, management fees of different types of mutual funds	

B

Table B.11. Structure and Performance of Other Financial Institutions[a]

	Annual data for recent periods
Number and total assets of	
Nonbank, non–deposit-taking financial institutions	
Leasing companies providing financial leasing facilities[b]	
Leasing companies providing operating leasing facilities[c]	
Factoring companies	
Institutions providing SME or microfinance	
Government-owned or joint (public–private) specialized banks or financial institutions	
Institution that specialize in primary housing loans	
Primary sources of funds (e.g., private or public equity, bond issues) for	
Nonbank non–deposit-taking financial institutions generally	
Leasing companies	
Factoring	
SME and microfinance providers	
Specialized institutions	

Note: SME = small and medium enterprise

a. See definition in chapter 6. It includes non-bank financial institutions—other than security market intermediaries, insurance firms, and pension funds—that are both deposit taking, and non–deposit-taking banks that provide a range of specialized financial services.

b. Financial leasing can be defined as a leasing arrangement wherein the lessee takes on most of the benefit and burden of ownership of the leased asset—lease payments make up a large part, if not all, of the leased asset's cost, and the title to the asset will most likely pass on to the lessee at the end of the lease.

c. Operating leasing is generally defined as a leasing arrangement wherein the lessor retains many of the benefits and burdens of ownership of the leased asset, such as the right to claim depreciation or other tax benefits of ownership. The term of the lease generally lasts for only a portion of the working life of the asset, and title is retained by the lessor.

B

Table B.12. Systemic Liquidity Infrastructure—Money, Exchange, and Debt Market

	Annual or higher frequency data for a recent period

Inter-bank money market[a]

Average daily volume of the transactions and the bid and offer interest rates (or average, maximum, and minimum interest rates) broken down by maturity (e.g., overnight, 1 week, 2 week) and by instruments (e.g., unsecured inter-bank loans, repos, and so forth)

Aggregate data on financial institution's exposure to the interbank money market by type of financial institution and by maturity (quarterly)

Average daily volume or end period volume and yield to maturity of central bank bills (if any), treasury bills, and commercial bank bills, and negotiable certificate of deposits sold on the primary issue market (by maturity)

Average daily volume (or total during a period) and yield to maturity of central bank bills, treasury bills, and bank bills, plus NCDs (of different residual maturities) transacted in the secondary markets

Ownership structure (e.g., domestic versus foreign, banks, nonbanks, public, private) of key money market instruments

Interbank foreign exchange markets

Average (or end of period) domestic currency or USD exchange rate on the spot market, bid, and offer spot exchange rates, and average daily volume of transactions (number and value) on the spot market

Average domestic currency or USD exchange rate and average and total volume (number and value) of forward transactions (by maturity)

Distribution of foreign exchange transactions by type of investor

Volume of central bank operations in the spot—and forward FX market

Central bank or monetary authority, liquidity management operations (excludes emergency lending)

Value and frequency of liquidity management operations (open market operations in specified money market or other market instruments) by the central bank

Aggregate (end of period stock) liquidity provided to or withdrawn from the banking system as a result of OMOs

LOLR activities (outstanding stock and rates) broken down by type of instrument, types of borrower, and currency, including standing and discretionary loan facilities, access limit per institution (average), and interest rates charged (by maturity structure and type of loan collateral)

Number of institutions that account for 50 percent or 70 percent of total liquidity provided through discount window or other liquidity adjustment facilities

Data on liquidity ratios (if any) imposed by Central Bank by type of authorized financial institutions

Foreign exchange SWAP arrangements with foreign central banks, monetary authorities, and commercial banks

Required reserves, excess reserves, and free reserves, and selected liquidity ratios

Public debt management and government bond markets

Public sector debt that is outstanding, broken down by issuer (central government, central bank, state-owned entities, state local governments), by instrument, by type of investor, and by maturity

Public sector holdings of liquid financial assets

Average duration or term to maturity of government debt outstanding

Note: NCDs = negotiable certificates of deposit; USD = U.S. dollars; FX = foreign exchange; OMOs = open market operations; LOLR = lender of last resort.

Table B.13. Systemic Liquidity Infrastructure—Payments and Securities Settlement Systems

	Annual or higher frequency data for a recent period

Volume and value of transactions processed in specified payment settlement systems, including

Number of participants

Daily average volume and value processed

Projected trends in volume or value

Breakdown of payment transactions by financial market transactions, commercial transactions, and consumer transactions

Frequency distribution of number of participants by value groupings

Netting ratio

Concentration ratio

Overnight or intraday credit—size and rates

Volume and type of transactions returned or not processed at the completion of clearing and settlement process

Average time to settle—for recent months and for 3 peak days—after payments enter the system for testing through the day for payment by size; number and value of payments in various "time to settle" bands

Average number and value of queued payments in recent months and on peak days

Total notes and coins issues, transferable deposits, narrow money supply, transferable deposits in foreign currency and broad money

Required reserves, portion of required reserves available for settlement, excess reserves, transferable interbank deposits, central bank credit to banks (both in domestic and foreign currency)

Volume and value of transactions by payment instrument:
- checks (domestic, foreign currency) and payment by cards (credit, debit, and stored value)
- Paper-based credit transfers (customer initiated, interbank large value)
- Paperless credit transfers (customer initiated, interbank or large value, direct debits, e-money, other)

Number of checking accounts, ATMs, POS, ATM-debit cards, credit cards.

Total volume and value (annual) of transactions in various interbank transfer systems (low-value systems, large-value systems, domestic and foreign currency transaction)

Volume and value of instructions handled by various securities settlement systems (government, securities, corporate shares, corporate debt, other)

Note: ATMs = automated teller machines; POS = point of sale.

B

Table B.14. Legal, Governance, and Information Infrastructure

Annual data for recent periods

Safety net and emergency

Size distribution of deposits for the banking system and for major banks, and the percentage of total deposits (and depositors) that is insured

Depositor payouts—amounts and number of depositors—by deposit protection fund

Timing, number of banks, value of assets, and duration of the operation for various types of bank intervention operation (e.g., statutory management, bank license withdrawals, liquidation, purchase and assumption, government takeover)

Size of operations and their timing for policy holder and investment protection funds

Volume and terms of emergency lending operations and their rationale

Insolvency regime and creditor rights

Volume and percentage of total of different types of lending (e.g., corporate, personal, real estate, automobile), connected lending, and large exposures in banks, NBFIs, and DFIs

Percentage of corporate loans that is securitized, classified by type of security

Level and percentage of NPL in banks, NBFIs, and DFIs, classified by type of lending and by industry; value and percentage of classified loans in each classification category

Number of credits, amounts, and percentages (as a percentage of total credit under collection or recovery) in each of the following:

- Sale of credit to a third party
- Debt rescheduling
- Informal workout
- Nonjudicial foreclosure or execution
- Judicial foreclosure (immoveable assets)
- Judicial proceedings and execution (moveable assets)
- Liquidation proceedings (bankruptcy)
- Rehabilitation proceedings (e.g., formal, court supervised) debt to-equity conversion
- Other (describe, country specific)

For each of the above categories of debt resolution, annual data on

- Average recovery rates (as a percentage of total credit, plus interest due)
- Average recovery rate (as a percentage of nominal value of credit)
- Average duration of recovery
- Average costs incurred in trying to collect the loans (e.g., costs of litigation, costs for external lawyers)

Corporate governance

Overview of capital markets (see table B.9)

Number, number of employees, sales, assets of companies by types of ownership and incorporation (e.g., proprietorship, partnership, limited liability company), and by listed and nonlisted separately

Percentage of the listed sector owned by state, foreign, domestic; institutional investors, holding companies, families, and so forth and items such as indicators of ownerships concentration and pyramid structures

Note: NBFI = nonbank financial institution; DFI = development finance institution.

B

Table B.15. Financial Sector Taxation

	Annual data for recent periods
Tax treatment—rate, withholding, deductions and exemptions if any—of incomes (interest, dividend, capital gain) from different categories of financial assets (e.g., deposits, stocks, bonds)	
Tax treatment—rate, deductible items such as loan loss provisions and other exclusion—of incomes, transactions or gross receipts (or other VAT and sales tax) of various classes of financial institutions	
Tax treatment of transactions in different financial markets	
Tax treatment of pension funds and life insurance—tax rates on premia or contributions—on earnings on the fund while invested and on withdrawals or pensions	
Remuneration of required reserves and excess reserves	

Note: VAT = value added tax.

Table B.16. Indicators of Access to Financial Services

	Annual or higher frequency data for a recent period
Financial institutions	
Number of branches, or other banking service outlets, for each bank, NBFI, and DFI and for each province (state and local jurisdictions)	
Number of ATMs for each bank, NBFI, and DFI and for each province	
Size distribution of loans for banks, NBFIs, and DFIs; similar distribution data for deposits	
Number of employees for each bank, NBFI, and DFI and for each province	
Payments[a]	
Percentages of households with transaction accounts, payment cards; total number of transaction accounts, payment cards in the system	
Savings[a]	
Percentages of households with savings accounts; total number of savings and time deposit accounts	
Allocation of funds[a]	
Percentage of households with residential mortgage; with other borrowings in last year (stock or flow)	
Percentage of enterprises (including unincorporated) with borrowing from formal financial intermediaries	
Percentages of enterprises reporting credit refusal in past year or discouraged borrowers	
Monitoring users[a]	
Number and percentage of loans covered by various credit registries	
Risk transformation[a]	
Percentage of households with life, motor, and household insurance	
Cost of financial services (banking charges)[a]	
Average or lowest quintile of the cost of maintaining standard transactions accounts (all inclusive cost) for financial intermediaries	
Cost of standard internal retail payment; cost of standard international remittance from a specified source country	
Percentage of households with more than 1 hour traveling distance from a bank branch by public transport	

Note: NBFI = nonbank financial institution; DFI = development finance institution; ATMs = automated teller machines.

a. These data were proposed by Honohan (2004) as basic national access indicators. Compilation of data will typically require surveys of households, financial service providers, and experts with knowledge of the field. Further breakdown of the proposed access information by socioeconomic classes of households or types of enterprises (e.g., microenterprises) would increase the value of available information for policy and research purposes. Such information can be combined with data on holdings of various financial assets and liabilities by households, nonfinancial corporates, and financial institutions for a more detailed assessment.

B

Appendix C

Data Sources for Financial Sector Assessments

C.1 Overview

Data sources for financial sector assessments can be broadly divided into national sources and commercial databases. National sources use supervisory and national accounts data, whereas commercial databases rely primarily on published financial statements. Data from national sources are usually made available through the bank supervisors' Web sites and publications, as well as through databases of international organizations, such as the Organisation for Economic Co-operation and Development (OECD) and Asia Regional Information Center (ARIC).

Data from national sources are usually aggregated for the entire banking system, although some supervisors also publish bank-level data. The databases usually include indicators of financial stability such as bank capital adequacy, asset quality, profitability, and liquidity, as well as indicators of financial system structure and development such as total financial assets and ratios of monetary aggregates to the gross domestic product (GDP). The main advantage of data obtained from national sources is that they cover the banking system in its entirety and often have higher frequency and better timeliness than commercial data providers. However, financial sector authorities in many countries do not disclose all available data to the public, especially when the data relate to financial sector soundness and stability. In addition, national supervisory data are not standardized across countries, and the data come in different formats and definitions. The OECD publishes standardized databases with annual bank, insurance, and institutional investors' soundness indicators and financial system structure data for 31 countries compiled from national sources, but data standardization requirements lead to delays in the processing and publishing of the data.

C

Commercial databases providing bank-level indicators draw mainly on published bank financial reports. Databases such as Bankscope and Thomson One Banker contain a large number of nonaggregated annual financial statements. Bankscope transforms the original data reported by the banking institutions into a standardized format that is used for the computation of bank-level soundness indicators. The database has the capacity to aggregate those indicators on a country basis. However, the availability of the underlying data for computing indicators and the coverage of the banking systems may vary by country and, if inadequate, may produce misleading results. In addition, the public reporting definitions of some of the indicators may differ from the definitions used by bank supervisors.

The Banker's Almanac database has a comprehensive coverage of the financial systems, including both banks and nonbank financial companies, but the number of published indicators is limited. Corporate-level soundness and development indicators for publicly traded companies not limited to banks, but including also nonbank financial and nonfinancial corporations, are available from Thomson One Banker, which also publishes company stock performance data. Other commercial databases, such as CEIC Asia and Haver Analytics, which specialize in economic statistics, tap into national sources and provide more timely and higher frequency aggregate-level bank indicators for some countries as well as country-level, market-based indicators, such as stock exchange capitalization, turnover, number of listed companies, and stock market indices. CEIC Asia provides some data on real estate prices. Information on bonds, equities, commodities, and derivative instruments (e.g., options, futures, swaps)—including prices, yields, spreads, market indices, and the like—are available from commercial data providers such as Bloomberg, Datastream, and Global Insight. In addition, Bloomberg provides some company-level financial statements and performance information for developed countries and for some emerging market countries. Thomson One Banker's company data are retrievable through Datastream.

The rating agencies that publish financial information on rated banks on their Web sites are another source of bank-level indicators. Moody's Investor Services compiles banking system statistical supplements for developed and emerging market countries. Fitch Research publishes special country reports on major banks' performance, banking system structure, and prudential regulations, which contain selected soundness indicators. Both Moody's and Fitch Research focus their attention on the larger banks in a country, and their coverage of the banking systems is not comprehensive. The indicators are more often not aggregated and may have a lag from 6 months to 1 year, depending on when the reports were issued. Along with the financial information, Moody's publishes the financial strength ratings of individual banks and aggregates the information into an overall banking system financial strength rating. Fitch rates individual banks in terms of potential support the banks may get in a crisis situation.

Additional details on those data sources are presented in the following sections.

C.2 National Data Sources

National bank supervisors publish on their Web sites some of the financial soundness indicators (FSIs) that they collect, either in the statistics section or as part of their bank supervision publications. Availability varies by country, and for some countries, disclosure is limited to monetary balance sheet data. Published supervisory data are updated more frequently than commercial sources—often quarterly—and cover the banking sector in its entirety. In some countries with large banking sectors, there is still a lag in the collection, aggregation, and reporting of the indicators. In countries where the bank supervisor is not the central bank but another stand-alone agency (e.g., many countries in Latin America where the bank supervisor is usually the banking commission), the Web sites contain more comprehensive banking sector data. In some cases, only the underlying data used for the FSIs computation are published and are in a raw data format.

Some of the countries publishing FSIs on their Web sites are as follows:

- Europe: Austria, Belgium, Iceland, Italy, Luxembourg
- Latin America: Argentina, Bolivia, Chile, Colombia, Ecuador, Mexico, Paraguay, Peru, República Bolivariana de Venezuela
- Emerging Europe: Bulgaria, Croatia, the Czech Republic, Estonia, Israel, Poland, Slovakia, Slovenia, Turkey, Ukraine
- Asia: Bangladesh, India, the Republic of Korea, Malaysia, Pakistan, Philippines, Thailand
- Middle East: the Arab Republic of Egypt
- Africa: Kenya, South Africa, Zimbabwe
- Other: Australia, Canada, New Zealand, United States

C.3 International Organizations

C.3.1 OECD Databases

The OECD Bank Profitability Statistics Database has three main components: (a) income statement and balance sheet statistics, (b) structure of financial system, and (c) classification of banks assets and liabilities.

Income statement and balance sheet statistics provide information on income statements, balance sheets, and capital adequacy by banking groups. Data relate to individual banking groups as defined by country (e.g., Germany: all banks, commercial banks, large commercial banks, savings banks, cooperative banks, regional giro institutions, regional institutions of cooperative banks). Data are provided in national currency and include the following:

- Years covered: 1979 onward, annual, latest update for 2001
- Countries covered: Australia, Austria, Belgium, Canada, the Czech Republic, Denmark, Iceland, Finland, France, Germany, Greece, Hungary, Iceland, Ireland, Italy, Japan, the Republic of Korea, Luxembourg, Mexico, the Netherlands, New Zealand, Norway, Poland, Portugal, the Slovak Republic, Spain, Sweden, Switzerland, Turkey, United Kingdom, United States

Structure of financial system provides information on the overall structure of the financial system by type of institution and their components: central banks, other monetary institutions, other financial institutions, and insurance institutions. Data relate to number of institutions, number of branches, number of employees, total assets and liabilities, and total financial assets. Data are provided in national currency, and they include the following:

- Years covered: 1995 onward, annual, (latest update for 2002)
- Countries covered: Same as in income statement and balance sheet statistics

Classification of banks assets and liabilities provides the composition of bank assets and liabilities of residents and nonresidents denominated in domestic and foreign currencies. Data are provided in national currency and they include the following:

- Years covered: 1995 onward, latest update for 2002
- Countries covered: Australia, Austria, Belgium, Canada, the Czech Republic, Finland, France, Germany, Greece, Hungary, Iceland, Ireland, Italy, Luxembourg, the Netherlands, New Zealand, Norway, Poland, Portugal, Spain, Sweden, Switzerland, Turkey, United Kingdom

The OECD insurance statistics have two main components: comparative insurance data and insurance statistics.

Comparative insurance data include gross premiums, market share in OECD, density, penetration, life insurance share, retention ration, ratio of reinsurance acceptance, and foreign company market share in the domestic market. Those statistics are provided for life insurance, nonlife insurance, and total. They include the following:

- Years covered: 1993 onward, annual, latest update for 2002
- Countries covered: Australia, Austria, Belgium, Canada, the Czech Republic, Denmark, Finland, France, Germany, Greece, Hungary, Iceland, Ireland, Italy, Japan, the Republic of Korea, Luxembourg, Mexico, the Netherlands, New Zealand, Norway, Poland, Portugal, Singapore, the Slovak Republic, Spain, Sweden, Switzerland, Turkey, United Kingdom, United States

Insurance statistics are statistics per country and are provided in the following areas: number of insurance companies, number of employees, business written, outstanding investment by direct insurance companies, breakdown of nonlife insurance premiums, gross claims payments, gross operating expenses, and commissions. They include the following:

- Years Covered: 1993 onward, annual, latest update for 2001
- Countries covered: Australia, Austria, Belgium, Canada, the Czech Republic, Denmark, Finland, France, Germany, Greece, Hungary, Iceland, Ireland, Italy, Japan, the Republic of Korea, Luxembourg, Mexico, the Netherlands, New Zealand, Norway, Poland, Portugal, Singapore, the Slovak Republic, Spain, Sweden, Switzerland, Turkey, United Kingdom, United States

The OECD institutional investors statistics provide the financial assets of institutional investors, insurance companies, pension funds, investment companies, and other forms of institutional investors as outstanding amounts in U.S. dollars and as a percentage of GDP. They include the following:

- Years covered: 1980 onward, annual, latest update for 2002
- Countries covered: Australia, Austria, Belgium, Canada, the Czech Republic, Denmark, Finland, France, Germany, Greece, Hungary, Iceland, Italy, Japan, the Republic of Korea, Luxembourg, Mexico, the Netherlands, Norway, Poland, Portugal, Spain, Sweden, Switzerland, Turkey, United Kingdom, United States

C.3.2 European Central Bank Monetary Statistics

The European Central Bank (ECB) publishes—as part of its monetary statistics—aggregated and consolidated balance sheets of the euro area monetary financial institutions, as well as details on national aggregated balance sheets of the euro area monetary institutions. Recently published series contain information on the cross-border positions of monetary financial institutions residing in the euro area vis-à-vis all financial institutions residing within and outside the euro area. Other monetary financial institutions statistics cover the number of institutions subject to minimum reserve requirement in each member and accession country, the number of mutual funds, and the number of foreign bank branches In addition, the ECB publishes the aggregated balance sheet of euro area investment funds and statistics on securities issuance, money market interest rates, government bond yields, and stock market indices. They include the following:

- Years covered: 1997 onward (1999 for some series)
- Countries covered: Euro area countries

C.3.3 Bank for International Settlements (BIS)

BIS publishes on its Web site the following databases that are of interest for financial sector assessments: consolidated banking statistics, international banking statistics, securities statistics, derivatives statistics, and payment and settlement system statistics.

Consolidated banking statistics include consolidated data on foreign and international claims by maturity and sector and by nationality of reporting bank. The data cover the following:

- Years covered: 1983 onward, quarterly frequency
- Countries covered: BIS reporting banks' claims on all countries

International banking statistics include locational statistics on external positions of BIS reporting banks by sector and by currency. Their coverage is as follows:

- Years covered: 1977 onward, quarterly frequency
- Countries covered: BIS reporting banks' claims on all countries

Securities statistics include domestic and international debt securities by sector, residence, and nationality of issuer. Their coverage is as follows:

- Years covered: 1987 onward, quarterly
- Countries covered: Developed and developing countries

C

Derivatives statistics include over-the-counter and exchange-traded derivatives statistics, and cover the following:

- Years covered: 1998 onward, semiannual
- Countries covered: aggregate data by risk category and instrument (regional breakdowns available for exchange-traded derivatives)

Payment and settlement system statistics include data on various settlement media; information on notes and coins; data on various noncash means of payments and transactions; and other information on different interbank funds transfer systems, payment cards, electronic payments, and automated teller machines, etc. The coverage of the data is as follows:

- Years covered :1995 onward, annually updated
- Countries covered: Belgium, Canada, France, Germany, Hong Kong (China), Italy, Japan, the Netherlands, Singapore, Sweden, Switzerland, United Kingdom, United States

C.3.4 Asia Regional Information Center

The Asia Regional Information Center (ARIC Database) includes capital adequacy and nonperforming loan indicators for the financial sector plus the debt-to-equity and return on equity indicators for the corporate sector. The database covers the following:

- Years covered: 1997 onward, frequency—monthly, quarterly, annual, varies by indicator and country
- Countries covered: Bangladesh, Brunei Darussalam, India, Indonesia, Malaysia, Pakistan, Philippines, the Republic of Korea, Singapore, Sri Lanka, Thailand

C.3.5 IMF

IMF produces the following databases of particular interest for financial sector assessments: international financial statistics (IFS) and bonds, equities, and loans database (BEL).

Produced by the IMF, the IFS provides international statistics on macroeconomic indicators and selected aspects of international and domestic finance from 1948 to the present. It contains approximately 32,000 time series covering more than 200 countries and areas.

The BEL database contains data on bond issuance, syndicated loans, and equity placements. Records are available for each individual transaction with several fields that provide the terms of those transactions. Data are also available through reports in an aggregated format at the country and regional levels. This database is internal to the IMF. Its coverage is as follows:

- Years covered: 1980 to present except for equities that span 1983 to present, annual, monthly, daily frequencies
- Countries covered: developing countries

C.3.6 International Finance Corporation (IFC)

IFC publishes the Emerging Markets Database (EMDB).

EMDB contains the latest figures for all IFC indices—global, investable, industry, and frontier—and on market data such as prices, corporate actions, and stock ID information. The database provides three levels of data: comprehensive data on individual stocks covered in all markets, data series for each index computed, and data series for each market covered. It also includes the following:

- Years covered: varies by country and indicator
- Countries covered: emerging market countries

C.3.7 World Bank

The World Bank produces the world development indicators database. It contains statistical data for more than 550 development indicators and time series data from 1960 onward, thus covering more than 200 countries and 18 country groups. Data are provided in both national currencies and U.S. dollars, and ratios are available where applicable. Financial sector data available include the following: bank liquid reserves, domestic banking credit, deposit and lending interest rates and spreads, stock market capitalization, value of stocks traded, system liquid liabilities, and so forth.

C.3.8 Commercial Databases

C.3.8.1 *Commercial Databases Providing Aggregate Financial Sector Data*

The CEIC Data Company Ltd. produces the CEIC Asia Database. This database provides, in addition to economic data, aggregate balance sheets by banking groups (e.g., all banks, commercial banks, and, in some cases, foreign banks and state-owned banks). For some countries, a limited number of FSIs are available, mainly bank lending and asset quality indicators. However, for some countries, available are bank capital adequacy indicators and, in some cases, a limited number of structural and insurance indicators (e.g., number of banks, some insurance data). For some countries, individual bank balance sheets are provided. In addition, the database has information on financial markets (e.g., stock market capitalization, indices, turnover ratios) and, for some countries, on real estate prices. Data also include the following:

- Years covered: vary by country (from 2–3 years to 5–6 years); frequency is usually monthly, quarterly,, and annually: the balance sheet and FSIs data have a lag of 1–2 quarters.
- Countries covered: Australia, Bangladesh, Cambodia, China, Hong Kong (China), India, Indonesia, Japan, the Republic of Korea, Malaysia, Pakistan, Philippines, Singapore, Sri Lanka, Taiwan (China), Thailand, Vietnam

CEIC's emerging Europe and emerging Americas databases provide, in addition to economic statistics, aggregate bank balance sheet data. In addition, the database has information on financial markets: stock market capitalization, indices, and turnover ratios. The data coverage is as follows:

- Years covered: varies by country (usually 5–6 years); frequency is usually monthly, quarterly, and annually
- Countries covered: emerging Europe (Bulgaria, Croatia, the Czech Republic, Hungary, Israel, Poland, Romania, Russia, the Slovak Republic, and Slovenia); South Africa; Turkey; and emerging Americas (Argentina, Brazil, Chile, Colombia, Ecuador, Mexico, Peru, República Bolivariana de Venezuela)

Haver Analytics provides—in addition to economic statistics—financial data, which, depending on the country, may include aggregate bank asset information, or capital markets data, data on domestic and external government debt, number of bankruptcies in the corporate sector, and the like. The data coverage is as follows:

- Years covered: Varies by country and indicator, monthly frequency for the market data
- Countries covered: Africa, Asia Pacific, Central America, Eastern Europe, G10+ countries, Latin America, Middle East, and Western Asia

Global Insight provides—in addition to economic statistics—data on bond indices, commodities, energy pricing, equities, equity indices, exchange rates, fixed income, futures, interest rates, money markets, and options. The data coverage is as follows:

- Years covered: varies by indicator and country, annual, semiannual, quarterly, monthly, weekly, daily frequencies
- Countries covered: worldwide coverage

C.3.8.2 *Commercial Databases Providing Bank-Level Data*

Bankscope provides financial data (financial statements and bank performance indicators) for more than 10,000 individual banks. Bank-level data can be aggregated automatically, but the prudential indicators are sometimes available only for a limited number of banks, thereby creating distortions in the aggregate indicators. Data can be filtered by banking groups (e.g., commercial banks, savings banks, cooperative banks, foreign banks, state-owned banks), although the ownership information is sometimes incomplete. The data coverage is as follows:

- Years covered: 1995 onward, annual frequency
- Countries covered: covers most of the countries in the world, but level of banking system coverage varies by country

Banker's Almanac provides a comprehensive list of all the financial institutions in a particular country with their ownership and some financial statement information: stylized balance sheet and income statement data for the past 5 years, plus three performance indicators (return on assets, return on equity, and equity capital to total assets). The data coverage is as follows:

- Years covered: 1999 onward, annual frequency
- Countries covered: worldwide coverage

Bloomberg provides company-level financial information (summary balance sheets, income statements, cash flow statements, and performance indicators) for large listed banks, other financial and nonfinancial companies, and a variety of capital markets data and market-based indicators, including information on bond spreads, derivative instruments, ratings, and the like. The data coverage is as follows:

- Years covered: varies by bank, usually about 10 years for the large international banks, annual figures, some quarterly figures available
- Countries covered: Global, covering about 126 countries; data coverage varies by country, more adequate coverage for the industrialized countries and large emerging markets

Thomson One Banker provides company-level financial information (annual reports and financial ratios covering leverage, profitability, liquidity, asset utilization including market indices, and stock performance data for publicly traded companies). Companies can be filtered by industry (market sector). Financial information for banks and financial services companies is also available, but coverage varies by country and is often limited for emerging market countries. Thomson One Banker data are also retrievable through DataStream Advance. The data coverage is as follows:

- Years covered: 1990 onward, annual frequency, quarterly for the United States
- Countries covered: countries with active stock exchanges

DataStream Advance provides data on equities, equity indices, bonds, bond indices, interest rates, futures, options, and commodities. Thomson One Banker's company information can also be accessed through DataStream Advance. The data coverage is as follows:

- Years covered: varies by country, indicator, and company, usually at least 10 years for market data
- Countries covered: primarily countries with active capital markets

C.3.8.3 Ratings Agencies

Moody's Investors Services publishes financial statements and selected FSIs for the rated banks in each country in a banking statistical supplement. Each supplement contains 5 years of annual bank-level data. For some countries, banking system aggregates are also available. Moody's also rates the financial strength of each bank, using bank performance and other country-specific indicators. The data coverage is as follows:

- Years covered: each statistical supplement covers 5 years of annual data
- Countries covered: rated banks in developed and emerging market countries, annual frequency; data timeliness varies depending on when the supplement was published and has up to 1 year of lag

Fitch Research publishes selected financial information for the top five to six banks in developed countries and in some emerging market countries as part of its special reports on rated banks' financial results. Some information on financial system structure and

C

bank regulations is also available from its reports on banking systems and prudential regulations. The data coverage is as follows:

- Years covered: each report usually covers 2 years of data
- Countries covered: developed and emerging market countries

References

Altman, Edward I., and Paul Narayanan. 1997. "Business Failure Classification Models: An International Survey." In *International Accounting and Finance Handbook*, 2nd ed., ed. Frederick D. S. Choi, chapter 10. New York: John Wiley and Sons.

Bank for International Settlements (BIS). 2001. "Structural Aspects of Market Liquidity from a Financial Stability Perspective." Available at http://www.bis.org/publ/cgfs_note01.pdf (a discussion note for a meeting of the Financial Stability Forum.

———. 2005. "Real Estate Indicators and Financial Stability." BIS Paper No. 21, Bank for International Settlements, Basel, Switzerland.

———. 1999. Market Liquidity: Research Findings and Selected Policy Implications. Committee on Global Financial System. Publications No. 11, Bank for International Settlements, Basel, Switzerland.

Begum, Jahanara, May Khamis, and Kal Wajid. 2001. *Usefulness of Sectoral Balance Sheets in Macroprudential Analysis*. Washington, DC: International Monetary Fund.

Borio, Claudio, and Patrick McGuire. 2004. "Twin Peaks in Equity and Prices?" *BIS Quarterly Review* (March):79–93. Available at http://www.bis.org/publ/qtrpdf/r_qt0403.pdf.

Das, Udabir S., Davies Nigel, and Podpiera Richard. 2003. "Insurance Issues in Financial Soundness." IMF Working Paper No. 03/138, International Monetary Fund, Washington, DC.

Debelle, Guy. 2004. "Household Debt and the Macroeconomy." *BIS Quarterly Review* (March): 51–64. Available at: http://www.bis.org/publ/qtrpdf/r_qt0403.pdf.

Evans, Owen, Alfredo Leone, Mahinder Gill, and Paul Hilbers. 2002. "Macroprudential Indicators of Financial System." IMF Occasional Paper No. 192, IMF, Washington, DC.

Honahan, Patrick. 2004. "Measuring Microfinance Access: Building on Existing Cross-Country Data." Paper presented at UNDP, World Bank, and IMF Workshop on Data on Access of Poor and Low Income People to Financial Services, Washington, DC.

International Monetary Fund. 2000. *Monetary and Financial Statistics Manual*. Washington, DC: International Monetary Fund.

———. 2002. *A Balance Sheet Approach to Financial Crisis*. Washington, DC: International Monetary Fund.

———. 2004. *Compilation Guide on Financial Soundness Indicators*. Washington DC: International Monetary Fund. Available at http://www.imf.org/external/nplstal/bsi/eng/2004/guide/index.htm.

Levine, R. 1997. "Financial Development and Economic Growth: Views and Agenda." *Journal of Economic Literature* 35: 688–726.

C

Miles, Colin. 2002. "Large Complex Financial Institutions (LCFIs): Issues to Be Considered in the Financial Sector Assessment Program." International Monetary Fund, Monetary and Exchange Affairs Department, Operational Paper 02/3, International Monetary Fund, Washington, DC.

Pomerleano, Michael. 1998. "The East Asia Crisis and Corporate Finances: The Untold Micro Story." World Bank Working Paper No. 1990, World Bank, Washington, DC. Available at http://econ.worldbank.org/docs/907.pdf.

United Nations, the Commission of the European Communities, the International Monetary Fund, the Organisation for Economic Co-operation and Development, and the World Bank. 1993. *System of National Accounts*, Series F, No. 2, New York: United Nations.

World Bank. 2004. *Access to Financial Services in Brazil*. Washington, DC: World Bank.

C

Appendix D

Stress Testing

This technical note is intended to answer some of the questions that may arise as part of the process of stress testing a financial system. The note is structured as follows: Section D.1 begins with a discussion of stress testing in a financial system context that highlights some of the differences between stress testing that is designed to identify systemic weaknesses and stress testing within individual portfolios. Section D.2 provides an overview of the process itself—from identifying vulnerabilities, to constructing scenarios, to interpreting the results. Section D.3 shows some examples of stress-testing calculations. Section D.4 draws on experience in conducting stress testing as part of the Financial Sector Assessment Program (FSAP).

D.1 Overview of Stress Testing[1]

A stress test is a rough estimate of how the value of a portfolio changes when there are large changes to some of its risk factors (such as asset prices). The term *rough estimate* is used to avoid the perception that stress testing is a precise tool that can be used with scientific accuracy. Stress testing is an analytical technique that can be used to produce a numerical estimate of a particular sensitivity. Stress tests usually produce a numerical estimate of the change in value of the portfolio that has been caused by exceptional, but plausible, shocks. This change is often expressed in terms of the effect on some measure of capital as a way of understanding the sensitivity of the net worth of the institution to the risk being considered. The stress-testing process, however, is more than just applying a set of formulas to spreadsheets of numbers; it involves a series of judgments and assumptions that can be as critical to producing meaningful results as the actual calculations themselves. Each assumption, aggregation, or analytical approximation made in the process can introduce wide margins of error to the results; therefore, much care should be taken in their estimation and interpretation.

The use of stress tests has broadened over time. Stress tests were originally developed for use at the portfolio level to understand the latent risks to a trading book from extreme movements in market prices. They have now become widely used as a risk management tool by financial institutions (see, e.g., Committee on the Global Financial System 2000). Gradually, the techniques have been applied in a broader context, with the aim of measuring the sensitivity of a group of institutions (such as commercial banks) or even an entire financial system to common shocks. Stress-testing results may be compared across institutions, and the aggregate effect may be viewed as a change in financial soundness indicators (FSIs) caused by a common shock. The dispersion of the estimated effect among institutions of a common shock by itself produces valuable information on the potential for systemic risk.

System-focused stress tests, as the name implies, have several important differences from portfolio-level stress tests. The ultimate intent of system-focused approaches is different, because they aim to identify common vulnerabilities across institutions that could undermine the overall stability of the financial system. The focus is also more macroeconomic in nature, because the investigator is often interested in understanding how major changes in the economic environment may affect the financial system. A second difference between system-focused and portfolio-level stress tests lies in the complexity and degree of aggregation. System-focused stress tests may involve aggregation and comparison of more heterogeneous portfolios, often on the basis of different assumptions and methods of calculation. This aggregation requires adding or comparing "apples" and "oranges" to a much greater extent than is the case for a single institution's portfolio.

System-focused stress tests can be classified according to two types: either simultaneous stress tests of multiple portfolios using a common scenario, or a single scenario applied to an aggregated portfolio or model of the entire system.[2] Constructing an aggregated portfolio or model with sufficient detail is often an arduous and complex task. Therefore, most system-focused stress tests have adopted the first approach of applying a common scenario to a variety of institutions. This approach has the advantage that it provides information on the overall effect of shocks, as well as their distribution throughout the system, which can be useful for understanding the potential for contagion and confidence effects on stability. If data availability allows, conducting both types of tests—on an aggregated portfolio, as well as on individual portfolios—will provide the maximum information on a system's vulnerabilities.

D.2 The Process

System-focused stress testing is best seen as a process: part investigative, part diagnostic, part numerical, and part interpretive. Ideally, this process begins with the identification of specific vulnerabilities or areas of concern, followed by the construction of a scenario in the context of a consistent macroeconomic framework. The next step is to map the outputs of the scenario into a form that is usable for an analysis of financial institutions' balance sheets and income statements, then performing the numerical analysis, considering any second-round effects, and finally summarizing and interpreting the results. Each stage of the process is important to understanding the sensitivity of a financial system to a particular shock or vulnerability. Those stages are not necessarily sequential, because some modification or review of each component of the process may be desirable as work progresses. The following subsections describe the key stages of the stress-testing process in more detail, with the intent of providing a better understanding of what is involved and of how to go about implementing them.

D.2.1 Identifying Vulnerabilities

The first stage in the stress-testing process is the identification of the main vulnerabilities. Narrowing the focus of the exercise permits a more refined analysis, because it is unrealistic to attempt to stress every possible risk factor for a portfolio or system. Focusing on the weak points in a financial system enables the assessor to tailor the stress-testing exercise more effectively and thus permits a richer understanding of inherent vulnerabilities and a more effective use of time and resources.

Isolating the key vulnerabilities to stress test is an iterative process that involves both qualitative and quantitative elements. System-focused stress tests can use a range of numerical indicators to help isolate potential weaknesses, including the "big picture" or macrolevel indicators, broad structural indicators, and institution-focused or microlevel indicators. Those measures should be seen as providing complementary information on potential vulnerabilities. This process may be facilitated by drawing on a range of expertise in the context of a dedicated working group.

Knowledge of the broader macroeconomic environment will provide an overall context for the performance of the financial system and will indicate potential sources of shocks. Understanding the macroeconomic picture aids the understanding of what is "normal" for an economy with respect to its own history and in comparison with other countries. This information provides a useful metric for understanding potential sources of shocks, because key macrovariables and financial variables that are the most volatile, misaligned, or out of equilibrium are often the most susceptible to major shocks or realignments. This analysis can also inform the macrosimulations described later. Such an analysis can use data about the real sector, the government sector, and the external sector and can draw on the existing sources of macroeconomic analysis from local or external sources, including IMF Article IV consultation reports.

A variety of indicators of the structure of the financial system can provide important insights into the location of risks in the financial system, including data on ownership and market shares, balance-sheet structures, and flow-of-fund accounts. Qualitative information on the institutional and regulatory frameworks that govern financial activities can also help to interpret developments in a range of indicators. Discussions with supervisors and regulators, private sector analysts, and market participants can be quite revealing as to the likely sources of vulnerability in a financial system. This type of information is often anecdotal in nature, which may make interpretation difficult, but it can provide important context to an assessment of potential financial sector vulnerabilities and can form the starting point for more quantitative assessments of vulnerabilities.

D

In addition to using the broad macroeconomic context and structural indicators, we can use a range of FSIs to narrow the focus and to understand the financial system's vulnerability to shocks and its capacity to absorb the resulting losses. The analysis of FSIs can be informed by the information gathered from the macroeconomic and structural indicators discussed earlier.

D.2.2 Constructing Scenarios—Use of Macroeconomic Models

Once the key questions or main vulnerabilities of interest have been identified, the next step is to construct a scenario that will form the basis of the stress test. This phase of the process involves an examination of the available data and models that can be used to understand the behavior of the system with respect to the main vulnerabilities. Using those data, one can construct a scenario in the context of some overall macroeconomic framework or model, depending on the complexity of the system and the availability of a suitable model.

The objective of using an explicit macroeconomic model is to link a particular set of shocks to key macrovariables and financial variables in a consistent and forward-looking framework. The use of a macroframework does not necessarily require a large research effort, but it can leverage existing expertise and research. The key reason for using this approach is to bring the discipline and consistency of an empirically based model and an explicit focus on the link between the macroeconomy and the main vulnerabilities.

Drawing on the main macroeconomic vulnerabilities, the analyst should arrive at a consensus for the key macrovariables and financial variables that are the most volatile, misaligned, or likely to have the greatest effect on the financial system. Typically, such misaligned variables are susceptible to major shocks or realignments and, thus, can form the basis of a realistic simulation scenario. Depending on the structure and features of the macromodel that is available, the simulation can produce a range of economic and financial variables as outputs.

Here are three illustrative examples of the process of developing a scenario:

- Example 1: Suppose that housing prices had risen sharply on the strength of rapid employment growth, rising household disposable incomes, and low interest rates, thereby fuelling a mortgage-lending boom. An analysis of bank balance sheets and income statements shows a strong dependence on mortgage lending both in the stock of assets and in the flow of income. A possible scenario could involve a rise in unemployment, a fall in disposable incomes, and a sharp rise in interest rates affecting the debt servicing capacity of households. The outputs from a macromodel could provide a range of information on employment, real incomes, prices, and interest rates, which could be used to formulate a specific stress test for bank balance sheets.

- Example 2: Suppose that the macrolevel analysis indicated an overvalued exchange rate caused by strong capital inflows with associated credit growth financing a surge in construction investment. An analysis of structural data on institutional balance sheets and income statements reveals a sharp increase in exposure to foreign-currency–denominated real estate loans, and microlevel indicators of FSIs. Individual balance-sheet information shows rising defaults on property loans. One scenario might include a sudden reversal of capital flows and a rapid depreciation of the exchange rate. Macrosimulations of this scenario could produce a range of outputs, including real gross domestic product (GDP) growth, price level, interest rates, and exchange rate. Those outputs could then form the basis of a stress test of balance sheets for individual institutions.

- Example 3: Suppose that financial deregulation and low interest rates, together with strong wage and economic growth, have fuelled a sharp rise in consumer (nonmortgage) lending. An analysis of balance sheets and income statements reveals banks and nonbanks now earn more than a quarter of their income from this lending, with exposures (and credit extended to consumers) growing rapidly. Furthermore, nonbanks are funding their lending largely through commercial paper placements. Although FSIs show only modest rises in delinquency rates and nonperforming assets, there are concerns about credit quality going forward. One possible scenario might involve a sharp rise in interest rates, increasing banks' funding costs and (temporarily) narrowing their margins, perhaps caused by a policy response to increased inflationary pressures or an external shock. The output of a macromodel could be used to analyze the possible effect on household incomes and the debt-servicing capacity.

Ideally, a macroeconometric or simulation model should form the basis of the stress-testing scenarios. One objective of system-focused stress tests is to understand the effect of major changes in the economic environment on the financial system. Using a macromodel provides a forward-looking and internally consistent framework for analyzing key linkages between the financial system and the real economy. The feasibility of this approach will vary according to the range of modeling expertise available, as well as the type of macromodel in place. Here are some of the considerations involved in using a macromodel:[3]

- *What are the baseline assumptions?* The baseline assumption could be either no change from the latest data, or the central forecast or most likely scenario from the most recent forecasting exercise.
- *What policy responses are assumed?* Depending on the model, different policy reaction functions may be imbedded in the model (such as a Taylor rule relating monetary policy instrument settings to deviations in inflation and output from their targets), or an assumption of no change in policies may be used. One can assume no policy response will typically imply a larger macroeconomic effect of any shock, but this conclusion will depend on the model and scenario.
- *What is the time horizon of the simulations?* If a quarterly model is available, it may be possible to produce forecasts over the next six to eight quarters. When one applies the scenarios to individual balance sheets, however, a shorter time horizon is desirable if no reaction by institutions to the specific shocks is assumed (i.e., if it is assumed that institutions do not adjust their balance sheets, then the results can be interpreted as a comparative static exercise).
- *Which variables are assumed to be fixed, and which are shocked?* Many macroeconomic models use a large number of exogenous variables. Implementing a particular scenario requires a judgment as to which variables are assumed to be constant.

D

Changing a large number of exogenous variables may make the scenario unnecessarily complex with little benefit in terms of realism and less acceptance of the results by participants.

- *What size of shocks should be used?* Shocks either can be calibrated on historical experience (e.g., largest change over the chosen time horizon seen in the past 10 years), or can be set on the basis of a hypothetical scenario (e.g., a 20 percent fall in the exchange rate). Historical experience may be more intuitive and easier to justify, but major structural changes may invalidate historical calibration (e.g., deregulation may change fundamental economic relations).

In the absence of a macromodel, it may be necessary to rely on more rudimentary approaches. Some authorities may not have a well-developed macromodel available. Even if a model is in place, there may be difficulties in using it to simulate relevant shocks. Some models may not be tractable for the type of economic shock that the analyst wishes to consider, whereas others may not incorporate a financial sector or may not allow for a policy reaction by authorities. Thus, it may not always be feasible to generate a macroscenario using a consistent macromodel. Even in those circumstances, it is still possible to frame the analysis in the context of an internally consistent, forward-looking macroeconomic scenario by using textbook macromodels, which are supplemented by existing empirical research, or by using models developed for another country that has a similar structure.

D.2.3 Balance-Sheet Implementation

Once a set of adjustment scenarios has been produced in a consistent macroframework, the next step is to translate the various outputs into the balance sheets and income statements of financial institutions. There are two main approaches to translating or "mapping" scenarios into balance sheets: the "bottom-up" approach, in which estimates are based on data for individual portfolios, which can then be aggregated, and the "top-down" approach, which uses aggregated or macrolevel data to estimate the effect.[4]

Under the bottom-up approach, the response to various shocks in a scenario is estimated at the portfolio level while using highly disaggregated data from individual financial institutions at a point in time. The results of the bottom-up approach can then be aggregated or compared to analyze the sensitivity of the entire sector or group of institutions. The bottom-up approach has the advantage of making better use of individual portfolio data; however, if individual institutions provide their own estimates, then the approach may introduce some inconsistencies about how each institution applies the scenario and produces its numerical estimates. The bottom-up approach also provides information on how the effect of shocks varies across institutions and on the variance or dispersion of this effect, which is an important statistic on financial stability of the system insofar as large losses in one institution can trigger contagion.

The top-down approach is used to estimate the responsiveness of a group of institutions to a particular scenario. Under this approach, a common parameter or estimate is applied to all institutions in the data set, (e.g., using a panel regression or a regression of aggregated information) to arrive at an estimate of the aggregate effect. The top-down approach is often easier to implement, because it requires only time series of aggregated data and is a consistent and uniform method that implicitly takes into account the responses of banks to shocks over time. However, aggregate historical relationships may not hold in the future. Ideally, both methods should be applied, but data limitations may preclude the application of both methods in many countries.

The remainder of this section discusses the various steps involved in implementing a system-focused stress test by addressing a series of key questions. The questions include the following: Who should perform the empirical analysis? Which institutions should be included? What are the data constraints? How large should the shocks be? How do we link the macroadjustment scenarios to individual balance sheets and income statements?

D.2.3.1 *Execution, Scope, and Coverage*

The first question to consider in implementing a system-focused stress test is who crunches the numbers: the supervisory agency or central bank, or the institutions themselves? Ideally, individual institutions should be as heavily involved in the process as possible—regardless of whether a top-down or bottom-up approach is used—because individual institutions will typically have the best access to data and knowledge of their own portfolios. For institutions with sophisticated risk management systems or significant international operations, most will have systems and stress-testing procedures in place as part of their internal risk monitoring processes.[5] For countries with financial institutions that have more rudimentary systems and have less expertise in modeling their portfolios, involvement in the process may be beneficial by expanding their knowledge. In those circumstances, it may be necessary for the central bank or supervisory agency to provide guidance or even to undertake parts of the empirical analysis, but this process should still involve individual institutions as much as possible. Having institutions cooperate in a stress-testing exercise may require some moral suasion or other incentives, including the ability to benchmark their own results against their peer groups or the ability to learn from other participants. At the same time, the supervisory agency or central bank needs to minimize conflicts of interest arising from the institutions' participation in the exercise. In particular, it needs to minimize incentives of institutions to project an overly optimistic picture, which could compromise the quality of the test. The supervisory or central bank staff may need to confirm the validity of the tests, including confirmation by carrying out independent tests as needed.

Implementing a stress test also requires addressing this question: Which institutions should be included in the exercise? The coverage of the stress-testing exercise should be broad enough to represent a meaningful critical mass of the financial system, while keeping the number of institutions covered at a feasible level (e.g., fewer than 20). The total market share of the institutions involved (in terms of assets, deposits, or some other criteria such as importance in the payment system) can be used to determine a cutoff point, because the exercise may become unwieldy if too many institutions are involved. Depending on their interlinkages, both banks and nonbank financial institutions should be included in the analysis, although this involvement may present some difficulties if they are supervised by different entities or have different balance-sheet reporting dates or practices.[6] In countries with a large number of small institutions, consideration could be given to either aggregating smaller institutions into a single balance sheet or taking a

D

representative sample of institutions, or even ignoring them if they are not systemically important.

Another important factor to consider in conducting a stress test is the data constraints. The availability and quality of data impose major constraints on the nature of stress tests that can be performed. Data limitations arise from the lack of basic data availability (especially in countries where information on balance-sheet exposures may not be available), difficulty in isolating specific exposures (especially in the case of large complex financial institutions, or financial institutions that are active in the derivative markets), lack of risk data (such as duration or default measures in countries where risk management systems are less sophisticated), and confidentiality issues (limitations on what supervisors are legally able to share with other parties).

If one is to overcome the data difficulties, it may be possible to work with the larger and more sophisticated institutions to get better data or to calibrate some parts of the exercise. For example, if the exposure of interest is the aggregate exposure to a specific borrower or sector, individual institutions may be able to produce information on that exposure from their internal risk monitoring systems, even if they do not report data to the authorities in that particular format. When confidentiality issues do arise, it may be possible for the institution with access to the data to conduct the stress testing while using agreed assumptions and methodologies and to share the results with the authorities in a form that is sufficiently informative of the risk exposures but that would not breach confidentiality laws or protocols.

The choice and implementation of stress-testing techniques in practice reflects the data quality and technical capacity available. In addition to the design of the stress-testing scenarios and the choice of top-down versus bottom-up approaches, an important part of the stress-testing process is the selection of technical tools to implement the stress-testing calculations. For each of the risk factors, there are several techniques or approaches to implementing the calculations. The techniques generally differ in the required volume of data and in their computational complexity. The choice, therefore, largely depends on the data availability (e.g., if no data are available on time to repricing of assets and liabilities, the interest rate risk can be assessed only by using very rough methods) and on the technical capacity available (e.g., software, staffing constraints, and time constraints).

D.2.3.2 The Calibration of Shocks

Another key question to address in implementing a system-focused stress test is how big are the shocks? Stress testing involves discovering the effect of exceptional but plausible events; therefore, the scenarios considered should be beyond the normal range of experience. Scenarios can be based on historical data (e.g., using the largest observed changes or extreme values over a specified period), or they can be hypothetical and may involve large movements thought to be plausible. Historical scenarios can be more intuitive because they were actually observed, but hypothetical scenarios may be more realistic, especially if the financial structure has changed significantly (e.g., with deregulation, liberalization, or changes in monetary policy operating procedures). Experiences of other countries can be a useful guide as well.

Although the object of stress testing is not to apply shocks until all major financial institutions fail, it is exceptional outcomes that precipitate financial instability.[7] Thus, when one is assessing the vulnerability of financial systems, it is important to consider a range of movements that is wide enough to capture such outcomes. For example, a simple sensitivity test can be calibrated according to the largest change in a risk factor over the past 10 years. It is important to bear in mind that the relevant empirical measure for scenarios is the joint probability of all factors moving simultaneously, which may be difficult to assess empirically. Because it is often difficult to attach a probability to hypothetical scenarios, some judgment is involved. However, this judgment can be guided by historical experience. In some circumstances, small changes in key variables may be sufficient to precipitate difficulties in some institutions.

D.2.3.3 *The Mapping of Macroscenarios to Balance Sheets: The Bottom-Up Approach*

Translating a macroeconomic framework into the balance sheet of a financial institution requires mapping macrovariables into a set of common risk factors that can be applied to stress individual balance sheets. Applying a stress to an individual balance sheet under the bottom-up approach involves shocking the risk factors that determine the underlying value of a portfolio and then revaluing that portfolio. Because most portfolios have numerous instruments, each with a unique price, the process of revaluing a portfolio may require knowledge of hundreds or thousands of market prices. Financial institutions typically simplify this process by mapping each element of a portfolio into a smaller set of common risk factors. Thus, two mappings are required to implement a system-focused stress test: one mapping from the macroadjustment scenarios to the set of common risk factors and another mapping from the common risk factors into all of the instruments in a portfolio.

For a financial institution, implementing a stress test typically requires a range of specific indicators. The indicators include interest rates (e.g., the term structure of the risk-free rate and credit quality spreads), exchange rates (e.g., spot and forward, bilateral, and trade-weighted), asset prices (e.g., market price indices), and credit exposures and quality. Thus, it may be necessary to supplement the output of the macromodel with additional estimates of what each scenario would imply in terms of the common risk factors.

Some financial institutions have their own internal models that link macroeconomic factors to the performance of their balance sheet, which can, in turn, be used to help calibrate this mapping to a set of common factors. Other potential sources of information to flesh out the details of this mapping could include either studies that are performed on the domestic economy and that address the term structure of interest rates, or models used to estimate the equilibrium real exchange rate. Two examples of this process may prove illustrative:

- Suppose the macro-model produces only two interest rates: an overnight cash rate and a 10-year bond rate. An empirical model of the term-structure of interest rates could be used to produce an estimated set of interest rates for a larger set of maturities. In turn, those data could be used to derive credit spreads.
- Suppose the macromodel produces only a trade-weighted exchange rate or a single bilateral exchange rate. If one is to get a broader range of exchange rates, it may

D

be possible to use the weightings implicit in the trade-weighted index to produce a set of bilateral exchange rates. Producing a range of exchange rates from a single bilateral exchange rate forecast from a macromodel can be accomplished by assuming some pattern of cross rates.

Once the macro-scenarios have been mapped into a set of common risk factors, the next step is to map the risk factors into the portfolios of individual institutions. The party that is usually best placed to construct such a mapping is the individual institution involved in the stress-testing exercise because it typically has the best access to expertise and detailed information on the portfolio itself. It may also have a well-developed risk management model that is capable of performing many of the calculations. The range of techniques that are typically used to estimate sensitivities of a balance sheet or income statement to shocks in specified risk factors can vary according to the complexities of the portfolio and the scope of risk management framework used by banks. The techniques also differ according to the type of risk being assessed, as illustrated in section D.3 of this technical note. As mentioned earlier, some financial institutions have macroframeworks that can be used to link the larger macroeconomic picture (e.g., unemployment rate, GDP growth, sectoral growth rates) to portfolio performance and so can map the adjustment scenarios directly into their own balance sheets and income statements by using their internal models.

In many circumstances, individual institutions will not have internal models capable of translating broad macroeconomic developments but will have their own internal models or expertise that can be used to construct an appropriate mapping. For example, many banks have internal models that use credit scores or default probabilities as key parameters in understanding the evolution of credit risk in their portfolio. Banks can estimate the effect of macroeconomic changes on those internal risk model parameters or can use the most recent economic downturn as a guiding rod for assessing the effect of broad economic changes on their portfolio. In some cases, it may be necessary to rely on the expert judgment of risk managers in adjusting the key parameters, particularly if the systems have been in place for only a relatively short period of time and thus have not spanned an entire economic cycle.

D.2.3.4 Top-Down Approach

Conducting a "top-down" approach to stress testing provides a useful check on the results on the basis of individual balance-sheet information (the bottom-up approach). Furthermore, financial institutions in some countries may not have the capacity to estimate the effect of a given set of shocks on their portfolio. In this case, the agency coordinating the stress-testing exercise could adopt a "top-down" approach and could apply adjustment parameters that are based on systemwide estimates. For example, a regression model of loan loss rates for the entire banking system could be used to estimate the effect of a macroadjustment scenario on the credit quality of an institution. Examples of this approach include the following:

- Frøyland and Larsen (2002) modeled losses for Norwegian banks on household loans as a function of household debt, wealth, and unemployment. They also modeled losses on loans to enterprises as a function of risk-weighted debt and collateral. Andreeva (2004) modeled the loan loss ratio (to assets) of loans to Norwegian enterprises as a function of bankruptcy probabilities and a variety of economic factors, including the unemployment rate and the real interest rate.

- Benito, Whitley, and Young (2001) extended the Bank of England's macromodel by incorporating household and corporate balance sheets. They then performed a stress test by incorporating a fall in housing prices and a rise in interest rates and by examining the effect on a variety of indicators, including mortgage arrears.

- Hoggarth and Whitley (2003) described the process of using the Bank of England's macromodel, as well as using the top-down approach, to estimate the effect of macrovariables on new provisions by banks.

- Arpa et al. (2000) estimated the effect of macroeconomic factors (real GDP, real estate prices, inflation, and real interest rates) on risk provisions and on earnings for Austrian banks. Kalirai and Scheicher (2002) modeled loan loss provisions in Austria as a function of various macroeconomic indicators and then used the model to conduct a series of sensitivity tests.

- Pesola (2001) examined the Nordic banking crisis by estimating a model of loan losses as a function of GDP, indebtedness, unexpected changes in income and interest rates, and deregulation.

The estimated equations from those papers are all examples of how the authorities or individual institutions can use the top-down approach to approximate the effect of economic developments on individual portfolios or to calibrate the parameters used in their stress tests. Regression-based estimates have their limitations, because they are often providing only a partial equilibrium estimate of some effect; therefore, care should be taken in interpreting the results of such estimates.

D.2.4 Interpretation and Publication

Experience in conducting stress tests suggests they are a useful tool for identifying the latent risk exposures and the likely significance of losses in a systematic and intuitive manner. Stress tests can be particularly useful when they are conducted on a regular basis, thereby providing information about changes in the risk profile of the system over time. Although stress test results are useful to evaluate effects of large movements (tail events) in key variables, care should be taken not to portray them as providing a precise measure of the magnitude of losses. Stress tests can indicate how much could be lost but not how much is likely to be lost.

Interpretation of stress tests needs to take into account their limitations. If the underlying model is incorrectly specified or estimated, the conclusions drawn from a stress-test may be invalid. Stress tests are also unlikely to capture the full range and interaction of risk exposures (such as operational risk and legal risk) and may give a misleading picture of the true nature of risk taking by participating institutions. Finally, stress tests typically consider only part of a bank's income-generating operations. Thus banks may have significant income flows that are unaffected in performance or value by the specific stress test scenarios analyzed.

D

An overview of the stress tests results can be conveyed by grouping the aggregate effect of the stress tests by type of risk or by scenario. The composition of expected losses (as a proportion of capital or income for instance) can be used to summarize the central results. For bottom-up approaches, descriptive statistics (e.g., mean, median, standard deviation, minimum, maximum, and number of institutions in each decile) and peer group analysis can be used to convey how the effect at the aggregate level is distributed across individual institutions.

Public dissemination of the results of stress tests can present some difficulties with regard to confidentiality and interpretation of results. Participating institutions may be reluctant to have any information disclosed that could identify specific firms. Some analysts may interpret the particular scenarios chosen as reflecting an official view on the most likely scenario or the most problematic, which may not be the case. Nevertheless, the publication of summary or aggregated information on stress test results by a wide variety of countries suggests that those difficulties can be overcome. Disclosure of some summary information on the results (such as the mean and the range) can be informative for financial markets and individual institutions wishing to benchmark their own results against their competitors without revealing the identities of individual institutions. Disclosure of the scenarios undertaken can also raise awareness of different risks for institutions to consider and incorporate into their own stress-testing programs.

D.3 Examples of Stress-Testing Calculations

Stress tests can be applied to both assets and liabilities and can be used to assess various risks: market risk (possibility of losses from changes in prices or yields), credit risk (potential for losses from borrower defaults or nonperformance on a contract), liquidity risk (possibility of depositor runs or losses from assets becoming illiquid), or contagion risk (possibility of losses resulting from failures in other financial institutions). Stress tests usually produce a numerical estimate of the portfolio's change in value—often expressed in terms of the effect on a measure such as the capital asset ratio or risk-weighted capital adequacy ratio—to illustrate the sensitivity of an institution's net worth to a given risk.

D.3.1 Exchange Rate Risk

Exchange rate risk is the risk that exchange rate changes can affect the value of an institution's assets and liabilities, as well as its off–balance-sheet items. Exchange rate risk can be direct (a financial institution takes or holds a position in foreign currency) or indirect (a foreign exchange position taken by one of the financial institution's borrowers or by counterparties may affect their creditworthiness). The most commonly used measure of foreign exchange exposure is an institution's net open foreign exchange position. Under the Basel methodology, a bank's net open position is calculated as the sum of the following items:[8] the net spot position (i.e., all asset items less all liability items, including accrued interest, which is denominated in the currency in question), the net forward-position, guarantees that are certain to be called and are likely to be irrecoverable, net future income or expenses not yet accrued but already fully hedged, any other item representing a profit or

D

loss in foreign currencies, and the net delta-based equivalent of the total book of foreign currency options. The resulting net open position in each currency can be stress tested against variations in the exchange rate of a particular currency (sensitivity analysis). For example, the change in net open position on account of a change in exchange rate can help determine the sensitivity of the position to exchange rate risk.

To illustrate the relation between the net open position and the direct exchange rate stress test, let F denote the net open position in foreign exchange, C be the capital, A_{RW} be the risk-weighted assets (all in domestic currency units), and e be the exchange rate in units of foreign currency per a unit of domestic currency. A depreciation (a decline) in the exchange rate leads to a proportional decline in the domestic currency value of the foreign exchange exposure, that is, $\Delta e/e = \Delta F/F$.[9] Assume, as is often done, that a decline in the value of the net open position translates directly into a decline in capital, that is, $\Delta C/\Delta F = 1$.[10] The effect of the exchange rate shock on the ratio of capital to risk-weighted assets would then be calculated as

$$\frac{\Delta[C(e)/A_{RW}(e)]}{\Delta e} \cong \frac{\dfrac{F}{e}A_{RW} - C\dfrac{\Delta A_{RW}}{\Delta C}\dfrac{F}{e}}{A_{RW}^2} \cong \frac{1}{e}\frac{F}{C}\frac{C}{A_{RW}}\left(1 - \frac{\Delta A_{RW}}{\Delta C}\frac{C}{A_{RW}}\right). \qquad (1)$$

where we used the fact that $\Delta C/\Delta e = \Delta F/\Delta e = F/e$. The operator Δ denotes change, and the symbol $\cong$ means that the equation holds only approximately for larger than infinitesimal changes. Equation 1 can be rewritten as

$$\Delta[C(e)/A_{RW}(e)] \cong \frac{\Delta e}{e}\frac{F}{C}\frac{C}{A_{RW}}\left(1 - \frac{\Delta A_{RW}}{\Delta C}\frac{C}{A_{RW}}\right), \qquad (2)$$

The straightforward relationship between the net open position and the direct exchange rate stress test holds only under certain assumptions. Equation 2 summarizes the relationship between the basic exchange rate stress test and the respective FSIs. The term $\Delta A_{RW}/\Delta C$ can have values from 0 to 1, reflecting the degree of co-movement of capital and the risk-weighted assets. In the special case of $\Delta A_{RW}/\Delta C = 0$, that is, if the risk-weighted assets do not change, then the change in the capital adequacy ratio (in percentage points) equals simply the exchange rate shock (in percent) times the exposure, which is measured as a product of the two core FSIs (F/C and C/A_{RW}). This relationship is sometimes used as a shorthand calculation of the direct exchange rate stress test. The calculation highlights the assumptions behind such approximations, in particular the assumption of no change in A_{RW}.[11] Also, equation 2 holds only as a linear approximation, which works well if foreign exchange portfolios are essentially linear, that is, the banking sector is not very active in options markets. If banks have large positions in foreign exchange options, the relation between the exchange rate change and the effect on capital can become highly nonlinear. In such cases, a stress test that is based on a more detailed decomposition of banks' positions in foreign exchange would be a clearly superior analytical tool.[12]

The net open position captures the direct foreign exchange risk. In practice, this risk tends to be rather small compared with other risks that banks face, given that the expo-

D

sure is relatively easy to measure and, therefore, to manage or regulate by setting limits. It is typically much more difficult to monitor foreign exchange vulnerabilities of banks' counterparties and, therefore, the aggregate risk banks would face through changes in credit risk resulting from changes in the exchange rate. The corporate sector's net foreign exchange exposure to equity is one of the encouraged indicators in the set endorsed by the Executive Board in June 2001. However, no FSAP mission so far has been able to provide this indicator, and only a few FSAP missions have been able to address the indirect foreign exchange risks in the stress-testing calculation. Several FSAP missions recommended improvements in the collection of data on foreign exchange exposures in the corporate sector.

It is important to incorporate the indirect exchange risk in the stability assessment. Although FSAP missions have not been able to collect comprehensive data on corporate sectors' foreign exchange exposure, several FSAP missions that analyzed the corporate sector in detail generally found that the banking sectors' indirect exchange rate risk was more important than its direct exchange rate risk. To illustrate the significance of the indirect risk in overall banking sector risk, denote the corporate sector's debt, equity, and open foreign exchange position as $D_C(e)$, $E_C(e)$, and $F_C(e)$, respectively.[13] Assume that, similar to the case of banks' net open position, a percentage change in the exchange rate will translate into the same percentage change in the domestic currency value of the net open position, which will, in turn, lead to an equivalent change in the corporate sector's equity, that is, $\Delta E_C/\Delta e = \Delta F_C/\Delta e = F/e$. The effect of the exchange rate on the corporate leverage (D_C/E_C) is then given by

$$\frac{\Delta[D_c(e)/E_c(e)]}{\Delta e} \cong \frac{\dfrac{\Delta D_c}{\Delta E_c}\dfrac{F_c}{e}E_c - D_c\dfrac{F_c}{e}}{E_c^2} \cong -\frac{1}{e}\frac{F_c}{E_c}\left(\frac{D_c}{E_c} - \frac{\Delta D_c}{\Delta E_c}\right). \tag{3}$$

Thus, if the corporate sector is short in foreign exchange, a depreciation (decline) in the exchange rate would lead to an increase in its leverage. Corporate leverage typically is positively correlated with the share of banks' nonperforming loans (NPL) in total loans (TL), denoted as NPL/TL, that is, $\Delta(\text{NPL/TL})/\Delta(D_C/E_C) = a > 0$.[14] The effect of a change in the exchange rate on the NPL/TL ratio can then be expressed as

$$\Delta(\text{NPL/TL}) \cong a\Delta[D_c(e)/E_c(e)] \cong -\frac{\Delta e}{e}\frac{F_c}{E_c}a\left(\frac{D_c}{E_c} - \frac{\Delta D_c}{\Delta E_c}\right). \tag{4}$$

In the special case when $\Delta D_C/\Delta E_C = 0$, the change in the NPL/TL ratio would equal the exchange rate change times the respective FSI (the net open position), times the parameter a, which can be estimated empirically, as shown in chapter 3. To find the effect on capital adequacy, we can assume—as done in several assessments—that the credit shock has the form of a transition of performing loans into the nonperforming category. By differentiating C/A_{RW} with respect to NPL/TL, and by substituting for NPL/TL from equation 4, we obtain

$$\Delta(C/A_{RW}) \cong \frac{\Delta e}{e} \frac{TL}{A_{RW}} \left(1 - \frac{C}{A_{RW}} \frac{\Delta A_{RW}}{\Delta C}\right) \pi \frac{F_c}{E_c} a\left(\frac{D_c}{E_c} - \frac{\Delta D_c}{\Delta E_c}\right), \qquad (5)$$

where we assume (as is commonly done) that provisions are expressed as a fixed percentage (π) of NPLs and that they are deducted directly from capital.

The incorporation of the indirect effect makes the analysis—and the relationship between the FSIs and the stress test calculations—more complex and dependent on additional assumptions or regression analysis. The presentation of the direct effect in equation 2 and the indirect effect in equation 5 may appear similar, given that in both cases, the change in the capital adequacy FSI is expressed as the shock times an FSI that characterizes the exposure (the net open position). However, the calculation of the indirect effect in equation 5 is perhaps the simplest possible expression for the indirect exchange rate effect using FSIs. It relies on additional assumptions and parameters that would need to be estimated or determined, such as the sensitivity parameter, reflecting the effect of the corporate sector on the banking sector, the provisioning rate, and the ratio of TLs to risk-weighted assets.

The complexity of the indirect exchange rate stress test is greater because it should include the effects on stocks as well as on flows. The calculation of the indirect effect shown in equation 5 would need to reflect the effect of exchange rate changes on the net present value of the corporate sector, which means taking into account changes in the net present value of future earnings. For example, in export-oriented companies, a depreciation could generally be expected to increase their future earnings. In terms of the net present value, the effect would be essentially equivalent to the effect of a long position in foreign currency. However, it may be more practical to calculate the effect on flows by estimating the elasticity of earnings to interest and principal expenses (an encouraged FSI) with respect to the exchange rate and then to estimate the relationship between this FSI and the NPL/TL ratio.

Alternatively, it would be useful to compile an indicator measuring the corporate sector's flow exposure, for example, a ratio of foreign exchange earnings to total earnings or (ideally) a ratio of earnings in foreign exchange to interest and principal expenses in foreign exchange. Subject to further developmental work and analysis, such an indicator could be included in the set of encouraged FSIs.

D.3.2 Interest Rate Risk

Duration is a key indicator for the measurement of the direct interest rate risk. The principal usefulness of duration stems from the fact that it approximates the elasticity of the market values of assets and liabilities to the respective rates of return,[15]

$$\frac{\Delta A(r_A)}{A(r_A)} \cong \frac{-D_A \Delta r_A}{(1 + r_A)}, \quad \frac{\Delta A(r_L)}{A(r_L)} \cong \frac{-D_L \Delta r_L}{(1 + r_L)}, \qquad (6)$$

where $A(r_A)$ and $L(r_L)$ are market values of assets and liabilities of a banking system, and where r_A and r_L are annual interest rates on assets and liabilities. This feature of duration can be used to summarize the effect of changes in interest rates on banks' capital. In particular, we can define capital as $A(r_A) - L(r_L)$, and can express it as a ratio to risk weighted assets.[16] Differentiating capital with respect to the interest rate on assets, and substituting from equation 6, the sensitivity of the C/A_{RW} ratio to interest rate changes can be expressed as

$$\frac{\Delta[C(r_A,r_L)/A_{RW}(r_A)]}{\Delta(r_A)} \cong -\frac{(L/A_{RW})}{1+r_A}\left(D_A - D_L\frac{1+r_A}{1+r_L}\frac{\Delta r_L}{\Delta r_A}\right)\frac{1-\dfrac{\Delta A_{RW}}{A_{RW}}\dfrac{C}{\Delta C}}{1-\dfrac{\Delta A}{A}\dfrac{C}{\Delta C}}. \qquad (7)$$

Assuming that the risk-weighted assets move proportionately to total assets, that is, $\Delta A_{RW}/A_{RW}=\Delta A/A$, equation 7 can be simplified to

$$\frac{\Delta[C(r_A,r_L)/A_{RW}(r_A)]}{\Delta(r_A)} \cong -\frac{(L/A_{RW})}{1+r_A}GAP_D, \qquad (8)$$

where GAP_D is the duration gap, defined as

$$GAP_D = D_A - D_L\frac{1+r_A}{1+r_L}\frac{\Delta r_L}{\Delta r_A}. \qquad (9)$$

The duration gap and the direct interest rate stress test are two analytical tools that can often be viewed as substitutes for each other. Equations 8 and 9 illustrate the relationship between the two duration FSIs and the capital adequacy FSI.[17] In particular, equation 8 characterizes the relationship between the "interest rate exposure FSI" and the corresponding stress test in a similar way as equation 2 for the exchange rate risk. The interest rate exposure FSI is the duration gap, which is a function of the two duration FSIs. In the special case when the interest rates for assets and liabilities move simultaneously, the duration gap can be approximated as a difference of the two durations: $D_A - D_L$. Similar to the exchange rate risk, the effect on capital adequacy can generally be expressed as a product of the shock and the "exposure FSI." In both cases, however, this shortcut formula is subject to simplifying assumptions, such as the one on the relationship between total and risk-weighted assets.

The duration gap is a reliable estimator of the effect of interest rate changes only for small shocks. Durations can change with changes in interest rates. Because stress tests typically involve large changes in interest rates, it is advisable to include second derivative terms to account for convexity. However, given the complexities involved in such calculations, FSAP stress tests so far have not been able to satisfactorily reflect possible changes in duration. In fact, most FSAP missions used much simpler approaches than

D

those based on duration.[18] A related issue is the calculation of a combined interest rate and exchange rate shock, when the combination of the aggregate duration and the aggregate net open position may give only an approximate indication of the overall effect. A currency breakdown of duration would help to identify maturity mismatches by currencies. Again, this analysis was typically not done in FSAP missions, mostly because of the lack of data.

The calculation of duration of total assets and total liabilities of a financial system can be a difficult computational task; however, alternative approaches are possible. In practice, alternative and less-costly approaches to measuring the interest rate risk are often used. Assets and liabilities can be lumped into groups that are based on common features, such as coupon rates (or comparable contractual rates), maturities, and credit risk. Within such cells, one can estimate the implied cash flow stream and the relevant market yields and can compute duration, which can then be aggregated across the cells.

A simplified measure of interest rate sensitivity that is often used in place of duration is based on the traditional "maturity gap analysis." Under this approach, expected payments on assets and liabilities are sorted into "buckets" according to the time to repricing or when payments are due (e.g., period until financial instruments are redeemed or the interest rates on them are reset or reindexed).[19] Similar to duration, the net difference (gap) in each time bucket can be multiplied by an assumed change in interest rates to gain an indication of the sensitivity of banks' income to changes in interest rates.

Maturity gap data are useful, but they are inferior to duration measures and could conceal actual risks in the system. Ahmed, Beatty, and Bettinghaus (1999), using empirical data on U.S. banks, 1991–99, found that maturity gaps reported by the banks were useful in assessing the loss potential of banks' interest rate risk positions, because there was a significant statistical relationship between the maturity gap and future changes in net interest income. However, it is possible that the maturities of financial assets and liabilities match, but the timing of the cash flows on assets and liabilities is not matched (i.e., their durations differ) and banks are, thereby, open to interest rate gains or losses. Bierwag (1987) showed practical examples of banks that have zero maturity gaps but that, in fact, have extremely risky positions (measured by duration).

Similar to the net open position in foreign exchange, duration gaps capture only the direct effect of an interest rate change on the bank. They do not reflect indirect effects, in particular the effect that an increase in lending interest rates is likely to have on the credit risk of banks' borrowers. This risk could be approximated by using the encouraged FSI of corporate earnings to interest and principal expenses. In practice, however, this indicator has so far been reported relatively infrequently, even though it has been used more frequently in the recent FSAP mission. Those FSAP missions that attempted to assess this type of risk typically estimated a regression model for the share of NPLs to TLs, with interest rates among the explanatory variables. The panel data estimate presented by IMF (2003) did not find a significant relationship between interest rates and the NPL/TL ratio, although this lack of relationship may reflect the limitation of the data set. However, for individual countries using time series data, the slope coefficient was often significantly negative.[20] Similar to the exchange rate risk, the integration of the direct and indirect interest rate risk is easier to implement with the help of stress tests.

D

In some stress-testing exercises, the values of a set of correlated risk factors (e.g., a set of prices, macrovariables, financial ratios, yield curve shifts) are simulated assuming a joint probability distribution of those factors, typically a joint normal distribution that is based on empirically determined parameters. The values drawn from the distribution—through Monte Carlo simulations—are used to stress the portfolio so that probability of specified extreme outcomes or the size of potential losses at specified probability level can be calculated.

D.3.3 Credit Risk

Credit risk is the risk that counterparties or obligors will default on their contractual obligations. It refers to the risk that the cash flows of an asset may not be paid in full, according to contractual agreements. Stress testing of credit risk typically begins with the collection of data on different credit qualities, usually the categories of performing loans and NPLs (e.g., substandard, doubtful, and loss) tracked by the supervisor.

Alternatively, if banks are providing their own data and estimates that are based on their internal models, then the different credit quality measures that they employ can be used. A variety of stress tests can be applied to those data, depending on the underlying quality of banking supervision. For example, if underprovisioning is an issue, a scenario that applies more stringent provisioning criteria to existing balance sheets can be performed.

For other countries, assumptions about the growth rate of different qualities of credit can be applied, or assumptions about the migration between categories can be made. Those scenarios can be based on previous recessions or episodes of rising defaults and increases in NPLs. Cross-sectional regressions of NPL ratios on various macroeconomic variables (e.g., interest rates, growth rates, exchange rates) can provide benchmark sensitivities of NPLs to different macroeconomic shocks. Once a set of adjusted data on credit quality is derived, existing provisioning rates can be applied to determine the effect on bank balance sheets.

An example of implementation of the credit risk stress test is given in the following paragraphs, which are based on a recent FSAP. The methodology proposed in Boss (2002) was used to link default frequencies and macroeconomic conditions. This model is particularly suited for macroeconomic stress testing because it explicitly models credit risk in relation to macroeconomic variables. Some models include a Monte Carlo simulation approach to calculate the loss distribution of a credit portfolio.[21] However, more frequently, including the case discussed here, a simpler regression approach was used to link historically observed default frequencies to macroeconomic variables.

The expected loss at time t, $E[L_t]$, is given by the volume of the credit portfolio at time t, V_t, times the average default probability in the economy at time t, p_t, times 1 minus the recovery rate, RR, which is typically assumed to be a fixed number.

$$E[L_t] = V_t p_t (1 - \mathrm{RR}) \tag{10}$$

The average default probability at time t is modeled as a logistic function of a macroeconomic index, which depends on the current values of the macroeconomic variables under observation:

$$p_t = \frac{1}{1 + e^{-y_t}}, \qquad (11)$$

where y_t denotes the macroeconomic index at time t. The p_t can be estimated directly (substituting y_t by a linear combination of macroeconomic variables and then using logistic regression in order to get estimated average default probabilities $\hat{p}_t$). Or it is possible to calculate first the "observed" values for the macroeconomic index y_t by taking the inverse of the logistic function using the historically observed default frequencies

$$y_t = -\ln\left(\frac{1}{p_t} - 1\right), \qquad (12)$$

and then use linear regression to explain the index y_t by a combination of macroeconomic variables. If one is to get estimated average default probabilities $\hat{p}_t$, the output of the macroeconomic model explaining yt has to be plugged into the logistic function of default probabilities. In the particular FSAP case, the following regression was estimated:

$$\Delta^l y_t = \ln\left(\frac{y_t}{y_{t-1}}\right) = \beta_0 + \beta_1 x_{1,t} + \beta_2 x_{2,t} + \dots + \beta_K x_{K,t} + \varepsilon_t \text{ with } \varepsilon_{s,t} \sim N(0, \sigma_\varepsilon), \qquad (13)$$

where

$$\Delta^l y_t = \ln\left(\frac{y_t}{y_{t-1}}\right)$$

is the logarithmic change or growth of the macroeconomic index, calculated according to the respective equation above and $x_{1,t}, x_{2,t}, \dots x_{K,t}$ denote the set of macroeconomic variables at time t and $\beta_0, \beta_1, \beta_2, \dots \beta_K$ stand for the parameters that determine the direction and extent of the effect that those factors have on the index or, eventually, the sector-specific default probability. The parameters are estimated by means of a linear regression, where the error term ε_t is assumed to be an independent, normally distributed random variable.

D

D.3.4 Other Risks

Stress tests can be performed on other risks, including liquidity risk, commodity risk, or equity price risk. Asset liquidity risk refers to the inability to conduct a transaction at current market prices because of the size of the transaction. Funding liquidity risk refers to the inability to access sufficient funds to meet payment obligations in a timely manner. Liquidity risk can be assessed by imposing a "haircut" on the liquid assets of an institution and by examining the effect on the liquid assets ratio (for asset liquidity risk). A conservative scenario would be to assume that only the cash held by banks (in domestic and foreign currency), as well as the reserve requirements, were always liquid.

The next step would be to add to the category of liquid assets those deposits that banks hold abroad. Deposits with local banks can become illiquid if the country is confronted with a systemic liquidity crisis. Similarly, domestic government or corporate bonds can rapidly become illiquid when enough banks are trying to sell the assets all at once. Conversely, to the extent that the liquidity crisis does not affect the main financial centers, banks could dispose of their foreign bonds to meet liquidity outflows at home. For funding liquidity risk, a stress test can be constructed on the basis of assumptions about the ability of an institution to continue attracting sources of funds. For example, the rate of withdrawal of deposits or other funding sources can be increased, or assumptions can be made about the withdrawal of credit lines and other funding sources to determine the effect on some measure of liquidity for the institution.

Commodity risk refers to the potential losses that may result from changes in the market price of bank assets and liabilities, as well as off–balance-sheet instruments caused by commodity price changes. Even if financial institutions do not take positions in commodities or commodity-linked instruments directly, they may be subject to commodity price risk indirectly through the effect on their loan portfolio. This risk occurs if their borrowers' ability to repay their debts is affected by shocks to commodity prices. This indirect source of commodity risk can be particularly important for many banks in developing countries that lend to exporters or to importers of commodities.

Commodity risk can be assessed by examining the effect of a fall in the value of the commodity (e.g., oil or copper) on the balance sheets of financial institutions. This assessment can be either through their direct holdings of the commodity or indirectly through an analysis of the effect on key customers. One can calculate the financial institution's net position in the most-relevant commodities by netting long and short positions, which are expressed in terms of the standard unit of measurement, in the same commodity. The net position can then be converted into the national currency at current spot rates for the commodity. Commodity derivatives should be converted into notional commodities positions and can be included in the framework in the same way. Assuming a price fall of 20 percent, for example, and estimating the dollar value of this shock show the sensitivity of the portfolio to this commodity.

Equity price risk is the risk that stock price changes affect the value of an institution's assets and liabilities and its off–balance-sheet items. Equity price risk consists of two components: specific equity price risk and general equity price risk. Specific equity price risk refers to the risk associated with movements in the price of an individual stock. General equity price risk is the risk associated with movements of the stock market as a whole. Similar to commodity price risk, the starting point for measuring sensitivity to equity price risk is to calculate the net open position, including on– and off–balance-sheet positions in each equity security, including equity derivatives, converted into notional equity positions (options are delta weighted).

If one is to stress test for specific market risk—that is, equity risk related to the individual issuer—the stress test would have to be applied to the net open position in the equity concerned. Such a stress test would primarily be relevant when the institution is known to hold a highly concentrated trading portfolio of equities. More commonly, stress tests are conducted for general market risk, that is, the risk related to a major change in the overall stock market, usually a market crash scenario. For this purpose, the net open positions of an institution in all equities would be aggregated, and the stress scenario would be applied to the institution's aggregate position.

D

Financial institutions that include equity risk factors in their internal models should conduct comprehensive stress tests using their own measurement techniques and should provide the results to regulators. For those institutions, the net open positions in each equity should still be available, before aggregation into the overall position, and the model should be able to stress test each equity separately. Internal models can also be used to implement scenario analysis, thus taking account of correlations among stock prices, or indices, although those correlations may break down during crises.

Equity exposures in the trading book may be subject to frequent and substantial swings, along with stock market developments. The results of stress tests can, therefore, be outdated fairly quickly. Whereas supervisory reports or published annual reports of financial institutions can give a reasonable "snapshot," it is preferable to obtain more current data on the composition of an institution's equity portfolio from the financial institution itself. Where such up-to-date data are unavailable, knowledge about the most frequently traded equities, as well as the stock exchange dealing and underwriting activities of the institution, can sometimes help in updating open position estimates.

D.3.5 Second Round Effects

Stress tests can be improved by including second-round effects. In particular, most stress tests assume no realignments of portfolios in response to risk factors. Stress tests are typically applied to balance sheets at a point in time or in conjunction with a forecast over a specific horizon, and the effect is calculated as if the shock were "marked-to-market" or were valued at market prices. This approach is valid if the time horizon is short or if changes in the portfolios take time to implement. For example, assuming only a limited behavioral response in a large loan portfolio over a 1-month horizon may be a reasonable assumption, because it is often difficult to restructure a portfolio in a short time without incurring losses from "fire-sale" prices.[22]

Such an assumption may also be justifiable for an individual institution that does not have a large effect on the financial system or the macroeconomy, that is, the feedback effects are relatively small. However, once the time horizon of a scenario or shock extends beyond a year or more, the assumption of no behavioral response becomes harder to justify. Similarly, for systemically important institutions or systems as a whole, the assumption of no feedback effects may be an oversimplification. The policy environment may also change over a longer horizon as monetary or supervisory authorities react to shocks.

One approach that is often used to consider second-round effects and linkages between institutions is the use of contagion models.[23] Those models attempt to estimate the effect of the failure of key institutions on other institutions and, hence, the overall financial system. The models have so far been used mostly for the analysis of risks arising from the interbank market, even though the same concept can be used for contagion analysis more broadly. The following example shows an analysis of interbank contagion.

There are two general types of interbank contagion stress tests: (a) pure interbank stress test, in which the shock is the failure of one bank, triggered, for example, by fraud, and the effect on other banks in the system is through the interbank exposures; and (b) integrated interbank stress test, in which the banking system is first subjected to macroeconomic shocks or scenarios. If those shocks or scenarios trigger a failure of a bank or

D

Table D.1. Matrix of Bank-to-Bank Exposures

	Bank 1	Bank 2	...	Bank $n-1$	Bank n
Bank 1	-- --	$E_{1,2}$	...	$E_{1,n-1}$	$E_{1,n}$
Bank 2					
.	.	.	-- --	.	.
Bank $n-1$	$E_{n,1}$	$E_{n-1,2}$	...	-- --	-- --
Bank n	E_n	$E_{n,2}$	...	$E_{n,n-1}$	-- --

Note: The diagonal elements of this $n \times n$ matrix marked "-- --" are zero; the off diagonal element E_{ij} indicates net uncollateralized lending from bank i to j.

a group of banks, the interbank stress test is run to assess the effect of additional failures through interbank exposures. The basic methodology of the two approaches is the same; the difference is that the integrated stress test is run through a system that is already weakened by an external shock.

The key input to the interbank contagion stress tests is a matrix of bilateral exposures (see table D.1). In this matrix, the cell in the ith row and jth column contains the net uncollateralized lending from bank i to bank j, E_{ij}, defined as a difference between all loans and similar exposures (including off–balance-sheet exposures) from bank i to bank j, minus all loans and similar exposures from bank j to bank i. Note that $E_{ij} = -E_{ji}$.

The "pure" interbank contagion stress test aims to estimate the effect of the failure of a bank or group of banks on the system. The test assumes that there is a failure in a bank (say, Bank 1), for instance, caused by a fraud. The first round of the contagion calculation would derive the direct effect of Bank 1's failure on each of the other banks, assuming Bank 1 would not repay its uncollateralized interbank exposures (or a part of the exposures). If some banks fail as a result of Bank 1's failure,[24] the second round of the calculation would derive the effect on each of the remaining banks of those newly failed banks' not repaying their uncollateralized interbank exposures. The process can be repeated for a third time if there are new failures after the second run, and so on. Concrete examples of such interbank contagion tests and their results can be found in Furfine (1999) for U.S. banks; in Wells (2002) for United Kingdom banks; in Blåvarg and Nimander (2002) for Swedish banks; and in Elsinger, Lehar, and Summer (2002) for Austrian banks. In the case of the United Kingdom, Sweden, and Austria, the tests presented in the articles are very similar to those carried out under the FSAP.

The results of the contagion calculations can be presented in a number of ways. Figure D.1 provides an example of such a presentation in a case of a system with four banks. For an interesting example of presenting the network structure of the interbank market with a large number of banks, see Boss et al. (2004). Two indicators of systemic risk can be calculated from the output of the pure interbank stress test: (a) a frequency of bank failure indicator, which is the ratio of the cumulative number of failures to the number of banks in the system, and (b) statistical measures of the effect on bank system capital (e.g., mean, distribution, and quartiles). Specifically, one can define a "systemic risk index," which is the average reduction in capital ratios of banks in the system triggered by a failure of a

D

Figure D.1. Example of Contagion Effects of a Counterparty Failure

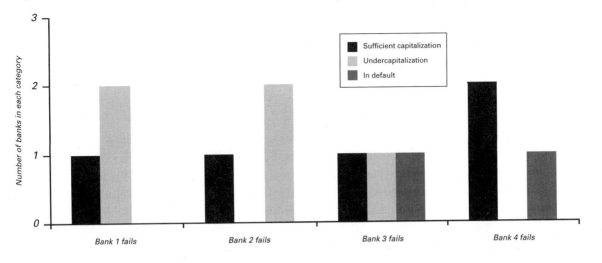

bank. Such a measure could be computed for all banks in the system and used to rank them by their systemic importance.

D.3.6 Stress Testing of Insurance Companies

Stress testing of insurance company balance sheets and income statements is not as well developed in financial stability analysis as in stress testing of banks. Insurance companies are generally considered to represent a lower level of systemic risk than banks, mainly because of the different character of their liabilities, which often have a longer duration than banks. However, distress in the insurance sector can have important systemic implications, including through ownership relations with the banking sector and its effect on confidence in the financial sector as a whole.

Because insurance companies have a different balance-sheet structure compared to banks, stress tests of their balance sheets present unique challenges. Insurance companies face underwriting risk, catastrophe risk, and risks on technical claims provisions. On the asset side, more or less similar to banks, they also face market risk, credit risk, liquidity risk, operational risk, group risk, and systemic risk in differing degrees to those faced by banks and other financial institutions. Thus, the stress testing of the risks could be based on methods similar to those used for banks. However, on the liability side, different types of shocks and methods of analysis would be needed. For an example, increase in mortality rates or probabilities of certain catastrophic events would increase claims, and those factors would have to be modeled.

The complexity of the contracts underlying insurance company balance sheets can create difficulties in revaluing liabilities and may require detailed data on a contract-by-contract basis to enable an accurate assessment of the effect of changes in risk factors. Stochastic techniques are sometimes used by insurers to assess their resilience to shock. Such techniques are complex and account for the probability of a range of possible outcomes. Alternatively, simple deterministic tests (for example, shifts in loss ratios or in

D

gauging the effect of specified catastrophic events), can reveal useful information about immunity to shocks. In some jurisdictions, insurance firms are required to report regularly on standardized stress test results to their supervisors. Recent FSAPs have begun to apply stress test scenarios affecting the liability side developments, in addition to the focus on asset values.

D.4 Summary of FSAP Experience[25]

Stress tests have been performed for every country participating in the FSAP. The tests are designed to provide a quantitative measure of the vulnerability of the financial system to different shocks and to complement the insights gathered from other components of the assessment. This analysis includes elements of the legal, institutional, regulatory, and supervisory framework; observance of key financial sector standards and codes; analysis of the financial system structure and key vulnerabilities; and empirical analysis of financial soundness indicators.

Data availability is a key factor in determining the approach and sophistication of stress tests performed as part of the FSAP. Most analyses are performed on a bank-by-bank (bottom-up) basis, which is based on single factor and scenario approaches. Contagion risks and second-round effects have typically not been addressed in many FSAPs, although some have incorporated elements of interbank contagion into the exercise. The involvement of the authorities has varied according to their expertise and ability or willingness to provide data, with some country authorities precluded from providing data on individual institutions by bank secrecy laws or conventions. For countries that have published the summary assessment of the FSAP mission, most have included a summary of the stress-testing results.[26]

The overall approach and implementation of stress tests as part of the FSAP has evolved over time. Some recent trends include the following:

- As familiarity and use of the techniques have spread, country authorities and individual financial institutions now play a greater role in the design and implementation of stress tests. Increased reliance is being placed on using the internal models of banks to evaluate the effect of shocks, including their off–balance-sheet exposures.
- The use of macrosimulation models to calibrate a macroscenario has increased, and several recent FSAPs have included interbank contagion calculations.
- Coverage of nonbank financial institutions has increased, with many insurance companies now being included in many cases as part of the analysis.
- Many country authorities are now implementing their own stress-testings programs as part of their macroprudential surveillance, partly as a result of FSAP-related work.

D

Notes

1. This section draws substantially on Jones, Hilbers, and Slack (2004). Useful overviews and surveys of the relevant literature are also contained in Blaschke et al. (2001), Čihák (2004a), and Sorge (2004).

2. System-focused stress tests can also take the form of sensitivity tests, in which only a single risk factor is shocked. In this paper, we focused on scenarios, but sensitivity tests can be considered in the same framework as a one-dimensional scenario.

3. For an interesting example of the use of macroeconomic modeling to assess the potential effect of specific vulnerabilities, see Gereben, Woolford, and Black (2003) for a scenario analysis for New Zealand.

4. See Hoggarth and Whitley (2003) for further details, and a discussion of how the approach was used for the U.K. FSAP.

5. Many large banks have value at risk frameworks in place for internal monitoring of risk positions [see Jorion (2001) for a survey of Value at Risk methods]. For an international review of stress testing practices in large banks, see Committee on the Global Financial System (2000). Banks that follow the Basel Committee's internal ratings–based approach are required by their supervisors to have a comprehensive stress-testing program in place (Basel Committee on Banking Supervision 2003). With the implementation of Basel II, stress tests are set to become more commonplace in banks.

6. See section D.3 for a discussion of stress testing of insurance companies.

7. In some cases, it may be useful to calibrate the size of shocks to cause one or more of the institutions involved to breach their minimum capital requirement so they can determine the magnitude of shocks necessary to cause such a "failure." However, as the size of the shocks increases, the accuracy of most estimation methods decreases, thereby increasing the potential margin of error.

8. For more details, see Basel Committee on Banking Supervision (1998).

9. This relation is valid if the net open position is long or short, that is, $F \neq 0$.

10. More realistically, we could deduct the effect of the shock first from profits and only then from capital. However, it would make the notation more complex without providing many additional insights.

11. Empirically, $\Delta A_{RW}/\Delta C$ could be estimated by a regression. In practice, FSAP stress tests have usually been based on simplifying assumptions, such as $\Delta A_{RW}/\Delta C = 1$ or 0.

12. So far, however, most stress tests in FSAP missions have not incorporated such non-linear effects. The *Compilation Guide on Financial Soundness Indicators* (IMF 2004) encourages the identification of the component elements of the net open position, including options in bought and sold positions.

13. Given the practical difficulties involved in obtaining empirical data on open positions in the household sector, for simplicity we refer here only to the corporate sector, even though the theoretical analysis would be essentially the same even if we included the household sector.

14. Chapter 3 shows that for a panel of 47 countries, a 10-percentage point rise in the corporate leverage was associated with a 1.1-percentage point rise in NPL/TL after a 1 year lag.

D

15. Duration is defined as the weighted average term-to-maturity of an asset's (liability's) cash flow, the weights being the present value of each future cash flow as a percentage of the asset's (liability's) full price. See the *Compilation Guide on FSIs* (IMF 2004, paragraph 3.52) for a formula that could be used to calculate duration.

16. The effects can also be expressed in terms of banks' profitability, which may be useful when branches of foreign banks, which typically do not have own capital, play an important role in the local economy. Bierwag (1987) derived the effect on profits in the case of a single bank.

17. The actual FSI may be somewhat different, because it refers to regulatory capital rather than the difference of market values of assets and liabilities.

18. Only about 20 percent of FSAPs conducted a duration-based stress test (see IMF and World Bank 2003). The rest typically used simplified methods such as maturity gaps or earnings at risk.

19. The *Compilation Guide on Financial Soundness Indicators* (IMF 2004) includes a table showing how such simplified measure can be calculated. An even simpler approach would be based on the average maturity of assets and liabilities.

20. For instance, in the case of Hong Kong SAR, it has been estimated that an increase in nominal interest rates by 1 percentage point leads to a rise in the classified loan ratio by 0.2 percentage points with a lag of two quarters (Shu 2002).

21. Barnhill, Papanagiotou, and Schumacher (2000) provide an example of such simulations for South African banks.

22. Although the increasingly widespread use of derivatives may permit a more rapid adjustment in exposures.

23. See Čihák (2004a,b) for further details. Upper and Worms (2002), Furfine (1999), Degryse and Nguyen (2004), and Gropp and Vesala (2004) also examine interbank contagion.

24. The simplest way to implement this is to assume that a bank fails if its capital becomes negative as a result of the shock. A more complex calculation could be based on a mapping from capital adequacy to the probability of failure, if such mapping could be estimated based on past data.

25. This section is based on International Monetary Fund and World Bank (2003) and International Monetary Fund and World Bank (2005).

26. See http://www.imf.org/external/np/fsap/fsap.asp#cp for copies of published reports.

References

Ahmed, Anwer S., Anne Beatty, and Bruce Bettinghaus. 1999. "Evidence on the Efficacy of Market Risk Disclosures by Commercial Banks." Mimeo, Syracuse University, NY.

Andreeva, Olga. 2004. "Aggregate Bankruptcy Probabilities and Their Role in Explaining Banks' Loan Losses." Norges Bank Working Paper ANO 2004/2, Norges Bank, Oslo, Norway. Available at http://www.norges-bank.no/publikasjoner/arbeidsnotater/pdf/arb-2004-02.pdf.

Arpa, Markus, Irene Giulini, Andreas Ittner, and Franz Pauer. 2000. "The Influence of Macroeconomic Developments on Austrian Banks: Implications for Banking

Supervision." BIS Papers, No. 1, Bank for International Settlements, Basel, Switzerland. Available at http://www.bis.org/publ/bispap01c.pdf.

Barnhill, Theodore M., Panagiotis Papanagiotou, and Liliana Schumacher. 2000. "Measuring Integrated Market and Credit Risks in Banking Portfolios: An Application to a Set of Hypothetical Banks Operating in South Africa." IMF Working Paper, WP/00/212, International Monetary Fund, Washington, DC. Available at http://www.imf.org/external/pubs/ft/wp/2000/wp00212.pdf.

Basel Committee on Banking Supervision. 1998. "Amendment to the Capital Accord to Incorporate Market Risks" (January 1996, updated in April 1998). Bank for International Settlement, Basel, Switzerland. Available at http://www.bis.org/publ/bcbsc222.pdf.

———. 2003. "The New Basel Capital Accord, Consultative Document." Bank for International Settlements, Basel, Switzerland. Available at http://www.bis.org/bcbs/cp3full.pdf.

Benito, Andrew, John Whitley, and Garry Young. 2001. "Analysing Corporate and Household Sector Balance Sheets." *Financial Stability Review 11*: 160–74. Available at http://www.bankofengland.co.uk/publications/fsr/2001/fsr11art5.pdf.

Bierwag, Gerald O. 1987. *Duration Analysis*. Cambridge, MA: Harper & Row.

Blaschke, Winfrid, Matthew T. Jones, Giovanni Majnoni, and Soledad Martínez Peria. 2001. "Stress Testing of Financial Systems: An Overview of Issues, Methodologies, and FSAP Experiences." IMF Working Paper, WP/01/88, International Monetary Fund, Washington, DC. Available at http://www.imf.org/external/pubs/ft/wp/2001/wp0188.pdf.

Blåvarg, M. and P. Nimander. 2002. "Inter-bank exposures and systemic risk." *Sveriges Riksbank Economic Review* 2. Stockholm: Sveriges Riksbank.

Boss, Michael. 2002. "A Macroeconomic Credit Risk Model for Stress Testing the Austrian Credit Portfolio." *Financial Stability Report 4*, 64–82. Vienna, Austria: Austrian National Bank.

Boss, Michael, Helmut Elsinger, Martin Summer, and Stefan Thurner. 2004. "An Empirical Analysis of the Network Structure of the Austrian Interbank Market." *Financial Stability Report 7*, 77–87. Vienna, Austria: Austrian National Bank.

Čihák, Martin. 2004a. "Stress Testing: A Review of Key Concepts, Research, and Policy Note." No. 2/2004, Czech National Bank, Prague, Czech Republic. Available at http://www.cnb.cz/en/pdf/IRPN_2_2004.pdf.

———. 2004b. "Designing Stress Tests for the Czech Banking System, Research and Policy Note." No. 3/2004, Czech National Bank, Prague, Czech Republic. Available at http://www.cnb.cz/en/pdf/IRPN_3_2004.pdf.

Committee on the Global Financial System. 2000. *Stress Testing by Large Financial Institutions: Current Practice and Aggregation Issues*. Basel, Switzerland: Bank for International Settlements. Available at http://www.bis.org/publ/cgfs14.htm.

Degryse, Hans, and Grégory Nguyen. 2004. "Interbank Exposures: An Empirical Examination of Systemic Risk in the Belgian Banking System." Paper presented at the Financial Intermediation Research Society Conference on Banking, Insurance, and Intermediation, Capri, Italy, May 13–15. Available at http://finance.wharton.upenn.edu/~allenf/capri/papers/082degryse.pdf.

D

Elsinger, Helmut, Alfred Lehar, and Martin Summer. 2002. "Risk Assessment for Banking Systems." Working Paper No. 79, Austrian National Bank, Vienna, Austria. Available at http://www2.oenb.at/workpaper/wp79.pdf.

Frøyland, Espen, and Kai Larsen. 2002. "How Vulnerable Are Financial Institutions to Macroeconomic Changes? An Analysis Based on Stress Testing." *Norges Bank Economic Bulletin* LXXIII (3). Norges Bank, Oslo, Norway. Available at http://www.norges-bank.no/english/publications/economic_bulletin/2002-03/froyland.pdf.

Furfine, Craig H. 1999. "Interbank Exposures: Quantifying the Risk of Contagion." BIS Working Papers, No. 70, Bank for International Settlements, Basel, Switzerland. Available at http://www.bis.org/publ/work70.pdf.

Gereben, Aron, Ian Woolford, and Melleny Black. 2003. "The Macroeconomic Impacts of a Foot-and-Mouth Disease Outbreak: an Information Paper for Department of the Prime Minister and Cabinet." Information Paper, Reserve Bank of New Zealand, Wellington, New Zealand. Available at http://www.rbnz.govt.nz/research/0130346_2.pdf.

Gropp, Reint, and Jukka Vesala. 2004. "Bank Contagion in Europe." Paper presented at the Financial Intermediation Research Society Conference on Banking, Insurance and Intermediation, Capri, Italy, May 13–15, 2004. Available at http://finance.wharton.upenn.edu/~allenf/capri/papers/159gropp.doc.

Hoggarth, Glenn, and John Whitley. 2003. "Assessing the Strength of UK Banks through Macroeconomic Stress Tests." *Financial Stability Review 14*: 91–103. Available at http://www.bankofengland.co.uk/publications/fsr/2003/fsr14art3.pdf.

International Monetary Fund (IMF). 2003a. "Financial Soundness Indicators—Background Paper." Paper prepared by the Staff of the Monetary and Financial Systems and Statistics Departments, International Monetary Fund, Washington, DC. Available at http://www.imf.org/external/np/sta/fsi/eng/2003/051403bp.pdf.

———. 2004. *Compilation Guide on Financial Soundness Indicators*. Washington, DC: International Monetary Fund. Available at http://www.imf.org/external/np/sta/fsi/eng/2004/guide.

International Monetary Fund (IMF) and World Bank. 2003. "Analytical Tools of the FSAP." Background paper prepared for March 14, 2003, IMF Executive Board meeting, International Monetary Fund, Washington, DC. Available at http://www.imf.org/external/np/fsap/2003/022403a.htm.

———. 2005. "Financial Sector Assessment Program—Background Paper." Background paper prepared for March 2005 Bank and Fund Executive Board Meetings, International Monetary Fund, Washington, DC. Available at http://www.imf.org/external/np/fsap/2005/022205a.pdf.

Jones, Matthew, Paul Hilbers, and Graham Slack. 2004. "Stress Testing Financial Systems: What to Do When the Governor Calls." Working Paper 04/127, International Monetary Fund, Washington, DC.

Jorion, Philippe. 2001. *Value at Risk: The New Benchmark for Managing Market Risk*. 2nd ed. New York: McGraw Hill.

Kalirai, Harvir, and Martin Scheicher. 2002. "Macroeconomic Stress Testing: Preliminary Evidence for Austria," In *Financial Stability Report 3*, Vienna, Austria, Austrian National Bank. Available at http://www2.oenb.at/english/download/pdf/fsr_3e.pdf.

D

Pesola, Jarmo. 2001. "The Role of Macroeconomic Shocks in Banking Crises." Bank of Finland Discussion Paper 6-2001, Bank of Finland, Helsinki, Finland. Available at http://www.bof.fi/eng/6_julkaisut/6.1_SPn_julkaisut/6.1.5_keskustelualoitteita/0106jp.pdf.

Shu, Chang. 2002. "The Impact of Macroeconomic Environment on the Asset Quality of Hong Kong's Banking Sector," Hong Kong Monetary Authority Research Memorandum No. 20/2002, December 2002. Available at http://www.info.gov.hk/hkma/eng/research/RM20-2002.pdf.

Sorge, Marco. 2004. "Stress-Testing Financial Systems: An Overview of Current Methodologies." BIS Working Paper No. 165, Bank for International Settlements, Basel, Switzerland.

Upper, Christian, and Andreas Worms. 2002. "Estimating Bilateral Exposures in the German Interbank Market: Is There a Danger of Contagion?" Discussion Paper 09/02, Economic Research Centre of the Deutsche Bundesbank, Frankfurt, Germany. Available at http://www.deutschebundesbank.de/vo/download/dkp/2002/09/200209dkp.pdf.

D

Appendix E

Benchmarking and Decomposing Interest Rate Spreads and Margins

The analysis of interest spreads and margins can assist assessors in benchmarking a country's banking system and in identifying and quantifying major deficiencies and impediments to depth, breadth, and efficiency of financial intermediation. As an illustration of how spreads and margins may be analyzed, even in an environment with limited data, this appendix uses Kenya to describe how interest spreads may be decomposed into contributory factors and how interest margins may be benchmarked against international comparators.

Although Kenya has high interest rate spreads and margins that are similar to other countries in the region, it has substantially higher spreads and margins than OECD countries (see table E.1). The term *spread* is used to mean the difference between lending and deposit rates, whereas *net interest margin* refers to the net interest actually received and expressed as a percentage of interest-bearing assets.

The most comprehensive international source for interest rates, and the one from which the data in table E.1 are drawn, is International Financial Statistics, which generally publishes just one representative deposit rate and one loan rate. For any given bank, the spread conceals a wide variation in both deposits and lending rates charged by any given bank, depending on the marginal operating costs (and the provision for likely loan loss) and its market power vis-à-vis the customer. The marginal loan will be priced to ensure that the bank's capital at risk is sufficiently remunerated, given the marginal cost of mobilized funds, including any taxes or reserve requirements that apply to the loan or to the mobilized funds. For a country's banking system as a whole, the use of a single representative rate blurs much of the detail. Nevertheless, it helps throw some light on the relative magnitude of different contributors to the cost.

E

For Kenya, data on the average interest rate spread were calculated from individual bank returns and were averaged over different classes of banks as shown in table E.2.[1] Then again for each bank, administrative costs and the additions to loan loss provisions were expressed as a percentage of loans. Finally, the opportunity cost of reserve requirements was calculated.[2] With before-tax profits as a residual (and a profits tax rate of 30 percent), the decomposition of table E.2.was arrived at. It points to overhead costs and the profit margin as the most important component of the interest rate spread in Kenya.

State-owned banks have the highest spread, followed by foreign-owned banks and privately owned Kenyan banks. High operating costs may suggest inefficiency or may imply the use of more costly staff personnel and systems. Despite their higher operating costs, the foreign banks, benefiting from reputational advantages that allow them to mobilize deposits at lower interest rates, enjoy higher profit margins and, therefore, higher spreads. Overhead costs and loan loss provisions constitute two-thirds of government-owned banks' spread, whereas overhead costs and the profit margin constitute two-thirds of the spread of privately owned banks. Although the profit margin seems relatively high, note that this is the profit on lending only, the most risky line of business for banks. The overall

Table E.1. Interest Rates, Spreads, and Margins in International Comparison

	Real lending rate	Real deposit rate	Interest spread	Interest margin
Kenya	16.5	3.5	13.0	9.2
Sub-Saharan Africa (total)	9.9	−1.5	11.5	8.1
Uganda	19.4	5.9	13.5	12.7
Tanzania	12.0	−1.2	13.1	7.5
Other low-income countries	10.8	−1.6	12.4	7.8
OECD countries	4.6	0.5	4.1	3.6

Source: The net interest margin is calculated as the actual net interest revenue relative to total earning assets. Data are from the World Bank Financial Structure Database based on raw data from Bankscope for 2001.

Note: OECD = Organisation for Economic Co-operation and Development; CPI = Consumer Price Index . Real lending (deposit) interest rates are the difference between average lending (deposit) interest rates for 2002 and the log of CPI inflation for 2002. The interest spread is the difference between deposit and lending rates quoted in International Financial Statistics.

Table E.2. Kenya: Decomposition of Interest Spreads

	All banks	State-owned banks	Domestic private	Foreign banks
Overhead cost	5.6	4.4	5.3	6.6
Loan loss provisions	2.5	4.9	1.5	1.8
Reserve requirements	0.3	0.3	0.4	0.2
Profit tax (30 percent)	1.9	2.2	1.6	2.1
After tax profit margin	4.5	5.2	3.7	4.9
Total spread	14.9	16.9	12.5	15.5
Return on assets (after tax)	1.4	−0.4	1.0	3.0

Source: Beck and Fuchs (2004), who used bank-by-bank data from the Central Bank of Kenya as explained in the text.

Note: All data are for 2002.

E

Table E.3. Bank Productivity in International Comparison

	Net interest/ employee	Assets/employee	Loans/employee	Deposits/ employee
Kenya	36	581	295	458
Other Sub-Saharan Africa	49	1,073	505	742
Emerging markets	60	2,040	911	1,620

Source: Authors' calculations using data from Bankscope.

Note: All data are from 2002 and in thousands of U.S. dollars.

Table E.4. Bank Productivity Across Different Kenyan Bank Groups

	Net interest/ employee	Assets/employee	Loans/employee	Deposits/ employee
State-owned banks	23	303	187	222
Private domestic banks	31	577	317	447
Foreign banks	50	770	349	625

Source: Authors' calculations using data from Central Bank of Kenya.

Note: All data are from 2002 and in thousands of U.S. dollars.

profitability for banks is significantly lower, as indicated by the return on assets, which is of a level comparable to other banking markets.

An analysis of the overhead costs shows that they are driven by wage costs, which constitute 50 percent of total overhead costs. Other factors relating to the costs of financial service provision in the local market include fraud, security costs, the inefficient payment system, and a heavy regulatory burden, as illustrated by the high reporting requirements, the annual re-licensing process, and the licensing procedures for the opening and closing of branches. Compared with banks in other sub-Saharan African countries and other emerging countries, Kenyan banks appear to be overstaffed, and their employees appear to be less productive (see table E.3). Kenyan banks have more than three times as many employees for a given amount of assets, loans, and deposits than other banks in emerging countries, and the average Kenyan bank employee earns only half of the net interest revenue as the average employee in emerging markets.

However, there are large differences in productivity across different ownership groups of Kenyan banks (see table E.4). Employees in state-owned banks earn only half of the net interest revenue of employees in foreign-owned banks. State-owned banks have twice as many employees relative to their assets, loans, and deposits as foreign-owned banks. The higher productivity of foreign-owned banks compensates for the higher wage costs of those banks when compared with domestic banks. Private domestic banks are less productive and more overstaffed than foreign-owned banks but are more productive and less overstaffed than state-owned banks. This disparity across ownership groups indicates significant potential gains from increased competition and the resulting productivity improvements.

E

Table E.5. Net Interest Margins and Overhead Costs in International Comparison

	Interest margin	Overhead cost
Kenya	7.0	5.9
Worldwide average	3.6	3.0
Difference	3.4	2.9
Protection of property rights	1.4	0.8
Bank size	0.9	0.7
Other bank characteristics	−0.3	0.5
Other country characteristics	0.1	0.0
Unexplained (Kenya residual)	1.2	0.8

Source: Beck and Fuchs (2004), using data and results from Demirgüç-Kunt, Laeven, and Levine (2004) and data from Central Bank of Kenya.

Instead of our looking at bank-level cost patterns, it is equally interesting to stand back and to examine what national structural features (and external characteristics of different banks, such as ownership) are associated with higher interest spreads and margins. A recent cross-country study of the determinants of net interest margins and overhead costs for banks in 72 countries (Demirgüç-Kunt, Laeven, and Levine, 2004) provided the material for such an analysis. The authors provided a regression equation that explains a reasonable proportion of the variation in net interest margins in terms of national and bank-level characteristics. Inserting local values for the explanatory variables allows a predicted value for any given country and, indeed, any given bank.

The difference between average Kenyan interest margins and those in the rest of the world for the period studied by Demirgüç-Kunt, Laeven, and Levine[3] was 3.4 percent (7.0 percent compared with 3.6 percent). About two-thirds of the difference can be explained by differences in the values of the explanatory variables in Kenya compared with the rest of the world. In particular, as shown in table E.5, Kenya's relatively weak protection of property rights and the small size of its banks are major contributors to the difference.[4] Those two factors also provide the most important explanation for the higher overhead costs in Kenya—accounting for 0.8 percentage points of the costs. The relative smaller size—thus the lack of scale economies—of Kenyan banks explains 0.9 percentage points of the higher net interest margin and 0.7 percentage points of the higher overhead costs.

The lack of a sound legal and institutional environment and the small size of Kenyan banks thus seem to be two of the most important factors explaining why net interest margins and overhead costs are almost twice as high in Kenya as in the rest of the world. Overall, this analysis of national structural features confirms the conclusions that are based on cost and profit decomposition. In particular, the deficient legal and institutional framework contributes to the need for high loan loss provisions. The benchmarking exercise clearly suggests a desirable direction of policy.

Notes

1. The calculations and discussion follow Beck and Fuchs (2004).
2. For large loans to risk-free borrowers funded on the wholesale deposit market quasi-taxes, such as unremunerated reserve requirements, may contribute most of the spread. Calculating the break-even spread on such loans is a good way of inferring the marginal contribution of reserve requirements to intermediation spreads.
3. Although Demirgüç-Kunt, Laeven, and Levine (2004) use data over 1995–1999 and have a limited sample of banks for each country, the data for Kenya is based on 38 Kenyan banks representing 98 percent of the banking system and is for the year 2002.
4. These calculations were obtained by multiplying the coefficient estimates from two regressions in that paper (Table 8, column 3 and Table 11, column 3) with the difference between values of the respective variables for Kenya and the mean value for all countries in the study.

References

Barth, James, Gerard Caprio, and Ross Levine. 2004. "Bank Supervision and Regulation: What Works Best?" *Journal of Financial Intermediation* 13 (2): 205–48.

Beck, Thorsten, Aslı Demirgüç-Kunt, and Ross Levine. 2000. "A New Database on the Structure and Development of the Financial Sector." World Bank Economic

———. 2003. "Law, Endowments and Finance." *Journal of Financial Economics* 70 (2): 137–81.

———. 2002. "Industry Growth and Capital Allocation: Does Having a Market- or Bank-based System Matter?" *Journal of Financial Economics* 64: 147–80.

Beck, Thorsten, and Michael Fuchs. 2004. "Structural Issues in the Kenyan Financial System: Improving Competition and Access." World Bank Policy Research Working Paper, World Bank, Washington, DC.

Beck, Thorsten, Ross Levine, and Norman Loayza. 2000. "Finance and the Sources of Growth." *Journal of Financial Economics* 58: 261–300.

Bossone, Biagio, Patrick Honohan, and Millard Long. 2002. "Policy for Small Financial Systems." In *Financial Sector Policy for Developing Countries—A Reader*, ed. G. Caprio, P. Honohan, and D. Vittas, pp. 95–128. New York: Oxford University Press. Available at http://wbln0018.worldbank.org/html/FinancialSectorWeb.nsf/(attachmentweb)/Fs06/$FILE/Fs06.pdf.

Christen, Robert Peck, Timothy R. Lyman, and Richard Rosenberg. 2003. *Microfinance Consensus Guidelines*. Washington, DC: Consultative Group to Assist the Poorest.

Claessens, Stijn, and Luc Laeven. 2004. "What Drives Bank Competition? Some International Evidence." *Journal of Money, Banking and Credit*. Volume 36, Number 3 (part2), June 2004, pp. 563–583.

Demirgüç-Kunt, Aslı, and Harry Huizinga. 1999. "Determinants of Commercial Bank Interest Margins and Profitability: Some International Evidence." *World Bank Economic Review* 13: 379–408.

E

Demirgüç-Kunt, Aslı, Luc Laeven, and Ross Levine. 2004. "Regulations, Market Structure, Institutions and the Cost of Financial Intermediation." *Journal of Money, Banking and Credit.* Volume 36, Number 3 (part2), June 2004, pp. 593–622.

Fazzari, Steven, Glenn Hubbard, and Bruce Petersen. 1988. "Financing Constraints and Corporate Investment." Brookings Papers on Economic Activity 1, pp. 141–95, Brookings Institute, Washington, DC.

Financial Stability Forum. *Compendium of Standards.*

Honohan, Patrick. 2003. "Avoiding the Pitfalls in Taxing Financial Intermediation." In *Taxation of Financial Intermediation: Theory and Practice for Emerging Economies,* ed. P. Honohan. New York: Oxford University Press.

———. 2004a. "Financial Development, Growth and Poverty: How Close Are the Links?" World Bank Policy Research Working Paper 3203, World Bank, Washington, DC.

———. 2004b. "Measuring Microfinance Access: Building on Existing Cross-country Data." Paper presented at the UNDP, World Bank, and IMF Workshop Data on the Access of Poor and Low Income People to Financial Services, Washington, DC, October 26.

Impavido, Gregorio, Alberto Musalem, and Dimitri Vittas. 2003. "Promoting Pension Funds." In *Globalization and National Financial Systems,* ed. J. A. Hanson, P. Honohan and G. Majnoni. New York: Oxford University Press.

International Monetary Fund and World Bank. 2001. *Guidelines for Public Debt Management.* Washington, DC: International Monetary Fund and World Bank. Available at http://www.imf.org/external/np/mae/pdebt/2000/eng/index.htm.

———. 2003. "Development issues in the FSAP." Mimeo.

La Porta, Rafael, Florencio Lopez-de-Silanes, and Andrei Shleifer. 2002. "Government Ownership of Commercial Banks." *Journal of Finance* 57: 265–301.

La Porta, Rafael, Florencio Lopez-de-Silanes, Andrei Shleifer, and Robert W. Vishny. 1997. "Legal Determinants of External Finance." *Journal of Finance* 52: 1131–1150.

———. 1998. "Law and Finance." Journal of Political Economy 106: 1113–55.

Levine, Ross. 1997. "Financial Development and Economic Growth: Views and Agenda." *Journal of Economic Literature* 35: 688–726.

Levine, Ross, Norman Loayza, and Thorsten Beck. 2000. "Financial Intermediation and Growth: Causality and Causes." *Journal of Monetary Economics* 46: 31–77.

Jaffee, Dwight M., and Betrand Renaud. 1996. "Strategies to Develop Mortgage Markets in Transition Economies," World Bank Policy Research Working Paper 1697, World Bank, Washington, DC.

Jappelli, Tullio, and Marco Pagano. 2002. "Information Sharing, Lending and Defaults: Cross-Country Evidence." *Journal of Banking and Finance* 26: 2017–45.

Miller, Margaret (ed). 2003. *Credit Reporting Systems and the International Economy.* Cambridge, MA: MIT Press.

Organisation for Economic Co-operation and Development. 2002. *Insurance and Private Pensions Compendium for Emerging Economies.* Paris: Organisation for Economic Co-operation and Development.

E

Vittas, Dimitri. 1998. "Regulatory Controversies of Private Pension Funds," World Bank Policy Research Working Paper 1893, World Bank, Washington, DC. Available at http://econ.worldbank.org/docs/824.pdf.

World Bank. 2001a. *Finance for Growth. Policy Choices in a Volatile World.* New York: Oxford University Press.

———. 2001b. *Developing Government Bond Markets.* Washington, DC: World Bank.

E

Appendix F

Institutional Structure of Financial Regulation and Supervision[1]

Overview

Around the world, many countries are reconsidering the institutional structure of regulatory and supervisory agencies in the financial sector. This reconsideration reflects the concern that the existing structures—which were often established in a markedly different market and institutional environment than exists today—may have become inappropriate to meet the key regulatory objectives effectively. These objectives include fostering market efficiency and promoting market confidence and stability. As countries reassess and then implement changes in their regulatory and supervisory architecture, a number of issues are raised in relation to both the developmental and stability aspects of the financial sector's evolution.

From the developmental perspective, the main question that arises is whether the existing organizational structure of the financial regulatory and supervisory function is adequate to oversee an often rapidly evolving financial sector that is characterized by new types of financial institutions and new institutional structure (such as financial conglomerates.) It is also feasible that a poorly structured supervisory function could impede financial innovation or encourage inappropriate forms of innovation. For instance, if the structure gives rise to significant supervisory gaps—that is, differences in regulation of activities that have a similar function but that are performed by different institutional types—market participants are likely to seek opportunities for regulatory arbitrage and to engage in financial operations that are not appropriate from a regulatory perspective. This regulatory arbitrage, in turn, will lead to a developmental outcome for the financial sector that is suboptimal.

F

From the stability perspective, several key issues pertain to the institutional structure of regulation. The question of regulatory gaps and the implications for regulatory arbitrage is pertinent in this context also. Unsupervised, or inadequately supervised, institutions can be a primary cause of financial instability, and weak institutions will likely try to seek out the lines of least supervisory resistance and to engage in overly risky types of financial behavior. There is always a possibility that a change in supervisory structure could lead to less-optimal outcomes from the stability point of view. Such a case could be, for instance, moving responsibility for supervising banks from a strong and independent central bank to a new agency that is perceived to be less robust. Another issue that has stability implications relates to the risks that arise in transitional phases. Specifically, if a country decides to change the institutional structure of its supervision, there is typically a transitional period during which responsibility is shifted from one set of supervisory bodies to another. During such a transitional phase, there is a risk that the stability of the financial system could be undermined, especially if a supervisory vacuum exists for an extended period.

Range of Financial Supervisory Structures

A wide variety of institutional structures for financial supervision exists around the world. There is a spectrum of alternatives rather than an "either–or" choice, and there is considerable variety within the spectrum and even within the same basic model. Although no universal pattern exists, there is a general trend toward (a) reducing the number of separate agencies, (b) integrating prudential supervisory arrangements, (c) reducing the role of the central bank in prudential oversight of financial institutions, (d) placing more emphasis on the role of the central bank in systemic stability, and, if a unified agency is created, (e) making this an agency other than the central bank.

National differences reflect a multitude of factors: historic evolution, structure of the financial system, political structure and traditions, and size of the country and financial sector. Table F.1 gives an indication of the range of models for supervisory structure that have been adopted around the world. The framework for organizing supervision functions is along sectoral lines (multiple supervisors), is integrated for two sectors regardless of the objectives of supervision, or is integrated across all sectors into unified agencies. In the unified model (i.e., integrated across all sectors) two variants have appeared: (a) a single integrated supervisor responsible for all objectives of supervision (except possibly competition issues) and (b) two integrated supervisors—one focusing on prudential regulation and supervision of financial institutions and another focusing on conduct of business supervision across all institutional types and markets. This model of integrating supervisory functions according to objectives of supervision is further discussed in the section below on types of unified supervision, drawing on the experience of the Netherlands.

Importance of Institutional Structure

The institutional structure of supervisory agencies is not simply an administrative matter; it is important to meet the objectives of financial supervision for several reasons. The

F

objectives of financial supervision are to promote efficiency and competition,[2] to maintain market confidence, to protect depositors or consumers (as appropriate), and to foster systemic stability. Supervisory capacity and the supervisory process itself are the critical elements in attaining those goals. Above all other considerations, institutional structure may have an effect on supervisory capacity and process and, hence, on the overall effectiveness of regulation and supervision, because of the expertise, experience, and culture that develop within particular regulatory agencies and with the approaches they adopt.

One school of thought argues that focused, rather than diversified or conglomerate, regulators are more effective simply because their mandates are clearly defined, which allows the buildup of expertise. There is a danger (although this risk is by no means inevitable) that expertise, collective memory, and experience can be lost when changes are made. Others argue that regulation is more likely to be effective if a single agency is responsible for all aspects of regulation and supervision.

Closely related to effectiveness is the clarity of responsibility for particular aspects or objectives of regulation. This clarity, in turn, raises the question of interagency rivalry and disputes and of the effectiveness of needed information exchange and coordination. Seldom does regulation have a single objective; when multiple objectives are set, conflicts can arise between them. Although this potential for conflict is true irrespective of institutional structure, different structures may be more or less efficient at handling conflicts and facilitating information exchange and cooperation. Specific country circumstances dictate whether conflicts could be better handled or whether cooperation could become easier within a single agency or between agencies if responsibilities for particular objectives are more clearly defined. It becomes a question of whether transaction costs are lower when conflicts are resolved internally (e.g., between different divisions of a single agency) rather than externally between different agencies.

Different structures have implications for the costs of regulation. On the one hand, if there are economies of scale and scope in regulation, there should be advantages to having a small number of agencies or even a single authority. On the other hand, if a single regulator (encompassing a wide variety of financial institutions) adopts an inappropriate regulatory regime (perhaps because its remit is too wide and unfocused), then the compliance and structural costs of regulation would rise—even though the purely institutional costs of regulatory agencies (i.e., the costs of running supervisory agencies) might be lower. The following considerations are relevant for the costs of regulation:

- A major issue relates to overlap and underlap and to whether a particular structure causes an unnecessary duplication of regulatory activity and, hence, places unnecessary costs on firms; it also relates to whether some aspects of business or some institutions fall through the net altogether.
- A multiple-agency regime, especially if it allows regulated institutions an element of choice, creates the potential for regulatory arbitrage and inconsistent regulation between different institutions conducting the same type of business.
- Public perceptions and credibility also may be a significant issue in that, with multiple agencies, it may not be clear to the consumer which agency is responsible for a particular issue of regulation or to whom complaints should be addressed.

F

Any change in supervisory architecture must take into account the likely effect on the governance of the agency or agencies concerned. There are four prerequisites for good regulatory governance in regulatory and supervisory agencies: accountability, independence, integrity, and transparency. Each may be affected by a structural change in the supervisory process.[3] The importance of corporate governance arrangements arises from several factors: (a) they determine the effectiveness and efficiency of the agencies' operations; (b) they have a powerful effect on the agency's credibility, authority, and public standing; and (c) they have an important effect on the authority and credibility of agency's attempt to encourage and to require effective corporate governance arrangements within regulated firms.

For all those reasons, the institutional structure of regulatory agencies is an issue of some significance. However, the importance should not be exaggerated. A crucial point is that institutional structure does not, in itself, guarantee what really matters: the effectiveness of regulation in achieving its objectives in an efficient and cost-effective manner. The arguments in favor of and against various supervisory structures can best be drawn out by considering the case for and against a fully unified prudential agency.

Case for the Fully Unified Model

The fully unified model is particularly relevant when regulated entities are increasingly consolidating their activities and turning into conglomerates with centralized risk management. Several arguments might favor the creation of a single unified agency for prudential regulation and supervision. Those arguments are as follows:

- There may be economies of scale within regulatory agencies (particularly with respect to skill requirements and recruitment of staff members with appropriate skills and qualifications). If so, the smaller the number of agencies, the lower the institutional costs should be. A single regulator might be more efficient because of shared resources and, in particular, shared information technology systems and support services. The argument for economies of scale might apply particularly to the "small-country" case.

- It is likely to be easier to achieve an optimal deployment of staff members within a unified agency than within a specialist and fragmented institutional structure.

- As noted, the distinction between functional and institutional regulation does not apply to a financial system made up of specialist institutions. For financial conglomerates, a unified agency enables a groupwide picture of the risks of an institution to be observed more clearly and thus to be supervised. This groupwide supervision of risks is especially important when financial conglomerates themselves adopt a centralized approach to risk management and risk taking. In such a case, there is merit in having an institutional structure of supervision that mirrors the practice of regulated institutions. As a result, a more rapid response to emerging groupwide problems should be possible.

- There is less scope for incomplete coverage, with some institutions or lines of business slipping through the regulatory and supervisory net because of confusion about which agency is responsible. There may even be damaging disputes between agencies in a multiple-agency structure.

F

- There might be merit in having a simple regulatory structure that is readily understood and recognized by regulated firms and consumers. Some of the traditional distinctions between different types of institutions have become increasingly blurred, which undermines some of the traditional arguments in favor of separate regulation and supervision of different types of financial institutions.

- There might be an advantage to having a structure that mirrors the business of regulated institutions. To the extent that financial institutions have steadily diversified, traditional functional divisions have been eroded. Although there are various ways of addressing overall prudential requirements for diversified institutions, a single, conglomerate regulator might be able to monitor the full range of institutions' business more effectively and be better able to detect potential solvency risks emanating from different parts of the business.

- Equally, the distinctions between certain types of financial products have become increasingly blurred, which raises questions about the case for regulating them differently. The potential danger of a fragmented institutional structure is that similar products (products providing the same or a similar service) are regulated differently because they are supplied by different types of financial firms. This difference in the regulation of similar products may impair competitive neutrality. It is more likely that a consistent approach to regulation and supervision of different types of institutions will emerge.

- A single agency should, in principle, avoid problems of competitive inequality, inconsistencies, duplication, overlap, and gaps that can arise with a regime that is based on several agencies. A singe regulator should make it easier for similar products offered by different types of institutions to be regulated and supervised in a consistent manner.

- A single agency also should minimize regulatory arbitrage. A potential danger with multiple agencies is that overall effectiveness may be impaired as financial firms engage in various forms of regulatory and supervisory arbitrage. This arbitrage can involve the placement of a particular financial service or product in that part of a given financial conglomerate where the supervisory costs are the lowest or where supervisory oversight is the least intrusive. It also may lead firms to design new financial institutions or to redesign existing ones strictly to minimize or avoid supervisory oversight. This regulatory arbitrage also can induce "competition in laxity," as different agencies compete to avoid the migration of institutions to competing agencies.

- If expertise in regulation is in short supply, expertise might be used more effectively if it is concentrated within a single agency. Such an agency also might offer better career prospects. Accountability of regulation also might be more certain with a simple structure if for no other reason than that it would be more difficult for different agencies to "pass the buck."

- The costs imposed on regulated firms might be reduced to the extent that firms would need to deal with only one agency. This issue was particularly significant in the United Kingdom when, before the creation of the Financial Services Authority (a fully unified agency), a financial conglomerate might be regulated and supervised by and required to report to nine regulatory agencies. There also can be economies, plus greater effectiveness, when all information about financial firms is lodged within a single agency.

Case Against the Fully Unified Model

There is clear merit in the arguments stated in the case for a unified model, and there is a certain prima facie appeal to the concept of a unified prudential regulator. However, several reservations may be voiced about such an agency:

- One of the arguments in favor of a single prudential agency—that as financial firms have increasingly diversified, the traditional functional distinctions between institutions have been eroded—is not applicable in many countries. Although this lack of applicability is generally the case in industrial countries, it may not be true of all countries or even of all institutions in industrial countries. In very many countries, there remain—and will remain for the foreseeable future—major differences among banks, securities firms, and insurance companies.

- Firms in all sub-sectors of the financial system have diversified, but their core business almost invariably remains dominant. The nature of the risks may be sufficiently different to warrant a differentiated approach to prudential regulation. Insurance companies have long-term liabilities with ill-defined value, whereas assets are generally marketable with readily ascertainable values. Banks, by contrast, tend to have relatively short-term liabilities with assets that are difficult to liquidate and to value. Consequently, the applicable prudential supervisory regimes are different, and there would be few (if any) efficiencies in bringing their supervision together.

- Accountability of the single agency might be more difficult, because of the problems of defining clear objectives for the agency. Accountability always has been difficult to implement for a supervisory agency—whether it be in a single agency or with multiple agencies—given the multiple objectives and the need to ensure a sufficient degree of confidentiality of supervisory actions on individual institutions. Nevertheless, accountability for objectives can be better implemented if cross-sectoral integration of supervisory functions is organized based on objectives of supervision, as in Australia and the Netherlands.

- There is a danger within a single agency that the necessary distinctions between different products and institutions will not be made. A single agency might not have a clear focus on the objectives and rationale of regulation and supervision and might not make the necessary differentiations between different types of institutions and businesses. Even if the different regulatory requirements of different types of firms are managed within specialist divisions of an integrated regulator, there is no guarantee that supervisors who are within the same organization (but who are responsible for different types of business) will necessarily communicate and coordinate more efficiently and closely than if they were within different, specialist regulatory agencies. Regardless of the institutional structure that is chosen in a particular country, the ultimate skill lies in balancing conflicting pressures.

- A potential moral hazard is that the public will believe that the spectrum of risks among financial institutions has disappeared or become blurred. In particular, the distinction could become obscured between deposits that are redeemable on demand at face value and certain investments where the value of an institution's liability is a function of the performance of the institution in managing its assets. There may be a tendency for the public to assume that all creditors of institutions supervised by a given supervisor will receive equal protection.

- A large unified regulator might become excessively bureaucratic in its procedures and might be slow to react to problems as they emerge.

- The creation of a single regulator might involve a loss of potentially valuable information because a single approach is adopted. In effect, there might be merit in having a degree of competition and diversity in regulation so that lessons can be learned from the experience of different approaches. In some respects, the case for not having a monopoly regulator is the same as with any monopolist.

- Further, there may not be any economies of scale to be derived from an integrated regulator. The economics literature demonstrates quite clearly that diseconomies of scale can arise in some circumstances. Put another way, what economists refer to as X-inefficiencies (that is, inefficiencies caused by suboptimal resource allocation and not by a lack of economies of scale) may arise in a monopolist regulator. It is not self-evident that a single, unified regulator would, in practice, be more efficient than a series of specialist regulators that are based on clearly defined objectives and are focused specifically on regulation to meet those clearly defined objectives. In addition, as in Ireland and Finland, economies of scale in infrastructure, information technology, and services can be achieved by locating separate agencies within the same building and by sharing common resources while, nevertheless, maintaining strict separation of regulatory and supervisory policy and execution.

- A single, all-embracing agency also may be subject to the hazards of the "Christmas tree" effect, in which a wide range of miscellaneous functions are loaded onto it, overburdening it with activities divorced from its primary function and objectives.

- Regardless of the nature of the change made to institutional structure, there are always potentially serious transaction costs to consider. There is a degree of unpredictability in the process of change itself. A bargaining process may be opened between different interest groups, the legislative process might be captured by vested interests, key personnel may be lost, and management may be diverted from the core activity of regulation and supervision.

The arguments for and against unified prudential agencies are finely balanced, and the optimal structure is likely to vary between countries, depending on the structure of their financial system (and, in particular, whether the system is populated by specialist or conglomerate institutions), the past traditions, the political environment, and the size of the country. If a single agency is created, the type of unified supervision and the issue of internal structure need further consideration.

Types of Unified Supervision

The decision on the type of unified supervision agencies—whether based on limited objectives or cross-sectoral unification of all objectives—also gives rise to complex trade-

F

Table F.1. Countries with a Single Supervisor, Semi-Integrated Supervisory Agencies and Multiple Supervisors in 2004

Single supervisor for the financial system	Agency supervising two types of financial intermediaries			Multiple supervisors[a]
	Banks and securities firms	Banks and insurers	Securities firms and insurers	
Austria	Finland	Australia	Bolivia	Albania*	Italy*
Bahrain*	Luxembourg	Belgium	Bulgaria*	Argentina*	Jordan*
Bermuda*	Mexico	Canada	Chile	Bahamas*	Lithuania*
Cayman Islands*	Switzerland	Colombia	Egypt, Arab Rep. of*	Barbados*	New Zealand*
Denmark	Uruguay	Ecuador	Jamaica*	Botswana*	Panama
Estonia		El Salvador	Mauritius*	Brazil*	Philippines*
Germany		Guatemala	Slovakia*	China	Poland*
Gibraltar		Malaysia*	South Africa*	Croatia*	Portugal*
Hungary		Peru	Ukraine*	Cyprus*	Russia*
Iceland		Venezuela, República Bolivariana de		Dominican Republic*	Slovenia*
Ireland*				Egypt*	Sri Lanka*
Japan				France*	Spain*
Kazakhstan*				Greece*	Thailand*
Latvia				Hong Kong (China)*	Tunisia*
Maldives*				India*	Turkey
Malta*				Indonesia*	Uganda*
Nicaragua				Israel*	United States*
Norway					
Singapore*					
Korea, Rep. of					
Sweden					
United Arab Emirates*					
Uruguay*					
United Kingdom					
Australia[b]					
Netherlands[b]					

As percentage of all countries in the sample

29%	6%	12%	11%	42%

*Banking supervision is conducted by the central bank.

Source: How Countries Supervise Their Banks, Insurers, and Securities Markets. 2004. Central Banking Publications, London: Sponsored by international law firm Freshfields Bruckaus and Beringer.

Note: Sample includes only countries that supervise all three types of intermediaries (banks, securities firms, and insurers).

a. At least one for banks, one for securities firms, and one for insurers.
b. Two integrated cross-sectoral supervisors, each focusing on specific objective of supervision: one for prudential supervision of institutions in all sectors; another for conduct of business supervision of all sectors and markets.

offs. In principle, a supervisory framework could be organized in line with basic policy objectives (or functions), regardless of the type of financial business (banking, insurance, securities trading, and non-bank financial business). The objectives (or functions) to be accommodated include prudential regulation, systemic stability, consumer or investor protection, and competition. Although the multiplicity of objectives and institutional types gives rise to a matrix of potential regulatory arrangements by objective and type of business, the normal approach in creating integrated supervisors has been (as seen in table F.1) to adopt cross-sectoral unification of all objectives and related functions (with the exception of competition objective) in a single agency.

Australia and the Netherlands are, however, unusual among integrated supervisors because they created two separate integrated supervisors: one focused on prudential supervision and one focused on the conduct-of-business supervision. Thus, each agency focuses on a specific objective of supervision. If the objectives of supervision were few and very distinct, it would be fairly straightforward to design a framework in which each institution was charged with achieving a distinct objective. In reality, a major complication is the fact that the various supervisory norms and instruments underpinning the objectives of supervision are not fully distinct. In general, the various supervisory domains will contain shared elements as well as inconsistent elements.

Consequently, the practical design of a supervision framework will face tradeoffs between maximizing synergies among the common elements and minimizing conflicts among the inconsistent elements. Because the importance of the various tradeoffs will vary across countries with different financial systems and legal arrangements, if follows that the appropriate arrangement of objective or functionally oriented supervision will vary across countries. For example, the Netherlands model differs from other cross-sectoral supervision frameworks in many ways: (a) consolidation of both microprudential and macroprudential supervision into a single body within the central bank (DNB-PVK); (b) the consolidation of all conduct-of-business supervision within a separate body, the Authority for Financial Markets (AFM); and (c) the establishment of agreements or "covenants" between main supervisors to ensure good coordination and cooperation. A council of financial supervisors (RFT) offers the two supervisors (DNB-PVK and AFM) a platform for the coordination and mutual fine-tuning of regulation and policy, especially on integrity supervision issues.

Consolidation of macroprudential and microprudential supervision in a single agency distinguishes the Netherlands model from cross-sectoral approaches in other countries. In both the United Kingdom and Australia, for example, macroprudential surveillance is conducted by the central bank, but microprudential surveillance has been taken over by separate agencies.[4] The combination of both aspects of prudential supervision in the Netherlands largely reflects the fact that its financial system is dominated by a handful of large, complex financial institutions. That being the case, the distinction between microprudential and macroprudential issues is blurred, at least in the case of the largest institutions.

There are both pros and cons associated with such consolidation. On the positive side, consolidation is likely to encourage taking greater account of macroeconomic and systemic stability considerations in microprudential analysis. Macroeconomic analysis is also likely to benefit by taking better account of the structure and characteristics of the

F

financial system at the microlevel. A single macroprudential and microprudential supervisor also is seen as advantageous in the event of a financial crisis, because it would facilitate rapid assembly of essential prudential information and facilitate speedy decision making.

At the same time, it is recognized that combining macroprudential and microprudential supervision under one roof could lead to conflicts between objectives. A particular concern is that microprudential considerations could put increased pressure on the central bank to provide generous lender-of-last-resort facilities and that knowledge of this support could encourage less-prudent behavior by banks. In principle, this concern is valid. However, in practice, it may not be a very significant issue in the Netherlands because the DNB is authorized to lend—including in emergency circumstances—only against acceptable collateral. In practical terms, the moral hazard is that the DNB might be willing to offer slightly better terms on offered collateral than it might otherwise do. That probability is unlikely to promote significantly riskier behavior by financial institutions.

An additional issue in relation to the consolidation of macroprudential and microprudential supervision is whether this supervisory role should be located within the central bank. The fact that the DNB is no longer responsible for conducting an independent monetary policy undercuts one of the traditional arguments in favor of locating prudential supervision outside the central bank, because the scope for conflict of interest between monetary policy and prudential policy objectives is largely eliminated.

Internal Structure of Unified Supervisory Agencies

Given the arguments that have been outlined, the objective within a single agency must be to create an internal organizational structure that maximizes the potential advantages (e.g., cost efficiency, less regulatory arbitrage), while at the same time guarding against the potential hazards (e.g., heavy bureaucracy, lack of focus). Internal organization could reflect different institutional types or different functional lines. For instance, some supervisory activities (e.g., licensing, prudential control) could be established to cover all institutional types. A number of variations are possible. Country experiences to date suggest that no one model for the internal organization of unified agencies has been notably more successful than any of the others.

Role of the Central Bank

A key issue in any institutional structure of regulatory and supervisory agencies is the position and role of the central bank. In the vast majority of countries, the central bank has historically been responsible for both the systemic stability and the prudential regulation and supervision of banks. In only a very small minority of cases has it also been responsible for the supervision of non-bank financial institutions. Even so, there are several alternative models for the role of the central bank, depending on whether it is involved in monitoring the payments system, providing emergency liquidity to the markets, supervising banks, managing deposit insurance, or playing a role in providing the safety net or crisis resolution.

Nevertheless, almost universally, the central bank is allocated at least some role in maintaining systemic stability, even if it is not involved in the prudential supervision of the banks that make up the system. However, its role raises a number of issues.

The first issue is that of power. If the central bank has independent powers to set interest rates, the combination of a widespread regulatory function with monetary control might appear to place excessive powers within the hands of unelected officials. It might create the public perception that any "safety net" that might apply to banks will also be extended to a wide range of financial institutions.

Another issue is that of possible conflicts of interest. These conflicts could arise, for example, because of monetary policy implications of bank resolution actions, thereby posing a tradeoff among conflicting objectives. This concern is frequently advanced by academic economists as the main argument against allowing the central bank to participate in regulation. Those economists believe that a central bank with responsibility for preventing systemic risk is more likely to loosen monetary policy on occasions of difficulty.[5]

The question of conflicts of interest might be an argument in favor of giving the central bank regulatory responsibilities. There are several questions: If not the central bank, then which other body should have such powers? What conflicts of interest might the body have? If the central bank does not play this role, will it then be given to a body more subject to direct political influence? If public policy conflicts do arise, they will do so regardless of whether supervision is a responsibility of the central bank. Such conflicts may arise no matter what institutional structure is created, and the conflicts must be resolved somehow. The key issue is whether the transaction costs of resolving them are higher or lower when they are resolved internally rather than externally. The advantages of having the central bank also serve as the supervisory agency of banks in the financial system may be summarized as follows:

Because the central bank has responsibility for oversight of the system as a whole and for stability of the payments system, there are powerful synergies in being the supervisory agency for the institutions that make up the system. Some analysts doubt that, in practice and when stability is under strain, it is feasible for an agency to be responsible for the system but not for the individual firms.

The central bank necessarily gains information about banks by virtue of its monetary policy operations. There are, therefore, information synergies between the conduct of monetary policy and the prudential supervision of banks. The central bank needs information about the solvency and liquidity of banks when considering its role as lender of last resort.

The central bank often has an independent status in the economy that might not be replicated by other regulatory or supervisory agencies. Moreover, the central bank usually has considerable authority in an economy, and that authority enhances the credibility of regulation and supervision—if it is allocated this task.

From time to time, conflicts of interest can arise between the requirements of monetary policy and the prudential position of banks. It can be argued that such conflicts are better resolved internally within a single agency than externally between different agencies. Monetary policy operates largely through interest rates that also affect the financial position of banks. In addition, economies of scale may be derived from combining responsibility for monetary policy and prudential supervision of banks. Moreover, the

F

status of the central bank may enhance its ability to recruit the necessary skills for bank supervision.

There are, however, arguments against having the central bank as the supervisory agency of banks. Such an arrangement may be viewed as concentrating excessive power in the hands of an unelected central bank whose accountability may be weak. Regulatory failures may compromise the authority of the central bank in other areas of its activity. For example, the central bank's objective of ensuring monetary stability may conflict with its objective of securing the safety and soundness of banks.

In a recent reform of institutional arrangements for financial regulation and supervision, the government of Ireland embedded prudential regulation of banks and other financial institutions within the central bank (which was already responsible for banks and securities) but at the same time changed the structure of the bank. Supervision and monetary stability are now separated and run as independent arms within the central bank. However, because Ireland is a member of the European Monetary Union, the monetary policy powers of the central bank are very limited. Similarly, as discussed earlier, the Netherlands Bank now combines prudential supervision of all sectors with its macroprudential surveillance responsibilities.

In practice, no bank regulator could, or should, ever be totally independent of the central bank. The central bank is the monopoly provider of the reserve base and the lender of last resort. Any serious banking problems are bound to lead to calls for the central bank to use its reserve-creating powers. Moreover, the central bank, in its macro-policy operational role, must have a direct concern with the payments and settlements system, the money markets, and the development of monetary aggregates. Any serious problem with the health of the banking system will touch on one or more of these concerns. Therefore, there are bound to be, and must be, very close relationships between the bank regulator and the monetary policy authority. Establishing such relationships is one of the priorities in structural reform.

Furthermore, with the growing international integration of financial institutions and markets, central banks are increasingly focused on macroprudential surveillance as part of their systemic stability responsibilities (which is reflected in the publication of financial stability reports by increasing numbers of countries). This top-down approach to analyzing financial soundness requires very close collaboration with supervisory bodies—within or outside the central bank (e.g., in data sharing, conducting aggregate stress tests, or providing transparency of aggregate information).

This need for coordination might suggest unifying the functions within the central bank. However, for a variety of reasons (including the need for confidentiality), when the central bank combines both roles, the supervisory department is usually separate from the monetary policy department. Coordination is regarded as necessary only between the top officials. Such regular meetings of senior officials can be organized just as easily whether their subordinates are in separate buildings or the same building and whether their organization is formally separate or not. Perhaps the only real difference is that disagreements between senior officials would be settled (quietly) within the central bank in the case of unification, and they would be settled outside the bank, presumably by the minister of finance, with more likelihood of publicity, in the case of separation. However, it is hard

F

to identify actual cases of publicly observed disagreement between the central bank and the bank regulator in countries where there is such a separation.

The bottom line is that banking realities will force considerable coordination and interaction between the senior officials dealing with monetary policy and with bank supervision. There must always be a close link between the central bank and the supervisory authority. The question of whether the banking supervisory body is formally within or outside the central bank is then essentially a subsidiary issue, depending on perceptions of the appropriate locus of power and responsibility. Those perceptions will vary depending on the accidents of history and culture. There is no single, best approach under all circumstances, as is clearly evidenced by the variety of regulatory structures in different countries.

Whatever institutional structure is created, there will always be an important need for effective coordination among the central bank, the regulatory agency (or agencies), and the ministry of finance. In particular, cooperation, coordination (especially when intervention is made), and (perhaps above all else) information sharing are needed around the world. Mechanisms are needed to ensure information sharing regardless of the type of institutional structure created for regulation and supervision.

The overall conclusion is that safeguarding financial stability is a core function of the modern central bank, even though it may not be responsible for regulating and supervising banks and other financial institutions. Irrespective of the decision about the role in regulation and the supervision of individual financial institutions, the central bank must necessarily be centrally involved in the safety net arrangements, the liquidity support, the payments system, and the maintenance of stability in the financial system as a whole. In cases where the central bank is not responsible for regulation and supervision, its responsibility for financial stability requires cooperation with and from those agencies that are responsible for regulation and supervision. This issue cannot be avoided, and explicit arrangements are needed.

Conclusions

International experience indicates a wide variety of institutional regulatory formats, suggesting that there is no universal ideal model. A key consideration is the extent to which regulatory structure affects the overall effectiveness and efficiency of regulation and supervision, because this consideration should be the ultimate one when choosing between alternative formats. This consideration is also the reason why the issue of institutional structure is important.

However, in itself, institutional structure does not guarantee effective regulation and supervision, and it would be wrong to assume that changing the structure of regulatory institutions is a panacea. What an institutional structure does is it establishes the framework in which to optimize a regulatory regime. In effect, institutional structure provides the architecture of regulation and supervision. More appropriate structures may help, but, fundamentally, better regulation comes from stronger laws, better-trained staff members, and better enforcement.

F

If effectiveness of supervision, as judged by the observance of various international standards and codes, is seen to be adversely affected, owing to weakness in specific areas (core principles), then the key issue for an assessor is the extent to which changes in the institutional structure could help overcome those weaknesses. If the lack of compliance with some of the core principles reflects either weak infrastructure or weak supervisory capacity of sectoral supervisors, then forming a unified supervisor may not be the answer. There is also additional risk that the existing weaknesses could be exacerbated by attempting to form a unified supervisory structure without addressing up front the problems at the sectoral level of supervisors. Moreover, when a change in institutional structure has been implemented, it is important to assess whether this change has adversely affected the quality of enforcement in a particular sector (e.g., because of a loss of skilled staff members in securities laws enforcement) or has weakened regulatory governance (e.g., because of weakened transparency or independence). The ultimate decision is fundamentally driven by the extent to which the financial services industry has integrated its functions and adopted centralized risk management.

With the emergence of mixed financial institutions, the case for unified agencies has strengthened as they more closely mirror the emerging structure of financial systems and the business of financial firms. Whatever decisions are made, it is important to recognize that a perfect institutional structure is a chimera, and it might be necessary to accept the inevitability of working within an imperfect structure.

Notes

1. This Appendix draws heavily on chapter 2 of Carmichael, Fleming, and Llewellyn (2004).
2. An important question is how to fit competition issues into the overall institutional structure of regulation and supervision and, in particular, the extent to which competition issues should be the responsibility of a supervisory agency or whether they should fall within the domain of an agency for competition policy for the economy as a whole. This issue has been the subject of much debate, and even controversy, and countries have solved this issue in a range of different ways.
3. For a recent discussion of the effect of regulatory governance on financial soundness, see Das, Quintyn, and Chenard (2004).
4. It may be noted that separation of macroprudential surveillance from microprudential supervision also occurs in some systems, such as Canada's, that are not explicitly based on a cross-sectoral approach.
5. In dollarized economies, such conflicts of interest are diminished because of the limited room for both lender of last resort and monetary policy operations. This reduced scope for conflicts might favor the case for having the central bank assume supervisory responsibilities.

F

References

Abrams, Richard K., and Michael Taylor. 2000. "Issues in the Unification of Financial Sector Supervision." MAE Operational Paper, International Monetary Fund, Washington, DC.

Briault, Clive. 1998. "A Single Regulator for the U.K. Financial Services Industry." *Financial Stability Review* 5 (Autumn): 19–25.

Brimmer, A. F. 1989. "Distinguished Lecture on Economics in Government: Central Banking and Systemic Risks in Capital Markets." *Journal of Economic Perspectives* 3 (2): 3–16.

Carmichael, Jeffrey. 2002. "Public Sector Governance and the Finance Sector." Ch. 5.in *Financial Sector Governance: The Role of the Public and Private Sectors*, ed. Robert Litan, Michael Pomerleano, and V. Sundararajan, pp. 121–62. Washington DC, Brookings Institutions Press.

Carmichael, Jeffrey, Alexander Fleming, and David T. Llewellyn. 2004. *Aligning Financial Supervisory Structure with Country Needs*. Washington, DC: World Bank.

Cukierman, Alex. 1992. *Central Bank Strategy, Credibility, and Independence*. Cambridge, MA: MIT Press.

Das, Udaibir S., and Marc Quintyn. 2002. "Crisis Prevention and Crisis Management: The Role of Regulatory Governance." In *Financial Sector Governance: The Role of the Public and Private Sectors*, ed. Robert Litan, Michael Pomerleano, and V. Sundararajan, pp. 163–208. Washington, DC: Brookings Institution Press.

Das, Udaibir S., Marc Quintyn, and Kina Chenard. 2004. "Does Regulatory Governance Matter for Financial System Stability? An Empirical Analysis." IMF working paper 04/89, International Monetary Fund, Washington, DC.

George, E. A. 1996. "Some Thoughts on Financial Regulation." *Bank of England Quarterly Bulletin* 36 (May).

Goodhart, Charles A. E. 1996. "Some Regulatory Concerns." *Swiss Journal of Economics and Statistics* 243 (4–2): 651–4.

Goodhart, Charles A., Philipp Hartmann, David T. Llewellyn, Liliana Rojas-Suárez, and Steven Weisbrod. 1999. *Financial Regulation: Why, How, and Where Now?* London: Routledge.

Goodhart, Charles A. E., and Dirk Schoenmaker. 1995. "Institutional Separation between Supervisory and Monetary Agencies." In *The Central Bank and the Financial System*, ed. Charles Goodhart, Ch.16, London: Macmillan.

Healey, Juliette. 2003. "Financial Stability and the Central Bank: International Evidence." In *Financial Stability and Central Banks*, ed. Peter Sinclair and Juliette Healy ed., 19–78. London: Routledge.

Heller, H. R. 1991. "Prudential Supervision and Monetary Policy." In *International Financial Policy: Essays in Honor of Jacques J. Polak*, ed. Jakob A. Frenkel and Morris Goldstein, 269–81. Washington, DC: International Monetary Fund.

International Monetary Fund, Financial Sector Assessment Program, The Kingdom of the Netherlands—Netherlands. 2004. "Technical Note: the Netherlands Model

F

of Financial Sector Supervision." International Monetary Fund, Washington DC. Available at http://www.imf.org.

Llewellyn, David T. 1998. "A Prospectus from the FSA: Its Approach to Regulation." *Journal of Financial Regulation and Compliance* (December).

————. 1999a. "The Economic Rationale of Financial Regulation." FSA Occasional Paper 1. London: Financial Services Authority.

————. 1999b. "Introduction: The Institutional Structure of Regulatory Agencies." In Neil Courtis, ed., *How Countries Supervise Their Banks, Insurers, and Securities Markets.* London: Central Bank Publications.

Luna Martínez, José, and Thomas A. Rose. 2003. "International Survey of Integrated Financial Sector Supervision." Policy Research Working Paper 3096. World Bank, Washington, DC.

Ministry of Finance of the Republic of Estonia. 2001. *Challenges for the Unified Financial Supervision in the New Millennium.* Tallinn, Estonia: Ministry of Finance of the Republic of Estonia.

Oosterloo, Sander, and Jakob de Haan. 2003. "A Survey of International Frameworks for Financial Stability." *Occasional Studies*, Vol. 1, No. 4. Amsterdam: De Nederlandsche Bank.

Sinclair, P. J. N. 2000. Central Banks and Financial Stability. *Bank of England Quarterly Bulletin* (November): 377–91.

Taylor, Michael. 1995. *Twin Peaks: A Regulatory Structure for the New Century.* London: Centre for Study of Financial Innovation.

————. 1996. *Peak Practice: How to Reform the U.K.'s Regulatory System.* London: Centre for the Study of Financial Innovation.

Taylor, Michael, and Alexander E. Fleming. 1999. "Integrated Financial Supervision: Lessons from Northern European Experience." Policy Research Working Paper 2223. World Bank, Washington, DC.

Thompson, Graeme. 1996. "Regulatory Policy Issues in Australia." In *Future of Financial System*, ed. Malcolm Edey, pp. 252–69. Sydney: Reserve Bank of Australia.

F

Appendix G

Banking Resolution and Insolvency—Emerging World Bank and International Monetary Fund Guidelines

G.1 Bank Insolvency Framework: Objectives and Scope

G.1.1 Objectives

In early 2002, the World Bank and the International Monetary Fund (IMF) in coordination with the Bank for International Settlements (BIS), Basel Committee on Banking Supervision (BCBS), Financial Stability Institute (FSI), Financial Stability Forum (FSF), and some regional financial institutions, launched the Global Bank Insolvency Initiative (GBII). Its main objectives are as follows:

- To identify the appropriate legal, institutional, and regulatory framework to address banks in distress (Bank Insolvency Framework)
- To progressively create an international consensus regarding the framework, including best practices and alternatives
- To design a methodology for the assessment of the countries' framework and to undertake voluntary country assessments as appropriate
- To facilitate the provision of technical assistance to countries for the improvement of their framework for addressing bank insolvency

G.1.2 Background

World Bank–IMF staff members have carried out a broad consultative process to prepare a draft report on the bank insolvency framework. A number of global and regional seminars, with participation of more than 90 countries, have been held as part of the GBII in the past three years to ensure a wide consultation process, including countries from all regions of the world, as well as representatives for the regulatory and legal professions. A joint World Bank–IMF drafting team prepared successive versions of a report on bank insolvency in consultation with a Core Consultative Group (CCG).[1] Since mid-2004, a number of pilot country reviews of the institutional, legal, and regulatory framework to address bank insolvency have been carried out for a number of systemically and regionally important countries. After those pilot reviews, a revised version of the main report is expected to be circulated for the information of World Bank and IMF Boards.

G.1.3 Scope

The initiative aims to identify internationally accepted principles regarding the legal and institutional framework necessary to address cases of bank failures, starting at the point at which the authorities need to assume control of the bank for the purpose of rehabilitating or, where appropriate, liquidating it in a structured and orderly fashion. In particular, the report covers the following areas:

- The institutional arrangements necessary for dealing with bank insolvency
- General legal issues arising in bank insolvency proceedings
- The legal framework empowering the banking authorities to assume control of a distressed bank (either in the context of official administration or by way of other arrangements), which allows them to conduct the restructuring of an insolvent bank
- The principles applicable to the restructuring of insolvent banks, the special problems associated with different restructuring techniques, and the legal approaches that may be followed to deal with them
- The legal underpinnings and modalities of bank liquidation proceedings
- Modifications to the legal and institutional framework in the event of a systemic crisis

G.1.4 Links with the Basel Core Principle

The "efficient resolution of problems in banks" is mentioned in the Core Principles for Effective Banking Supervision (BCP) issued by the BCBS as one of the key preconditions for effective banking supervision. Other preconditions are jointly the sound and sustainable macroeconomic policies, a well-developed public infrastructure, an effective market discipline, and the mechanisms for providing appropriate systemic protection. In addition, earlier reviews of lessons from BCP assessments by World Bank and IMF staff members have recommended that, in view of their importance, adequate procedures for the resolution of problem banks should be made an integral part of the BCP assessments.[2] In addition, compliance with BCP 22 on remedial measures depends critically on a strong framework for bank insolvency.[3]

G.2 Key Institutional Aspects of the Bank Insolvency Regime

A set of key features of the broader legal and institutional environment for bank regulation and contract enforcement will affect the effectiveness of any bank insolvency regime. Many of those features are included as part of BCPs, and others may be viewed as part of the preconditions for effective supervision and robust bank exit policies. The features include the following:

- A clear legal framework for banking supervision, including operational autonomy of banking authorities, and specific decision making powers and procedures (part of BCP 1)
- Well-defined property and contractual rights (part of preconditions of BCP)
- Effective enforcement procedures (for expeditions and effective collection of claims and enforcement of security interests)
- Integrity and transparency of official decision making process

G.3 General Issues in Bank Insolvency Proceedings

G.3.1 Choice of Bank Insolvency Regime

The choice of legal arrangement should be conducive to achieving financial stability while also preserving the value of bank assets.[4] A primary choice must be made between a system based on the type of proceedings generally applicable to insolvent corporations, with any appropriate modifications,[5] and a special regime that is designed exclusively for banks.[6] A special regime for bank insolvency—or adequate modifications to the corporate insolvency regime—is needed because of (a) the potential systemic effects of bank failures, (b) the objective of safeguarding financial stability in the course of bank insolvency, and (c) the special role of banking authorities in bank insolvency.

The choice between the two systems has implications for the institutional framework for bank insolvency. There is no dominant model; countries share features of both systems to varying degrees. Either system—dominant general insolvency model with adaptations to deal with banks or special regime for bank insolvency—can work effectively.[7] A country's choice will depend on a variety of institutional, legal, and practical factors, including the quality and effectiveness of the country's existing corporate insolvency legislation, the ability of the insolvency courts to reach decisions in the short timeframe necessary for bank restructuring, the skills and integrity of the judiciary in comparison with the banking authorities, and the quality of supporting professions such as accountants and lawyers.

G.3.2 Administrative or Court-Based Special Bank Insolvency Regime

When a country seeks to address cases of bank insolvency through the corporate insolvency framework (with appropriate modifications), insolvency proceedings are invariably conducted in the courts. By contrast, the adoption of a special bank insolvency regime

G

separate from corporate insolvency law offers two main possibilities: first, the insolvency proceedings may be initiated and conducted.by a banking authority, or, second, the proceedings may remain under the jurisdiction of the insolvency courts even if the banking supervisory authorities retain a number of key functions, which are, in most cases, related to the commencement and the supervision of certain key aspects of the proceedings.

In some jurisdictions, there would be significant opposition to the introduction of purely administrative proceedings. Constitutional principles may preclude any official action involving the removal or extinction of property rights, unless it is sanctioned by court order or accompanied by appropriate compensation. Where the supervisory authority is given the responsibility to declare insolvency and to control the administration or liquidation, the relevant administrative decisions are typically subject to judicial review by the administrative courts or an equivalent mechanism of control. Judicial review ensures the legality of the authorities' actions and avoids unjustifiable interference with private interests.

Overall, the establishment of a special bank insolvency regime (in particular, an administrative one) can be designed to ensure speed and consistency between the supervisory and insolvency-related functions. However, the success of such a system depends on careful legislative drafting and implementation, so it can ensure the greatest possible compatibility with other branches of the law, avoid distortions and arbitrage arising from the uneven treatment of banks and non-bank financial institutions, and resolve the problems of jurisdictional scope and institutional competence resulting from the emergence of financial conglomerates.

G.3.3 Commencement of Bank Insolvency Proceedings

Banking authorities have an informational advantage and are, thus, better placed than creditors to assess a bank's true situation and to detect insolvency at an early stage. It is, therefore, generally accepted that the supervisory authority must have the power to initiate insolvency proceedings against a bank.[8]

Many jurisdictions go further and grant to their supervisors exclusive competence to commence proceedings. Two justifications are usually put forward in support of this approach: First, the declaration of a bank's insolvency may have systemic implications, which the bank's creditors would fail to take into account. Second, the decentralized initiation of proceedings might allow frivolous or malicious creditors to initiate proceedings against solvent banks. In other countries, however, a bank's owners, management, or creditors also are entitled to bring proceedings before the insolvency courts on the usual grounds of corporate insolvency law. This approach seeks to preserve the rights of parties who have a financial stake in the bank to bring proceedings, and it assumes that the procedural requirements of court-based proceedings will provide sufficient safeguards against abuses. It also recognizes that those parties may ensure that insolvency proceedings are launched against insolvent banks even if the supervisors are unjustifiably reluctant to take action.

Where other parties are allowed to bring insolvency proceedings before the insolvency courts, the law should require prior consultation with the supervisory authority before proceedings are filed. Subsequently, the supervisory authority should be fully entitled to

G

participate in all stages of the proceedings. In particular, the authority should have a right to be heard before the original decision on the declaration of insolvency. The supervisory authority—or a member of its staff or other person proposed by the authority—could also be eligible for appointment as official administrator, liquidator, or both. The supervisory authority should be given full access to an insolvent bank's records. It should receive documents and notifications as if it were a creditor. It should be entitled to submit restructuring plans and other proposals to the court, raise objections to the proposals of other parties, and participate in all hearings and shareholders' or creditors' meetings. It also should retain the power to control the timing and manner (including the content) of public announcements relating to the original filing of proceedings and subsequent actions, as well as to take other appropriate measures (e.g., to declare a short "bank holiday") to enhance the quality and credibility of information available to the market and to prevent a crisis of confidence.

In an administrative system, where the commencement of insolvency proceedings takes the form of a decision of the supervisory authority, the law should grant to the bank's owners an opportunity to appeal against the decision to a special tribunal or to seek judicial review in the general administrative courts. In all cases, the available remedy should be specified in the legislation, and the procedure should be expeditious. It is, however, of singular importance that the exercise of any rights of appeal or review does not automatically lead to an interim restoration of the old owners and directors in the bank's management. It is also important that the system for the exercise of any right of appeal or judicial review should include safeguards for the avoidance of abuse by interested parties and should not result in the provision of interim relief by way of staying of the administrative proceedings.

G.3.4 Licensing Implication of Bank Insolvency

The law should clearly specify the relationship between the declaration of a bank's insolvency and its status as a licensed institution. In a number of countries, the withdrawal of an institution's banking license automatically results in its placement in liquidation. Elsewhere, this approach is considered draconian and unwarranted to the extent that it could lead to the mandatory termination of institutions that are not marred by criminality, that are otherwise solvent, and that could continue to operate as non-bank enterprises.[9] In some countries, it is the commencement of insolvency proceedings that triggers the automatic or discretionary withdrawal of the bank's license. However, the automatic withdrawal of authorization is not advisable unless the bank has already been placed in liquidation.[10] If liquidation proceedings have not been commenced and if an attempt is being made under official administration to restructure the bank, the loss of the bank's license could rule out many forms of open-bank restructuring.

Finally, some jurisdictions with court-based bank insolvency systems dissociate the decisions concerning licensing from the insolvency process. There, the power of the supervisor to revoke a bank's license operates in parallel to—and independently of—the procedure for declaring insolvency. Accordingly, the supervisory authority may seek to close an insolvent bank either by applying to the courts for its liquidation or by withdrawing its license.[11]

G

G.3.5 Rights of Shareholders and Creditors in the Context of Bank Insolvency

The survival of shareholders' governance rights can significantly complicate the search for an effective bank resolution. To avoid this eventuality, a sound bank insolvency regime can transfer control over the institution to the official administrator, in particular, through the suspension of the governance rights of shareholders. Where bank insolvency proceedings take place within the general framework of corporate insolvency law, the possibility of appropriate exceptions should be considered.

When official administration and liquidation are organized as distinct legal proceedings that are subject to separate rules, the commencement of liquidation will imply that the survival of the bank is no longer possible and will generally result in the outright termination of shareholders' governance rights (although shareholders will retain a residual, purely financial interest in the estate's assets, in the event that those assets prove sufficient for the satisfaction of all remaining liabilities).

By contrast, in the case of official administration (or of single-stream proceedings, in which rehabilitation and liquidation are alternative results), many legal systems seek to ensure that the restructuring will not be conducted in ways that violate shareholders' property rights, including their continuing stake in a potentially viable enterprise. For the same reason, some jurisdictions continue to recognize shareholders' governance rights during the official administration, even though this recognition can make the process more cumbersome and potentially inefficient. The property-rights-based rationale for the continuing participation of shareholders in the governance of an insolvent bank is stronger when the bank still has a positive net worth (e.g., because it has crossed the threshold of regulatory insolvency but is not insolvent in a balance-sheet sense). Nonetheless, to provide appropriate safeguards for shareholders' property rights without undermining the effectiveness of the insolvency proceedings, alternative solutions can be used.

For instance, the law could enable the official administrator to seek a special court order for the approval of restructuring plans if the consent of shareholders is not forthcoming. Alternatively, the official administrator could be empowered to formally invite shareholders to participate in the bank's recapitalization and to expel them only if they fail to do so in time. In any event, the recognition of any shareholders' rights in the context of official administration (including their preemptive rights of participation in the bank's recapitalization) should not affect the powers of the banking supervisory authority to take swift action as needed, including the power to decide on the fitness of large shareholders of banking institutions.

A more difficult question concerns the dilution or expropriation of the shareholders' financial participation in the bank as part of a restructuring plan that involves recapitalization with public funds, with outside private capital, or both. If the bank has a positive net worth, dilution or expropriation should not be done without compensation, whether at the time of the relevant action or at a later point. Nonetheless, because of constitutional or other considerations, dilution or expropriation—with or without compensation—may not be possible in some countries other than by order of an insolvency court. If dilution or expropriation is possible, the relevant corporate actions should be conducted in a legally secure way and should be based on an explicit ordering of potentially conflicting rules so that the old shareholders do not have surviving claims on the restructured bank (e.g., under general rules of commercial or company law).

Whatever the domestic legal position, under no circumstances should shareholders' rights provide an excuse to allow shareholders to appropriate the benefits of outside financial support to an insolvent bank. For instance, when a bank is successfully restructured with public financial assistance, the old shareholders should not be restored (after the termination of the official administration) to ownership rights beyond the measure justified by the bank's net worth immediately before the commencement of the restructuring effort. To do otherwise would have the effect of transferring the value of the public assistance from the taxpayer to the bank's preexisting shareholders.

G.4 Official Administration of Banks

G.4.1 Definition

In this report, official administration of banks refers to those forms of insolvency proceedings in which an official authority (e.g., a court-appointed administrator, a banking authority, an administrator appointed by a banking authority) assumes direct managerial control of an insolvent bank, with a view to (a) protecting its assets, (b) assessing its true financial condition, and (c) then either conducting all the necessary restructuring operations or placing the bank in liquidation. Official administration continues until the institution has been restored to soundness or placed in liquidation.

G.4.2 Basic Principles

An effective framework for official administration needs to be built on a number of basic premises, including the following:

- *Speed:* The threat of bank insolvency needs a quick and decisive response.
- *Autonomy:* The official administrator must have sufficient autonomy in taking action.
- *Proportionality:* The powers of the official administrator need to be sufficient to protect creditors', depositors', and systemic interest while avoiding unnecessary interference with the property rights of owners.
- *Flexibility:* The option to close the bank and proceed with liquidation must never be excluded.
- *Accountability:* The broad powers of official administrator need to be balanced by transparency and accountability.
- *Professionalism:* The official administration should be conducted by experienced, fit, and proper official administrators, with specific experience in managing a bank.

G

G.4.3 Basic Elements of the Official Administration Regime

The report describes sound practices in relation to triggers for official administration and for the phases of official administration, including diagnosis and restructuring of insolvent banks. The report also discusses basic legal features of official administration:

- Appointment, replacement, and discharge of the official administrator
- Temporary protection against creditors' rights
- Protection of assets, containment of liabilities, and pursuit of claims
- Preparation of an inventory of assets and liabilities
- Decisions on restructuring or liquidation
- Cost of official administration
- Termination of official administration

Some of the principles to govern the framework for official administration are as follows:

- The law should identify which institution appoints a temporary administrator (for a limited time) and the rights and responsibilities of an administrator.
- The law should indicate the treatment of depositors during the temporary administration.
- The temporary administrator should have the authority to take over the day-to-day operations of the bank while the bank's financial conditions are being evaluated. During temporary administration, shareholder rights should be suspended.
- The temporary administrator should have sufficient authority to prevent asset stripping, to reverse asset transfers that have taken place just prior to suspension of the shareholders, and, in general, to keep credit discipline. The temporary administrator may also have authority to halt certain actions against the bank, pending the completion of due process.
- Shareholders may be able to protest the actions of the temporary administrator through the court system, but any appeal should not halt the resolution activities of the administrator.

G.5 Bank Restructuring

G.5.1 Definition

Bank restructuring is used in an economic sense to signify a set of actions designed to substantially modify the operations and financial structure of a banking institution. From a legal perspective, restructuring will, in some cases, result in the bank's survival as a legal entity, whereas, in other cases, the bank's legal personality will be dissolved—even if most of the bank's economic operations will continue (as a consequence, for example, of a merger or of a purchase-and-assumption operation).

G

G.5.2 Key Objectives

The purpose of restructuring is to ensure the continuation of the bank's business, in whole or in part, as an economic unit ("going concern") on a financially sound basis. A country's laws need to establish the objectives and basic principles to be followed by the authorities in restructuring a bank in the context of insolvency proceedings.

G.5.3 Basic Principles

Drawing on international experience and practices, certain principles for bank restructuring are outlined in the following paragraphs.

G.5.3.1 *Limit Moral Hazard*

In a sound and efficient financial system, only well-administered institutions should remain in business. It is not the role of authorities to prevent bank failure; rather their role is to facilitate the rapid exit of insolvent institutions from the financial system. Exceptions to this principle should be allowed only on the basis of justifiable considerations directly related to the stability of the financial system.

G.5.3.2 *Least Cost Solution*

In choosing between alternative schemes, the authorities should engage in restructuring operations that minimize restructuring costs. Restructuring costs are defined as the cost of recapitalization and of other operations by the government, after deducting the subsequent proceeds from re-privatization and asset recovery.

G.5.3.3 *Expeditious Bank Restructuring*

Insolvent banks should be restructured quickly to minimize the eventual costs to depositors, creditors, and taxpayers. The longer a bank or banking asset is held by an administrator, the more value it is likely to lose. Experience has shown that, if left unchecked, the restructuring of insolvent banks may drag on for a long time (especially in the context of a weak institutional environment). In countries where an official administration scheme exists, the relevant provisions should limit the time a bank under official administration is kept operating when no resolution scheme can be arranged.[12]

G.5.3.4 *Operational as Well as Financial Restructuring*

Bank restructuring must aim at addressing the causes, not just the symptoms, of bank insolvency. The new owners and directors of the bank must eliminate nonprofitable branches, must lay off redundant staff members, and must refocus the bank's business operations on profitable activities. Moreover, they must ensure that the bank complies with sound financial and prudential ratios. Thus, any restructuring scheme that allows an insolvent bank to survive as a separate entity should ensure that the bank is restored not only to solvency, but also and more important, to profitability so that it can operate on a sound basis over the medium and long term.

G

G.5.3.5 *Maintenance of Competitive Conditions*

Bank restructuring should not distort competition, subsidize failure, or penalize the more efficient banks in the system. This principle may be contained in competition law and enforced by the relevant authorities, though often in cooperation with the banking authorities.

G.5.3.6 *Accountability and Transparency of Process*

Bank restructuring should be carried out in a framework of fairness and transparency. Autonomous banking authorities should be held accountable for their actions. In particular, information should be made public about the rationale for important decisions, such as those involving the use and allocation of public funds, government assumption of control and ownership of a weak bank on systemic stability grounds (see section G.5.5 below for a discussion), the sale of banks to private investors, or the definitive closure and liquidation of insolvent institutions. Nonetheless, the authorities should retain sufficient flexibility to make decisions rapidly and without having to disclose relevant information in advance. In particular, they should be able to negotiate and implement in confidence certain actions, such as the sale of the bank under insolvency proceedings to a solvent acquirer or the transfer of its assets and liabilities to other institutions in the context of purchase-and-assumption transactions. In those cases, public disclosure of all relevant information should occur once the relevant transactions have been completed.

G.5.4 Bank Restructuring and Cases with Actual or Potential Systemic Implications

Although legislation should require the authorities to observe the principles whenever they deal with an insolvent bank, the law should also provide flexibility to the banking authorities to handle exceptional cases, such as bank failures with systemic implications that may cause disruptions or even the collapse of the payment and settlement systems, may trigger bank runs, or may cause other widespread disruptions in the financial system. If the authorities deem that the failure of a bank has serious systemic implications, they will need to use a restructuring technique that minimizes any systemic risks, even if some of the above principles cannot be fully observed.[13]

To prevent bank failures without systemic consequences from being treated as cases of a systemic nature, the law should establish the requirements that the authorities must comply with before they can use exceptional legal provisions.

G.5.5 Publicly Assisted Bank Restructuring

More recently, there has been broad international convergence on the principle that the discretionary, open-ended application of public funds to keep afloat insolvent banks and to make good their losses is unjustifiable. This practice transfers commercial losses to the taxpayer, validates bad bank management, and prevents the operation of the financial sector under conditions of market discipline and undistorted competition.

Generally, in situations of individual bank failure, no public funds should be used in the bank's restructuring or liquidation, except in relation to payments under state-guaranteed deposit insurance schemes. However, to facilitate the continuation of the viable part of insolvent banks on a going-concern basis and to minimize the cost of bank failure, the laws of some countries should authorize (or even require) that the deposit protection agency—or another agency with restructuring functions and powers—must provide limited financial assistance for the restructuring of insolvent banks in official administration. That provision must be to the extent that it is likely to result in a least-cost resolution from the perspective of the agency (as distinct from that of the bank or its stakeholders).

More specifically, a public agency may be empowered to assist bank-restructuring operations whenever the value of its assistance does not exceed, on its estimation, the amount that it would have to pay out against insured deposits in the event of closure and liquidation. The forms that the agency's assistance can take may vary and may include the subsidization of the sale of impaired assets, loss-sharing arrangements, or direct transfers of cash funds to the insolvent institution or its acquirers to absorb losses. Invariably, however, it will be aimed at making possible the bank's merger with a solvent institution or a purchase-and-assumption transaction, in circumstances where this change would not be commercially feasible otherwise.

A fundamental principle underpinning any type of publicly assisted bank restructuring is that recapitalization with public funds (accompanied by government assumption of control and ownership, or government approved restructuring plan) should be attempted only in situations where the bank's existing owners are made to absorb all accumulated past losses. This principle means that the shareholders' net position in the bank should be verified and recognized through appropriate write-downs of the own-fund items. For banks that are under insolvency proceedings and that are not yet completely insolvent in the balance-sheet sense, shareholders' participation in the restructured institution should be diluted. For balance-sheet insolvent banks, public funds should be forthcoming only after the shareholders have surrendered their shares or the shares have been otherwise eliminated in recognition of accumulated past losses. More generally, the shareholders should not gain any benefit from a bank's restructuring except to the extent that they have directly participated in its costs.[14]

G.5.6 Main Restructuring Techniques and Basic Applicable Principles

The guidelines include the appropriate treatment of the legal issues involved in different bank restructuring techniques, such as mergers or acquisitions, good-bank and bad-bank separation, bridge banks, and purchase-and-assumptions transactions. Key legal issues include the following:

- Need for supervisory approval of the restructuring
- Mechanisms to protect property rights and dilute shareholders' rights
- Rules for negotiations with prospective investors
- Rules affecting the transfer of assets and liabilities
- Rules on the use of a bank's proprietary information

G

The key principles to govern the legal and regulatory framework for bank restructuring are as follows:

- The agency responsible for bank resolution should be clearly identified. The rights and responsibilities should be clearly described.
- The treatment of shareholders must be clearly laid out in the law. In principle, shareholders who do not participate in the recapitalization of the bank should lose their investment in the bank. Shareholders participating in the bank's recapitalization must first be judged to be "fit and proper."
- Actions that can be taken in bank resolution must be described in the law and could include bank mergers, sale of the bank, and purchase and assumption of bank assets (which may include a branch network) by another bank.
- If the authorities wish to establish an asset management company to manage some portion of the nonperforming loans of problem banks, explicit legal authority must be established, including how the assets will be transferred, what the valuation is of transferred assets, what the problem bank will receive in exchange, and what the methods are for asset workout.
- If an agreement is reached with a majority of the creditors of the bank to share in the restructuring and recapitalization costs, a minority of creditors should not have the ability either to prevent such actions or to avoid participating (there should be a "cram down" provision.)

G.6 Bank Liquidation

In liquidation, an insolvent bank is dissolved after a liquidator assumes legal control of its estate, collects and realizes its assets, and distributes the proceeds to creditors—in full or partial satisfaction of their claims—in accordance with the principle of equal (pari passu) treatment of similarly situated creditors and the applicable rules on priority. Liquidation will be appropriate if the bank's restructuring does not appear feasible or if the restructuring involves the spinning off of the viable operations of the bank, thus leaving only its residual, nonviable part with the original legal entity. On the commencement of liquidation and until the final act of dissolution, the bank will continue to exist as a legal entity but will no longer be a going concern. However, bundles of assets may be sold as part of a business, rather than on a piecemeal basis, to ensure the maximization of their economic value.

The primary objective in a liquidation is to ensure the preservation and optimal collection of the bank's assets so that creditors (including depositors) receive as much as possible of what is owed to them. Effective bank liquidation presupposes that the legal system provides satisfactory answers to certain special problems, which may not be present in a non-financial firm. Accordingly, a jurisdiction must have a complete legal framework in place to handle the liquidation of banks. The absence of such a framework will not only result in disorderly closure of individual insolvent banks but also increase the risk of spillover effects, with potential systemic implications.

G

In particular, the liquidation framework should comprise clear rules for formally placing the insolvent bank in liquidation, terminating its banking activities, and assigning to a qualified agency the tasks related to the liquidation of its estate. With regard to the latter, the liquidation framework must contain provisions that ensure immediate and effective protection of the assets, including an automatic moratorium or suspension of all collection activity against the bank to prevent a race between creditors for the seizure of assets and to ensure the orderly realization of assets and equitable distribution of proceeds. It is also of vital importance that the rules provide sufficient flexibility to enable the liquidator to achieve the realization of assets in the most cost-effective way and that they ensure that proceeds are distributed to the various classes of creditors (including depositors) in a fair and transparent manner, which does not violate their relative priority. Some of the key principles to govern the legal and regulatory framework for bank liquidation are as follows:

- Bank shareholders must be held responsible for the losses of the bank. When a bank is found to be insolvent, the supervisory agency must be in a position to write down shareholder equity and to eliminate shareholder rights.
- The supervisory agency should be given the responsibility to establish the list of qualified liquidators.
- The supervisory authority must have the right to appoint a bank liquidator to replace the shareholders. The bank liquidator must have the authority to sell all or part of the bank's assets including branches.
- The law must determine the priorities for distributing resources from asset sales among creditors.

G.7 Key Features of the Legal Framework in the Context of Systemic Crises

Despite the fact that systemic banking crises and their resolution are qualitatively different from individual cases of bank insolvency, there are at least two benefits to having in place an adequate legal and institutional framework to address bank insolvency in normal times for managing systemic banking crisis situations:

- First, a good legal and institutional framework could play a mitigating role. A legal framework that comprises many of the critical principles discussed in this report could allow the authorities to ensure that weak-bank problems or insolvency cases are addressed before they can cause systemic problems.
- Second, if the legal and regulatory framework is adequate enough to handle single bank failures, the same framework also could provide a basis for the implementation of most operational aspects of a restructuring strategy, thereby smoothening and expediting the systemic bank restructuring phase.

Nonetheless, modifications to both the legal and institutional framework may still be needed (and in most cases are) to deal with systemic crises. Modifications to the legal framework would help address (a) special institutional arrangements for systemic

G

crisis management (e.g., bank restructuring agency), (b) the need for coordination and exchange of information among all government agencies (e.g., high-level financial stability policy committee), (c) clear legal authority to take the measures that may be required, (d) systemic bank restructuring, (e) asset management and resolution, (f) general conditions and key legal issues for the use of public funds, (g) financial instruments and techniques, (g) role of the central bank, (h) reestablishment of regulatory compliance after a crisis, and (i) treatment of depositors. However, changes to the institutional framework, which would be needed at times of crisis, should be temporary and should respect the basic institutional structure of the country's governmental arrangements.

Notes

1. The CCG consisted of 20 country representatives and representatives from all the international financial institutions involved, as well as a few independent experts. Its main task was to review and provide comments on the different versions of the main report to ensure that a basic level of international consensus is reflected in the report. The World Bank Board considered the report at a technical briefing in January 8, 2004.

2. See IMF (2002b).

3. A recent IMF study (IMF 2004a) concluded that insufficient legal basis, ineffective enforcement, forbearance, limited range of measures available, and excessive court intervention have been factors that impede appropriate compliance with BCP 22 by a significant number of countries. This study highlighted the importance of developing a strong bank insolvency framework. The GBII would help in fostering such a framework.

4. An effective bank insolvency framework should enable the resolution of a troubled bank in a way that (a) does not unduly increase moral hazard and, thus, maintains market discipline; (b) does not unduly raise the risk of contagion; and (c) avoids the unnecessary destruction of the value of the bank's assets.

5. In jurisdictions where the general insolvency legislation is also applied to banks, the law in most cases requires a special role for the banking regulatory authorities in relation to the commencement of the proceedings. In some countries, the special role of the banking regulatory authorities includes the appointment of a trustee or liquidator or other key aspects of the proceedings.

6. Because one of the main arguments for the appropriateness of having a special regime for banks is frequently predicated on the need to give special protection to deposits from the general public, in many jurisdictions, the special insolvency regime is not applied to non–deposit-taking financial entities.

7. For example, the United Kingdom has no special statutory regime to address insolvency of financial institutions. They are subject to the same formal insolvency procedures as unregulated companies, but the law allows for exceptions to grant the Financial Services Authority various rights in insolvency proceedings and does not allow banks certain rescue or rehabilitation procedures that are available to small unregulated companies. Together with other powers of Financial Services Authority and Financial

Services Compensation Scheme, the system provides an effective insolvency regime. (See IMF Country Report No. 03/46 on UK).

8. Depending on whether the jurisdiction follows the court-based or the administrative approach, the supervisory authority will need to either petition the insolvency court or declare the insolvency itself in the form of an autonomous decision in public law.

9. In certain jurisdictions, however, the justification for automatic liquidation as a consequence of de-licensing will be precisely that banks are organized as special-purpose companies and would not constitutionally be able to continue operating as non-bank entities.

10. In countries in which banks are subject to special liquidation proceedings, logic requires that the automatic withdrawal of an institution's banking authorization as a result of the commencement of liquidation proceedings should not affect its continuing characterization as a bank for the purposes of these proceedings.

11. In some cases, the supervisory authority retains the discretionary power to withdraw the license even after the commencement of insolvency proceedings. It would be clearly anomalous, however, if a supervisory authority were permitted to use this power to effectively veto a restructuring plan that it was unable to oppose successfully before the insolvency court.

12. In many cases, countries with a weak institutional environment have encountered serious problems in implementing any scheme of official administration whereby banks are kept open. In those cases, it may be desirable to implement the restructuring operations in an extremely quick manner to avoid loss of value of insolvent banks' assets.

13. For example, in some cases with clear systemic implication, emergency assistance involving the use of public funds may be needed, and it may be unavoidable to go over the least-cost principle, especially when it has been formulated in a very rigid manner. Nevertheless, in those special cases, a decision-making process that ensures proper assessment of the systemic consequences involved and that properly limits the moral hazard effects is needed. For example, provisions requiring a previous joint pronouncement from the highest authorities involved could be necessary before any kind of exception to the general norms could be made.

14. One reason why publicly assisted restructuring may not be effectively carried out by means of voluntary transactions outside the formal bank insolvency framework is that once the shareholders become apprised of the likelihood of assistance, they will be unwilling to approve the dilution of their own interest in the bank and will hold out for some additional benefit.

G

Appendix H

Assessment of Pension Schemes from a Financial Sector Perspective

A pension plan is a long-term financial contract that promises to pay a retiring worker a sum of money intended to support old age consumption (Mitchell 2002, p. 2). Pension plans are generally classified as either a defined contribution (DC) plan or a defined benefit (DB) plan. Those two plans have significantly different characteristics. In a DC plan, the sponsor promises to periodically deposit a specified contribution into the plan (e.g., per pay period), which is then invested in capital market instruments of various risk levels. An individual's total pension is based on amount contributed, length of employment, and investment return. By contrast, a DB plan is based on a promise by the sponsor to pay the retiree a specified benefit, usually based on the employee's wage plus the length of service. In that case, the market risk associated with the investment returns is borne by the employer (sponsor), who must set aside sufficient funds to pay the promised benefits. In a DC scheme, market risk is borne by the employee.

Hybrid pension schemes that have the features of a DB plan but require a greater sharing of risks by beneficiaries (as in DC schemes) are emerging in several countries, partly in response to rising costs of DB plans in an environment of increasing longevity of retirees. Similar to traditional DB plans, the employer or trustee invests the plan assets and typically bears some of the investment risk. At the same time, the employee has an individual account—a notional account maintained for record-keeping purposes—and receives the account balance at separation as a lump sum or annuity, thereby assuming more longevity risk.[1]

Pension plans can be either funded or unfunded. In funded plans, pension liabilities are paid out from the accumulated assets. Essentially, benefits are paid out from a fund built over a period of years from the contributions of its members (i.e., on the basis of accumulation of financial assets), plus investment income. Most DC plans are funded.

H

449

Unfunded pensions also are financed directly from the contributions of the plan provider or sponsor, the plan's participant, or both, but unlike funded schemes, they are not fully backed by assets to pay the future promised benefits, although they may still have associated reserves to cover immediate expenses (Yermo 2002). Generally, in unfunded schemes, resources are transferred directly from the currently working generation to the retired generation. For example, in pay-as-you-go (PAYG) schemes, contributions by present workers through payroll deductions are used to pay the current benefits of retirees.

National pension systems are usually represented by a multi-pillar structure, whereby the sources of retirement benefits are a mixture of government, employment, and individual savings. Although there are various definitions, the three pillars can be identified by their sources of savings as follows: Pillar I is the government, usually a combination of a universal entitlement and an earnings-related component; Pillar II is occupational (employer) pension funds, increasingly funded; and Pillar III is private savings and individual plans, often tax advantaged.[2]

The assessment of pensions from the perspective of financial sector stability focuses on the financial management and financial markets aspects. The assessment process cannot follow a strict framework, in part because pension systems vary greatly across countries and are marked by different contribution and payout characteristics. Accordingly, each assessment is guided by the individual country's level of pension system development. The process is further complicated by the fact that pensions are intrinsically complex forms of long-term savings linked to capital markets, insurance, and social security (Whitehouse 2002).

H.1 Assessment Framework

Despite the cross-country variations, assessments typically cover the following:

- *Structure and Performance of the Pension Sector:* number and types of providers; portfolio compositions; investment regimes; asset growth; gross and net rates of return; fees, costs, and profits; payouts and replacement ratios; coverage of the labor force; and contribution to capital markets development
- *Regulatory Framework:*[3] pension laws, licensing criteria, governance structures, accounting and auditing rules and practices, custodian rules and arrangements, disclosure, investment regulations, outsourcing regulations, and the voluntary pension system
- *Supervisory Framework:* approach to supervision (proactive vs. reactive), legal status and internal structure of the supervisory agency, regulatory and enforcement powers of supervisor, ability to carry out early interventions, and relationship with other supervisors

Within the assessment of the structure and performance of the pension sector, the focus on the effect on capital markets development is of great importance. Pension systems also have significant effects on poverty alleviation, labor markets, fiscal soundness, fairness and adequacy, and intergenerational and intra-generational redistributive effects, but those issues are typically beyond the scope of the financial sector assessment.

H

H.2 Importance of Regulating and Supervising Pension Systems

Effective oversight of pension systems is an integral component of financial sector stability because of the social, fiscal, and global financial ramifications of pension fund management. Sections H.2.1 to H.2.4 highlight the following considerations:

H.2.1 Income and Household Security

Pensions provide a critical source of income security for workers in their retirement years. The pensions are often long term in nature (60 years or more). The significance of well-managed and well-regulated funds extends beyond the elderly to current workers, who contribute on the basis of an expected future revenue stream. In addition, the increasing transition from DB to DC and to hybrid plans, plus the decrease in state pensions, bears financially on the household sector, which is now more exposed to retirement risks (e.g., investment, market, longevity). Therefore, to date, much of pension fund regulation has focused on the protection of pensioner and employee rights.

Effective oversight in this regard is predicated on ensuring that individual investors have confidence that their savings are secure.[4] Notably, trust and confidence on the part of both participants toward the integrity of the provider—be it government or a private entity—are essential components of a well-functioning system. A sound regulatory and supervisory framework can also significantly enhance pensioner security by increasing the long-term security of the funds, ensuring efficiency, and providing considerable freedom of choice in planning options.

H.2.2 Issues of Funding

As populations mature, the relative size of pension liabilities and the related investment risks have grown accordingly and have, in many instances, exceeded expectations. Consequently, greater attention is being called to managing and maintaining funding levels and to meeting payment obligations, which is reflected in greater emphasis on regulatory and supervisory structures.

H.2.3 Fiscal Management

If one considers the risks of politically motivated misallocation of funds and the fiscal implications of mismanagement, regulatory and supervisory attention must be given to publicly managed funds (see section H.3 below).

H.2.4 Financial Markets

The focus on ensuring the soundness of pension sectors also attests to their growing role in, and influence on, global financial markets. The effect of pension funds on the stability of financial markets is transmitted in a number of ways, most notably through their investment behavior. The pension fund sector, especially in Organisation for Economic Co-operation and Development (OECD) countries, is an investor class on its own whose global size and

H

projected growth means that it can unilaterally move markets through any reallocation of funds. Known as institutional investors, pension funds (along with insurance companies) hold not only tremendous amounts of domestic and international fixed income but also equity assets.

There is no uniform approach to pension supervision, only fundamental elements that guide the oversight framework in many countries. Those prudential and protective rules encompass the following:

- Establishing a "fit and proper" test for funds and managers
- Segregating, diversifying, and performing a valuation of assets
- Imposing checks and balances on fund governance, custodians, actuaries, and auditors
- Guaranteeing extensive disclosure and high transparency on the part of funds through regular financial reporting (on a quarterly basis)
- Ensuring the financial soundness of funds, sometimes by imposing restrictions on certain investments and asset holdings
- Protecting beneficiaries from misconduct and misallocation of funds
- Establishing strong supervisory capacities for financial analysis and frequent inspection, as well as providing an early action tool to contain losses and to protect members
- Shielding supervisors from political pressure

H.3 Regulation and Supervision of Public and Government Pension Funds: Risks and Regulatory Responses[5]

Public pension plans are schemes, social security or similar, whereby the government administers the payment of pension benefits. The basic goal is to provide benefits for the population at large. Traditionally, public plans have been PAYG, although some countries have prefunded pension liabilities or private plans.

Oversight of government-run plans is required for numerous reasons, particularly the fiscal implications of mismanagement. The risks associated with DC schemes managed by the public sector arise namely from the government's control over a large pool of funds. Such control can be problematic because those funds are frequently subject to political manipulation and pressures to, among other things, increase benefits, lower contributions, and hide problems. Moreover, government officials can be tempted to direct the investment of such funds either into government securities to help fund the budget or into politically attractive projects, disregarding the interests of pension investors. Risks also arise when fund management is outsourced to the private sector, including the possibility that the funds will not be optimally managed.

Under-funded pension systems can impose a heavy fiscal burden. Recent Financial Sector Assessment Programs have found that many government plans are under-funded and sometimes insolvent. The main culprit is the mismatch of funds, whereby often generous benefits are not matched by adequate contributions. Short working years and early

Table H.1. The Core Principles of Occupational Pension Regulation (OECD 2004)

1.	Conditions for effective regulation and supervision	• Legal and regulatory framework should be comprehensive and flexible to protect soundness of pension plans and overall stability. • Financial Market infrastructure should be developed to support diversified investments of pension funds.. • The regulatory framework should promote a level playing field between different operators and not impose excessive burdens on pension markets, institutions or employers
2.	Establishment of pension plans, pension funds, and pension fund managing companies	• Pension funds must meet proper legal, accounting, technical, and financial criteria. • A clear statement of pension funds objectives, parameters, responsibilities, and beneficiaries rights needs formal documentation. • Pension plan assets need to be legally separated from the assets of plan sponsor.
3.	Pension plan liabilities, funding rules, winding up, and insurance	• Adequate funding of pension liabilities is required for defined benefit pension plans. • Appropriate calculation methods to measure liabilities and value assets, including actuarial techniques are necessary. • Proper winding-up mechanisms must be put in place to recognize creditors' rights and to ensure payment of contributions due from employers in the event of insolvency.
4.	Asset management	• Proper disclosure is necessary for valuation of pension assets. • Pension fund governing body should be subject to prudent person standard. • Pension funds must mitigate risk by imposing portfolio limits that maintain the proper diversification of assets. • Self-investment and investment abroad should be prohibited. • A governing body is required to set and follow investment policy.
5.	Rights of members and beneficiaries and adequacy of benefits	• There should be nondiscriminatory access to private pension schemes, regardless of age, race, salary, gender, and terms of employment. • The portability of pension rights and beneficiary protection should be ensured in the event of early departure. • Adequate disclosure and education should be given to a beneficiary with regard to fee structure, plan performance, and benefit conditions.
6.	Supervision	• Effective supervisory bodies need to be established with appropriate powers to conduct on and off-site supervision and examine individual plans when relevant. • The supervisory body should have comprehensive investigatory and enforcement powers to obtain relevant data, take action to ensure compliance, impose sanctions, and initiate matters for criminal prosecution.

Source: OECD (2004).

retirements, which are common and sometimes encouraged, contribute to the mismatch problem.

A range of appropriate regulations can be established to oversee public pensions:

- Profitability rules (or minimum return requirements) can be imposed on private suppliers to reduce the risk that the funds will under-perform the industry average. This regulation also reflects the moral obligation imposed on a government to ensure an adequate pension income for individuals with no control over their investments.
- Restrictions on portfolio composition of pension funds can ensure a high probability that their performance will fall within a narrow range.
- A guarantee fund can be established to supplement shortfalls.
- A strong government commitment is needed to the disclosure of both the composition and performance of the portfolio.
- A strong and publicly disclosed set of internal governance standards should be required.
- Public pension schemes must show a commitment to regular audit for compliance and efficiency by an independent audit agency.

H

- Public pension schemes must report against publicly agreed benchmarks for performance.

Strong regulatory standards are also necessary for DB schemes to ensure that the promise of a specific payout is honored, especially when management is privatized or contracted to the private sector. Regulation usually takes the form of periodic actuarial reviews of the funds to assess the capacity of the fund to meet its payment obligations.

H.4 Regulation and Supervision of Private Funds

Private pension plans are schemes administered by an employer, a pension entity, or a private sector provider. They may either complement or substitute for social security systems and may include plans for public sector workers (Yermo 2002, p. 3). The regulation and supervision of privately run pension funds is equally as important as that of public plans and increasingly so as more countries move toward a mix of public and privately run plans. In addition, governments have moved toward contracting out the investment arm of their pension programs to private fund management companies.

Privately managed or independent funds rely heavily on professional asset management. As such, "trust" in the integrity of managers and the solvency of funds is fundamental to securing the confidence of both sponsors (government, private company) and employees that their retirement savings are not mismanaged (Carmichael and Pomerleano 2002). Accordingly, the focus of supervision is on ensuring high transparency plus strong reporting and conduct rules.

The primary regulatory tools for managing private pensions are (a) licensing requirements to ensure the high quality of asset managers, (b) disclosure standards, (c) governance standards, and (d) minimum capital requirements (Carmichael and Pomerleano 2002, p. 113). Because the investment decision is out of the control of employees, the strength of the regulations regarding investment regimes and their enforcement is particularly relevant.

The OECD, recognizing the importance of protecting pensions provided by employers, developed guidelines for regulation, which are summarized in the following paragraphs.

Occupational pension plans have raised regulatory concerns, because of the inherent risk they bear from their exposure to capital market volatility. Any unexpected declines in equity or bond prices have the potential to cause significant losses in a fund, thereby posing serious threats to a worker's expected retirement funds. The rise in occupational pension schemes has called attention to requiring greater accountability on the part of private entities. In recognition of those risks, the OECD has established the six Core Principles of Occupational Pension Regulation (see table H.1). The goal of those recommendations is to mitigate the risk of pensioners and to provide standards for the funding of company pension schemes.

H.5 Regulatory Oversight

The methods of pension regulation and supervision differ across countries, reflecting individual national standards and structures. For example, some OECD countries have

H

established independent, separate pension fund supervisory agencies. Elsewhere, pension funds can fall under the insurance regulator, a universal financial services supervisor, or the ministry of finance. Nevertheless, despite country differences, there are broadly two models of supervision: proactive and reactive.

- Proactive supervision involves detailed specification of the activities of pension fund managers, as well as tight supervision and audit to enforce the rules.
- Reactive supervision allows for a greater degree of self-regulation within the sector.

Supervision can cover institutional controls (authorization and licensing of managers and funds); financial tasks (e.g., ensuring financial reporting, valuing portfolios, and supervising restrictions on asset holdings); membership; and benefits controls (e.g., enrollment, marketing and transfer between funds, and monitoring the calculation of entitlements).

Concern over insufficient regulatory attention to solvency and risk management issues has directed focus on greater risk-based supervision and on greater attention to asset–liability management by pension funds. For example, several pension guarantee funds take portfolio risks into account when establishing premiums. In some countries, risk-based capital or funding requirements have been introduced into the pension system.[6] The OECD Core Principles of Occupational Pension Regulation propose principles related to the full funding of pension schemes and the enhancement of portability.

H.6   The Regulation of Investment Regimes[7]

The means by which investment regimes, and thus asset allocation, related to public and private pensions are regulated will vary across and within countries (e.g., each individual U.S. state has its own investment regime). Regulatory (and tax) constraints on investment behavior and national funding rules significantly influence pension fund strategies. For example, in the case of Chile,[8] the pension sector is regulated by a highly complex investment regime, with limits by instruments, instrument characteristics, issuers, and issuer types. By comparison, the investment regime for pension funds in OECD countries is considered relatively much simpler.

OECD countries are typically classified in two groups, adhering to either the prudent man rule or the quantitative restrictions regime. The former states that pension funds should manage their portfolios as a prudent man, implying a proper diversification of the portfolio and few direct restrictions. The lack of restrictions is countered by a heavy reliance on the presence of competent and honest managers to ensure the implementation of relevant standards, as well as on the assurance of an adequate level of ability and integrity. This assurance requires the development of strict criteria comparable across firms or of legislating criteria regarding the expertise of fund managers. Prudent man rules also require that greater financial and legal responsibility be attached to any imprudent action by corporate officers. Such rules can vary across countries, sectors, and companies, but the OECD recommends a flexible general framework that can be applicable across borders.

A quantitative restrictions regime involves direct restrictions on the portfolio, both by instrument and user, including foreign asset and concentration limits. Despite variations across countries, general principles for the regulation of investment portfolios have been articulated by OECD (2000). The purpose of regulation is to ensure both the security and

H

the profitability of the funds invested. Basic principles of portfolio management focus on (and differentiate between) both assets and liabilities, especially asset–liability management (ensuring that liabilities are sufficiently covered by suitable assets). Another important principle is that they differentiate between each institution, thus taking a comprehensive view of each institution's structure and the range of risks to which it is exposed.

Basic standards of portfolio management outlined by the OECD include the following:

- Diversification (between categories) and dispersion (within a given category) of assets
- Maturity matching (including a liquidity principle) of assets and liabilities
- Currency matching applied comprehensively (derivatives can be used in this regard)
- Pension assets invested primarily in long-term securities that provide for a prudent risk–return profile
- Schemes managed in a way that is consistent with the risk tolerance profile of stakeholders

Quantitative restrictions outlined by the OECD include the following:

- No minimum level of investment should be placed on the portfolio, except on an exceptional and temporary basis.
- Maximum levels of investment by category may be justified on prudential grounds, in which case it may be advisable to

  - allow firms to exceed such conditions under certain circumstances,
  - differentiate between maxima and allow ceilings to be exceeded on the basis of that differentiation, and
  - take account of how such investments are valued and of the actual effect of that valuation.

- Investment in an asset must be limited to a proportion of the fund's total portfolio and even restricted if that asset involves special risks.
- Certain categories of investments may need to be strictly limited (e.g., loans without appropriate guarantees, unquoted shares, and company shares that raise risks of conflict of interest).
- Limits should be placed on investments by insurance companies and pension funds in companies or on investments holding a large volume of such categories of assets.
- The use of financial derivatives as management instruments may be useful or effective if done prudently and in accordance with established rules that ensure consistency with appropriate risk management systems.
- Appropriate and compatible accounting methods may be set up so that information on investments is sufficiently transparent.

H

H.7 Government Guarantee Funds[9]

In several countries, government guarantee funds have been established to ensure DC private pension plans. The goal of such guarantees is to reduce an individual's exposure to investment and other risks associated with private plans and to diversify the risk of pension fund failures among the general population of pension plans. In developing countries, especially in Latin America where they have sprouted, government guarantee schemes have helped to ease the transition from government sponsored DB plans to privately run DC plans. It is expected that guarantee funds will grow in importance as more countries shift to greater emphasis on private plans.

Government pension guarantees, as illustrated by the practices in the Latin American region, have commonly been of two forms:

- A guarantee that ensures that each DC fund earns an annual rate of return greater than a pre-specified minimum
- A guarantee that directly ensures each individual return on pension savings, rather than the guarantee on each pension fund (guarantees that participants receive a minimum benefit payment throughout their retirement years, even if their retirement savings are exhausted)

Nonetheless, the structure of government pension guarantees varies across countries. The United States, Germany, and Switzerland have long-standing institutions to insure pension benefits. For example, in the United States, the key role of the Pension Benefit Guarantee Corporation, whose funds are contributed by private firms, is to ensure private pension plans and to protect the retirement benefits of workers whose companies fail or go out of business. In Chile, by contrast, the government has established a minimum pension guarantee that promises to keep pension benefits above a certain level. Only workers who have contributed for at least 20 years are eligible, and the guarantee is intended to reduce the risk that workers will outlive their savings.

The presence of insurance funds is not without inherent risks, including moral hazard and poor design and operation. For example, a fund may carry an investment portfolio similar to that of covered pension funds, which can limit its ability to act in times of crisis. The use of more risk-based elements in the design of guarantee funds, such as risk-based premiums would reduce moral hazard.

Notes

1. See Green (2003), Francis (2004), Johnson and Steuerle (2003), and Scheiber (2003), for a discussion of hybrid plans.
2. For a discussion of various types of pension systems, see Yermo (2002) and Carmichael and Pomerleano (2002).
3. Analyzing the regulatory framework depends heavily on the level of government involvement in pension provision.
4. Several recent corporate failures have underlined the importance of transparency and the diversification of pensions fund assets, regardless of type (e.g., the collapse of U.S.-based Enron saw the loss by workers of their entire occupational pension savings, which had been invested largely in company stocks. Losses are estimated between US$5 billion and US$10 billion. The employees were encouraged to buy stocks, which were hugely overpriced and were based on false financial statements that grossly inflated earnings.)

H

5. This section is based on Carmichael and Pomerleano (2002), pp. 115–17.
6. For an interesting case study in the development of a risk-based capital system, see the IMF (2004) box 3.4 on the Netherlands, p. 104.
7. Investment strategies are typically based on the size and depth of domestic capital markets, as well as access to international capital markets, which is important for diversification and possibly higher rates of return. Size and depth of markets determine the availability of instruments of varying risk, return and maturity, and liquidity characteristics. In many developing countries, shallow capital markets result in heavy investment in government bonds and bank deposits.
8. Chile's pension fund sector, one of the most developed among emerging markets, is a fully funded system operated by the private sector (which insulates it from political pressures). The Chilean investment regime includes limits specified for each instrument, each class of instrument (variable and fixed income), different combinations of instruments and also sub-limits, depending on risk, liquidity, characteristics, and company age. The limits by issuer are divided into three main categories aimed at (a) portfolio diversification, (b) restricting investments in related companies, and (c) limiting ownership concentration.
9. Section is based on Pennacchi (1998).

References

Carmichael, Jefferey, and Michael Pomerleano. 2002. *The Development and Regulation of Non-Bank Financial Institutions*. Washington, DC: World Bank.

Green, L. Bernard. 2003. *What Is a Pension Equity Plan?* Washington, DC: U.S. Department of Labor.

Francis, David. 2004. "As Pensions Fade, Some Firms Try Hybrid Plans." *Christian Science Monitor*, October 25, 2004.

International Monetary Fund. 2004. *Global Financial Stability Report*. Washington, DC: International Monetary Fund.

Johnson, Richard, and Eugene Steuerle 2003. "Promoting Work at Older Ages: The Role of Hybrid Pension Plans in an Aging Population." Pension Research Council WP 2003-26. The Wharton School, University of Pennsylvania, Philadelphia, PA. Available at http://rider.wharton.upenn.edu/~prc/PRC/WP/WP2003-26.pdf.

Mitchell, Olivia. 2002. "Redesigning Public Sector Pensions in Developing Countries." Pension Research Council WP 2002-9, The Wharton School, University of Pennsylvania, Philadelphia, PA.

OECD. 2000. *Selected Principles for the Regulation of Investments by Insurance Companies and Pension Funds*. OECD: Paris.

———. 2004. *Recommendation on Core Principles of Occupational Pension Regulation*. OECD: Paris.

Pennacchi, George. 1998. "Government Guarantees on Pension Fund Returns." WB Social Protection Discussion Paper No. 9806, World Bank, Washington, DC.

Scheiber, Sylvester J. 2003. "The Shift to Hybrid Pensions by US Employers." Pension Research Council Working Paper 2003-23, The Wharton School, University of

H

Pennsylvania, Philadelphia, PA. Available at http://rider.wharton.upenn.edu/~prc/PRC/WP/WP2003-23.pdf.

Whitehouse, Edward. 1999. *Pension Reform Primer—Supervision: Building Public Confidence in Mandatory Funded Pensions*. Washington, DC: World Bank.

Yermo, Juan. 2002. *Revised Taxonomy for Pension Plans, Pension Funds and Pension Entities*. A Paper prepared for the OECD Working Party On Private Pensions, OECD (October 2002): Paris.

H

ECO-AUDIT

Environmental Benefits Statement

The World Bank is committed to preserving endangered forests and natural resources. We have chosen to print *Financial Sector Assessment: A Handbook* on 30% post-consumer recycled fiber paper, processed chlorine free. The World Bank has formally agreed to follow the recommended standards for paper usage set by the Green Press Initiative—a nonprofit program supporting publishers in using fiber that is not sourced from endangered forests. For more information, visit www.greenpressinitiative.org.

The printing of these books on recycled paper saved the following:

Trees*	Solid Waste	Water	Net Greenhouse Gases	Electricity
46	2,158	19,575	4,239	7,872
*40' in height and 6–8" in diameter	Pounds	Gallons	Pounds	KWH